Presented to

_____

by

_____

_____

_____

on

_____

HOLY BIBLE

NEW TESTAMENT AND PSALMS

Contemporary English Version

CANADIAN BIBLE SOCIETY

10 Carnforth Road
Toronto, Ontario
M4A 2S4

Holy Bible

New Testament and Psalms
in the
Contemporary English Version

New Testament: ©American Bible Society, 1995
Psalms: ©American Bible Society, 1995

CEV352NTP New Testament and Psalms
Typeset by Canadian Bible Society, 1995
Printed in Korea

21737 CEV352NTP
ISBN 0-88834-284-5

CBS-1997-20M

Welcome to
The Contemporary English Version

L anguages are spoken before they are written. And far more communication is done through the spoken word than through the written word. In fact, more people *hear* the Bible read than read it for themselves. Traditional translations of the Bible count on the *reader's* ability to understand a *written* text. But the *Contemporary English Version* differs from all other English Bibles—past and present—in that it takes into consideration the needs of the *hearer,* as well as those of the reader, who may not be familiar with traditional biblical language.

The *Contemporary English Version* has been described as a "user-friendly" and a "mission-driven" translation that can be *read aloud* without stumbling, *heard* without misunderstanding, and *listened to* with enjoyment and appreciation, because the language is contemporary and the style is lucid and lyrical.

The *Contemporary English Version* invites you to *read,* to *hear,* to *understand* and to *share the Word of God now as never before!*

The Contemporary English Version

Translation it is that opens the window, to let in the light; that breaks the shell, that we may eat the kernel; that puts aside the curtain, that we may look into the most holy place; that removes the cover of the well, that we may come by the water ("The Translators to the Reader," King James Version, 1611).

The most important document in the history of the English language is the King James Version of the Bible. To measure its spiritual impact on the English speaking world would be more impossible than counting the grains of sand along the ocean shores. Historically, many Bible translators have attempted in some measure to *retain the form* of the King James Version. But the translators of the Contemporary English Version of the Bible have diligently sought to *capture the spirit* of the King James Version by following certain principles set forth by its translators in the document "The Translators to the Reader," which was printed in the earliest editions.

This is the Word of God, which we translate

Accuracy, beauty, clarity, and dignity—all of these can and must be achieved in the translation of the Bible. After all, as the translators of the King James Version stated, "This is the Word of God, which we translate."

v

Every attempt has been made to produce a text that is faithful to the *meaning* of the original. In order to assure the *accuracy* of the Contemporary English Version, the Old Testament was translated directly from the Hebrew and Aramaic texts published by the United Bible Societies (*Biblia Hebraica Stuttgartensia,* fourth edition corrected). And the New Testament was translated directly from the Greek text published by the United Bible Societies (third edition corrected and compared with the fourth revised edition).

The drafts in their earliest stages were sent for review and comment to a number of biblical scholars, theologians, and educators representing a wide variety of church traditions. In addition, drafts were sent for review and comment to all English-speaking Bible Societies and to more than forty United Bible Societies translation consultants around the world. Final approval of the text was given by the American Bible Society Board of Trustees on the recommendation of its Translations Subcommittee.

We desire that the Scripture … may be understood

That the Scripture may be understood even by ordinary people was a primary goal of the translators of the King James Version. And they raised the question, "What can be more available thereto than to deliver God's book unto God's people in a tongue which they understand?" Martin Luther also did his translation for the common people, and he established the following guidelines:

> We do not have to inquire of the literal Latin, how we are to speak German…. Rather we must inquire about this of the mother in the home, the

children on the street, the common man in the marketplace. *We must be guided by their language, the way they speak, and do our translating accordingly.*

Today more people *hear* the Bible read aloud than read it for themselves! And statistics released by the National Center for Education indicate that "almost half of U.S. adults have very limited reading and writing skills." If this is the case, a contemporary translation must be a text that an inexperienced reader can *read aloud* without stumbling, that someone unfamiliar with traditional biblical terminology can *hear without misunderstanding,* and that everyone can *listen to with enjoyment* because the style is lucid and lyrical.

In order to attain these goals of clarity, beauty, and dignity, the translators of the Contemporary English Version carefully studied every word, phrase, clause, and paragraph of the original. Then, with equal care, they struggled to discover the best way to translate the text, so that it would be suitable both for *private* and *public* reading, and for *memorizing.* The result is an English text that is enjoyable and easily understood by the vast majority of English speakers, regardless of their religious or educational background.

In the *hearing* of a translation, even the inclusion of a simple word like "and" can make a significant difference. Matthew 2.9 of the Contemporary English Version reads as follows: "The wise men listened to what the king said and then left. *And* the star they had seen in the east went on ahead of them until it stopped over the place where the child was."

"And" at the beginning of the second sentence assists both the person who reads the text aloud and those who must depend upon hearing it read. Like all other punctuation marks, the period after "left" is silent, and so the text without "And" could possibly be *heard* as, "The wise men listened to what the king said and then left the star they had seen in the east." However, as the text now stands, the oral reader must pause briefly for a breath before "And," which will signal the hearer that a new sentence has begun.

As another example, try reading the following two sentences aloud: "You yourselves admit, then, that you agree with what your ancestors did" and "for it was better with me then than now." Both suffer from potential tongue twisters ("admit, then, that" and "then than"). But the first is doubly difficult because it consists of a lengthy series of unaccented syllables that do not allow the reader to take a breath. In the Contemporary English Version every attempt has been made to avoid these and other kinds of constructions that could possibly prove problematic for oral reading.

According to the rules of English grammar, the pronoun *he* must refer back to *God* in the following sentence: "The other, however, rebuked him saying, 'Don't you fear *God?* You received the same sentence *he* did.'" But the reference is actually to Jesus, who is mentioned earlier in the passage. Traditional translations assume that the reader can study the printed text and finally figure out the meaning, but the Contemporary English Version is concerned equally with the reader and the *hearer.* And in many situations, the hearer may have only *one* chance to understand what is read aloud.

In poetry, the *appearance of the text on the page* is important, since in oral reading there is a tendency to stress the last word on a line and to pause momentarily before going to the next line, especially if the second line is indented. Compare the three following examples, where the lines of the same text have been broken improperly (a) and properly (b):

1. (a) He brought me out into a broad
          place.
   (b) He brought me out
          into a broad place.

2. (a) With the loyal you show yourself
          loyal.
   (b) With the loyal
          you show yourself loyal.

3. (a) The Lord my God lights up
          my darkness.
   (b) The Lord my God
          lights up my darkness.

No fault is to be found with the translation itself. Yet there is a significant difference in the *appearance* of the text on the page, because the lines on the right have been *measured,* in order to prevent unfortunate runovers. In this form, the text not only looks better on the page, but it is easier to read and memorize, and it avoids such disastrous combinations as "He brought me out into a broad" or "With the loyal you show yourself" or "The Lord my God lights up." Moreover, both formats require exactly the same amount of lines.

The first translation in the history of the English Bible to develop a text with measured poetry lines is the Contemporary English Version, in which the translators have consciously created a text that will not suffer from unfortunate line breaks when published in double columns. *Accuracy* is the main concern of translators, but it must be realized that in the translation of biblical poetry, what the reader *sees* is what will be *said,* and what others will *hear.* This means that lines improperly broken can easily lead to a misunderstanding of the text, especially for those who must depend upon *hearing* the Scriptures read.

Hebrew poetry has its own systems of sound, rhyme, and rhythm, as well as a *form* that involves much repetition. It is impossible in English to retain the sounds, rhymes, and rhythms of the Hebrew text, but traditional translations have attempted to reproduce the frequent repetition, in which a second line will repeat or expand, either negatively or positively, the thoughts of the previous line. However, this repetition is often ineffective for those English speakers who are unaccustomed to the poetic style of the biblical authors. And so, the translators of the Contemporary English Version have followed the example of Martin Luther in the translation of poetry:

> Whoever would speak German *must not use Hebrew style.* Rather he must see to it—once he understands the Hebrew author—that he concentrates on the *sense* of the text, asking himself, "Pray tell, what do the Germans say in such a situation?" Once he has the German words to serve his purpose, let him drop the Hebrew words and *express the meaning freely* in the best German he knows.

The qualities that many critics value most in modern poetry are effortless *economy* and *exactness* of language. It is hoped that readers will discover similar features in the poetry of the Contemporary English Version, which strives for beauty and dignity, as much as for accuracy and clarity. In this translation, the poetry often requires fewer lines than do traditional translations, but the *integrity, intent,* and *impact* of the original are consistently maintained. Note, for example, the rendering of Job 38.14, 15:

> Early dawn outlines the hills
> like stitches on clothing
> or sketches on clay.
> But its light is too much
> for those who are evil,
> and their power is broken.

In everyday speech, "gender generic" or "inclusive" language is used, because it sounds most natural to people today. This means that where the biblical languages require masculine nouns or pronouns when both men and women are intended, this intention must be reflected in translation, though the English *form* may be very different from that of the original. The Greek text of Matthew 16.24 is literally, "If anyone wants to follow me, *he* must deny *himself* and take up *his* cross and follow me." The Contemporary English Version shifts to a form which is still accurate, and at the same time more effective in English: "If any of *you* want to be my followers, *you* must forget about *yourself. You* must take up *your* cross and follow me."

Variety of translations is profitable

The translators of the King James Version said, "... variety of translations is profitable for the finding out of the sense of the Scriptures" and "We affirm and avow that the very meanest translation of the Bible in English, set forth by men of our profession…contains the Word of God, nay is the Word of God." They even stated, "No cause therefore why the Word translated should be denied to be the Word, or forbidden to be current, notwithstanding that some imperfections and blemishes may be noted in the setting forth of it."

Each English translation is, in its own right, the Word of God, yet each translation serves to meet the needs of a different audience. In this regard, the Contemporary English Version should be considered a *companion*—the *mission* arm—of traditional translations, because it takes seriously the words of the apostle Paul that "faith comes by *hearing*."

It has pleased God in his divine providence

Translating the Bible may be compared to living the life of faith. God has not given us all the answers for our pilgrim journey, but we have been provided with all that we need to know in order to be saved. As the translators of the King James Version observed:

> …it has pleased God in His divine providence here and there to scatter those words and sentences of that difficulty and doubtfulness, not in doctrinal points that concern salvation (for in such it has been vouched that the Scriptures are plain), but in matters of less moment, that fearfulness would better beseem us than confidence….
>
> For as it is a fault of incredulity, to doubt of those things that are evident; so to determine of such things that the Spirit of God has left (even

in the mind of the judicious) questionable, can be no less than presumption.

Bible translators do not have the privilege and luxury of working from the original manuscripts of either the Old or New Testament. Indeed, there are numerous difficult passages where decisions must be made concerning what word or words actually belong in the text, and what these words may, in fact, mean. At such places, the best a translator can do is to give what seems to be one possible meaning for the difficult text and to indicate this by a note, which was also what the King James translators did: "...so diversity of signification and sense in the margin, where the text is not clear, must needs be good; yea, is necessary, as we are persuaded." Fortunately, these "words and sentences of that difficulty and doubtfulness" do not in any way leave unclear the central message of the Bible or any of its major doctrines.

Having and using as great helps as were needful

The translators of the Contemporary English Version have not created new or novel interpretations of the text. Rather, it was their goal to express mainstream interpretations of the text in current, everyday English. To do so required *listening* carefully to each word of the biblical text, to the way in which English is spoken today, to the remarks of their reviewers, and especially to the Spirit of God. Once again the comments of the translators of the King James Version are appropriate:

Neither did we think much to consult the translators or commentators ... but neither did we disdain to revise that which we had done, and to bring to the anvil that which we had hammered; but having and using as great helps as were needful, and fearing no reproach for slowness, nor coveting praise for expedition, we have at the length, through the good hand of the Lord upon us, brought forth the work to that pass that you see.

Accordingly, the translators of the Contemporary English Version are indebted to all translators and biblical scholars who have gone before them and have made it possible to understand something of the languages, cultures, and history of biblical times. And, together with the apostle Paul, they confess: *We don't have the right to claim that we have done anything on our own. God gives us what it takes to do all that we do.* (2 Corinthians 3.5)

> *Offer praise to God our Savior*
> *because of our Lord Jesus Christ!*
> (Jude 24 and 25)

About the New Testament

In the first century A.D., Christians and Jews used the same Scriptures, which Christians later called the Old Testament. Both of these communities of faith usually used the Scriptures in a Greek translation (called the Septuagint) instead of in the original languages of Hebrew and Aramaic. This collection of sacred writings in Greek was the Bible of the early Christians. They found proof in these writings that Jesus was the Messiah and the Son of God, and they also found there how God wanted them to live.

Later in the first century, Christians started writing the books that would become the New Testament. These were the books about the life and teaching of Jesus (called Gospels), the letters of Paul and others, and the books of the Acts of the Apostles and Revelation. All of these were written in Greek, which was a language that people all over the Roman empire could understand. By the second century, these books were widely used by Christians for preaching, teaching, worshipping, and telling about their faith.

The writings of the New Testament are arranged in an order that gives the greatest value to the four books (Gospels) about Jesus, since they tell about his life and teaching, his miracles, his saving death on a cross, and his rising to life. These four Gospels (Matthew, Mark, Luke, and John) take up almost half of the New Testament, which is another reason why they are placed first.

The Acts of the Apostles follows the four Gospels. It actually continues the Gospel of Luke and shows the connection between the ministry of Jesus and the mission of the early church. Acts also shows how the followers of Jesus answered the question of whether Gentiles could also become Christians.

The letters of Paul follow next, and they are arranged roughly in order of their length (from Romans to Philemon). Most of these letters were written to churches Paul had started, and in them he deals with problems that had come up. Paul's letters are then followed by a group of writings called known as the "general letters", because they are mostly addressed to a general audience and were to be circulated to other followers. These letters are also arranged roughly in order of their length (from Hebrews to 3 John and Jude).

Revelation is the last book in the New Testament, and it was written to give hope and encouragement to Christians who were suffering because of their faith. It is also a prophecy and contains visions of how God will punish evil people and reward his faithful followers.

The New Testament is the world's most widely read book! More than 70 million copies are printed throughout the world each year, and the complete New Testament has been translated into more than eight hundred languages.

How can a book that is almost two thousand years old be in such demand and influence so many lives today? Why are people so interested in a young

Jewish carpenter named Jesus, who lived his short life without going more than seventy miles from the small village where he was born? The New Testament is in demand because it tells the good news about Jesus Christ! And this good news is God's powerful way of saving *everyone* who has faith in Jesus. In the New Testament we learn that God is kind and that he loved the people of this world so much that he sent Jesus Christ into the world to save us all.

For these reasons, and many more, people keep coming to the New Testament for the light and power it gives for daily living. Jesus promised that God's Spirit would always guide them to understand the message of the Scriptures. And so, in the New Testament we are not reading dead words from the past. Here we meet Jesus Christ, the living Word of God.

NEW TESTAMENT
AND PSALMS

Contents

Contents

Matthew Tells the Good News

The Sermon on the Mount (5.1–7.28), the Lord's Prayer (6.9-13), and the Golden Rule (7.12: "Treat others as you want them to treat you") are all in this book. It is perhaps the best known and the most quoted of all the books that have ever been written about Jesus. That is one reason why Matthew was placed first among the four books about Jesus called Gospels.

One of the most important ideas found here is that God expects his people to obey him, and this is what is meant by the Greek word that appears in many translations as righteousness. It is used seven times by Matthew, but only once by Luke, and not at all by Mark. So it is an important clue to much of what Matthew wants his readers to understand about the teaching of Jesus.

Jesus first uses this word at his own baptism, when he tells John the Baptist, "We must do all that God wants us to do" (3.15). Then, during his Sermon on the Mount, he speaks five more times of what God's people must do to obey him (5.6, 10, 20; 6.1, 33). And finally, he reminds the chief priests and leaders of the people, "John the Baptist showed you how to do right" (21.32).

Matthew wanted to provide for the people of his time a record of Jesus' message and ministry. It is clear that the Old Testament Scriptures were very important to these people. And Matthew never fails to

1

show when these texts point to the coming of Jesus as the Messiah sent from God. Matthew wrote this book to make sure Christians knew that their faith in Jesus as the Messiah was well anchored in the Old Testament Scriptures, and to help them grow in faith.

Matthew ends his story with the words of Jesus to his followers, which tell what they are to do after he leaves them:

I have been given all authority in heaven and on earth! Go to the people of all nations and make them my disciples. Baptize them in the name of the Father, the Son, and the Holy Spirit, and teach them to do everything I have told you. I will be with you always, even until the end of the world. (28.18b-20)

A QUICK LOOK AT THIS BOOK

The Ancestors of Jesus
(Luke 3.23-38)

1 Jesus Christ came from the family of King David and also from the family of Abraham. And this is a list of his ancestors. 2-6aFrom Abraham to King David, his ancestors were:

Abraham, Isaac, Jacob, Judah and his brothers (Judah's sons were Perez and Zerah, and their mother was Tamar), Hezron;

Ram, Amminadab, Nahshon, Salmon, Boaz (his mother was Rahab), Obed (his mother was Ruth), Jesse, and King David.

6b-11 From David to the time of the exile in Babylonia, the ancestors of Jesus were:

David, Solomon (his mother had been Uriah's wife), Rehoboam, Abijah, Asa, Jehoshaphat, Jehoram;

Uzziah, Jotham, Ahaz, Hezekiah, Manasseh, Amon, Josiah, and Jehoiachin and his brothers.

12-16 From the exile to the birth of Jesus, his ancestors were:

Jehoiachin, Shealtiel, Zerubbabel, Abiud, Eliakim, Azor, Zadok, Achim;

Eliud, Eleazar, Matthan, Jacob, and Joseph, the husband of Mary, the mother of Jesus, who is called the Messiah.

17 There were fourteen generations from Abraham to David. There were also fourteen from David to the exile in Babylonia and fourteen more to the birth of the Messiah.

The Birth of Jesus
(Luke 2.1-7)

18 This is how Jesus Christ was born. A young woman named Mary was engaged to Joseph from King David's family. But before they were married, she learned that she was going to have a baby by God's Holy Spirit. [19] Joseph was a good man[a] and did not want to embarrass Mary in front of everyone. So he decided to quietly call off the wedding.

---

[a] good man: Or "kind man," or "man who always did the right thing."

20 While Joseph was thinking about this, an angel from the Lord came to him in a dream. The angel said, "Joseph, the baby that Mary will have is from the Holy Spirit. Go ahead and marry her. 21 Then after her baby is born, name him Jesus,[b] because he will save his people from their sins."

22 So the Lord's promise came true, just as the prophet had said, 23 "A virgin will have a baby boy, and he will be called Immanuel," which means "God is with us."

24 After Joseph woke up, he and Mary were soon married, just as the Lord's angel had told him to do. 25 But they did not sleep together before her baby was born. Then Joseph named him Jesus.

The Wise Men

2 When Jesus was born in the village of Bethlehem in Judea, Herod was king. During this time some wise men[c] from the east came to Jerusalem 2 and said, "Where is the child born to be king of the Jews? We saw his star in the east[d] and have come to worship him."

3 When King Herod heard about this, he was worried, and so was everyone else in Jerusalem. 4 Herod brought together the chief priests and the teachers of the Law of Moses and asked them, "Where will the Messiah be born?"

5 They told him, "He will be born in Bethlehem, just as the prophet wrote,

---

[b] name him Jesus: In Hebrew the name "Jesus" means "the Lord saves."

[c] wise men: People famous for studying the stars.

[d] his star in the east: Or "his star rise."

6 'Bethlehem in the land of Judea,
        you are very important
        among the towns of Judea.
    From your town will come a leader,
        who will be like a shepherd
        for my people Israel.'"

7 Herod secretly called in the wise men and asked them when they had first seen the star. 8He told them, "Go to Bethlehem and search carefully for the child. As soon as you find him, let me know. I want to go and worship him too."

9 The wise men listened to what the king said and then left. And the star they had seen in the east went on ahead of them until it stopped over the place where the child was. 10They were thrilled and excited to see the star.

11 When the men went into the house and saw the child with Mary, his mother, they knelt down and worshiped him. They took out their gifts of gold, frankincense, and myrrh*e* and gave them to him. 12Later they were warned in a dream not to return to Herod, and they went back home by another road.

The Escape to Egypt

13 After the wise men had gone, an angel from the Lord appeared to Joseph in a dream and said, "Get up! Hurry and take the child and his mother to Egypt!

---

e frankincense, and myrrh: Frankincense was a valuable powder that was burned to make a sweet smell. Myrrh was a valuable sweet-smelling powder often used in perfume.

Stay there until I tell you to return, because Herod is looking for the child and wants to kill him."

14 That night, Joseph got up and took his wife and the child to Egypt, 15where they stayed until Herod died. So the Lord's promise came true, just as the prophet had said, "I called my son out of Egypt."

The Killing of the Children

16 When Herod found out that the wise men from the east had tricked him, he was very angry. He gave orders for his men to kill all the boys who lived in or near Bethlehem and were two years old and younger. This was based on what he had learned from the wise men.

17 So the Lord's promise came true, just as the prophet Jeremiah had said,

18 "In Ramah a voice was heard
     crying and weeping loudly.
Rachel was mourning for her children,
     and she refused to be comforted,
     because they were dead."

The Return from Egypt

19 After King Herod died, an angel from the Lord appeared in a dream to Joseph while he was still in Egypt. 20The angel said, "Get up and take the child and his mother back to Israel. The people who wanted to kill him are now dead."

21 Joseph got up and left with them for Israel. 22But when he heard that Herod's son Archelaus was now ruler of Judea, he was afraid to go there. Then in a dream he was told to go to Galilee, 23and they went to live there in the town of Nazareth. So the Lord's

promise came true, just as the prophet had said, "He will be called a Nazarene." *f*

The Preaching of John the Baptist
(Mark 1.1-8; Luke 3.1-18; John 1.19-28)

3 Years later, John the Baptist started preaching in the desert of Judea. ²He said, "Turn back to God! The kingdom of heaven *g* will soon be here." *h*

3 John was the one the prophet Isaiah was talking about, when he said,

"In the desert someone is shouting,
    'Get the road ready for the Lord!
    Make a straight path for him.' "

4 John wore clothes made of camel's hair. He had a leather strap around his waist and ate grasshoppers and wild honey.

5 From Jerusalem and all Judea and from the Jordan River Valley crowds of people went to John. ⁶They told how sorry they were for their sins, and he baptized them in the river.

7 Many Pharisees and Sadducees also came to be baptized. But John said to them:

You bunch of snakes! Who warned you to run from the coming judgment? ⁸Do something to show that you have really given up your sins. ⁹And don't start telling yourselves that you

---

f *He will be called a Nazarene*: The prophet who said this is not known.

g *kingdom of heaven*: In the Gospel of Matthew "kingdom of heaven" is used with the same meaning as "God's kingdom" in Mark and Luke.

h *will soon be here*: Or "is already here."

belong to Abraham's family. I tell you that God can turn these stones into children for Abraham. ¹⁰An ax is ready to cut the trees down at their roots. Any tree that doesn't produce good fruit will be chopped down and thrown into a fire.

11 I baptize you with water so that you will give up your sins.ⁱ But someone more powerful is going to come, and I am not good enough even to carry his sandals.ʲ He will baptize you with the Holy Spirit and with fire. ¹²His threshing fork is in his hand, and he is ready to separate the wheat from the husks.ᵏ He will store the wheat in a barn and burn the husks in a fire that never goes out.

The Baptism of Jesus
(Mark 1.9-11; Luke 3.21,22)

13 Jesus left Galilee and went to the Jordan River to be baptized by John. ¹⁴But John kept objecting and said, "I ought to be baptized by you. Why have you come to me?"

15 Jesus answered, "For now this is how it should be, because we must do all that God wants us to do." Then John agreed.

ⁱ *so that you will give up your sins*: Or "because you have given up your sins."

ʲ *carry his sandals*: This was one of the duties of a slave.

ᵏ *His threshing fork is in his hand, and he is ready to separate the wheat from the husks*: After Jewish farmers had trampled out the grain, they used a large fork to pitch the grain and the husks into the air. Wind would blow away the light husks, and the grain would fall back to the ground, where it could be gathered up.

16 So Jesus was baptized. And as soon as he came out of the water, the sky opened, and he saw the Spirit of God coming down on him like a dove. 17Then a voice from heaven said, "This is my own dear Son, and I am pleased with him."

Jesus and the Devil
(Mark 1.12, 13; Luke 4.1-13)

4 The Holy Spirit led Jesus into the desert, so that the devil could test him. 2After Jesus had gone without eating[1] for forty days and nights, he was very hungry. 3Then the devil came to him and said, "If you are God's Son, tell these stones to turn into bread."

4 Jesus answered, "The Scriptures say:

> 'No one can live only on food.
> People need every word
>   that God has spoken.'"

5 Next, the devil took Jesus to the holy city and had him stand on the highest part of the temple. 6The devil said, "If you are God's Son, jump off. The Scriptures say:

> 'God will give his angels orders about you.
> They will catch you in their arms,
>   and you won't hurt your feet on the stones.'"

7 Jesus answered, "The Scriptures also say, 'Don't try to test the Lord your God!'"

8 Finally, the devil took Jesus up on a very high mountain and showed him all the kingdoms on earth

---

[1] *went without eating*: The Jewish people sometimes went without eating (also called "fasting") to show their love for God or to show sorrow for their sins.

and their power. 9The devil said to him, "I will give all this to you, if you will bow down and worship me."

10 Jesus answered, "Go away Satan! The Scriptures say:

> 'Worship the Lord your God
> and serve only him.'"

11 Then the devil left Jesus, and angels came to help him.

Jesus Begins His Work
(Mark 1.14, 15; Luke 4.14, 15)

12 When Jesus heard that John had been put in prison, he went to Galilee. 13But instead of staying in Nazareth, Jesus moved to Capernaum. This town was beside Lake Galilee in the territory of Zebulun and Naphtali.*m* 14So God's promise came true, just as the prophet Isaiah had said,

> 15 "Listen, lands of Zebulun and Naphtali,
> lands along the road to the sea
> and east of the Jordan!
> Listen Galilee, land of the Gentiles!
> 16 Although your people live in darkness,
> they will see a bright light.
> Although they live in the shadow of death,
> a light will shine on them."

17 Then Jesus started preaching, "Turn back to God! The kingdom of heaven will soon be here."*n*

---

m *Zebulun and Naphtali*: In Old Testament times these tribes were in northern Palestine, and in New Testament times many Gentiles lived where these tribes had once been.

n *The kingdom of heaven will soon be here*: See the two notes at 3.2.

Jesus Chooses Four Fishermen
(Mark 1.16-20; Luke 5.1-11)

18 While Jesus was walking along the shore of Lake Galilee, he saw two brothers. One was Simon, also known as Peter, and the other was Andrew. They were fishermen, and they were casting their net into the lake. 19Jesus said to them, "Come with me! I will teach you how to bring in people instead of fish." 20Right then the two brothers dropped their nets and went with him.

21 Jesus walked on until he saw James and John, the sons of Zebedee. They were in a boat with their father, mending their nets. Jesus asked them to come with him too. 22Right away they left the boat and their father and went with Jesus.

Jesus Teaches, Preaches, and Heals
(Luke 6.17-19)

23 Jesus went all over Galilee, teaching in the Jewish meeting places and preaching the good news about God's kingdom. He also healed every kind of disease and sickness. 24News about him spread all over Syria, and people with every kind of sickness or disease were brought to him. Some of them had a lot of demons in them, others were thought to be crazy,*o* and still others could not walk. But Jesus healed them all.

25 Large crowds followed Jesus from Galilee and the region around the ten cities known as

---

o thought to be crazy: In ancient times people with epilepsy were thought to be crazy.

Decapolis.*p* They also came from Jerusalem, Judea, and from across the Jordan River.

The Sermon on the Mount

5 When Jesus saw the crowds, he went up on the side of a mountain and sat down.*q*

Blessings

(Luke 6.20-23)

Jesus' disciples gathered around him, ²and he taught them:

³ God blesses those people
who depend only on him.
They belong to the kingdom of heaven!*r*
⁴ God blesses those people
who grieve.
They will find comfort!
⁵ God blesses those people
who are humble.
The earth will belong to them!
⁶ God blesses those people
who want to obey him*s*
more than to eat or drink.
They will be given what they want!

---

p the ten cities known as Decapolis: A group of ten cities east of Samaria and Galilee, where the people followed the Greek way of life.

q sat down: Teachers in the ancient world, including Jewish teachers, usually sat down when they taught.

r They belong to the kingdom of heaven: Or "The kingdom of heaven belongs to them."

s who want to obey him: Or "who want to do right" or "who want everyone to be treated right."

7 God blesses those people
who are merciful.
They will be treated with mercy!

8 God blesses those people
whose hearts are pure.
They will see him!

9 God blesses those people
who make peace.
They will be called his children!

10 God blesses those people
who are treated badly for doing right.
They belong to the kingdom of heaven.[1]

11 God will bless you when people insult you, mistreat you, and tell all kinds of evil lies about you because of me. 12Be happy and excited! You will have a great reward in heaven. People did these same things to the prophets who lived long ago.

Salt and Light
(Mark 9.50; Luke 14.34,35)

13 You are like salt for everyone on earth. But if salt no longer tastes like salt, how can it make food salty? All it is good for is to be thrown out and walked on.

14 You are like light for the whole world. A city built on top of a hill cannot be hidden, 15and no one would light a lamp and put it under a clay pot. A lamp is placed on a lampstand, where it can give light to everyone in the house. 16Make your light shine, so that others will see

---

[1] *They belong to the kingdom of heaven*: See the note at 5.3.

the good that you do and will praise your Father
in heaven.

The Law of Moses

17 Don't suppose that I came to do away
with the Law and the Prophets.*u* I did not come
to do away with them, but to give them their full
meaning. 18 Heaven and earth may disappear.
But I promise you that not even a period or
comma will ever disappear from the Law.
Everything written in it must happen.

19 If you reject even the least important command in the Law and teach others to do the
same, you will be the least important person in
the kingdom of heaven. But if you obey and
teach others its commands, you will have an
important place in the kingdom. 20 You must
obey God's commands better than the Pharisees
and the teachers of the Law obey them. If you
don't, I promise you that you will never get into
the kingdom of heaven.

Anger

21 You know that our ancestors were told, "Do
not murder" and "A murderer must be brought
to trial." 22 But I promise you that if you are
angry with someone,*v* you will have to stand
trial. If you call someone a fool, you will be

---

u the Law and the Prophets: The Jewish Scriptures, that is,
the Old Testament.
v someone: In verses 22-24 the Greek text has "brother,"
which may refer to people in general or to other followers.

taken to court. And if you say that someone is worthless, you will be in danger of the fires of hell.

23 So if you are about to place your gift on the altar and remember that someone is angry with you, 24leave your gift there in front of the altar. Make peace with that person, then come back and offer your gift to God.

25 Before you are dragged into court, make friends with the person who has accused you of doing wrong. If you don't, you will be handed over to the judge and then to the officer who will put you in jail. 26I promise you that you will not get out until you have paid the last cent you owe.

Marriage

27 You know the commandment which says, "Be faithful in marriage." 28But I tell you that if you look at another woman and want her, you are already unfaithful in your thoughts. 29If your right eye causes you to sin, poke it out and throw it away. It is better to lose one part of your body, than for your whole body to end up in hell. 30If your right hand causes you to sin, chop it off and throw it away! It is better to lose one part of your body, than for your whole body to be thrown into hell.

Divorce
(Matthew 19.9; Mark 10.11,12; Luke 16.18)

31 You have been taught that a man who divorces his wife must write out divorce papers

for her.ᵂ ³²But I tell you not to divorce your wife
unless she has committed some terrible sexual
sin.ˣ If you divorce her, you will cause her to be
unfaithful, just as any man who marries her is
guilty of taking another man's wife.

Promises

33 You know that our ancestors were told,
"Don't use the Lord's name to make a promise
unless you are going to keep it." ³⁴But I tell you
not to swear by anything when you make a
promise! Heaven is God's throne, so don't swear
by heaven. ³⁵The earth is God's footstool, so
don't swear by the earth. Jerusalem is the city of
the great king, so don't swear by it. ³⁶Don't
swear by your own head. You cannot make one
hair white or black. ³⁷When you make a
promise, say only "Yes" or "No." Anything else
comes from the devil.

Revenge
(Luke 6.29,30)

38 You know that you have been taught, "An
eye for an eye and a tooth for a tooth." ³⁹But I

ᵂ *write out divorce papers for her*: Jewish men could
divorce their wives, but the women could not divorce
their husbands. The purpose of writing these papers was
to make it harder for a man to divorce his wife. Before
this law was made, all a man had to do was to send his
wife away and say that she was no longer his wife.

ˣ *some terrible sexual sin*: This probably refers to the laws
about the wrong kinds of marriages that are forbidden in
Leviticus 18.6-18 or to some serious sexual sin.

tell you not to try to get even with a person who has done something to you. When someone slaps your right cheek,[y] turn and let that person slap your other cheek. 40If someone sues you for your shirt, give up your coat as well. 41If a soldier forces you to carry his pack one mile, carry it two miles.[z] 42When people ask you for something, give it to them. When they want to borrow money, lend it to them.

Love
(Luke 6.27,28,32-36)

43 You have heard people say, "Love your neighbors and hate your enemies." 44But I tell you to love your enemies and pray for anyone who mistreats you. 45Then you will be acting like your Father in heaven. He makes the sun rise on both good and bad people. And he sends rain for the ones who do right and for the ones who do wrong. 46If you love only those people who love you, will God reward you for that? Even tax collectors[a] love their friends. 47If you greet only your friends, what's so great about that? Don't even unbelievers do that? 48But you must always act like your Father in heaven.

---

[y] *right cheek*: A slap on the right cheek was a bad insult.

[z] *two miles*: A Roman soldier had the right to force a person to carry his pack as far as one mile.

[a] *tax collectors*: These were usually Jewish people who paid the Romans for the right to collect taxes. They were hated by other Jews who thought of them as traitors to their country and to their religion.

Giving

6 When you do good deeds, don't try to show off. If you do, you won't get a reward from your Father in heaven.

2 When you give to the poor, don't blow a loud horn. That's what show-offs do in the meeting places and on the street corners, because they are always looking for praise. I can assure you that they already have their reward.

3 When you give to the poor, don't let anyone know about it.[b] 4Then your gift will be given in secret. Your Father knows what is done in secret, and he will reward you.

Prayer
(Luke 11.2-4)

5 When you pray, don't be like those show-offs who love to stand up and pray in the meeting places and on the street corners. They do this just to look good. I can assure you that they already have their reward.

6 When you pray, go into a room alone and close the door. Pray to your Father in private. He knows what is done in private, and he will reward you.

7 When you pray, don't talk on and on as people do who don't know God. They think God likes to hear long prayers. 8Don't be like them. Your Father knows what you need before you ask.

---

[b] *don't let anyone know about it*: The Greek text has, "Don't let your left hand know what your right hand is doing."

9 You should pray like this:
> Our Father in heaven,
>   help us to honor your name.
> 10 Come and set up your kingdom,
>   so that everyone on earth will obey you,
>   as you are obeyed in heaven.
> 11 Give us our food for today.[c]
> 12 Forgive us for doing wrong,
>   as we forgive others.
> 13 Keep us from being tempted
>   and protect us from evil.[d]

14 If you forgive others for the wrongs they do to you, your Father in heaven will forgive you. 15But if you don't forgive others, your Father will not forgive your sins.

Worshiping God by Going without Eating

16 When you go without eating,[e] don't try to look gloomy as those show-offs do when they go without eating. I can assure you that they already have their reward. 17Instead, comb your hair and wash your face. 18Then others won't know that you are going without eating. But your Father sees what is done in private, and he will reward you.

---

c *our food for today*: Or "the food that we need" or "our food for the coming day."

d *evil*: Or "the evil one," that is, the devil. Some manuscripts add, "The kingdom, the power, and the glory are yours forever. Amen."

e *without eating*: See the note at 4.2.

Treasures in Heaven
(Luke 12.33,34)

19 Don't store up treasures on earth! Moths and rust can destroy them, and thieves can break in and steal them. 20Instead, store up your treasures in heaven, where moths and rust cannot destroy them, and thieves cannot break in and steal them. 21Your heart will always be where your treasure is.

Light
(Luke 11.34-36)

22 Your eyes are like a window for your body. When they are good, you have all the light you need. 23But when your eyes are bad, everything is dark. If the light inside you is dark, you surely are in the dark.

Money
(Luke 16.13)

24 You cannot be the slave of two masters! You will like one more than the other or be more loyal to one than the other. You cannot serve both God and money.

Worry
(Luke 12.22-31)

25 I tell you not to worry about your life. Don't worry about having something to eat, drink, or wear. Isn't life more than food or clothing? 26Look at the birds in the sky! They don't plant or harvest. They don't even store grain in

barns. Yet your Father in heaven takes care of them. Aren't you worth more than birds?

27 Can worry make you live longer?[f] 28 Why worry about clothes? Look how the wild flowers grow. They don't work hard to make their clothes. 29 But I tell you that Solomon with all his wealth[g] wasn't as well clothed as one of them. 30 God gives such beauty to everything that grows in the fields, even though it is here today and thrown into a fire tomorrow. He will surely do even more for you! Why do you have such little faith?

31 Don't worry and ask yourselves, "Will we have anything to eat? Will we have anything to drink? Will we have any clothes to wear?" 32 Only people who don't know God are always worrying about such things. Your Father in heaven knows that you need all of these. 33 But more than anything else, put God's work first and do what he wants. Then the other things will be yours as well.

34 Don't worry about tomorrow. It will take care of itself. You have enough to worry about today.

Judging Others
(Luke 6.37,38,41,42)

7 Don't condemn others, and God won't condemn you. 2 God will be as hard on you as you are on others! He will treat you exactly as you treat them.

---

[f] *live longer*: Or "grow taller."

[g] *Solomon with all his wealth*: The Jewish people thought that Solomon was the richest person who had ever lived.

3 You can see the speck in your friend's eye, but you don't notice the log in your own eye. 4How can you say, "My friend, let me take the speck out of your eye," when you don't see the log in your own eye? 5You're nothing but show-offs! First, take the log out of your own eye. Then you can see how to take the speck out of your friend's eye.

6 Don't give to dogs what belongs to God. They will only turn and attack you. Don't throw pearls down in front of pigs. They will trample all over them.

Ask, Search, Knock
(Luke 11.9-13)

7 Ask, and you will receive. Search, and you will find. Knock, and the door will be opened for you. 8Everyone who asks will receive. Everyone who searches will find. And the door will be opened for everyone who knocks. 9Would any of you give your hungry child a stone, if the child asked for some bread? 10Would you give your child a snake if the child asked for a fish? 11As bad as you are, you still know how to give good gifts to your children. But your heavenly Father is even more ready to give good things to people who ask.

12 Treat others as you want them to treat you. This is what the Law and the Prophets[h] are all about.

---

[h] *the Law and the Prophets*: See the note at 5.17.

The Narrow Gate
(Luke 13.24)

13 Go in through the narrow gate. The gate to destruction is wide, and the road that leads there is easy to follow. A lot of people go through that gate. 14But the gate to life is very narrow. The road that leads there is so hard to follow that only a few people find it.

A Tree and Its Fruit
(Luke 6.43-45)

15 Watch out for false prophets! They dress up like sheep, but inside they are wolves who have come to attack you. 16You can tell what they are by what they do. No one picks grapes or figs from thornbushes. 17A good tree produces good fruit, and a bad tree produces bad fruit. 18A good tree cannot produce bad fruit, and a bad tree cannot produce good fruit. 19Every tree that produces bad fruit will be chopped down and burned. 20You can tell who the false prophets are by their deeds.

A Warning
(Luke 13.26,27)

21 Not everyone who calls me their Lord will get into the kingdom of heaven. Only the ones who obey my Father in heaven will get in. 22On the day of judgment many will call me their Lord. They will say, "We preached in your name, and in your name we forced out demons and worked many miracles." 23But I will tell

them, "I will have nothing to do with you! Get out of my sight, you evil people!"

Two Builders
(Luke 6.47-49)

24 Anyone who hears and obeys these teachings of mine is like a wise person who built a house on solid rock. 25Rain poured down, rivers flooded, and winds beat against that house. But it did not fall, because it was built on solid rock.

26 Anyone who hears my teachings and doesn't obey them is like a foolish person who built a house on sand. 27The rain poured down, the rivers flooded, and the winds blew and beat against that house. Finally, it fell with a crash.

28 When Jesus finished speaking, the crowds were surprised at his teaching. 29He taught them like someone with authority, and not like their teachers of the Law of Moses.

Jesus Heals a Man
(Mark 1.40-45; Luke 5.12-16)

8 As Jesus came down the mountain, he was followed by large crowds. 2Suddenly a man with leprosy*i* came and knelt in front of Jesus. He said, "Lord, you have the power to make me well, if only you wanted to."

3 Jesus put his hand on the man and said, "I want to! Now you are well." At once the man's leprosy disappeared. 4Jesus told him, "Don't tell anyone about

---

i *leprosy:* In biblical times the word "leprosy" was used for many different kinds of skin diseases.

this, but go and show the priest that you are well. Then take a gift to the temple just as Moses commanded, and everyone will know that you have been healed."[j]

Jesus Heals an Army Officer's Servant
(Luke 7.1-10; John 4.43-54)

5 When Jesus was going into the town of Capernaum, an army officer came up to him and said, 6"Lord, my servant is at home in such terrible pain that he can't even move."

7 "I will go and heal him," Jesus replied.

8 But the officer said, "Lord, I'm not good enough for you to come into my house. Just give the order, and my servant will get well. 9I have officers who give orders to me, and I have soldiers who take orders from me. I can say to one of them, 'Go!' and he goes. I can say to another, 'Come!' and he comes. I can say to my servant, 'Do this!' and he will do it."

10 When Jesus heard this, he was so surprised that he turned and said to the crowd following him, "I tell you that in all of Israel I've never found anyone with this much faith! 11Many people will come from everywhere to enjoy the feast in the kingdom of heaven with Abraham, Isaac, and Jacob. 12But the ones who should have been in the kingdom will be

---

j *everyone will know that you have been healed*: People with leprosy had to be examined by a priest and told that they were well (that is, "clean") before they could once again live a normal life in the Jewish community. The gift that Moses commanded was the sacrifice of some lambs together with flour mixed with olive oil.

thrown out into the dark. They will cry and grit their teeth in pain."

13 Then Jesus said to the officer, "You may go home now. Your faith has made it happen."

Right then his servant was healed.

Jesus Heals Many People

(Mark 1.29-34; Luke 4.38-41)

14 Jesus went to the home of Peter, where he found that Peter's mother-in-law was sick in bed with fever. 15He took her by the hand, and the fever left her. Then she got up and served Jesus a meal.

16 That evening many people with demons in them were brought to Jesus. And with only a word he forced out the evil spirits and healed everyone who was sick. 17So God's promise came true, just as the prophet Isaiah had said,

"He healed our diseases
      and made us well."

Some Who Wanted To Go with Jesus

(Luke 9.57-62)

18 When Jesus saw the crowd,*k* he went across Lake Galilee. 19A teacher of the Law of Moses came up to him and said, "Teacher, I'll go anywhere with you!"

20 Jesus replied, "Foxes have dens, and birds have nests. But the Son of Man doesn't have a place to call his own."

21 Another disciple said to Jesus, "Lord, let me wait till I bury my father."

---

k saw the crowd: Some manuscripts have "large crowd."
  Others have "large crowds."

22 Jesus answered, "Come with me, and let the dead bury their dead."[l]

A Storm
(Mark 4.35-41; Luke 8.22-25)

23 After Jesus left in a boat with his disciples, 24a terrible storm suddenly struck the lake, and waves started splashing into their boat.

Jesus was sound asleep, 25so the disciples went over to him and woke him up. They said, "Lord, save us! We're going to drown!"

26 But Jesus replied, "Why are you so afraid? You surely don't have much faith." Then he got up and ordered the wind and the waves to calm down. And everything was calm.

27 The men in the boat were amazed and said, "Who is this? Even the wind and the waves obey him."

Two Men with Demons in Them
(Mark 5.1-20; Luke 8.26-39)

28 After Jesus had crossed the lake, he came to shore near the town of Gadara[m] and started down the road. Two men with demons in them came to him from the tombs.[n] They were so fierce that no one could travel that way. 29Suddenly they shouted,

---

[l] *let the dead bury their dead*: For the Jewish people a proper burial of their dead was a very important duty. But Jesus teaches that following him is even more important.

[m] *Gadara*: Some manuscripts have "Gergesa." Others have "Gerasa."

[n] *tombs*: It was thought that demons and evil spirits lived in tombs and in caves that were used for burying the dead.

"Jesus, Son of God, what do you want with us? Have you come to punish us before our time?"

30 Not far from there a large herd of pigs was feeding. 31So the demons begged Jesus, "If you force us out, please send us into those pigs!" 32Jesus told them to go, and they went out of the men and into the pigs. All at once the pigs rushed down the steep bank into the lake and drowned.

33 The people taking care of the pigs ran to the town and told everything, especially what had happened to the two men. 34Everyone in town came out to meet Jesus. When they saw him, they begged him to leave their part of the country.

Jesus Heals a Crippled Man
(Mark 2.1-12; Luke 5.17-26)

9 Jesus got into a boat and crossed back over to the town where he lived.*o* 2Some people soon brought to him a crippled man lying on a mat. When Jesus saw how much faith they had, he said to the crippled man, "My friend, don't worry! Your sins are forgiven."

3 Some teachers of the Law of Moses said to themselves, "Jesus must think he is God!"

4 But Jesus knew what was in their minds, and he said, "Why are you thinking such evil things? 5Is it easier for me to tell this crippled man that his sins are forgiven or to tell him to get up and walk? 6But I will show you that the Son of Man has the right to forgive sins here on earth." So Jesus said to the man, "Get up! Pick up your mat and go on home." 7The man got up

---

o *where he lived*: Capernaum (see 4.13).

and went home. ⁸When the crowds saw this, they were afraid*p* and praised God for giving such authority to people.

Jesus Chooses Matthew
(Mark 2.13-17; Luke 5.27-32)

9 As Jesus was leaving, he saw a tax collector*q* named Matthew sitting at the place for paying taxes. Jesus said to him, "Come with me." Matthew got up and went with him.

10 Later, Jesus and his disciples were having dinner at Matthew's house.*r* Many tax collectors and other sinners were also there. ¹¹Some Pharisees asked Jesus' disciples, "Why does your teacher eat with tax collectors and other sinners?"

12 Jesus heard them and answered, "Healthy people don't need a doctor, but sick people do. ¹³Go and learn what the Scriptures mean when they say, 'Instead of offering sacrifices to me, I want you to be merciful to others.' I didn't come to invite good people to be my followers. I came to invite sinners."

People Ask about Going without Eating
(Mark 2.18-22; Luke 5.33-39)

14 One day some followers of John the Baptist came and asked Jesus, "Why do we and the Pharisees often go without eating,*s* while your disciples never do?"

---

p afraid: Some manuscripts have "amazed."
q tax collector: See the note at 5.46.
r Matthew's house: Or "Jesus' house."
s without eating: See the note at 4.2.

15 Jesus answered:

The friends of a bridegroom don't go without eating while he is still with them. But the time will come when he will be taken from them. Then they will go without eating.

16 No one uses a new piece of cloth to patch old clothes. The patch would shrink and tear a bigger hole.

17 No one pours new wine into old wineskins. The wine would swell and burst the old skins.[t] Then the wine would be lost, and the skins would be ruined. New wine must be put into new wineskins. Both the skins and the wine will then be safe.

A Dying Girl and a Sick Woman

(Mark 5.21-43; Luke 8.40-56)

18 While Jesus was still speaking, an official came and knelt in front of him. The man said, "My daughter has just now died! Please come and place your hand on her. Then she will live again."

19 Jesus and his disciples got up and went with the man.

20 A woman who had been bleeding for twelve years came up behind Jesus and barely touched his clothes. 21 She had said to herself, "If I can just touch his clothes, I will get well."

22 Jesus turned. He saw the woman and said, "Don't worry! You are now well because of your faith." At that moment she was healed.

---

[t] *swell and burst the old skins*: While the juice from grapes was becoming wine, it would swell and stretch the skins in which it had been stored. If the skins were old and stiff, they would burst.

23 When Jesus went into the home of the official and saw the musicians and the crowd of mourners,[u] [24]he said, "Get out of here! The little girl isn't dead. She is just asleep." Everyone started laughing at Jesus. [25]But after the crowd had been sent out of the house, Jesus went to the girl's bedside. He took her by the hand and helped her up.

26 News about this spread all over that part of the country.

Jesus Heals Two Blind Men

27 As Jesus was walking along, two blind men began following him and shouting, "Son of David,[v] have pity on us!"

28 After Jesus had gone indoors, the two blind men came up to him. He asked them, "Do you believe I can make you well?"

"Yes, Lord," they answered.

29 Jesus touched their eyes and said, "Because of your faith, you will be healed." [30]They were able to see, and Jesus strictly warned them not to tell anyone about him. [31]But they left and talked about him to everyone in that part of the country.

Jesus Heals a Man Who Could Not Talk

32 As Jesus and his disciples were on their way, some people brought to him a man who could not

---

[u] *the crowd of mourners*: The Jewish people often hired mourners for funerals.

[v] *Son of David*: The Jewish people expected the Messiah to be from the family of King David, and for this reason the Messiah was often called the "Son of David."

talk because a demon was in him. [33] After Jesus had forced the demon out, the man started talking. The crowds were so amazed that they began saying, "Nothing like this has ever happened in Israel!"

34 But the Pharisees said, "The leader of the demons gives him the power to force out demons."

Jesus Has Pity on People

35 Jesus went to every town and village. He taught in their meeting places and preached the good news about God's kingdom. Jesus also healed every kind of disease and sickness. [36] When he saw the crowds, he felt sorry for them. They were confused and helpless, like sheep without a shepherd. [37] He said to his disciples, "A large crop is in the fields, but there are only a few workers. [38] Ask the Lord in charge of the harvest to send out workers to bring it in."

Jesus Chooses His Twelve Apostles
(Mark 3.13-19; Luke 6.12-16)

10 Jesus called together his twelve disciples. He gave them the power to force out evil spirits and to heal every kind of disease and sickness. [2] The first of the twelve apostles was Simon, better known as Peter. His brother Andrew was an apostle, and so were James and John, the two sons of Zebedee. [3] Philip, Bartholomew, Thomas, Matthew the tax collector,[w] James the son of Alphaeus, and Thaddaeus were also apostles. [4] The others were Simon, known

---

[w] *tax collector*: See the note at 5.46.

as the Eager One,^{x} and Judas Iscariot,^{y} who later betrayed Jesus.

Instructions for the Twelve Apostles
(Mark 6.7-13; Luke 9.1-6)

5 Jesus sent out the twelve apostles with these instructions:

Stay away from the Gentiles and don't go to any Samaritan town. ^{6}Go only to the people of Israel, because they are like a flock of lost sheep. ^{7}As you go, announce that the kingdom of heaven will soon be here.^{z} ^{8}Heal the sick, raise the dead to life, heal people who have leprosy,^{a} and force out demons. You received without paying, now give without being paid. ^{9}Don't take along any gold, silver, or copper coins. ^{10}And don't carry^b a traveling bag or an extra shirt or sandals or a walking stick.

Workers deserve their food. ^{11}So when you go to a town or a village, find someone worthy enough to have you as their guest and stay with

---

^{x} *known as the Eager One*: The Greek text has "Cananaean," which probably comes from a Hebrew word meaning "zealous" (see Luke 6.15). "Zealot" was the name later given to the members of a Jewish group that resisted and fought against the Romans.

^{y} *Iscariot*: This may mean "a man from Kerioth" (a place in Judea). But more probably it means "a man who was a liar" or "a man who was a betrayer."

^{z} *will soon be here*: Or "is already here."

^{a} *leprosy*: See the note at 8.2.

^{b} *Don't take along...don't carry*: Or "Don't accept...don't accept."

them until you leave. 12When you go to a home, give it your blessing of peace. 13If the home is deserving, let your blessing remain with them. But if the home isn't deserving, take back your blessing of peace. 14If someone won't welcome you or listen to your message, leave their home or town. And shake the dust from your feet at them.[c] 15I promise you that the day of judgment will be easier for the towns of Sodom and Gomorrah[d] than for that town.

Warning about Trouble
(Mark 13.9-13; Luke 21.12-17)

16 I am sending you like lambs into a pack of wolves. So be as wise as snakes and as innocent as doves. 17Watch out for people who will take you to court and have you beaten in their meeting places. 18Because of me, you will be dragged before rulers and kings to tell them and the Gentiles about your faith. 19But when someone arrests you, don't worry about what you will say or how you will say it. At that time you will be given the words to say. 20But you will not really be the one speaking. The Spirit from your Father will tell you what to say.

---

[c] shake the dust from your feet at them: This was a way of showing rejection (see Acts 13.51).

[d] Sodom and Gomorrah: During the time of Abraham the Lord destroyed these towns because the people there were so evil.

21 Brothers and sisters will betray one another and have each other put to death. Parents will betray their own children, and children will turn against their parents and have them killed. 22Everyone will hate you because of me. But if you remain faithful until the end, you will be saved. 23When people mistreat you in one town, hurry to another one. I promise you that before you have gone to all the towns of Israel, the Son of Man will come.

24 Disciples are not better than their teacher, and slaves are not better than their master. 25It is enough for disciples to be like their teacher and for slaves to be like their master. If people call the head of the family Satan, what will they say about the rest of the family?

The One To Fear
(Luke 12.2-7)

26 Don't be afraid of anyone! Everything that is hidden will be found out, and every secret will be known. 27Whatever I say to you in the dark, you must tell in the light. And you must announce from the housetops whatever I have whispered to you. 28Don't be afraid of people. They can kill you, but they cannot harm your soul. Instead, you should fear God who can destroy both your body and your soul in hell. 29Aren't two sparrows sold for only a penny? But your Father knows when any one of them falls to the ground. 30Even the hairs on your head are counted. 31So don't be afraid! You are worth much more than many sparrows.

Telling Others about Christ
(Luke 12.8,9)

32 If you tell others that you belong to me, I will tell my Father in heaven that you are my followers. 33But if you reject me, I will tell my Father in heaven that you don't belong to me.

Not Peace, but Trouble
(Luke 12.51-53; 14.26,27)

34 Don't think that I came to bring peace to the earth! I came to bring trouble, not peace. 35I came to turn sons against their fathers, daughters against their mothers, and daughters-in-law against their mothers-in-law. 36Your worst enemies will be in your own family.

37 If you love your father or mother or even your sons and daughters more than me, you are not fit to be my disciples. 38And unless you are willing to take up your cross and come with me, you are not fit to be my disciples. 39If you try to save your life, you will lose it. But if you give it up for me, you will surely find it.

Rewards
(Mark 9.41)

40 Anyone who welcomes you welcomes me. And anyone who welcomes me also welcomes the one who sent me. 41Anyone who welcomes a prophet, just because that person is a prophet, will be given the same reward as a prophet. Anyone who welcomes a good person, just because that person is good, will be given the same reward as a

good person. 42And anyone who gives one of my most humble followers a cup of cool water, just because that person is my follower, will surely be rewarded.

John the Baptist
(Luke 7.18-35)

11 After Jesus had finished instructing his twelve disciples, he left and began teaching and preaching in the towns.*

2 John was in prison when he heard what Christ was doing. So John sent some of his followers 3to ask Jesus, "Are you the one we should be looking for? Or must we wait for someone else?"

4 Jesus answered, "Go and tell John what you have heard and seen. 5The blind are now able to see, and the lame can walk. People with leprosy* are being healed, and the deaf can hear. The dead are raised to life, and the poor are hearing the good news. 6God will bless everyone who doesn't reject me because of what I do."

7 As John's followers were going away, Jesus spoke to the crowds about John:

What sort of person did you go out into the desert to see? Was he like tall grass blown about by the wind? 8What kind of man did you go out to see? Was he someone dressed in fine clothes? People who dress like that live in the king's

---

e the towns: The Greek text has "their towns," which may refer to the towns of Galilee or to the towns where Jesus' disciples had lived.

f leprosy: See the note at 8.2.

palace. ⁹What did you really go out to see? Was he a prophet? He certainly was. I tell you that he was more than a prophet. ¹⁰In the Scriptures God says about him, "I am sending my messenger ahead of you to get things ready for you." ¹¹I tell you that no one ever born on this earth is greater than John the Baptist. But whoever is least in the kingdom of heaven is greater than John.

12 From the time of John the Baptist until now, violent people have been trying to take over the kingdom of heaven by force. ¹³All the Books of the Prophets and the Law of Moses ᵍ told what was going to happen up to the time of John. ¹⁴And if you believe them, John is Elijah, the prophet you are waiting for. ¹⁵If you have ears, pay attention!

16 You people are like children sitting in the market and shouting to each other,

¹⁷ "We played the flute,
        but you would not dance!
    We sang a funeral song,
        but you would not mourn!"

¹⁸John the Baptist did not go around eating and drinking, and you said, "That man has a demon in him!" ¹⁹But the Son of Man goes around eating and drinking, and you say, "That man eats and drinks too much! He is even a friend of tax collectors ʰ and sinners." Yet Wisdom is shown to be right by what it does.

ᵍ *the Books of the Prophets and the Law of Moses*: The Jewish Scriptures, that is, the Old Testament.

ʰ *tax collectors*: See the note at 5.46.

The Unbelieving Towns
(Luke 10.13-15)

20 In the towns where Jesus had worked most of his miracles, the people refused to turn to God. So Jesus was upset with them and said:

21 You people of Chorazin are in for trouble! You people of Bethsaida are in for trouble too! If the miracles that took place in your towns had happened in Tyre and Sidon, the people there would have turned to God long ago. They would have dressed in sackcloth and put ashes on their heads.[i] 22I tell you that on the day of judgment the people of Tyre and Sidon will get off easier than you will.

23 People of Capernaum, do you think you will be honored in heaven? You will go down to hell! If the miracles that took place in your town had happened in Sodom, that town would still be standing. 24So I tell you that on the day of judgment the people of Sodom will get off easier than you.

Come to Me and Rest
(Luke 10.21,22)

25 At that moment Jesus said:

My Father, Lord of heaven and earth, I am grateful that you hid all this from wise and educated people and showed it to ordinary people. 26Yes, Father, that is what pleased you.

---

[i] *sackcloth...ashes on their heads*: This was one way that people showed how sorry they were for their sins.

27 My Father has given me everything, and he is the only one who knows the Son. The only one who truly knows the Father is the Son. But the Son wants to tell others about the Father, so that they can know him too.

28 If you are tired from carrying heavy burdens, come to me and I will give you rest. ²⁹Take the yoke^j I give you. Put it on your shoulders and learn from me. I am gentle and humble, and you will find rest. ³⁰This yoke is easy to bear, and this burden is light.

A Question about the Sabbath
(Mark 2.23-28; Luke 6.1-5)

12 One Sabbath, Jesus and his disciples were walking through some wheat fields.^k His disciples were hungry and began picking and eating grains of wheat. ²Some Pharisees noticed this and said to Jesus, "Why are your disciples picking grain on the Sabbath? They are not supposed to do that!"

3 Jesus answered:

You surely must have read what David did when he and his followers were hungry. ⁴He went into the house of God, and then they ate the sacred loaves of bread that only priests are supposed to eat. ⁵Haven't you read in the Law of Moses that the priests are allowed to work in

---

^j *yoke*: Yokes were put on the necks of animals, so that they could pull a plow or wagon. A yoke was a symbol of obedience and hard work.

^k *walking through some wheat fields*: It was the custom to let hungry travelers pick grains of wheat.

the temple on the Sabbath? But no one says that they are guilty of breaking the law of the Sabbath. 6I tell you that there is something here greater than the temple. 7Don't you know what the Scriptures mean when they say, "Instead of offering sacrifices to me, I want you to be merciful to others?" If you knew what this means, you would not condemn these innocent disciples of mine. 8So the Son of Man is Lord over the Sabbath.

A Man with a Crippled Hand
(Mark 3.1-6; Luke 6.6-11)

9 Jesus left and went into one of the Jewish meeting places, 10where there was a man whose hand was crippled. Some Pharisees wanted to accuse Jesus of doing something wrong, and they asked him, "Is it right to heal someone on the Sabbath?"

11 Jesus answered, "If you had a sheep that fell into a ditch on the Sabbath, wouldn't you lift it out? 12People are worth much more than sheep, and so it is right to do good on the Sabbath." 13Then Jesus told the man, "Hold out your hand." The man did, and it became as healthy as the other one.

14 The Pharisees left and started making plans to kill Jesus.

God's Chosen Servant

15 When Jesus found out what was happening, he left there and large crowds followed him. He healed all of their sick, 16but warned them not to tell anyone about him. 17So God's promise came true, just as Isaiah the prophet had said,

¹⁸ "Here is my chosen servant!
    I love him, and he pleases me.
 I will give him my Spirit,
    and he will bring justice to the nations.
¹⁹ He won't shout or yell
    or call out in the streets.
²⁰ He won't break off a bent reed
    or put out a dying flame,
 but he will make sure that justice is done.
²¹ All nations will place their hope in him."

Jesus and the Ruler of the Demons
(Mark 3.20-30; Luke 11.14-23; 12.10)

22 Some people brought to Jesus a man who was blind and could not talk because he had a demon in him. Jesus healed the man, and then he was able to talk and see. ²³The crowds were so amazed that they asked, "Could Jesus be the Son of David?"¹

24 When the Pharisees heard this, they said, "He forces out demons by the power of Beelzebul, the ruler of the demons!"

25 Jesus knew what they were thinking, and he said to them:

Any kingdom where people fight each other will end up ruined. And a town or family that fights will soon destroy itself. ²⁶So if Satan fights against himself, how can his kingdom last? ²⁷If I use the power of Beelzebul to force out demons, whose power do your own followers use to force them out? Your followers are the

---

¹ *Could Jesus be the Son of David*: Or "Does Jesus think he is the Son of David?" See the note at 9.27.

ones who will judge you. 28But when I force out demons by the power of God's Spirit, it proves that God's kingdom has already come to you. 29How can anyone break into a strong man's house and steal his things, unless he first ties up the strong man? Then he can take everything.

30 If you are not on my side, you are against me. If you don't gather in the harvest with me, you scatter it. 31-32I tell you that any sinful thing you do or say can be forgiven. Even if you speak against the Son of Man, you can be forgiven. But if you speak against the Holy Spirit, you can never be forgiven, either in this life or in the life to come.

A Tree and Its Fruit
(Luke 6.43-45)

33 A good tree produces only good fruit, and a bad tree produces bad fruit. You can tell what a tree is like by the fruit it produces. 34You are a bunch of evil snakes, so how can you say anything good? Your words show what is in your hearts. 35Good people bring good things out of their hearts, but evil people bring evil things out of their hearts. 36I promise you that on the day of judgment, everyone will have to account for every careless word they have spoken. 37On that day they will be told that they are either innocent or guilty because of the things they have said.

A Sign from Heaven
(Mark 8.11, 12; Luke 11.29-32)

38 Some Pharisees and teachers of the Law of

Moses said, "Teacher, we want you to show us a sign from heaven."

39 But Jesus replied:

You want a sign because you are evil and won't believe! But the only sign you will get is the sign of the prophet Jonah. [40]He was in the stomach of a big fish for three days and nights, just as the Son of Man will be deep in the earth for three days and nights. [41]On the day of judgment the people of Nineveh[m] will stand there with you and condemn you. They turned to God when Jonah preached, and yet here is something far greater than Jonah. [42]The Queen of the South[n] will also stand there with you and condemn you. She traveled a long way to hear Solomon's wisdom, and yet here is something much greater than Solomon.

Return of an Evil Spirit
(Luke 11.24-26)

43 When an evil spirit leaves a person, it travels through the desert, looking for a place to rest. But when the demon doesn't find a place, [44]it says, "I will go back to the home I left." When it gets there and finds the place empty, clean, and fixed up, [45]it goes off and finds seven other evil spirits even worse than itself. They all come and

---

[m] *Nineveh*: During the time of Jonah this city was the capital of the Assyrian Empire, which was Israel's worst enemy. But Jonah was sent there to preach, so that the people would turn to the Lord and be saved.

[n] *Queen of the South*: Sheba, probably a country in southern Arabia.

make their home there, and the person ends up in worse shape than before. That's how it will be with you evil people of today.

Jesus' Mother and Brothers
(Mark 3.31-35; Luke 8.19-21)

46 While Jesus was still speaking to the crowds, his mother and brothers came and stood outside because they wanted to talk with him. 47Someone told Jesus, "Your mother and brothers are standing outside and want to talk with you."*o*

48 Jesus answered, "Who is my mother and who are my brothers?" 49Then he pointed to his disciples and said, "These are my mother and my brothers! 50Anyone who obeys my Father in heaven is my brother or sister or mother."

A Story about a Farmer
(Mark 4.1-9; Luke 8.4-8)

13 That same day Jesus left the house and went out beside Lake Galilee, where he sat down to teach.*p* 2Such large crowds gathered around him that he had to sit in a boat, while the people stood on the shore. 3Then he taught them many things by using stories. He said:

A farmer went out to scatter seed in a field. 4While the farmer was scattering the seed, some of it fell along the road and was eaten by birds. 5Other seeds fell on thin, rocky ground and quickly started

---

o with you: Some manuscripts do not have verse 47.

p sat down to teach: Teachers in the ancient world, including Jewish teachers, usually sat down when they taught.

growing because the soil wasn't very deep. ⁶But when the sun came up, the plants were scorched and dried up, because they did not have enough roots. ⁷Some other seeds fell where thornbushes grew up and choked the plants. ⁸But a few seeds did fall on good ground where the plants produced a hundred or sixty or thirty times as much as was scattered. ⁹If you have ears, pay attention!

Why Jesus Used Stories
(Mark 4.10-12; Luke 8.9,10)

10 Jesus' disciples came to him and asked, "Why do you use nothing but stories when you speak to the people?"

11 Jesus answered:

I have explained the secrets about the kingdom of heaven to you, but not to others. ¹²Everyone who has something will be given more. But people who don't have anything will lose even what little they have. ¹³I use stories when I speak to them because when they look, they cannot see, and when they listen, they cannot hear or understand. ¹⁴So God's promise came true, just as the prophet Isaiah had said,

"These people will listen and listen,
but never understand.

They will look and look, but never see.

¹⁵ All of them have stubborn minds!

Their ears are stopped up,
and their eyes are covered.

They cannot see or hear or understand.

If they could, they would turn to me,
and I would heal them."

16 But God has blessed you, because your eyes can see and your ears can hear! 17Many prophets and good people were eager to see what you see and to hear what you hear. But I tell you that they did not see or hear.

Jesus Explains the Story about the Farmer
(Mark 4.13-20; Luke 8.11-15)

18 Now listen to the meaning of the story about the farmer:

19 The seeds that fell along the road are the people who hear the message about the kingdom, but don't understand it. Then the evil one comes and snatches the message from their hearts. 20The seeds that fell on rocky ground are the people who gladly hear the message and accept it right away. 21But they don't have deep roots, and they don't last very long. As soon as life gets hard or the message gets them in trouble, they give up.

22 The seeds that fell among the thornbushes are also people who hear the message. But they start worrying about the needs of this life and are fooled by the desire to get rich. So the message gets choked out, and they never produce anything. 23The seeds that fell on good ground are the people who hear and understand the message. They produce as much as a hundred or sixty or thirty times what was planted.

Weeds among the Wheat

24 Jesus then told them this story:

The kingdom of heaven is like what happened when a farmer scattered good seed in a field.

²⁵But while everyone was sleeping, an enemy came and scattered weed seeds in the field and then left.

26 When the plants came up and began to ripen, the farmer's servants could see the weeds. ²⁷The servants came and asked, "Sir, didn't you scatter good seed in your field? Where did these weeds come from?"

28 "An enemy did this," he replied.

His servants then asked, "Do you want us to go out and pull up the weeds?"

29 "No!" he answered. "You might also pull up the wheat. ³⁰Leave the weeds alone until harvest time. Then I'll tell my workers to gather the weeds and tie them up and burn them. But I'll have them store the wheat in my barn."

Stories about a Mustard Seed and Yeast
(Mark 4.30-32; Luke 13.18-21)

31 Jesus told them another story:

The kingdom of heaven is like what happens when a farmer plants a mustard seed in a field. ³²Although it is the smallest of all seeds, it grows larger than any garden plant and becomes a tree. Birds even come and nest on its branches.

33 Jesus also said:

The kingdom of heaven is like what happens when a woman mixes a little yeast into three big batches of flour. Finally, all the dough rises.

The Reason for Teaching with Stories
(Mark 4.33,34)

34 Jesus used stories when he spoke to the people.

In fact, he did not tell them anything without using stories. 35So God's promise came true, just as the prophet*q* had said,

> "I will use stories to speak my message
> and to explain things that have been hidden
> since the creation of the world."

Jesus Explains the Story about the Weeds

36 After Jesus left the crowd and went inside,*r* his disciples came to him and said, "Explain to us the story about the weeds in the wheat field."

37 Jesus answered:

The one who scattered the good seed is the Son of Man. 38The field is the world, and the good seeds are the people who belong to the kingdom. The weed seeds are those who belong to the evil one, 39and the one who scattered them is the devil. The harvest is the end of time, and angels are the ones who bring in the harvest.

40 Weeds are gathered and burned. That's how it will be at the end of time. 41The Son of Man will send out his angels, and they will gather from his kingdom everyone who does wrong or causes others to sin. 42Then he will throw them into a flaming furnace, where people will cry and grit their teeth in pain. 43But everyone who has done right will shine like the sun in their Father's kingdom. If you have ears, pay attention!

---

q the prophet: Some manuscripts have "the prophet Isaiah."
r went inside: Or "went home."

A Hidden Treasure

44 The kingdom of heaven is like what happens when someone finds treasure hidden in a field and buries it again. A person like that is happy and goes and sells everything in order to buy that field.

A Valuable Pearl

45 The kingdom of heaven is like what happens when a shop owner is looking for fine pearls. 46After finding a very valuable one, the owner goes and sells everything in order to buy that pearl.

A Fish Net

47 The kingdom of heaven is like what happens when a net is thrown into a lake and catches all kinds of fish. 48When the net is full, it is dragged to the shore, and the fishermen sit down to separate the fish. They keep the good ones, but throw the bad ones away. 49That's how it will be at the end of time. Angels will come and separate the evil people from the ones who have done right. 50Then those evil people will be thrown into a flaming furnace, where they will cry and grit their teeth in pain.

New and Old Treasures

51 Jesus asked his disciples if they understood all these things. They said, "Yes, we do."

52 So he told them, "Every student of the Scriptures who becomes a disciple in the kingdom of heaven is

like someone who brings out new and old treasures from the storeroom."

The People of Nazareth Turn against Jesus
(Mark 6.1-6; Luke 4.16-30)

53 When Jesus had finished telling these stories, he left 54and went to his hometown. He taught in their meeting place, and the people were so amazed that they asked, "Where does he get all this wisdom and the power to work these miracles? 55Isn't he the son of the carpenter? Isn't Mary his mother, and aren't James, Joseph, Simon, and Judas his brothers? 56Don't his sisters still live here in our town? How can he do all this?" 57So the people were very unhappy because of what he was doing.

But Jesus said, "Prophets are honored by everyone, except the people of their hometown and their own family." 58And because the people did not have any faith, Jesus did not work many miracles there.

The Death of John the Baptist
(Mark 6.14-29; Luke 9.7-9)

14 About this time Herod the ruler[s] heard the news about Jesus 2and told his officials, "This is John the Baptist! He has come back from death, and that's why he has the power to work these miracles."

3-4 Herod had earlier arrested John and had him chained and put in prison. He did this because John had told him, "It isn't right for you to take Herodias,

---

[s] *Herod the ruler*: Herod Antipas, the son of Herod the Great (see 2.1).

the wife of your brother Philip." [5]Herod wanted to kill John. But the people thought John was a prophet, and Herod was afraid of what they might do.

6 When Herod's birthday came, the daughter of Herodias danced for the guests. She pleased Herod [7]so much that he swore to give her whatever she wanted. [8]But the girl's mother told her to say, "Here on a platter I want the head of John the Baptist!"

9 The king was sorry for what he had said. But he did not want to break the promise he had made in front of his guests. So he ordered a guard [10]to go to the prison and cut off John's head. [11]It was taken on a platter to the girl, and she gave it to her mother. [12]John's followers took his body and buried it. Then they told Jesus what had happened.

Jesus Feeds Five Thousand
(Mark 6.30-44; Luke 9.10-17; John 6.1-14)

13 After Jesus heard about John, he crossed Lake Galilee[t] to go to some place where he could be alone. But the crowds found out and followed him on foot from the towns. [14]When Jesus got out of the boat, he saw the large crowd. He felt sorry for them and healed everyone who was sick.

15 That evening the disciples came to Jesus and said, "This place is like a desert, and it is already late. Let the crowds leave, so they can go to the villages and buy some food."

16 Jesus replied, "They don't have to leave. Why don't you give them something to eat?"

17 But they said, "We have only five small loaves

---

[t] *crossed Lake Galilee*: To the east side.

of bread" and two fish." 18 Jesus asked his disciples to bring the food to him, 19 and he told the crowd to sit down on the grass. Jesus took the five loaves and the two fish. He looked up toward heaven and blessed the food. Then he broke the bread and handed it to his disciples, and they gave it to the people.

20 After everyone had eaten all they wanted, Jesus' disciples picked up twelve large baskets of leftovers.

21 There were about five thousand men who ate, not counting the women and children.

Jesus Walks on the Water
(Mark 6.45-52; John 6.15-21)

22 Right away, Jesus made his disciples get into a boat and start back across the lake." But he stayed until he had sent the crowds away. 23 Then he went up on a mountain where he could be alone and pray. Later that evening, he was still there.

24 By this time the boat was a long way from the shore. It was going against the wind and was being tossed around by the waves. 25 A little while before morning, Jesus came walking on the water toward his disciples. 26 When they saw him, they thought he was a ghost. They were terrified and started screaming.

27 At once, Jesus said to them, "Don't worry! I am Jesus. Don't be afraid."

28 Peter replied, "Lord, if it is really you, tell me to come to you on the water."

" small loaves of bread: These would have been flat and round or in the shape of a bun.
" back across the lake: To the west side.

29 "Come on!" Jesus said. Peter then got out of the boat and started walking on the water toward him.

30 But when Peter saw how strong the wind was, he was afraid and started sinking. "Save me, Lord!" he shouted.

31 Right away, Jesus reached out his hand. He helped Peter up and said, "You surely don't have much faith. Why do you doubt?"

32 When Jesus and Peter got into the boat, the wind died down. 33 The men in the boat worshiped Jesus and said, "You really are the Son of God!"

Jesus Heals Sick People in Gennesaret
(Mark 6.53-56)

34 Jesus and his disciples crossed the lake and came to shore near the town of Gennesaret. 35 The people found out that he was there, and they sent word to everyone who lived in that part of the country. So they brought all the sick people to Jesus. 36 They begged him just to let them touch his clothes, and everyone who did was healed.

The Teaching of the Ancestors
(Mark 7.1-13)

15 About this time some Pharisees and teachers of the Law of Moses came from Jerusalem. They asked Jesus, 2 "Why don't your disciples obey what our ancestors taught us to do? They don't even wash their hands[w] before they eat."

---

[w] wash their hands: The Jewish people had strict laws about washing their hands before eating, especially if they had been out in public.

3 Jesus answered:

Why do you disobey God and follow your own teaching? 4Didn't God command you to respect your father and mother? Didn't he tell you to put to death all who curse their parents? 5But you let people get by without helping their parents when they should. You let them say that what they have has been offered to God.[x] 6Is this any way to show respect to your parents? You ignore God's commands in order to follow your own teaching. 7And you are nothing but show-offs! Isaiah the prophet was right when he wrote that God had said,

8 "All of you praise me with your words,
but you never really think about me.

9 It is useless for you to worship me,
when you teach rules
made up by humans."

What Really Makes People Unclean
(Mark 7.14-23)

10 Jesus called the crowd together and said, "Pay attention and try to understand what I mean. 11The food that you put into your mouth doesn't make you unclean and unfit to worship God. The bad words that come out of your mouth are what make you unclean."

12 Then his disciples came over to him and asked, "Do you know that you insulted the Pharisees by what you said?"

---

[x] has been offered to God: According to Jewish custom, when people said something was offered to God, it belonged to him and could not be used for anyone else, not even for their own parents.

13 Jesus answered, "Every plant that my Father in heaven did not plant will be pulled up by the roots. 14 Stay away from those Pharisees! They are like blind people leading other blind people, and all of them will fall into a ditch."

15 Peter replied, "What did you mean when you talked about the things that make people unclean?"

16 Jesus then said:

Don't any of you know what I am talking about by now? 17 Don't you know that the food you put into your mouth goes into your stomach and then out of your body? 18 But the words that come out of your mouth come from your heart. And they are what make you unfit to worship God. 19 Out of your heart come evil thoughts, murder, unfaithfulness in marriage, vulgar deeds, stealing, telling lies, and insulting others. 20 These are what make you unclean. Eating without washing your hands will not make you unfit to worship God.

A Woman's Faith
(Mark 7.24-30)

21 Jesus left and went to the territory near the cities of Tyre and Sidon. 22 Suddenly a Canaanite woman *y* from there came out shouting, "Lord and Son of David,*z* have pity on me! My daughter is full of demons." 23 Jesus did not say a word. But the woman kept following along and shouting, so his disciples came up and asked him to send her away.

---

y Canaanite woman: This woman was not Jewish.
z Son of David: See the note at 9.27.

24 Jesus said, "I was sent only to the people of Israel! They are like a flock of lost sheep."

25 The woman came closer. Then she knelt down and begged, "Please help me, Lord!"

26 Jesus replied, "It isn't right to take food away from children and feed it to dogs."*a*

27 "Lord, that's true," the woman said, "but even dogs get the crumbs that fall from their owner's table."

28 Jesus answered, "Dear woman, you really do have a lot of faith, and you will be given what you want." At that moment her daughter was healed.

Jesus Heals Many People

29 From there, Jesus went along Lake Galilee. Then he climbed a hill and sat down. 30Large crowds came and brought many people who were crippled or blind or lame or unable to talk. They placed them, and many others, in front of Jesus, and he healed them all. 31Everyone was amazed at what they saw and heard. People who had never spoken could now speak. The lame were healed, the crippled could walk, and the blind were able to see. Everyone was praising the God of Israel.

Jesus Feeds Four Thousand
(Mark 8.1-10)

32 Jesus called his disciples together and told them, "I feel sorry for these people. They have been with me for three days, and they don't have anything to eat. I don't want to send them away hungry. They might faint on their way home."

---

a feed it to dogs: The Jewish people sometimes referred to
Gentiles as dogs.

33 His disciples said, "This place is like a desert. Where can we find enough food to feed such a crowd?"

34 Jesus asked them how much food they had. They replied, "Seven small loaves of bread[b] and a few little fish."

35 After Jesus had told the people to sit down, 36he took the seven loaves of bread and the fish and gave thanks. He then broke them and handed them to his disciples, who passed them around to the crowds.

37 Everyone ate all they wanted, and the leftovers filled seven large baskets.

38 There were four thousand men who ate, not counting the women and children.

39 After Jesus had sent the crowds away, he got into a boat and sailed across the lake. He came to shore near the town of Magadan.[c]

A Demand for a Sign from Heaven
(Mark 8.11-13; Luke 12.54-56)

16 The Pharisees and Sadducees came to Jesus and tried to test him by asking for a sign from heaven. 2He told them:

If the sky is red in the evening, you say the weather will be good. 3But if the sky is red and gloomy in the morning, you say it is going to rain. You can tell what the weather will be like by looking at the sky. But you don't understand what is happening now.[d] 4You want a sign

[b] small loaves of bread: See the note at 14.17.

[c] Magadan: The location is unknown.

[d] If the sky is red...what is happening now: The words of Jesus in verses 2 and 3 are not in some manuscripts.

because you are evil and won't believe! But the only sign you will be given is what happened to Jonah.*

Then Jesus left.

The Yeast of the Pharisees and Sadducees
(Mark 8.14-21)

5 The disciples had forgotten to bring any bread when they crossed the lake. *f* 6Jesus then warned them, "Watch out! Guard against the yeast of the Pharisees and Sadducees."

7 The disciples talked this over and said to each other, "He must be saying this because we didn't bring along any bread."

8 Jesus knew what they were thinking and said:

You surely don't have much faith! Why are you talking about not having any bread? 9Don't you understand? Have you forgotten about the five thousand people and all those baskets of leftovers from just five loaves of bread? 10And what about the four thousand people and all those baskets of leftovers from only seven loaves of bread? 11Don't you know by now that I am not talking to you about bread? Watch out for the yeast of the Pharisees and Sadducees!

12 Finally, the disciples understood that Jesus wasn't talking about the yeast used to make bread, but about the teaching of the Pharisees and Sadducees.

---

e what happened to Jonah: Jonah was in the stomach of a big fish for three days and nights (see 12.40).
f crossed the lake: To the east side.

Who Is Jesus?

(Mark 8.27-30; Luke 9.18-21)

13 When Jesus and his disciples were near the town of Caesarea Philippi, he asked them, "What do people say about the Son of Man?"

14 The disciples answered, "Some people say you are John the Baptist or maybe Elijah[g] or Jeremiah or some other prophet."

15 Then Jesus asked them, "But who do you say I am?"

16 Simon Peter spoke up, "You are the Messiah, the Son of the living God."

17 Jesus told him:

Simon, son of Jonah, you are blessed! You didn't discover this on your own. It was shown to you by my Father in heaven. 18 So I will call you Peter, which means "a rock." On this rock I will build my church, and death itself will not have any power over it. 19 I will give you the keys to the kingdom of heaven, and God in heaven will allow whatever you allow on earth. But he will not allow anything that you don't allow.

20 Jesus told his disciples not to tell anyone that he was the Messiah.

Jesus Speaks about His Suffering and Death

(Mark 8.31–9.1; Luke 9.22-27)

21 From then on, Jesus began telling his disciples what would happen to him. He said, "I must go to

---

g Elijah: Many of the Jewish people expected the prophet Elijah to come and prepare the way for the Messiah.

Jerusalem. There the nation's leaders, the chief priests, and the teachers of the Law of Moses will make me suffer terribly. I will be killed, but three days later I will rise to life."

22 Peter took Jesus aside and told him to stop talking like that. He said, "God would never let this happen to you, Lord!"

23 Jesus turned to Peter and said, "Satan, get away from me! You're in my way because you think like everyone else and not like God."

24 Then Jesus said to his disciples:

If any of you want to be my followers, you must forget about yourself. You must take up your cross and follow me. 25If you want to save your life,[h] you will destroy it. But if you give up your life for me, you will find it. 26What will you gain, if you own the whole world but destroy yourself? What would you give to get back your soul?

27 The Son of Man will soon come in the glory of his Father and with his angels to reward all people for what they have done. 28I promise you that some of those standing here will not die before they see the Son of Man coming with his kingdom.

The True Glory of Jesus
(Mark 9.2-13; Luke 9.28-36)

17 Six days later Jesus took Peter and the brothers James and John with him. They went up on a very high mountain where they could be alone. 2There

---

[h] *life*: In verses 25 and 26 the same Greek word is translated "life," "yourself," and "soul."

in front of the disciples, Jesus was completely changed. His face was shining like the sun, and his clothes became white as light.

3 All at once Moses and Elijah were there talking with Jesus. 4So Peter said to him, "Lord, it is good for us to be here! Let us make three shelters, one for you, one for Moses, and one for Elijah."

5 While Peter was still speaking, the shadow of a bright cloud passed over them. From the cloud a voice said, "This is my own dear Son, and I am pleased with him. Listen to what he says!" 6When the disciples heard the voice, they were so afraid that they fell flat on the ground. 7But Jesus came over and touched them. He said, "Get up and don't be afraid!" 8When they opened their eyes, they saw only Jesus.

9 On their way down from the mountain, Jesus warned his disciples not to tell anyone what they had seen until after the Son of Man had been raised from death.

10 The disciples asked Jesus, "Don't the teachers of the Law of Moses say that Elijah must come before the Messiah does?"

11 Jesus told them, "Elijah certainly will come and get everything ready. 12In fact, he has already come. But the people did not recognize him and treated him just as they wanted to. They will soon make the Son of Man suffer in the same way." 13Then the disciples understood that Jesus was talking to them about John the Baptist.

Jesus Heals a Boy
(Mark 9.14-29; Luke 9.37-43a)

14 Jesus and his disciples returned to the crowd. A man knelt in front of him 15and said, "Lord, have pity on my son! He has a bad case of epilepsy and often

falls into a fire or into water. [16]I brought him to your disciples, but none of them could heal him."

17 Jesus said, "You people are too stubborn to have any faith! How much longer must I be with you? Why do I have to put up with you? Bring the boy here." [18]Then Jesus spoke sternly to the demon. It went out of the boy, and right then he was healed.

19 Later the disciples went to Jesus in private and asked him, "Why couldn't we force out the demon?"

20-21 Jesus replied:

It is because you don't have enough faith! But I can promise you this. If you had faith no larger than a mustard seed, you could tell this mountain to move from here to there. And it would. Everything would be possible for you.[i]

Jesus Again Speaks about His Death
(Mark 9.30-32; Luke 9.43b-45)

22 While Jesus and his disciples were going from place to place in Galilee, he told them, "The Son of Man will be handed over to people [23]who will kill him. But three days later he will rise to life." All of this made the disciples very sad.

Paying the Temple Tax

24 When Jesus and the others arrived in Capernaum, the collectors for the temple tax came to Peter and asked, "Does your teacher pay the temple tax?"

25 "Yes, he does," Peter answered.

---

[i] *for you*: Some manuscripts add, "But the only way to force out that kind of demon is by praying and going without eating."

After they had returned home, Jesus went up to Peter and asked him, "Simon, what do you think? Do the kings of this earth collect taxes and fees from their own people or from foreigners?"*j*

26 Peter answered, "From foreigners."

Jesus replied, "Then their own people*k* don't have to pay. 27But we don't want to cause trouble. So go cast a line into the lake and pull out the first fish you hook. Open its mouth, and you will find a coin. Use it to pay your taxes and mine."

Who Is the Greatest?
(Mark 9.33-37; Luke 9.46-48)

18 About this time the disciples came to Jesus and asked him who would be the greatest in the kingdom of heaven. 2Jesus called a child over and had the child stand near him. 3Then he said:

I promise you this. If you don't change and become like a child, you will never get into the kingdom of heaven. 4But if you are as humble as this child, you are the greatest in the kingdom of heaven. 5And when you welcome one of these children because of me, you welcome me.

Temptations To Sin
(Mark 9.42-48; Luke 17.1,2)

6 It will be terrible for people who cause even one of my little followers to sin. Those people

---

j from their own people or from foreigners: Or "from their children or from others."

k From foreigners…their own people: Or "From other people…their children."

would be better off thrown into the deepest part of the ocean with a heavy stone tied around their necks! [7]The world is in for trouble because of the way it causes people to sin. There will always be something to cause people to sin, but anyone who does this will be in for trouble.

[8] If your hand or foot causes you to sin, chop it off and throw it away! You would be better off to go into life crippled or lame than to have two hands or two feet and be thrown into the fire that never goes out. [9]If your eye causes you to sin, poke it out and get rid of it. You would be better off to go into life with only one eye than to have two eyes and be thrown into the fires of hell.

The Lost Sheep
(Luke 15.3-7)

[10-11] Don't be cruel to any of these little ones! I promise you that their angels are always with my Father in heaven.[l] [12]Let me ask you this. What would you do if you had a hundred sheep and one of them wandered off? Wouldn't you leave the ninety-nine on the hillside and go look for the one that had wandered away? [13]I am sure that finding it would make you happier than having the ninety-nine that never wandered off. [14]That's how it is with your Father in heaven. He doesn't want any of these little ones to be lost.

---

[l] *in heaven*: Some manuscripts add, "The Son of Man came to save people who are lost."

When Someone Sins
(Luke 17.3)

15 If one of my followers*m* sins against you,
go and point out what was wrong. But do it in
private, just between the two of you. If that
person listens, you have won back a follower.
16But if that one refuses to listen, take along one
or two others. The Scriptures teach that every
complaint must be proven true by two or more
witnesses. 17If the follower refuses to listen to
them, report the matter to the church. Anyone
who refuses to listen to the church must be
treated like an unbeliever or a tax collector.*n*

Allowing and Not Allowing

18 I promise you that God in heaven will
allow whatever you allow on earth, but he will
not allow anything you don't allow. 19I promise
that when any two of you on earth agree about
something you are praying for, my Father in
heaven will do it for you. 20Whenever two or
three of you come together in my name,*o* I am
there with you.

An Official Who Refused To Forgive

21 Peter came up to the Lord and asked, "How

---

m followers: The Greek text has "brother," which is used
here and elsewhere in this chapter to refer to a follower
of Christ.

n tax collector: See the note at 5.46.

o in my name: Or "as my followers."

many times should I forgive someone[p] who does something wrong to me? Is seven times enough?"

22 Jesus answered:

Not just seven times, but seventy-seven times![q] 23 This story will show you what the kingdom of heaven is like:

One day a king decided to call in his officials and ask them to give an account of what they owed him. 24 As he was doing this, one official was brought in who owed him fifty million silver coins. 25 But he didn't have any money to pay what he owed. The king ordered him to be sold, along with his wife and children and all he owned, in order to pay the debt.

26 The official got down on his knees and began begging, "Have pity on me, and I will pay you every cent I owe!" 27 The king felt sorry for him and let him go free. He even told the official that he did not have to pay back the money.

28 As the official was leaving, he happened to meet another official, who owed him a hundred silver coins. So he grabbed the man by the throat. He started choking him and said, "Pay me what you owe!"

29 The man got down on his knees and began begging, "Have pity on me, and I will pay you back." 30 But the first official refused to have

---

p *someone*: Or "a follower." See the note at 18.15.

q *seventy-seven times*: Or "seventy times seven." The large number means that one follower should never stop forgiving another.

pity. Instead, he went and had the other official put in jail until he could pay what he owed.

31 When some other officials found out what had happened, they felt sorry for the man who had been put in jail. Then they told the king what had happened. 32The king called the first official back in and said, "You're an evil man! When you begged for mercy, I said you did not have to pay back a cent. 33Don't you think you should show pity to someone else, as I did to you?" 34The king was so angry that he ordered the official to be tortured until he could pay back everything he owed. 35That is how my Father in heaven will treat you, if you don't forgive each of my followers with all your heart.

Teaching about Divorce
(Mark 10.1-12)

19 When Jesus finished teaching, he left Galilee and went to the part of Judea that is east of the Jordan River. 2Large crowds followed him, and he healed their sick people.

3 Some Pharisees wanted to test Jesus. They came up to him and asked, "Is it right for a man to divorce his wife for just any reason?"

4 Jesus answered, "Don't you know that in the beginning the Creator made a man and a woman? 5That's why a man leaves his father and mother and gets married. He becomes like one person with his wife. 6Then they are no longer two people, but one. And no one should separate a couple that God has joined together."

7 The Pharisees asked Jesus, "Why did Moses say that a man could write out divorce papers and send his wife away?"

8 Jesus replied, "You are so heartless! That's why Moses allowed you to divorce your wife. But from the beginning God did not intend it to be that way. 9I say that if your wife has not committed some terrible sexual sin,*r* you must not divorce her to marry someone else. If you do, you are unfaithful."

10 The disciples said, "If that's how it is between a man and a woman, it's better not to get married."

11 Jesus told them, "Only those people who have been given the gift of staying single can accept this teaching. 12Some people are unable to marry because of birth defects or because of what someone has done to their bodies. Others stay single in order to serve God better. Anyone who can accept this teaching should do so."

Jesus Blesses Little Children
(Mark 10.13-16; Luke 18.15-17)

13 Some people brought their children to Jesus, so that he could place his hands on them and pray for them. His disciples told the people to stop bothering him. 14But Jesus said, "Let the children come to me, and don't try to stop them! People who are like these children belong to God's kingdom."*s* 15After Jesus had placed his hands on the children, he left.

---

r some terrible sexual sin: See the note at 5.32.

s People who are like these children belong to God's kingdom: Or "God's kingdom belongs to people who are like
  these children."

A Rich Young Man

(Mark 10.17-31; Luke 18.18-30)

16 A man came to Jesus and asked, "Teacher, what good thing must I do to have eternal life?"

17 Jesus said to him, "Why do you ask me about what is good? Only God is good. If you want to have eternal life, you must obey his commandments."

18 "Which ones?" the man asked.

Jesus answered, "Do not murder. Be faithful in marriage. Do not steal. Do not tell lies about others. 19Respect your father and mother. And love others as much as you love yourself." 20The young man said, "I have obeyed all of these. What else must I do?"

21 Jesus replied, "If you want to be perfect, go sell everything you own! Give the money to the poor, and you will have riches in heaven. Then come and be my follower." 22When the young man heard this, he was sad, because he was very rich.

23 Jesus said to his disciples, "It's terribly hard for rich people to get into the kingdom of heaven! 24In fact, it's easier for a camel to go through the eye of a needle than for a rich person to get into God's kingdom."

25 When the disciples heard this, they were greatly surprised and asked, "How can anyone ever be saved?"

26 Jesus looked straight at them and said, "There are some things that people cannot do, but God can do anything."

27 Peter replied, "Remember, we have left everything to be your followers! What will we get?"

28 Jesus answered:

Yes, all of you have become my followers. And so in the future world, when the Son of Man sits on his glorious throne, I promise that you will sit on twelve thrones to judge the twelve tribes of Israel. 29All who have given up home or brothers and sisters or father and mother or children or land for me will be given a hundred times as much. They will also have eternal life. 30But many who are now first will be last, and many who are last will be first.

Workers in a Vineyard

20 As Jesus was telling what the kingdom of heaven would be like, he said:

Early one morning a man went out to hire some workers for his vineyard. 2After he had agreed to pay them the usual amount for a day's work, he sent them off to his vineyard.

3 About nine that morning, the man saw some other people standing in the market with nothing to do. 4He said he would pay them what was fair, if they would work in his vineyard. 5So they went.

At noon and again about three in the afternoon he returned to the market. And each time he made the same agreement with others who were loafing around with nothing to do.

6 Finally, about five in the afternoon the man went back and found some others standing there. He asked them, "Why have you been standing here all day long doing nothing?"

7 "Because no one has hired us," they answered. Then he told them to go work in his vineyard.

8 That evening the owner of the vineyard told the man in charge of the workers to call them in

and give them their money. He also told the man
to begin with the ones who were hired last.
9When the workers arrived, the ones who had
been hired at five in the afternoon were given a
full day's pay.

10 The workers who had been hired first
thought they would be given more than the others.
But when they were given the same, 11they began
complaining to the owner of the vineyard. 12They
said, "The ones who were hired last worked for
only one hour. But you paid them the same that
you did us. And we worked in the hot sun all day
long!"

13 The owner answered one of them, "Friend,
I didn't cheat you. I paid you exactly what we
agreed on. 14Take your money now and go!
What business is it of yours if I want to pay
them the same that I paid you? 15Don't I have
the right to do what I want with my own
money? Why should you be jealous, if I want to
be generous?"

16 Jesus then said, "So it is. Everyone who is now
first will be last, and everyone who is last will be
first."

Jesus Again Tells about His Death
(Mark 10.32-34; Luke 18.31-34)

17 As Jesus was on his way to Jerusalem, he took
his twelve disciples aside and told them in private:

18 We are now on our way to Jerusalem,
where the Son of Man will be handed over to
the chief priests and the teachers of the Law of
Moses. They will sentence him to death, 19and

then they will hand him over to foreigners*t* who will make fun of him. They will beat him and nail him to a cross. But on the third day he will rise from death.

A Mother's Request
(Mark 10.35-45)

20 The mother of James and John*u* came to Jesus with her two sons. She knelt down and started begging him to do something for her. 21 Jesus asked her what she wanted, and she said, "When you come into your kingdom, please let one of my sons sit at your right side and the other at your left."*v*

22 Jesus answered, "Not one of you knows what you are asking. Are you able to drink from the cup*w* that I must soon drink from?"

James and John said, "Yes, we are!"

23 Jesus replied, "You certainly will drink from my cup! But it isn't for me to say who will sit at my right side and at my left. That is for my Father to say."

24 When the ten other disciples heard this, they were angry with the two brothers. 25 But Jesus called the disciples together and said:

You know that foreign rulers like to order their people around. And their great leaders have full

---

t foreigners: The Romans, who ruled Judea at this time.

u mother of James and John: The Greek text has "mother of the sons of Zebedee" (see 26.37).

v right side … left: The most powerful people in a kingdom sat at the right and left side of the king.

w drink from the cup: In the Scriptures a cup is sometimes used as a symbol of suffering. To "drink from the cup" is to suffer.

power over everyone they rule. 26But don't act like them. If you want to be great, you must be the servant of all the others. 27And if you want to be first, you must be the slave of the rest. 28The Son of Man did not come to be a slave master, but a slave who will give his life to rescue*x* many people.

Jesus Heals Two Blind Men
(Mark 10.46-52; Luke 18.35-43)

29 Jesus was followed by a large crowd as he and his disciples were leaving Jericho. 30Two blind men were sitting beside the road. And when they heard that Jesus was coming their way, they shouted, "Lord and Son of David,*y* have pity on us!"

31 The crowd told them to be quiet, but they shouted even louder, "Lord and Son of David, have pity on us!"

32 When Jesus heard them, he stopped and asked, "What do you want me to do for you?"

33 They answered, "Lord, we want to see!"

34 Jesus felt sorry for them and touched their eyes. Right away they could see, and they became his followers.

Jesus Enters Jerusalem
(Mark 11.1-11; Luke 19.28-38; John 12.12-19)

21 When Jesus and his disciples came near Jerusalem, he went to Bethphage on the Mount of Olives and sent two of them on ahead. 2He told

---

x rescue: The Greek word often, though not always, means the payment of a price to free a slave or a prisoner.

y Son of David: See the note at 9.27.

them, "Go into the next village, where you will at once find a donkey and her colt. Untie the two donkeys and bring them to me. ³If anyone asks why you are doing that, just say, 'The Lord*z* needs them.' Right away he will let you have the donkeys."

4 So God's promise came true, just as the prophet had said,

⁵ "Announce to the people of Jerusalem:
'Your king is coming to you!
He is humble and rides on a donkey.
He comes on the colt of a donkey.'"

6 The disciples left and did what Jesus had told them to do. ⁷They brought the donkey and its colt and laid some clothes on their backs. Then Jesus got on.

8 Many people spread clothes in the road, while others put down branches*a* which they had cut from trees. ⁹Some people walked ahead of Jesus and others followed behind. They were all shouting,

"Hooray*b* for the Son of David!*c*
God bless the one who comes
in the name of the Lord.
Hooray for God in heaven above!"

10 When Jesus came to Jerusalem, everyone in the city was excited and asked, "Who can this be?"

11 The crowd answered, "This is Jesus, the prophet from Nazareth in Galilee."

---

z The Lord: Or "The master of the donkeys."

a spread clothes…put down branches: This was one way that the Jewish people welcomed a famous person.

b Hooray: This translates a word that can mean "please save us." But it is most often used as a shout of praise to God.

c Son of David: See the note at 9.27.

Jesus in the Temple
(Mark 11.15-19; Luke 19.45-48; John 2.13-22)

12 Jesus went into the temple and chased out everyone who was selling or buying. He turned over the tables of the moneychangers and the benches of the ones who were selling doves. 13He told them, "The Scriptures say, 'My house should be called a place of worship.' But you have turned it into a place where robbers hide."

14 Blind and lame people came to Jesus in the temple, and he healed them. 15But the chief priests and the teachers of the Law of Moses were angry when they saw his miracles and heard the children shouting praises to the Son of David.*d* 16The men said to Jesus, "Don't you hear what those children are saying?"

"Yes, I do!" Jesus answered. "Don't you know that the Scriptures say, 'Children and infants will sing praises'?" 17Then Jesus left the city and went out to the village of Bethany, where he spent the night.

Jesus Puts a Curse on a Fig Tree
(Mark 11.12-14, 20-24)

18 When Jesus got up the next morning, he was hungry. He started out for the city, 19and along the way he saw a fig tree. But when he came to it, he found only leaves and no figs. So he told the tree, "You will never again grow any fruit!" Right then the fig tree dried up.

20 The disciples were shocked when they saw how quickly the tree had dried up. 21But Jesus said to

---

d Son of David: See the note at 9.27.

them, "If you have faith and don't doubt, I promise that you can do what I did to this tree. And you will be able to do even more. You can tell this mountain to get up and jump into the sea, and it will. 22If you have faith when you pray, you will be given whatever you ask for."

A Question about Jesus' Authority
(Mark 11.27-33; Luke 20.1-8)

23 Jesus gone into the temple and was teaching when the chief priests and the leaders of the people came up to him. They asked, "What right do you have to do these things? Who gave you this authority?"

24 Jesus answered, "I have just one question to ask you. If you answer it, I will tell you where I got the right to do these things. 25Who gave John the right to baptize? Was it God in heaven or merely some human being?"

They thought it over and said to each other, "We can't say that God gave John this right. Jesus will ask us why we didn't believe John. 26On the other hand, these people think that John was a prophet, and we are afraid of what they might do to us. That's why we can't say that it was merely some human who gave John the right to baptize." 27So they told Jesus, "We don't know."

Jesus said, "Then I won't tell you who gave me the right to do what I do."

A Story about Two Sons

28 Jesus said:
I will tell you a story about a man who had two sons. Then you can tell me what you think.

The father went to the older son and said, "Go work in the vineyard today!" 29His son told him that he would not do it, but later he changed his mind and went. 30The man then told his younger son to go work in the vineyard. The boy said he would, but he didn't go. 31Which one of the sons obeyed his father?

"The older one," the chief priests and leaders answered.

Then Jesus told them:

You can be sure that tax collectors*e* and prostitutes will get into the kingdom of God before you ever will! 32When John the Baptist showed you how to do right, you would not believe him. But these evil people did believe. And even when you saw what they did, you still would not change your minds and believe.

Renters of a Vineyard
(Mark 12.1-12; Luke 20,9-19)

33 Jesus told the chief priests and leaders to listen to this story:

A land owner once planted a vineyard. He built a wall around it and dug a pit to crush the grapes in. He also built a lookout tower. Then he rented out his vineyard and left the country.

34 When it was harvest time, the owner sent some servants to get his share of the grapes. 35But the renters grabbed those servants. They beat up one, killed one, and stoned one of them to death. 36He then sent more servants than he

---

e tax collectors: See the note at 5.46.

did the first time. But the renters treated them in the same way.

37 Finally, the owner sent his own son to the renters, because he thought they would respect him. ³⁸But when they saw the man's son, they said, "Someday he will own the vineyard. Let's kill him! Then we can have it all for ourselves." ³⁹So they grabbed him, threw him out of the vineyard, and killed him.

40 Jesus asked, "When the owner of that vineyard comes, what do you suppose he will do to those renters?"

41 The chief priests and leaders answered, "He will kill them in some horrible way. Then he will rent out his vineyard to people who will give him his share of grapes at harvest time."

42 Jesus replied, "You surely know that the Scriptures say,

'The stone that the builders tossed aside
    is now the most important stone of all.
This is something the Lord has done,
    and it is amazing to us.'

⁴³I tell you that God's kingdom will be taken from you and given to people who will do what he demands. ⁴⁴Anyone who stumbles over this stone will be crushed, and anyone it falls on will be smashed to pieces."ᶠ

45 When the chief priests and the Pharisees heard these stories, they knew that Jesus was talking about them. ⁴⁶So they looked for a way to arrest Jesus. But they were afraid to, because the people thought he was a prophet.

---

f *pieces*: Verse 44 is not in some manuscripts.

The Great Banquet
(Luke 14.15-24)

22 Once again Jesus used stories to teach the people:

2 The kingdom of heaven is like what happened when a king gave a wedding banquet for his son. ³The king sent some servants to tell the invited guests to come to the banquet, but the guests refused. ⁴He sent other servants to say to the guests, "The banquet is ready! My cattle and prize calves have all been prepared. Everything is ready. Come to the banquet!"

5 But the guests did not pay any attention. Some of them left for their farms, and some went to their places of business. ⁶Others grabbed the servants, then beat them up and killed them.

7 This made the king so furious that he sent an army to kill those murderers and burn down their city. ⁸Then he said to the servants, "It is time for the wedding banquet, and the invited guests don't deserve to come. ⁹Go out to the street corners and tell everyone you meet to come to the banquet." ¹⁰They went out on the streets and brought in everyone they could find, good and bad alike. And the banquet room was filled with guests.

11 When the king went in to meet the guests, he found that one of them wasn't wearing the right kind of clothes for the wedding. ¹²The king asked, "Friend, why didn't you wear proper clothes for the wedding?" But the guest had no

excuse. 13 So the king gave orders for that person to be tied hand and foot and to be thrown outside into the dark. That's where people will cry and grit their teeth in pain. 14 Many are invited, but only a few are chosen.

Paying Taxes
(Mark 12.13-17; Luke 20.20-26)

15 The Pharisees got together and planned how they could trick Jesus into saying something wrong. 16 They sent some of their followers and some of Herod's followers[g] to say to him, "Teacher, we know that you are honest. You teach the truth about what God wants people to do. And you treat everyone with the same respect, no matter who they are. 17 Tell us what you think! Should we pay taxes to the Emperor or not?"

18 Jesus knew their evil thoughts and said, "Why are you trying to test me? You show-offs! 19 Let me see one of the coins used for paying taxes." They brought him a silver coin, 20 and he asked, "Whose picture and name are on it?"

21 "The Emperor's," they answered.

Then Jesus told them, "Give the Emperor what belongs to him and give God what belongs to God." 22 His answer surprised them so much that they walked away.

---

g Herod's followers: People who were political followers of the family of Herod the Great (see 2.1) and his son Herod Antipas (see 14.1), and who wanted Herod to be king in Jerusalem.

Life in the Future World
(Mark 12.18-27; Luke 20.27-40)

23 The Sadducees did not believe that people would rise to life after death. So that same day some of the Sadducees came to Jesus and said:

24 Teacher, Moses wrote that if a married man dies and has no children, his brother should marry the widow. Their first son would then be thought of as the son of the dead brother.

25 Once there were seven brothers who lived here. The first one married, but died without having any children. So his wife was left to his brother. 26 The same thing happened to the second and third brothers and finally to all seven of them. 27 At last the woman died. 28 When God raises people from death, whose wife will this woman be? She had been married to all seven brothers.

29 Jesus answered:

You are completely wrong! You don't know what the Scriptures teach. And you don't know anything about the power of God. 30 When God raises people to life, they won't marry. They will be like the angels in heaven. 31 And as for people being raised to life, God was speaking to you when he said, 32 "I am the God worshiped by Abraham, Isaac, and Jacob." *h* He isn't the God of the dead, but of the living.

33 The crowds were surprised to hear what Jesus was teaching.

---

h I am the God worshiped by Abraham, Isaac, and Jacob: Jesus argues that if God is worshiped by these three, they must still be alive, because he is the God of the living.

The Most Important Commandment

(Mark 12.28-34; Luke 10.25-28)

34 After Jesus had made the Sadducees look foolish, the Pharisees heard about it and got together. 35 One of them was an expert in the Jewish Law. So he tried to test Jesus by asking, 36 "Teacher, what is the most important commandment in the Law?"

37 Jesus answered:

Love the Lord your God with all your heart, soul, and mind. 38 This is the first and most important commandment. 39 The second most important commandment is like this one. And it is, "Love others as much as you love yourself." 40 All the Law of Moses and the Books of the Prophets[i] are based on these two commandments.

About David's Son

(Mark 12.35-37; Luke 20.41-44)

41 While the Pharisees were still there, Jesus asked them, 42 "What do you think about the Messiah? Whose family will he come from?"

They answered, "He will be a son of King David."[j]

43 Jesus replied, "How then could the Spirit have David call the Messiah his Lord? David said,

44 'The Lord said to my Lord:
Sit at my right side[k] until I make your enemies
into a footstool for you.'

---

[i] the Law of Moses and the Books of the Prophets: The Jewish Scriptures, that is, the Old Testament.

[j] son of King David: See the note at 9.27.

[k] right side: The place of power and honor.

⁴⁵If David called the Messiah his Lord, how can the Messiah be a son of King David?" ⁴⁶No one was able to give Jesus an answer, and from that day on, no one dared ask him any more questions.

Jesus Condemns the Pharisees and the Teachers of the Law of Moses
(Mark 12.38-40; Luke 11.37-52; 20.45-47)

23 Jesus said to the crowds and to his disciples: 2 The Pharisees and the teachers of the Law are experts in the Law of Moses. ³So obey everything they teach you, but don't do as they do. After all, they say one thing and do something else.

4 They pile heavy burdens on people's shoulders and won't lift a finger to help. ⁵Everything they do is just to show off in front of others. They even make a big show of wearing Scripture verses on their foreheads and arms, and they wear big tassels[1] for everyone to see. ⁶They love the best seats at banquets and the front seats in the meeting places. ⁷And when they are in the market, they like to have people greet them as their teachers.

8 But none of you should be called a teacher. You have only one teacher, and all of you are like

---

[1] *wearing Scripture verses on their foreheads and arms ... tassels*: As a sign of their love for the Lord and his teachings, the Jewish people had started wearing Scripture verses in small leather boxes. But the Pharisees tried to show off by making the boxes bigger than necessary. The Jewish people were also taught to wear tassels on the four corners of their robes to show their love for God.

brothers and sisters. 9Don't call anyone on earth your father. All of you have the same Father in heaven. 10None of you should be called the leader. The Messiah is your only leader. 11Whoever is the greatest should be the servant of the others. 12If you put yourself above others, you will be put down. But if you humble yourself, you will be honored.

13-14 You Pharisees and teachers of the Law of Moses are in for trouble! You're nothing but show-offs. You lock people out of the kingdom of heaven. You won't go in yourselves, and you keep others from going in.*m*

15 You Pharisees and teachers of the Law of Moses are in for trouble! You're nothing but show-offs. You travel over land and sea to win one follower. And when you have done so, you make that person twice as fit for hell as you are.

16 You are in for trouble! You are supposed to lead others, but you are blind. You teach that it doesn't matter if a person swears by the temple. But you say that it does matter if someone swears by the gold in the temple. 17You blind fools! Which is greater, the gold or the temple that makes the gold sacred?

18 You also teach that it doesn't matter if a person swears by the altar. But you say that it

---

m from going in: Some manuscripts add, "You Pharisees and teachers are in for trouble! And you're nothing but show-offs! You cheat widows out of their homes and then pray long prayers just to show off. So you will be punished most of all."

does matter if someone swears by the gift on the altar. [19]Are you blind? Which is more important, the gift or the altar that makes the gift sacred? [20]Anyone who swears by the altar also swears by everything on it. [21]And anyone who swears by the temple also swears by God, who lives there. [22]To swear by heaven is the same as swearing by God's throne and by the one who sits on that throne.

23 You Pharisees and teachers are show-offs, and you're in for trouble! You give God a tenth of the spices from your garden, such as mint, dill, and cumin. Yet you neglect the more important matters of the Law, such as justice, mercy, and faithfulness. These are the important things you should have done, though you should not have left the others undone either. [24]You blind leaders! You strain out a small fly but swallow a camel.

25 You Pharisees and teachers are show-offs, and you're in for trouble! You wash the outside of your cups and dishes, while inside there is nothing but greed and selfishness. [26]You blind Pharisee! First clean the inside of a cup, and then the outside will also be clean.

27 You Pharisees and teachers are in for trouble! You're nothing but show-offs. You're like tombs that have been whitewashed.[n] On the outside they

---

[n] *whitewashed*: Tombs were whitewashed to keep anyone from accidentally touching them. A person who touched a dead body or a tomb was considered unclean and could not worship with the rest of the Jewish people.

are beautiful, but inside they are full of bones and filth. 28That's what you are like. Outside you look good, but inside you are evil and only pretend to be good.

29 You Pharisees and teachers are nothing but show-offs, and you're in for trouble! You build monuments for the prophets and decorate the tombs of good people. 30And you claim that you would not have taken part with your ancestors in killing the prophets. 31But you prove that you really are the relatives of the ones who killed the prophets. 32So keep on doing everything they did. 33You are nothing but snakes and the children of snakes! How can you escape going to hell?

34 I will send prophets and wise people and experts in the Law of Moses to you. But you will kill them or nail them to a cross or beat them in your meeting places or chase them from town to town. 35That's why you will be held guilty for the murder of every good person, beginning with the good man Abel. This also includes Barachiah's son Zechariah,*o* the man you murdered between the temple and the altar. 36I can promise that you people living today will be punished for all these things!

-----

o Zechariah: Genesis is the first book in the Jewish Scriptures, and it tells that Abel was the first person to be murdered. Second Chronicles is the last book in the Jewish Scriptures, and the last murder that it tells about is that of Zechariah.

Jesus Loves Jerusalem
(Luke 13.34,35)

37 Jerusalem, Jerusalem! Your people have killed the prophets and have stoned the messengers who were sent to you. I have often wanted to gather your people, as a hen gathers her chicks under her wings. But you wouldn't let me. 38 And now your temple will be deserted. 39 You won't see me again until you say,

"Blessed is the one
    who comes in the name of the Lord."

The Temple Will Be Destroyed
(Mark 13.1,2; Luke 21.5,6)

24 After Jesus left the temple, his disciples came over and said, "Look at all these buildings!"

2 Jesus replied, "Do you see these buildings? They will certainly be torn down! Not one stone will be left in place."

Warning about Trouble
(Mark 13.3-13; Luke 21.7-19)

3 Later, as Jesus was sitting on the Mount of Olives, his disciples came to him in private and asked, "When will this happen? What will be the sign of your coming and of the end of the world?"

4 Jesus answered:

Don't let anyone fool you. 5 Many will come and claim to be me. They will say that they are the Messiah, and they will fool many people.

6 You will soon hear about wars and threats of wars, but don't be afraid. These things will have

to happen first, but that isn't the end. 7Nations and kingdoms will go to war against each other. People will starve to death, and in some places there will be earthquakes. 8But this is just the beginning of troubles.

9 You will be arrested, punished, and even killed. Because of me, you will be hated by people of all nations. 10Many will give up and will betray and hate each other. 11Many false prophets will come and fool a lot of people. 12Evil will spread and cause many people to stop loving others. 13But if you keep on being faithful right to the end, you will be saved. 14When the good news about the kingdom has been preached all over the world and told to all nations, the end will come.

The Horrible Thing
(Mark 13.14-23; Luke 21.20-24)

15 Someday you will see that "Horrible Thing" in the holy place, just as the prophet Daniel said. Everyone who reads this must try to understand! 16If you are living in Judea at that time, run to the mountains. 17If you are on the roofp of your house, don't go inside to get anything. 18If you are out in the field, don't go back for your coat. 19It will be a terrible time for women who are expecting babies or nursing young children. 20And pray that you won't have

---

p roof: In Palestine the houses usually had a flat roof. Stairs on the outside led up to the roof, which was made of beams and boards covered with packed earth.

to escape in winter or on a Sabbath.[q] 21This will
be the worst time of suffering since the beginning of the world, and nothing this terrible will
ever happen again. 22If God doesn't make the
time shorter, no one will be left alive. But
because of God's chosen ones, he will make the
time shorter.

23 Someone may say, "Here is the Messiah!"
or "There he is!" But don't believe it. 24False
messiahs and false prophets will come and work
great miracles and signs. They will even try to
fool God's chosen ones. 25But I have warned
you ahead of time. 26If you are told that the
Messiah is out in the desert, don't go there!
And if you are told that he is in some secret
place, don't believe it! 27The coming of the Son
of Man will be like lightning that can be seen
from east to west. 28Where there is a corpse,
there will always be buzzards.[r]

---

[q] *in winter or on a Sabbath*: In Palestine the winters are
cold and rainy and make travel difficult. The Jewish
people were not allowed to travel much more than half a
mile on the Sabbath. For these reasons it was hard for
them to escape from their enemies in the winter or on a
Sabbath.

[r] *Where there is a corpse, there will always be buzzards*:
This saying may mean that when anything important
happens, people soon know about it. Or the saying may
mean that whenever something bad happens, curious
people gather around and stare. But the word translated
"buzzard" also means "eagle" and may refer to the
Roman army, which had an eagle as its symbol.

When the Son of Man Appears
(Mark 13.24-27; Luke 21.25-28)

29 Right after those days of suffering,

"The sun will become dark,
  and the moon will no longer shine.
The stars will fall,
  and the powers in the sky*s*
    will be shaken."

30 Then a sign will appear in the sky. And there will be the Son of Man.*t* All nations on earth will weep when they see the Son of Man coming on the clouds of heaven with power and great glory. 31 At the sound of a loud trumpet, he will send his angels to bring his chosen ones together from all over the earth.

A Lesson from a Fig Tree
(Mark 13.28-31; Luke 21.29-33)

32 Learn a lesson from a fig tree. When its branches sprout and start putting out leaves, you know that summer is near. 33 So when you see all these things happening, you will know that the time has almost come.*u* 34 I can promise you that some of the people of this generation will still be alive when all this happens. 35 The

---

s *the powers in the sky*: In ancient times people thought that the stars were spiritual powers.

t *And there will be the Son of Man*: Or "And it will be the Son of Man."

u *the time has almost come*: Or "he (that is, the Son of Man) will soon be here."

sky and the earth won't last forever, but my words will.

No One Knows the Day or Time
(Mark 13.32-37; Luke 17.26-30, 34-36)

36 No one knows the day or hour. The angels in heaven don't know, and the Son himself doesn't know.[v] Only the Father knows. 37 When the Son of Man appears, things will be just as they were when Noah lived. 38 People were eating, drinking, and getting married right up to the day that the flood came and Noah went into the big boat. 39 They didn't know anything was happening until the flood came and swept them all away. That is how it will be when the Son of Man appears.

40 Two men will be in the same field, but only one will be taken. The other will be left. 41 Two women will be together grinding grain, but only one will be taken. The other will be left. 42 So be on your guard! You don't know when your Lord will come. 43 Homeowners never know when a thief is coming, and they are always on guard to keep one from breaking in. 44 Always be ready! You don't know when the Son of Man will come.

Faithful and Unfaithful Servants
(Luke 12.35-48)

45 Who are faithful and wise servants? Who are the ones the master will put in charge of giving the other servants their food supplies at the proper

---

[v] and the Son himself doesn't know: These words are not in some manuscripts.

time? ⁴⁶Servants are fortunate if their master comes and finds them doing their job. ⁴⁷You may be sure that a servant who is always faithful will be put in charge of everything the master owns. ⁴⁸But suppose one of the servants thinks that the master won't return until late. ⁴⁹Suppose that evil servant starts beating the other servants and eats and drinks with people who are drunk. ⁵⁰If that happens, the master will surely come on a day and at a time when the servant least expects him. ⁵¹That servant will then be punished and thrown out with the ones who only pretended to serve their master. There they will cry and grit their teeth in pain.

A Story about Ten Girls

25 The kingdom of heaven is like what happened one night when ten girls took their oil lamps and went to a wedding to meet the groom.ʷ ²Five of the girls were foolish and five were wise. ³The foolish ones took their lamps, but no extra oil. ⁴The ones who were wise took along extra oil for their lamps.

5 The groom was late arriving, and the girls became drowsy and fell asleep. ⁶Then in the middle of the night someone shouted, "Here's the groom! Come to meet him!"

ʷ *to meet the groom*: Some manuscripts add "and the bride." It was the custom for the groom to go to the home of the bride's parents to get his bride. Young girls and other guests would then go with them to the home of the groom's parents, where the wedding feast would take place.

7 When the girls got up and started getting their lamps ready, 8the foolish ones said to the others, "Let us have some of your oil! Our lamps are going out."

9 The girls who were wise answered, "There's not enough oil for all of us! Go and buy some for yourselves."

10 While the foolish girls were on their way to get some oil, the groom arrived. The girls who were ready went into the wedding, and the doors were closed. 11Later the other girls returned and shouted, "Sir, sir! Open the door for us!"

12 But the groom replied, "I don't even know you!"

13 So, my disciples, always be ready! You don't know the day or the time when all this will happen.

A Story about Three Servants
(Luke 19.11-27)

14 The kingdom is also like what happened when a man went away and put his three servants in charge of all he owned. 15The man knew what each servant could do. So he handed five thousand coins to the first servant, two thousand to the second, and one thousand to the third. Then he left the country.

16 As soon as the man had gone, the servant with the five thousand coins used them to earn five thousand more. 17The servant who had two thousand coins did the same with his money and earned two thousand more. 18But the servant with one thousand coins dug a hole and hid his master's money in the ground.

19 Some time later the master of those servants returned. He called them in and asked what they had done with his money. 20 The servant who had been given five thousand coins brought them in with the five thousand that he had earned. He said, "Sir, you gave me five thousand coins, and I have earned five thousand more."

21 "Wonderful!" his master replied. "You are a good and faithful servant. I left you in charge of only a little, but now I will put you in charge of much more. Come and share in my happiness!"

22 Next, the servant who had been given two thousand coins came in and said, "Sir, you gave me two thousand coins, and I have earned two thousand more."

23 "Wonderful!" his master replied. "You are a good and faithful servant. I left you in charge of only a little, but now I will put you in charge of much more. Come and share in my happiness!"

24 The servant who had been given one thousand coins then came in and said, "Sir, I know that you are hard to get along with. You harvest what you don't plant and gather crops where you haven't scattered seed. 25 I was frightened and went out and hid your money in the ground. Here is every single coin!"

26 The master of the servant told him, "You are lazy and good-for-nothing! You know that I harvest what I don't plant and gather crops where I haven't scattered seed. 27 You could have at least put my money in the bank, so that I could have earned interest on it."

28 Then the master said, "Now your money will be taken away and given to the servant with ten thousand coins! 29Everyone who has something will be given more, and they will have more than enough. But everything will be taken from those who don't have anything. 30You are a worthless servant, and you will be thrown out into the dark where people will cry and grit their teeth in pain."

The Final Judgment

31 When the Son of Man comes in his glory with all of his angels, he will sit on his royal throne. 32The people of all nations will be brought before him, and he will separate them, as shepherds separate their sheep from their goats.

33 He will place the sheep on his right and the goats on his left. 34Then the king will say to those on his right, "My father has blessed you! Come and receive the kingdom that was prepared for you before the world was created. 35When I was hungry, you gave me something to eat, and when I was thirsty, you gave me something to drink. When I was a stranger, you welcomed me, 36and when I was naked, you gave me clothes to wear. When I was sick, you took care of me, and when I was in jail, you visited me."

37 Then the ones who pleased the Lord will ask, "When did we give you something to eat or drink? 38When did we welcome you as a stranger or give you clothes to wear 39or visit you while you were sick or in jail?"

40 The king will answer, "Whenever you did it for any of my people, no matter how unimportant they seemed, you did it for me."

41 Then the king will say to those on his left, "Get away from me! You are under God's curse. Go into the everlasting fire prepared for the devil and his angels! 42I was hungry, but you did not give me anything to eat, and I was thirsty, but you did not give me anything to drink. 43I was a stranger, but you did not welcome me, and I was naked, but you did not give me any clothes to wear. I was sick and in jail, but you did not take care of me."

44 Then the people will ask, "Lord, when did we fail to help you when you were hungry or thirsty or a stranger or naked or sick or in jail?"

45 The king will say to them, "Whenever you failed to help any of my people, no matter how unimportant they seemed, you failed to do it for me."

46 Then Jesus said, "Those people will be punished forever. But the ones who pleased God will have eternal life."

The Plot To Kill Jesus
(Mark 14.1,2; Luke 22.1,2; John 11.45-53)

26 When Jesus had finished teaching, he told his disciples, 2"You know that two days from now will be Passover. That is when the Son of Man will be handed over to his enemies and nailed to a cross."

3 At that time the chief priests and the nation's leaders were meeting at the home of Caiaphas the high priest. 4They planned how they could sneak

around and have Jesus arrested and put to death. 5But they said, "We must not do it during Passover, because the people will riot."

At Bethany
(Mark 14.3-9; John 12.1-8)

6 Jesus was in the town of Bethany, eating at the home of Simon, who had leprosy.x 7A woman came in with a bottle of expensive perfume and poured it on Jesus' head. 8But when his disciples saw this, they became angry and complained, "Why such a waste? 9We could have sold this perfume for a lot of money and given it to the poor."

10 Jesus knew what they were thinking, and he said:

Why are you bothering this woman? She has done a beautiful thing for me. 11You will always have the poor with you, but you won't always have me. 12She has poured perfume on my body to prepare it for burial.y 13You may be sure that wherever the good news is told all over the world, people will remember what she has done. And they will tell others.

Judas and the Chief Priests
(Mark 14.10, 11; Luke 22.3-6)

14 Judas Iscariotz was one of the twelve disciples. He went to the chief priests 15and asked, "How much

---

x *leprosy*: See the note at 8.2.
y *poured perfume on my body to prepare it for burial*: The Jewish people taught that giving someone a proper burial was even more important than helping the poor.
z *Iscariot*: See the note at 10.4.

will you give me if I help you arrest Jesus?" They paid Judas thirty silver coins, 16and from then on he started looking for a good chance to betray Jesus.

Jesus Eats the Passover Meal with His Disciples
(Mark 14.12-21; Luke 22.7-13; John 13.21-30)

17 On the first day of the Festival of Thin Bread, Jesus' disciples came to him and asked, "Where do you want us to prepare the Passover meal?"

18 Jesus told them to go to a certain man in the city and tell him, "Our teacher says, 'My time has come! I want to eat the Passover meal with my disciples in your home.'" 19They did as Jesus told them and prepared the meal.

20-21 When Jesus was eating with his twelve disciples that evening, he said, "One of you will surely hand me over to my enemies."

22 The disciples were very sad, and each one said to Jesus, "Lord, you can't mean me!"

23 He answered, "One of you men who has eaten with me from this dish will betray me. 24The Son of Man will die, as the Scriptures say. But it's going to be terrible for the one who betrays me! That man would be better off if he had never been born."

25 Judas said, "Teacher, you surely don't mean me!"

"That's what you say!" Jesus replied. But later, Judas did betray him.

The Lord's Supper
(Mark 14.22-26; Luke 22.14-23; 1 Corinthians 11.23-25)

26 During the meal Jesus took some bread in his hands. He blessed the bread and broke it. Then he

gave it to his disciples and said, "Take this and eat it. This is my body."

27 Jesus picked up a cup of wine and gave thanks to God. He then gave it to his disciples and said, "Take this and drink it. 28This is my blood, and with it God makes his agreement with you. It will be poured out, so that many people will have their sins forgiven. 29From now on I am not going to drink any wine, until I drink new wine with you in my Father's kingdom." 30Then they sang a hymn and went out to the Mount of Olives.

Peter's Promise

(Mark 14.27-31; Luke 22.31-34; John 13.36-38)

31 Jesus said to his disciples, "During this very night, all of you will reject me, as the Scriptures say,

'I will strike down the shepherd,
    and the sheep will be scattered.'

32But after I am raised to life, I will go to Galilee ahead of you."

33 Peter spoke up, "Even if all the others reject you, I never will!"

34 Jesus replied, "I promise you that before a rooster crows tonight, you will say three times that you don't know me." 35But Peter said, "Even if I have to die with you, I will never say I don't know you."

All the others said the same thing.

Jesus Prays

(Mark 14.32-42; Luke 22.39-46)

36 Jesus went with his disciples to a place called Gethsemane. When they got there, he told them, "Sit here while I go over there and pray."

37 Jesus took along Peter and the two brothers, James and John.[a] He was very sad and troubled, 38and he said to them, "I am so sad that I feel as if I am dying. Stay here and keep awake with me."

39 Jesus walked on a little way. Then he knelt with his face to the ground and prayed, "My Father, if it is possible, don't make me suffer by having me drink from this cup.[b] But do what you want, and not what I want."

40 He came back and found his disciples sleeping. So he said to Peter, "Can't any of you stay awake with me for just one hour? 41Stay awake and pray that you won't be tested. You want to do what is right, but you are weak."

42 Again Jesus went to pray and said, "My Father, if there is no other way, and I must suffer, I will still do what you want."

43 Jesus came back and found them sleeping again. They simply could not keep their eyes open. 44He left them and prayed the same prayer once more.

45 Finally, Jesus returned to his disciples and said, "Are you still sleeping and resting?[c] The time has come for the Son of Man to be handed over to sinners. 46Get up! Let's go. The one who will betray me is already here."

---

[a] *the two brothers, James and John*: The Greek text has "the two sons of Zebedee" (see 27.56).

[b] *having me drink from this cup*: In the Scriptures "to drink from a cup" sometimes means to suffer (see the note at 20.22).

[c] *Are you still sleeping and resting?*: Or "You may as well keep on sleeping and resting."

Jesus Is Arrested

(Mark 14.43-50; Luke 22.47-53; John 18.3-12)

47 Jesus was still speaking, when Judas the betrayer came up. He was one of the twelve disciples, and a large mob armed with swords and clubs was with him. They had been sent by the chief priests and the nation's leaders. 48Judas had told them ahead of time, "Arrest the man I greet with a kiss."*d*

49 Judas walked right up to Jesus and said, "Hello, teacher." Then Judas kissed him.

50 Jesus replied, "My friend, why are you here?"*e*

The men grabbed Jesus and arrested him. 51One of Jesus' followers pulled out a sword. He struck the servant of the high priest and cut off his ear.

52 But Jesus told him, "Put your sword away. Anyone who lives by fighting will die by fighting. 53Don't you know that I could ask my Father, and right away he would send me more than twelve armies of angels? 54But then, how could the words of the Scriptures come true, which say that this must happen?"

55 Jesus said to the mob, "Why do you come with swords and clubs to arrest me like a criminal? Day after day I sat and taught in the temple, and you didn't arrest me. 56But all this happened, so that what the prophets wrote would come true."

All of Jesus' disciples left him and ran away.

---

d *the man I greet with a kiss*: It was the custom for people to greet each other with a kiss on the cheek.

e *why are you here?*: Or "do what you came for."

Jesus Is Questioned by the Council
(Mark 14.53-65; Luke 22.54,55,63-71;
John 18.13,14,19-24)

57 After Jesus had been arrested, he was led off to the house of Caiaphas the high priest. The nation's leaders and the teachers of the Law of Moses were meeting there. 58But Peter followed along at a distance and came to the courtyard of the high priest's palace. He went in and sat down with the guards to see what was going to happen.

59 The chief priests and the whole council wanted to put Jesus to death. So they tried to find some people who would tell lies about him in court.*f* 60But they could not find any, even though many did come and tell lies. At last, two men came forward 61and said, "This man claimed that he would tear down God's temple and build it again in three days."

62 The high priest stood up and asked Jesus, "Why don't you say something in your own defense? Don't you hear the charges they are making against you?" 63But Jesus did not answer. So the high priest said, "With the living God looking on, you must tell the truth. Tell us, are you the Messiah, the Son of God?"*g*

64 "That is what you say!" Jesus answered. "But I tell all of you,

---

f *some people who would tell lies about him in court*: The Law of Moses taught that two witnesses were necessary before a person could be put to death (see verse 60).

g *Son of God*: One of the titles used for the kings of Israel.

'Soon you will see the Son of Man
   sitting at the right side[h] of God All-Powerful
   and coming on the clouds of heaven.'"

65 The high priest then tore his robe and said, "This man claims to be God! We don't need any more witnesses! You have heard what he said. 66 What do you think?"

They answered, "He is guilty and deserves to die!" 67 Then they spit in his face and hit him with their fists. Others slapped him 68 and said, "You think you are the Messiah! So tell us who hit you!"

Peter Says He Doesn't Know Jesus
(Mark 14.66-72; Luke 22.56-62; John 18.15-18, 25-27)

69 While Peter was sitting out in the courtyard, a servant girl came up to him and said, "You were with Jesus from Galilee."

70 But in front of everyone Peter said, "That isn't so! I don't know what you are talking about!"

71 When Peter had gone out to the gate, another servant girl saw him and said to some people there, "This man was with Jesus from Nazareth."

72 Again Peter denied it, and this time he swore, "I don't even know that man!"

73 A little while later some people standing there walked over to Peter and said, "We know that you are one of them. We can tell it because you talk like someone from Galilee."

74 Peter began to curse and swear, "I don't know that man!"

Right then a rooster crowed, 75 and Peter remembered

[h] right side: See the note at 22.44.

that Jesus had said, "Before a rooster crows, you will say three times that you don't know me." Then Peter went out and cried hard.

Jesus Is Taken to Pilate
(Mark 15.1; Luke 23.1,2; John 18.28-32)

27 Early the next morning all the chief priests and the nation's leaders met and decided that Jesus should be put to death. ²They tied him up and led him away to Pilate the governor.

The Death of Judas
(Acts 1.18,19)

3 Judas had betrayed Jesus, but when he learned that Jesus had been sentenced to death, he was sorry for what he had done. He returned the thirty silver coins to the chief priests and leaders ⁴and said, "I have sinned by betraying a man who has never done anything wrong."

"So what? That's your problem," they replied. ⁵Judas threw the money into the temple and then went out and hanged himself.

6 The chief priests picked up the money and said, "This money was paid to have a man killed. We can't put it in the temple treasury." ⁷Then they had a meeting and decided to buy a field that belonged to someone who made clay pots. They wanted to use it as a grave-yard for foreigners. ⁸That's why people still call that place "Field of Blood." ⁹So the words of the prophet Jeremiah came true,

"They took the thirty silver coins,
    the price of a person
        among the people of Israel.

¹⁰ They paid it for a potter's field,[i]
as the Lord had commanded me."

Pilate Questions Jesus

(Mark 15.2-5; Luke 23.3-5; John 18.33-38)

11 Jesus was brought before Pilate the governor, who asked him, "Are you the king of the Jews?"

"Those are your words!" Jesus answered. ¹²And when the chief priests and leaders brought their charges against him, he did not say a thing.

13 Pilate asked him, "Don't you hear what crimes they say you have done?" ¹⁴But Jesus did not say anything, and the governor was greatly amazed.

The Death Sentence

(Mark 15.6-15; Luke 23.13-26; John 18.39–19.16)

15 During Passover the governor always freed a prisoner chosen by the people. ¹⁶At that time a well-known terrorist named Jesus Barabbas[j] was in jail. ¹⁷So when the crowd came together, Pilate asked them, "Which prisoner do you want me to set free? Do you want Jesus Barabbas or Jesus who is called the Messiah?" ¹⁸Pilate knew that the leaders had brought Jesus to him because they were jealous.

19 While Pilate was judging the case, his wife sent him a message. It said, "Don't have anything to do

---

[i] *a potter's field*: Perhaps a field owned by someone who made clay pots. But it may have been a field where potters came to get clay or to make pots or to throw away their broken pieces of pottery.

[j] *Jesus Barabbas*: Here and in verse 17 many manuscripts have "Barabbas."

with that innocent man. I have had nightmares because of him."

20 But the chief priests and the leaders convinced the crowds to ask for Barabbas to be set free and for Jesus to be killed. 21Pilate asked the crowd again, "Which of these two men do you want me to set free?"

"Barabbas!" they replied.

22 Pilate asked them, "What am I to do with Jesus, who is called the Messiah?"

They all yelled, "Nail him to a cross!"

23 Pilate answered, "But what crime has he done?"

"Nail him to a cross!" they yelled even louder.

24 Pilate saw that there was nothing he could do and that the people were starting to riot. So he took some water and washed his hands*k* in front of them and said, "I won't have anything to do with killing this man. You are the ones doing it!"

25 Everyone answered, "We and our own families will take the blame for his death!"

26 Pilate set Barabbas free. Then he ordered his soldiers to beat Jesus with a whip and nail him to a cross.

Soldiers Make Fun of Jesus
(Mark 15.16-21; John 19.2,3)

27 The governor's soldiers led Jesus into the fortress*l* and brought together the rest of the troops. 28They

---

k *washed his hands*: To show that he was innocent.

l *fortress*: The place where the Roman governor stayed. It was probably at Herod's palace west of Jerusalem, though it may have been Fortress Antonia north of the temple, where the Roman troops were stationed.

stripped off Jesus' clothes and put a scarlet robe[m] on him. 29They made a crown out of thorn branches and placed it on his head, and they put a stick in his right hand. The soldiers knelt down and pretended to worship him. They made fun of him and shouted, "Hey, you king of the Jews!" 30Then they spit on him. They took the stick from him and beat him on the head with it.

Jesus Is Nailed to a Cross
(Mark 15.22-32; Luke 23.27-43; John 19.17-27)

31 When the soldiers had finished making fun of Jesus, they took off the robe. They put his own clothes back on him and led him off to be nailed to a cross. 32On the way they met a man from Cyrene named Simon, and they forced him to carry Jesus' cross.

33 They came to a place named Golgotha, which means "Place of a Skull."[n] 34There they gave Jesus some wine mixed with a drug to ease the pain. But when Jesus tasted what it was, he refused to drink it.

35 The soldiers nailed Jesus to a cross and gambled to see who would get his clothes. 36Then they sat down to guard him. 37Above his head they put a sign that told why he was nailed there. It read, "This is Jesus, the King of the Jews." 38The soldiers also nailed two criminals on crosses, one to the right of Jesus and the other to his left.

39 People who passed by said terrible things about

---

[m] *scarlet robe*: This was probably a Roman soldier's robe.
[n] *Place of a Skull*: The place was probably given this name because it was near a large rock in the shape of a human skull.

Jesus. They shook their heads and [40]shouted, "So you're the one who claimed you could tear down the temple and build it again in three days! If you are God's Son, save yourself and come down from the cross!"

41 The chief priests, the leaders, and the teachers of the Law of Moses also made fun of Jesus. They said, [42]"He saved others, but he can't save himself. If he is the king of Israel, he should come down from the cross! Then we will believe him. [43]He trusted God, so let God save him, if he wants to. He even said he was God's Son." [44]The two criminals also said cruel things to Jesus.

The Death of Jesus
(Mark 15.33-41; Luke 23.44-49; John 19.28-30)

45 At noon the sky turned dark and stayed that way until three o'clock. [46]Then about that time Jesus shouted, "Eli, Eli, lema sabachthani?"[o] which means "My God, my God, why have you deserted me?"

47 Some of the people standing there heard Jesus and said, "He's calling for Elijah."[p] [48]One of them at once ran and grabbed a sponge. He soaked it in wine, then put it on a stick and held it up to Jesus.

49 Others said, "Wait! Let's see if Elijah will come[q] and save him." [50]Once again Jesus shouted, and then he died.

---

[o] Eli...sabachthani: These words are in Aramaic, a language spoken in Palestine during the time of Jesus.

[p] Elijah: In Aramaic the name "Elijah" sounds like "Eli," which means "my God."

[q] Elijah will come: See the note at 16.14.

51 At once the curtain in the temple[r] was torn in two from top to bottom. The earth shook, and rocks split apart. [52]Graves opened, and many of God's people were raised to life. [53]They left their graves, and after Jesus had risen to life, they went into the holy city, where they were seen by many people.

54 The officer and the soldiers guarding Jesus felt the earthquake and saw everything else that happened. They were frightened and said, "This man really was God's Son!"

55 Many women had come with Jesus from Galilee to be of help to him, and they were there, looking on at a distance. [56]Mary Magdalene, Mary the mother of James and Joseph, and the mother of James and John[s] were some of these women.

Jesus Is Buried

(Mark 15.42-47; Luke 23.50-56; John 19.38-42)

57 That evening a rich disciple named Joseph from the town of Arimathea [58]went and asked for Jesus' body. Pilate gave orders for it to be given to Joseph, [59]who took the body and wrapped it in a clean linen cloth. [60]Then Joseph put the body in his own tomb that had been cut into solid rock[t] and had never been used. He

---

[r] *curtain in the temple*: There were two curtains in the temple. One was at the entrance, and the other separated the holy place from the most holy place that the Jewish people thought of as God's home on earth. The second curtain is probably the one that is meant.

[s] *of James and John*: The Greek text has "of Zebedee's sons" (see 26.37).

[t] *tomb... solid rock*: Some of the Jewish people buried their dead in rooms carved into solid rock. A heavy stone was rolled against the entrance.

rolled a big stone against the entrance to the tomb and went away.

61 All this time Mary Magdalene and the other Mary were sitting across from the tomb.

62 On the next day, which was a Sabbath, the chief priests and the Pharisees went together to Pilate. 63They said, "Sir, we remember what that liar said while he was still alive. He claimed that in three days he would come back from death. 64So please order the tomb to be carefully guarded for three days. If you don't, his disciples may come and steal his body. They will tell the people that he has been raised to life, and this last lie will be worse than the first one."*u*

65 Pilate said to them, "All right, take some of your soldiers and guard the tomb as well as you know how." 66So they sealed it tight and placed soldiers there to guard it.

Jesus Is Alive
(Mark 16.1-8; Luke 24.1-12; John 20.1-10)

28 The Sabbath was over, and it was almost daybreak on Sunday when Mary Magdalene and the other Mary went to see the tomb. 2Suddenly a strong earthquake struck, and the Lord's angel came down from heaven. He rolled away the stone and sat on it. 3The angel looked as bright as lightning, and his clothes were white as snow. 4The guards shook from fear and fell down, as though they were dead.

5 The angel said to the women, "Don't be afraid! I know you are looking for Jesus, who was nailed to a cross. 6He isn't here! God has raised him to life, just

---

u the first one: Probably the belief that Jesus is the Messiah.

as Jesus said he would. Come, see the place where his body was lying. ⁷Now hurry! Tell his disciples that he has been raised to life and is on his way to Galilee. Go there, and you will see him. That is what I came to tell you."

8 The women were frightened and yet very happy, as they hurried from the tomb and ran to tell his disciples. ⁹Suddenly Jesus met them and greeted them. They went near him, held on to his feet, and worshiped him. ¹⁰Then Jesus said, "Don't be afraid! Tell my followers to go to Galilee. They will see me there."

Report of the Guard

11 While the women were on their way, some soldiers who had been guarding the tomb went into the city. They told the chief priests everything that had happened. ¹²So the chief priests met with the leaders and decided to bribe the soldiers with a lot of money. ¹³They said to the soldiers, "Tell everyone that Jesus' disciples came during the night and stole his body while you were asleep. ¹⁴If the governorᵛ hears about this, we will talk to him. You won't have anything to worry about." ¹⁵The soldiers took the money and did what they were told. The people of Judea still tell each other this story.

What Jesus' Followers Must Do
(Mark 16.14-18; Luke 24.36-49; John 20.19-23; Acts 1.6-8)

16 Jesus' eleven disciples went to a mountain in Galilee, where Jesus had told them to meet him. ¹⁷They saw him and worshiped him, but some of them doubted.

ᵛ *governor*: Pontius Pilate.

18 Jesus came to them and said:

I have been given all authority in heaven and on earth! 19Go to the people of all nations and make them my disciples. Baptize them in the name of the Father, the Son, and the Holy Spirit, 20and teach them to do everything I have told you. I will be with you always, even until the end of the world.

Mark Tells the Good News

ABOUT THIS BOOK

This is the shortest of the four New Testament books that tell about the life and teachings of Jesus, but it is also the most action-packed. From the very beginning of his ministry, Jesus worked mighty wonders. After choosing four followers (1.16-20), he immediately performed many miracles of healing. Among those healed were a man with an evil spirit in him (1.21-28), Simon's mother-in-law (1.30,31), crowds of sick people (1.32-34), and a man with leprosy (1.40-45). Over and over Mark tells how Jesus healed people, but always in such a way as to show that he did these miracles by the power of God.

The religious leaders refused to accept Jesus. This led to conflicts (2.2-3.6) that finally made them start looking for a way to kill him (11.18). But the demons saw the power of Jesus, and they knew that he was the Son of God, although Jesus would not let them tell anyone.

This book is full of miracles that amazed the crowds and Jesus' followers. But, according to Mark, the most powerful miracle of Jesus is his suffering and death. The first person to understand this miracle was the Roman soldier who saw Jesus die on the cross and said, "This man really was the Son of God!" (15.39).

This Gospel is widely thought to be the first one written. The many explanations of Aramaic words and

Jewish customs in Mark suggest that Mark wrote to Gentile or non-Jewish Christians. He wants to tell about Jesus and to encourage readers to believe in the power of Jesus to rescue them from sickness, demons, and death. He also wants to remind them that the new life of faith is not an easy life, and that they must follow Jesus by serving others and being ready to suffer as he did.

The first followers of Jesus to discover the empty tomb were three women, and the angel told them:

Don't be alarmed! You are looking for Jesus from Nazareth, who was nailed to a cross. God has raised him to life, and he isn't here. (16.6)

A QUICK LOOK AT THIS BOOK

The Preaching of John the Baptist
(Matthew 3.1-12; Luke 3.1-18; John 1.19-28)

1 This is the good news about Jesus Christ, the Son of God.[a] 2It began just as God had said in the book written by Isaiah the prophet,

"I am sending my messenger
    to get the way ready for you.
    3 In the desert someone is shouting,

---

[a] *the Son of God*: These words are not in some manuscripts.

'Get the road ready for the Lord!
Make a straight path for him.' "

4 So John the Baptist showed up in the desert and told everyone, "Turn back to God and be baptized! Then your sins will be forgiven."

5 From all Judea and Jerusalem crowds of people went to John. They told how sorry they were for their sins, and he baptized them in the Jordan River.

6 John wore clothes made of camel's hair. He had a leather strap around his waist and ate grasshoppers and wild honey.

7 John also told the people, "Someone more powerful is going to come. And I am not good enough even to stoop down and untie his sandals.[b] 8 I baptize you with water, but he will baptize you with the Holy Spirit!"

The Baptism of Jesus
(Matthew 3.13-17; Luke 3.21,22)

9 About that time Jesus came from Nazareth in Galilee, and John baptized him in the Jordan River. 10 As soon as Jesus came out of the water, he saw the sky open and the Holy Spirit coming down to him like a dove. 11 A voice from heaven said, "You are my own dear Son, and I am pleased with you."

Jesus and Satan
(Matthew 4.1-11; Luke 4.1-13)

12 Right away God's Spirit made Jesus go into the desert. 13 He stayed there for forty days while Satan tested him. Jesus was with the wild animals, but angels took care of him.

---

[b] *untie his sandals*: This was the duty of a slave.

Jesus Begins His Work
(Matthew 4.12-17; Luke 4.14,15)

14 After John was arrested, Jesus went to Galilee and told the good news that comes from God.[c] 15He said, "The time has come! God's kingdom will soon be here.[d] Turn back to God and believe the good news!"

Jesus Chooses Four Fishermen
(Matthew 4.18-22; Luke 5.1-11)

16 As Jesus was walking along the shore of Lake Galilee, he saw Simon and his brother Andrew. They were fishermen and were casting their nets into the lake. 17Jesus said to them, "Come with me! I will teach you how to bring in people instead of fish." 18Right then the two brothers dropped their nets and went with him.

19 Jesus walked on and soon saw James and John, the sons of Zebedee. They were in a boat, mending their nets. 20At once Jesus asked them to come with him. They left their father in the boat with the hired workers and went with him.

A Man with an Evil Spirit
(Luke 4.31-37)

21 Jesus and his disciples went to the town of Capernaum. Then on the next Sabbath he went into the Jewish meeting place and started teaching. 22Everyone was amazed at his teaching. He taught with authority,

---

[c] *that comes from God*: Or "that is about God."
[d] *will soon be here*: Or "is already here."

and not like the teachers of the Law of Moses. 23Suddenly a man with an evil spirit[e] in him entered the meeting place and yelled, 24"Jesus from Nazareth, what do you want with us? Have you come to destroy us? I know who you are! You are God's Holy One."

25 Jesus told the evil spirit, "Be quiet and come out of the man!"26The spirit shook him. Then it gave a loud shout and left.

27 Everyone was completely surprised and kept saying to each other, "What is this? It must be some new kind of powerful teaching! Even the evil spirits obey him." 28News about Jesus quickly spread all over Galilee.

Jesus Heals Many People
(Matthew 8.14-17; Luke 4.38-41)

29 As soon as Jesus left the meeting place with James and John, they went home with Simon and Andrew. 30When they got there, Jesus was told that Simon's mother-in-law was sick in bed with fever. 31Jesus went to her. He took hold of her hand and helped her up. The fever left her, and she served them a meal.

32 That evening after sunset,[f] all who were sick or had demons in them were brought to Jesus. 33In fact, the whole town gathered around the door of the house. 34Jesus healed all kinds of terrible diseases and forced out a lot of demons. But the demons knew who he was, and he did not let them speak.

---

[e] *evil spirit*: A Jewish person who had an evil spirit was considered "unclean" and was not allowed to eat or worship with other Jewish people.

[f] *after sunset*: The Sabbath was over, and a new day began at sunset.

35 Very early the next morning, Jesus got up and went to a place where he could be alone and pray. 36 Simon and the others started looking for him. 37 And when they found him, they said, "Everyone is looking for you!"

38 Jesus replied, "We must go to the nearby towns, so that I can tell the good news to those people. This is why I have come." 39 Then Jesus went to Jewish meeting places everywhere in Galilee, where he preached and forced out demons.

Jesus Heals a Man
(Matthew 8.1-4; Luke 5.12-16)

40 A man with leprosy[g] came to Jesus and knelt down.[h] He begged, "You have the power to make me well, if only you wanted to."

41 Jesus felt sorry for[i] the man. So he put his hand on him and said, "I want to! Now you are well." 42 At once the man's leprosy disappeared, and he was well.

43 After Jesus strictly warned the man, he sent him on his way. 44 He said, "Don't tell anyone about this. Just go and show the priest that you are well. Then take a gift to the temple as Moses commanded, and everyone will know that you have been healed."[j]

---

[g] *leprosy*: In biblical times the word "leprosy" was used for many different kinds of skin diseases.

[h] *and knelt down*: These words are not in some manuscripts.

[i] *felt sorry for*: Some manuscripts have "was angry with."

[j] *everyone will know that you have been healed*: People with leprosy had to be examined by a priest and told that they were well (that is, "clean") before they could once again live a normal life in the Jewish community. The gift that Moses commanded was the sacrifice of some lambs together with flour mixed with olive oil.

45 The man talked about it so much and told so many people, that Jesus could no longer go openly into a town. He had to stay away from the towns, but people still came to him from everywhere.

Jesus Heals a Crippled Man
(Matthew 9.1-8; Luke 5.17-26)

2 Jesus went back to Capernaum, and a few days later people heard that he was at home.[k] 2Then so many of them came to the house that there wasn't even standing room left in front of the door.

Jesus was still teaching 3when four people came up, carrying a crippled man on a mat. 4But because of the crowd, they could not get him to Jesus. So they made a hole in the roof[l] above him and let the man down in front of everyone.

5 When Jesus saw how much faith they had, he said to the crippled man, "My friend, your sins are forgiven."

6 Some of the teachers of the Law of Moses were sitting there. They started wondering, 7"Why would he say such a thing? He must think he is God! Only God can forgive sins."

8 Right away, Jesus knew what they were thinking, and he said, "Why are you thinking such things? 9Is it easier for me to tell this crippled man that his sins are forgiven or to tell him to get up and pick up his mat and go on home? 10I will show you that the Son of Man has the right to forgive sins here on earth." So

---

[k] at home: Or "in the house" (perhaps Simon Peter's home).
[l] roof: In Palestine the houses usually had a flat roof. Stairs on the outside led up to the roof that was made of beams and boards covered with packed earth.

Jesus said to the man, [11]"Get up! Pick up your mat and go on home."

12 The man got right up. He picked up his mat and went out while everyone watched in amazement. They praised God and said, "We have never seen anything like this!"

Jesus Chooses Levi
(Matthew 9.9-13; Luke 5.27-32)

13 Once again, Jesus went to the shore of Lake Galilee. A large crowd gathered around him, and he taught them. [14]As he walked along, he saw Levi, the son of Alphaeus. Levi was sitting at the place for paying taxes, and Jesus said to him, "Come with me!" So he got up and went with Jesus.

15 Later, Jesus and his disciples were having dinner at Levi's house.[m] Many tax collectors[n] and other sinners had become followers of Jesus, and they were also guests at the dinner.

16 Some of the teachers of the Law of Moses were Pharisees, and they saw that Jesus was eating with sinners and tax collectors. So they asked his disciples, "Why does he eat with tax collectors and sinners?"

17 Jesus heard them and answered, "Healthy people don't need a doctor, but sick people do. I didn't come to invite good people to be my followers. I came to invite sinners."

---

[m] *Levi's house*: Or "Jesus' house."

[n] *tax collectors*: These were usually Jewish people who paid the Romans for the right to collect taxes. They were hated by other Jews who thought of them as traitors to their country and to their religion.

People Ask about Going without Eating

(Matthew 9.14-17; Luke 5.33-39)

18 The followers of John the Baptist and the Pharisees often went without eating.[o] Some people came and asked Jesus, "Why do the followers of John and those of the Pharisees often go without eating, while your disciples never do?"

19 Jesus answered:

The friends of a bridegroom don't go without eating while he is still with them. 20But the time will come when he will be taken from them. Then they will go without eating.

21 No one patches old clothes by sewing on a piece of new cloth. The new piece would shrink and tear a bigger hole.

22 No one pours new wine into old wineskins. The wine would swell and burst the old skins.[p] Then the wine would be lost, and the skins would be ruined. New wine must be put into new wineskins.

A Question about the Sabbath

(Matthew 12.1-8; Luke 6.1-5)

23 One Sabbath Jesus and his disciples were walking through some wheat fields. His disciples were

---

[o] without eating: The Jewish people sometimes went without eating (also called "fasting") to show their love for God or to show sorrow for their sins.

[p] swell and burst the old skins: While the juice from grapes was becoming wine, it would swell and stretch the skins in which it had been stored. If the skins were old and stiff, they would burst.

picking grains of wheat as they went along.[q] 24Some Pharisees asked Jesus, "Why are your disciples picking grain on the Sabbath? They are not supposed to do that!"

25 Jesus answered, "Haven't you read what David did when he and his followers were hungry and in need? 26It was during the time of Abiathar the high priest. David went into the house of God and ate the sacred loaves of bread that only priests are allowed to eat. He also gave some to his followers."

27 Jesus finished by saying, "People were not made for the good of the Sabbath. The Sabbath was made for the good of people. 28So the Son of Man is Lord over the Sabbath."

A Man with a Crippled Hand
(Matthew 12.9-14; Luke 6.6-11)

3 The next time that Jesus went into the meeting place, a man with a crippled hand was there. 2The Pharisees[r] wanted to accuse Jesus of doing something wrong, and they kept watching to see if Jesus would heal him on the Sabbath.

3 Jesus told the man to stand up where everyone could see him. 4Then he asked, "On the Sabbath should we do good deeds or evil deeds? Should we save someone's life or destroy it?" But no one said a word.

5 Jesus was angry as he looked around at the people. Yet he felt sorry for them because they were

---

[q] went along: It was the custom to let hungry travelers pick grains of wheat.

[r] Pharisees: The Greek text has "they" (but see verse 6).

so stubborn. Then he told the man, "Stretch out your hand." He did, and his bad hand was healed.

6 The Pharisees left. And right away they started making plans with Herod's followers[s] to kill Jesus.

Large Crowds Come to Jesus

7 Jesus led his disciples down to the shore of the lake. Large crowds followed him from Galilee, Judea, [8]and Jerusalem. People came from Idumea, as well as other places east of the Jordan River. They also came from the region around the cities of Tyre and Sidon. All of these crowds came because they had heard what Jesus was doing. [9]He even had to tell his disciples to get a boat ready to keep him from being crushed by the crowds.

10 After Jesus had healed many people, the other sick people begged him to let them touch him. [11]And whenever any evil spirits saw Jesus, they would fall to the ground and shout, "You are the Son of God!" [12]But Jesus warned the spirits not to tell who he was.

Jesus Chooses His Twelve Apostles
(Matthew 10.1-4; Luke 6.12-16)

13 Jesus decided to ask some of his disciples to go up on a mountain with him, and they went. [14]Then he chose twelve of them to be his apostles,[t] so that they could be with him. He also wanted to send them out to preach [15]and to force out demons. [16]Simon was one of the twelve, and Jesus named him Peter. [17]There were

---

[s] *Herod's followers*: People who were political followers of the family of Herod the Great and his son Herod Antipas.

[t] *to be his apostles*: These words are not in some manuscripts.

also James and John, the two sons of Zebedee. Jesus called them Boanerges, which means "Thunderbolts." 18 Andrew, Philip, Bartholomew, Matthew, Thomas, James son of Alphaeus, and Thaddaeus were also apostles. The others were Simon, known as the Eager One,[u] 19 and Judas Iscariot,[v] who later betrayed Jesus.

Jesus and the Ruler of Demons
(Matthew 12.22-32; Luke 11.14-23; 12.10)

20 Jesus went back home,[w] and once again such a large crowd gathered that there was no chance even to eat. 21 When Jesus' family heard what he was doing, they thought he was crazy and went to get him under control.

22 Some teachers of the Law of Moses came from Jerusalem and said, "This man is under the power of Beelzebul, the ruler of demons! He is even forcing out demons with the help of Beelzebul."

23 Jesus told the people to gather around him. Then he spoke to them in riddles and said:

How can Satan force himself out? 24 A nation whose people fight each other won't last very long. 25 And a family that fights won't last long

---

[u] *known as the Eager One*: The Greek text has "Cananaean," which probably comes from a Hebrew word meaning "zealous" (see Luke 6.15). "Zealot" was the name later given to the members of a Jewish group which resisted and fought against the Romans.

[v] *Iscariot*: This may mean "a man from Kerioth" (a place in Judea). But more probably it means "a man who was a liar" or "a man who was a betrayer."

[w] *went back home*: Or "entered a house" (perhaps the home of Simon Peter).

either. 26So if Satan fights against himself, that will be the end of him.

27 How can anyone break into the house of a strong man and steal his things, unless he first ties up the strong man? Then he can take everything.

28 I promise you that any of the sinful things you say or do can be forgiven, no matter how terrible those things are. 29But if you speak against the Holy Spirit, you can never be forgiven. That sin will be held against you forever.

30 Jesus said this because the people were saying that he had an evil spirit in him.

Jesus' Mother and Brothers
(Matthew 12.46-50; Luke 8.19-21)

31 Jesus' mother and brothers came and stood outside. Then they sent someone with a message for him to come out to them. 32The crowd that was sitting around Jesus told him, "Your mother and your brothers and sisters *x* are outside and want to see you."

33 Jesus asked, "Who is my mother and who are my brothers?" 34Then he looked at the people sitting around him and said, "Here are my mother and my brothers. 35Anyone who obeys God is my brother or sister or mother."

A Story about a Farmer
(Matthew 13.1-9; Luke 8.4-8)

4 The next time Jesus taught beside Lake Galilee, a big crowd gathered. It was so large that he had

---

x and sisters: These words are not in some manuscripts.

to sit in a boat out on the lake, while the people stood on the shore. ²He used stories to teach them many things, and this is part of what he taught:

3 Now listen! A farmer went out to scatter seed in a field. ⁴While the farmer was scattering the seed, some of it fell along the road and was eaten by birds. ⁵Other seeds fell on thin, rocky ground and quickly started growing because the soil wasn't very deep. ⁶But when the sun came up, the plants were scorched and dried up, because they did not have enough roots. ⁷Some other seeds fell where thornbushes grew up and choked out the plants. So they did not produce any grain. ⁸But a few seeds did fall on good ground where the plants grew and produced thirty or sixty or even a hundred times as much as was scattered.

9 Then Jesus said, "If you have ears, pay attention."

Why Jesus Used Stories
(Matthew 13.10-17; Luke 8.9,10)

10 When Jesus was alone with the twelve apostles and some others, they asked him about these stories. ¹¹He answered:

I have explained the secret about God's kingdom to you, but for others I can use only stories. ¹²The reason is,

"These people will look and look,
    but never see.
They will listen and listen,
    but never understand.
If they did, they would turn to God,
    and he would forgive them."

Jesus Explains the Story about the Farmer
(Matthew 13.18-23; Luke 8.11-15)

13 Jesus told them:

If you don't understand this story, you won't understand any others. 14What the farmer is spreading is really the message about the kingdom. 15The seeds that fell along the road are the people who hear the message. But Satan soon comes and snatches it away from them. 16The seeds that fell on rocky ground are the people who gladly hear the message and accept it right away. 17But they don't have any roots, and they don't last very long. As soon as life gets hard or the message gets them in trouble, they give up.

18 The seeds that fell among the thornbushes are also people who hear the message. 19But they start worrying about the needs of this life. They are fooled by the desire to get rich and to have all kinds of other things. So the message gets choked out, and they never produce anything. 20The seeds that fell on good ground are the people who hear and welcome the message. They produce thirty or sixty or even a hundred times as much as was planted.

Light
(Luke 8.16-18)

21 Jesus also said:

You don't light a lamp and put it under a clay pot or under a bed. Don't you put a lamp on a lampstand? 22There is nothing hidden that will not be made public. There is no secret that will not be well known. ²³If you have ears, pay attention!

24 Listen carefully to what you hear! The way you treat others will be the way you will be treated—and even worse. ²⁵Everyone who has something will be given more. But people who don't have anything will lose what little they have.

Another Story about Seeds

26 Again Jesus said:

God's kingdom is like what happens when a farmer scatters seed in a field. ²⁷The farmer sleeps at night and is up and around during the day. Yet the seeds keep sprouting and growing, and he doesn't understand how. ²⁸It is the ground that makes the seeds sprout and grow into plants that produce grain. ²⁹Then when harvest season comes and the grain is ripe, the farmer cuts it with a sickle. *y*

A Mustard Seed
(Matthew 13.31,32; Luke 13.18,19)

30 Finally, Jesus said:

What is God's kingdom like? What story can I use to explain it? ³¹It is like what happens when a mustard seed is planted in the ground. It is the smallest seed in all the world. ³²But once it is planted, it grows larger than any garden plant.

---

y sickle: A knife with a long curved blade, used to cut grain and other crops.

It even puts out branches that are big enough for birds to nest in its shade.

The Reason for Teaching with Stories
(Matthew 13.34,35)

33 Jesus used many other stories when he spoke to the people, and he taught them as much as they could understand. 34 He did not tell them anything without using stories. But when he was alone with his disciples, he explained everything to them.

A Storm
(Matthew 8.23-27; Luke 8.22-25)

35 That evening, Jesus said to his disciples, "Let's cross to the east side." 36 So they left the crowd, and his disciples started across the lake with him in the boat. Some other boats followed along. 37 Suddenly a windstorm struck the lake. Waves started splashing into the boat, and it was about to sink.

38 Jesus was in the back of the boat with his head on a pillow, and he was asleep. His disciples woke him and said, "Teacher, don't you care that we're about to drown?"

39 Jesus got up and ordered the wind and the waves to be quiet. The wind stopped, and everything was calm.

40 Jesus asked his disciples, "Why were you afraid? Don't you have any faith?"

41 Now they were more afraid than ever and said to each other, "Who is this? Even the wind and the waves obey him!"

A Man with Evil Spirits
(Matthew 8.28-34; Luke 8.26-39)

5 Jesus and his disciples crossed Lake Galilee and came to shore near the town of Gerasa.ᶻ ²When he was getting out of the boat, a man with an evil spirit quickly ran to him ³from the graveyardᵃ where he had been living. No one was able to tie the man up anymore, not even with a chain. ⁴He had often been put in chains and leg irons, but he broke the chains and smashed the leg irons. No one could control him. ⁵Night and day he was in the graveyard or on the hills, yelling and cutting himself with stones.

6 When the man saw Jesus in the distance, he ran up to him and knelt down. ⁷He shouted, "Jesus, Son of God in heaven, what do you want with me? Promise me in God's name that you won't torture me!" ⁸The man said this because Jesus had already told the evil spirit to come out of him.

9 Jesus asked, "What is your name?"

The man answered, "My name is Lots, because I have 'lots' of evil spirits." ¹⁰He then begged Jesus not to send them away.

11 Over on the hillside a large herd of pigs was feeding. ¹²So the evil spirits begged Jesus, "Send us into those pigs! Let us go into them." ¹³Jesus let them go, and they went out of the man and into the pigs.

ᶻ *Gerasa*: Some manuscripts have "Gadara," and others have "Gergesa."

ᵃ *graveyard*: It was thought that demons and evil spirits lived in graveyards.

The whole herd of about two thousand pigs rushed down the steep bank into the lake and drowned.

14 The men taking care of the pigs ran to the town and the farms to spread the news. Then the people came out to see what had happened. ¹⁵When they came to Jesus, they saw the man who had once been full of demons. He was sitting there with his clothes on and in his right mind, and they were terrified.

16 Everyone who had seen what had happened told about the man and the pigs. ¹⁷Then the people started begging Jesus to leave their part of the country.

18 When Jesus was getting into the boat, the man begged to go with him. ¹⁹But Jesus would not let him. Instead, he said, "Go home to your family and tell them how much the Lord has done for you and how good he has been to you."

20 The man went away into the region near the ten cities known as Decapolis[b] and began telling everyone how much Jesus had done for him. Everyone who heard what had happened was amazed.

A Dying Girl and a Sick Woman
(Matthew 9.18-26; Luke 8.40-56)

21 Once again Jesus got into the boat and crossed Lake Galilee.[c] Then as he stood on the shore, a large crowd gathered around him. ²²The person in charge of the Jewish meeting place was also there. His name was Jairus, and when he saw Jesus, he went over to

---

[b] the ten cities known as Decapolis: A group of ten cities east of Samaria and Galilee, where the people followed the Greek way of life.
[c] crossed Lake Galilee: To the west side.

him. He knelt at Jesus' feet 23 and started begging him for help. He said, "My daughter is about to die! Please come and touch her, so she will get well and live." 24 Jesus went with Jairus. Many people followed along and kept crowding around.

25 In the crowd was a woman who had been bleeding for twelve years. 26 She had gone to many doctors, and they had not done anything except cause her a lot of pain. She had paid them all the money she had. But instead of getting better, she only got worse.

27 The woman had heard about Jesus, so she came up behind him in the crowd and barely touched his clothes. 28 She had said to herself, "If I can just touch his clothes, I will get well." 29 As soon as she touched them, her bleeding stopped, and she knew she was well.

30 At that moment Jesus felt power go out from him. He turned to the crowd and asked, "Who touched my clothes?"

31 His disciples said to him, "Look at all these people crowding around you! How can you ask who touched you?" 32 But Jesus turned to see who had touched him.

33 The woman knew what had happened to her. She came shaking with fear and knelt down in front of Jesus. Then she told him the whole story.

34 Jesus said to the woman, "You are now well because of your faith. May God give you peace! You are healed, and you will no longer be in pain."

35 While Jesus was still speaking, some men came from Jairus' home and said, "Your daughter has died! Why bother the teacher anymore?"

36 Jesus heard[d] what they said, and he said to Jairus, "Don't worry. Just have faith!"

37 Jesus did not let anyone go with him except Peter and the two brothers, James and John. 38 They went home with Jairus and saw the people crying and making a lot of noise.[e] 39 Then Jesus went inside and said to them, "Why are you crying and carrying on like this? The child isn't dead. She is just asleep." 40 But the people laughed at him.

After Jesus had sent them all out of the house, he took the girl's father and mother and his three disciples and went to where she was. 41-42 He took the twelve-year-old girl by the hand and said, "Talitha, koum!"[f] which means "Little girl, get up!" The girl got right up and started walking around.

Everyone was greatly surprised. 43 But Jesus ordered them not to tell anyone what had happened. Then he said, "Give her something to eat."

The People of Nazareth Turn against Jesus
(Matthew 13.53-58; Luke 4.16-30)

6 Jesus left and returned to his hometown[g] with his disciples. 2 The next Sabbath he taught in the Jewish meeting place. Many of the people who heard him were amazed and asked, "How can he do all this? Where did he get such wisdom and the power to

---

[d] heard: Or "ignored."

[e] crying and making a lot of noise: The Jewish people often hired mourners for funerals.

[f] Talitha, koum: These words are in Aramaic, a language spoken in Palestine during the time of Jesus.

[g] hometown: Nazareth.

work these miracles? [h] Isn't he the carpenter, [h] the son of Mary? Aren't James, Joseph, Judas, and Simon his brothers? Don't his sisters still live here in our town?" The people were very unhappy because of what he was doing.

4 But Jesus said, "Prophets are honored by everyone, except the people of their hometown and their relatives and their own family." 5 Jesus could not work any miracles there, except to heal a few sick people by placing his hands on them. 6 He was surprised that the people did not have any faith.

Instructions for the Twelve Apostles
(Matthew 10.5-15; Luke 9.1-6)

Jesus taught in all the neighboring villages. 7 Then he called together his twelve apostles and sent them out two by two with power over evil spirits. 8 He told them, "You may take along a walking stick. But don't carry food or a traveling bag or any money. 9 It's all right to wear sandals, but don't take along a change of clothes. 10 When you are welcomed into a home, stay there until you leave that town. 11 If any place won't welcome you or listen to your message, leave and shake the dust from your feet [i] as a warning to them."

12 The apostles left and started telling everyone to turn to God. 13 They forced out many demons and

---

[h] *carpenter*: The Greek word may also mean someone who builds or works with stone or brick.

[i] *shake the dust from your feet*: This was a way of showing rejection.

healed a lot of sick people by putting olive oil[j] on them.

The Death of John the Baptist
(Matthew 14.1-12; Luke 9.7-9)

14 Jesus became so well-known that Herod the ruler[k] heard about him. Some people thought he was John the Baptist, who had come back to life with the power to work miracles. [15]Others thought he was Elijah[l] or some other prophet who had lived long ago. [16]But when Herod heard about Jesus, he said, "This must be John! I had his head cut off, and now he has come back to life."

17-18 Herod had earlier married Herodias, the wife of his brother Philip. But John had told him, "It isn't right for you to take your brother's wife!" So, in order to please Herodias, Herod arrested John and put him in prison.

19 Herodias had a grudge against John and wanted to kill him. But she could not do it [20]because Herod was afraid of John and protected him. He knew that John was a good and holy man. Even though Herod was confused by what John said,[m] he was glad to listen to him. And he often did.

---

[j] *olive oil*: The Jewish people used olive oil as a way of healing people. Sometimes olive oil is a symbol for healing by means of a miracle (see James 5.14).

[k] *Herod the ruler*: Herod Antipas, the son of Herod the Great.

[l] *Elijah*: Many of the Jewish people expected the prophet Elijah to come and prepare the way for the Messiah.

[m] *was confused by what John said*: Some manuscripts have "did many things because of what John said."

21 Finally, Herodias got her chance when Herod gave a great birthday celebration for himself and invited his officials, his army officers, and the leaders of Galilee. 22 The daughter of Herodias[n] came in and danced for Herod and his guests. She pleased them so much that Herod said, "Ask for anything, and it's yours! 23 I swear that I will give you as much as half of my kingdom, if you want it."

24 The girl left and asked her mother, "What do you think I should ask for?"

Her mother answered, "The head of John the Baptist!"

25 The girl hurried back and told Herod, "Right now on a platter I want the head of John the Baptist!"

26 The king was very sorry for what he had said. But he did not want to break the promise he had made in front of his guests. 27 At once he ordered a guard to cut off John's head there in prison. 28 The guard put the head on a platter and took it to the girl. Then she gave it to her mother.

29 When John's followers learned that he had been killed, they took his body and put it in a tomb.

Jesus Feeds Five Thousand
(Matthew 14.13-21; Luke 9.10-17; John 6.1-14)

30 After the apostles returned to Jesus,[o] they told him everything they had done and taught. 31 But so many people were coming and going that Jesus and the apostles did not even have a chance to eat. Then

---

[n] *Herodias*: Some manuscripts have "Herod."

[o] *the apostles returned to Jesus*: From the mission on which he had sent them (see 6.7,12,13).

Jesus said, "Let's go to a place*p* where we can be alone and get some rest." ³²They left in a boat for a place where they could be alone. ³³But many people saw them leave and figured out where they were going. So people from every town ran on ahead and got there first.

34 When Jesus got out of the boat, he saw the large crowd that was like sheep without a shepherd. He felt sorry for the people and started teaching them many things.

35 That evening the disciples came to Jesus and said, "This place is like a desert, and it is already late. ³⁶Let the crowds leave, so they can go to the farms and villages near here and buy something to eat."

37 Jesus replied, "You give them something to eat."

But they asked him, "Don't you know that it would take almost a year's wages*q* to buy all of these people something to eat?"

38 Then Jesus said, "How much bread do you have? Go and see!"

They found out and answered, "We have five small loaves of bread*r* and two fish." ³⁹Jesus told his disciples to have the people sit down on the green grass. ⁴⁰They sat down in groups of a hundred and groups of fifty.

---

p a place: This was probably northeast of Lake Galilee (see verse 45).

q almost a year's wages: The Greek text has "two hundred silver coins." Each coin was the average day's wage for a worker.

r small loaves of bread: These would have been flat and round or in the shape of a bun.

41 Jesus took the five loaves and the two fish. He looked up toward heaven and blessed the food. Then he broke the bread and handed it to his disciples to give to the people. He also divided the two fish, so that everyone could have some.

42 After everyone had eaten all they wanted, 43 Jesus' disciples picked up twelve large baskets of leftover bread and fish.

44 There were five thousand men who ate the food.

Jesus Walks on the Water
(Matthew 14.22-33; John 6.15-21)

45 Right away, Jesus made his disciples get into the boat and start back across to Bethsaida. But he stayed until he had sent the crowds away. 46 Then he told them good-by and went up on the side of a mountain to pray.

47 Later that evening he was still there by himself, and the boat was somewhere in the middle of the lake. 48 He could see that the disciples were struggling hard, because they were rowing against the wind. Not long before morning, Jesus came toward them. He was walking on the water and was about to pass the boat.

49 When the disciples saw Jesus walking on the water, they thought he was a ghost, and they started screaming. 50 All of them saw him and were terrified. But at that same time he said, "Don't worry! I am Jesus. Don't be afraid." 51 He then got into the boat with them, and the wind died down. The disciples were completely confused. 52 Their minds were closed, and they could not understand the true meaning of the loaves of bread.

Jesus Heals Sick People in Gennesaret
(Matthew 14.34-36)

53 Jesus and his disciples crossed the lake and brought the boat to shore near the town of Gennesaret. 54 As soon as they got out of the boat, the people recognized Jesus. 55 So they ran all over that part of the country to bring their sick people to him on mats. They brought them each time they heard where he was. 56 In every village or farm or marketplace where Jesus went, the people brought their sick to him. They begged him to let them just touch his clothes, and everyone who did was healed.

The Teaching of the Ancestors
(Matthew 15.1-9)

7 Some Pharisees and several teachers of the Law of Moses from Jerusalem came and gathered around Jesus. 2 They noticed that some of his disciples ate without first washing their hands.*s*

3 The Pharisees and many others obey the teachings of their ancestors. They always wash their hands in the proper way*t* before eating. 4 None of them will eat anything they buy in the market until it is washed. They also follow a lot of other teachings, such as washing cups, pitchers, and bowls.*u*

---

s *without first washing their hands*: The Jewish people had strict laws about washing their hands before eating, especially if they had been out in public.

t *in the proper way*: The Greek text has "with the fist," but the exact meaning is not clear. It could mean "to the wrist" or "to the elbow."

u *bowls*: Some manuscripts add "and sleeping mats."

5 The Pharisees and teachers asked Jesus, "Why don't your disciples obey what our ancestors taught us to do? Why do they eat without washing their hands?"

6 Jesus replied:

You are nothing but show-offs! The prophet Isaiah was right when he wrote that God had said,

"All of you praise me with your words,
    but you never really think about me.
7 It is useless for you to worship me,
    when you teach rules
        made up by humans."

8 You disobey God's commands in order to obey what humans have taught. 9 You are good at rejecting God's commands so that you can follow your own teachings! 10 Didn't Moses command you to respect your father and mother? Didn't he tell you to put to death all who curse their parents? 11 But you let people get by without helping their parents when they should. You let them say that what they own has been offered to God.*v* 12 You won't let those people help their parents. 13 And you ignore God's commands in order to follow your own teaching. You do a lot of other things that are just as bad.

What Really Makes People Unclean
(Matthew 15.10-20)

14 Jesus called the crowd together again and said, "Pay attention and try to understand what I mean.

---

v *has been offered to God*: According to Jewish custom, when anything was offered to God, it could not be used for anyone else, not even for a person's parents.

15-16The food that you put into your mouth doesn't make you unclean and unfit to worship God. The bad words that come out of your mouth are what make you unclean."[w]

17 After Jesus and his disciples had left the crowd and had gone into the house, they asked him what these sayings meant. 18He answered, "Don't you know what I am talking about by now? You surely know that the food you put into your mouth cannot make you unclean. 19It doesn't go into your heart, but into your stomach, and then out of your body." By saying this, Jesus meant that all foods were fit to eat.

20 Then Jesus said:

What comes from your heart is what makes you unclean. 21Out of your heart come evil thoughts, vulgar deeds, stealing, murder, 22unfaithfulness in marriage, greed, meanness, deceit, indecency, envy, insults, pride, and foolishness. 23All of these come from your heart, and they are what make you unfit to worship God.

A Woman's Faith
(Matthew 15.21-28)

24 Jesus left and went to the region near the city of Tyre, where he stayed in someone's home. He did not want people to know he was there, but they found out anyway. 25A woman whose daughter had an evil spirit in her heard where Jesus was. And right away she came and knelt down at his feet. 26The woman was Greek and had been born in the part of Syria known

---

[w] unclean: Some manuscripts add, "If you have ears, pay attention."

as Phoenicia. She begged Jesus to force the demon out of her daughter. 27But Jesus said, "The children must first be fed! It isn't right to take away their food and feed it to dogs."ˣ

28 The woman replied, "Lord, even dogs eat the crumbs that children drop from the table."

29 Jesus answered, "That's true! You may go now. The demon has left your daughter." 30When the woman got back home, she found her child lying on the bed. The demon had gone.

Jesus Heals a Man Who Was Deaf and Could Hardly Talk

31 Jesus left the region around Tyre and went by way of Sidon toward Lake Galilee. He went through the land near the ten cities known as Decapolis.ʸ 32Some people brought to him a man who was deaf and could hardly talk. They begged Jesus just to touch him.

33 After Jesus had taken him aside from the crowd, he stuck his fingers in the man's ears. Then he spit and put it on the man's tongue. 34Jesus looked up toward heaven, and with a groan he said, "Effatha!"ᶻ which means "Open up!" 35At once the man could hear, and he had no more trouble talking clearly.

36 Jesus told the people not to say anything about what he had done. But the more he told them, the

---

ˣ *feed it to dogs*: The Jewish people often referred to Gentiles as dogs.

ʸ *the ten cities known as Decapolis*: See the note at 5.20.

ᶻ *Effatha*: This word is in Aramaic, a language spoken in Palestine during the time of Jesus.

more they talked about it. ³⁷They were completely amazed and said, "Everything he does is good! He even heals people who cannot hear or talk."

Jesus Feeds Four Thousand
(Matthew 15.32-39)

8 One day another large crowd gathered around Jesus. They had not brought along anything to eat. So Jesus called his disciples together and said, ²"I feel sorry for these people. They have been with me for three days, and they don't have anything to eat. ³Some of them live a long way from here. If I send them away hungry, they might faint on their way home."

4 The disciples said, "This place is like a desert. Where can we find enough food to feed such a crowd?"

5 Jesus asked them how much food they had. They replied, "Seven small loaves of bread."ᵃ

6 After Jesus told the crowd to sit down, he took the seven loaves and blessed them. He then broke the loaves and handed them to his disciples, who passed them out to the crowd. ⁷They also had a few little fish, and after Jesus had blessed these, he told the disciples to pass them around.

8-9 The crowd of about four thousand people ate all they wanted, and the leftovers filled seven large baskets.

As soon as Jesus had sent the people away, ¹⁰he got into the boat with the disciples and crossed to the territory near Dalmanutha.ᵇ

ᵃ *small loaves of bread*: See the note at 6.38.
ᵇ *Dalmanutha*: The place is unknown.

A Sign from Heaven
(Matthew 16.1-4)

11 The Pharisees came out and started an argument with Jesus. They wanted to test him by asking for a sign from heaven. 12Jesus groaned and said, "Why are you always looking for a sign? I can promise you that you will not be given one!" 13Then he left them. He again got into a boat and crossed over to the other side of the lake.

The Yeast of the Pharisees and of Herod
(Matthew 16.5-12)

14 The disciples had forgotten to bring any bread, and they had only one loaf with them in the boat. 15Jesus warned them, "Watch out! Guard against the yeast of the Pharisees and of Herod."[c]

16 The disciples talked this over and said to each other, "He must be saying this because we don't have any bread."

17 Jesus knew what they were thinking and asked, "Why are you talking about not having any bread? Don't you understand? Are your minds still closed? 18Are your eyes blind and your ears deaf? Don't you remember 19how many baskets of leftovers you picked up when I fed those five thousand people with only five small loaves of bread?"

"Yes," the disciples answered. "There were twelve baskets."

20 Jesus then asked, "And how many baskets of leftovers did you pick up when I broke seven small loaves of bread for those four thousand people?"

---

[c] *Herod*: Herod Antipas, the son of Herod the Great.

"Seven," they answered.

21 "Don't you know what I am talking about by now?" Jesus asked.

Jesus Heals a Blind Man at Bethsaida

22 As Jesus and his disciples were going into Bethsaida, some people brought a blind man to him and begged him to touch the man. 23 Jesus took him by the hand and led him out of the village, where he spit into the man's eyes. He placed his hands on the blind man and asked him if he could see anything. 24 The man looked up and said, "I see people, but they look like trees walking around."

25 Once again Jesus placed his hands on the man's eyes, and this time the man stared. His eyes were healed, and he saw everything clearly. 26 Jesus said to him, "You may return home now, but don't go into the village."

Who Is Jesus?
(Matthew 16.13-20; Luke 9.18-21)

27 Jesus and his disciples went to the villages near the town of Caesarea Philippi. As they were walking along, he asked them, "What do people say about me?"

28 The disciples answered, "Some say you are John the Baptist or maybe Elijah.[d] Others say you are one of the prophets."

29 Then Jesus asked them, "But who do you say I am?"

"You are the Messiah!" Peter replied.

---

[d] *Elijah*: See the note at 6.15.

30 Jesus warned the disciples not to tell anyone about him.

Jesus Speaks about His Suffering and Death
(Matthew 16.21-28; Luke 9.22-27)

31 Jesus began telling his disciples what would happen to him. He said, "The nation's leaders, the chief priests, and the teachers of the Law of Moses will make the Son of Man suffer terribly. He will be rejected and killed, but three days later he will rise to life." 32Then Jesus explained clearly what he meant.

Peter took Jesus aside and told him to stop talking like that. 33But when Jesus turned and saw the disciples, he corrected Peter. He said to him, "Satan, get away from me! You are thinking like everyone else and not like God."

34 Jesus then told the crowd and the disciples to come closer, and he said:

If any of you want to be my followers, you must forget about yourself. You must take up your cross and follow me. 35If you want to save your life,[e] you will destroy it. But if you give up your life for me and for the good news, you will save it. 36What will you gain, if you own the whole world but destroy yourself? 37What could you give to get back your soul?

38 Don't be ashamed of me and my message among these unfaithful and sinful people! If you

---

[e] *life*: In verses 35-37 the same Greek word is translated "life," "yourself," and "soul."

are, the Son of Man will be ashamed of you when he comes in the glory of his Father with the holy angels. [1] I can assure you that some of the people standing here will not die before they see God's kingdom come with power.

The True Glory of Jesus
(Matthew 17.1-13; Luke 9.28-36)

2 Six days later Jesus took Peter, James, and John with him. They went up on a high mountain, where they could be alone. There in front of the disciples, Jesus was completely changed. [3] And his clothes became much whiter than any bleach on earth could make them. [4] Then Moses and Elijah were there talking with Jesus.

5 Peter said to Jesus, "Teacher, it is good for us to be here! Let us make three shelters, one for you, one for Moses, and one for Elijah." [6] But Peter and the others were terribly frightened, and he did not know what he was talking about.

7 The shadow of a cloud passed over and covered them. From the cloud a voice said, "This is my Son, and I love him. Listen to what he says!" [8] At once the disciples looked around, but they saw only Jesus.

9 As Jesus and his disciples were coming down the mountain, he told them not to say a word about what they had seen, until the Son of Man had been raised from death. [10] So they kept it to themselves. But they wondered what he meant by the words "raised from death."

11 The disciples asked Jesus, "Don't the teachers of the Law of Moses say that Elijah must come before the Messiah does?"

12 Jesus answered:

Elijah certainly will come[f] to get everything ready. But don't the Scriptures also say that the Son of Man must suffer terribly and be rejected? 13I can assure you that Elijah has already come. And people treated him just as they wanted to, as the Scriptures say they would.

Jesus Heals a Boy
(Matthew 17.14-20; Luke 9.37-43a)

14 When Jesus and his three disciples came back down, they saw a large crowd around the other disciples. The teachers of the Law of Moses were arguing with them.

15 The crowd was really surprised to see Jesus, and everyone hurried over to greet him.

16 Jesus asked, "What are you arguing about?"

17 Someone from the crowd answered, "Teacher, I brought my son to you. A demon keeps him from talking. 18Whenever the demon attacks my son, it throws him to the ground and makes him foam at the mouth and grit his teeth in pain. Then he becomes stiff. I asked your disciples to force out the demon, but they couldn't do it."

19 Jesus said, "You people don't have any faith! How much longer must I be with you? Why do I have to put up with you? Bring the boy to me."

20 They brought the boy, and as soon as the demon saw Jesus, it made the boy shake all over. He fell down and began rolling on the ground and foaming at the mouth.

---

f *Elijah certainly will come*: See the note at 6.15.

21 Jesus asked the boy's father, "How long has he been like this?"

The man answered, "Ever since he was a child. 22 The demon has often tried to kill him by throwing him into a fire or into water. Please have pity and help us if you can!"

23 Jesus replied, "Why do you say 'if you can'? Anything is possible for someone who has faith!"

24 Right away the boy's father shouted, "I do have faith! Please help me to have even more."

25 When Jesus saw that a crowd was gathering fast, he spoke sternly to the evil spirit that had kept the boy from speaking or hearing. He said, "I order you to come out of the boy! Don't ever bother him again."

26 The spirit screamed and made the boy shake all over. Then it went out of him. The boy looked dead, and almost everyone said he was. 27 But Jesus took hold of his hand and helped him stand up.

28 After Jesus and the disciples had gone back home and were alone, they asked him, "Why couldn't we force out that demon?"

29 Jesus answered, "Only prayer can force out that kind of demon."

Jesus Again Speaks about His Death
(Matthew 17.22,23; Luke 9.43b-45)

30 Jesus left with his disciples and started through Galilee. He did not want anyone to know about it, 31 because he was teaching the disciples that the Son of Man would be handed over to people who would kill him. But three days later he would rise to life. 32 The disciples did not understand what Jesus meant, and they were afraid to ask.

Who Is the Greatest?
(Matthew 18.1-5; Luke 9.46-48)

33 Jesus and his disciples went to his home in Capernaum. After they were inside the house, Jesus asked them, "What were you arguing about along the way?" 34They had been arguing about which one of them was the greatest, and so they did not answer.

35 After Jesus sat down and told the twelve disciples to gather around him, he said, "If you want the place of honor, you must become a slave and serve others!"

36 Then Jesus had a child stand near him. He put his arm around the child and said, 37"When you welcome even a child because of me, you welcome me. And when you welcome me, you welcome the one who sent me."

For or against Jesus
(Luke 9.49,50)

38 John said, "Teacher, we saw a man using your name to force demons out of people. But he wasn't one of us, and we told him to stop."

39 Jesus said to his disciples:

Don't stop him! No one who works miracles in my name will soon turn and say something bad about me. 40Anyone who isn't against us is for us. 41And anyone who gives you a cup of water in my name, just because you belong to me, will surely be rewarded.

Temptations To Sin
(Matthew 18.6-9; Luke 17.1,2)

42 It will be terrible for people who cause even one of my little followers to sin. Those people

would be better off thrown into the ocean with a heavy stone tied around their necks. [43-44]So if your hand causes you to sin, cut it off! You would be better off to go into life crippled than to have two hands and be thrown into the fires of hell that never go out.[g] [45-46]If your foot causes you to sin, chop it off. You would be better off to go into life lame than to have two feet and be thrown into hell.[h] [47]If your eye causes you to sin, get rid of it. You would be better off to go into God's kingdom with only one eye than to have two eyes and be thrown into hell. [48]The worms there never die, and the fire never stops burning.

[49]Everyone must be salted with fire.[i]

[50]Salt is good. But if it no longer tastes like salt, how can it be made salty again? Have salt among you and live at peace with each other.[j]

Teaching about Divorce
(Matthew 19.1-12; Luke 16.18)

10 After Jesus left, he went to Judea and then on to the other side of the Jordan River. Once again

---

[g] *never go out*: Some manuscripts add, "The worms there never die, and the fire never stops burning."

[h] *thrown into hell*: Some manuscripts add, "The worms there never die, and the fire never stops burning."

[i] *salted with fire*: Some manuscripts add "and every sacrifice will be seasoned with salt." The verse may mean that Christ's followers must suffer because of their faith.

[j] *Have salt among you and live at peace with each other*: This may mean that when Christ's followers have to suffer because of their faith, they must still try to live at peace with each other.

large crowds came to him, and as usual, he taught them.

2 Some Pharisees wanted to test Jesus. So they came up to him and asked if it was right for a man to divorce his wife. 3Jesus asked them, "What does the Law of Moses say about that?"

4 They answered, "Moses allows a man to write out divorce papers and send his wife away."

5 Jesus replied, "Moses gave you this law because you are so heartless. 6But in the beginning God made a man and a woman. 7That's why a man leaves his father and mother and gets married. 8He becomes like one person with his wife. Then they are no longer two people, but one. 9And no one should separate a couple that God has joined together."

10 When Jesus and his disciples were back in the house, they asked him about what he had said. 11He told them, "A man who divorces his wife and marries someone else is unfaithful to his wife. 12A woman who divorces her husband[k] and marries again is also unfaithful."

Jesus Blesses Little Children
(Matthew 19.13-15; Luke 18.15-17)

13 Some people brought their children to Jesus so that he could bless them by placing his hands on them. But his disciples told the people to stop bothering him.

14 When Jesus saw this, he became angry and said, "Let the children come to me! Don't try to stop

---

[k] *A woman who divorces her husband*: Roman law let a woman divorce her husband, but Jewish law did not let a woman do this.

them. People who are like these little children belong to the kingdom of God.[1] 15I promise you that you cannot get into God's kingdom, unless you accept it the way a child does." 16Then Jesus took the children in his arms and blessed them by placing his hands on them.

A Rich Man
(Matthew 19.16-30; Luke 18.18-30)

17 As Jesus was walking down a road, a man ran up to him. He knelt down, and asked, "Good teacher, what can I do to have eternal life?"

18 Jesus replied, "Why do you call me good? Only God is good. 19You know the commandments. 'Do not murder. Be faithful in marriage. Do not steal. Do not tell lies about others. Do not cheat. Respect your father and mother.'"

20 The man answered, "Teacher, I have obeyed all these commandments since I was a young man."

21 Jesus looked closely at the man. He liked him and said, "There's one thing you still need to do. Go sell everything you own. Give the money to the poor, and you will have riches in heaven. Then come with me."

22 When the man heard Jesus say this, he went away gloomy and sad because he was very rich.

23 Jesus looked around and said to his disciples, "It's hard for rich people to get into God's kingdom!" 24The disciples were shocked to hear this. So Jesus

---

[1] *People who are like these little children belong to the kingdom of God*: Or "The kingdom of God belongs to people who are like these little children."

told them again, "It's terribly hard*m* to get into God's kingdom! 25In fact, it's easier for a camel to go through the eye of a needle than for a rich person to get into God's kingdom."

26 Jesus' disciples were even more amazed. They asked each other, "How can anyone ever be saved?"

27 Jesus looked at them and said, "There are some things that people cannot do, but God can do anything."

28 Peter replied, "Remember, we left everything to be your followers!"

29 Jesus told him:

You can be sure that anyone who gives up home or brothers or sisters or mother or father or children or land for me and for the good news 30will be rewarded. In this world they will be given a hundred times as many houses and brothers and sisters and mothers and children and pieces of land, though they will also be mistreated. And in the world to come, they will have eternal life. 31But many who are now first will be last, and many who are now last will be first.

Jesus Again Tells about His Death
(Matthew 20.17-19; Luke 18.31-34)

32 The disciples were confused as Jesus led them toward Jerusalem, and his other followers were afraid. Once again, Jesus took the twelve disciples aside and told them what was going to happen to him. He said:

---

m hard: Some manuscripts add "for people who trust in their wealth." Others add "for the rich."

33 We are now on our way to Jerusalem where the Son of Man will be handed over to the chief priests and the teachers of the Law of Moses. They will sentence him to death and hand him over to foreigners,[n] 34who will make fun of him and spit on him. They will beat him and kill him. But three days later he will rise to life.

The Request of James and John
(Matthew 20.20-28)

35 James and John, the sons of Zebedee, came up to Jesus and asked, "Teacher, will you do us a favor?"

36 Jesus asked them what they wanted, 37and they answered, "When you come into your glory, please let one of us sit at your right side and the other at your left."[o]

38 Jesus told them, "You don't really know what you're asking! Are you able to drink from the cup[p] that I must soon drink from or be baptized as I must be baptized?"[q]

39 "Yes, we are!" James and John answered.

Then Jesus replied, "You certainly will drink from the cup from which I must drink. And you will be baptized just as I must! 40But it isn't for me to say who will sit at my right side and at my left. That is for God to decide."

---

[n] *foreigners*: The Romans who ruled Judea at this time.

[o] *right side… left*: The most powerful people in a kingdom sat at the right and left side of the king.

[p] *drink from the cup*: In the Scriptures a "cup" is sometimes used as a symbol of suffering. To "drink from the cup" would be to suffer.

[q] *as I must be baptized*: Baptism is used with the same meaning that "cup" has in this verse.

41 When the ten other disciples heard this, they were angry with James and John. 42But Jesus called the disciples together and said:

You know that those foreigners who call themselves kings like to order their people around. And their great leaders have full power over the people they rule. 43But don't act like them. If you want to be great, you must be the servant of all the others. 44And if you want to be first, you must be everyone's slave. 45The Son of Man did not come to be a slave master, but a slave who will give his life to rescue[r] many people.

Jesus Heals Blind Bartimaeus
(Matthew 20.29-34; Luke 18.35-43)

46 Jesus and his disciples went to Jericho. And as they were leaving, they were followed by a large crowd. A blind beggar by the name of Bartimaeus son of Timaeus was sitting beside the road. 47When he heard that it was Jesus from Nazareth, he shouted, "Jesus, Son of David,[s] have pity on me!" 48Many people told the man to stop, but he shouted even louder, "Son of David, have pity on me!"

49 Jesus stopped and said, "Call him over!"

They called out to the blind man and said, "Don't be afraid! Come on! He is calling for you." 50The man threw off his coat as he jumped up and ran to Jesus.

---

r rescue: The Greek word often, though not always, means the payment of a price to free a slave or a prisoner.

s Son of David: The Jewish people expected the Messiah to be from the family of King David, and for this reason the Messiah was often called the "Son of David."

51 Jesus asked, "What do you want me to do for you?" The blind man answered, "Master,[t] I want to see!"

52 Jesus told him, "You may go. Your eyes are healed because of your faith."

Right away the man could see, and he went down the road with Jesus.

Jesus Enters Jerusalem

(Matthew 21.1-11; Luke 19.28-40; John 12.12-19)

11 Jesus and his disciples reached Bethphage and Bethany near the Mount of Olives. When they were getting close to Jerusalem, Jesus sent two of them on ahead. 2He told them, "Go into the next village. As soon as you enter it, you will find a young donkey that has never been ridden. Untie the donkey and bring it here. 3If anyone asks why you are doing that, say, 'The Lord[u] needs it and will soon bring it back.'"

4 The disciples left and found the donkey tied near a door that faced the street. While they were untying it, 5some of the people standing there asked, "Why are you untying the donkey?" 6They told them what Jesus had said, and the people let them take it.

7 The disciples led the donkey to Jesus. They put some of their clothes on its back, and Jesus got on. 8Many people spread clothes on the road, while others went to cut branches from the fields.[v]

9 In front of Jesus and behind him, people went along shouting,

---

[t] *Master*: A Hebrew word that may also mean "Teacher."

[u] *The Lord*: Or "The master of the donkey."

[v] *spread...branches from the fields*: This was one way that the Jewish people welcomed a famous person.

"Hooray!*w* God bless the one
    who comes in the name of the Lord!
10 God bless the coming kingdom
    of our ancestor David.
    Hooray for God in heaven above!"

11 After Jesus had gone to Jerusalem, he went into
the temple and looked around at everything. But since
it was already late in the day, he went back to Bethany
with the twelve disciples.

Jesus Puts a Curse on a Fig Tree
(Matthew 21.18, 19)

12 When Jesus and his disciples left Bethany the
next morning, he was hungry. 13From a distance
Jesus saw a fig tree covered with leaves, and he went
to see if there were any figs on the tree. But there
were not any, because it wasn't the season for figs.
14So Jesus said to the tree, "Never again will anyone
eat fruit from this tree!" The disciples heard him say
this.

Jesus in the Temple
(Matthew 21.12-17; Luke 19.45-48; John 2.13-22)

15 After Jesus and his disciples reached Jerusalem,
he went into the temple and began chasing out everyone who was selling and buying. He turned over the
tables of the moneychangers and the benches of those
who were selling doves. 16Jesus would not let anyone
carry things through the temple. 17Then he taught the
people and said, "The Scriptures say, 'My house should

---

w Hooray: This translates a word that can mean "please save
us." But it is most often used as a shout of praise to God.

be called a place of worship for all nations.' But you have made it a place where robbers hide!"

18 The chief priests and the teachers of the Law of Moses heard what Jesus said, and they started looking for a way to kill him. They were afraid of him, because the crowds were completely amazed at his teaching.

19 That evening, Jesus and the disciples went outside the city.

A Lesson from the Fig Tree
(Matthew 21.20-22)

20 As the disciples walked past the fig tree the next morning, they noticed that it was completely dried up, roots and all. [21]Peter remembered what Jesus had said to the tree. Then Peter said, "Teacher, look! The tree you put a curse on has dried up."

22 Jesus told his disciples:

Have faith in God! [23]If you have faith in God and don't doubt, you can tell this mountain to get up and jump into the sea, and it will. [24]Everything you ask for in prayer will be yours, if you only have faith.

25-26 Whenever you stand up to pray, you must forgive what others have done to you. Then your Father in heaven will forgive your sins.[x]

A Question about Jesus' Authority
(Matthew 21.23-27; Luke 20.1-8)

27 Jesus and his disciples returned to Jerusalem. And as he was walking through the temple, the chief

---

[x] *your sins:* Some manuscripts add, "But if you do not forgive others, God will not forgive you."

priests, the nation's leaders, and the teachers of the Law of Moses came over to him. 28They asked, "What right do you have to do these things? Who gave you this authority?"

29 Jesus answered, "I have just one question to ask you. If you answer it, I will tell you where I got the right to do these things. 30Who gave John the right to baptize? Was it God in heaven or merely some human being?"

31 They thought it over and said to each other, "We can't say that God gave John this right. Jesus will ask us why we didn't believe John. 32On the other hand, these people think that John was a prophet. So we can't say that it was merely some human who gave John the right to baptize."

They were afraid of the crowd 33and told Jesus, "We don't know."

Jesus replied, "Then I won't tell you who gave me the right to do what I do."

Renters of a Vineyard
(Matthew 21.33-46; Luke 20.9-19)

12 Jesus then told them this story:
A farmer once planted a vineyard. He built a wall around it and dug a pit to crush the grapes in. He also built a lookout tower. Then he rented out his vineyard and left the country.

2 When it was harvest time, he sent a servant to get his share of the grapes. 3The renters grabbed the servant. They beat him up and sent him away without a thing.

4 The owner sent another servant, but the renters beat him on the head and insulted him

terribly. 5Then the man sent another servant, and they killed him. He kept sending servant after servant. They beat some of them and killed others.

6 The owner had a son he loved very much. Finally, he sent his son to the renters because he thought they would respect him. 7But they said to themselves, "Someday he will own this vineyard. Let's kill him! That way we can have it all for ourselves." 8So they grabbed the owner's son and killed him. Then they threw his body out of the vineyard.

9 Jesus asked, "What do you think the owner of the vineyard will do? He will come and kill those renters and let someone else have his vineyard. 10You surely know that the Scriptures say,

'The stone that the builders tossed aside
    is now the most important stone of all.
11 This is something the Lord has done,
    and it is amazing to us.'"

12 The leaders knew that Jesus was really talking about them, and they wanted to arrest him. But because they were afraid of the crowd, they let him alone and left.

Paying Taxes
(Matthew 22.15-22; Luke 20.20-26)

13 The Pharisees got together with Herod's followers.y Then they sent some men to trick Jesus into saying something wrong. 14They went to him and

---

y *Herod's followers*: People who were political followers of the family of Herod the Great and his son Herod Antipas.

said, "Teacher, we know that you are honest. You treat everyone with the same respect, no matter who they are. And you teach the truth about what God wants people to do. Tell us, should we pay taxes to the Emperor or not?"

15 Jesus knew what they were up to, and he said, "Why are you trying to test me? Show me a coin!"

16 They brought him a silver coin, and he asked, "Whose picture and name are on it?"

"The Emperor's," they answered.

17 Then Jesus told them, "Give the Emperor what belongs to him and give God what belongs to God." The men were amazed at Jesus.

Life in the Future World
(Matthew 22.23-33; Luke 20.27-40)

18 The Sadducees did not believe that people would rise to life after death. So some of them came to Jesus and said:

19 Teacher, Moses wrote that if a married man dies and has no children, his brother should marry the widow. Their first son would then be thought of as the son of the dead brother. 20There were once seven brothers. The first one married, but died without having any children. 21The second brother married his brother's widow, and he also died without having children. The same thing happened to the third brother, 22and finally to all seven brothers. At last the woman died. 23When God raises people from death, whose wife will this woman be? After all, she had been married to all seven brothers.

24 Jesus answered:

You are completely wrong! You don't know what the Scriptures teach. And you don't know anything about the power of God. 25When God raises people to life, they won't marry. They will be like the angels in heaven. 26You surely know about people being raised to life. You know that in the story about Moses and the burning bush, God said, "I am the God worshiped by Abraham, Isaac, and Jacob."z 27He isn't the God of the dead, but of the living. You Sadducees are all wrong.

The Most Important Commandment
(Matthew 22.34-40; Luke 10.25-28)

28 One of the teachers of the Law of Moses came up while Jesus and the Sadducees were arguing. When he heard Jesus give a good answer, he asked him, "What is the most important commandment?"

29 Jesus answered, "The most important one says: 'People of Israel, you have only one Lord and God. 30You must love him with all your heart, soul, mind, and strength.' 31The second most important commandment says: 'Love others as much as you love yourself.' No other commandment is more important than these."

32 The man replied, "Teacher, you are certainly right to say there is only one God. 33It is also true that we must love God with all our heart, mind, and

---

z "I am the God worshiped by Abraham, Isaac, and Jacob": Jesus argues that if God is worshiped by these three, they must still be alive, because he is the God of the living.

strength, and that we must love others as much as we love ourselves. These commandments are more important than all the sacrifices and offerings that we could possibly make."

34 When Jesus saw that the man had given a sensible answer, he told him, "You are not far from God's kingdom." After this, no one dared ask Jesus any more questions.

About David's Son
(Matthew 22.41-46; Luke 20.41-44)

35 As Jesus was teaching in the temple, he said, "How can the teachers of the Law of Moses say that the Messiah will come from the family of King David? 36 The Holy Spirit had David say,

'The Lord said to my Lord:
    Sit at my right side *a*
    until I make your enemies
        into a footstool for you.'

37 If David called the Messiah his Lord, how can the Messiah be his son?" *b*

The large crowd enjoyed listening to Jesus teach.

Jesus Condemns the Pharisees and the Teachers of the Law of Moses
(Matthew 23.1-36; Luke 20.45-47)

38 As Jesus was teaching, he said:

Guard against the teachers of the Law of Moses! They love to walk around in long robes and be greeted in the market. 39 They like the

---

a right side: The place of power and honor.
b David...his son: See the note at 10.47.

front seats in the meeting places and the best seats at banquets. 40But they cheat widows out of their homes and pray long prayers just to show off. They will be punished most of all.

A Widow's Offering
(Luke 21.1-4)

41 Jesus was sitting in the temple near the offering box and watching people put in their gifts. He noticed that many rich people were giving a lot of money. 42Finally, a poor widow came up and put in two coins that were worth only a few pennies. 43Jesus told his disciples to gather around him. Then he said:

I tell you that this poor widow has put in more than all the others. 44Everyone else gave what they didn't need. But she is very poor and gave everything she had. Now she doesn't have a cent to live on.

The Temple Will Be Destroyed
(Matthew 24.1,2; Luke 21.5,6)

13 As Jesus was leaving the temple, one of his disciples said to him, "Teacher, look at these beautiful stones and wonderful buildings!"

2 Jesus replied, "Do you see these huge buildings? They will certainly be torn down! Not one stone will be left in place."

Warning about Trouble
(Matthew 24.3-14; Luke 21.7-19)

3 Later, as Jesus was sitting on the Mount of Olives across from the temple, Peter, James, John, and Andrew

came to him in private. 4They asked, "When will these things happen? What will be the sign that they are about to take place?"

5 Jesus answered:

Watch out and don't let anyone fool you! 6Many will come and claim to be me. They will use my name and fool many people.

7 When you hear about wars and threats of wars, don't be afraid. These things will have to happen first, but that isn't the end. 8Nations and kingdoms will go to war against each other. There will be earthquakes in many places, and people will starve to death. But this is just the beginning of troubles.

9 Be on your guard! You will be taken to courts and beaten with whips in their meeting places. And because of me, you will have to stand before rulers and kings to tell about your faith. 10But before the end comes, the good news must be preached to all nations.

11 When you are arrested, don't worry about what you will say. You will be given the right words when the time comes. But you will not really be the ones speaking. Your words will come from the Holy Spirit.

12 Brothers and sisters will betray each other and have each other put to death. Parents will betray their own children, and children will turn against their parents and have them killed. 13Everyone will hate you because of me. But if you keep on being faithful right to the end, you will be saved.

The Horrible Thing
(Matthew 24.15-21; Luke 21.20-24)

14 Someday you will see that "Horrible Thing" where it should not be.[c] Everyone who reads this must try to understand! If you are living in Judea at that time, run to the mountains. 15If you are on the roof[d] of your house, don't go inside to get anything. 16If you are out in the field, don't go back for your coat. 17It will be an awful time for women who are expecting babies or nursing young children. 18Pray that it won't happen in winter.[e] 19This will be the worst time of suffering since God created the world, and nothing this terrible will ever happen again. 20If the Lord doesn't make the time shorter, no one will be left alive. But because of his chosen and special ones, he will make the time shorter.

21 If someone should say, "Here is the Messiah!" or "There he is!" don't believe it. 22False messiahs and false prophets will come and work miracles and signs. They will even try to fool God's chosen ones. 23But be on your guard! That's why I am telling you these things now.

When the Son of Man Appears
(Matthew 24.29-31; Luke 21.25-28)

24 In those days, right after that time of suffering,

---

[c] *where it should not be*: Probably the holy place in the temple.
[d] *roof*: See the note at 2.4.
[e] *in winter*: In Palestine the winters are cold and rainy and make travel difficult.

"The sun will become dark,
   and the moon will no longer shine.
   25 The stars will fall,
   and the powers in the sky*f*
   will be shaken."

26 Then the Son of Man will be seen coming in the clouds with great power and glory. 27 He will send his angels to gather his chosen ones from all over the earth.

A Lesson from a Fig Tree
(Matthew 24.32-35; Luke 21.29-33)

28 Learn a lesson from a fig tree. When its branches sprout and start putting out leaves, you know summer is near. 29 So when you see all these things happening, you will know that the time has almost come.*g* 30 You can be sure that some of the people of this generation will still be alive when all this happens. 31 The sky and the earth will not last forever, but my words will.

No One Knows the Day or Time
(Matthew 24.36-44)

32 No one knows the day or the time. The angels in heaven don't know, and the Son himself doesn't know. Only the Father knows. 33 So watch out and be ready! You don't know when

---

f the powers in the sky: In ancient times people thought that the stars were spiritual powers.

g the time has almost come: Or "he (that is, the Son of Man) will soon be here."

the time will come. 34It is like what happens when a man goes away for a while and places his servants in charge of everything. He tells each of them what to do, and he orders the guard to keep alert. 35So be alert! You don't know when the master of the house will come back. It could be in the evening or at midnight or before dawn or in the morning. 36But if he comes suddenly, don't let him find you asleep. 37I tell everyone just what I have told you. Be alert!

A Plot To Kill Jesus
(Matthew 26.1-5; Luke 22.1,2; John 11.45-53)

14 It was now two days before Passover and the Festival of Thin Bread. The chief priests and the teachers of the Law of Moses were planning how they could sneak around and have Jesus arrested and put to death. 2They were saying, "We must not do it during the festival, because the people will riot."

At Bethany
(Matthew 26.6-13; John 12.1-8)

3 Jesus was eating in Bethany at the home of Simon, who once had leprosy,[h] when a woman came in with a very expensive bottle of sweet-smelling perfume.[i] After breaking it open, she poured the perfume on

---

[h] *leprosy*: In biblical times the word "leprosy" was used for many different skin diseases.

[i] *sweet-smelling perfume*: The Greek text has "perfume made of pure spikenard," a plant used to make perfume.

Jesus' head. ⁴This made some of the guests angry, and they complained, "Why such a waste? ⁵We could have sold this perfume for more than three hundred silver coins and given the money to the poor!" So they started saying cruel things to the woman.

6 But Jesus said:

Leave her alone! Why are you bothering her? She has done a beautiful thing for me. ⁷You will always have the poor with you. And whenever you want to, you can give to them. But you won't always have me here with you. ⁸She has done all she could by pouring perfume on my body to prepare it for burial. ⁹You may be sure that wherever the good news is told all over the world, people will remember what she has done. And they will tell others.

Judas and the Chief Priests
(Matthew 26.14-16; Luke 22.3-6)

10 Judas Iscariot*j* was one of the twelve disciples. He went to the chief priests and offered to help them arrest Jesus. ¹¹They were glad to hear this, and they promised to pay him. So Judas started looking for a good chance to betray Jesus.

Jesus Eats with His Disciples
(Matthew 26.17-25; Luke 22.7-14, 21-23; John 13.21-30)

12 It was the first day of the Festival of Thin Bread, and the Passover lambs were being killed. Jesus' disciples asked him, "Where do you want us to prepare the Passover meal?"

---

j Iscariot: See the note at 3.19.

13 Jesus said to two of the disciples, "Go into the city, where you will meet a man carrying a jar of water.[k] Follow him, 14and when he goes into a house, say to the owner, 'Our teacher wants to know if you have a room where he can eat the Passover meal with his disciples.' 15The owner will take you upstairs and show you a large room furnished and ready for you to use. Prepare the meal there."

16 The two disciples went into the city and found everything just as Jesus had told them. So they prepared the Passover meal.

17-18 While Jesus and the twelve disciples were eating together that evening, he said, "The one who will betray me is now eating with me."

19 This made the disciples sad, and one after another they said to Jesus, "You surely don't mean me!"

20 He answered, "It is one of you twelve men who is eating from this dish with me. 21The Son of Man will die, just as the Scriptures say. But it is going to be terrible for the one who betrays me. That man would be better off if he had never been born."

The Lord's Supper
(Matthew 26.26-30; Luke 22.14-23; 1 Corinthians 11.23-25)

22 During the meal Jesus took some bread in his hands. He blessed the bread and broke it. Then he gave it to his disciples and said, "Take this. It is my body."

23 Jesus picked up a cup of wine and gave thanks to God. He gave it to his disciples, and they all drank

---

[k] *a man carrying a jar of water*: A male slave carrying water could mean that the family was rich.

some. 24Then he said, "This is my blood, which is poured out for many people, and with it God makes his agreement. 25From now on I will not drink any wine, until I drink new wine in God's kingdom." 26Then they sang a hymn and went out to the Mount of Olives.

Peter's Promise
(Matthew 26.31-35; Luke 22.31-34; John 13.36-38)

27 Jesus said to his disciples, "All of you will reject me, as the Scriptures say,

'I will strike down the shepherd,
    and the sheep will be scattered.'

28But after I am raised to life, I will go ahead of you to Galilee."

29 Peter spoke up, "Even if all the others reject you, I never will!"

30 Jesus replied, "This very night before a rooster crows twice, you will say three times that you don't know me."

31 But Peter was so sure of himself that he said, "Even if I have to die with you, I will never say that I don't know you!"

All the others said the same thing.

Jesus Prays
(Matthew 26.36-46; Luke 22.39-46)

32 Jesus went with his disciples to a place called Gethsemane, and he told them, "Sit here while I pray."

33 Jesus took along Peter, James, and John. He was sad and troubled and 34told them, "I am so sad that I feel as if I am dying. Stay here and keep awake with me."

35-36 Jesus walked on a little way. Then he knelt down on the ground and prayed, "Father,[l] if it is possible, don't let this happen to me! Father, you can do anything. Don't make me suffer by having me drink from this cup.[m] But do what you want, and not what I want."

37 When Jesus came back and found the disciples sleeping, he said to Simon Peter, "Are you asleep? Can't you stay awake for just one hour? 38 Stay awake and pray that you won't be tested. You want to do what is right, but you are weak."

39 Jesus went back and prayed the same prayer. 40 But when he returned to the disciples, he found them sleeping again. They simply could not keep their eyes open, and they did not know what to say.

41 When Jesus returned to the disciples the third time, he said, "Are you still sleeping and resting?[n] Enough of that! The time has come for the Son of Man to be handed over to sinners. 42 Get up! Let's go. The one who will betray me is already here."

Jesus Is Arrested
(Matthew 26.47-56; Luke 22.47-53; John 18.3-12)

43 Jesus was still speaking, when Judas the betrayer came up. He was one of the twelve disciples, and a mob of men armed with swords and clubs were with him. They had been sent by the chief priests, the

---

[l] *Father*: The Greek text has "Abba," which is an Aramaic word meaning "father."

[m] *by having me drink from this cup*: See the note at 10.38.

[n] *Are you still sleeping and resting?*: Or "You may as well keep on sleeping and resting."

nation's leaders, and the teachers of the Law of Moses. 44Judas had told them ahead of time, "Arrest the man I greet with a kiss.º Tie him up tight and lead him away."

45 Judas walked right up to Jesus and said, "Teacher!" Then Judas kissed him, 46and the men grabbed Jesus and arrested him.

47 Someone standing there pulled out a sword. He struck the servant of the high priest and cut off his ear.

48 Jesus said to the mob, "Why do you come with swords and clubs to arrest me like a criminal? 49Day after day I was with you and taught in the temple, and you didn't arrest me. But what the Scriptures say must come true."

50 All of Jesus' disciples ran off and left him. 51One of them was a young man who was wearing only a linen cloth. And when the men grabbed him, 52he left the cloth behind and ran away naked.

Jesus Is Questioned by the Council
(Matthew 26.57-68; Luke 22.54,55,63-71; John 18.13,14,19-24)

53 Jesus was led off to the high priest. Then the chief priests, the nation's leaders, and the teachers of the Law of Moses all met together. 54Peter had followed at a distance. And when he reached the courtyard of the high priest's house, he sat down with the guards to warm himself beside a fire.

55 The chief priests and the whole council tried to

º *greet with a kiss*: It was the custom for people to greet each other with a kiss on the cheek.

find someone to accuse Jesus of a crime, so they could put him to death. But they could not find anyone to accuse him. ⁵⁶Many people did tell lies against Jesus, but they did not agree on what they said. ⁵⁷Finally, some men stood up and lied about him. They said, ⁵⁸"We heard him say he would tear down this temple that we built. He also claimed that in three days he would build another one without any help." ⁵⁹But even then they did not agree on what they said.

60 The high priest stood up in the council and asked Jesus, "Why don't you say something in your own defense? Don't you hear the charges they are making against you?" ⁶¹But Jesus kept quiet and did not say a word. The high priest asked him another question, "Are you the Messiah, the Son of the glorious God?"ᵖ

62 "Yes, I am!" Jesus answered.

"Soon you will see the Son of Man
　　sitting at the right side�q of God All-Powerful,
　　and coming with the clouds of heaven."

63 At once the high priest ripped his robe apart and shouted, "Why do we need more witnesses? ⁶⁴You heard him claim to be God! What is your decision?" They all agreed that he should be put to death.

65 Some of the people started spitting on Jesus. They blindfolded him, hit him with their fists, and said, "Tell us who hit you!" Then the guards took charge of Jesus and beat him.

ᵖ *Son of the glorious God*: "Son of God" was one of the
　　titles used for the kings of Israel.
q *right side*: See the note at 12.36.

Peter Says He Doesn't Know Jesus
(Matthew 26.69-75; Luke 22.56-62; John 18.15-18,25-27)

66 While Peter was still in the courtyard, a servant girl of the high priest came up 67 and saw Peter warming himself by the fire. She stared at him and said, "You were with Jesus from Nazareth!"

68 Peter replied, "That isn't true! I don't know what you're talking about. I don't have any idea what you mean." He went out to the gate, and a rooster crowed.[r]

69 The servant girl saw Peter again and said to the people standing there, "This man is one of them!"

70 "No, I'm not!" Peter replied.

A little while later some of the people said to Peter, "You certainly are one of them. You're a Galilean!"

71 This time Peter began to curse and swear, "I don't even know the man you're talking about!"

72 Right away the rooster crowed a second time. Then Peter remembered that Jesus had told him, "Before a rooster crows twice, you will say three times that you don't know me." So Peter started crying.

Pilate Questions Jesus
(Matthew 27.1,2, 11-14; Luke 23.1-5; John 18.28-38)

15 Early the next morning the chief priests, the nation's leaders, and the teachers of the Law of Moses met together with the whole Jewish council. They tied up Jesus and led him off to Pilate.

---

[r] *a rooster crowed*: These words are not in some manuscripts.

2 He asked Jesus, "Are you the king of the Jews?"

"Those are your words," Jesus answered.

3 The chief priests brought many charges against Jesus. 4Then Pilate questioned him again, "Don't you have anything to say? Don't you hear what crimes they say you have done?" 5But Jesus did not answer, and Pilate was amazed.

The Death Sentence
(Matthew 27.15-26; Luke 23.13-25; John 18.39–19.16)

6 During Passover, Pilate always freed one prisoner chosen by the people. 7And at that time there was a prisoner named Barabbas. He and some others had been arrested for murder during a riot. 8The crowd now came and asked Pilate to set a prisoner free, just as he usually did.

9 Pilate asked them, "Do you want me to free the king of the Jews?" 10Pilate knew that the chief priests had brought Jesus to him because they were jealous.

11 But the chief priests told the crowd to ask Pilate to free Barabbas.

12 Then Pilate asked the crowd, "What do you want me to do with this man you say is[s] the king of the Jews?"

13 They yelled, "Nail him to a cross!"

14 Pilate asked, "But what crime has he done?"

"Nail him to a cross!" they yelled even louder.

15 Pilate wanted to please the crowd. So he set Barabbas free. Then he ordered his soldiers to beat Jesus with a whip and nail him to a cross.

---

[s] *this man you say is*: These words are not in some manuscripts.

Soldiers Make Fun of Jesus
(Matthew 27.27-30; John 19.2,3)

16 The soldiers led Jesus inside the courtyard of the fortress*ᵗ* and called together the rest of the troops. ¹⁷They put a purple robe*ᵘ* on him, and on his head they placed a crown that they had made out of thorn branches. ¹⁸They made fun of Jesus and shouted, "Hey, you king of the Jews!" ¹⁹Then they beat him on the head with a stick. They spit on him and knelt down and pretended to worship him.

20 When the soldiers had finished making fun of Jesus, they took off the purple robe. They put his own clothes back on him and led him off to be nailed to a cross. ²¹Simon from Cyrene happened to be coming in from a farm, and they forced him to carry Jesus' cross. Simon was the father of Alexander and Rufus.

Jesus Is Nailed to a Cross
(Matthew 27.31-44; Luke 23.27-43; John 19.17-27)

22 The soldiers took Jesus to Golgotha, which means "Place of a Skull."*ᵛ* ²³There they gave him some wine mixed with a drug to ease the pain, but he refused to drink it.

ᵗ fortress: The place where the Roman governor stayed. It was probably at Herod's palace west of Jerusalem, though it may have been Fortress Antonia, north of the temple, where the Roman troops were stationed.
ᵘ purple robe: This was probably a Roman soldier's robe.
ᵛ Place of a Skull: The place was probably given this name because it was near a large rock in the shape of a human skull.

24 They nailed Jesus to a cross and gambled to see who would get his clothes. 25It was about nine o'clock in the morning when they nailed him to the cross. 26On it was a sign that told why he was nailed there. It read, "This is the King of the Jews." 27-28The soldiers also nailed two criminals on crosses, one to the right of Jesus and the other to his left.*w*

29 People who passed by said terrible things about Jesus. They shook their heads and shouted, "Ha! So you're the one who claimed you could tear down the temple and build it again in three days. 30Save yourself and come down from the cross!"

31 The chief priests and the teachers of the Law of Moses also made fun of Jesus. They said to each other, "He saved others, but he can't save himself. 32If he is the Messiah, the king of Israel, let him come down from the cross! Then we will see and believe." The two criminals also said cruel things to Jesus.

The Death of Jesus
(Matthew 27.45-56; Luke 23.44-49; John 19.28-30)

33 About noon the sky turned dark and stayed that way until around three o'clock. 34Then about that time Jesus shouted, "Eloi, Eloi, lema sabachthani?"*x* which means "My God, my God, why have you deserted me?"

35 Some of the people standing there heard Jesus and said, "He is calling for Elijah."*y* 36One of them

---

w *left*: Some manuscripts add, "So the Scriptures came true which say, 'He was accused of being a criminal.'"

x *Eloi...sabachthani*: These words are in Aramaic, a language spoken in Palestine during the time of Jesus.

y *Elijah*: The name "Elijah" sounds something like "Eloi," which means "my God."

ran and grabbed a sponge. After he had soaked it in wine, he put it on a stick and held it up to Jesus. He said, "Let's wait and see if Elijah will come[z] and take him down!" [37]Jesus shouted and then died.

38 At once the curtain in the temple[a] tore in two from top to bottom.

39 A Roman army officer was standing in front of Jesus. When the officer saw how Jesus died, he said, "This man really was the Son of God!"

40-41 Some women were looking on from a distance. They had come with Jesus to Jerusalem. But even before this they had been his followers and had helped him while he was in Galilee. Mary Magdalene and Mary the mother of the younger James and of Joseph were two of these women. Salome was also one of them.

Jesus Is Buried
(Matthew 27.57-61; Luke 23.50-56; John 19.38-42)

42 It was now the evening before the Sabbath, and the Jewish people were getting ready for that sacred day. [43]A man named Joseph from Arimathea was brave enough to ask Pilate for the body of Jesus. Joseph was a highly respected member of the Jewish council, and he was also waiting for God's kingdom to come.

---

[z] *see if Elijah will come*: See the note at 6.15.

[a] *curtain in the temple*: There were two curtains in the temple. One was at the entrance, and the other separated the holy place from the most holy place that the Jewish people thought of as God's home on earth. The second curtain is probably the one which is meant.

44 Pilate was surprised to hear that Jesus was already dead, and he called in the army officer to find out if Jesus had been dead very long. 45After the officer told him, Pilate let Joseph have Jesus' body.

46 Joseph bought a linen cloth and took the body down from the cross. He had it wrapped in the cloth, and he put it in a tomb that had been cut into solid rock. Then he rolled a big stone against the entrance to the tomb.

47 Mary Magdalene and Mary the mother of Joseph were watching and saw where the body was placed.

Jesus Is Alive
(Matthew 28.1-8; Luke 24.1-12; John 20.1-10)

16 After the Sabbath, Mary Magdalene, Salome, and Mary the mother of James bought some spices to put on Jesus' body. 2Very early on Sunday morning, just as the sun was coming up, they went to the tomb. 3On their way, they were asking one another, "Who will roll the stone away from the entrance for us?" 4But when they looked, they saw that the stone had already been rolled away. And it was a huge stone!

5 The women went into the tomb, and on the right side they saw a young man in a white robe sitting there. They were alarmed.

6 The man said, "Don't be alarmed! You are looking for Jesus from Nazareth, who was nailed to a cross. God has raised him to life, and he isn't here. You can see the place where they put his body. 7Now go and tell his disciples, and especially Peter, that he will go ahead of you to Galilee. You will see him there, just as he told you."

8 When the women ran from the tomb, they were confused and shaking all over. They were too afraid to tell anyone what had happened.

ONE OLD ENDING TO MARK'S GOSPEL *b*

Jesus Appears to Mary Magdalene
(Matthew 28.9,10; John 20.11-18)

9 Very early on the first day of the week, after Jesus had risen to life, he appeared to Mary Magdalene. Earlier he had forced seven demons out of her. 10She left and told his friends, who were crying and mourning. 11Even though they heard that Jesus was alive and that Mary had seen him, they would not believe it.

Jesus Appears to Two Disciples
(Luke 24.13-35)

12 Later, Jesus appeared in another form to two disciples, as they were on their way out of the city. 13But when these disciples told what had happened, the others would not believe.

What Jesus' Followers Must Do
(Matthew 28.16-20; Luke 24.36-49; John 20.19-23; Acts 1.6-8)

14 Afterwards, Jesus appeared to his eleven disciples as they were eating. He scolded them because they were too stubborn to believe the ones who had seen him after he had been raised to life. 15Then he told them:

---

b One Old Ending to Mark's Gospel: Verses 9-20 are not in some manuscripts.

Go and preach the good news to everyone in the world. ¹⁶Anyone who believes me and is baptized will be saved. But anyone who refuses to believe me will be condemned. ¹⁷Everyone who believes me will be able to do wonderful things. By using my name they will force out demons, and they will speak new languages. ¹⁸They will handle snakes and will drink poison and not be hurt. They will also heal sick people by placing their hands on them.

Jesus Returns to Heaven
(Luke 24.50-53; Acts 1.9-11)

19 After the Lord Jesus had said these things to the disciples, he was taken back up to heaven where he sat down at the right side[c] of God. ²⁰Then the disciples left and preached everywhere. The Lord was with them, and the miracles they worked proved that their message was true.

ANOTHER OLD ENDING TO MARK'S GOSPEL[d]

9-10 The women quickly told Peter and his friends what had happened. Later, Jesus sent the disciples to the east and to the west with his sacred and everlasting message of how people can be saved forever.

---

[c] *right side*: See the note at 12.36.

[d] *Another Old Ending to Mark's Gospel*: Some manuscripts and early translations have both this shorter ending and the longer one (verses 9-20).

Luke Tells the Good News

God's love is for everyone! Jesus came into the world to be the Savior of all people! These are two of the main thoughts in this book. Several of the best known stories that Jesus used for teaching about God's love are found only in Luke's Gospel: The Good Samaritan (10.25-37), A Lost Sheep (15.1-7), and A Lost Son (15.11-32). Only Luke tells how Jesus visited in the home of a hated tax collector (19.1-10) and promised life in paradise to a dying criminal (23.39-43).

Luke mentions God's Spirit more than any of the other New Testament writers. For example, the power of the Spirit was with John the Baptist from the time he was born (1.15). And the angel promised Mary, "The Holy Spirit will come down to you.... So your child will be called the holy Son of God" (1.35). Jesus followed the Spirit (4.1, 14, 18; 10.21) and taught that the Spirit is God's greatest gift (11.13).

Luke shows how important prayer was to Jesus. Jesus prayed often: after being baptized (3.21), before choosing the disciples (6.12), before asking his disciples who they thought he was (9.18), and before giving up his life on the cross (23.34, 46). From Luke we learn of three stories that Jesus told to teach about prayer (11.5-9; 18.1-8, 9-14).

An important part of Luke's story is the way in which he shows the concern of Jesus for the poor: the good news is preached to them (4.18; 7.22), they receive God's blessings (6.20), they are invited to the great feast (14.13, 21), the poor man Lazarus is taken to heaven by angels (16.20, 22), and Jesus commands his disciples to sell what they have and give the money to the poor (12.33).

To make sure that readers would understand that Jesus was raised physically from death, Luke reports that the risen Jesus ate a piece of fish (24.42, 43). There could be no mistake about the risen Jesus: he was not a ghost. His being raised from death was real and not someone's imagination. Luke also wrote another book—the Acts of the Apostles—to show what happened to Jesus' followers after he was raised from death and taken up to heaven. No other Gospel has a second volume that continues the story.

Luke closes this first book that he wrote by telling that Jesus returned to heaven. But right before Jesus leaves, he tells his disciples:

The Scriptures say that the Messiah must suffer, then three days later he will rise from death. They also say that all people of every nation must be told in my name to turn to God, in order to be forgiven. So beginning in Jerusalem, you must tell everything that has happened. (24.46-48)

A QUICK LOOK AT THIS BOOK

1 Many people have tried to tell the story of what God has done among us. [2]They wrote what we had been told by the ones who were there in the beginning and saw what happened. [3]So I made a careful study[a] of everything and then decided to write and tell you exactly what took place. Honorable Theophilus, [4]I have done this to let you know the truth about what you have heard.

An Angel Tells about the Birth of John

5 When Herod was king of Judea, there was a priest by the name of Zechariah from the priestly group of Abijah. His wife Elizabeth was from the family of Aaron.[b] [6]Both of them were good people and pleased the Lord God by obeying all that he had commanded. [7]But they did not have children. Elizabeth could not have any, and both Zechariah and Elizabeth were already old.

8 One day Zechariah's group of priests were on duty, and he was serving God as a priest. [9]According to the custom of the priests, he had been chosen to go into the Lord's temple that day and to burn incense,[c] [10]while the people stood outside praying.

11 All at once an angel from the Lord appeared to Zechariah at the right side of the altar. [12]Zechariah

---

[a] *a careful study*: Or "a study from the beginning."
[b] *Aaron*: The brother of Moses and the first priest.
[c] *burn incense*: This was done twice a day, once in the morning and again in the late afternoon.

was confused and afraid when he saw the angel. ¹³But the angel told him:

Don't be afraid, Zechariah! God has heard your prayers. Your wife Elizabeth will have a son, and you must name him John. ¹⁴His birth will make you very happy, and many people will be glad. ¹⁵Your son will be a great servant of the Lord. He must never drink wine or beer, and the power of the Holy Spirit will be with him from the time he is born.

16 John will lead many people in Israel to turn back to the Lord their God. ¹⁷He will go ahead of the Lord with the same power and spirit that Elijah*d* had. And because of John, parents will be more thoughtful of their children. And people who now disobey God will begin to think as they ought to. That is how John will get people ready for the Lord.

18 Zechariah said to the angel, "How will I know this is going to happen? My wife and I are both very old."

19 The angel answered, "I am Gabriel, God's servant, and I was sent to tell you this good news. ²⁰You have not believed what I have said. So you will not be able to say a thing until all this happens. But everything will take place when it is supposed to."

21 The crowd was waiting for Zechariah and kept wondering why he was staying so long in the temple. ²²When he did come out, he could not speak, and they knew he had seen a vision. He motioned to them with his hands, but did not say a thing.

---

d Elijah: The prophet Elijah was known for his power to work miracles.

23 When Zechariah's time of service in the temple was over, he went home. 24Soon after that, his wife was expecting a baby, and for five months she did not leave the house. She said to herself, 25"What the Lord has done for me will keep people from looking down on me."[e]

An Angel Tells about the Birth of Jesus

26 One month later God sent the angel Gabriel to the town of Nazareth in Galilee 27with a message for a virgin named Mary. She was engaged to Joseph from the family of King David. 28The angel greeted Mary and said, "You are truly blessed! The Lord is with you."

29 Mary was confused by the angel's words and wondered what they meant. 30Then the angel told Mary, "Don't be afraid! God is pleased with you, 31and you will have a son. His name will be Jesus. 32He will be great and will be called the Son of God Most High. The Lord God will make him king, as his ancestor David was. 33He will rule the people of Israel forever, and his kingdom will never end."

34 Mary asked the angel, "How can this happen? I am not married!"

35 The angel answered, "The Holy Spirit will come down to you, and God's power will come over you. So your child will be called the holy Son of God. 36Your relative Elizabeth is also going to have a son, even though she is old. No one thought she could ever

---

[e] keep people from looking down on me: When a married woman could not have children, it was thought that the Lord was punishing her.

have a baby, but in three months she will have a son.
³⁷Nothing is impossible for God!"

38 Mary said, "I am the Lord's servant! Let it happen as you have said." And the angel left her.

Mary Visits Elizabeth

39 A short time later Mary hurried to a town in the hill country of Judea. ⁴⁰She went into Zechariah's home, where she greeted Elizabeth. ⁴¹When Elizabeth heard Mary's greeting, her baby moved within her.

The Holy Spirit came upon Elizabeth. ⁴²Then in a loud voice she said to Mary:

God has blessed you more than any other woman! He has also blessed the child you will have. ⁴³Why should the mother of my Lord come to me? ⁴⁴As soon as I heard your greeting, my baby became happy and moved within me. ⁴⁵The Lord has blessed you because you believed that he will keep his promise.

Mary's Song of Praise

46 Mary said:

With all my heart ⁴⁷ I praise the Lord,
    and I am glad because of God my Savior.
⁴⁸ God cares for me, his humble servant.
    From now on, all people will say
        God has blessed me.
⁴⁹ God All-Powerful has done great things for me,
    and his name is holy.
⁵⁰ He always shows mercy
    to everyone who worships him.
⁵¹ The Lord has used his powerful arm
    to scatter those who are proud.

⁵² God drags strong rulers from their thrones
and puts humble people
in places of power.
⁵³ God gives the hungry good things to eat,
and sends the rich away with nothing.
⁵⁴ God helps his servant Israel
and is always merciful to his people.
⁵⁵ The Lord made this promise
to our ancestors,
to Abraham and his family forever!

56 Mary stayed with Elizabeth about three months.
Then she went back home.

The Birth of John the Baptist

57 When Elizabeth's son was born, ⁵⁸her neighbors
and relatives heard how kind the Lord had been to
her, and they too were glad.

59 Eight days later they did for the child what the
Law of Moses commands.ᶠ They were going to
name him Zechariah, after his father. ⁶⁰But Elizabeth
said, "No! His name is John."

61 The people argued, "No one in your family has
ever been named John." ⁶²So they motioned to
Zechariah to find out what he wanted to name his son.

63 Zechariah asked for a writing tablet. Then he
wrote, "His name is John." Everyone was amazed.
⁶⁴Right away, Zechariah started speaking and praising
God.

ᶠ *what the Law of Moses commands*: This refers to circumcision. It is the cutting off of skin from the private part of
Jewish boys eight days after birth to show that they
belong to the Lord.

65 All the neighbors were frightened because of what had happened, and everywhere in the hill country people kept talking about these things. 66Everyone who heard about this wondered what this child would grow up to be. They knew that the Lord was with him.

Zechariah Praises the Lord

67 The Holy Spirit came upon Zechariah, and he began to speak:

> 68 Praise the Lord, the God of Israel!
>   He has come to save his people.
> 69 Our God has given us a mighty Savior[g]
>   from the family of David his servant.
> 70 Long ago the Lord promised
>   by the words of his holy prophets
> 71 to save us from our enemies
>   and from everyone who hates us.
> 72 God said he would be kind to our people
>   and keep his sacred promise.
> 73 He told our ancestor Abraham
> 74   that he would rescue us from our enemies.
> Then we could serve him without fear,
> 75   by being holy and good as long as we live.
> 76 You, my son, will be called
>   a prophet of God in heaven above.
> You will go ahead of the Lord
>   to get everything ready for him.

---

[g] *a mighty Savior*: The Greek text has "a horn of salvation." In the Scriptures animal horns are often a symbol of great strength.

77 You will tell his people that they can be saved
when their sins are forgiven.

78 God's love and kindness will shine upon us
like the sun that rises in the sky.[h]

79 On us who live in the dark shadow of death
this light will shine
to guide us into a life of peace.

80 As John grew up, God's Spirit gave him great
power. John lived in the desert until the time he was
sent to the people of Israel.

The Birth of Jesus
(Matthew 1.18-25)

2 About that time Emperor Augustus gave orders
for the names of all the people to be listed in
record books.[i] 2These first records were made when
Quirinius was governor of Syria.[j]

3 Everyone had to go to their own hometown to be
listed. 4So Joseph had to leave Nazareth in Galilee
and go to Bethlehem in Judea. Long ago Bethlehem
had been King David's hometown, and Joseph went
there because he was from David's family.

5 Mary was engaged to Joseph and traveled with
him to Bethlehem. She was soon going to have a
baby, 6and while they were there, 7she gave birth to

---

[h] *like the sun that rises in the sky*: Or "like the Messiah
coming from heaven."

[i] *names ... listed in record books*: This was done so that
everyone could be made to pay taxes to the Emperor.

[j] *Quirinius was governor of Syria*: It is known that Quirinius
made a record of the people in A.D. 6 or 7. But the exact
date of the record taking that Luke mentions is not known.

her first-born[k] son. She dressed him in baby clothes[l] and laid him on a bed of hay, because there was no room for them in the inn.

The Shepherds

8 That night in the fields near Bethlehem some shepherds were guarding their sheep. 9All at once an angel came down to them from the Lord, and the brightness of the Lord's glory flashed around them. The shepherds were frightened. 10But the angel said, "Don't be afraid! I have good news for you, which will make everyone happy. 11This very day in King David's hometown a Savior was born for you. He is Christ the Lord. 12You will know who he is, because you will find him dressed in baby clothes and lying on a bed of hay."

13 Suddenly many other angels came down from heaven and joined in praising God. They said:

14 "Praise God in heaven!
    Peace on earth
        to everyone who pleases God."

15 After the angels had left and gone back to heaven, the shepherds said to each other, "Let's go to Bethlehem and see what the Lord has told us about." 16They hurried off and found Mary and Joseph, and they saw the baby lying on a bed of hay.

17 When the shepherds saw Jesus, they told his

---

[k] *first-born*: The Jewish people said that the first-born son in each of their families belonged to the Lord.

[l] *dressed him in baby clothes*: The Greek text has "wrapped him in wide strips of cloth," which was how young babies were dressed.

parents what the angel had said about him. [18]Everyone
listened and was surprised. [19]But Mary kept thinking
about all this and wondering what it meant.

20 As the shepherds returned to their sheep, they
were praising God and saying wonderful things about
him. Everything they had seen and heard was just as
the angel had said.

21 Eight days later Jesus' parents did for him what
the Law of Moses commands.[m] And they named him
Jesus, just as the angel had told Mary when he
promised she would have a baby.

Simeon Praises the Lord

22 The time came for Mary and Joseph to do what
the Law of Moses says a mother is supposed to do
after her baby is born.[n]

They took Jesus to the temple in Jerusalem and presented him to the Lord, [23]just as the Law of the Lord
says, "Each first-born[o] baby boy belongs to the Lord."
[24]The Law of the Lord also says that parents have to
offer a sacrifice, giving at least a pair of doves or two
young pigeons. So that is what Mary and Joseph did.

25 At this time a man named Simeon was living in
Jerusalem. Simeon was a good man. He loved God
and was waiting for God to save the people of Israel.

---

[m] *what the Law of Moses commands*: See the note at 1.59.
[n] *after her baby is born*: After a Jewish mother gave birth
     to a son, she was considered "unclean" and had to stay
     home until he was circumcised (see the note at 1.59).
     Then she had to stay home for another 33 days, before
     offering a sacrifice to the Lord.
[o] *first-born*: See the note at 2.7.

God's Spirit came to him 26and told him that he would not die until he had seen Christ the Lord.

27 When Mary and Joseph brought Jesus to the temple to do what the Law of Moses says should be done for a new baby, the Spirit told Simeon to go into the temple. 28Simeon took the baby Jesus in his arms and praised God,

29 "Lord, I am your servant,
    and now I can die in peace,
        because you have kept your promise to me.
30 With my own eyes I have seen
    what you have done to save your people,
31   and foreign nations will also see this.
32 Your mighty power is a light for all nations,
        and it will bring honor
            to your people Israel."

33 Jesus' parents were surprised at what Simeon had said. 34Then he blessed them and told Mary, "This child of yours will cause many people in Israel to fall and others to stand. The child will be like a warning sign. Many people will reject him, 35and you, Mary, will suffer as though you had been stabbed by a dagger. But all this will show what people are really thinking."

Anna Speaks about the Child Jesus

36 The prophet Anna was also there in the temple. She was the daughter of Phanuel from the tribe of Asher, and she was very old. In her youth she had been married for seven years, but her husband died. 37And now she was eighty-four years old.p Night and

---

p *And now she was eighty-four years old*: Or "And now she had been a widow for eighty-four years."

day she served God in the temple by praying and often going without eating.[q]

38 At that time Anna came in and praised God. She spoke about the child Jesus to everyone who hoped for Jerusalem to be set free.

The Return to Nazareth

39 After Joseph and Mary had done everything that the Law of the Lord commands, they returned home to Nazareth in Galilee. 40The child Jesus grew. He became strong and wise, and God blessed him.

The Boy Jesus in the Temple

41 Every year Jesus' parents went to Jerusalem for Passover. 42And when Jesus was twelve years old, they all went there as usual for the celebration. 43After Passover his parents left, but they did not know that Jesus had stayed on in the city. 44They thought he was traveling with some other people, and they went a whole day before they started looking for him. 45When they could not find him with their relatives and friends, they went back to Jerusalem and started looking for him there.

46 Three days later they found Jesus sitting in the temple, listening to the teachers and asking them questions. 47Everyone who heard him was surprised at how much he knew and at the answers he gave.

48 When his parents found him, they were amazed. His mother said, "Son, why have you done this to us?

---

q *without eating*: The Jewish people sometimes went without eating (also called "fasting") to show their love for God or to show sorrow for their sins.

Your father and I have been very worried, and we have been searching for you!"

49 Jesus answered, "Why did you have to look for me? Didn't you know that I would be in my Father's house?"[r] 50But they did not understand what he meant.

51 Jesus went back to Nazareth with his parents and obeyed them. His mother kept on thinking about all that had happened.

52 Jesus became wise, and he grew strong. God was pleased with him and so were the people.

The Preaching of John the Baptist
(Matthew 3.1-12; Mark 1.1-8; John 1.19-28)

3 For fifteen years[s] Emperor Tiberius had ruled that part of the world. Pontius Pilate was governor of Judea, and Herod[t] was the ruler of Galilee. Herod's brother, Philip, was the ruler in the countries of Iturea and Trachonitis, and Lysanias was the ruler of Abilene. 2Annas and Caiaphas were the Jewish high priests.[u]

At that time God spoke to Zechariah's son John, who was living in the desert. 3So John went along the Jordan Valley, telling the people, "Turn back to God and be baptized! Then your sins will be forgiven." 4Isaiah the prophet wrote about John when he said,

---

[r] *in my Father's house*: Or "doing my Father's work."

[s] *For fifteen years*: This was either A.D. 28 or 29, and Jesus was about thirty years old (see 3.23).

[t] *Herod*: Herod Antipas, the son of Herod the Great.

[u] *Annas and Caiaphas...high priests*: Annas was high priest from A.D. 6 until 15. His son-in-law Caiaphas was high priest from A.D. 18 until 37.

"In the desert someone is shouting,
'Get the road ready for the Lord!
Make a straight path for him.
 5 Fill up every valley
    and level every mountain and hill.
Straighten the crooked paths
    and smooth out the rough roads.
 6 Then everyone will see
    the saving power of God.'"

7 Crowds of people came out to be baptized, but John said to them, "You bunch of snakes! Who warned you to run from the coming judgment? 8 Do something to show that you really have given up your sins. Don't start saying that you belong to Abraham's family. God can turn these stones into children for Abraham.ᵛ 9 An ax is ready to cut the trees down at their roots. Any tree that doesn't produce good fruit will be cut down and thrown into a fire."

10 The crowds asked John, "What should we do?"

11 John told them, "If you have two coats, give one to someone who doesn't have any. If you have food, share it with someone else."

12 When tax collectorsʷ came to be baptized, they asked John, "Teacher, what should we do?"

ᵛ *children for Abraham*: The Jewish people thought they were God's chosen people because of God's promises to their ancestor Abraham.

ʷ *tax collectors*: These were usually Jewish people who paid the Romans for the right to collect taxes. They were hated by other Jews who thought of them as traitors to their country and to their religion.

13 John told them, "Don't make people pay more than they owe."

14 Some soldiers asked him, "And what about us? What do we have to do?"

John told them, "Don't force people to pay money to make you leave them alone. Be satisfied with your pay."

15 Everyone became excited and wondered, "Could John be the Messiah?"

16 John said, "I am just baptizing with water. But someone more powerful is going to come, and I am not good enough even to untie his sandals.^{x} He will baptize you with the Holy Spirit and with fire. 17His threshing fork ^{y} is in his hand, and he is ready to separate the wheat from the husks. He will store the wheat in his barn and burn the husks with a fire that never goes out."

18 In many different ways John preached the good news to the people. 19But to Herod the ruler, he said, "It was wrong for you to take Herodias, your brother's wife." John also said that Herod had done many other bad things. 20Finally, Herod put John in jail, and this was the worst thing he had done.

The Baptism of Jesus
(Matthew 3.13-17; Mark 1.9-11)

21 While everyone else was being baptized, Jesus

---

^{x} *untie his sandals*: This was the duty of a slave.

^{y} *threshing fork*: After Jewish farmers had trampled out the grain, they used a large fork to pitch the grain and the husks into the air. Wind would blow away the light husks, and the grain would fall back to the ground, where it could be gathered up.

himself was baptized. Then as he prayed, the sky opened up, [22]and the Holy Spirit came down upon him in the form of a dove. A voice from heaven said, "You are my own dear Son, and I am pleased with you."

The Ancestors of Jesus
(Matthew 1.1-17)

23 When Jesus began to preach, he was about thirty years old. Everyone thought he was the son of Joseph. But his family went back through Heli, [24]Matthat, Levi, Melchi, Jannai, Joseph, [25]Mattathias, Amos, Nahum, Esli, Naggai, [26]Maath, Mattathias, Semein, Josech, Joda;

27 Joanan, Rhesa, Zerubbabel, Shealtiel, Neri, [28]Melchi, Addi, Cosam, Elmadam, Er, [29]Joshua, Eliezer, Jorim, Matthat, Levi;

30 Simeon, Judah, Joseph, Jonam, Eliakim, [31]Melea, Menna, Mattatha, Nathan, David, [32]Jesse, Obed, Boaz, Salmon, Nahshon;

33 Amminadab, Admin, Arni, Hezron, Perez, Judah, [34]Jacob, Isaac, Abraham, Terah, Nahor, [35]Serug, Reu, Peleg, Eber, Shelah;

36 Cainan, Arphaxad, Shem, Noah, Lamech, [37]Methuselah, Enoch, Jared, Mahalaleel, Kenan, [38]Enosh, and Seth.

The family of Jesus went all the way back to Adam and then to God.

Jesus and the Devil
(Matthew 4.1-11; Mark 1.12, 13)

4 When Jesus returned from the Jordan River, the power of the Holy Spirit was with him, and the Spirit led him into the desert. [2]For forty days Jesus

was tested by the devil, and during that time he went without eating.[z] When it was all over, he was hungry.

3 The devil said to Jesus, "If you are God's Son, tell this stone to turn into bread."

4 Jesus answered, "The Scriptures say, 'No one can live only on food.'"

5 Then the devil led Jesus up to a high place and quickly showed him all the nations on earth. 6The devil said, "I will give all this power and glory to you. It has been given to me, and I can give it to anyone I want to. 7Just worship me, and you can have it all."

8 Jesus answered, "The Scriptures say:

'Worship the Lord your God
    and serve only him!'"

9 Finally, the devil took Jesus to Jerusalem and had him stand on top of the temple. The devil said, "If you are God's Son, jump off. 10-11The Scriptures say:

'God will tell his angels to take care of you.
    They will catch you in their arms,
    and you will not hurt your feet
        on the stones.'"

12 Jesus answered, "The Scriptures also say, 'Don't try to test the Lord your God!'"

13 After the devil had finished testing Jesus in every way possible, he left him for a while.

Jesus Begins His Work
(Matthew 4.12-17; Mark 1.14,15)

14 Jesus returned to Galilee with the power of the Spirit. News about him spread everywhere. 15He taught in the Jewish meeting places, and everyone praised him.

---

[z] went without eating: See the note at 2.37.

The People of Nazareth Turn against Jesus
(Matthew 13.53-58; Mark 6.1-6)

16 Jesus went back to Nazareth, where he had been brought up, and as usual he went to the meeting place on the Sabbath. When he stood up to read from the Scriptures, 17he was given the book of Isaiah the prophet. He opened it and read,

18 "The Lord's Spirit has come to me,
       because he has chosen me
           to tell the good news to the poor.
       The Lord has sent me
           to announce freedom for prisoners,
           to give sight to the blind,
           to free everyone who suffers,
19 and to say, 'This is the year
       the Lord has chosen.'"

20 Jesus closed the book, then handed it back to the man in charge and sat down. Everyone in the meeting place looked straight at Jesus.

21 Then Jesus said to them, "What you have just heard me read has come true today."

22 All the people started talking about Jesus and were amazed at the wonderful things he said. They kept on asking, "Isn't he Joseph's son?"

23 Jesus answered:

You will certainly want to tell me this saying, "Doctor, first make yourself well." You will tell me to do the same things here in my own hometown that you heard I did in Capernaum. 24But you can be sure that no prophets are liked by the people of their own hometown.

25 Once during the time of Elijah there was

no rain for three and a half years, and people everywhere were starving. There were many widows in Israel, 26but Elijah was sent only to a widow in the town of Zarephath near the city of Sidon. 27During the time of the prophet Elisha, many men in Israel had leprosy.*a* But no one was healed, except Naaman who lived in Syria.

28 When the people in the meeting place heard Jesus say this, they became so angry 29that they got up and threw him out of town. They dragged him to the edge of the cliff on which the town was built, because they wanted to throw him down from there. 30But Jesus slipped through the crowd and got away.

A Man with an Evil Spirit
(Mark 1.21-28)

31 Jesus went to the town of Capernaum in Galilee and taught the people on the Sabbath. 32His teaching amazed them because he spoke with power. 33There in the Jewish meeting place was a man with an evil spirit. He yelled out, 34 "Hey, Jesus of Nazareth, what do you want with us? Are you here to get rid of us? I know who you are! You are God's Holy One."

35 Jesus ordered the evil spirit to be quiet and come out. The demon threw the man to the ground in front of everyone and left without harming him.

36 They all were amazed and kept saying to each other, "What kind of teaching is this? He has power to

---

a *leprosy*: In biblical times the word "leprosy" was used for many different kinds of skin diseases.

order evil spirits out of people!" ³⁷News about Jesus spread all over that part of the country.

Jesus Heals Many People
(Matthew 8.14-17; Mark 1.29-34)

38 Jesus left the meeting place and went to Simon's home. When Jesus got there, he was told that Simon's mother-in-law was sick with a high fever. ³⁹So Jesus went over to her and ordered the fever to go away. Right then she was able to get up and serve them a meal.

40 After the sun had set, people with all kinds of diseases were brought to Jesus. He put his hands on each one of them and healed them. ⁴¹Demons went out of many people and shouted, "You are the Son of God!" But Jesus ordered the demons not to speak because they knew he was the Messiah.

42 The next morning Jesus went out to a place where he could be alone, and crowds came looking for him. When they found him, they tried to stop him from leaving. ⁴³But Jesus said, "People in other towns must hear the good news about God's kingdom. That's why I was sent." ⁴⁴So he kept on preaching in the Jewish meeting places in Judea.[b]

Jesus Chooses His First Disciples
(Matthew 4.18-22; Mark 1.16-20)

5 Jesus was standing on the shore of Lake Gennesaret,[c] teaching the people as they crowded around him to hear God's message. ²Near the shore

---

[b] *Judea:* Some manuscripts have "Galilee."

[c] *Lake Gennesaret:* Another name for Lake Galilee.

he saw two boats left there by some fishermen who had gone to wash their nets. ³Jesus got into the boat that belonged to Simon and asked him to row it out a little way from the shore. Then Jesus sat down[d] in the boat to teach the crowd.

4 When Jesus had finished speaking, he told Simon, "Row the boat out into the deep water and let your nets down to catch some fish."

5 "Master," Simon answered, "we have worked hard all night long and have not caught a thing. But if you tell me to, I will let the nets down." ⁶They did it and caught so many fish that their nets began ripping apart. ⁷Then they signaled for their partners in the other boat to come and help them. The men came, and together they filled the two boats so full that they both began to sink.

8 When Simon Peter saw this happen, he knelt down in front of Jesus and said, "Lord, don't come near me! I am a sinner." ⁹Peter and everyone with him were completely surprised at all the fish they had caught. ¹⁰His partners James and John, the sons of Zebedee, were surprised too.

Jesus told Simon, "Don't be afraid! From now on you will bring in people instead of fish." ¹¹The men pulled their boats up on the shore. Then they left everything and went with Jesus.

Jesus Heals a Man
(Matthew 8.1-4; Mark 1.40-45)

12 Jesus came to a town where there was a man

---

[d] *sat down*: Teachers in the ancient world, including Jewish teachers, usually sat down when they taught.

who had leprosy.*e* When the man saw Jesus, he knelt down to the ground in front of Jesus and begged, "Lord, you have the power to make me well, if only you wanted to."

13 Jesus put his hand on him and said, "I want to! Now you are well." At once the man's leprosy disappeared. 14Jesus told him, "Don't tell anyone about this, but go and show yourself to the priest. Offer a gift to the priest, just as Moses commanded, and everyone will know that you have been healed."*f*

15 News about Jesus kept spreading. Large crowds came to listen to him teach and to be healed of their diseases. 16But Jesus would often go to some place where he could be alone and pray.

Jesus Heals a Crippled Man
(Matthew 9.1-8; Mark 2.1-12)

17 One day some Pharisees and experts in the Law of Moses sat listening to Jesus teach. They had come from every village in Galilee and Judea and from Jerusalem.

God had given Jesus the power to heal the sick, 18and some people came carrying a crippled man on a mat. They tried to take him inside the house and put him in front of Jesus. 19But because of the crowd, they

---

e leprosy: See the note at 4.27.

f everyone will know that you have been healed: People with leprosy had to be examined by a priest and told that they were well (that is, "clean") before they could once again live a normal life in the Jewish community. The gift that Moses commanded was the sacrifice of some lambs together with flour mixed with olive oil.

could not get him to Jesus. So they went up on the roof,[g] where they removed some tiles and let the mat down in the middle of the room.

20 When Jesus saw how much faith they had, he said to the crippled man, "My friend, your sins are forgiven."

21 The Pharisees and the experts began arguing, "Jesus must think he is God! Only God can forgive sins."

22 Jesus knew what they were thinking, and he said, "Why are you thinking that? 23Is it easier for me to tell this crippled man that his sins are forgiven or to tell him to get up and walk? 24But now you will see that the Son of Man has the right to forgive sins here on earth." Jesus then said to the man, "Get up! Pick up your mat and walk home."

25 At once the man stood up in front of everyone. He picked up his mat and went home, giving thanks to God. 26Everyone was amazed and praised God. What they saw surprised them, and they said, "We have seen a great miracle today!"

Jesus Chooses Levi

(Matthew 9.9-13; Mark 2.13-17)

27 Later, Jesus went out and saw a tax collector[h] named Levi sitting at the place for paying taxes. Jesus said to him, "Come with me." 28Levi left everything and went with Jesus.

---

[g] *roof*: In Palestine the houses usually had a flat roof. Stairs on the outside led up to the roof, which was made of beams and boards covered with packed earth. Luke says that the roof was made of (clay) tiles, which were also used for making roofs in New Testament times.

[h] *tax collector*: See the note at 3.12.

29 In his home Levi gave a big dinner for Jesus. Many tax collectors and other guests were also there.

30 The Pharisees and some of their teachers of the Law of Moses grumbled to Jesus' disciples, "Why do you eat and drink with those tax collectors and other sinners?"

31 Jesus answered, "Healthy people don't need a doctor, but sick people do. 32I didn't come to invite good people to turn to God. I came to invite sinners."

People Ask about Going without Eating
(Matthew 9.14-17; Mark 2.18-22)

33 Some people said to Jesus, "John's followers often pray and go without eating,[i] and so do the followers of the Pharisees. But your disciples never go without eating or drinking."

34 Jesus told them, "The friends of a bridegroom don't go without eating while he is still with them. 35But the time will come when he will be taken from them. Then they will go without eating."

36 Jesus then told them these sayings:

No one uses a new piece of cloth to patch old clothes. The patch would shrink and make the hole even bigger.

37 No one pours new wine into old wineskins. The new wine would swell and burst the old skins.[j] Then the wine would be lost, and the

---

[i] *without eating*: See the note at 2.37.

[j] *swell and burst the old skins*: While the juice from grapes was becoming wine, it would swell and stretch the skins in which it had been stored. If the skins were old and stiff, they would burst.

skins would be ruined. 38New wine must be put only into new wineskins.

39 No one wants new wine after drinking old wine. They say, "The old wine is better."

A Question about the Sabbath
(Matthew 12.1-8; Mark 2.23-28)

6 One Sabbath when Jesus and his disciples were walking through some wheat fields,k the disciples picked some wheat. They rubbed the husks off with their hands and started eating the grain.

2 Some Pharisees said, "Why are you picking grain on the Sabbath? You're not supposed to do that!"

3 Jesus answered, "You surely have read what David did when he and his followers were hungry. 4He went into the house of God and took the sacred loaves of bread that only priests were supposed to eat. He not only ate some himself, but even gave some to his followers."

5 Jesus finished by saying, "The Son of Man is Lord over the Sabbath."

A Man with a Crippled Hand
(Matthew 12.9-14; Mark 3.1-6)

6 On another Sabbathl Jesus was teaching in a Jewish meeting place, and a man with a crippled right hand was there. 7Some Pharisees and teachers of the Law of Moses kept watching Jesus to see if he would

---

k *walking through some wheat fields*: It was the custom to let hungry travelers pick grains of wheat.
l *On another Sabbath*: Some manuscripts have a reading which may mean "the Sabbath after the next."

heal the man. They did this because they wanted to accuse Jesus of doing something wrong.

8 Jesus knew what they were thinking. So he told the man to stand up where everyone could see him. And the man stood up. ⁹Then Jesus asked, "On the Sabbath should we do good deeds or evil deeds? Should we save someone's life or destroy it?"

10 After he had looked around at everyone, he told the man, "Stretch out your hand." He did, and his bad hand became completely well.

11 The teachers and the Pharisees were furious and started saying to each other, "What can we do about Jesus?"

Jesus Chooses His Twelve Apostles
(Matthew 10.1-4; Mark 3.13-19)

12 About that time Jesus went off to a mountain to pray, and he spent the whole night there. ¹³The next morning he called his disciples together and chose twelve of them to be his apostles. ¹⁴One was Simon, and Jesus named him Peter. Another was Andrew, Peter's brother. There were also James, John, Philip, Bartholomew, ¹⁵Matthew, Thomas, and James the son of Alphaeus. The rest of the apostles were Simon, known as the Eager One,ᵐ ¹⁶Jude, who was the son of James, and Judas Iscariot,ⁿ who later betrayed Jesus.

ᵐ *known as the Eager One*: The word "eager" translates the Greek word "zealot," which was a name later given to the members of a Jewish group that resisted and fought against the Romans.

ⁿ *Iscariot*: This may mean "a man from Kerioth" (a place in Judea). But more probably it means "a man who was a liar" or "a man who was a betrayer."

Jesus Teaches, Preaches, and Heals
(Matthew 4.23-25)

17 Jesus and his apostles went down from the mountain and came to some flat, level ground. Many other disciples were there to meet him. Large crowds of people from all over Judea, Jerusalem, and the coastal cities of Tyre and Sidon were there too. ¹⁸These people had come to listen to Jesus and to be healed of their diseases. All who were troubled by evil spirits were also healed. ¹⁹Everyone was trying to touch Jesus, because power was going out from him and healing them all.

Blessings and Troubles
(Matthew 5.1-12)

20 Jesus looked at his disciples and said:

God will bless you people who are poor.
His kingdom belongs to you!
   ²¹ God will bless you hungry people.
You will have plenty to eat!
God will bless you people who are crying.
You will laugh!

22 God will bless you when others hate you and won't have anything to do with you. God will bless you when people insult you and say cruel things about you, all because you are a follower of the Son of Man. ²³Long ago your own people did these same things to the prophets. So when this happens to you, be happy and jump for joy! You will have a great reward in heaven.

   ²⁴ But you rich people are in for trouble.
You have already had an easy life!

25 You well-fed people are in for trouble.
    You will go hungry!
You people who are laughing now
    are in for trouble.
You are going to cry and weep!

26 You are in for trouble when everyone says good things about you. That is what your own people said about those prophets who told lies.

Love for Enemies
(Matthew 5.38-48; 7.12a)

27 This is what I say to all who will listen to me:
    Love your enemies, and be good to everyone who hates you. 28 Ask God to bless anyone who curses you, and pray for everyone who is cruel to you. 29 If someone slaps you on one cheek, don't stop that person from slapping you on the other cheek. If someone wants to take your coat, don't try to keep back your shirt. 30 Give to everyone who asks and don't ask people to return what they have taken from you. 31 Treat others just as you want to be treated.

32 If you love only someone who loves you, will God praise you for that? Even sinners love people who love them. 33 If you are kind only to someone who is kind to you, will God be pleased with you for that? Even sinners are kind to people who are kind to them. 34 If you lend money only to someone you think will pay you back, will God be pleased with you for that? Even sinners lend to sinners because they think they will get it all back.

35 But love your enemies and be good to them. Lend without expecting to be paid back.[o] Then you will get a great reward, and you will be the true children of God in heaven. He is good even to people who are unthankful and cruel. 36 Have pity on others, just as your Father has pity on you.

Judging Others
(Matthew 7.1-5)

37 Jesus said:

Don't judge others, and God won't judge you. Don't be hard on others, and God won't be hard on you. Forgive others, and God will forgive you. 38 If you give to others, you will be given a full amount in return. It will be packed down, shaken together, and spilling over into your lap. The way you treat others is the way you will be treated.

39 Jesus also used some sayings as he spoke to the people. He said:

Can one blind person lead another blind person? Won't they both fall into a ditch? 40 Are students better than their teacher? But when they are fully trained, they will be like their teacher.

41 You can see the speck in your friend's eye. But you don't notice the log in your own eye. 42 How can you say, "My friend, let me take the speck out of your eye," when you don't see the log in your own eye? You show-offs! First, get

---

[o] *without expecting to be paid back*: Some manuscripts have "without giving up on anyone."

the log out of your own eye. Then you can see how to take the speck out of your friend's eye.

A Tree and Its Fruit
(Matthew 7.17-20; 12.34b,35)

43 A good tree cannot produce bad fruit, and a bad tree cannot produce good fruit. 44 You can tell what a tree is like by the fruit it produces. You cannot pick figs or grapes from thorn-bushes. 45 Good people do good things because of the good in their hearts. Bad people do bad things because of the evil in their hearts. Your words show what is in your heart.

Two Builders
(Matthew 7.24-27)

46 Why do you keep on saying that I am your Lord, when you refuse to do what I say? 47 Anyone who comes and listens to me and obeys me 48 is like someone who dug down deep and built a house on solid rock. When the flood came and the river rushed against the house, it was built so well that it didn't even shake. 49 But anyone who hears what I say and doesn't obey me is like someone whose house wasn't built on solid rock. As soon as the river rushed against that house, it was smashed to pieces!

Jesus Heals an Army Officer's Servant
(Matthew 8.5-13; John 4.43-54)

7 After Jesus had finished teaching the people, he went to Capernaum. 2 In that town an army officer's servant was sick and about to die. The officer

liked this servant very much. ³And when he heard about Jesus, he sent some Jewish leaders to ask him to come and heal the servant.

4 The leaders went to Jesus and begged him to do something. They said, "This man deserves your help! ⁵He loves our nation and even built us a meeting place." ⁶So Jesus went with them.

When Jesus wasn't far from the house, the officer sent some friends to tell him, "Lord, don't go to any trouble for me! I am not good enough for you to come into my house. ⁷And I am certainly not worthy to come to you. Just say the word, and my servant will get well. ⁸I have officers who give orders to me, and I have soldiers who take orders from me. I can say to one of them, 'Go!' and he goes. I can say to another, 'Come!' and he comes. I can say to my servant, 'Do this!' and he will do it."

9 When Jesus heard this, he was so surprised that he turned and said to the crowd following him, "In all of Israel I've never found anyone with this much faith!"

10 The officer's friends returned and found the servant well.

A Widow's Son

11 Soon Jesus and his disciples were on their way to the town of Nain, and a big crowd was going along with them. ¹²As they came near the gate of the town, they saw people carrying out the body of a widow's only son. Many people from the town were walking along with her.

13 When the Lord saw the woman, he felt sorry for her and said, "Don't cry!"

14 Jesus went over and touched the stretcher on which the people were carrying the dead boy. They stopped, and Jesus said, "Young man, get up!" 15The boy sat up and began to speak. Jesus then gave him back to his mother.

16 Everyone was frightened and praised God. They said, "A great prophet is here with us! God has come to his people."

17 News about Jesus spread all over Judea and everywhere else in that part of the country.

John the Baptist
(Matthew 11.1-19)

18-19 John's followers told John everything that was being said about Jesus. So he sent two of them to ask the Lord, "Are you the one we should be looking for? Or must we wait for someone else?"

20 When these messengers came to Jesus, they said, "John the Baptist sent us to ask, 'Are you the one we should be looking for? Or are we supposed to wait for someone else?'"

21 At that time Jesus was healing many people who were sick or in pain or were troubled by evil spirits, and he was giving sight to a lot of blind people. 22Jesus said to the messengers sent by John, "Go and tell John what you have seen and heard. Blind people are now able to see, and the lame can walk. People who have leprosy*p* are being healed, and the deaf can now hear. The dead are raised to life, and the poor are hearing the good news. 23God will bless everyone who doesn't reject me because of what I do."

---

p leprosy: See the note at 4.27.

24 After John's messengers had gone, Jesus began speaking to the crowds about John:

What kind of person did you go out to the desert to see? Was he like tall grass blown about by the wind? 25 What kind of man did you really go out to see? Was he someone dressed in fine clothes? People who wear expensive clothes and live in luxury are in the king's palace. 26 What then did you go out to see? Was he a prophet? He certainly was! I tell you that he was more than a prophet. 27 In the Scriptures, God calls John his messenger and says, "I am sending my messenger ahead of you to get things ready for you." 28 No one ever born on this earth is greater than John. But whoever is least important in God's kingdom is greater than John.

29 Everyone had been listening to John. Even the tax collectors[q] had obeyed God and had done what was right by letting John baptize them. 30 But the Pharisees and the experts in the Law of Moses refused to obey God and be baptized by John.

31 Jesus went on to say:

What are you people like? What kind of people are you? 32 You are like children sitting in the market and shouting to each other,

"We played the flute,
   but you would not dance!
We sang a funeral song,
   but you would not cry!"

33 John the Baptist did not go around eating and drinking, and you said, "John has a demon in

---

q *tax collectors*: See the note at 3.12.

him!" 34But because the Son of Man goes around eating and drinking, you say, "Jesus eats and drinks too much! He is even a friend of tax collectors and sinners." 35Yet Wisdom is shown to be right by what its followers do.

Simon the Pharisee

36 A Pharisee invited Jesus to have dinner with him. So Jesus went to the Pharisee's home and got ready to eat.*r*

37 When a sinful woman in that town found out that Jesus was there, she bought an expensive bottle of perfume. 38Then she came and stood behind Jesus. She cried and started washing his feet with her tears and drying them with her hair. The woman kissed his feet and poured the perfume on them.

39 The Pharisee who had invited Jesus saw this and said to himself, "If this man really were a prophet, he would know what kind of woman is touching him! He would know that she is a sinner."

40 Jesus said to the Pharisee, "Simon, I have something to say to you."

"Teacher, what is it?" Simon replied.

41 Jesus told him, "Two people were in debt to a moneylender. One of them owed him five hundred silver coins, and the other owed him fifty. 42Since

---

r *got ready to eat*: On special occasions the Jewish people often followed the Greek and Roman custom of lying down on their left side and leaning on their left elbow, while eating with their right hand. This is how the woman could come up behind Jesus and wash his feet (see verse 38).

neither of them could pay him back, the moneylender said that they didn't have to pay him anything. Which one of them will like him more?"

43 Simon answered, "I suppose it would be the one who had owed more and didn't have to pay it back."

"You are right," Jesus said.

44 He turned toward the woman and said to Simon, "Have you noticed this woman? When I came into your home, you didn't give me any water so I could wash my feet. But she has washed my feet with her tears and dried them with her hair. ⁴⁵You didn't greet me with a kiss, but from the time I came in, she has not stopped kissing my feet. ⁴⁶You didn't even pour olive oil on my head,^s but she has poured expensive perfume on my feet. ⁴⁷So I tell you that all her sins are forgiven, and that is why she has shown great love. But anyone who has been forgiven for only a little will show only a little love."

48 Then Jesus said to the woman, "Your sins are forgiven."

49 Some other guests started saying to one another, "Who is this who dares to forgive sins?"

50 But Jesus told the woman, "Because of your faith, you are now saved.^t May God give you peace!"

---

^s *washed my feet … greet me with a kiss … pour olive oil on my head*: Guests in a home were usually offered water so they could wash their feet, because most people either went barefoot or wore sandals and would come in the house with very dusty feet. Guests were also greeted with a kiss on the cheek, and special ones often had sweet-smelling olive oil poured on their head.

^t *saved*: Or "healed." The Greek word may have either meaning.

Women Who Helped Jesus

8 Soon after this, Jesus was going through towns and villages, telling the good news about God's kingdom. His twelve apostles were with him, ²and so were some women who had been healed of evil spirits and all sorts of diseases. One of the women was Mary Magdalene,ᵘ who once had seven demons in her. ³Joanna, Susanna, and many others had also used what they owned to help Jesusᵛ and his disciples. Joanna's husband Chuza was one of Herod's officials.ʷ

A Story about a Farmer
(Matthew 13.1-9; Mark 4.1-9)

4 When a large crowd from several towns had gathered around Jesus, he told them this story:

5 A farmer went out to scatter seed in a field. While the farmer was doing it, some of the seeds fell along the road and were stepped on or eaten by birds. ⁶Other seeds fell on rocky ground and started growing. But the plants did not have enough water and soon dried up. ⁷Some other seeds fell where thornbushes grew up and choked the plants. ⁸The rest of the seeds

---

ᵘ *Magdalene*: Meaning "from Magdala," a small town on the western shore of Lake Galilee. There is no hint that she is the sinful woman in 7.36-50.

ᵛ *used what they owned to help Jesus*: Women often helped Jewish teachers by giving them money.

ʷ *Herod's officials*: Herod Antipas, the son of Herod the Great.

fell on good ground where they grew and produced a hundred times as many seeds.

When Jesus had finished speaking, he said, "If you have ears, pay attention!"

Why Jesus Used Stories
(Matthew 13.10-17; Mark 4.10-12)

9 Jesus' disciples asked him what the story meant. [10]So he answered:

I have explained the secrets about God's kingdom to you, but for others I can only use stories. These people look, but they don't see, and they hear, but they don't understand.

Jesus Explains the Story about a Farmer
(Matthew 13.18-23; Mark 4.13-20)

11 This is what the story means: The seed is God's message, [12]and the seeds that fell along the road are the people who hear the message. But the devil comes and snatches the message out of their hearts, so that they will not believe and be saved. [13]The seeds that fell on rocky ground are the people who gladly hear the message and accept it. But they don't have deep roots, and they believe only for a little while. As soon as life gets hard, they give up.

14 The seeds that fell among the thornbushes are also people who hear the message. But they are so eager for riches and pleasures that they never produce anything. [15]Those seeds that fell on good ground are the people who listen to the message and keep it in good and honest hearts. They last and produce a harvest.

Light
(Mark 4.21-25)

16 No one lights a lamp and puts it under a bowl or under a bed. A lamp is always put on a lampstand, so that people who come into a house will see the light. 17There is nothing hidden that will not be found. There is no secret that will not be well known. 18Pay attention to how you listen! Everyone who has something will be given more, but people who have nothing will lose what little they think they have.

Jesus' Mother and Brothers
(Matthew 12.46-50; Mark 3.31-35)

19 Jesus' mother and brothers went to see him, but because of the crowd they could not get near him. 20Someone told Jesus, "Your mother and brothers are standing outside and want to see you."

21 Jesus answered, "My mother and my brothers are those people who hear and obey God's message."

A Storm
(Matthew 8.23-27; Mark 4.35-41)

22 One day, Jesus and his disciples got into a boat, and he said, "Let's cross the lake."ˣ They started out, 23and while they were sailing across, he went to sleep.

Suddenly a windstorm struck the lake, and the boat started sinking. They were in danger. 24So they went

---

ˣ *cross the lake*: To the eastern shore of Lake Galilee, where most of the people were not Jewish.

to Jesus and woke him up, "Master, Master! We are about to drown!"

Jesus got up and ordered the wind and waves to stop. They obeyed, and everything was calm. [25]Then Jesus asked the disciples, "Don't you have any faith?"

But they were frightened and amazed. They said to each other, "Who is this? He can give orders to the wind and the waves, and they obey him!"

A Man with Demons in Him
(Matthew 8.28-34; Mark 5.1-20)

26 Jesus and his disciples sailed across Lake Galilee and came to shore near the town of Gerasa.[y] [27]As Jesus was getting out of the boat, he was met by a man from that town. The man had demons in him. He had gone naked for a long time and no longer lived in a house, but in the graveyard.[z]

28 The man saw Jesus and screamed. He knelt down in front of him and shouted, "Jesus, Son of God in heaven, what do you want with me? I beg you not to torture me!" [29]He said this because Jesus had already told the evil spirit to go out of him.

The man had often been attacked by the demon. And even though he had been bound with chains and leg irons and kept under guard, he smashed whatever bound him. Then the demon would force him out into lonely places.

30 Jesus asked the man, "What is your name?"

He answered, "My name is Lots." He said this

---

[y] *Gerasa*: Some manuscripts have "Gergesa."
[z] *graveyard*: It was thought that demons and evil spirits lived in graveyards.

because there were 'lots' of demons in him. ³¹They begged Jesus not to send them to the deep pit,^a where they would be punished.

32 A large herd of pigs was feeding there on the hillside. So the demons begged Jesus to let them go into the pigs, and Jesus let them go. ³³Then the demons left the man and went into the pigs. The whole herd rushed down the steep bank into the lake and drowned.

34 When the men taking care of the pigs saw this, they ran to spread the news in the town and on the farms. ³⁵The people went out to see what had happened, and when they came to Jesus, they also found the man. The demons had gone out of him, and he was sitting there at the feet of Jesus. He had clothes on and was in his right mind. But the people were terrified.

36 Then all who had seen the man healed told about it. ³⁷Everyone from around Gerasa^b begged Jesus to leave, because they were so frightened.

When Jesus got into the boat to start back, ³⁸the man who had been healed begged to go with him. But Jesus sent him off and said, ³⁹"Go back home and tell everyone how much God has done for you." The man then went all over town, telling everything that Jesus had done for him.

A Dying Girl and a Sick Woman
(Matthew 9.18-26; Mark 5.21-43)

40 Everyone had been waiting for Jesus, and when

---

^a *deep pit*: The place where evil spirits are kept and punished.
^b *Gerasa*: See the note at 8.26.

he came back, a crowd was there to welcome him.
⁴¹Just then the man in charge of the Jewish meeting place came and knelt down in front of Jesus. His name was Jairus, and he begged Jesus to come to his home ⁴²because his twelve-year-old child was dying. She was his only daughter.

While Jesus was on his way, people were crowding all around him. ⁴³In the crowd was a woman who had been bleeding for twelve years. She had spent everything she had on doctors,ᶜ but none of them could make her well.

44 As soon as she came up behind Jesus and barely touched his clothes, her bleeding stopped.

45 "Who touched me?" Jesus asked.

While everyone was denying it, Peter said, "Master, people are crowding all around and pushing you from every side."ᵈ

46 But Jesus answered, "Someone touched me, because I felt power going out from me." ⁴⁷The woman knew that she could not hide, so she came trembling and knelt down in front of Jesus. She told everyone why she had touched him and that she had been healed right away.

48 Jesus said to the woman, "You are now well because of your faith. May God give you peace!"

49 While Jesus was speaking, someone came from Jairus' home and said, "Your daughter has died! Why bother the teacher anymore?"

ᶜ *She had spent everything she had on doctors*: Some manuscripts do not have these words.

ᵈ *from every side*: Some manuscripts add "and you ask, 'Who touched me?'"

50 When Jesus heard this, he told Jairus, "Don't worry! Have faith, and your daughter will get well."

51 Jesus went into the house, but he did not let anyone else go with him, except Peter, John, James, and the girl's father and mother. 52Everyone was crying and weeping for the girl. But Jesus said, "The child isn't dead. She is just asleep." 53The people laughed at him because they knew she was dead.

54 Jesus took hold of the girl's hand and said, "Child, get up!" 55She came back to life and got right up. Jesus told them to give her something to eat. 56Her parents were surprised, but Jesus ordered them not to tell anyone what had happened.

Instructions for the Twelve Apostles
(Matthew 10.5-15; Mark 6.7-13)

9 Jesus called together his twelve apostles and gave them complete power over all demons and diseases. 2Then he sent them to tell about God's kingdom and to heal the sick. 3He told them, "Don't take anything with you! Don't take a walking stick or a traveling bag or food or money or even a change of clothes. 4When you are welcomed into a home, stay there until you leave that town. 5If people won't welcome you, leave the town and shake the dust from your feet*e* as a warning to them."

6 The apostles left and went from village to village, telling the good news and healing people everywhere.

---

e shake the dust from your feet: This was a way of showing rejection.

Herod Is Worried

(Matthew 14.1-12; Mark 6.14-29)

7 Herod[f] the ruler heard about all that was happening, and he was worried. Some people were saying that John the Baptist had come back to life. [8] Others were saying that Elijah had come[g] or that one of the prophets from long ago had come back to life. [9] But Herod said, "I had John's head cut off! Who is this I hear so much about?" Herod was eager to meet Jesus.

Jesus Feeds Five Thousand

(Matthew 14.13-21; Mark 6.30-44; John 6.1-14)

10 The apostles came back and told Jesus everything they had done. He then took them with him to the village of Bethsaida, where they could be alone. [11] But a lot of people found out about this and followed him. Jesus welcomed them. He spoke to them about God's kingdom and healed everyone who was sick.

12 Late in the afternoon the twelve apostles came to Jesus and said, "Send the crowd to the villages and farms around here. They need to find a place to stay and something to eat. There is nothing in this place. It is like a desert!"

13 Jesus answered, "You give them something to eat."

---

[f] *Herod*: Herod Antipas, the son of Herod the Great.

[g] *Elijah had come*: Many of the Jewish people expected the prophet Elijah to come and prepare the way for the Messiah.

But they replied, "We have only five small loaves of bread[h] and two fish. If we are going to feed all these people, we will have to go and buy food." 14There were about five thousand men in the crowd.

Jesus said to his disciples, "Have the people sit in groups of fifty." 15They did this, and all the people sat down. 16Jesus took the five loaves and the two fish. He looked up toward heaven and blessed the food. Then he broke the bread and fish and handed them to his disciples to give to the people.

17 Everyone ate all they wanted. What was left over filled twelve baskets.

Who Is Jesus?
(Matthew 16.13-19; Mark 8.27-29)

18 When Jesus was alone praying, his disciples came to him, and he asked them, "What do people say about me?"

19 They answered, "Some say that you are John the Baptist or Elijah[i] or a prophet from long ago who has come back to life."

20 Jesus then asked them, "But who do you say I am?"

Peter answered, "You are the Messiah sent from God."

21 Jesus strictly warned his disciples not to tell anyone about this.

Jesus Speaks about His Suffering and Death
(Matthew 16.20-28; Mark 8.30-9.1)

22 Jesus told his disciples, "The nation's leaders, the

---

[h] small loaves of bread: These would have been flat and round or in the shape of a bun.

[i] Elijah: See the note at 9.8.

chief priests, and the teachers of the Law of Moses
will make the Son of Man suffer terribly. They will
reject him and kill him, but three days later he will rise
to life."

23 Then Jesus said to all the people:

If any of you want to be my followers, you
must forget about yourself. You must take up
your cross each day and follow me. 24If you
want to save your life,^{j} you will destroy it. But if
you give up your life for me, you will save it.
25What will you gain, if you own the whole
world but destroy yourself or waste your life?
26If you are ashamed of me and my message, the
Son of Man will be ashamed of you when he
comes in his glory and in the glory of his Father
and the holy angels. 27You can be sure that some
of the people standing here will not die before
they see God's kingdom.

The True Glory of Jesus
(Matthew 17.1-8; Mark 9.2-8)

28 About eight days later Jesus took Peter, John,
and James with him and went up on a mountain to
pray. 29While he was praying, his face changed, and
his clothes became shining white. 30Suddenly Moses
and Elijah were there speaking with him. 31They
appeared in heavenly glory and talked about all that
Jesus' death^k in Jerusalem would mean.

---

^{j} *life*: In verses 24 and 25 a Greek word which often means
"soul" is translated "life" and "yourself."

^{k} *Jesus' death*: In Greek this is "his departure," which
probably includes his rising to life and his return to heaven.

32 Peter and the other two disciples had been sound asleep. All at once they woke up and saw how glorious Jesus was. They also saw the two men who were with him.

33 Moses and Elijah were about to leave, when Peter said to Jesus, "Master, it is good for us to be here! Let us make three shelters, one for you, one for Moses, and one for Elijah." But Peter did not know what he was talking about.

34 While Peter was still speaking, a shadow from a cloud passed over them, and they were frightened as the cloud covered them. 35From the cloud a voice spoke, "This is my chosen Son. Listen to what he says!"

36 After the voice had spoken, Peter, John, and James saw only Jesus. For some time they kept quiet and did not say anything about what they had seen.

Jesus Heals a Boy
(Matthew 17.14-18; Mark 9.14-27)

37 The next day Jesus and his three disciples came down from the mountain and were met by a large crowd. 38Just then someone in the crowd shouted, "Teacher, please do something for my son! He is my only child! 39A demon often attacks him and makes him scream. It shakes him until he foams at the mouth, and it won't leave him until it has completely worn the boy out. 40I begged your disciples to force out the demon, but they couldn't do it."

41 Jesus said to them, "You people are stubborn and don't have any faith! How much longer must I be with you? Why do I have to put up with you?"

Then Jesus said to the man, "Bring your son to me." 42While the boy was being brought, the demon attacked him and made him shake all over. Jesus ordered the demon to stop. Then he healed the boy and gave him back to his father. 43Everyone was amazed at God's great power.

Jesus Again Speaks about His Death
(Matthew 17.22,23; Mark 9.30-32)

While everyone was still amazed at what Jesus was doing, he said to his disciples, 44"Pay close attention to what I am telling you! The Son of Man will be handed over to his enemies." 45But the disciples did not know what he meant. The meaning was hidden from them. They could not understand it, and they were afraid to ask.

Who Is the Greatest?
(Matthew 18.1-5; Mark 9.33-37)

46 Jesus' disciples were arguing about which one of them was the greatest. 47Jesus knew what they were thinking, and he had a child stand there beside him. 48Then he said to his disciples, "When you welcome even a child because of me, you welcome me. And when you welcome me, you welcome the one who sent me. Whichever one of you is the most humble is the greatest."

For or against Jesus
(Mark 9.38-40)

49 John said, "Master, we saw a man using your name to force demons out of people. But we told him to stop, because he isn't one of us."

50 "Don't stop him!" Jesus said. "Anyone who isn't against you is for you."

A Samaritan Village Refuses To Receive Jesus

51 Not long before it was time for Jesus to be taken up to heaven, he made up his mind to go to Jerusalem. 52 He sent some messengers on ahead to a Samaritan village to get things ready for him. 53 But he was on his way to Jerusalem, so the people there refused to welcome him. 54 When the disciples James and John saw what was happening, they asked, "Lord, do you want us to call down fire from heaven to destroy these people?"[l]

55 But Jesus turned and corrected them for what they had said.[m] 56 Then they all went on to another village.

Three People Who Wanted To Be Followers
(Matthew 8.19-22)

57 Along the way someone said to Jesus, "I'll go anywhere with you!"

58 Jesus said, "Foxes have dens, and birds have nests, but the Son of Man doesn't have a place to call his own."

59 Jesus told someone else to come with him. But the man said, "Lord, let me wait until I bury my father."[n]

---

[l] *to destroy these people*: Some manuscripts add "as Elijah did."

[m] *what they had said*: Some manuscripts add, "and said, 'Don't you know what spirit you belong to? The Son of Man did not come to destroy people's lives, but to save them.'"

[n] *bury my father*: The Jewish people taught that giving someone a proper burial was even more important than helping the poor.

60 Jesus answered, "Let the dead take care of the dead, while you go and tell about God's kingdom."

61 Then someone said to Jesus, "I want to go with you, Lord, but first let me go back and take care of things at home."

62 Jesus answered, "Anyone who starts plowing and keeps looking back isn't worth a thing to God's kingdom!"

The Work of the Seventy-Two Followers

10 Later the Lord chose seventy-two*o* other followers and sent them out two by two to every town and village where he was about to go. ²He said to them:

A large crop is in the fields, but there are only a few workers. Ask the Lord in charge of the harvest to send out workers to bring it in. ³Now go, but remember, I am sending you like lambs into a pack of wolves. ⁴Don't take along a moneybag or a traveling bag or sandals. And don't waste time greeting people on the road.*p* ⁵As soon as you enter a home, say, "God bless this home with peace." ⁶If the people living there are peace-loving, your prayer for peace will bless them. But if they are not peace-loving,

---

o seventy-two: Some manuscripts have "seventy." According to the book of Genesis, there were seventy nations on earth. But the ancient Greek translation of the Old Testament has "seventy-two" in place of "seventy." Jesus probably chose this number of followers to show that his message was for everyone in the world.

p waste time greeting people on the road: In those days a polite greeting could take a long time.

your prayer will return to you. [7]Stay with the same family, eating and drinking whatever they give you, because workers are worth what they earn. Don't move around from house to house.

8 If the people of a town welcome you, eat whatever they offer. [9]Heal their sick and say, "God's kingdom will soon be here!"[q]

10 But if the people of a town refuse to welcome you, go out into the street and say, [11]"We are shaking the dust from our feet[r] as a warning to you. And you can be sure that God's kingdom will soon be here!"[s] [12]I tell you that on the day of judgment the people of Sodom will get off easier than the people of that town!

The Unbelieving Towns
(Matthew 11.20-24)

13 You people of Chorazin are in for trouble! You people of Bethsaida are also in for trouble! If the miracles that took place in your towns had happened in Tyre and Sidon, the people there would have turned to God long ago. They would have dressed in sackcloth and put ashes on their heads.[t] [14]On the day of judgment the people of Tyre and Sidon will get

---

q *will soon be here*: Or "is already here."
r *shaking the dust from our feet*: This was a way of showing rejection.
s *will soon be here*: Or "is already here."
t *dressed in sackcloth...ashes on their heads*: This was one way that people showed how sorry they were for their sins.

off easier than you will. 15People of Capernaum, do you think you will be honored in heaven? Well, you will go down to hell!

16 My followers, whoever listens to you is listening to me. Anyone who says "No" to you is saying "No" to me. And anyone who says "No" to me is really saying "No" to the one who sent me.

The Return of the Seventy-Two

17 When the seventy-two[u] followers returned, they were excited and said, "Lord, even the demons obeyed when we spoke in your name!"

18 Jesus told them:

I saw Satan fall from heaven like a flash of lightning. 19I have given you the power to trample on snakes and scorpions and to defeat the power of your enemy Satan. Nothing can harm you. 20But don't be happy because evil spirits obey you. Be happy that your names are written in heaven!

Jesus Thanks His Father
(Matthew 11.25-27; 13.16,17)

21 At that same time, Jesus felt the joy that comes from the Holy Spirit,[v] and he said:

My Father, Lord of heaven and earth, I am grateful that you hid all this from wise and educated people and showed it to ordinary people. Yes, Father, that is what pleased you.

22 My Father has given me everything, and

---

[u] *seventy-two*: See the note at 10.1.

[v] *the Holy Spirit*: Some manuscripts have "his spirit."

he is the only one who knows the Son. The only one who really knows the Father is the Son. But the Son wants to tell others about the Father, so that they can know him too.

23 Jesus then turned to his disciples and said to them in private, "You are really blessed to see what you see! 24Many prophets and kings were eager to see what you see and to hear what you hear. But I tell you that they did not see or hear."

The Good Samaritan

25 An expert in the Law of Moses stood up and asked Jesus a question to see what he would say. "Teacher," he asked, "what must I do to have eternal life?"

26 Jesus answered, "What is written in the Scriptures? How do you understand them?"

27 The man replied, "The Scriptures say, 'Love the Lord your God with all your heart, soul, strength, and mind.' They also say, 'Love your neighbors as much as you love yourself.'"

28 Jesus said, "You have given the right answer. If you do this, you will have eternal life."

29 But the man wanted to show that he knew what he was talking about. So he asked Jesus, "Who are my neighbors?"

30 Jesus replied:

As a man was going down from Jerusalem to Jericho, robbers attacked him and grabbed everything he had. They beat him up and ran off, leaving him half dead.

31 A priest happened to be going down the same road. But when he saw the man, he walked

by on the other side. ³²Later a temple helper*ʷ*
came to the same place. But when he saw the
man who had been beaten up, he also went by on
the other side.

33 A man from Samaria then came traveling
along that road. When he saw the man, he felt
sorry for him ³⁴and went over to him. He treated his wounds with olive oil and wine*ˣ* and
bandaged them. Then he put him on his own
donkey and took him to an inn, where he took
care of him. ³⁵The next morning he gave the
innkeeper two silver coins and said, "Please
take care of the man. If you spend more than
this on him, I will pay you when I return."

36 Then Jesus asked, "Which one of these three
people was a real neighbor to the man who was beaten
up by robbers?"

37 The teacher answered, "The one who showed
pity."

Jesus said, "Go and do the same!"

Martha and Mary

38 The Lord and his disciples were traveling along
and came to a village. When they got there, a woman
named Martha welcomed him into her home. ³⁹She
had a sister named Mary, who sat down in front
of the Lord and was listening to what he said.

ʷ temple helper: A man from the tribe of Levi, whose job
it was to work around the temple.

ˣ olive oil and wine: In New Testament times these were
used as medicine. Sometimes olive oil is a symbol for
healing by means of a miracle (see James 5.14).

⁴⁰Martha was worried about all that had to be done. Finally, she went to Jesus and said, "Lord, doesn't it bother you that my sister has left me to do all the work by myself? Tell her to come and help me!"

41 The Lord answered, "Martha, Martha! You are worried and upset about so many things, ⁴²but only one thing is necessary. Mary has chosen what is best, and it will not be taken away from her."

Prayer
(Matthew 6.9-13; 7.7-11)

11 When Jesus had finished praying, one of his disciples said to him, "Lord, teach us to pray, just as John taught his followers to pray."

2 So Jesus told them, "Pray in this way:

'Father, help us to honor your name.
  Come and set up your kingdom.
  3 Give us each day the food we need.ʸ
  4 Forgive our sins,
    as we forgive everyone
      who has done wrong to us.
    And keep us from being tempted.'"

5 Then Jesus went on to say:

Suppose one of you goes to a friend in the middle of the night and says, "Let me borrow three loaves of bread. ⁶A friend of mine has dropped in, and I don't have a thing for him to eat." ⁷And suppose your friend answers, "Don't bother me! The door is bolted, and my children

---

ʸ *the food we need*: Or "food for today" or "food for the coming day."

and I are in bed. I cannot get up to give you something."

8 He may not get up and give you the bread, just because you are his friend. But he will get up and give you as much as you need, simply because you are not ashamed to keep on asking.

9 So I tell you to ask and you will receive, search and you will find, knock and the door will be opened for you. 10Everyone who asks will receive, everyone who searches will find, and the door will be opened for everyone who knocks. 11Which one of you fathers would give your hungry child a snake if the child asked for a fish? 12 Which one of you would give your child a scorpion if the child asked for an egg? 13As bad as you are, you still know how to give good gifts to your children. But your heavenly Father is even more ready to give the Holy Spirit to anyone who asks.

Jesus and the Ruler of Demons
(Matthew 12.22-30; Mark 3.20-27)

14 Jesus forced a demon out of a man who could not talk. And after the demon had gone out, the man started speaking, and the crowds were amazed. 15But some people said, "He forces out demons by the power of Beelzebul, the ruler of the demons!"

16 Others wanted to put Jesus to the test. So they asked him to show them a sign from God. 17Jesus knew what they were thinking, and he said:

A kingdom where people fight each other will end up in ruin. And a family that fights will break up. 18If Satan fights against himself, how can his kingdom last? Yet you say that I force out demons by the power of Beelzebul. 19If I use his power to force out demons, whose power do your own followers use to force them out? They are the ones who will judge you. 20But if I use God's power to force out demons, it proves that God's kingdom has already come to you.

21 When a strong man arms himself and guards his home, everything he owns is safe. 22But if a stronger man comes and defeats him, he will carry off the weapons in which the strong man trusted. Then he will divide with others what he has taken. 23If you are not on my side, you are against me. If you don't gather in the crop with me, you scatter it.

Return of an Evil Spirit
(Matthew 12.43-45)

24 When an evil spirit leaves a person, it travels through the desert, looking for a place to rest. But when it doesn't find a place, it says, "I will go back to the home I left." 25When it gets there and finds the place clean and fixed up, 26it goes off and finds seven other evil spirits even worse than itself. They all come and make their home there, and that person ends up in worse shape than before.

Being Really Blessed

27 While Jesus was still talking, a woman in the crowd spoke up, "The woman who gave birth to you and nursed you is blessed!"

28 Jesus replied, "That's true, but the people who are really blessed are the ones who hear and obey God's message!"[z]

A Sign from God
(Matthew 12.38-42; Mark 8.12)

29 As crowds were gathering around Jesus, he said:

You people of today are evil! You keep looking for a sign from God. But what happened to Jonah[a] is the only sign you will be given. 30Just as Jonah was a sign to the people of Nineveh, the Son of Man will be a sign to the people of today. 31When the judgment comes, the Queen of the South[b] will stand there with you and condemn you. She traveled a long way to hear Solomon's wisdom, and yet here is something far greater than Solomon. 32The people of Nineveh will also stand there with you and condemn you. They turned to God when Jonah preached, and yet here is something far greater than Jonah.

Light
(Matthew 5.15; 6.22,23)

33 No one lights a lamp and then hides it or puts it under a clay pot. A lamp is put on a lampstand,

---

[z] "That's true, but the people who are really blessed ...message": Or "That's not true, the people who are blessed...message.'"

[a] what happened to Jonah: Jonah was in the stomach of a big fish for three days and nights (see Matthew 12.40).

[b] Queen of the South: Sheba, probably a country in southern Arabia.

so that everyone who comes into the house can see the light. 34 Your eyes are the lamp for your body. When your eyes are good, you have all the light you need. But when your eyes are bad, everything is dark. 35 So be sure that your light isn't darkness. 36 If you have light, and nothing is dark, then light will be everywhere, as when a lamp shines brightly on you.

Jesus Condemns the Pharisees and Teachers of the Law of Moses
(Matthew 23.1-36; Mark 12.38-40; Luke 20.45-47)

37 When Jesus finished speaking, a Pharisee invited him home for a meal. Jesus went and sat down to eat.*c* 38 The Pharisee was surprised that he did not wash his hands *d* before eating. 39 So the Lord said to him:

You Pharisees clean the outside of cups and dishes, but on the inside you are greedy and evil. 40 You fools! Didn't God make both the outside and the inside?*e* 41 If you would only give what you have to the poor, everything you do would please God.

42 You Pharisees are in for trouble! You give God a tenth of the spices from your gardens,

---

c sat down to eat: See the note at 7.36.

d did not wash his hands: The Jewish people had strict laws about washing their hands before eating, especially if they had been out in public.

e Didn't God make both the outside and the inside?: Or "Doesn't the person who washes the outside always wash the inside too?"

such as mint and rue. But you cheat people, and you don't love God. You should be fair and kind to others and still give a tenth to God.

43 You Pharisees are in for trouble! You love the front seats in the meeting places, and you like to be greeted with honor in the market. ⁴⁴But you are in for trouble! You are like unmarked graves*f* that people walk on without even knowing it.

45 A teacher of the Law of Moses spoke up, "Teacher, you said cruel things about us."

46 Jesus replied:

You teachers are also in for trouble! You load people down with heavy burdens, but you won't lift a finger to help them carry the loads. ⁴⁷Yes, you are really in for trouble. You build monuments to honor the prophets your own people murdered long ago. ⁴⁸You must think that was the right thing for your people to do, or else you would not have built monuments for the prophets they murdered.

49 Because of your evil deeds, the Wisdom of God said, "I will send prophets and apostles to you. But you will murder some and mistreat others." ⁵⁰You people living today will be punished for all the prophets who have been murdered since the beginning of the world. ⁵¹This includes every prophet from the time of

---

f *unmarked graves*: Tombs were whitewashed to keep anyone from accidentally touching them. A person who touched a dead body or a tomb was considered unclean and could not worship with other Jewish people.

Abel to the time of Zechariah,[g] who was murdered between the altar and the temple. You people will certainly be punished for all of this.

52 You teachers of the Law of Moses are really in for trouble! You carry the keys to the door of knowledge about God. But you never go in, and you keep others from going in.

53 Jesus was about to leave, but the teachers and the Pharisees wanted to get even with him. They tried to make him say what he thought about other things, [54]so that they could catch him saying something wrong.

Warnings

12 As thousands of people crowded around Jesus and were stepping on each other, he told his disciples:

Be sure to guard against the dishonest teaching[h] of the Pharisees! It is their way of fooling people. [2]Everything that is hidden will be found out, and every secret will be known. [3]Whatever you say in the dark will be heard when it is day. Whatever you whisper in a closed room will be shouted from the housetops.

---

[g] *from the time of Abel...Zechariah:* Genesis is the first book in the Jewish Scriptures, and it tells that Abel was the first person to be murdered. Second Chronicles is the last book in the Jewish Scriptures, and the last murder that it tells about is that of Zechariah.

[h] *dishonest teaching:* The Greek text has "yeast," which is used here of a teaching that is not true (see Matthew 16.6, 12).

The One To Fear
(Matthew 10.28-31)

4 My friends, don't be afraid of people. They can kill you, but after that, there is nothing else they can do. 5God is the one you must fear. Not only can he take your life, but he can throw you into hell. God is certainly the one you should fear!

6 Five sparrows are sold for just two pennies, but God doesn't forget a one of them. 7Even the hairs on your head are counted. So don't be afraid! You are worth much more than many sparrows.

Telling Others about Christ
(Matthew 10.32,33; 12.32; 10.19,20)

8 If you tell others that you belong to me, the Son of Man will tell God's angels that you are my followers. 9But if you reject me, you will be rejected in front of them. 10If you speak against the Son of Man, you can be forgiven, but if you speak against the Holy Spirit, you cannot be forgiven.

11 When you are brought to trial in the Jewish meeting places or before rulers or officials, don't worry about how you will defend yourselves or what you will say. 12At that time the Holy Spirit will tell you what to say.

A Rich Fool

13 A man in a crowd said to Jesus, "Teacher, tell my brother to give me my share of what our father left us when he died."

14 Jesus answered, "Who gave me the right to settle arguments between you and your brother?"

15 Then he said to the crowd, "Don't be greedy! Owning a lot of things won't make your life safe."

16 So Jesus told them this story:

A rich man's farm produced a big crop, 17and he said to himself, "What can I do? I don't have a place large enough to store everything."

18 Later, he said, "Now I know what I'll do. I'll tear down my barns and build bigger ones, where I can store all my grain and other goods. 19Then I'll say to myself, 'You have stored up enough good things to last for years to come. Live it up! Eat, drink, and enjoy yourself.'"

20 But God said to him, "You fool! Tonight you will die. Then who will get what you have stored up?"

21 "This is what happens to people who store up everything for themselves, but are poor in the sight of God."

Worry
(Matthew 6.25-34)

22 Jesus said to his disciples:

I tell you not to worry about your life! Don't worry about having something to eat or wear. 23Life is more than food or clothing. 24Look at the crows! They don't plant or harvest, and they don't have storehouses or barns. But God takes care of them. You are much more important than any birds. 25Can worry make you live longer?*i* 26If you don't have power over small things, why worry about everything else?

---

i *live longer*: Or "grow taller."

27 Look how the wild flowers grow! They don't work hard to make their clothes. But I tell you that Solomon with all his wealth[j] wasn't as well clothed as one of these flowers. 28 God gives such beauty to everything that grows in the fields, even though it is here today and thrown into a fire tomorrow. Won't he do even more for you? You have such little faith!

29 Don't keep worrying about having something to eat or drink. 30 Only people who don't know God are always worrying about such things. Your Father knows what you need. 31 But put God's work first, and these things will be yours as well.

Treasures in Heaven
(Matthew 6.19-21)

32 My little group of disciples, don't be afraid! Your Father wants to give you the kingdom. 33 Sell what you have and give the money to the poor. Make yourselves moneybags that never wear out. Make sure your treasure is safe in heaven, where thieves cannot steal it and moths cannot destroy it. 34 Your heart will always be where your treasure is.

Faithful and Unfaithful Servants
(Matthew 24.45-51)

35 Be ready and keep your lamps burning 36 just like those servants who wait up for their

---

[j] *Solomon with all his wealth*: The Jewish people thought that Solomon was the richest person who had ever lived.

master to return from a wedding feast. As soon as he comes and knocks, they open the door for him. 37Servants are fortunate if their master finds them awake and ready when he comes! I promise you that he will get ready and have his servants sit down so he can serve them. 38Those servants are really fortunate if their master finds them ready, even though he comes late at night or early in the morning. 39 You would surely not let a thief break into your home, if you knew when the thief was coming. 40So always be ready! You don't know when the Son of Man will come.

41 Peter asked Jesus, "Did you say this just for us or for everyone?"

42 The Lord answered:

Who are faithful and wise servants? Who are the ones the master will put in charge of giving the other servants their food supplies at the proper time? 43Servants are fortunate if their master comes and finds them doing their job. 44A servant who is always faithful will surely be put in charge of everything the master owns.

45 But suppose one of the servants thinks that the master won't return until late. Suppose that servant starts beating all the other servants and eats and drinks and gets drunk. 46If that happens, the master will come on a day and at a time when the servant least expects him. That servant will then be punished and thrown out with the servants who cannot be trusted.

47 If servants are not ready or willing to do what their master wants them to do, they will be

beaten hard. ⁴⁸But servants who don't know what their master wants them to do will not be beaten so hard for doing wrong. If God has been generous with you, he will expect you to serve him well. But if he has been more than generous, he will expect you to serve him even better.

Not Peace, but Trouble
(Matthew 10.34-36)

49 I came to set fire to the earth, and I wish it were already on fire! ⁵⁰I am going to be put to a hard test. And I will have to suffer a lot of pain until it is over. ⁵¹Do you think that I came to bring peace to earth? No indeed! I came to make people choose sides. ⁵²A family of five will be divided, with two of them against the other three. ⁵³Fathers and sons will turn against one another, and mothers and daughters will do the same. Mothers-in-law and daughters-in-law will also turn against each other.

Knowing What To Do
(Matthew 16.2,3; 5.25,26)

54 Jesus said to all the people:

As soon as you see a cloud coming up in the west, you say, "It's going to rain," and it does. ⁵⁵When the south wind blows, you say, "It's going to get hot," and it does. ⁵⁶Are you trying to fool someone? You can predict the weather by looking at the earth and sky, but you don't really know what's going on right now. ⁵⁷Why don't you understand the right thing to do?

⁵⁸When someone accuses you of something, try to settle things before you are taken to court. If you don't, you will be dragged before the judge. Then the judge will hand you over to the jailer, and you will be locked up. ⁵⁹You won't get out until you have paid the last cent you owe.

Turn Back to God

13 About this same time Jesus was told that Pilate had given orders for some people from Galilee to be killed while they were offering sacrifices. ²Jesus replied:

Do you think that these people were worse sinners than everyone else in Galilee just because of what happened to them? ³Not at all! But you can be sure that if you don't turn back to God, every one of you will also be killed. ⁴What about those eighteen people who died when the tower in Siloam fell on them? Do you think they were worse than everyone else in Jerusalem? ⁵Not at all! But you can be sure that if you don't turn back to God, every one of you will also die.

A Story about a Fig Tree

6 Jesus then told them this story:

A man had a fig tree growing in his vineyard. One day he went out to pick some figs, but he didn't find any. ⁷So he said to the gardener, "For three years I have come looking for figs on this tree, and I haven't found any yet. Chop it down! Why should it take up space?"

8 The gardener answered, "Master, leave it for another year. I'll dig around it and put some manure on it to make it grow. 9Maybe it will have figs on it next year. If it doesn't, you can have it cut down."

Healing a Woman on the Sabbath

10 One Sabbath, Jesus was teaching in a Jewish meeting place, 11and a woman was there who had been crippled by an evil spirit for eighteen years. She was completely bent over and could not straighten up. 12When Jesus saw the woman, he called her over and said, "You are now well." 13He placed his hands on her, and right away she stood up straight and praised God.

14 The man in charge of the meeting place was angry because Jesus had healed someone on the Sabbath. So he said to the people, "Each week has six days when we can work. Come and be healed on one of those days, but not on the Sabbath."

15 The Lord replied, "Are you trying to fool someone? Won't any one of you untie your ox or donkey and lead it out to drink on a Sabbath? 16This woman belongs to the family of Abraham, but Satan has kept her bound for eighteen years. Isn't it right to set her free on the Sabbath?" 17Jesus' words made his enemies ashamed. But everyone else in the crowd was happy about the wonderful things he was doing.

A Mustard Seed and Yeast
(Matthew 13.31-33; Mark 4.30-32)

18 Jesus said, "What is God's kingdom like? What can I compare it with? 19It is like what happens when

someone plants a mustard seed in a garden. The seed grows as big as a tree, and birds nest in its branches."

20 Then Jesus said, "What can I compare God's kingdom with? 21It is like what happens when a woman mixes yeast into three batches of flour. Finally, all the dough rises."

The Narrow Door
(Matthew 7.13, 14, 21-23)

22 As Jesus was on his way to Jerusalem, he taught the people in the towns and villages. 23Someone asked him, "Lord, are only a few people going to be saved?"

Jesus answered:

24 Do all you can to go in by the narrow door! A lot of people will try to get in, but will not be able to. 25Once the owner of the house gets up and locks the door, you will be left standing outside. You will knock on the door and say, "Sir, open the door for us!"

But the owner will answer, "I don't know a thing about you!"

26 Then you will start saying, "We dined with you, and you taught in our streets."

27 But he will say, "I really don't know who you are! Get away from me, you evil people!"

28 Then when you have been thrown outside, you will weep and grit your teeth because you will see Abraham and Isaac and all the prophets in God's kingdom. 29People will come from all directions and sit down to feast in God's kingdom. 30There the ones who are now least important will be the most important, and

those who are now most important will be least important.

Jesus and Herod

31 At that time some Pharisees came to Jesus and said, "You had better get away from here! Herod*k* wants to kill you."

32 Jesus said to them:

Go tell that fox, "I am going to force out demons and heal people today and tomorrow, and three days later I'll be through." 33But I am going on my way today and tomorrow and the next day. After all, Jerusalem is the place where prophets are killed.

Jesus Loves Jerusalem

(Matthew 23.37-39)

34 Jerusalem, Jerusalem! Your people have killed the prophets and have stoned the messengers who were sent to you. I have often wanted to gather your people, as a hen gathers her chicks under her wings. But you wouldn't let me. 35Now your temple will be deserted. You won't see me again until the time when you say,

"Blessed is the one who comes
in the name of the Lord."

Jesus Heals a Sick Man

14 One Sabbath, Jesus was having dinner in the home of an important Pharisee, and everyone was carefully watching Jesus. 2All of a sudden a man

---

k Herod: Herod Antipas, the son of Herod the Great.

with swollen legs stood up in front of him. ³Jesus turned and asked the Pharisees and the teachers of the Law of Moses, "Is it right to heal on the Sabbath?" ⁴But they did not say a word.

Jesus took hold of the man. Then he healed him and sent him away. ⁵Afterwards, Jesus asked the people, "If your son or ox falls into a well, wouldn't you pull him out right away, even on the Sabbath?" ⁶There was nothing they could say.

How To Be a Guest

7 Jesus saw how the guests had tried to take the best seats. So he told them:

8 When you are invited to a wedding feast, don't sit in the best place. Someone more important may have been invited. ⁹Then the one who invited you will come and say, "Give your place to this other guest!" You will be embarrassed and will have to sit in the worst place.

10 When you are invited to be a guest, go and sit in the worst place. Then the one who invited you may come and say, "My friend, take a better seat!" You will then be honored in front of all the other guests. ¹¹If you put yourself above others, you will be put down. But if you humble yourself, you will be honored.

12 Then Jesus said to the man who had invited him:

When you give a dinner or a banquet, don't invite your friends and family and relatives and rich neighbors. If you do, they will invite you in return, and you will be paid back. ¹³When you give a feast, invite the poor, the crippled, the lame, and the blind. [14]They cannot pay you back. But God will bless you and reward you when his people rise from death.

The Great Banquet
(Matthew 22.1-10)

15 After Jesus had finished speaking, one of the guests said, "The greatest blessing of all is to be at the banquet in God's kingdom!"

16 Jesus told him:

A man once gave a great banquet and invited a lot of guests. [17]When the banquet was ready, he sent a servant to tell the guests, "Everything is ready! Please come."

18 One guest after another started making excuses. The first one said, "I bought some land, and I've got to look it over. Please excuse me."

19 Another guest said, "I bought five teams of oxen, and I need to try them out. Please excuse me."

20 Still another guest said, "I have just gotten married, and I can't be there."

21 The servant told his master what happened, and the master became so angry that he said, "Go as fast as you can to every street and alley in town! Bring in everyone who is poor or crippled or blind or lame."

22 When the servant returned, he said, "Master, I've done what you told me, and there is still plenty of room for more people."

23 His master then told him, "Go out along the back roads and fence rows and make people come in, so that my house will be full. [24]Not one

of the guests I first invited will get even a bite of my food!"

Being a Disciple
(Matthew 10.37,38)

25 Large crowds were walking along with Jesus, when he turned and said:

26 You cannot be my disciple, unless you love me more than you love your father and mother, your wife and children, and your brothers and sisters. You cannot come with me unless you love me more than you love your own life.

27 You cannot be my disciple unless you carry your own cross and come with me.

28 Suppose one of you wants to build a tower. What is the first thing you will do? Won't you sit down and figure out how much it will cost and if you have enough money to pay for it? 29Otherwise, you will start building the tower, but not be able to finish. Then everyone who sees what is happening will laugh at you. 30They will say, "You started building, but could not finish the job."

31 What will a king do if he has only ten thousand soldiers to defend himself against a king who is about to attack him with twenty thousand soldiers? Before he goes out to battle, won't he first sit down and decide if he can win? 32If he thinks he won't be able to defend himself, he will send messengers and ask for peace while the other king is still a long way off. 33So then, you cannot be my disciple unless you give away everything you own.

Salt and Light
(Matthew 5.13; Mark 9.50)

34 Salt is good, but if it no longer tastes like salt, how can it be made to taste salty again? 35 It is no longer good for the soil or even for the manure pile. People simply throw it out. If you have ears, pay attention!

One Sheep
(Matthew 18.12-14)

15 Tax collectors[1] and sinners were all crowding around to listen to Jesus. 2 So the Pharisees and the teachers of the Law of Moses started grumbling, "This man is friendly with sinners. He even eats with them."

3 Then Jesus told them this story:

4 If any of you has a hundred sheep, and one of them gets lost, what will you do? Won't you leave the ninety-nine in the field and go look for the lost sheep until you find it? 5 And when you find it, you will be so glad that you will put it on your shoulder 6 and carry it home. Then you will call in your friends and neighbors and say, "Let's celebrate! I've found my lost sheep."

7 Jesus said, "In the same way there is more happiness in heaven because of one sinner who turns to God than over ninety-nine good people who don't need to."

One Coin

8 Jesus told the people another story:

---

[1] Tax collectors: See the note at 3.12.

What will a woman do if she has ten silver coins and loses one of them? Won't she light a lamp, sweep the floor, and look carefully until she finds it? ⁹Then she will call in her friends and neighbors and say, "Let's celebrate! I've found the coin I lost."

10 Jesus said, "In the same way God's angels are happy when even one person turns to him."

Two Sons

11 Jesus also told them another story:

Once a man had two sons. ¹²The younger son said to his father, "Give me my share of the property." So the father divided his property between his two sons.

13 Not long after that, the younger son packed up everything he owned and left for a foreign country, where he wasted all his money in wild living. ¹⁴He had spent everything, when a bad famine spread through that whole land. Soon he had nothing to eat.

15 He went to work for a man in that country, and the man sent him out to take care of his pigs.ᵐ ¹⁶He would have been glad to eat what the pigs were eating,ⁿ but no one gave him a thing.

ᵐ *pigs*: The Jewish religion taught that pigs were not fit to eat or even to touch. A Jewish man would have felt terribly insulted if he had to feed pigs, much less eat with them.

ⁿ *what the pigs were eating*: The Greek text has "(bean) pods," which came from a tree in Palestine. These were used to feed animals. Poor people sometimes ate them too.

17 Finally, he came to his senses and said, "My father's workers have plenty to eat, and here I am, starving to death! 18 I will go to my father and say to him, 'Father, I have sinned against God in heaven and against you. 19 I am no longer good enough to be called your son. Treat me like one of your workers.'"

20 The younger son got up and started back to his father. But when he was still a long way off, his father saw him and felt sorry for him. He ran to his son and hugged and kissed him.

21 The son said, "Father, I have sinned against God in heaven and against you. I am no longer good enough to be called your son."

22 But his father said to the servants, "Hurry and bring the best clothes and put them on him. Give him a ring for his finger and sandals *o* for his feet. 23 Get the best calf and prepare it, so we can eat and celebrate. 24 This son of mine was dead, but has now come back to life. He was lost and has now been found." And they began to celebrate.

25 The older son had been out in the field. But when he came near the house, he heard the music and dancing. 26 So he called one of the servants over and asked, "What's going on here?"

27 The servant answered, "Your brother has come home safe and sound, and your father ordered us to kill the best calf." 28 The older

---

o ring…sandals: These show that the young man's father fully accepted him as his son. A ring was a sign of high position in the family. Sandals showed that he was a son instead of a slave, since slaves did not usually wear sandals.

brother got so angry that he would not even go into the house.

His father came out and begged him to go in. 29But he said to his father, "For years I have worked for you like a slave and have always obeyed you. But you have never even given me a little goat, so that I could give a dinner for my friends. 30This other son of yours wasted your money on prostitutes. And now that he has come home, you ordered the best calf to be killed for a feast."

31 His father replied, "My son, you are always with me, and everything I have is yours. 32But we should be glad and celebrate! Your brother was dead, but he is now alive. He was lost and has now been found."

A Dishonest Manager

16 Jesus said to his disciples:
A rich man once had a manager to take care of his business. But he was told that his manager was wasting money. 2So the rich man called him in and said, "What is this I hear about you? Tell me what you have done! You are no longer going to work for me."

3 The manager said to himself, "What shall I do now that my master is going to fire me? I can't dig ditches, and I'm ashamed to beg. 4I know what I'll do, so that people will welcome me into their homes after I've lost my job."

5 Then one by one he called in the people who were in debt to his master. He asked the first one, "How much do you owe my master?"

6 "A hundred barrels of olive oil," the man answered.

So the manager said, "Take your bill and sit down and quickly write 'fifty'."

7 The manager asked someone else who was in debt to his master, "How much do you owe?"

"A thousand bushels*p* of wheat," the man replied.

The manager said, "Take your bill and write 'eight hundred'."

8 The master praised his dishonest manager for looking out for himself so well. That's how it is! The people of this world look out for themselves better than the people who belong to the light.

9 My disciples, I tell you to use wicked wealth to make friends for yourselves. Then when it is gone, you will be welcomed into an eternal home. 10Anyone who can be trusted in little matters can also be trusted in important matters. But anyone who is dishonest in little matters will be dishonest in important matters. 11If you cannot be trusted with this wicked wealth, who will trust you with true wealth? 12And if you cannot be trusted with what belongs to someone else, who will give you something that will be your own? 13You cannot be the slave of two masters. You will like one more than the other or be more loyal to one than to the other. You cannot serve God and money.

---

p A thousand bushels: The Greek text has "A hundred measures," and each measure is about ten or twelve bushels.

Some Sayings of Jesus

(Matthew 11,12,13; 5.31,32; Mark 10,11,12)

14 The Pharisees really loved money. So when they heard what Jesus said, they made fun of him. 15But Jesus told them:

You are always making yourselves look good, but God sees what is in your heart. The things that most people think are important are worthless as far as God is concerned.

16 Until the time of John the Baptist, people had to obey the Law of Moses and the Books of the Prophets.*q* But since God's kingdom has been preached, everyone is trying hard to get in. 17Heaven and earth will disappear before the smallest letter of the Law does.

18 It is a terrible sin*r* for a man to divorce his wife and marry another woman. It is also a terrible sin for a man to marry a divorced woman.

Lazarus and the Rich Man

19 There was once a rich man who wore expensive clothes and every day ate the best food. 20But a poor beggar named Lazarus was brought to the gate of the rich man's house. 21He was happy just to eat the scraps that fell from the rich man's table. His body was covered with sores, and dogs kept coming up to lick

---

q the Law of Moses and the Books of the Prophets: The Jewish Scriptures, that is, the Old Testament.

r a terrible sin: The Greek text uses a word that means the sin of being unfaithful in marriage.

them. [22]The poor man died, and angels took him to the place of honor next to Abraham.[s]

The rich man also died and was buried. [23]He went to hell[t] and was suffering terribly. When he looked up and saw Abraham far off and Lazarus at his side, [24]he said to Abraham, "Have pity on me! Send Lazarus to dip his finger in water and touch my tongue. I'm suffering terribly in this fire."

25 Abraham answered, "My friend, remember that while you lived, you had everything good, and Lazarus had everything bad. Now he is happy, and you are in pain. [26]And besides, there is a deep ditch between us, and no one from either side can cross over."

27 But the rich man said, "Abraham, then please send Lazarus to my father's home. [28]Let him warn my five brothers, so they won't come to this horrible place."

29 Abraham answered, "Your brothers can read what Moses and the prophets[u] wrote. They should pay attention to that."

30 Then the rich man said, "No, that's not enough! If only someone from the dead would go to them, they would listen and turn to God."

---

[s] *the place of honor next to Abraham*: The Jewish people thought that heaven would be a banquet that God would give for them. Abraham would be the most important person there, and the guest of honor would sit next to him.

[t] *hell*: The Greek text has "hades," which the Jewish people often thought of as the place where the dead wait for the final judgment.

[u] *Moses and the prophets*: The Jewish Scriptures, that is, the Old Testament.

31 So Abraham said, "If they won't pay attention to Moses and the prophets, they won't listen even to someone who comes back from the dead."

Faith and Service
(Matthew 18.6, 7, 21, 22; Mark 9.42)

17 Jesus said to his disciples:
There will always be something that causes people to sin. But anyone who causes them to sin is in for trouble. A person who causes even one of my little followers to sin 2 would be better off thrown into the ocean with a heavy stone tied around their necks. 3 So be careful what you do.

Correct any followers *v* of mine who sin, and forgive the ones who say they are sorry. 4 Even if one of them mistreats you seven times in one day and says, "I am sorry," you should still forgive that person.

5 The apostles said to the Lord, "Make our faith stronger!"

6 Jesus replied:
If you had faith no bigger than a tiny mustard seed, you could tell this mulberry tree to pull itself up, roots and all, and to plant itself in the ocean. And it would!

7 If your servant comes in from plowing or from taking care of the sheep, would you say, "Welcome! Come on in and have something to eat"? 8 No, you wouldn't say that. You would say, "Fix me something to eat. Get ready to serve me,

---

v followers: The Greek text has "brothers," which is often used in the New Testament for followers of Jesus.

so I can have my meal. Then later on you can eat and drink." ⁹Servants don't deserve special thanks for doing what they are supposed to do. ¹⁰And that's how it should be with you. When you've done all you should, then say, "We are merely servants, and we have simply done our duty."

Ten Men with Leprosy

11 On his way to Jerusalem, Jesus went along the border between Samaria and Galilee. ¹²As he was going into a village, ten men with leprosy *w* came toward him. They stood at a distance ¹³and shouted, "Jesus, Master, have pity on us!"

14 Jesus looked at them and said, "Go show yourselves to the priests." *x*

On their way they were healed. ¹⁵When one of them discovered that he was healed, he came back, shouting praises to God. ¹⁶He bowed down at the feet of Jesus and thanked him. The man was from the country of Samaria.

17 Jesus asked, "Weren't ten men healed? Where are the other nine? ¹⁸Why was this foreigner the only one who came back to thank God?" ¹⁹Then Jesus told the man, "You may get up and go. Your faith has made you well."

God's Kingdom
(Matthew 24.23-28, 37-41)

20 Some Pharisees asked Jesus when God's kingdom would come. He answered, "God's kingdom isn't

---

w *leprosy*: See the note at 4.27.

x *show yourselves to the priests*: See the note at 5.14.

something you can see. ²¹There is no use saying, 'Look! Here it is' or 'Look! There it is.' God's kingdom is here with you."ʸ

22 Jesus said to his disciples:

The time will come when you will long to see one of the days of the Son of Man, but you will not. ²³When people say to you, "Look there," or "Look here," don't go looking for him. ²⁴The day of the Son of Man will be like lightning flashing across the sky. ²⁵But first he must suffer terribly and be rejected by the people of today. ²⁶When the Son of Man comes, things will be just as they were when Noah lived. ²⁷People were eating, drinking, and getting married right up to the day when Noah went into the big boat. Then the flood came and drowned everyone on earth.

28 When Lotᶻ lived, people were also eating and drinking. They were buying, selling, planting, and building. ²⁹But on the very day Lot left Sodom, fiery flames poured down from the sky and killed everyone. ³⁰The same will happen on the day when the Son of Man appears.

31 At that time no one on a rooftopᵃ should go down into the house to get anything. No one

---

ʸ *here with you*: Or "in your hearts."

ᶻ *Noah...Lot*: When God destroyed the earth by a flood, he saved Noah and his family. And when God destroyed the cities of Sodom and Gomorrah and the evil people who lived there, he rescued Lot and his family (see Genesis 19.1-29).

ᵃ *rooftop*: See the note at 5.19.

in a field should go back to the house for anything. 32Remember what happened to Lot's wife.[b]

33 People who try to save their lives will lose them, and those who lose their lives will save them. 34On that night two people will be sleeping in the same bed, but only one will be taken. The other will be left. 35-36Two women will be together grinding wheat, but only one will be taken. The other will be left.[c]

37 Then Jesus' disciples spoke up, "But where will this happen, Lord?"

Jesus said, "Where there is a corpse, there will always be buzzards."[d]

A Widow and a Judge

18 Jesus told his disciples a story about how they should keep on praying and never give up:

2 In a town there was once a judge who didn't fear God or care about people. 3In that same town there was a widow who kept going to the

---

[b] *what happened to Lot's wife*: She turned to a block of salt when she disobeyed God (see Genesis 19.26).

[c] *will be left*: Some manuscripts add, "Two men will be in the same field, but only one will be taken. The other will be left."

[d] *Where there is a corpse, there will always be buzzards*: This saying may mean that when anything important happens, people soon know about it. Or the saying may mean that whenever something bad happens, curious people gather around and stare. But the word translated "buzzard" also means "eagle" and may refer to the Roman army, which had an eagle as its symbol.

judge and saying, "Make sure that I get fair treatment in court."

4 For a while the judge refused to do anything. Finally, he said to himself, "Even though I don't fear God or care about people, ⁵I will help this widow because she keeps on bothering me. If I don't help her, she will wear me out."

6 The Lord said:

Think about what that crooked judge said. ⁷Won't God protect his chosen ones who pray to him day and night? Won't he be concerned for them? ⁸He will surely hurry and help them. But when the Son of Man comes, will he find on this earth anyone with faith?

A Pharisee and a Tax Collector

9 Jesus told a story to some people who thought they were better than others and who looked down on everyone else:

10 Two men went into the temple to pray.ᵉ One was a Pharisee and the other a tax collector.ᶠ ¹¹The Pharisee stood over by himself and prayed,ᵍ "God, I thank you that I am not greedy, dishonest, and unfaithful in marriage like other people. And I am really glad that I am not like that tax collector over there. ¹²I go without

---

ᵉ *into the temple to pray*: Jewish people usually prayed there early in the morning and late in the afternoon.

ᶠ *tax collector*: See the note at 3.12.

ᵍ *stood over by himself and prayed*: Some manuscripts have "stood up and prayed to himself."

eating[h] for two days a week, and I give you one tenth of all I earn."

13 The tax collector stood off at a distance and did not think he was good enough even to look up toward heaven. He was so sorry for what he had done that he pounded his chest and prayed, "God, have pity on me! I am such a sinner."

14 Then Jesus said, "When the two men went home, it was the tax collector and not the Pharisee who was pleasing to God. If you put yourself above others, you will be put down. But if you humble yourself, you will be honored."

Jesus Blesses Little Children
(Matthew 19.13-15; Mark 10.13-16)

15 Some people brought their little children for Jesus to bless. But when his disciples saw them doing this, they told the people to stop bothering him. 16So Jesus called the children over to him and said, "Let the children come to me! Don't try to stop them. People who are like these children belong to God's kingdom.[i] 17You will never get into God's kingdom unless you enter it like a child!"

A Rich and Important Man
(Matthew 19.16-30; Mark 10.17-31)

18 An important man asked Jesus, "Good Teacher, what must I do to have eternal life?"

---

[h] *without eating*: See the note at 2.37.
[i] *People who are like these children belong to God's kingdom*: Or "God's kingdom belongs to people who are like these children."

19 Jesus said, "Why do you call me good? Only God is good. 20 You know the commandments: 'Be faithful in marriage. Do not murder. Do not steal. Do not tell lies about others. Respect your father and mother.'"

21 He told Jesus, "I have obeyed all these commandments since I was a young man."

22 When Jesus heard this, he said, "There is one thing you still need to do. Go and sell everything you own! Give the money to the poor, and you will have riches in heaven. Then come and be my follower." 23 When the man heard this, he was sad, because he was very rich.

24 Jesus saw how sad the man was. So he said, "It's terribly hard for rich people to get into God's kingdom! 25 In fact, it's easier for a camel to go through the eye of a needle than for a rich person to get into God's kingdom."

26 When the crowd heard this, they asked, "How can anyone ever be saved?"

27 Jesus replied, "There are some things that people cannot do, but God can do anything."

28 Peter said, "Remember, we left everything to be your followers!"

29 Jesus answered, "You can be sure that anyone who gives up home or wife or brothers or family or children because of God's kingdom 30 will be given much more in this life. And in the future world they will have eternal life."

Jesus Again Tells about His Death
(Matthew 20.17-19; Mark 10.32-34)

31 Jesus took the twelve apostles aside and said:

We are now on our way to Jerusalem. Everything that the prophets wrote about the Son of

Man will happen there. ³²He will be handed over to foreigners,ʲ who will make fun of him, mistreat him, and spit on him. ³³They will beat him and kill him, but three days later he will rise to life.

34 The apostles did not understand what Jesus was talking about. They could not understand, because the meaning of what he said was hidden from them.

Jesus Heals a Blind Beggar
(Matthew 20.29-34; Mark 10.46-52)

35 When Jesus was coming close to Jericho, a blind man sat begging beside the road. ³⁶The man heard the crowd walking by and asked what was happening. ³⁷Some people told him that Jesus from Nazareth was passing by. ³⁸So the blind man shouted, "Jesus, Son of David,ᵏ have pity on me!" ³⁹The people who were going along with Jesus told the man to be quiet. But he shouted even louder, "Son of David, have pity on me!"

40 Jesus stopped and told some people to bring the blind man over to him. When the blind man was getting near, Jesus asked, ⁴¹"What do you want me to do for you?"

"Lord, I want to see!" he answered.

42 Jesus replied, "Look and you will see! Your eyes are healed because of your faith." ⁴³Right away the man could see, and he went with Jesus and started

---

ʲ *foreigners*: The Romans, who ruled Judea at this time.
ᵏ *Son of David*: The Jewish people expected the Messiah to be from the family of King David, and for this reason the Messiah was often called the "Son of David."

thanking God. When the crowds saw what happened, they praised God.

Zacchaeus

19 Jesus was going through Jericho, 2where a man named Zacchaeus lived. He was in charge of collecting taxes *l* and was very rich. 3-4Jesus was heading his way, and Zacchaeus wanted to see what he was like. But Zacchaeus was a short man and could not see over the crowd. So he ran ahead and climbed up into a sycamore tree.

5 When Jesus got there, he looked up and said, "Zacchaeus, hurry down! I want to stay with you today." 6Zacchaeus hurried down and gladly welcomed Jesus.

7 Everyone who saw this started grumbling, "This man Zacchaeus is a sinner! And Jesus is going home to eat with him."

8 Later that day Zacchaeus stood up and said to the Lord, "I will give half of my property to the poor. And I will now pay back four times as much *m* to everyone I have ever cheated."

9 Jesus said to Zacchaeus, "Today you and your family have been saved, *n* because you are a true son of Abraham. *o* 10The Son of Man came to look for and to save people who are lost."

---

l in charge of collecting taxes: See the note at 3.12.

m pay back four times as much: Both Jewish and Roman law said that a person must pay back four times the amount that was taken.

n saved: Zacchaeus was Jewish, but it is only now that he is rescued from sin and placed under God's care.

o son of Abraham: As used in this verse, the words mean that Zacchaeus is truly one of God's special people.

A Story about Ten Servants
(Matthew 25.14-30)

11 The crowd was still listening to Jesus as he was getting close to Jerusalem. Many of them thought that God's kingdom would soon appear, 12and Jesus told them this story:

A prince once went to a foreign country to be crowned king and then to return. 13But before leaving, he called in ten servants and gave each of them some money. He told them, "Use this to earn more money until I get back."

14 But the people of his country hated him, and they sent messengers to the foreign country to say, "We don't want this man to be our king."

15 After the prince had been made king, he returned and called in his servants. He asked them how much they had earned with the money they had been given.

16 The first servant came and said, "Sir, with the money you gave me I have earned ten times as much."

17 "That's fine, my good servant!" the king said. "Since you have shown that you can be trusted with a small amount, you will be given ten cities to rule."

18 The second one came and said, "Sir, with the money you gave me, I have earned five times as much."

19 The king said, "You will be given five cities."

20 Another servant came and said, "Sir, here is your money. I kept it safe in a handkerchief. 21You are a hard man, and I was afraid of you.

You take what isn't yours, and you harvest crops you didn't plant."

22 "You worthless servant!" the king told him. "You have condemned yourself by what you have just said. You knew that I am a hard man, taking what isn't mine and harvesting what I've not planted. 23Why didn't you put my money in the bank? On my return, I could have had the money together with interest."

24 Then he said to some other servants standing there, "Take the money away from him and give it to the servant who earned ten times as much."

25 But they said, "Sir, he already has ten times as much!"

26 The king replied, "Those who have something will be given more. But everything will be taken away from those who don't have anything. 27Now bring me the enemies who didn't want me to be their king. Kill them while I watch!"

Jesus Enters Jerusalem
(Matthew 21.1-11; Mark 11.1-11; John 12.12-19)

28 When Jesus had finished saying all this, he went on toward Jerusalem. 29As he was getting near Bethphage and Bethany on the Mount of Olives, he sent two of his disciples on ahead. 30He told them, "Go into the next village, where you will find a young donkey that has never been ridden. Untie the donkey and bring it here. 31If anyone asks why you are doing that, just say, 'The Lord[p] needs it.'"

---

[p] The Lord: Or "The master of the donkey."

32 They went off and found everything just as Jesus had said. 33 While they were untying the donkey, its owners asked, "Why are you doing that?"

34 They answered, "The Lord[q] needs it."

35 Then they led the donkey to Jesus. They put some of their clothes on its back and helped Jesus get on. 36 And as he rode along, the people spread clothes on the road[r] in front of him. 37 When Jesus was starting down the Mount of Olives, his large crowd of disciples were happy and praised God because of all the miracles they had seen. 38 They shouted,

"Blessed is the king
    who comes in the name of the Lord!
Peace in heaven and glory to God."

39 Some Pharisees in the crowd said to Jesus, "Teacher, make your disciples stop shouting!"

40 But Jesus answered, "If they keep quiet, these stones will start shouting."

41 When Jesus came closer and could see Jerusalem, he cried 42 and said:

It is too bad that today your people don't know what will bring them peace! Now it is hidden from them. 43 Jerusalem, the time will come when your enemies will build walls around you to attack you. Armies will surround you and close in on you from every side. 44 They will level you to the ground and kill your people. Not one stone in your buildings will be left on

---

[q] *The Lord*: Or "The master of the donkey."

[r] *spread clothes on the road*: This was one way that the Jewish people welcomed a famous person.

top of another. This will happen because you did not see that God had come to save you.[s]

Jesus in the Temple
(Matthew 21.12-17; Mark 11.15-19; John 2.13-22)

45 When Jesus entered the temple, he started chasing out the people who were selling things. 46He told them, "The Scriptures say, 'My house should be a place of worship.' But you have made it a place where robbers hide!"

47 Each day, Jesus kept on teaching in the temple. So the chief priests, the teachers of the Law of Moses, and some other important people tried to have him killed. 48But they could not find a way to do it, because everyone else was eager to listen to him.

A Question about Jesus' Authority
(Matthew 21.23-27; Mark 11.27-33)

20 One day, Jesus was teaching in the temple and telling the good news. So the chief priests, the teachers, and the nation's leaders 2asked him, "What right do you have to do these things? Who gave you this authority?"

3 Jesus replied, "I want to ask you a question. 4Who gave John the right to baptize? Was it God in heaven or merely some human being?"

5 They talked this over and said to each other, "We can't say that God gave John this right. Jesus will ask

---

[s] that God had come to save you: The Jewish people looked for the time when God would come and rescue them from their enemies. But when Jesus came, many of them refused to obey him.

us why we didn't believe John. 6And we can't say that it was merely some human who gave John the right to baptize. The crowd will stone us to death, because they think John was a prophet."

7 So they told Jesus, "We don't know who gave John the right to baptize."

8 Jesus replied, "Then I won't tell you who gave me the right to do what I do."

Renters of a Vineyard
(Matthew 21.33-46; Mark 12.1-12)

9 Jesus told the people this story:

A man once planted a vineyard and rented it out. Then he left the country for a long time. 10When it was time to harvest the crop, he sent a servant to ask the renters for his share of the grapes. But they beat up the servant and sent him away without anything. 11So the owner sent another servant. The renters also beat him up. They insulted him terribly and sent him away without a thing. 12The owner sent a third servant. He was also beaten terribly and thrown out of the vineyard.

13 The owner then said to himself, "What am I going to do? I know what. I'll send my son, the one I love so much. They will surely respect him!"

14 When the renters saw the owner's son, they said to one another, "Someday he will own the vineyard. Let's kill him! Then we can have it all for ourselves." 15So they threw him out of the vineyard and killed him.

Jesus asked, "What do you think the owner of the vineyard will do? 16I'll tell you what. He will come and kill those renters and let someone else have his vineyard."

When the people heard this, they said, "This must never happen!"

17 But Jesus looked straight at them and said, "Then what do the Scriptures mean when they say, 'The stone that the builders tossed aside is now the most important stone of all'? 18 Anyone who stumbles over this stone will get hurt, and anyone it falls on will be smashed to pieces."

19 The chief priests and the teachers of the Law of Moses knew that Jesus was talking about them when he was telling this story. They wanted to arrest him right then, but they were afraid of the people.

Paying Taxes
(Matthew 22.15-22; Mark 12.13-17)

20 Jesus' enemies kept watching him closely, because they wanted to hand him over to the Roman governor. So they sent some men who pretended to be good. But they were really spies trying to catch Jesus saying something wrong. 21 The spies said to him, "Teacher, we know that you teach the truth about what God wants people to do. And you treat everyone with the same respect, no matter who they are. 22 Tell us, should we pay taxes to the Emperor or not?"

23 Jesus knew that they were trying to trick him. So he told them, 24 "Show me a coin." Then he asked, "Whose picture and name are on it?"

"The Emperor's," they answered.

25 Then he told them, "Give the Emperor what belongs to him and give God what belongs to God."

26Jesus' enemies could not catch him saying anything wrong there in front of the people. They were amazed at his answer and kept quiet.

Life in the Future World
(Matthew 22.23-33; Mark 12.18-27)

27 The Sadducees did not believe that people would rise to life after death. So some of them came to Jesus 28and said:

Teacher, Moses wrote that if a married man dies and has no children, his brother should marry the widow. Their first son would then be thought of as the son of the dead brother.

29 There were once seven brothers. The first one married, but died without having any children. 30The second one married his brother's widow, and he also died without having any children. 31The same thing happened to the third one. Finally, all seven brothers married that woman and died without having any children. 32At last the woman died. 33When God raises people from death, whose wife will this woman be? All seven brothers had married her.

34 Jesus answered:

The people in this world get married. 35But in the future world no one who is worthy to rise from death will either marry 36or die. They will be like the angels and will be God's children, because they have been raised to life.

37 In the story about the burning bush, Moses clearly shows that people will live again. He said, "The Lord is the God worshiped by Abraham,

Isaac, and Jacob." [t] 38So the Lord isn't the God of the dead, but of the living. This means that everyone is alive as far as God is concerned.

39 Some of the teachers of the Law of Moses said, "Teacher, you have given a good answer!" 40From then on, no one dared to ask Jesus any questions.

About David's Son
(Matthew 22.41-46; Mark 12.35-37)

41 Jesus asked, "Why do people say that the Messiah will be the son of King David? [u] 42In the book of Psalms, David himself says,

'The Lord said to my Lord,
    Sit at my right side [v]
    43 until I make your enemies
        into a footstool for you.'

44David spoke of the Messiah as his Lord, so how can the Messiah be his son?"

Jesus and the Teachers of the Law of Moses
(Matthew 23.1-36; Mark 12.38-40; Luke 11.37-54)

45 While everyone was listening to Jesus, he said to his disciples:

46 Guard against the teachers of the Law of Moses! They love to walk around in long robes, and they like to be greeted in the market. They

---

[t] "The Lord is the God worshiped by Abraham, Isaac, and Jacob": Jesus argues that if God is worshiped by these three, they must be alive, because he is the God of the living.

[u] the son of King David: See the note at 18.38.

[v] right side: The place of power and honor.

want the front seats in the meeting places and the best seats at banquets. 47But they cheat widows out of their homes and then pray long prayers just to show off. These teachers will be punished most of all.

A Widow's Offering
(Mark 12.41-44)

21 Jesus looked up and saw some rich people tossing their gifts into the offering box. 2He also saw a poor widow putting in two pennies. 3And he said, "I tell you that this poor woman has put in more than all the others. 4Everyone else gave what they didn't need. But she is very poor and gave everything she had."

The Temple Will Be Destroyed
(Matthew 24.1,2; Mark 13.1,2)

5 Some people were talking about the beautiful stones used to build the temple and about the gifts that had been placed in it. Jesus said, 6"Do you see these stones? The time is coming when not one of them will be left in place. They will all be knocked down."

Warning about Trouble
(Matthew 24.3-14; Mark 13.3-13)

7 Some people asked, "Teacher, when will all this happen? How can we know when these things are about to take place?"

8 Jesus replied:

Don't be fooled by those who will come and claim to be me. They will say, "I am Christ!" and "Now is the time!" But don't follow them.

⁹When you hear about wars and riots, don't be afraid. These things will have to happen first, but that isn't the end.

10 Nations will go to war against one another, and kingdoms will attack each other. ¹¹There will be great earthquakes, and in many places people will starve to death and suffer terrible diseases. All sorts of frightening things will be seen in the sky.

12 Before all this happens, you will be arrested and punished. You will be tried in your meeting places and put in jail. Because of me you will be placed on trial before kings and governors. ¹³But this will be your chance to tell about your faith.

14 Don't worry about what you will say to defend yourselves. ¹⁵I will give you the wisdom to know what to say. None of your enemies will be able to oppose you or to say that you are wrong. ¹⁶You will be betrayed by your own parents, brothers, family, and friends. Some of you will even be killed. ¹⁷Because of me, you will be hated by everyone. ¹⁸But don't worry!ʷ ¹⁹You will be saved by being faithful to me.

Jerusalem Will Be Destroyed
(Matthew 24.15-21; Mark 13.14-19)

20 When you see Jerusalem surrounded by soldiers, you will know that it will soon be destroyed. ²¹If you are living in Judea at that time, run to the mountains. If you are in the city,

---

ʷ *But don't worry*: The Greek text has "Not a hair of your head will be lost," which means "There's no need to worry."

leave it. And if you are out in the country, don't go back into the city. ²²This time of punishment is what is written about in the Scriptures. ²³It will be an awful time for women who are expecting babies or nursing young children! Everywhere in the land people will suffer horribly and be punished. ²⁴Some of them will be killed by swords. Others will be carried off to foreign countries. Jerusalem will be overrun by foreign nations until their time comes to an end.

When the Son of Man Appears
(Matthew 24.29-31; Mark 13.24-27)

25 Strange things will happen to the sun, moon, and stars. The nations on earth will be afraid of the roaring sea and tides, and they won't know what to do. ²⁶People will be so frightened that they will faint because of what is happening to the world. Every power in the sky will be shaken.ˣ ²⁷Then the Son of Man will be seen, coming in a cloud with great power and glory. ²⁸When all of this starts happening, stand up straight and be brave. You will soon be set free.

A Lesson from a Fig Tree
(Matthew 24.32-35; Mark 13.28-31)

29 Then Jesus told them a story:

When you see a fig tree or any other tree ³⁰putting out leaves, you know that summer will soon come. ³¹So, when you see these things

---

ˣ *Every power in the sky will be shaken*: In ancient times people thought that the stars were spiritual powers.

happening, you know that God's kingdom will soon be here. [32] You can be sure that some of the people of this generation will still be alive when all of this takes place. [33] The sky and the earth won't last forever, but my words will.

A Warning

34 Don't spend all of your time thinking about eating or drinking or worrying about life. If you do, the final day will suddenly catch you [35] like a trap. That day will surprise everyone on earth. [36] Watch out and keep praying that you can escape all that is going to happen and that the Son of Man will be pleased with you.

37 Jesus taught in the temple each day, and he spent each night on the Mount of Olives. [38] Everyone got up early and came to the temple to hear him teach.

A Plot To Kill Jesus
(Matthew 26.1-5, 14, 16; Mark 14.1, 2, 10, 11; John 11.45-53)

22 The Festival of Thin Bread, also called Passover, was near. [2] The chief priests and the teachers of the Law of Moses were looking for a way to get rid of Jesus, because they were afraid of what the people might do. [3] Then Satan entered the heart of Judas Iscariot,[y] who was one of the twelve apostles.

4 Judas went to talk with the chief priests and the officers of the temple police about how he could help them arrest Jesus. [5] They were very pleased and

y *Iscariot*: See the note at 6.16.

offered to pay Judas some money. ⁶He agreed and started looking for a good chance to betray Jesus when the crowds were not around.

Jesus Eats with His Disciples
(Matthew 26.17-25; Mark 14.12-21; John 13.21-30)

7 The day had come for the Festival of Thin Bread, and it was time to kill the Passover lambs. ⁸So Jesus said to Peter and John, "Go and prepare the Passover meal for us to eat."

9 But they asked, "Where do you want us to prepare it?"

10 Jesus told them, "As you go into the city, you will meet a man carrying a jar of water.ᶻ Follow him into the house ¹¹and say to the owner, 'Our teacher wants to know where he can eat the Passover meal with his disciples.' ¹²The owner will take you upstairs and show you a large room ready for you to use. Prepare the meal there."

13 Peter and John left. They found everything just as Jesus had told them, and they prepared the Passover meal.

The Lord's Supper
(Matthew 26.26-30; Mark 14.22-26; 1 Corinthians 11.23-25)

14 When the time came for Jesus and the apostles to eat, ¹⁵he said to them, "I have very much wanted to eat this Passover meal with you before I suffer. ¹⁶I tell you that I will not eat another Passover meal until it is finally eaten in God's kingdom."

ᶻ *a man carrying a jar of water*: A male slave carrying water would probably mean that the family was rich.

17 Jesus took a cup of wine in his hands and gave thanks to God. Then he told the apostles, "Take this wine and share it with each other. 18I tell you that I will not drink any more wine until God's kingdom comes."

19 Jesus took some bread in his hands and gave thanks for it. He broke the bread and handed it to his apostles. Then he said, "This is my body, which is given for you. Eat this as a way of remembering me!"

20 After the meal he took another cup of wine in his hands. Then he said, "This is my blood. It is poured out for you, and with it God makes his new agreement. 21The one who will betray me is here at the table with me! 22The Son of Man will die in the way that has been decided for him, but it will be terrible for the one who betrays him!"

23 Then the apostles started arguing about who would ever do such a thing.

An Argument about Greatness

24 The apostles got into an argument about which one of them was the greatest. 25So Jesus told them:

Foreign kings order their people around, and powerful rulers call themselves everyone's friends.ª 26But don't be like them. The most important one of you should be like the least important, and your leader should be like a servant. 27Who do people think is the greatest, a

---

ª everyone's friends: This translates a Greek word that rulers sometimes used as a title for themselves or for special friends.

person who is served or one who serves? Isn't it the one who is served? But I have been with you as a servant.

28 You have stayed with me in all my troubles. 29So I will give you the right to rule as kings, just as my Father has given me the right to rule as a king. 30You will eat and drink with me in my kingdom, and you will each sit on a throne to judge the twelve tribes of Israel.

Jesus' Disciples Will Be Tested
(Matthew 26.31-35; Mark 14.27-31; John 13.36-38)

31 Jesus said, "Simon, listen to me! Satan has demanded the right to test each one of you, as a farmer does when he separates wheat from the husks.[b] 32But Simon, I have prayed that your faith will be strong. And when you have come back to me, help the others."

33 Peter said, "Lord, I am ready to go with you to jail and even to die with you."

34 Jesus replied, "Peter, I tell you that before a rooster crows tomorrow morning, you will say three times that you don't know me."

Moneybags, Traveling Bags, and Swords

35 Jesus asked his disciples, "When I sent you out without a moneybag or a traveling bag or sandals, did you need anything?"

"No!" they answered.

36 Jesus told them, "But now, if you have a moneybag, take it with you. Also take a traveling bag, and if

---

[b] *separates wheat from the husks*: See the note at 3.17.

you don't have a sword,^{c} sell some of your clothes and buy one. ^{37}Do this because the Scriptures say, 'He was considered a criminal.' This was written about me, and it will soon come true."

38 The disciples said, "Lord, here are two swords!"

"Enough of that!" Jesus replied.

Jesus Prays
(Matthew 26.36-46; Mark 14.32-42)

39 Jesus went out to the Mount of Olives, as he often did, and his disciples went with him. ^{40}When they got there, he told them, "Pray that you won't be tested."

41 Jesus walked on a little way before he knelt down and prayed, ^{42}"Father, if you will, please don't make me suffer by having me drink from this cup.^{d} But do what you want, and not what I want."

43 Then an angel from heaven came to help him. ^{44}Jesus was in great pain and prayed so sincerely that his sweat fell to the ground like drops of blood.^{e}

45 Jesus got up from praying and went over to his disciples. They were asleep and worn out from being so sad. ^{46}He said to them, "Why are you asleep? Wake up and pray that you won't be tested."

---

^{c} *moneybag...traveling bag...sword*: These were things that someone would take on a dangerous journey. Jesus was telling his disciples to be ready for anything that might happen. They seem to have understood what he meant (see 22.49-51).

^{d} *having me drink from this cup*: In the Scriptures "to drink from a cup" sometimes means to suffer.

^{e} *Then an angel...like drops of blood*: Verses 43 and 44 are not in some manuscripts.

Jesus Is Arrested

(Matthew 26.47-56; Mark 14.43-50; John 18.3-11)

47 While Jesus was still speaking, a crowd came up. It was led by Judas, one of the twelve apostles. He went over to Jesus and greeted him with a kiss.*f*

48 Jesus asked Judas, "Are you betraying the Son of Man with a kiss?"

49 When Jesus' disciples saw what was about to happen, they asked, "Lord, should we attack them with a sword?" 50One of the disciples even struck at the high priest's servant with his sword and cut off the servant's right ear.

51 "Enough of that!" Jesus said. Then he touched the servant's ear and healed it.

52 Jesus spoke to the chief priests, the temple police, and the leaders who had come to arrest him. He said, "Why do you come out with swords and clubs and treat me like a criminal? 53I was with you every day in the temple, and you didn't arrest me. But this is your time, and darkness*g* is in control."

Peter Says He Doesn't Know Jesus

(Matthew 26.57,58,67-75; Mark 14.53,54,66-72;
John 18.12-18,25-27)

54 Jesus was arrested and led away to the house of the high priest, while Peter followed at a distance. 55Some people built a fire in the middle of the court-yard and were sitting around it. Peter sat there with

---

f greeted him with a kiss: It was the custom for people to greet each other with a kiss on the cheek.

g darkness: Darkness stands for the power of the devil.

them, 56and a servant girl saw him. Then after she had looked at him carefully, she said, "This man was with Jesus!"

57 Peter said, "Woman, I don't even know that man!"

58 A little later someone else saw Peter and said, "You are one of them!"

"No, I'm not!" Peter replied.

59 About an hour later another man insisted, "This man must have been with Jesus. They both come from Galilee."

60 Peter replied, "I don't know what you are talking about!" Right then, while Peter was still speaking, a rooster crowed.

61 The Lord turned and looked at Peter. And Peter remembered that the Lord had said, "Before a rooster crows tomorrow morning, you will say three times that you don't know me." 62Then Peter went out and cried hard.

63 The men who were guarding Jesus made fun of him and beat him. 64They put a blindfold on him and said, "Tell us who struck you!" 65They kept on insulting Jesus in many other ways.

Jesus Is Questioned by the Council
(Matthew 26.59-66; Mark 14.55-64; John 18.19-24)

66 At daybreak the nation's leaders, the chief priests, and the teachers of the Law of Moses got together and brought Jesus before their council. 67They said, "Tell us! Are you the Messiah?"

Jesus replied, "If I said so, you wouldn't believe me. 68And if I asked you a question, you wouldn't answer. 69But from now on, the Son of Man will be seated at the right side of God All-Powerful."

70 Then they asked, "Are you the Son of God?"[h] Jesus answered, "You say I am!"[i]

71 They replied, "Why do we need more witnesses? He said it himself!"

Pilate Questions Jesus

(Matthew 27.1,2,11-14; Mark 15.1-5; John 18.28-38)

23 Everyone in the council got up and led Jesus off to Pilate. 2They started accusing him and said, "We caught this man trying to get our people to riot and to stop paying taxes to the Emperor. He also claims that he is the Messiah, our king."

3 Pilate asked Jesus, "Are you the king of the Jews?"

"Those are your words," Jesus answered.

4 Pilate told the chief priests and the crowd, "I don't find him guilty of anything."

5 But they all kept on saying, "He has been teaching and causing trouble all over Judea. He started in Galilee and has now come all the way here."

Jesus Is Brought before Herod

6 When Pilate heard this, he asked, "Is this man from Galilee?" 7After Pilate learned that Jesus came from the region ruled by Herod,[j] he sent him to Herod, who was in Jerusalem at that time.

8 For a long time Herod had wanted to see Jesus and was very happy because he finally had this chance.

---

[h] *Son of God*: This was one of the titles used for the kings of Israel.

[i] *You say I am*: Or "That's what you say."

[j] *Herod*: Herod Antipas, the son of Herod the Great.

He had heard many things about Jesus and hoped to see him work a miracle.

9 Herod asked him a lot of questions, but Jesus did not answer. ¹⁰Then the chief priests and the teachers of the Law of Moses stood up and accused him of all kinds of bad things.

11 Herod and his soldiers made fun of Jesus and insulted him. They put a fine robe on him and sent him back to Pilate. ¹²That same day Herod and Pilate became friends, even though they had been enemies before this.

The Death Sentence
(Matthew 27.15-26; Mark 15.6-15; John 18.39–19.16)

13 Pilate called together the chief priests, the leaders, and the people. ¹⁴He told them, "You brought Jesus to me and said he was a troublemaker. But I have questioned him here in front of you, and I have not found him guilty of anything that you say he has done. ¹⁵Herod didn't find him guilty either and sent him back. This man doesn't deserve to be put to death! ¹⁶⁻¹⁷I will just have him beaten with a whip and set free."ᵏ

18 But the whole crowd shouted, "Kill Jesus! Give us Barabbas!" ¹⁹Now Barabbas was in jail because he had started a riot in the city and had murdered someone.

20 Pilate wanted to set Jesus free, so he spoke again to the crowds. ²¹But they kept shouting, "Nail him to a cross! Nail him to a cross!"

ᵏ *set free*: Some manuscripts add, "Pilate said this, because at every Passover he was supposed to set one prisoner free for the Jewish people."

22 Pilate spoke to them a third time, "But what crime has he done? I have not found him guilty of anything for which he should be put to death. I will have him beaten with a whip and set free."

23 The people kept on shouting as loud as they could for Jesus to be put to death. 24Finally, Pilate gave in. 25He freed the man who was in jail for rioting and murder, because he was the one the crowd wanted to be set free. Then Pilate handed Jesus over for them to do what they wanted with him.

Jesus Is Nailed to a Cross
(Matthew 27.31-44; Mark 15.21-32; John 19.17-27)

26 As Jesus was being led away, some soldiers grabbed hold of a man from Cyrene named Simon. He was coming in from the fields, but they put the cross on him and made him carry it behind Jesus.

27 A large crowd was following Jesus, and in the crowd a lot of women were crying and weeping for him. 28Jesus turned to the women and said:

Women of Jerusalem, don't cry for me! Cry for yourselves and for your children. 29Someday people will say, "Women who never had children are really fortunate!" 30At that time everyone will say to the mountains, "Fall on us!" They will say to the hills, "Hide us!" 31If this can happen when the wood is green, what do you think will happen when it is dry?*l*

---

l *If this can happen when the wood is green, what do you think will happen when it is dry?*: This saying probably means, "If this can happen to an innocent person, what do you think will happen to one who is guilty?"

32 Two criminals were led out to be put to death with Jesus. 33 When the soldiers came to the place called "The Skull,"*m* they nailed Jesus to a cross. They also nailed the two criminals to crosses, one on each side of Jesus.

34-35 Jesus said, "Father, forgive these people! They don't know what they're doing."*n*

While the crowd stood there watching Jesus, the soldiers gambled for his clothes. The leaders insulted him by saying, "He saved others. Now he should save himself, if he really is God's chosen Messiah!"

36 The soldiers made fun of Jesus and brought him some wine. 37 They said, "If you are the king of the Jews, save yourself!"

38 Above him was a sign that said, "This is the King of the Jews."

39 One of the criminals hanging there also insulted Jesus by saying, "Aren't you the Messiah? Save yourself and save us!"

40 But the other criminal told the first one off, "Don't you fear God? Aren't you getting the same punishment as this man? 41 We got what was coming to us, but he didn't do anything wrong." 42 Then he said to Jesus, "Remember me when you come into power!"

---

m *"The Skull"*: The place was probably given this name because it was near a large rock in the shape of a human skull.

n *Jesus said, "Father, forgive these people! They don't know what they're doing."*: These words are not in some manuscripts.

43 Jesus replied, "I promise that today you will be with me in paradise."*o*

The Death of Jesus
(Matthew 27.45-56; Mark 15.33-41; John 19.28-30)

44 Around noon the sky turned dark and stayed that way until the middle of the afternoon. 45The sun stopped shining, and the curtain in the temple*p* split down the middle. 46Jesus shouted, "Father, I put myself in your hands!" Then he died.

47 When the Roman officer saw what had happened, he praised God and said, "Jesus must really have been a good man!"

48 A crowd had gathered to see the terrible sight. Then after they had seen it, they felt brokenhearted and went home. 49All of Jesus' close friends and the women who had come with him from Galilee stood at a distance and watched.

Jesus Is Buried
(Matthew 27.57-61; Mark 15.42-47; John 19.38-42)

50-51 There was a man named Joseph, who was from Arimathea in Judea. Joseph was a good and honest

---

o paradise: In the Greek translation of the Old Testament, this word is used for the Garden of Eden. In New Testament times it was sometimes used for the place where God's people are happy and at rest, as they wait for the final judgment.

p curtain in the temple: There were two curtains in the temple. One was at the entrance, and the other separated the holy place from the most holy place that the Jewish people thought of as God's home on earth. The second curtain is probably the one which is meant.

man, and he was eager for God's kingdom to come. He was also a member of the council, but he did not agree with what they had decided.

52 Joseph went to Pilate and asked for Jesus' body. 53He took the body down from the cross and wrapped it in fine cloth. Then he put it in a tomb that had been cut out of solid rock and had never been used. 54It was Friday, and the Sabbath was about to begin.*q*

55 The women who had come with Jesus from Galilee followed Joseph and watched how Jesus' body was placed in the tomb. 56Then they went to prepare some sweet-smelling spices for his burial. But on the Sabbath they rested, as the Law of Moses commands.

Jesus Is Alive
(Matthew 28.1-10; Mark 16.1-8; John 20.1-10)

24 Very early on Sunday morning the women went to the tomb, carrying the spices that they had prepared. 2When they found the stone rolled away from the entrance, 3they went in. But they did not find the body of the Lord*r* Jesus, 4and they did not know what to think.

Suddenly two men in shining white clothes stood beside them. 5The women were afraid and bowed to the ground. But the men said, "Why are you looking in the place of the dead for someone who is alive? 6Jesus isn't here! He has been raised from death. Remember that while he was still in Galilee, he told

q the Sabbath was about to begin: The Sabbath begins at sunset on Friday.
r the Lord: These words are not in some manuscripts.

you, [7] 'The Son of Man will be handed over to sinners who will nail him to a cross. But three days later he will rise to life.'" [8] Then they remembered what Jesus had said.

9-10 Mary Magdalene, Joanna, Mary the mother of James, and some other women were the ones who had gone to the tomb. When they returned, they told the eleven apostles and the others what had happened. [11] The apostles thought it was all nonsense, and they would not believe.

12 But Peter ran to the tomb. And when he stooped down and looked in, he saw only the burial clothes. Then he returned, wondering what had happened.[s]

Jesus Appears to Two Disciples
(Mark 16.12,13)

13 That same day two of Jesus' disciples were going to the village of Emmaus, which was about seven miles from Jerusalem. [14] As they were talking and thinking about what had happened, [15] Jesus came near and started walking along beside them. [16] But they did not know who he was.

17 Jesus asked them, "What were you talking about as you walked along?"

The two of them stood there looking sad and gloomy. [18] Then the one named Cleopas asked Jesus, "Are you the only person from Jerusalem who didn't know what was happening there these last few days?"

19 "What do you mean?" Jesus asked.

---

[s] *what had happened*: Verse 12 is not in some manuscripts.

They answered:

Those things that happened to Jesus from Nazareth. By what he did and said he showed that he was a powerful prophet, who pleased God and all the people. ²⁰Then the chief priests and our leaders had him arrested and sentenced to die on a cross. ²¹We had hoped that he would be the one to set Israel free! But it has already been three days since all this happened.

22 Some women in our group surprised us. They had gone to the tomb early in the morning, ²³but did not find the body of Jesus. They came back, saying that they had seen a vision of angels who told them that he is alive. ²⁴Some men from our group went to the tomb and found it just as the women had said. But they didn't see Jesus either.

25 Then Jesus asked the two disciples, "Why can't you understand? How can you be so slow to believe all that the prophets said? ²⁶Didn't you know that the Messiah would have to suffer before he was given his glory?" ²⁷Jesus then explained everything written about himself in the Scriptures, beginning with the Law of Moses and the Books of the Prophets.^t

28 When the two of them came near the village where they were going, Jesus seemed to be going farther. ²⁹They begged him, "Stay with us! It's already late, and the sun is going down." So Jesus went into the house to stay with them.

---

^t *the Law of Moses and the Books of the Prophets*: The Jewish Scriptures, that is, the Old Testament.

30 After Jesus sat down to eat, he took some bread. He blessed it and broke it. Then he gave it to them. 31 At once they knew who he was, but he disappeared. 32 They said to each other, "When he talked with us along the road and explained the Scriptures to us, didn't it warm our hearts?" 33 So they got right up and returned to Jerusalem.

The two disciples found the eleven apostles and the others gathered together. 34 And they learned from the group that the Lord was really alive and had appeared to Peter. 35 Then the disciples from Emmaus told what happened on the road and how they knew he was the Lord when he broke the bread.

What Jesus' Followers Must Do

(Matthew 28.16-20; Mark 16.14-18; John 20.19-23; Acts 1.6-8)

36 While Jesus' disciples were talking about what had happened, Jesus appeared and greeted them. 37 They were frightened and terrified because they thought they were seeing a ghost.

38 But Jesus said, "Why are you so frightened? Why do you doubt? 39 Look at my hands and my feet and see who I am! Touch me and find out for yourselves. Ghosts don't have flesh and bones as you see I have."

40 After Jesus said this, he showed them his hands and his feet. 41 The disciples were so glad and amazed that they could not believe it. Jesus then asked them, "Do you have something to eat?" 42 They gave him a piece of baked fish. 43 He took it and ate it as they watched.

44 Jesus said to them, "While I was still with you, I told you that everything written about me in the Law

of Moses, the Books of the Prophets, and in the Psalms*u* had to happen."

45 Then he helped them understand the Scriptures. 46He told them:

The Scriptures say that the Messiah must suffer, then three days later he will rise from death. 47They also say that all people of every nation must be told in my name to turn to God, in order to be forgiven. So beginning in Jerusalem, 48you must tell everything that has happened. 49I will send you the one my Father has promised,*v* but you must stay in the city until you are given power from heaven.

Jesus Returns to Heaven
(Mark 16.19,20; Acts 1.9-11)

50 Jesus led his disciples out to Bethany, where he raised his hands and blessed them. 51As he was doing this, he left and was taken up to heaven.*w* 52After his disciples had worshiped him,*x* they returned to Jerusalem and were very happy. 53They spent their time in the temple, praising God.

---

u *Psalms*: The Jewish Scriptures were made up of three parts: (1) the Law of Moses, (2) the Books of the Prophets, (3) and the Writings, which included the Psalms. Sometimes the Scriptures were just called the Law or the Law (of Moses) and the Books of the Prophets.

v *the one my Father has promised*: Jesus means the Holy Spirit.

w *and was taken up to heaven*: These words are not in some manuscripts.

x *After his disciples had worshiped him*: These words are not in some manuscripts.

John Tells the Good News

Who is Jesus Christ? John answers this question in the first chapter of his Gospel. Using the words of an early Christian hymn, he calls Jesus the "Word" by which God created everything and by which he gave life to everyone (1.3,4). He shows how John the Baptist announced Jesus' coming, "Here is the Lamb of God who takes away the sin of the world" (1.29). When Philip met Jesus he knew Jesus was "the one that Moses and the Prophets wrote about" (1.45). And, in the words of Nathanael, Jesus is "the Son of God and the King of Israel" (1.49).

In John's Gospel we learn a lot about who Jesus is by observing what he said and did when he was with other people. These include a Samaritan woman who received Jesus' offer of life-giving water, a woman who had been caught in sin, his friend Lazarus who was brought back to life by Jesus, and his follower Thomas who doubted that Jesus was raised from death. Jesus also refers to himself as "I am", a phrase which translates the most holy name for God in the Hebrew Scriptures. He uses this name for himself when he makes his claim to be the life-giving bread, the light of the world, the good shepherd, and the true vine.

Jesus performs seven miracles that are more than miracles. Each of them is a "sign" that tells us something about Jesus as the Son of God. For example, by healing a lame man (5.1-8), Jesus shows that he is just like his Father, who never stops working (5.17). This sign also teaches that the Son does only what he sees his Father doing (5.19), and that like the Father "the Son gives life to anyone he wants to" (5.21).

The way John tells the story of Jesus is quite different from the other three Gospels. Here, Jesus has long conversations with people about who he is and what God sent him to do. In these conversations he teaches many important things—for example, that he is the way, the truth and the life.

Why did John write? John himself tells us, "So that you will put your faith in Jesus as the Messiah and the Son of God" (20.31). How is this possible? Jesus answers that question in his words to Nicodemus:

God loved the people of this world so much that he gave his only Son, so that everyone who has faith in him will have eternal life and never really die. (3.16)

A QUICK LOOK AT THIS BOOK

The Word of Life

1 In the beginning was the one
       who is called the Word.
   The Word was with God and was truly God.
2 From the very beginning
       the Word was with God.

³ And with this Word, God created all things.
      Nothing was made without the Word.
Everything that was created
⁴ received its life from him,
      and his life gave light to everyone.
⁵ The light keeps shining in the dark,
      and darkness has never put it out.ᵃ

⁶ God sent a man named John,
⁷ who came to tell about the light
      and to lead all people to have faith.
⁸ John wasn't that light.
      He came only to tell about the light.

⁹ The true light that shines on everyone
      was coming into the world.
¹⁰ The Word was in the world,
      but no one knew him,
though God had made the world with his Word.
¹¹ He came into his own world,
      but his own nation did not welcome him.
¹² Yet some people accepted him
      and put their faith in him.
So he gave them the right
      to be the children of God.
¹³ They were not God's children by nature
      or because of any human desires.
God himself was the one
      who made them his children.

¹⁴ The Word became a human being
      and lived here with us.

ᵃ *put it out*: Or "understood it."

We saw his true glory,
    the glory of the only Son of the Father.
From him all the kindness
and all the truth of God
    have come down to us.

15 John spoke about him and shouted, "This is the one I told you would come! He is greater than I am, because he was alive before I was born."

16 Because of all that the Son is, we have been given one blessing after another.[b] 17The Law was given by Moses, but Jesus Christ brought us undeserved kindness and truth. 18No one has ever seen God. The only Son, who is truly God and is closest to the Father, has shown us what God is like.

John the Baptist Tells about Jesus
(Matthew 3.1-12; Mark 1.1-8; Luke 3.15-17)

19-20 The leaders in Jerusalem sent priests and temple helpers to ask John who he was. He told them plainly, "I am not the Messiah." 21Then when they asked him if he were Elijah, he said, "No, I am not!" And when they asked if he were the Prophet,[c] he also said "No!"

22 Finally, they said, "Who are you then? We have to give an answer to the ones who sent us. Tell us who you are!"

23 John answered in the words of the prophet Isaiah,

---

[b] one blessing after another: Or "one blessing in place of another."

[c] the Prophet: Many of the Jewish people expected God to send them a prophet who would be like Moses, but with even greater power (see Deuteronomy 18.15, 18).

"I am only someone shouting in the desert, 'Get the road ready for the Lord!'"

24 Some Pharisees had also been sent to John. 25They asked him, "Why are you baptizing people, if you are not the Messiah or Elijah or the Prophet?"

26 John told them, "I use water to baptize people. But here with you is someone you don't know. 27Even though I came first, I am not good enough to untie his sandals." 28John said this as he was baptizing east of the Jordan River in Bethany.*d*

The Lamb of God

29 The next day, John saw Jesus coming toward him and said:

Here is the Lamb of God who takes away the sin of the world! 30He is the one I told you about when I said, "Someone else will come. He is greater than I am, because he was alive before I was born." 31I didn't know who he was. But I came to baptize you with water, so that everyone in Israel would see him.

32 I was there and saw the Spirit come down on him like a dove from heaven. And the Spirit stayed on him. 33Before this I didn't know who he was. But the one who sent me to baptize with water had told me, "You will see the Spirit come down and stay on someone. Then you will know that he is the one who will baptize with the Holy Spirit." 34I saw this happen, and I tell you that he is the Son of God.

---

d Bethany: An unknown village east of the Jordan with the same name as the village near Jerusalem.

The First Disciples of Jesus

35 The next day, John was there again, and two of his followers were with him. 36When he saw Jesus walking by, he said, "Here is the Lamb of God!" 37John's two followers heard him, and they went with Jesus.

38 When Jesus turned and saw them, he asked, "What do you want?"

They answered, "Rabbi, where do you live?" The Hebrew word "Rabbi" means "Teacher."

39 Jesus replied, "Come and see!" It was already about four o'clock in the afternoon when they went with him and saw where he lived. So they stayed on for the rest of the day.

40 One of the two men who had heard John and had gone with Jesus was Andrew, the brother of Simon Peter. 41The first thing Andrew did was to find his brother and tell him, "We have found the Messiah!" The Hebrew word "Messiah" means the same as the Greek word "Christ."

42 Andrew brought his brother to Jesus. And when Jesus saw him, he said, "Simon son of John, you will be called Cephas." This name can be translated as "Peter."*e*

Jesus Chooses Philip and Nathanael

43-44 The next day Jesus decided to go to Galilee. There he met Philip, who was from Bethsaida, the hometown of Andrew and Peter. Jesus said to Philip, "Come with me."

---

e *Peter*: The Aramaic name "Cephas" and the Greek name "Peter" each mean "rock."

45 Philip then found Nathanael and said, "We have found the one that Moses and the Prophets *f* wrote about. He is Jesus, the son of Joseph from Nazareth."

46 Nathanael asked, "Can anything good come from Nazareth?"

Philip answered, "Come and see."

47 When Jesus saw Nathanael coming toward him, he said, "Here is a true descendant of our ancestor Israel. And he isn't deceitful." *g*

48 "How do you know me?" Nathanael asked.

Jesus answered, "Before Philip called you, I saw you under the fig tree."

49 Nathanael said, "Rabbi, you are the Son of God and the King of Israel!"

50 Jesus answered, "Did you believe me just because I said that I saw you under the fig tree? You will see something even greater. ⁵¹I tell you for certain that you will see heaven open and God's angels going up and coming down on the Son of Man." *h*

Jesus at a Wedding in Cana

2 Three days later Mary, the mother of Jesus, was at a wedding feast in the village of Cana in Galilee.

---

f *Moses and the Prophets*: The Jewish Scriptures, that is, the Old Testament.

g *Israel…not deceitful*: Israel (meaning "a man who wrestled with God" or "a prince of God") was the name that the Lord gave to Jacob (meaning "cheater" or "deceiver"), the famous ancestor of the Jewish people.

h *going up and coming down on the Son of Man*: When Jacob (see the note at verse 47) was running from his brother Esau, he had a dream in which he saw angels going up and down on a ladder from earth to heaven (see Genesis 32.22-32).

2Jesus and his disciples had also been invited and were there.

3 When the wine was all gone, Mary said to Jesus, "They don't have any more wine."

4 Jesus replied, "Mother, my time hasn't yet come!*i* You must not tell me what to do."

5 Mary then said to the servants, "Do whatever Jesus tells you to do."

6 At the feast there were six stone water jars that were used by the people for washing themselves in the way that their religion said they must. Each jar held about twenty or thirty gallons. 7Jesus told the servants to fill them to the top with water. Then after the jars had been filled, 8he said, "Now take some water and give it to the man in charge of the feast."

The servants did as Jesus told them, 9and the man in charge drank some of the water that had now turned into wine. He did not know where the wine had come from, but the servants did. He called the bridegroom over 10and said, "The best wine is always served first. Then after the guests have had plenty, the other wine is served. But you have kept the best until last!"

11 This was Jesus' first miracle,*j* and he did it in the village of Cana in Galilee. There Jesus showed his glory, and his disciples put their faith in him. 12After

---

i *my time hasn't yet come!*: The time when the true glory of Jesus would be seen, and he would be recognized as God's Son (see 12.23).

j *miracle*: The Greek text has "sign." In the Gospel of John the word "sign" is used for the miracle itself and as a way of pointing to Jesus as the Son of God.

this, he went with his mother, his brothers, and his disciples to the town of Capernaum, where they stayed for a few days.

Jesus in the Temple
(Matthew 21.12,13; Mark 11.15-17; Luke 19.45,46)

13 Not long before the Jewish festival of Passover, Jesus went to Jerusalem. ¹⁴There he found people selling cattle, sheep, and doves in the temple. He also saw moneychangers sitting at their tables. ¹⁵So he took some rope and made a whip. Then he chased everyone out of the temple, together with their sheep and cattle. He turned over the tables of the money-changers and scattered their coins.

16 Jesus said to the people who had been selling doves, "Get those doves out of here! Don't make my Father's house a marketplace."

17 The disciples then remembered that the Scriptures say, "My love for your house burns in me like a fire."

18 The Jewish leaders asked Jesus, "What miracle[k] will you work to show us why you have done this?"

19 "Destroy this temple," Jesus answered, "and in three days I will build it again!"

20 The leaders replied, "It took forty-six years to build this temple. What makes you think you can rebuild it in three days?"

21 But Jesus was talking about his body as a temple. ²²And when he was raised from death, his disciples remembered what he had told them. Then they believed the Scriptures and the words of Jesus.

---

[k] miracle: See the note at 2.11.

Jesus Knows What People Are Like

23 In Jerusalem during Passover many people put their faith in Jesus, because they saw him work miracles.[l] 24But Jesus knew what was in their hearts, and he would not let them have power over him. 25No one had to tell him what people were like. He already knew.

Jesus and Nicodemus

3 There was a man named Nicodemus who was a Pharisee and a Jewish leader. 2One night he went to Jesus and said, "Sir, we know that God has sent you to teach us. You could not work these miracles, unless God were with you."

3 Jesus replied, "I tell you for certain that you must be born from above[m] before you can see God's kingdom!"

4 Nicodemus asked, "How can a grown man ever be born a second time?"

5 Jesus answered:

I tell you for certain that before you can get into God's kingdom, you must be born not only by water, but by the Spirit. 6Humans give life to their children. Yet only God's Spirit can change you into a child of God. 7Don't be surprised when I say that you must be born from above. 8Only God's Spirit gives new life. The Spirit is like the wind that blows wherever it wants to.

---

[l] miracles: See the note at 2.11.

[m] from above: Or "in a new way." The same Greek word is used in verses 7 and 31.

You can hear the wind, but you don't know where it comes from or where it is going.

9 "How can this be?" Nicodemus asked.

10 Jesus replied:

How can you be a teacher of Israel and not know these things? [11]I tell you for certain that we know what we are talking about because we have seen it ourselves. But none of you will accept what we say. [12]If you don't believe when I talk to you about things on earth, how can you possibly believe if I talk to you about things in heaven?

13 No one has gone up to heaven except the Son of Man, who came down from there. [14]And the Son of Man must be lifted up, just as that metal snake was lifted up by Moses in the desert.[n] [15]Then everyone who has faith in the Son of Man will have eternal life.

16 God loved the people of this world so much that he gave his only Son, so that everyone who has faith in him will have eternal life and never really die. [17]God did not send his Son into the world to condemn its people. He sent him to save them! [18]No one who has faith in God's Son will be condemned. But everyone who doesn't have faith in him has already been condemned for not having faith in God's only Son.

---

[n] *just as that metal snake was lifted up by Moses in the desert*: When the Lord punished the people of Israel by sending snakes to bite them, he told Moses to hold a metal snake up on a pole. Everyone who looked at the snake was cured of the snake bites (see Numbers 21.4-9).

19 The light has come into the world, and people who do evil things are judged guilty because they love the dark more than the light. ²⁰People who do evil hate the light and won't come to the light, because it clearly shows what they have done. ²¹But everyone who lives by the truth will come to the light, because they want others to know that God is really the one doing what they do.

Jesus and John the Baptist

22 Later, Jesus and his disciples went to Judea, where he stayed with them for a while and was baptizing people.

23-24 John had not yet been put in jail. He was at Aenon near Salim, where there was a lot of water, and people were coming there for John to baptize them.

25 John's followers got into an argument with a Jewish man *ᵒ* about a ceremony of washing.*ᵖ* ²⁶They went to John and said, "Rabbi, you spoke about a man when you were with him east of the Jordan. He is now baptizing people, and everyone is going to him."

27 John replied:

No one can do anything unless God in heaven allows it. ²⁸You surely remember how I told you that I am not the Messiah. I am only the one sent ahead of him.

29 At a wedding the groom is the one who gets married. The best man is glad just to be there

---

ᵒ a Jewish man: Some manuscripts have "some Jewish men."
ᵖ about a ceremony of washing: The Jewish people had many rules about washing themselves and their dishes, in order to make themselves fit to worship God.

and to hear the groom's voice. That's why I am
so glad. ³⁰Jesus must become more important,
while I become less important.

The One Who Comes from Heaven

31 God's Son comes from heaven and is
above all others. Everyone who comes from the
earth belongs to the earth and speaks about
earthly things. The one who comes from heaven
is above all others. ³²He speaks about what he
has seen and heard, and yet no one believes
him. ³³But everyone who does believe him has
shown that God is truthful. ³⁴The Son was sent
to speak God's message, and he has been given
the full power of God's Spirit.

35 The Father loves the Son and has given
him everything. ³⁶Everyone who has faith in
the Son has eternal life. But no one who rejects
him will ever share in that life, and God will be
angry with them forever.

4 Jesus knew that the Pharisees had heard that he
was winning and baptizing more followers than
John was. ²But Jesus' disciples were really the ones
doing the baptizing, and not Jesus himself.

Jesus and the Samaritan Woman

3 Jesus left Judea and started for Galilee again.
⁴This time he had to go through Samaria, ⁵and on his
way he came to the town of Sychar. It was near the
field that Jacob had long ago given to his son Joseph.
⁶⁻⁸The well that Jacob had dug was still there, and
Jesus sat down beside it because he was tired from
traveling. It was noon, and after Jesus' disciples had

gone into town to buy some food, a Samaritan woman came to draw water from the well.

Jesus asked her, "Would you please give me a drink of water?"

9 "You are a Jew," she replied, "and I am a Samaritan woman. How can you ask me for a drink of water when Jews and Samaritans won't have anything to do with each other?"*q*

10 Jesus answered, "You don't know what God wants to give you, and you don't know who is asking you for a drink. If you did, you would ask me for the water that gives life."

11 "Sir," the woman said, "you don't even have a bucket, and the well is deep. Where are you going to get this life-giving water? 12Our ancestor Jacob dug this well for us, and his family and animals got water from it. Are you greater than Jacob?"

13 Jesus answered, "Everyone who drinks this water will get thirsty again. 14But no one who drinks the water I give will ever be thirsty again. The water I give is like a flowing fountain that gives eternal life."

15 The woman replied, "Sir, please give me a drink of that water! Then I won't get thirsty and have to come to this well again."

16 Jesus told her, "Go and bring your husband."

17-18 The woman answered, "I don't have a husband."

"That's right," Jesus replied, "you're telling the truth. You don't have a husband. You have already been married

---

q won't have anything to do with each other: Or "won't use the same cups." The Samaritans lived in the land between Judea and Galilee. They worshiped God differently from the Jews and did not get along with them.

five times, and the man you are now living with isn't your husband."

19 The woman said, "Sir, I can see that you are a prophet. 20My ancestors worshiped on this mountain,[r] but you Jews say Jerusalem is the only place to worship."

21 Jesus said to her:

Believe me, the time is coming when you won't worship the Father either on this mountain or in Jerusalem. 22You Samaritans don't really know the one you worship. But we Jews do know the God we worship, and by using us, God will save the world. 23But a time is coming, and it is already here! Even now the true worshipers are being led by the Spirit to worship the Father according to the truth. These are the ones the Father is seeking to worship him. 24God is Spirit, and those who worship God must be led by the Spirit to worship him according to the truth.

25 The woman said, "I know that the Messiah will come. He is the one we call Christ. When he comes, he will explain everything to us."

26 "I am that one," Jesus told her, "and I am speaking to you now."

27 The disciples returned about this time and were surprised to find Jesus talking with a woman. But none of them asked him what he wanted or why he was talking with her.

28 The woman left her water jar and ran back into town. She said to the people, 29"Come and see a man who told me everything I have ever done! Could he be the Messiah?" 30Everyone in town went out to see Jesus.

---

[r] *this mountain*: Mount Gerizim, near the city of Shechem.

31 While this was happening, Jesus' disciples were saying to him, "Teacher, please eat something."

32 But Jesus told them, "I have food that you don't know anything about."

33 His disciples started asking each other, "Has someone brought him something to eat?"

34 Jesus said:

My food is to do what God wants! He is the one who sent me, and I must finish the work that he gave me to do. 35 You may say that there are still four months until harvest time. But I tell you to look, and you will see that the fields are ripe and ready to harvest.

36 Even now the harvest workers are receiving their reward by gathering a harvest that brings eternal life. Then everyone who planted the seed and everyone who harvests the crop will celebrate together. 37 So the saying proves true, "Some plant the seed, and others harvest the crop." 38 I am sending you to harvest crops in fields where others have done all the hard work.

39 A lot of Samaritans in that town put their faith in Jesus because the woman had said, "This man told me everything I have ever done." 40 They came and asked him to stay in their town, and he stayed on for two days.

41 Many more Samaritans put their faith in Jesus because of what they heard him say. 42 They told the woman, "We no longer have faith in Jesus just because of what you told us. We have heard him ourselves, and we are certain that he is the Savior of the world!"

Jesus Heals an Official's Son
(Matthew 8.5-13; Luke 7.1-10)

43-44 Jesus had said, "Prophets are honored everywhere, except in their own country." Then two days later he left [45]and went to Galilee. The people there welcomed him, because they had gone to the festival in Jerusalem and had seen everything he had done.

46 While Jesus was in Galilee, he returned to the village of Cana, where he had turned the water into wine. There was an official in Capernaum whose son was sick. [47]And when the man heard that Jesus had come from Judea, he went and begged him to keep his son from dying.

48 Jesus told the official, "You won't have faith unless you see miracles and wonders!"

49 The man replied, "Lord, please come before my son dies!"

50 Jesus then said, "Your son will live. Go on home to him." The man believed Jesus and started back home.

51 Some of the official's servants met him along the road and told him, "Your son is better!" [52]He asked them when the boy got better, and they answered, "The fever left him yesterday at one o'clock."

53 The boy's father realized that at one o'clock the day before, Jesus had told him, "Your son will live!" So the man and everyone in his family put their faith in Jesus.

54 This was the second miracle [s] that Jesus worked after he left Judea and went to Galilee.

---

[s] miracle: See the note at 2.11.

Jesus Heals a Sick Man

5 Later, Jesus went to Jerusalem for another Jewish festival.[t] 2In the city near the sheep gate was a pool with five porches, and its name in Hebrew was Bethzatha.[u]

3-4 Many sick, blind, lame, and crippled people were lying close to the pool.[v]

5 Beside the pool was a man who had been sick for thirty-eight years. 6When Jesus saw the man and realized that he had been crippled for a long time, he asked him, "Do you want to be healed?"

7 The man answered, "Lord, I don't have anyone to put me in the pool when the water is stirred up. I try to get in, but someone else always gets there first."

8 Jesus told him, "Pick up your mat and walk!" 9Right then the man was healed. He picked up his mat and started walking around. The day on which this happened was a Sabbath.

10 When the Jewish leaders saw the man carrying his mat, they said to him, "This is the Sabbath! No one is allowed to carry a mat on the Sabbath."

11 But he replied, "The man who healed me told me to pick up my mat and walk."

12 They asked him, "Who is this man that told you to pick up your mat and walk?" 13But he did not know

---

[t] another Jewish festival: Either the Festival of Shelters or Passover.

[u] Bethzatha: Some manuscripts have "Bethesda" and others have "Bethsaida."

[v] pool: Some manuscripts add, "They were waiting for the water to be stirred, because an angel from the Lord would sometimes come down and stir it. The first person to get into the pool after that would be healed."

who Jesus was, and Jesus had left because of the crowd.

14 Later, Jesus met the man in the temple and told him, "You are now well. But don't sin anymore or something worse might happen to you." 15The man left and told the leaders that Jesus was the one who had healed him. 16They started making a lot of trouble for Jesus because he did things like this on the Sabbath.

17 But Jesus said, "My Father has never stopped working, and that is why I keep on working." 18Now the leaders wanted to kill Jesus for two reasons. First, he had broken the law of the Sabbath. But even worse, he had said that God was his Father, which made him equal with God.

The Son's Authority

19 Jesus told the people:

I tell you for certain that the Son cannot do anything on his own. He can do only what he sees the Father doing, and he does exactly what he sees the Father do. 20The Father loves the Son and has shown him everything he does. The Father will show him even greater things, and you will be amazed. 21Just as the Father raises the dead and gives life, so the Son gives life to anyone he wants to.

22 The Father doesn't judge anyone, but he has made his Son the judge of everyone. 23The Father wants all people to honor the Son as much as they honor him. When anyone refuses to honor the Son, that is the same as refusing to honor the Father who sent him. 24I tell you for

certain that everyone who hears my message and has faith in the one who sent me has eternal life and will never be condemned. They have already gone from death to life.

25 I tell you for certain that the time will come, and it is already here, when all of the dead will hear the voice of the Son of God. And those who listen to it will live! 26 The Father has the power to give life, and he has given that same power to the Son. 27 And he has given his Son the right to judge everyone, because he is the Son of Man.

28 Don't be surprised! The time will come when all of the dead will hear the voice of the Son of Man, 29 and they will come out of their graves. Everyone who has done good things will rise to life, but everyone who has done evil things will rise and be condemned.

30 I cannot do anything on my own. The Father sent me, and he is the one who told me how to judge. I judge with fairness, because I obey him, and I don't just try to please myself.

Witnesses to Jesus

31 If I speak for myself, there is no way to prove I am telling the truth. 32 But there is someone else who speaks for me, and I know what he says is true. 33 You sent messengers to John, and he told them the truth. 34 I don't depend on what people say about me, but I tell you these things so that you may be saved. 35 John was a lamp that gave a lot of light, and you were glad to enjoy his light for a while.

36 But something more important than John speaks for me. I mean the things that the Father has given me to do! All of these speak for me and prove that the Father sent me.

37 The Father who sent me also speaks for me, but you have never heard his voice or seen him face to face. 38You have not believed his message, because you refused to have faith in the one he sent.

39 You search the Scriptures, because you think you will find eternal life in them. The Scriptures tell about me, 40but you refuse to come to me for eternal life.

41 I don't care about human praise, 42but I do know that none of you love God. 43I have come with my Father's authority, and you have not welcomed me. But you will welcome people who come on their own. 44How could you possibly believe? You like to have your friends praise you, and you don't care about praise that the only God can give!

45 Don't think that I will be the one to accuse you to the Father. You have put your hope in Moses, yet he is the very one who will accuse you. 46Moses wrote about me, and if you had believed Moses, you would have believed me. 47But if you don't believe what Moses wrote, how can you believe what I say?

Feeding Five Thousand

(Matthew 14.13-21; Mark 6.30-44; Luke 9.10-17)

6 Jesus crossed Lake Galilee, which was also known as Lake Tiberias. 2A large crowd had seen

him work miracles to heal the sick, and those people went with him. ³⁻⁴It was almost time for the Jewish festival of Passover, and Jesus went up on a mountain with his disciples and sat down.ʷ

5 When Jesus saw the large crowd coming toward him, he asked Philip, "Where will we get enough food to feed all these people?" ⁶He said this to test Philip, since he already knew what he was going to do.

7 Philip answered, "Don't you know that it would take almost a year's wagesˣ just to buy only a little bread for each of these people?"

8 Andrew, the brother of Simon Peter, was one of the disciples. He spoke up and said, ⁹"There is a boy here who has five small loaves ʸ of barley bread and two fish. But what good is that with all these people?"

10 The ground was covered with grass, and Jesus told his disciples to have everyone sit down. About five thousand men were in the crowd. ¹¹Jesus took the bread in his hands and gave thanks to God. Then he passed the bread to the people, and he did the same with the fish, until everyone had plenty to eat.

12 The people ate all they wanted, and Jesus told his disciples to gather up the leftovers, so that nothing would be wasted. ¹³The disciples gathered them up

---

ʷ *sat down*: Possibly to teach. Teachers in the ancient world, including Jewish teachers, usually sat down to teach.

ˣ *almost a year's wages*: The Greek text has "two hundred silver coins." Each coin was worth the average day's wages for a worker.

ʸ *small loaves*: These would have been flat and round or in the shape of a bun.

and filled twelve large baskets with what was left over from the five barley loaves.

14 After the people had seen Jesus work this miracle,[z] they began saying, "This must be the Prophet[a] who is to come into the world!" 15 Jesus realized that they would try to force him to be their king. So he went up on a mountain, where he could be alone.

Jesus Walks on the Water
(Matthew 14.22-27; Mark 6.45-52)

16 That evening, Jesus' disciples went down to the lake. 17 They got into a boat and started across for Capernaum. Later that evening Jesus had still not come to them, 18 and a strong wind was making the water rough. 19 When the disciples had rowed for three or four miles, they saw Jesus walking on the water. He kept coming closer to the boat, and they were terrified. 20 But he said, "I am Jesus![b] Don't be afraid!" 21 The disciples wanted to take him into the boat, but suddenly the boat reached the shore where they were headed.

The Bread That Gives Life

22 The people who had stayed on the east side of the lake knew that only one boat had been there. They also knew that Jesus had not left in it with his disciples. But the next day 23 some boats from Tiberias sailed near the place where the crowd had eaten the bread for which the Lord had given thanks. 24 They saw that Jesus and his disciples had left. Then they

---

[z] *miracle*: See the note at 2.11.
[a] *the Prophet*: See the note at 1.21.
[b] *I am Jesus*: The Greek text has "I am" (see the note at 8.24).

got into the boats and went to Capernaum to look for Jesus. 25They found him on the west side of the lake and asked, "Rabbi, when did you get here?"

26 Jesus answered, "I tell you for certain that you are not looking for me because you saw the miracles,[c] but because you ate all the food you wanted. 27Don't work for food that spoils. Work for food that gives eternal life. The Son of Man will give you this food, because God the Father has given him the right to do so."

28 "What exactly does God want us to do?" the people asked.

29 Jesus answered, "God wants you to have faith in the one he sent."

30 They replied, "What miracle will you work, so that we can have faith in you? What will you do? 31For example, when our ancestors were in the desert, they were given manna[d] to eat. It happened just as the Scriptures say, 'God gave them bread from heaven to eat.'"

32 Jesus then told them, "I tell you for certain that Moses wasn't the one who gave you bread from heaven. My Father is the one who gives you the true bread from heaven. 33And the bread that God gives is the one who came down from heaven to give life to the world."

---

[c] miracles: The Greek text has "signs" here and "sign" in verse 30 (see the note at 2.11).

[d] manna: When the people of Israel were wandering through the desert, the Lord gave them a special kind of food to eat. It tasted like a wafer and was called "manna," which in Hebrew means, "What is this?"

34 The people said, "Lord, give us this bread and don't ever stop!"

35 Jesus replied:

I am the bread that gives life! No one who comes to me will ever be hungry. No one who has faith in me will ever be thirsty. ³⁶I have told you already that you have seen me and still do not have faith in me. ³⁷Everything and everyone that the Father has given me will come to me, and I won't turn any of them away.

38 I didn't come from heaven to do what I want! I came to do what the Father wants me to do. He sent me, ³⁹and he wants to make certain that none of the ones he has given me will be lost. Instead, he wants me to raise them to life on the last day.ᵉ ⁴⁰My Father wants everyone who sees the Son to have faith in him and to have eternal life. Then I will raise them to life on the last day.

41 The people started grumbling because Jesus had said he was the bread that had come down from heaven. ⁴²They were asking each other, "Isn't he Jesus, the son of Joseph? Don't we know his father and mother? How can he say that he has come down from heaven?"

43 Jesus told them:

Stop grumbling! ⁴⁴No one can come to me, unless the Father who sent me makes them want to come. But if they do come, I will raise them to life on the last day. ⁴⁵One of the prophets wrote, "God will teach all of them." And so everyone

---

ᵉ *the last day*: When God will judge all people.

who listens to the Father and learns from him
will come to me.

46 The only one who has seen the Father is the
one who has come from him. No one else has
ever seen the Father. 47I tell you for certain that
everyone who has faith in me has eternal life.

48 I am the bread that gives life! 49Your
ancestors ate manna*f* in the desert, and later
they died. 50But the bread from heaven has
come down, so that no one who eats it will ever
die. 51I am that bread from heaven! Everyone
who eats it will live forever. My flesh is the life-
giving bread that I give to the people of this
world.

52 They started arguing with each other and asked,
"How can he give us his flesh to eat?"

53 Jesus answered:

I tell you for certain that you won't live
unless you eat the flesh and drink the blood of
the Son of Man. 54But if you do eat my flesh and
drink my blood, you will have eternal life, and
I will raise you to life on the last day. 55My flesh
is the true food, and my blood is the true drink.
56If you eat my flesh and drink my blood, you
are one with me, and I am one with you.

57 The living Father sent me, and I have life
because of him. Now everyone who eats my
flesh will live because of me. 58The bread that
comes down from heaven isn't like what your
ancestors ate. They died, but whoever eats this
bread will live forever.

---

f manna: See the note at 6.31.

59 Jesus was teaching in a Jewish place of worship in Capernaum when he said these things.

The Words of Eternal Life

60 Many of Jesus' disciples heard him and said, "This is too hard for anyone to understand."

61 Jesus knew that his disciples were grumbling. So he asked, "Does this bother you? 62 What if you should see the Son of Man go up to heaven where he came from? 63 The Spirit is the one who gives life! Human strength can do nothing. The words that I have spoken to you are from that life-giving Spirit. 64 But some of you refuse to have faith in me." Jesus said this, because from the beginning he knew who would have faith in him. He also knew which one would betray him.

65 Then Jesus said, "You cannot come to me, unless the Father makes you want to come. That is why I have told these things to all of you."

66 Because of what Jesus said, many of his disciples turned their backs on him and stopped following him. 67 Jesus then asked his twelve disciples if they were going to leave him. 68 Simon Peter answered, "Lord, there is no one else that we can go to! Your words give eternal life. 69 We have faith in you, and we are sure that you are God's Holy One."

70 Jesus told his disciples, "I chose all twelve of you, but one of you is a demon!" 71 Jesus was talking about Judas, the son of Simon Iscariot.[8] He would later betray Jesus, even though he was one of the twelve disciples.

---

[8] *Iscariot*: This may mean "a man from Kerioth" (a place in Judea). But more probably it means "a man who was a liar" or "a man who was a betrayer."

Jesus' Brothers Don't Have Faith in Him

7 Jesus decided to leave Judea and to start going through Galilee because the leaders of the people wanted to kill him. ²It was almost time for the Festival of Shelters, ³and Jesus' brothers said to him, "Why don't you go to Judea? Then your disciples can see what you are doing. ⁴No one does anything in secret, if they want others to know about them. So let the world know what you are doing!" ⁵Even Jesus' own brothers had not yet become his followers.

6 Jesus answered, "My time hasn't yet come,ʰ but your time is always here. ⁷The people of this world cannot hate you. They hate me, because I tell them that they do evil things. ⁸Go on to the festival. My time hasn't yet come, and I am not going." ⁹Jesus said this and stayed on in Galilee.

Jesus at the Festival of Shelters

10 After Jesus' brothers had gone to the festival, he went secretly, without telling anyone.

11 During the festival the leaders looked for Jesus and asked, "Where is he?" ¹²The crowds even got into an argument about him. Some were saying, "Jesus is a good man," while others were saying, "He is lying to everyone." ¹³But the people were afraid of their leaders, and none of them talked in public about him.

14 When the festival was about half over, Jesus went into the temple and started teaching. ¹⁵The leaders

---

ʰ *My time hasn't yet come*: See the note at 2.4.

were surprised and said, "How does this man know so much? He has never been taught!"

16 Jesus replied:

I am not teaching something that I thought up. What I teach comes from the one who sent me. 17If you really want to obey God, you will know if what I teach comes from God or from me. 18If I wanted to bring honor to myself, I would speak for myself. But I want to honor the one who sent me. That is why I tell the truth and not a lie. 19Didn't Moses give you the Law? Yet none of you obey it! So why do you want to kill me?

20 The crowd replied, "You're crazy! What makes you think someone wants to kill you?"

21 Jesus answered:

I worked one miracle,[i] and it amazed you. 22Moses commanded you to circumcise your sons. But it wasn't really Moses who gave you this command. It was your ancestors, and even on the Sabbath your ancestors circumcise your sons 23in order to obey the Law of Moses. Why are you angry with me for making someone completely well on the Sabbath? 24Don't judge by appearances. Judge by what is right.

25 Some of the people from Jerusalem were saying, "Isn't this the man they want to kill? 26Yet here he is, speaking for everyone to hear. And no one is arguing with him. Do you suppose the authorities know that he is the Messiah? 27But how could that be? No one

---

[i] *one miracle*: The healing of the lame man (5.1-18) (see the note at 2.11).

knows where the Messiah will come from, but we know where this man comes from."

28 As Jesus was teaching in the temple, he shouted, "Do you really think you know me and where I came from? I didn't come on my own! The one who sent me is truthful, and you don't know him. 29 But I know the one who sent me, because I came from him."

30 Some of the people wanted to arrest Jesus right then. But no one even laid a hand on him, because his time had not yet come.[j] 31 A lot of people in the crowd put their faith in him and said, "When the Messiah comes, he surely won't perform more miracles[k] than this man has done!"

Officers Sent To Arrest Jesus

32 When the Pharisees heard the crowd arguing about Jesus, they got together with the chief priests and sent some temple police to arrest him. 33 But Jesus told them, "I will be with you a little while longer, and then I will return to the one who sent me. 34 You will look for me, but you won't find me. You cannot go where I am going."

35 The people asked each other, "Where can he go to keep us from finding him? Is he going to some foreign country where our people live? Is he going there to teach the Greeks?[l] 36 What did he mean by saying that we will look for him, but won't find him? Why can't we go where he is going?"

---

j *his time had not yet come*: See the note at 2.4.

k *miracles*: See the note at 2.11.

l *Greeks*: Perhaps Gentiles or Jews who followed Greek customs.

Streams of Life-Giving Water

37 On the last and most important day of the festival, Jesus stood up and shouted, "If you are thirsty, come to me and drink! [38] Have faith in me, and you will have life-giving water flowing from deep inside you, just as the Scriptures say." [39] Jesus was talking about the Holy Spirit, who would be given to everyone that had faith in him. The Spirit had not yet been given to anyone, since Jesus had not yet been given his full glory.[m]

The People Take Sides

40 When the crowd heard Jesus say this, some of them said, "He must be the Prophet!"[n] [41] Others said, "He is the Messiah!" Others even said, "Can the Messiah come from Galilee? [42] The Scriptures say that the Messiah will come from the family of King David. Doesn't this mean that he will be born in David's hometown of Bethlehem?" [43] The people started taking sides against each other because of Jesus. [44] Some of them wanted to arrest him, but no one laid a hand on him.

The Leaders Refuse To Have Faith in Jesus

45 When the temple police returned to the chief priests and Pharisees, they were asked, "Why didn't you bring Jesus here?"

---

[m] *had not yet been given his full glory*: In the Gospel of John, Jesus is given his full glory both when he is nailed to the cross and when he is raised from death to sit beside his Father in heaven.

[n] *the Prophet*: See the note at 1.21.

46 They answered, "No one has ever spoken like that man!"

47 The Pharisees said to them, "Have you also been fooled? 48Not one of the chief priests or the Pharisees has faith in him. 49And these people who don't know the Law are under God's curse anyway."

50 Nicodemus was there at the time. He was a member of the council, and was the same one who had earlier come to see Jesus.º He said, 51"Our Law doesn't let us condemn people before we hear what they have to say. We cannot judge them before we know what they have done."

52 Then they said, "Nicodemus, you must be from Galilee! Read the Scriptures, and you will find that no prophet is to come from Galilee."

A Woman Caught in Sin

8 53Everyone else went home, 1but Jesus walked out to the Mount of Olives. 2Then early the next morning he went to the temple. The people came to him, and he sat downᵖ and started teaching them.

3 The Pharisees and the teachers of the Law of Moses brought in a woman who had been caught in bed with a man who wasn't her husband. They made her stand in the middle of the crowd. 4Then they said, "Teacher, this woman was caught sleeping with a man who isn't her husband. 5The Law of Moses teaches that a woman like this should be stoned to death! What do you say?"

º *who had earlier come to see Jesus*: See 3.1-21.
ᵖ *sat down*: See the note at 6.3,4.

6 They asked Jesus this question, because they wanted to test him and bring some charge against him. But Jesus simply bent over and started writing on the ground with his finger.

7 They kept on asking Jesus about the woman. Finally, he stood up and said, "If any of you have never sinned, then go ahead and throw the first stone at her!" 8 Once again he bent over and began writing on the ground. 9 The people left one by one, beginning with the oldest. Finally, Jesus and the woman were there alone.

10 Jesus stood up and asked her, "Where is everyone? Isn't there anyone left to accuse you?"

11 "No sir," the woman answered.

Then Jesus told her, "I am not going to accuse you either. You may go now, but don't sin anymore."[q]

Jesus Is the Light for the World

12 Once again Jesus spoke to the people. This time he said, "I am the light for the world! Follow me, and you won't be walking in the dark. You will have the light that gives life."

13 The Pharisees objected, "You are the only one speaking for yourself, and what you say isn't true!"

14 Jesus replied:

Even if I do speak for myself, what I say is true! I know where I came from and where I am going. But you don't know where I am from or

---

[q] don't sin anymore: Verses 1-11 are not in some manuscripts. In other manuscripts these verses are placed after 7.36 or after 21.25 or after Luke 21.38, with some differences in the text.

where I am going. ¹⁵You judge in the same way that everyone else does, but I don't judge anyone. ¹⁶If I did judge, I would judge fairly, because I would not be doing it alone. The Father who sent me is here with me. ¹⁷Your Law requires two witnesses to prove that something is true. ¹⁸I am one of my witnesses, and the Father who sent me is the other one.

19 "Where is your Father?" they asked.

"You don't know me or my Father!" Jesus answered. "If you knew me, you would know my Father."

20 Jesus said this while he was still teaching in the place where the temple treasures were stored. But no one arrested him, because his time had not yet come.ʳ

You Cannot Go Where I Am Going

21 Jesus also told them, "I am going away, and you will look for me. But you cannot go where I am going, and you will die with your sins unforgiven."

22 The people asked, "Does he intend to kill himself? Is that what he means by saying we cannot go where he is going?"

23 Jesus answered, "You are from below, but I am from above. You belong to this world, but I don't. ²⁴That is why I said you will die with your sins unforgiven. If you don't have faith in me for who I am,ˢ you will die, and your sins will not be forgiven."

ʳ *his time had not yet come*: See the note at 2.4.

ˢ *I am*: For the Jewish people the most holy name of God is "Yahweh," which may be translated "I am." In the Gospel of John "I am" is sometimes used by Jesus to show that he is that one.

25 "Who are you?" they asked Jesus.

Jesus answered, "I am exactly who I told you at the beginning. 26There is a lot more I could say to condemn you. But the one who sent me is truthful, and I tell the people of this world only what I have heard from him."

27 No one understood that Jesus was talking to them about the Father.

28 Jesus went on to say, "When you have lifted up the Son of Man,[t] you will know who I am. You will also know that I don't do anything on my own. I say only what my Father taught me. 29The one who sent me is with me. I always do what pleases him, and he will never leave me."

30 After Jesus said this, many of the people put their faith in him.

The Truth Will Set You Free

31 Jesus told the people who had faith in him, "If you keep on obeying what I have said, you truly are my disciples. 32You will know the truth, and the truth will set you free."

33 They answered, "We are Abraham's children! We have never been anyone's slaves. How can you say we will be set free?"

34 Jesus replied:

I tell you for certain that anyone who sins is a slave of sin! 35And slaves don't stay in the family forever, though the Son will always remain in the family. 36If the Son gives you freedom, you are free! 37I know that you are

---

[t] *lifted up the Son of Man*: See the note at 7.39.

from Abraham's family. Yet you want to kill me, because my message isn't really in your hearts. 38I am telling you what my Father has shown me, just as you are doing what your father has taught you.

Your Father Is the Devil

39 The people said to Jesus, "Abraham is our father!" Jesus replied, "If you were Abraham's children, you would do what Abraham did. 40Instead, you want to kill me for telling you the truth that God gave me. Abraham never did anything like that. 41But you are doing exactly what your father does."

"Don't accuse us of having someone else as our father!" they said. "We just have one father, and he is God."

42 Jesus answered:

If God were your Father, you would love me, because I came from God and only from him. He sent me. I did not come on my own. 43Why can't you understand what I am talking about? Can't you stand to hear what I am saying? 44Your father is the devil, and you do exactly what he wants. He has always been a murderer and a liar. There is nothing truthful about him. He speaks on his own, and everything he says is a lie. Not only is he a liar himself, but he is also the father of all lies.

45 Everything I have told you is true, and you still refuse to have faith in me. 46Can any of you accuse me of sin? If you cannot, why won't you have faith in me? After all, I am telling you the truth. 47Anyone who belongs to God will listen

to his message. But you refuse to listen, because you don't belong to God.

Jesus and Abraham

48 The people told Jesus, "We were right to say that you are a Samaritan[u] and that you have a demon in you!"

49 Jesus answered, "I don't have a demon in me. I honor my Father, and you refuse to honor me. 50I don't want honor for myself. But there is one who wants me to be honored, and he is also the one who judges. 51I tell you for certain that if you obey my words, you will never die."

52 Then the people said, "Now we are sure that you have a demon. Abraham is dead, and so are the prophets. How can you say that no one who obeys your words will ever die? 53Are you greater than our father Abraham? He died, and so did the prophets. Who do you think you are?"

54 Jesus replied, "If I honored myself, it would mean nothing. My Father is the one who honors me. You claim that he is your God, 55even though you don't really know him. If I said I didn't know him, I would be a liar, just like all of you. But I know him, and I do what he says. 56Your father Abraham was really glad to see me."

57 "You are not even fifty years old!" they said. "How could you have seen Abraham?"

58 Jesus answered, "I tell you for certain that even before Abraham was, I was, and I am."[v] 59The people

---

[u] *Samaritan*: See 4.9 and the note there.

[v] *I am*: See the note at 8.24.

picked up stones to kill Jesus, but he hid and left the temple.

Jesus Heals a Man Born Blind

9 As Jesus walked along, he saw a man who had been blind since birth. ²Jesus' disciples asked, "Teacher, why was this man born blind? Was it because he or his parents sinned?"

3 "No, it wasn't!" Jesus answered. "But because of his blindness, you will see God work a miracle for him. ⁴As long as it is day, we must do what the one who sent me wants me to do. When night comes, no one can work. ⁵While I am in the world, I am the light for the world."

6 After Jesus said this, he spit on the ground. He made some mud and smeared it on the man's eyes. ⁷Then he said, "Go and wash off the mud in Siloam Pool." The man went and washed in Siloam, which means "One Who Is Sent." When he had washed off the mud, he could see.

8 The man's neighbors and the people who had seen him begging wondered if he really could be the same man. ⁹Some of them said he was the same beggar, while others said he only looked like him. But he told them, "I am that man."

10 "Then how can you see?" they asked.

11 He answered, "Someone named Jesus made some mud and smeared it on my eyes. He told me to go and wash it off in Siloam Pool. When I did, I could see."

12 "Where is he now?" they asked.

"I don't know," he answered.

The Pharisees Try To Find Out What Happened

13-14 The day when Jesus made the mud and healed the man was a Sabbath. So the people took the man to the Pharisees. ¹⁵They asked him how he was able to see, and he answered, "Jesus made some mud and smeared it on my eyes. Then after I washed it off, I could see."

16 Some of the Pharisees said, "This man Jesus doesn't come from God. If he did, he would not break the law of the Sabbath."

Others asked, "How could someone who is a sinner work such a miracle?"^w

Since the Pharisees could not agree among themselves, ¹⁷they asked the man, "What do you say about this one who healed your eyes?"

"He is a prophet!" the man told them.

18 But the Jewish leaders would not believe that the man had once been blind. They sent for his parents ¹⁹and asked, "Is this the son that you said was born blind? How can he now see?"

20 The man's parents answered, "We are certain that he is our son, and we know that he was born blind. ²¹But we don't know how he got his sight or who gave it to him. Ask him! He is old enough to speak for himself."

22-23 The man's parents said this because they were afraid of their leaders. The leaders had already agreed that no one was to have anything to do with anyone who said Jesus was the Messiah.

24 The leaders called the man back and said,

---

^w *miracle*: See the note at 2.11.

"Swear by God to tell the truth! We know that Jesus is a sinner."

25 The man replied, "I don't know if he is a sinner or not. All I know is that I used to be blind, but now I can see!"

26 "What did he do to you?" they asked. "How did he heal your eyes?"

27 The man answered, "I have already told you once, and you refused to listen. Why do you want me to tell you again? Do you also want to become his disciples?"

28 The leaders insulted the man and said, "You are his follower! We are followers of Moses. 29 We are sure that God spoke to Moses, but we don't even know where Jesus comes from."

30 "How strange!" the man replied. "He healed my eyes, and yet you don't know where he comes from. 31 We know that God listens only to people who love and obey him. God doesn't listen to sinners. 32 And this is the first time in history that anyone has ever given sight to someone born blind. 33 Jesus could not do anything unless he came from God."

34 The leaders told the man, "You have been a sinner since the day you were born! Do you think you can teach us anything?" Then they said, "You can never come back into any of our meeting places!"

35 When Jesus heard what had happened, he went and found the man. Then Jesus asked, "Do you have faith in the Son of Man?"

36 He replied, "Sir, if you will tell me who he is, I will put my faith in him."

37 "You have already seen him," Jesus answered, "and right now he is talking with you."

38 The man said, "Lord, I put my faith in you!" Then he worshiped Jesus.

39 Jesus told him, "I came to judge the people of this world. I am here to give sight to the blind and to make blind everyone who can see."

40 When the Pharisees heard Jesus say this, they asked, "Are we blind?"

41 Jesus answered, "If you were blind, you would not be guilty. But now that you claim to see, you will keep on being guilty."

A Story about Sheep

10 Jesus said:

I tell you for certain that only thieves and robbers climb over the fence instead of going in through the gate to the sheep pen. 2-3But the gatekeeper opens the gate for the shepherd, and he goes in through it. The sheep know their shepherd's voice. He calls each of them by name and leads them out.

4 When he has led out all of his sheep, he walks in front of them, and they follow, because they know his voice. 5The sheep will not follow strangers. They don't recognize a stranger's voice, and they run away.

6 Jesus told the people this story. But they did not understand what he was talking about.

Jesus Is the Good Shepherd

7 Jesus said:

I tell you for certain that I am the gate for the sheep. 8Everyone who came before me was a thief or a robber, and the sheep did not listen to any of them. ⁹I am the gate. All who come in through me will be saved. Through me they will come and go and find pasture.

10 A thief comes only to rob, kill, and destroy. I came so that everyone would have life, and have it in its fullest. ¹¹I am the good shepherd, and the good shepherd gives up his life for his sheep. ¹²Hired workers are not like the shepherd. They don't own the sheep, and when they see a wolf coming, they run off and leave the sheep. Then the wolf attacks and scatters the flock. ¹³Hired workers run away because they don't care about the sheep.

14 I am the good shepherd. I know my sheep, and they know me. ¹⁵Just as the Father knows me, I know the Father, and I give up my life for my sheep. ¹⁶I have other sheep that are not in this sheep pen. I must bring them together too, when they hear my voice. Then there will be one flock of sheep and one shepherd.

17 The Father loves me, because I give up my life, so that I may receive it back again. ¹⁸No one takes my life from me. I give it up willingly! I have the power to give it up and the power to receive it back again, just as my Father commanded me to do.

19 The people took sides because of what Jesus had told them. ²⁰Many of them said, "He has a demon in him! He is crazy! Why listen to him?"

21 But others said, "How could anyone with a demon in him say these things? No one like that could give sight to a blind person!"

Jesus Is Rejected

22 That winter, Jesus was in Jerusalem for the Temple Festival. 23One day he was walking in that part of the temple known as Solomon's Porch,^x 24and the people gathered all around him. They said, "How long are you going to keep us guessing? If you are the Messiah, tell us plainly!"

25 Jesus answered:

I have told you, and you refused to believe me. The things I do by my Father's authority show who I am. 26But since you are not my sheep, you don't believe me. 27My sheep know my voice, and I know them. They follow me, 28and I give them eternal life, so that they will never be lost. No one can snatch them out of my hand. 29My Father gave them to me, and he is greater than all others.^y No one can snatch them from his hands, 30and I am one with the Father.

31 Once again the people picked up stones in order to kill Jesus. 32But he said, "I have shown you many good things that my Father sent me to do. Which one are you going to stone me for?"

33 They answered, "We are not stoning you because of any good thing you did. We are stoning you because you did a terrible thing. You are just a man, and here you are claiming to be God!"

---

^x *Solomon's Porch*: A public place with tall columns along the east side of the temple.

^y *he is greater than all others*: Some manuscripts have "they are greater than all others."

34 Jesus replied:

In your Scriptures doesn't God say, "You are gods"? 35 You can't argue with the Scriptures, and God spoke to those people and called them gods. 36 So why do you accuse me of a terrible sin for saying that I am the Son of God? After all, it is the Father who prepared me for this work. He is also the one who sent me into the world. 37 If I don't do as my Father does, you should not believe me. 38 But if I do what my Father does, you should believe because of that, even if you don't have faith in me. Then you will know for certain that the Father is one with me, and I am one with the Father.

39 Again they wanted to arrest Jesus. But he escaped 40 and crossed the Jordan to the place where John had earlier been baptizing. While Jesus was there, 41 many people came to him. They were saying, "John didn't work any miracles, but everything he said about Jesus is true." 42 A lot of those people also put their faith in Jesus.

The Death of Lazarus

11 1-2 A man by the name of Lazarus was sick in the village of Bethany. He had two sisters, Mary and Martha. This was the same Mary who later poured perfume on the Lord's head and wiped his feet with her hair. 3 The sisters sent a message to the Lord and told him that his good friend Lazarus was sick.

4 When Jesus heard this, he said, "His sickness won't end in death. It will bring glory to God and his Son."

5 Jesus loved Martha and her sister and brother. 6 But he stayed where he was for two more days.

7Then he said to his disciples, "Now we will go back to Judea."

8 "Teacher," they said, "the people there want to stone you to death! Why do you want to go back?"

9 Jesus answered, "Aren't there twelve hours in each day? If you walk during the day, you will have light from the sun, and you won't stumble. 10But if you walk during the night, you will stumble, because you don't have any light." 11Then he told them, "Our friend Lazarus is asleep, and I am going there to wake him up."

12 They replied, "Lord, if he is asleep, he will get better." 13Jesus really meant that Lazarus was dead, but they thought he was talking only about sleep.

14 Then Jesus told them plainly, "Lazarus is dead! 15I am glad that I wasn't there, because now you will have a chance to put your faith in me. Let's go to him."

16 Thomas, whose nickname was "Twin," said to the other disciples, "Come on. Let's go, so we can die with him."

Jesus Brings Lazarus to Life

17 When Jesus got to Bethany, he found that Lazarus had already been in the tomb four days. 18Bethany was only about two miles from Jerusalem, 19and many people had come from the city to comfort Martha and Mary because their brother had died.

20 When Martha heard that Jesus had arrived, she went out to meet him, but Mary stayed in the house. 21Martha said to Jesus, "Lord, if you had been here, my brother would not have died. 22Yet even now I know that God will do anything you ask."

23 Jesus told her, "Your brother will live again!"

24 Martha answered, "I know that he will be raised to life on the last day,ᶻ when all the dead are raised."

25 Jesus then said, "I am the one who raises the dead to life! Everyone who has faith in me will live, even if they die. 26 And everyone who lives because of faith in me will never really die. Do you believe this?"

27 "Yes, Lord!" she replied. "I believe that you are Christ, the Son of God. You are the one we hoped would come into the world."

28 After Martha said this, she went and privately said to her sister Mary, "The Teacher is here, and he wants to see you." 29 As soon as Mary heard this, she got up and went out to Jesus. 30 He was still outside the village where Martha had gone to meet him. 31 Many people had come to comfort Mary, and when they saw her quickly leave the house, they thought she was going out to the tomb to cry. So they followed her.

32 Mary went to where Jesus was. Then as soon as she saw him, she knelt at his feet and said, "Lord, if you had been here, my brother would not have died."

33 When Jesus saw that Mary and the people with her were crying, he was terribly upset 34 and asked, "Where have you put his body?"

They replied, "Lord, come and you will see."

35 Jesus started crying, 36 and the people said, "See how much he loved Lazarus."

ᶻ *the last day*: When God will judge all people.

37 Some of them said, "He gives sight to the blind. Why couldn't he have kept Lazarus from dying?"

38 Jesus was still terribly upset. So he went to the tomb, which was a cave with a stone rolled against the entrance. ³⁹Then he told the people to roll the stone away. But Martha said, "Lord, you know that Lazarus has been dead four days, and there will be a bad smell."

40 Jesus replied, "Didn't I tell you that if you had faith, you would see the glory of God?"

41 After the stone had been rolled aside, Jesus looked up toward heaven and prayed, "Father, I thank you for answering my prayer. ⁴²I know that you always answer my prayers. But I said this, so that the people here would believe that you sent me."

43 When Jesus had finished praying, he shouted, "Lazarus, come out!" ⁴⁴The man who had been dead came out. His hands and feet were wrapped with strips of burial cloth, and a cloth covered his face.

Jesus then told the people, "Untie him and let him go."

The Plot To Kill Jesus
(Matthew 26.1-5; Mark 14.1,2; Luke 22.1,2)

45 Many of the people who had come to visit Mary saw the things that Jesus did, and they put their faith in him. ⁴⁶Others went to the Pharisees and told what Jesus had done. ⁴⁷Then the chief priests and the Pharisees called the council together and said, "What should we do? This man is working a lot of miracles:ᵃ ⁴⁸If we don't stop him now, everyone will put their

ᵃ miracles: See the note at 2.11.

faith in him. Then the Romans will come and destroy our temple and our nation."[b]

49 One of the council members was Caiaphas, who was also high priest that year. He spoke up and said, "You people don't have any sense at all! [50]Don't you know it is better for one person to die for the people than for the whole nation to be destroyed?" [51]Caiaphas did not say this on his own. As high priest that year, he was prophesying that Jesus would die for the nation. [52]Yet Jesus would not die just for the Jewish nation. He would die to bring together all of God's scattered people. [53]From that day on, the council started making plans to put Jesus to death.

54 Because of this plot against him, Jesus stopped going around in public. He went to the town of Ephraim, which was near the desert, and he stayed there with his disciples.

55 It was almost time for Passover. Many of the Jewish people who lived out in the country had come to Jerusalem to get themselves ready[c] for the festival. [56]They looked around for Jesus. Then when they were in the temple, they asked each other, "You don't think he will come here for Passover, do you?"

57 The chief priests and the Pharisees told the people to let them know if any of them saw Jesus. That is how they hoped to arrest him.

---

b *destroy our temple and our nation*: The Jewish leaders were afraid that Jesus would lead his followers to rebel against Rome and that the Roman army would then destroy their nation.

c *get themselves ready*: The Jewish people had to do certain things to prepare themselves to worship God.

At Bethany

(Matthew 26.6-13; Mark 14.3-9)

12 Six days before Passover Jesus went back to Bethany, where he had raised Lazarus from death. [2] A meal had been prepared for Jesus. Martha was doing the serving, and Lazarus himself was there.

3 Mary took a very expensive bottle of perfume[d] and poured it on Jesus' feet. She wiped them with her hair, and the sweet smell of the perfume filled the house.

4 A disciple named Judas Iscariot[e] was there. He was the one who was going to betray Jesus, and he asked, [5] "Why wasn't this perfume sold for three hundred silver coins and the money given to the poor?" [6] Judas did not really care about the poor. He asked this because he carried the moneybag and sometimes would steal from it.

7 Jesus replied, "Leave her alone! She has kept this perfume for the day of my burial. [8] You will always have the poor with you, but you won't always have me."

A Plot To Kill Lazarus

9 A lot of people came when they heard that Jesus was there. They also wanted to see Lazarus, because Jesus had raised him from death. [10] So the chief

---

[d] *very expensive bottle of perfume*: The Greek text has "expensive perfume made of pure spikenard," a plant used to make perfume.

[e] *Iscariot*: See the note at 6.71.

priests made plans to kill Lazarus. [11]He was the reason that many of the people were turning from them and putting their faith in Jesus.

Jesus Enters Jerusalem
(Matthew 21.1-11; Mark 11.1-11; Luke 19.28-40)

12 The next day a large crowd was in Jerusalem for Passover. When they heard that Jesus was coming for the festival, [13]they took palm branches and went out to greet him.[f] They shouted,

> "Hooray![g]
> God bless the one
>   who comes in the name of the Lord!
> God bless the King of Israel!"

14 Jesus found a donkey and rode on it, just as the Scriptures say,

[15] "People of Jerusalem, don't be afraid!
> Your King is now coming,
>   and he is riding on a donkey."

16 At first, Jesus' disciples did not understand. But after he had been given his glory,[h] they remembered all this. Everything had happened exactly as the Scriptures said it would.

17-18 A crowd had come to meet Jesus because they had seen him call Lazarus out of the tomb. They kept talking about him and this miracle.[i] [19]But the

---

f *took palm branches and went out to greet him*: This was one way that the Jewish people welcomed a famous person.

g *Hooray*: This translates a word that can mean "please save us." But it is most often used as a shout of praise to God.

h *had been given his glory*: See the note at 7.39.

i *miracle*: See the note at 2.11.

Pharisees said to each other, "There is nothing that can be done! Everyone in the world is following Jesus."

Some Greeks Want To Meet Jesus

20 Some Greeks[j] had gone to Jerusalem to worship during Passover. 21Philip from Bethsaida in Galilee was there too. So they went to him and said, "Sir, we would like to meet Jesus." 22Philip told Andrew. Then the two of them went to Jesus and told him.

The Son of Man Must Be Lifted Up

23 Jesus said:

The time has come for the Son of Man to be given his glory.[k] 24I tell you for certain that a grain of wheat that falls on the ground will never be more than one grain unless it dies. But if it dies, it will produce lots of wheat. 25If you love your life, you will lose it. If you give it up in this world, you will be given eternal life. 26If you serve me, you must go with me. My servants will be with me wherever I am. If you serve me, my Father will honor you.

27 Now I am deeply troubled, and I don't know what to say. But I must not ask my Father to keep me from this time of suffering. In fact, I came into the world to suffer. 28So Father, bring glory to yourself.

---

[j] Greeks: Perhaps Gentiles who worshiped with the Jews. See the note at 7.35.

[k] be given his glory: See the note at 7.39.

A voice from heaven then said, "I have already brought glory to myself, and I will do it again!" 29When the crowd heard the voice, some of them thought it was thunder. Others thought an angel had spoken to Jesus.

30 Then Jesus told the crowd, "That voice spoke to help you, not me. 31This world's people are now being judged, and the ruler of this world[l] is already being thrown out! 32If I am lifted up above the earth, I will make everyone want to come to me." 33Jesus was talking about the way he would be put to death.

34 The crowd said to Jesus, "The Scriptures teach that the Messiah will live forever. How can you say that the Son of Man must be lifted up? Who is this Son of Man?"

35 Jesus answered, "The light will be with you for only a little longer. Walk in the light while you can. Then you won't be caught walking blindly in the dark. 36Have faith in the light while it is with you, and you will be children of the light."

The People Refuse To Have Faith in Jesus

After Jesus had said these things, he left and went into hiding. 37He had worked a lot of miracles[m] among the people, but they were still not willing to have faith in him. 38This happened so that what the prophet Isaiah had said would come true,

"Lord, who has believed our message?
And who has seen your mighty strength?"

---

[l] *world*: In the Gospel of John "world" sometimes refers to the people who live in this world and to the evil forces that control their lives.

[m] *miracles*: See the note at 2.11.

39The people could not have faith in Jesus, because Isaiah had also said,

> 40 "The Lord has blinded the eyes of the people,
>   and he has made the people stubborn.
> He did this so that they could not see
>   or understand,
>   and so that they would not turn to the Lord
>   and be healed."

41 Isaiah said this, because he saw the glory of Jesus and spoke about him.[n] 42Even then, many of the leaders put their faith in Jesus, but they did not tell anyone about it. The Pharisees had already given orders for the people not to have anything to do with anyone who had faith in Jesus. 43And besides, the leaders liked praise from others more than they liked praise from God.

Jesus Came To Save the World

44 In a loud voice Jesus said:

Everyone who has faith in me also has faith in the one who sent me. 45And everyone who has seen me has seen the one who sent me. 46I am the light that has come into the world. No one who has faith in me will stay in the dark.

47 I am not the one who will judge those who refuse to obey my teachings. I came to save the people of this world, not to be their judge. 48But everyone who rejects me and my teachings will be judged on the last day[o] by what I have said.

---

[n] he saw the glory of Jesus and spoke about him: Or "he saw the glory of God and spoke about Jesus."

[o] the last day: When God will judge all people.

⁴⁹I don't speak on my own. I say only what the Father who sent me has told me to say. ⁵⁰I know that his commands will bring eternal life. That is why I tell you exactly what the Father has told me.

Jesus Washes the Feet of His Disciples

13 It was before Passover, and Jesus knew that the time had come for him to leave this world and to return to the Father. He had always loved his followers in this world, and he loved them to the very end.

2 Even before the evening meal started, the devil had made Judas, the son of Simon Iscariot,ᵖ decide to betray Jesus.

3 Jesus knew that he had come from God and would go back to God. He also knew that the Father had given him complete power. ⁴So during the meal Jesus got up, removed his outer garment, and wrapped a towel around his waist. ⁵He put some water into a large bowl. Then he began washing his disciples' feet and drying them with the towel he was wearing.

6 But when he came to Simon Peter, that disciple asked, "Lord, are you going to wash my feet?"

7 Jesus answered, "You don't really know what I am doing, but later you will understand."

8 "You will never wash my feet!" Peter replied.

"If I don't wash you," Jesus told him, "you don't really belong to me."

9 Peter said, "Lord, don't wash just my feet. Wash my hands and my head."

10 Jesus answered, "People who have bathed and are clean all over need to wash just their feet. And you,

---

ᵖ *Iscariot*: See the note at 6.71.

my disciples, are clean, except for one of you."
[11]Jesus knew who would betray him. That is why he said, "except for one of you."

12 After Jesus had washed his disciples' feet and had put his outer garment back on, he sat down again.[q] Then he said:

Do you understand what I have done? [13]You call me your teacher and Lord, and you should, because that is who I am. [14]And if your Lord and teacher has washed your feet, you should do the same for each other. [15]I have set the example, and you should do for each other exactly what I have done for you. [16]I tell you for certain that servants are not greater than their master, and messengers are not greater than the one who sent them. [17]You know these things, and God will bless you, if you do them.

18 I am not talking about all of you. I know the ones I have chosen. But what the Scriptures say must come true. And they say, "The man who ate with me has turned against me!" [19]I am telling you this before it all happens. Then when it does happen, you will believe who I am.[r] [20]I tell you for certain that anyone who welcomes my messengers also welcomes me, and anyone who welcomes me welcomes the one who sent me.

---

[q] *sat down again*: On special occasions the Jewish people followed the Greek and Roman custom of lying down on their left side and leaning on their left elbow, while eating with their right hand.

[r] *I am*: See the note at 8.24.

Jesus Tells What Will Happen to Him

(Matthew 26.20-25; Mark 14.17-21; Luke 22.21-23)

21 After Jesus had said these things, he was deeply troubled and told his disciples, "I tell you for certain that one of you will betray me." 22They were confused about what he meant. And they just stared at each other.

23 Jesus' favorite disciple was sitting next to him at the meal, 24and Simon motioned for that disciple to find out which one Jesus meant. 25So the disciple leaned toward Jesus and asked, "Lord, which one of us are you talking about?"

26 Jesus answered, "I will dip this piece of bread in the sauce and give it to the one I was talking about."

Then Jesus dipped the bread and gave it to Judas, the son of Simon Iscariot.^{s} 27Right then Satan took control of Judas.

Jesus said, "Judas, go quickly and do what you have to do." 28No one at the meal understood what Jesus meant. 29But because Judas was in charge of the money, some of them thought that Jesus had told him to buy something they needed for the festival. Others thought that Jesus had told him to give some money to the poor. 30Judas took the piece of bread and went out.

It was already night.

The New Command

31 After Judas had gone, Jesus said:

Now the Son of Man will be given glory, and

---

^{s} *Iscariot*: See the note at 6.71.

he will bring glory to God. 32Then, after God is given glory because of him, God will bring glory to him, and God will do it very soon.

33 My children, I will be with you for a little while longer. Then you will look for me, but you won't find me. I tell you just as I told the people, "You cannot go where I am going." 34But I am giving you a new command. You must love each other, just as I have loved you. 35If you love each other, everyone will know that you are my disciples.

Peter's Promise

(Matthew 26.31-35; Mark 14.27-31; Luke 22.31-34)

36 Simon Peter asked, "Lord, where are you going?" Jesus answered, "You can't go with me now, but later on you will."

37 Peter asked, "Lord, why can't I go with you now? I would die for you!"

38 "Would you really die for me?" Jesus asked. "I tell you for certain that before a rooster crows, you will say three times that you don't even know me."

Jesus Is the Way to the Father

14 Jesus said to his disciples, "Don't be worried! Have faith in God and have faith in me.[t] 2There are many rooms in my Father's house. I wouldn't tell you this, unless it was true. I am going there to prepare a place for each of you. 3After I have done this, I will come back and take you with me.

---

[t] *Have faith in God and have faith in me*: Or "You have faith in God, so have faith in me."

Then we will be together. [4] You know the way to where I am going."

[5] Thomas said, "Lord, we don't even know where you are going! How can we know the way?"

[6] "I am the way, the truth, and the life!" Jesus answered. "Without me, no one can go to the Father. [7] If you had known me, you would have known the Father. But from now on, you do know him, and you have seen him."

[8] Philip said, "Lord, show us the Father. That is all we need."

[9] Jesus replied:

Philip, I have been with you for a long time. Don't you know who I am? If you have seen me, you have seen the Father. How can you ask me to show you the Father? [10] Don't you believe that I am one with the Father and that the Father is one with me? What I say isn't said on my own. The Father who lives in me does these things.

[11] Have faith in me when I say that the Father is one with me and that I am one with the Father. Or else have faith in me simply because of the things I do. [12] I tell you for certain that if you have faith in me, you will do the same things that I am doing. You will do even greater things, now that I am going back to the Father. [13] Ask me, and I will do whatever you ask. This way the Son will bring honor to the Father. [14] I will do whatever you ask me to do.

The Holy Spirit Is Promised

[15] Jesus said to his disciples:

If you love me, you will do as I command.

¹⁶Then I will ask the Father to send you the Holy Spirit who will help*ᵘ* you and always be with you. ¹⁷The Spirit will show you what is true. The people of this world cannot accept the Spirit, because they don't see or know him. But you know the Spirit, who is with you and will keep on living in you.

18 I won't leave you like orphans. I will come back to you. ¹⁹In a little while the people of this world won't be able to see me, but you will see me. And because I live, you will live. ²⁰Then you will know that I am one with the Father. You will know that you are one with me, and I am one with you. ²¹If you love me, you will do what I have said, and my Father will love you. I will also love you and show you what I am like.

22 The other Judas, not Judas Iscariot,ᵛ then spoke up and asked, "Lord, what do you mean by saying that you will show us what you are like, but you will not show the people of this world?"

23 Jesus replied:

If anyone loves me, they will obey me. Then my Father will love them, and we will come to them and live in them. ²⁴But anyone who doesn't love me, won't obey me. What they have heard me say doesn't really come from me, but from the Father who sent me.

25 I have told you these things while I am still with you. ²⁶But the Holy Spirit will come and

---

ᵘ help: The Greek word may mean "comfort," "encourage," or "defend."

ᵛ Iscariot: See the note at 6.71.

help*w* you, because the Father will send the Spirit to take my place. The Spirit will teach you everything and will remind you of what I said while I was with you.

27 I give you peace, the kind of peace that only I can give. It isn't like the peace that this world can give. So don't be worried or afraid.

28 You have already heard me say that I am going and that I will also come back to you. If you really love me, you should be glad that I am going back to the Father, because he is greater than I am.

29 I am telling you this before I leave, so that when it does happen, you will have faith in me. 30I cannot speak with you much longer, because the ruler of this world is coming. But he has no power over me. 31I obey my Father, so that everyone in the world might know that I love him.

It is time for us to go now.

Jesus Is the True Vine

15 Jesus said to his disciples:
I am the true vine, and my Father is the gardener. 2He cuts away every branch of mine that doesn't produce fruit. But he trims clean every branch that does produce fruit, so that it will produce even more fruit. 3You are already clean because of what I have said to you.

4 Stay joined to me, and I will stay joined to you. Just as a branch cannot produce fruit unless it stays joined to the vine, you cannot produce

---

w help: See the note at 14.16.

fruit unless you stay joined to me. ⁵I am the vine, and you are the branches. If you stay joined to me, and I stay joined to you, then you will produce lots of fruit. But you cannot do anything without me. ⁶If you don't stay joined to me, you will be thrown away. You will be like dry branches that are gathered up and burned in a fire.

7 Stay joined to me and let my teachings become part of you. Then you can pray for whatever you want, and your prayer will be answered. ⁸When you become fruitful disciples of mine, my Father will be honored. ⁹I have loved you, just as my Father has loved me. So remain faithful to my love for you. ¹⁰If you obey me, I will keep loving you, just as my Father keeps loving me, because I have obeyed him.

11 I have told you this to make you as completely happy as I am. ¹²Now I tell you to love each other, as I have loved you. ¹³The greatest way to show love for friends is to die for them. ¹⁴And you are my friends, if you obey me. ¹⁵Servants don't know what their master is doing, and so I don't speak to you as my servants. I speak to you as my friends, and I have told you everything that my Father has told me.

16 You did not choose me. I chose you and sent you out to produce fruit, the kind of fruit that will last. Then my Father will give you whatever you ask for in my name.ˣ ¹⁷So I command you to love each other.

ˣ *in my name*: Or "because you are my followers."

The World's Hatred

18 If the people of this world [y] hate you, just remember that they hated me first. ¹⁹If you belonged to the world, its people would love you. But you don't belong to the world. I have chosen you to leave the world behind, and that is why its people hate you. ²⁰Remember how I told you that servants are not greater than their master. So if people mistreat me, they will mistreat you. If they do what I say, they will do what you say.

21 People will do to you exactly what they did to me. They will do it because you belong to me, and they don't know the one who sent me. ²²If I had not come and spoken to them, they would not be guilty of sin. But now they have no excuse for their sin.

23 Everyone who hates me also hates my Father. ²⁴I have done things that no one else has ever done. If they had not seen me do these things, they would not be guilty. But they did see me do these things, and they still hate me and my Father too. ²⁵That is why the Scriptures are true when they say, "People hated me for no reason."

26 I will send you the Spirit who comes from the Father and shows what is true. The Spirit will help [z] you and will tell you about me. ²⁷Then you will also tell others about me, because you have been with me from the beginning.

---

y *world*: See the note at 12.31.
z *help*: See the note at 14.16.

16 I am telling you this to keep you from being afraid. [2]You will be chased out of the Jewish meeting places. And the time will come when people will kill you and think they are doing God a favor. [3]They will do these things because they don't know either the Father or me. [4]I am saying this to you now, so that when the time comes, you will remember what I have said.

The Work of the Holy Spirit

I was with you at the first, and so I didn't tell you these things. [5]But now I am going back to the Father who sent me, and none of you asks me where I am going. [6]You are very sad from hearing all of this. [7]But I tell you that I am going to do what is best for you. That is why I am going away. The Holy Spirit cannot come to help*[a]* you until I leave. But after I am gone, I will send the Spirit to you.

8 The Spirit will come and show the people of this world the truth about sin and God's justice and the judgment. [9]The Spirit will show them that they are wrong about sin, because they didn't have faith in me. [10]They are wrong about God's justice, because I am going to the Father, and you won't see me again. [11]And they are wrong about the judgment, because God has already judged the ruler of this world.

12 I have much more to say to you, but right now it would be more than you could understand. [13]The Spirit shows what is true and will

---

a help: See the note at 14.16.

come and guide you into the full truth. The Spirit doesn't speak on his own. He will tell you only what he has heard from me, and he will let you know what is going to happen. 14The Spirit will bring glory to me by taking my message and telling it to you. 15Everything that the Father has is mine. That is why I have said that the Spirit takes my message and tells it to you.

Sorrow Will Turn into Joy

16 Jesus told his disciples, "For a little while you won't see me, but after a while you will see me."

17 They said to each other, "What does Jesus mean by saying that for a little while we won't see him, but after a while we will see him? What does he mean by saying that he is going to the Father? 18What is this 'little while' that he is talking about? We don't know what he means."

19 Jesus knew that they had some questions, so he said:

You are wondering what I meant when I said that for a little while you won't see me, but after a while you will see me. 20I tell you for certain that you will cry and be sad, but the world will be happy. You will be sad, but later you will be happy.

21 When a woman is about to give birth, she is in great pain. But after it is all over, she forgets the pain and is happy, because she has brought a child into the world. 22You are now very sad. But later I will see you, and you will be so happy that no one will be able to change the way

you feel. 23When that time comes, you won't have to ask me about anything. I tell you for certain that the Father will give you whatever you ask for in my name. 24You have not asked for anything in this way before, but now you must ask in my name.*b* Then it will be given to you, so that you will be completely happy.

25 I have used examples to explain to you what I have been talking about. But the time will come when I will speak to you plainly about the Father and will no longer use examples like these. 26You will ask the Father in my name,*c* and I won't have to ask him for you. 27God the Father loves you because you love me, and you believe that I have come from him. 28I came from the Father into the world, but I am leaving the world and returning to the Father.

29 The disciples said, "Now you are speaking plainly to us! You are not using examples. 30At last we know that you understand everything, and we don't have any more questions. Now we believe that you truly have come from God."

31 Jesus replied:

Do you really believe me? 32The time will come and is already here when all of you will be scattered. Each of you will go back home and leave me by myself. But the Father will be with me, and I won't be alone. 33I have told you this, so that you might have peace in your hearts

---

b *in my name ... in my name*: Or "as my disciples ... as my disciples."

c *in my name*: Or "because you are my followers."

because of me. While you are in the world, you will have to suffer. But cheer up! I have defeated the world.[d]

Jesus Prays

17 After Jesus had finished speaking to his disciples, he looked up toward heaven and prayed: Father, the time has come for you to bring glory to your Son, in order that he may bring glory to you. [2]And you gave him power over all people, so that he would give eternal life to everyone you give him. [3]Eternal life is to know you, the only true God, and to know Jesus Christ, the one you sent. [4]I have brought glory to you here on earth by doing everything you gave me to do. [5]Now, Father, give me back the glory that I had with you before the world was created.

[6] You have given me some followers from this world, and I have shown them what you are like. They were yours, but you gave them to me, and they have obeyed you. [7]They know that you gave me everything I have. [8]I told my followers what you told me, and they accepted it. They know that I came from you, and they believe that you are the one who sent me. [9]I am praying for them, but not for those who belong to this world.[d] My followers belong to you, and I am praying for them. [10]All that I have is yours, and all that you have is mine, and they will bring glory to me.

---

[d] *world*: See the note at 12.31.

11 Holy Father, I am no longer in the world. I am coming to you, but my followers are still in the world. So keep them safe by the power of the name that you have given me. Then they will be one with each other, just as you and I are one. 12While I was with them, I kept them safe by the power you have given me. I guarded them, and not one of them was lost, except the one who had to be lost. This happened so that what the Scriptures say would come true.

13 I am on my way to you. But I say these things while I am still in the world, so that my followers will have the same complete joy that I do. 14I have told them your message. But the people of this world hate them, because they don't belong to this world, just as I don't.

15 Father, I don't ask you to take my followers out of the world, but keep them safe from the evil one. 16They don't belong to this world, and neither do I. 17Your word is the truth. So let this truth make them completely yours. 18I am sending them into the world, just as you sent me. 19I have given myself completely for their sake, so that they may belong completely to the truth.

20 I am not praying just for these followers. I am also praying for everyone else who will have faith because of what my followers will say about me. 21I want all of them to be one with each other, just as I am one with you and you are one with me. I also want them to be one with us. Then the people of this world will believe that you sent me.

22 I have honored my followers in the same way that you honored me, in order that they may be one with each other, just as we are one. 23I am one with them, and you are one with me, so that they may become completely one. Then this world's people will know that you sent me. They will know that you love my followers as much as you love me.

24 Father, I want everyone you have given me to be with me, wherever I am. Then they will see the glory that you have given me, because you loved me before the world was created. 25Good Father, the people of this world don't know you. But I know you, and my followers know that you sent me. 26I told them what you are like, and I will tell them even more. Then the love that you have for me will become part of them, and I will be one with them.

Jesus Is Betrayed and Arrested
(Matthew 26.47-56; Mark 14.43-50; Luke 22.47-53)

18 When Jesus had finished praying, he and his disciples crossed the Kidron Valley and went into a garden.*e* 2Jesus had often met there with his disciples, and Judas knew where the place was.

3-5 Judas had promised to betray Jesus. So he went to the garden with some Roman soldiers and temple police, who had been sent by the chief priests and the Pharisees. They carried torches, lanterns, and weapons. Jesus already knew everything that

---

e *garden*: The Greek word is usually translated "garden," but probably referred to an olive orchard.

was going to happen, but he asked, "Who are you looking for?"

They answered, "We are looking for Jesus from Nazareth!"

Jesus told them, "I am Jesus!"*f* 6At once they all backed away and fell to the ground.

7 Jesus again asked, "Who are you looking for?"

"We are looking for Jesus from Nazareth," they answered.

8 This time Jesus replied, "I have already told you that I am Jesus. If I am the one you are looking for, let these others go. 9Then everything will happen, just as the Scriptures say, 'I did not lose anyone you gave me.'"

10 Simon Peter had brought along a sword. He now pulled it out and struck at the servant of the high priest. The servant's name was Malchus, and Peter cut off his right ear. 11Jesus told Peter, "Put your sword away. I must drink from the cup*g* that the Father has given me."

Jesus Is Brought to Annas

(Matthew 26.57, 58; Mark 14.53, 54; Luke 22.54)

12 The Roman officer and his men, together with the temple police, arrested Jesus and tied him up. 13They took him first to Annas, who was the father-in-law of Caiaphas, the high priest that year. 14This was the same Caiaphas who had told the Jewish leaders, "It is better if one person dies for the people."

---

f I am Jesus: The Greek text has "I am" (see the note at 8.24).
g drink from the cup: In the Scriptures a cup is sometimes used as a symbol of suffering. To "drink from the cup" is to suffer.

Peter Says He Doesn't Know Jesus
(Matthew 26.69, 70; Mark 14.66-68; Luke 22.55-57)

15 Simon Peter and another disciple followed Jesus. That disciple knew the high priest, and he followed Jesus into the courtyard of the high priest's house. 16Peter stayed outside near the gate. But the other disciple came back out and spoke to the girl at the gate. She let Peter go in, 17but asked him, "Aren't you one of that man's followers?"

"No, I am not!" Peter answered.

18 It was cold, and the servants and temple police had made a charcoal fire. They were warming themselves around it, when Peter went over and stood near the fire to warm himself.

Jesus Is Questioned by the High Priest
(Matthew 26.59-66; Mark 14.55-64; Luke 22.66-71)

19 The high priest questioned Jesus about his followers and his teaching. 20But Jesus told him, "I have spoken freely in front of everyone. And I have always taught in our meeting places and in the temple, where all of our people come together. I have not said anything in secret. 21Why are you questioning me? Why don't you ask the people who heard me? They know what I have said."

22 As soon as Jesus said this, one of the temple police hit him and said, "That's no way to talk to the high priest!"

23 Jesus answered, "If I have done something wrong, say so. But if not, why did you hit me?" 24Jesus was still tied up, and Annas sent him to Caiaphas the high priest.

Peter Again Denies that He Knows Jesus
(Matthew 26.71-75; Mark 14.69-72; Luke 22.58-62)

25 While Simon Peter was standing there warming himself, someone asked him, "Aren't you one of Jesus' followers?"

Again Peter denied it and said, "No, I am not!"

26 One of the high priest's servants was there. He was a relative of the servant whose ear Peter had cut off, and he asked, "Didn't I see you in the garden with that man?"

27 Once more Peter denied it, and right then a rooster crowed.

Jesus Is Tried by Pilate
(Matthew 27.1,2, 11-14; Mark 15.1-5; Luke 23.1-5)

28 It was early in the morning when Jesus was taken from Caiaphas to the building where the Roman governor stayed. But the crowd waited outside. Any of them who had gone inside would have become unclean and would not be allowed to eat the Passover meal.[h]

29 Pilate came out and asked, "What charges are you bringing against this man?"

30 They answered, "He is a criminal! That's why we brought him to you."

31 Pilate told them, "Take him and judge him by your own laws."

---

[h] would have become unclean and would not be allowed to eat the Passover meal: Jewish people who came in close contact with foreigners right before Passover were not allowed to eat the Passover meal.

The crowd replied, "We are not allowed to put anyone to death." 32 And so what Jesus said about his death *i* would soon come true.

33 Pilate then went back inside. He called Jesus over and asked, "Are you the king of the Jews?"

34 Jesus answered, "Are you asking this on your own or did someone tell you about me?"

35 "You know I'm not a Jew!" Pilate said. "Your own people and the chief priests brought you to me. What have you done?"

36 Jesus answered, "My kingdom doesn't belong to this world. If it did, my followers would have fought to keep me from being handed over to our leaders. No, my kingdom doesn't belong to this world."

37 "So you are a king," Pilate replied.

"You are saying that I am a king," Jesus told him. "I was born into this world to tell about the truth. And everyone who belongs to the truth knows my voice."

38 Pilate asked Jesus, "What is truth?"

Jesus Is Sentenced to Death
(Matthew 27.15-31; Mark 15.6-20; Luke 23.13-25)

Pilate went back out and said, "I don't find this man guilty of anything! 39 And since I usually set a prisoner free for you at Passover, would you like for me to set free the king of the Jews?"

---

i *about his death*: Jesus had said that he would die by being "lifted up," which meant that he would die on a cross. The Romans killed criminals by nailing them on a cross, but they did not let the Jews kill anyone in this way.

40 They shouted, "No, not him! We want Barabbas." Now Barabbas was a terrorist.[j]

19 Pilate gave orders for Jesus to be beaten with a whip. [2] The soldiers made a crown out of thorn branches and put it on Jesus. Then they put a purple robe on him. [3] They came up to him and said, "Hey, you king of the Jews!" They also hit him with their fists.

4 Once again Pilate went out. This time he said, "I will have Jesus brought out to you again. Then you can see for yourselves that I have not found him guilty."

5 Jesus came out, wearing the crown of thorns and the purple robe. Pilate said, "Here is the man!"[k]

6 When the chief priests and the temple police saw him, they yelled, "Nail him to a cross! Nail him to a cross!"

Pilate told them, "You take him and nail him to a cross! I don't find him guilty of anything."

7 The crowd replied, "He claimed to be the Son of God! Our Law says that he must be put to death."

8 When Pilate heard this, he was terrified. [9] He went back inside and asked Jesus, "Where are you from?" But Jesus did not answer.

10 "Why won't you answer my question?" Pilate asked. "Don't you know that I have the power to let you go free or to nail you to a cross?"

11 Jesus replied, "If God had not given you the

---

j *terrorist*: Someone who stirred up trouble against the Romans in the hope of gaining freedom for the Jewish people.

k *"Here is the man!"*: Or "Look at the man!"

power, you couldn't do anything at all to me. But the one who handed me over to you did something even worse."

12 Then Pilate wanted to set Jesus free. But the crowd again yelled, "If you set this man free, you are no friend of the Emperor! Anyone who claims to be a king is an enemy of the Emperor."

13 When Pilate heard this, he brought Jesus out. Then he sat down on the judge's bench at the place known as "The Stone Pavement." In Aramaic this pavement is called "Gabbatha." 14It was about noon on the day before Passover, and Pilate said to the crowd, "Look at your king!"

15 "Kill him! Kill him!" they yelled. "Nail him to a cross!"

"So you want me to nail your king to a cross?" Pilate asked.

The chief priests replied, "The Emperor is our king!" 16Then Pilate handed Jesus over to be nailed to a cross.

Jesus Is Nailed to a Cross
(Matthew 27.32-44; Mark 15.21-32; Luke 23.26-43)

Jesus was taken away, 17and he carried his cross to a place known as "The Skull."[1] In Aramaic this place is called "Golgotha." 18There Jesus was nailed to the cross, and on each side of him a man was also nailed to a cross.

19 Pilate ordered the charge against Jesus to be written on a board and put above the cross. It read,

---

[1] *The Skull*: The place was probably given this name because it was near a large rock in the shape of a human skull.

"Jesus of Nazareth, King of the Jews." 20The words were written in Hebrew, Latin, and Greek.

The place where Jesus was taken wasn't far from the city, and many of the people read the charge against him. 21So the chief priests went to Pilate and said, "Why did you write that he is King of the Jews? You should have written, 'He claimed to be King of the Jews.'"

22 But Pilate told them, "What is written will not be changed!"

23 After the soldiers had nailed Jesus to the cross, they divided up his clothes into four parts, one for each of them. But his outer garment was made from a single piece of cloth, and it did not have any seams. 24The soldiers said to each other, "Let's not rip it apart. We will gamble to see who gets it." This happened so that the Scriptures would come true, which say,

"They divided up my clothes
    and gambled for my garments."

The soldiers then did what they had decided.

25 Jesus' mother stood beside his cross with her sister and Mary the wife of Clopas. Mary Magdalene was standing there too.[m] 26When Jesus saw his mother and his favorite disciple with her, he said to his mother,

---

[m] Jesus' mother stood beside his cross with her sister and Mary the wife of Clopas. Mary Magdalene was standing there too: The Greek text may also be understood to include only three women ("Jesus' mother stood beside the cross with her sister, Mary the mother of Clopas. Mary Magdalene was standing there too.") or merely two women ("Jesus' mother was standing there with her sister Mary of Clopas, that is, Mary Magdalene."). "Of Clopas" may mean "daughter of" or "mother of."

"This man is now your son." 27Then he said to the disciple, "She is now your mother." From then on, that disciple took her into his own home.

The Death of Jesus
(Matthew 27.45-56; Mark 15.33-41; Luke 23.44-49)

28 Jesus knew that he had now finished his work. And in order to make the Scriptures come true, he said, "I am thirsty!" 29A jar of cheap wine was there. Someone then soaked a sponge with the wine and held it up to Jesus' mouth on the stem of a hyssop plant. 30After Jesus drank the wine, he said, "Everything is done!" He bowed his head and died.

A Spear Is Stuck in Jesus' Side

31 The next day would be both a Sabbath and the Passover. It was a special day for the Jewish people,[n] and they did not want the bodies to stay on the crosses during that day. So they asked Pilate to break the men's legs[o] and take their bodies down. 32The soldiers first broke the legs of the other two men who were nailed there. 33But when they came to Jesus, they saw that he was already dead, and they did not break his legs.

34 One of the soldiers stuck his spear into Jesus' side, and blood and water came out. 35We know this

---

[n] *a special day for the Jewish people*: Passover could be any day of the week. But according to the Gospel of John, Passover was on a Sabbath in the year that Jesus was nailed to a cross.

[o] *break the men's legs*: This was the way that the Romans sometimes speeded up the death of a person who had been nailed to a cross.

is true, because it was told by someone who saw it happen. Now you can have faith too. 36All this happened so that the Scriptures would come true, which say, "No bone of his body will be broken" 37and, "They will see the one in whose side they stuck a spear."

Jesus Is Buried

(Matthew 27.57-61; Mark 15.42-47; Luke 23.50-56)

38 Joseph from Arimathea was one of Jesus' disciples. He had kept it secret though, because he was afraid of the Jewish leaders. But now he asked Pilate to let him have Jesus' body. Pilate gave him permission, and Joseph took it down from the cross.

39 Nicodemus also came with about seventy-five pounds of spices made from myrrh and aloes. This was the same Nicodemus who had visited Jesus one night.*p* 40The two men wrapped the body in a linen cloth, together with the spices, which was how the Jewish people buried their dead. 41In the place where Jesus had been nailed to a cross, there was a garden with a tomb that had never been used. 42The tomb was nearby, and since it was the time to prepare for the Sabbath, they were in a hurry to put Jesus' body there.

Jesus Is Alive

(Matthew 28.1-10; Mark 16.1-8; Luke 24.1-12)

20 On Sunday morning while it was still dark, Mary Magdalene went to the tomb and saw that the stone had been rolled away from the entrance.

---

p Nicodemus who had visited Jesus one night: See 3.1-21.

2She ran to Simon Peter and to Jesus' favorite disciple and said, "They have taken the Lord from the tomb! We don't know where they have put him."

3 Peter and the other disciple started for the tomb. 4They ran side by side, until the other disciple ran faster than Peter and got there first. 5He bent over and saw the strips of linen cloth lying inside the tomb, but he did not go in.

6 When Simon Peter got there, he went into the tomb and saw the strips of cloth. 7He also saw the piece of cloth that had been used to cover Jesus' face. It was rolled up and in a place by itself. 8The disciple who got there first then went into the tomb, and when he saw it, he believed. 9At that time Peter and the other disciple did not know that the Scriptures said Jesus would rise to life. 10So the two of them went back to the other disciples.

Jesus Appears to Mary Magdalene
(Mark 16.9-11)

11 Mary Magdalene stood crying outside the tomb. She was still weeping, when she stooped down 12and saw two angels inside. They were dressed in white and were sitting where Jesus' body had been. One was at the head and the other was at the foot. 13The angels asked Mary, "Why are you crying?"

She answered, "They have taken away my Lord's body! I don't know where they have put him."

14 As soon as Mary said this, she turned around and saw Jesus standing there. But she did not know who he was. 15Jesus asked her, "Why are you crying? Who are you looking for?"

She thought he was the gardener and said, "Sir, if you have taken his body away, please tell me, so I can go and get him."

16 Then Jesus said to her, "Mary!"

She turned and said to him, "Rabboni." The Aramaic word "Rabboni" means "Teacher."

17 Jesus told her, "Don't hold on to me! I have not yet gone to the Father. But tell my disciples that I am going to the one who is my Father and my God, as well as your Father and your God." 18Mary Magdalene then went and told the disciples that she had seen the Lord. She also told them what he had said to her.

Jesus Appears to His Disciples
(Matthew 28.16-20; Mark 16.14-18; Luke 24.36-49)

19 The disciples were afraid of the Jewish leaders, and on the evening of that same Sunday they locked themselves in a room. Suddenly, Jesus appeared in the middle of the group. He greeted them 20and showed them his hands and his side. When the disciples saw the Lord, they became very happy.

21 After Jesus had greeted them again, he said, "I am sending you, just as the Father has sent me." 22Then he breathed on them and said, "Receive the Holy Spirit. 23If you forgive anyone's sins, they will be forgiven. But if you don't forgive their sins, they will not be forgiven."

Jesus and Thomas

24 Although Thomas the Twin was one of the twelve disciples, he wasn't with the others when Jesus appeared to them. 25So they told him, "We have seen the Lord!"

But Thomas said, "First, I must see the nail scars in his hands and touch them with my finger. I must put my hand where the spear went into his side. I won't believe unless I do this!"

26 A week later the disciples were together again. This time, Thomas was with them. Jesus came in while the doors were still locked and stood in the middle of the group. He greeted his disciples 27 and said to Thomas, "Put your finger here and look at my hands! Put your hand into my side. Stop doubting and have faith!"

28 Thomas replied, "You are my Lord and my God!"

29 Jesus said, "Thomas, do you have faith because you have seen me? The people who have faith in me without seeing me are the ones who are really blessed!"

Why John Wrote His Book

30 Jesus worked many other miracles*q* for his disciples, and not all of them are written in this book. 31 But these are written so that you will put your faith in Jesus as the Messiah and the Son of God. If you have faith in*r* him, you will have true life.

Jesus Appears to Seven Disciples

21 Jesus later appeared to his disciples along the shore of Lake Tiberias. 2 Simon Peter, Thomas the Twin, Nathanael from Cana in Galilee, and the brothers James and John,*s* were there, together with

---

q miracles: See the note at 2.11.

r put your faith in... have faith in: Some manuscripts have "keep on having faith in... keep on having faith in."

s the brothers James and John: Greek "the two sons of Zebedee."

two other disciples. ³Simon Peter said, "I'm going fishing!"

The others said, "We will go with you." They went out in their boat. But they didn't catch a thing that night.

4 Early the next morning Jesus stood on the shore, but the disciples did not realize who he was. ⁵Jesus shouted, "Friends, have you caught anything?"

"No!" they answered.

6 So he told them, "Let your net down on the right side of your boat, and you will catch some fish."

They did, and the net was so full of fish that they could not drag it up into the boat.

7 Jesus' favorite disciple told Peter, "It's the Lord!" When Simon heard that it was the Lord, he put on the clothes that he had taken off while he was working. Then he jumped into the water. ⁸The boat was only about a hundred yards from shore. So the other disciples stayed in the boat and dragged in the net full of fish.

9 When the disciples got out of the boat, they saw some bread and a charcoal fire with fish on it. ¹⁰Jesus told his disciples, "Bring some of the fish you just caught." ¹¹Simon Peter got back into the boat and dragged the net to shore. In it were one hundred fifty-three large fish, but still the net did not rip.

12 Jesus said, "Come and eat!" But none of the disciples dared ask who he was. They knew he was the Lord. ¹³Jesus took the bread in his hands and gave some of it to his disciples. He did the same with the fish. ¹⁴This was the third time that Jesus appeared to his disciples after he was raised from death.

Jesus and Peter

15 When Jesus and his disciples had finished eating, he asked, "Simon son of John, do you love me more than the others do?"[t]

Simon Peter answered, "Yes, Lord, you know I do!"

"Then feed my lambs," Jesus said.

16 Jesus asked a second time, "Simon son of John, do you love me?"

Peter answered, "Yes, Lord, you know I love you!"

"Then take care of my sheep," Jesus told him.

17 Jesus asked a third time, "Simon son of John, do you love me?"

Peter was hurt because Jesus had asked him three times if he loved him. So he told Jesus, "Lord, you know everything. You know I love you."

Jesus replied, "Feed my sheep. 18I tell you for certain that when you were a young man, you dressed yourself and went wherever you wanted to go. But when you are old, you will hold out your hands. Then others will wrap your belt around you and lead you where you don't want to go."

19 Jesus said this to tell how Peter would die and bring honor to God. Then he said to Peter, "Follow me!"

Jesus and His Favorite Disciple

20 Peter turned and saw Jesus' favorite disciple following them. He was the same one who had sat

---

[t] *more than the others do?*: Or "more than you love these things?"

next to Jesus at the meal and had asked, "Lord, who is going to betray you?" 21When Peter saw that disciple, he asked Jesus, "Lord, what about him?"

22 Jesus answered, "What is it to you, if I want him to live until I return? You must follow me." 23So the rumor spread among the other disciples that this disciple would not die. But Jesus did not say he would not die. He simply said, "What is it to you, if I want him to live until I return?"

24 This disciple is the one who told all of this. He wrote it, and we know he is telling the truth.

25 Jesus did many other things. If they were all written in books, I don't suppose there would be room enough in the whole world for all the books.

The Acts of the Apostles

This is the second book written by Luke. His first one
is commonly known as the Gospel of Luke. In it he
told "all that Jesus did and taught from the very first
until he was taken up to heaven" (1.1,2). In this book
Luke continues the story by describing some of the
struggles the disciples faced as they tried to obey the
command of Jesus: "You will tell everyone about me
in Jerusalem, in all Judea, in Samaria, and everywhere in the world" (1.8).

So many different countries are mentioned in Acts
that the book may seem to have been written only to
tell about the spread of the Christian message. But
that is only part of the story. After Jesus was taken up
to heaven, one of the big problems for his followers
was deciding who could belong to God's people. And
since Jesus and his first followers were Jews, it was
only natural for many of them to think that his message was only for Jews. But in Acts the Spirit is
always present to show that Jesus came to save both
Jews and Gentiles, and that God wants followers
from every nation and race to be part of his people.

The first conflict between Christians and Jews took
place when some of the Jewish religious leaders
rejected the message about Jesus (4.1-31; 7.1-59). But
the most serious problems for the early church happened because the disciples at first failed to understand
that anyone could become a follower of Jesus without

first becoming a Jew. This began to change when
Philip dared to take the message to the Samaritans
(8.7-25), and when Peter went to the home of
Cornelius, a captain in the Roman army (10.1-48).

Finally, Peter reported to the church in Jerusalem
(11.1-18) and a meeting was held there (15.3-35) to
discuss the question of who could become followers
of Christ. Before the meeting was over, everyone
agreed that the Spirit of God was leading them to
reach out to Gentiles as well as Jews with the good
news of Jesus.

The one who did the most for the spread of the
faith was a man named Paul, and much of the book
tells about his preaching among the Gentiles. Finally,
he took the message to Rome, the world's most
important city at that time (28.16-31). One of Luke's
main reasons for writing was to show that nothing
could keep the Christian message from spreading
everywhere:

> For two years Paul stayed in a rented house and
> welcomed everyone who came to see him. He
> bravely preached about God's kingdom and taught
> about the Lord Jesus Christ, and no one tried to
> stop him. (28.30, 31)

A QUICK LOOK AT THIS BOOK

1. Telling the Good News in Jerusalem   (1.1-8.3)
2. The Good News in Judea and Samaria   (8.4-12.25)
3. Paul's First Journey to Tell the Good News
      (13.1-14.28)
4. An Important Decision in Jerusalem   (15.1-35)
5. Paul's Second Journey to Tell the Good News
      (15.36-18.22)

1 Theophilus, I first wrote to you*a* about all that Jesus did and taught from the very first ²until he was taken up to heaven. But before he was taken up, he gave orders to the apostles he had chosen with the help of the Holy Spirit.

3 For forty days after Jesus had suffered and died, he proved in many ways that he had been raised from death. He appeared to his apostles and spoke to them about God's kingdom. ⁴While he was still with them, he said:

Don't leave Jerusalem yet. Wait here for the Father to give you the Holy Spirit, just as I told you he has promised to do. ⁵John baptized with water, but in a few days you will be baptized with the Holy Spirit.

Jesus Is Taken to Heaven

6 While the apostles were still with Jesus, they asked him, "Lord, are you now going to give Israel its own king again?"*b*

7 Jesus said to them, "You don't need to know the time of those events that only the Father controls. ⁸But the Holy Spirit will come upon you and give you power.

---

a *I first wrote to you*: The Gospel of Luke.
b *are you now going to give Israel its own king again?*:
  Or "are you now going to rule Israel as its king?"

Then you will tell everyone about me in Jerusalem, in all Judea, in Samaria, and everywhere in the world." [9]After Jesus had said this and while they were watching, he was taken up into a cloud. They could not see him, [10]but as he went up, they kept looking up into the sky.

Suddenly two men dressed in white clothes were standing there beside them. [11]They said, "Why are you men from Galilee standing here and looking up into the sky? Jesus has been taken to heaven. But he will come back in the same way that you have seen him go."

Someone To Take the Place of Judas

[12-13] The Mount of Olives was about half a mile from Jerusalem. The apostles who had gone there were Peter, John, James, Andrew, Philip, Thomas, Bartholomew, Matthew, James the son of Alphaeus, Simon, known as the Eager One,[c] and Judas the son of James.

After the apostles returned to the city, they went upstairs to the room where they had been staying.

[14] The apostles often met together and prayed with a single purpose in mind.[d] The women and Mary the mother of Jesus would meet with them, and so would his brothers. [15]One day there were about one

---

[c] known as the Eager One: The Greek text has "Cananaean," which probably comes from a Hebrew word meaning "zealous" (see Luke 6.15). "Zealot" was the name later given to the members of a Jewish group which resisted and fought against the Romans.

[d] met together and prayed with a single purpose in mind: Or "met together in a special place for prayer."

hundred twenty of the Lord's followers meeting together, and Peter stood up to speak to them. [16-17]He said:

My friends, long ago by the power of the Holy Spirit, David said something about Judas, and what he said has now happened. Judas was one of us and had worked with us, but he brought the mob to arrest Jesus. [18]Then Judas bought some land with the money he was given for doing that evil thing. He fell headfirst into the field. His body burst open, and all his insides came out. [19]When the people of Jerusalem found out about this, they called the place Akeldama, which in the local language means "Field of Blood."

20 In the book of Psalms it says,

"Leave his house empty,
    and don't let anyone live there."

It also says,

"Let someone else have his job."

21-22 So we need someone else to help us tell others that Jesus has been raised from death. He must also be one of the men who was with us from the very beginning. He must have been with us from the time the Lord Jesus was baptized by John until the day he was taken to heaven.

23 Two men were suggested: One of them was Joseph Barsabbas, known as Justus, and the other was Matthias. [24]Then they all prayed, "Lord, you know what everyone is like! Show us the one you have chosen [25]to be an apostle and to serve in place of

Judas, who got what he deserved." 26They drew names, and Matthias was chosen to join the group of the eleven apostles.

The Coming of the Holy Spirit

2 On the day of Pentecost*e* all the Lord's followers were together in one place. 2Suddenly there was a noise from heaven like the sound of a mighty wind! It filled the house where they were meeting. 3Then they saw what looked like fiery tongues moving in all directions, and a tongue came and settled on each person there. 4The Holy Spirit took control of everyone, and they began speaking whatever languages the Spirit let them speak.

5 Many religious Jews from every country in the world were living in Jerusalem. 6And when they heard this noise, a crowd gathered. But they were surprised, because they were hearing everything in their own languages. 7They were excited and amazed, and said:

Don't all these who are speaking come from Galilee? 8Then why do we hear them speaking our very own languages? 9Some of us are from Parthia, Media, and Elam. Others are from Mesopotamia, Judea, Cappadocia, Pontus, Asia, 10Phrygia, Pamphylia, Egypt, parts of Libya near Cyrene, Rome, 11Crete, and Arabia. Some of us were born Jews, and others of us have

---

e *Pentecost*: A Jewish festival that came fifty days after Passover and celebrated the wheat harvest. Jews later celebrated Pentecost as the time when they were given the Law of Moses.

chosen to be Jews. Yet we all hear them using our own languages to tell the wonderful things God has done.

12 Everyone was excited and confused. Some of them even kept asking each other, "What does all this mean?"

13 Others made fun of the Lord's followers and said, "They are drunk."

Peter Speaks to the Crowd

14 Peter stood with the eleven apostles and spoke in a loud and clear voice to the crowd:

Friends and everyone else living in Jerusalem, listen carefully to what I have to say! 15 You are wrong to think that these people are drunk. After all, it is only nine o'clock in the morning. 16 But this is what God had the prophet Joel say,

17 "When the last days come,
    I will give my Spirit to everyone.
  Your sons and daughters will prophesy.
  Your young men will see visions,
    and your old men will have dreams.
18 In those days I will give my Spirit
    to my servants, both men and women,
  and they will prophesy.

19 I will work miracles in the sky above
    and wonders on the earth below.
    There will be blood and fire
    and clouds of smoke.
20 The sun will turn dark,
    and the moon will be as red as blood

before the great and wonderful day
of the Lord appears.

21 Then the Lord will save everyone
who asks for his help."

22 Now, listen to what I have to say about Jesus from Nazareth. God proved that he sent Jesus to you by having him work miracles, wonders, and signs. All of you know this. 23God had already planned and decided that Jesus would be handed over to you. So you took him and had evil men put him to death on a cross. 24But God set him free from death and raised him to life. Death could not hold him in its power. 25What David said are really the words of Jesus,

"I always see the Lord near me,
and I will not be afraid
with him at my right side.

26 Because of this, my heart will be glad,
my words will be joyful,
and I will live in hope.

27 The Lord won't leave me in the grave.
I am his holy one,
and he won't let my body decay.

28 He has shown me the path to life,
and he makes me glad
by being near me."

29 My friends, it is right for me to speak to you about our ancestor David. He died and was buried, and his tomb is still here. 30But David was a prophet, and he knew that God had made a promise he would not break. He had told David that someone from his own family would someday be king.

31 David knew this would happen, and so he told us that Christ would be raised to life. He said that God would not leave him in the grave or let his body decay. 32All of us can tell you that God has raised Jesus to life!

33 Jesus was taken up to sit at the right side *f* of God, and he was given the Holy Spirit, just as the Father had promised. Jesus is also the one who has given the Spirit to us, and that is what you are now seeing and hearing.

34 David didn't go up to heaven. So he wasn't talking about himself when he said, "The Lord told my Lord to sit at his right side, 35until he made my Lord's enemies into a footstool for him." 36Everyone in Israel should then know for certain that God has made Jesus both Lord and Christ, even though you put him to death on a cross.

37 When the people heard this, they were very upset. They asked Peter and the other apostles, "Friends, what shall we do?"

38 Peter said, "Turn back to God! Be baptized in the name of Jesus Christ, so that your sins will be forgiven. Then you will be given the Holy Spirit. 39This promise is for you and your children. It is for everyone our Lord God will choose, no matter where they live."

40 Peter told them many other things as well. Then he said, "I beg you to save yourselves from what will happen to all these evil people." 41On that day about three thousand believed his message and were baptized. 42They spent their time learning from the

---

f *right side*: The place of honor and power.

apostles, and they were like family to each other. They also broke bread^g and prayed together.

Life among the Lord's Followers

43 Everyone was amazed by the many miracles and wonders that the apostles worked. ^{44}All the Lord's followers often met together, and they shared everything they had. ^{45}They would sell their property and possessions and give the money to whoever needed it. ^{46}Day after day they met together in the temple. They broke bread^g together in different homes and shared their food happily and freely, ^{47}while praising God. Everyone liked them, and each day the Lord added to their group others who were being saved.

Peter and John Heal a Lame Man

3 The time of prayer^h was about three o'clock in the afternoon, and Peter and John were going into the temple. ^{2}A man who had been born lame was being carried to the temple door. Each day he was placed beside this door, known as the Beautiful Gate. He sat there and begged from the people who were going in.

3 The man saw Peter and John entering the temple, and he asked them for money. ^{4}But they looked straight at him and said, "Look up at us!"

5 The man stared at them and thought he was going to get something. ^{6}But Peter said, "I don't have any silver or

---

^{g} *broke bread*: They ate together and celebrated the Lord's Supper.

^{h} *The time of prayer*: Many of the Jewish people prayed in their homes at regular times each day (see Daniel 6.11), and on special occasions they prayed in the temple.

gold! But I will give you what I do have. In the name of Jesus Christ from Nazareth, get up and start walking." ⁷Peter then took him by the right hand and helped him up.

At once the man's feet and ankles became strong, ⁸and he jumped up and started walking. He went with Peter and John into the temple, walking and jumping and praising God. ⁹Everyone saw him walking around and praising God. ¹⁰They knew that he was the beggar who had been lying beside the Beautiful Gate, and they were completely surprised. They could not imagine what had happened to the man.

Peter Speaks in the Temple

11 While the man kept holding on to Peter and John, the whole crowd ran to them in amazement at the place known as Solomon's Porch.*ⁱ* ¹²Peter saw that a crowd had gathered, and he said:

Friends, why are you surprised at what has happened? Why are you staring at us? Do you think we have some power of our own? Do you think we were able to make this man walk because we are so religious? ¹³The God that Abraham, Isaac, Jacob, and our other ancestors worshiped has brought honor to his Servant*ʲ* Jesus. He is the one you betrayed. You turned against him when he was being tried by Pilate, even though Pilate wanted to set him free.

14 You rejected Jesus, who was holy and good. You asked for a murderer to be set free,

---

ⁱ Solomon's Porch: A public place with tall columns along the east side of the temple.

ʲ Servant: Or "Son."

15and you killed the one who leads people to life. But God raised him from death, and all of us can tell you what he has done. 16You see this man, and you know him. He put his faith in the name of Jesus and was made strong. Faith in Jesus made this man completely well while everyone was watching.

17 My friends, I am sure that you and your leaders didn't know what you were doing. 18But God had his prophets tell that his Messiah would suffer, and now he has kept that promise. 19So turn to God! Give up your sins, and you will be forgiven. 20Then that time will come when the Lord will give you fresh strength. He will send you Jesus, his chosen Messiah. 21But Jesus must stay in heaven until God makes all things new, just as his holy prophets promised long ago.

22 Moses said, "The Lord your God will choose one of your own people to be a prophet, just as he chose me. Listen to everything he tells you. 23No one who disobeys that prophet will be one of God's people any longer."

24 Samuel and all the other prophets who came later also spoke about what is now happening. 25You are really the ones God told his prophets to speak to. And you were given the promise that God made to your ancestors. He said to Abraham, "All nations on earth will be blessed because of someone from your family." 26God sent his chosen Son*k* to you first, because

k Son: Or "Servant."

God wanted to bless you and make each one of you turn away from your sins.

Peter and John Are Brought in Front of the Council

4 The apostles were still talking to the people, when some priests, the captain of the temple guard, and some Sadducees arrived. ²These men were angry because the apostles were teaching the people that the dead would be raised from death, just as Jesus had been raised from death. ³It was already late in the afternoon, and they arrested Peter and John and put them in jail for the night. ⁴But a lot of people who had heard the message believed it. So by now there were about five thousand followers of the Lord.

5 The next morning the leaders, the elders, and the teachers of the Law of Moses met in Jerusalem. ⁶The high priest Annas was there, as well as Caiaphas, John, Alexander, and other members of the high priest's family. ⁷They brought in Peter and John and made them stand in the middle while they questioned them. They asked, "By what power and in whose name have you done this?"

8 Peter was filled with the Holy Spirit and told the nation's leaders and the elders:

9 You are questioning us today about a kind deed in which a crippled man was healed. ¹⁰But there is something we must tell you and everyone else in Israel. This man is standing here completely well because of the power of Jesus Christ from Nazareth. You put Jesus to death on a cross, but God raised him to life. ¹¹He is the stone that you builders thought was worthless,

and now he is the most important stone of all. ¹²Only Jesus has the power to save! His name is the only one in all the world that can save anyone.

13 The officials were amazed to see how brave Peter and John were, and they knew that these two apostles were only ordinary men and not well educated. The officials were certain that these men had been with Jesus. ¹⁴But they could not deny what had happened. The man who had been healed was standing there with the apostles.

15 The officials commanded them to leave the council room. Then the officials said to each other, ¹⁶"What can we do with these men? Everyone in Jerusalem knows about this miracle, and we cannot say it didn't happen. ¹⁷But to keep this thing from spreading, we will warn them never again to speak to anyone about the name of Jesus." ¹⁸So they called the two apostles back in and told them that they must never, for any reason, teach anything about the name of Jesus.

19 Peter and John answered, "Do you think God wants us to obey you or to obey him? ²⁰We cannot keep quiet about what we have seen and heard."

21-22 The officials could not find any reason to punish Peter and John. So they threatened them and let them go. The man who was healed by this miracle was more than forty years old, and everyone was praising God for what had happened.

Peter and Others Pray for Courage

23 As soon as Peter and John had been set free, they went back and told the others everything that the

chief priests and the leaders had said to them. 24When the rest of the Lord's followers heard this, they prayed together and said:

Master, you created heaven and earth, the sea, and everything in them. 25And by the Holy Spirit you spoke to our ancestor David. He was your servant, and you told him to say:

"Why are all the Gentiles so furious?
    Why do people make foolish plans?
26 The kings of earth prepare for war,
    and the rulers join together
        against the Lord and his Messiah."

27 Here in Jerusalem, Herod[l] and Pontius Pilate got together with the Gentiles and the people of Israel. Then they turned against your holy Servant[m] Jesus, your chosen Messiah. 28They did what you in your power and wisdom had already decided would happen.

29 Lord, listen to their threats! We are your servants. So make us brave enough to speak your message. 30Show your mighty power, as we heal people and work miracles and wonders in the name of your holy Servant[m] Jesus.

31 After they had prayed, the meeting place shook. They were all filled with the Holy Spirit and bravely spoke God's message.

Sharing Possessions

32 The group of followers all felt the same way about everything. None of them claimed that their

---

[l] *Herod*: Herod Antipas, the son of Herod the Great.
[m] *Servant*: See the note at 3.13.

possessions were their own, and they shared everything they had with each other. [33]In a powerful way the apostles told everyone that the Lord Jesus was now alive. God greatly blessed his followers,[n] [34]and no one went in need of anything. Everyone who owned land or houses would sell them and bring the money [35]to the apostles. Then they would give the money to anyone who needed it.

36-37 Joseph was one of the followers who had sold a piece of property and brought the money to the apostles. He was a Levite from Cyprus, and the apostles called him Barnabas, which means "one who encourages others."

Peter Condemns Ananias and Sapphira

5 Ananias and his wife Sapphira also sold a piece of property. [2]But they agreed to cheat and keep some of the money for themselves.

So when Ananias took the rest of the money to the apostles, [3]Peter said, "Why has Satan made you keep back some of the money from the sale of the property? Why have you lied to the Holy Spirit? [4]The property was yours before you sold it, and even after you sold it, the money was still yours. What made you do such a thing? You didn't lie to people. You lied to God!"

5 As soon as Ananias heard this, he dropped dead, and everyone who heard about it was frightened. [6]Some young men came in and wrapped up his body. Then they took it out and buried it.

---

[n] *God greatly blessed his followers*: Or "Everyone highly respected his followers."

7 Three hours later Sapphira came in, but she did not know what had happened to her husband. 8Peter asked her, "Tell me, did you sell the property for this amount?"

"Yes," she answered, "that's the amount."

9 Then Peter said, "Why did the two of you agree to test the Lord's Spirit? The men who buried Ananias are by the door, and they will carry you out!" 10At once she fell at Peter's feet and died.

When the young men came back in, they found Sapphira lying there dead. So they carried her out and buried her beside her husband. 11The church members were afraid, and so was everyone else who heard what had happened.

Peter's Unusual Power

12 The apostles worked many miracles and wonders among the people. All of the Lord's followers often met in the part of the temple known as Solomon's Porch.o 13No one outside their group dared join them, even though everyone liked them very much.

14 Many men and women started having faith in the Lord. 15Then sick people were brought out to the road and placed on cots and mats. It was hoped that Peter would walk by, and his shadow would fall on them and heal them. 16A lot of people living in the towns near Jerusalem brought those who were sick or troubled by evil spirits, and they were all healed.

Trouble for the Apostles

17 The high priest and all the other Sadducees who were with him became jealous. 18They arrested

---

o Solomon's Porch: See the note at 3.11.

the apostles and put them in the city jail. [19]But that night an angel from the Lord opened the doors of the jail and led the apostles out. The angel said, [20]"Go to the temple and tell the people everything about this new life." [21]So they went into the temple before sunrise and started teaching.

The high priest and his men called together their council, which included all of Israel's leaders. Then they ordered the apostles to be brought to them from the jail. [22]The temple police who were sent to the jail did not find the apostles. They returned and said, [23]"We found the jail locked tight and the guards standing at the doors. But when we opened the doors and went in, we didn't find anyone there." [24]The captain of the temple police and the chief priests listened to their report, but they did not know what to think about it.

[25] Just then someone came in and said, "Right now those men you put in jail are in the temple, teaching the people!" [26]The captain went with some of the temple police and brought the apostles back. But they did not use force. They were afraid that the people might start throwing stones at them.

[27] When the apostles were brought before the council, the high priest said to them, [28]"We told you plainly not to teach in the name of Jesus. But look what you have done! You have been teaching all over Jerusalem, and you are trying to blame us for his death."

[29] Peter and the apostles replied:

We don't obey people. We obey God. [30]You killed Jesus by nailing him to a cross. But the God our ancestors worshiped raised him to life [31]and made him our Leader and Savior. Then

God gave him a place at his right side,[p] so that the people of Israel would turn back to him and be forgiven. [32]We are here to tell you about all this, and so is the Holy Spirit, who is God's gift to everyone who obeys God.

33 When the council members heard this, they became so angry that they wanted to kill the apostles. [34]But one of the members was the Pharisee Gamaliel, a highly respected teacher. He ordered the apostles to be taken out of the room for a little while. [35]Then he said to the council:

Be careful what you do with these men. [36]Not long ago Theudas claimed to be someone important, and about four hundred men joined him. But he was killed. All his followers were scattered, and that was the end of that.

37 Later, when the people of our nation were being counted, Judas from Galilee showed up. A lot of people followed him, but he was killed, and all his followers were scattered.

38 So I advise you to stay away from these men. Leave them alone. If what they are planning is something of their own doing, it will fail. [39]But if God is behind it, you cannot stop it anyway, unless you want to fight against God.

The council members agreed with what he said, [40]and they called the apostles back in. They had them beaten with a whip and warned them not to speak in the name of Jesus. Then they let them go.

41 The apostles left the council and were happy, because God had considered them worthy to suffer

---

[p] *right side*: See the note at 2.33.

for the sake of Jesus. [42]Every day they spent time in the temple and in one home after another. They never stopped teaching and telling the good news that Jesus is the Messiah.

Seven Leaders for the Church

6 A lot of people were now becoming followers of the Lord. But some of the ones who spoke Greek started complaining about the ones who spoke Aramaic. They complained that the Greek-speaking widows were not given their share when the food supplies were handed out each day.

2 The twelve apostles called the whole group of followers together and said, "We should not give up preaching God's message in order to serve at tables.[q] [3]My friends, choose seven men who are respected and wise and filled with God's Spirit. We will put them in charge of these things. [4]We can spend our time praying and serving God by preaching."

5 This suggestion pleased everyone, and they began by choosing Stephen. He had great faith and was filled with the Holy Spirit. Then they chose Philip, Prochorus, Nicanor, Timon, Parmenas, and also Nicolaus, who worshiped with the Jewish people[r] in Antioch. [6]These men were brought to the apostles.

---

[q] *to serve at tables*: This may mean either that they were in charge of handing out food to the widows or that they were in charge of the money, since the Greek word "table" may also mean "bank."

[r] *worshiped with the Jewish people*: This translates the Greek word "proselyte" that means a Gentile who had accepted the Jewish religion.

Then the apostles prayed and placed their hands on the men to show that they had been chosen to do this work. 7God's message spread, and many more people in Jerusalem became followers. Even a large number of priests put their faith in the Lord.

Stephen Is Arrested

8 God gave Stephen the power to work great miracles and wonders among the people. 9But some men from Cyrene and Alexandria were members of a group who called themselves "Free Men."[s] They started arguing with Stephen. Some others from Cilicia and Asia also argued with him. 10But they were no match for Stephen, who spoke with the great wisdom that the Spirit gave him. 11So they talked some men into saying, "We heard Stephen say terrible things against Moses and God!"

12 They turned the people and their leaders and the teachers of the Law of Moses against Stephen. Then they all grabbed Stephen and dragged him in front of the council.

13 Some men agreed to tell lies about Stephen, and they said, "This man keeps on saying terrible things about this holy temple and the Law of Moses. 14We have heard him claim that Jesus from Nazareth will destroy this place and change the customs that Moses gave us." 15Then all the council members stared at Stephen. They saw that his face looked like the face of an angel.

---

s *Free Men*: A group of Jewish men who had once been slaves, but had been freed.

Stephen's Speech

7 The high priest asked Stephen, "Are they telling the truth about you?"

2 Stephen answered:

Friends, listen to me. Our glorious God appeared to our ancestor Abraham while he was still in Mesopotamia, before he had moved to Haran. ³God told him, "Leave your country and your relatives and go to a land that I will show you." ⁴Then Abraham left the land of the Chaldeans and settled in Haran.

After his father died, Abraham came and settled in this land where you now live. ⁵God didn't give him any part of it, not even a square foot. But God did promise to give it to him and his family forever, even though Abraham didn't have any children. ⁶God said that Abraham's descendants would live for a while in a foreign land. There they would be slaves and would be mistreated four hundred years. ⁷But he also said, "I will punish the nation that makes them slaves. Then later they will come and worship me in this place."

8 God said to Abraham, "Every son in each family must be circumcised to show that you have kept your agreement with me." So when Isaac was eight days old, Abraham circumcised him. Later, Isaac circumcised his son Jacob, and Jacob circumcised his twelve sons. ⁹These men were our ancestors.

Joseph was also one of our famous ancestors. His brothers were jealous of him and sold him as a slave to be taken to Egypt. But God was with him ¹⁰and rescued him from all his troubles. God made him so wise that the Egyptian king thought highly of him. The king even made Joseph governor over Egypt and put him in charge of everything he owned.

11 Everywhere in Egypt and Canaan the grain crops failed. There was terrible suffering, and our ancestors could not find enough to eat. ¹²But when Jacob heard that there was grain in Egypt, he sent our ancestors there for the first time. ¹³It was on their second trip that Joseph told his brothers who he was, and the king learned about Joseph's family.

14 Joseph sent for his father and his relatives. In all, there were seventy-five of them. ¹⁵His father went to Egypt and died there, just as our ancestors did. ¹⁶Later their bodies were taken back to Shechem and placed in the tomb that Abraham had bought from the sons of Hamor.

17 Finally, the time came for God to do what he had promised Abraham. By then the number of our people in Egypt had greatly increased. ¹⁸Another king was ruling Egypt, and he didn't know anything about Joseph. ¹⁹He tricked our ancestors and was cruel to them. He even made them leave their babies outside, so they would die.

20 During this time Moses was born. He was a very beautiful child, and for three months his parents took care of him in their home. ²¹Then when they were forced to leave him outside, the king's daughter found him and

raised him as her own son. 22Moses was given the best education in Egypt. He was a strong man and a powerful speaker.

23 When Moses was forty years old, he wanted to help the Israelites because they were his own people. 24One day he saw an Egyptian mistreating one of them. So he rescued the man and killed the Egyptian. 25Moses thought the rest of his people would realize that God was going to use him to set them free. But they didn't understand.

26 The next day Moses saw two of his own people fighting, and he tried to make them stop. He said, "Men, you are both Israelites. Why are you so cruel to each other?"

27 But the man who had started the fight pushed Moses aside and asked, "Who made you our ruler and judge? 28Are you going to kill me, just as you killed that Egyptian yesterday?" 29When Moses heard this, he ran away to live in the country of Midian. His two sons were born there.

30 Forty years later, an angel appeared to Moses from a burning bush in the desert near Mount Sinai. 31Moses was surprised by what he saw. He went closer to get a better look, and the Lord said, 32"I am the God who was worshiped by your ancestors, Abraham, Isaac, and Jacob." Moses started shaking all over and didn't dare to look at the bush.

33 The Lord said to him, "Take off your sandals. The place where you are standing is holy. 34With my own eyes I have seen the suffering

of my people in Egypt. I have heard their groans and have come down to rescue them. Now I am sending you back to Egypt."

35 This was the same Moses that the people rejected by saying, "Who made you our leader and judge?" God's angel had spoken to Moses from the bush. And God had even sent the angel to help Moses rescue the people and be their leader.

36 In Egypt and at the Red Sea[1] and in the desert, Moses rescued the people by working miracles and wonders for forty years. 37Moses is the one who told the people of Israel, "God will choose one of your people to be a prophet, just as he chose me." 38Moses brought our people together in the desert, and the angel spoke to him on Mount Sinai. There he was given these life-giving words to pass on to us. 39But our ancestors refused to obey Moses. They rejected him and wanted to go back to Egypt.

40 The people said to Aaron, "Make some gods to lead us! Moses led us out of Egypt, but we don't know what's happened to him now." 41Then they made an idol in the shape of a calf. They offered sacrifices to the idol and were pleased with what they had done.

---

[1] *Red Sea*: This name comes from the Bible of the early Christians, a translation made into Greek about 200 B.C. It refers to the body of water that the Israelites crossed and was one of the marshes or fresh water lakes near the eastern part of the Nile Delta, where they lived and where the towns of Exodus 13.17–14.9 were located.

42 God turned his back on his people and left them. Then they worshiped the stars in the sky, just as it says in the Book of the Prophets, "People of Israel, you didn't offer sacrifices and offerings to me during those forty years in the desert. ⁴³Instead, you carried the tent where the god Molech is worshiped, and you took along the star of your god Rephan. You made those idols and worshiped them. So now I will have you carried off beyond Babylonia."

44 The tent where our ancestors worshiped God was with them in the desert. This was the same tent that God had commanded Moses to make. And it was made like the model that Moses had seen. ⁴⁵Later it was given to our ancestors, and they took it with them when they went with Joshua. They carried the tent along as they took over the land from those people that God had chased out for them. Our ancestors used this tent until the time of King David. ⁴⁶He pleased God and asked him if he could build a house of worship for the people*u* of Israel. ⁴⁷And it was finally King Solomon who built a house for God.*v*

48 But the Most High God doesn't live in houses made by humans. It is just as the prophet said, when he spoke for the Lord,

49 "Heaven is my throne,
    and the earth is my footstool.
 What kind of house
    will you build for me?

---

u the people: Some manuscripts have "God."
v God: Or "the people."

In what place will I rest?
50   I have made everything."

51 You stubborn and hardheaded people! You are always fighting against the Holy Spirit, just as your ancestors did. 52Is there one prophet that your ancestors didn't mistreat? They killed the prophets who told about the coming of the One Who Obeys God. *w* And now you have turned against him and killed him. 53Angels gave you God's Law, but you still don't obey it.

Stephen Is Stoned to Death

54 When the council members heard Stephen's speech, they were angry and furious. 55But Stephen was filled with the Holy Spirit. He looked toward heaven, where he saw our glorious God and Jesus standing at his right side.*x* 56Then Stephen said, "I see heaven open and the Son of Man standing at the right side of God!"

57 The council members shouted and covered their ears. At once they all attacked Stephen 58and dragged him out of the city. Then they started throwing stones at him. The men who had brought charges against him put their coats at the feet of a young man named Saul.*y*

---

w One Who Obeys God: That is, Jesus.
x standing at his right side: The "right side" is the place of honor and power. "Standing" may mean that Jesus is welcoming Stephen (see verse 59).
y Saul: Better known as Paul, who became a famous follower of Jesus.

59 As Stephen was being stoned to death, he called out, "Lord Jesus, please welcome me!" 60He knelt down and shouted, "Lord, don't blame them for what they have done." Then he died. 1-2Saul approved the stoning of Stephen. Some faithful followers of the Lord buried Stephen and mourned very much for him.

Saul Makes Trouble for the Church

At that time the church in Jerusalem suffered terribly. All of the Lord's followers, except the apostles, were scattered everywhere in Judea and Samaria. 3Saul started making a lot of trouble for the church. He went from house to house, arresting men and women and putting them in jail.

The Good News Is Preached in Samaria

4 The Lord's followers who had been scattered went from place to place, telling the good news. 5Philip went to the city of Samaria and told the people about Christ. 6They crowded around Philip because they were eager to hear what he was saying and to see him work miracles. 7Many people with evil spirits were healed, and the spirits went out of them with a shout. A lot of crippled and lame people were also healed. 8Everyone in that city was very glad because of what was happening.

9 For some time a man named Simon had lived in the city of Samaria and had amazed the people. He practiced witchcraft and claimed to be somebody great. 10Everyone, rich and poor, crowded around him. They said, "This man is the power of God called 'The Great Power.'"

11 For a long time, Simon had used witchcraft to amaze the people, and they kept crowding around him. 12But when they believed what Philip was saying about God's kingdom and about the name of Jesus Christ, they were all baptized. 13Even Simon believed and was baptized. He stayed close to Philip, because he marveled at all the miracles and wonders.

14 The apostles in Jerusalem heard that some people in Samaria had accepted God's message, and they sent Peter and John. 15When the two apostles arrived, they prayed that the people would be given the Holy Spirit. 16Before this, the Holy Spirit had not been given to anyone in Samaria, though some of them had been baptized in the name of the Lord Jesus. 17Peter and John then placed their hands on everyone who had faith in the Lord, and they were given the Holy Spirit.

18 Simon noticed that the Spirit was given only when the apostles placed their hands on the people. So he brought money 19and said to Peter and John, "Let me have this power too! Then anyone I place my hands on will also be given the Holy Spirit."

20 Peter said to him, "You and your money will both end up in hell if you think you can buy God's gift! 21You don't have any part in this, and God sees that your heart isn't right. 22Get rid of these evil thoughts and ask God to forgive you. 23I can see that you are jealous and bound by your evil ways."

24 Simon said, "Please pray to the Lord, so that what you said won't happen to me."

25 After Peter and John had preached about the Lord, they returned to Jerusalem. On their way they told the good news in many villages of Samaria.

Philip and an Ethiopian Official

26 The Lord's angel said to Philip, "Go south[z]
along the desert road that leads from Jerusalem to
Gaza."[a] 27 So Philip left.

An important Ethiopian official happened to be
going along that road in his chariot. He was the chief
treasurer for Candace, the Queen of Ethiopia. The
official had gone to Jerusalem to worship 28 and was
now on his way home. He was sitting in his chariot,
reading the book of the prophet Isaiah.

29 The Spirit told Philip to catch up with the chariot.
30 Philip ran up close and heard the man reading aloud
from the book of Isaiah. Philip asked him, "Do you
understand what you are reading?"

31 The official answered, "How can I understand
unless someone helps me?" He then invited Philip to
come up and sit beside him.

32 The man was reading the passage that said,

"He was led like a sheep
    on its way to be killed.
He was silent as a lamb
    whose wool is being cut off,
    and he did not say a word.
    33 He was treated like a nobody
        and did not receive a fair trial.
    How can he have children,
        if his life is snatched away?"

[z] Go south: Or "About noon go."
[a] the desert road that leads from Jerusalem to Gaza:
    Or "the road that leads from Jerusalem to Gaza in the
    desert."

34 The official said to Philip, "Tell me, was the prophet talking about himself or about someone else?" 35 So Philip began at this place in the Scriptures and explained the good news about Jesus.

36-37 As they were going along the road, they came to a place where there was some water. The official said, "Look! Here is some water. Why can't I be baptized?"[b] 38 He ordered the chariot to stop. Then they both went down into the water, and Philip baptized him.

39 After they had come out of the water, the Lord's Spirit took Philip away. The official never saw him again, but he was very happy as he went on his way.

40 Philip later appeared in Azotus. He went from town to town, all the way to Caesarea, telling people about Jesus.

Saul Becomes a Follower of the Lord
(Acts 22.6-16; 26.12-18)

9 Saul kept on threatening to kill the Lord's followers. He even went to the high priest 2 and asked for letters to their leaders in Damascus. He did this because he wanted to arrest and take to Jerusalem any man or woman who had accepted the Lord's Way.[c] 3 When Saul had almost reached Damascus, a bright light from heaven suddenly flashed around him.

---

b *Why can't I be baptized*: Some manuscripts add, "Philip replied, 'You can, if you believe with all your heart.' "The official answered, 'I believe that Jesus Christ is the Son of God.'"

c *accepted the Lord's Way*: In the book of Acts, this means to become a follower of the Lord Jesus.

[4]He fell to the ground and heard a voice that said, "Saul! Saul! Why are you so cruel to me?"

5 "Who are you?" Saul asked.

"I am Jesus," the Lord answered. "I am the one you are so cruel to. [6]Now get up and go into the city, where you will be told what to do."

7 The men with Saul stood there speechless. They had heard the voice, but they had not seen anyone. [8]Saul got up from the ground, and when he opened his eyes, he could not see a thing. Someone then led him by the hand to Damascus, [9]and for three days he was blind and did not eat or drink.

10 A follower named Ananias lived in Damascus, and the Lord spoke to him in a vision. Ananias answered, "Lord, here I am."

11 The Lord said to him, "Get up and go to the house of Judas on Straight Street. When you get there, you will find a man named Saul from the city of Tarsus. Saul is praying, [12]and he has seen a vision. He saw a man named Ananias coming to him and putting his hands on him, so that he could see again."

13 Ananias replied, "Lord, a lot of people have told me about the terrible things this man has done to your followers in Jerusalem. [14]Now the chief priests have given him the power to come here and arrest anyone who worships in your name."

15 The Lord said to Ananias, "Go! I have chosen him to tell foreigners, kings, and the people of Israel about me. [16]I will show him how much he must suffer for worshiping in my name."

17 Ananias left and went into the house where Saul was staying. Ananias placed his hands on him and said, "Saul, the Lord Jesus has sent me. He is the same

one who appeared to you along the road. He wants you to be able to see and to be filled with the Holy Spirit."

18 Suddenly something like fish scales fell from Saul's eyes, and he could see. He got up and was baptized. 19Then he ate and felt much better.

Saul Preaches in Damascus

For several days Saul stayed with the Lord's followers in Damascus. 20Soon he went to the Jewish meeting places and started telling people that Jesus is the Son of God. 21Everyone who heard Saul was amazed and said, "Isn't this the man who caused so much trouble for those people in Jerusalem who worship in the name of Jesus? Didn't he come here to arrest them and take them to the chief priests?"

22 Saul preached with such power that he completely confused the Jewish people in Damascus, as he tried to show them that Jesus is the Messiah.

23 Later some of them made plans to kill Saul, 24but he found out about it. He learned that they were guarding the gates of the city day and night in order to kill him. 25Then one night his followers let him down over the city wall in a large basket.

Saul in Jerusalem

26 When Saul arrived in Jerusalem, he tried to join the followers. But they were all afraid of him, because they did not believe he was a true follower. 27Then Barnabas helped him by taking him to the apostles. He explained how Saul had seen the Lord and how the Lord had spoken to him. Barnabas also said that when Saul was in Damascus, he had spoken bravely in the name of Jesus.

28 Saul moved about freely with the followers in Jerusalem and told everyone about the Lord. 29He was always arguing with the Jews who spoke Greek, and so they tried to kill him. 30But the followers found out about this and took Saul to Caesarea. From there they sent him to the city of Tarsus.

31 The church in Judea, Galilee, and Samaria now had a time of peace and kept on worshiping the Lord. The church became stronger, as the Holy Spirit encouraged it and helped it grow.

Peter Heals Aeneas

32 While Peter was traveling from place to place, he visited the Lord's followers who lived in the town of Lydda. 33There he met a man named Aeneas, who for eight years had been sick in bed and could not move. 34Peter said to Aeneas, "Jesus Christ has healed you! Get up and make up your bed."*d* Right away he stood up.

35 Many people in the towns of Lydda and Sharon saw Aeneas and became followers of the Lord.

Peter Brings Dorcas Back to Life

36 In Joppa there was a follower named Tabitha. Her Greek name was Dorcas, which means "deer." She was always doing good things for people and had given much to the poor. 37But she got sick and died, and her body was washed and placed in an upstairs room. 38Joppa wasn't far from Lydda, and the followers heard that Peter was there. They sent two men to say to him, "Please come with us as quickly as you can!" 39Right away, Peter went with them.

---

d and make up your bed: Or "and fix something to eat."

The men took Peter upstairs into the room. Many widows were there crying. They showed him the coats and clothes that Dorcas had made while she was still alive.

40 After Peter had sent everyone out of the room, he knelt down and prayed. Then he turned to the body of Dorcas and said, "Tabitha, get up!" The woman opened her eyes, and when she saw Peter, she sat up. 41 He took her by the hand and helped her to her feet.

Peter called in the widows and the other followers and showed them that Dorcas had been raised from death. 42 Everyone in Joppa heard what had happened, and many of them put their faith in the Lord. 43 Peter stayed on for a while in Joppa in the house of a man named Simon, who made leather.

Peter and Cornelius

10 In Caesarea there was a man named Cornelius, who was the captain of a group of soldiers called "The Italian Unit." 2 Cornelius was a very religious man. He worshiped God, and so did everyone else who lived in his house. He had given a lot of money to the poor and was always praying to God.

3 One afternoon at about three o'clock,[e] Cornelius had a vision. He saw an angel from God coming to him and calling him by name. 4 Cornelius was surprised and stared at the angel. Then he asked, "What is this all about?"

The angel answered, "God has heard your prayers and knows about your gifts to the poor. 5 Now send

_____

[e] *at about three o'clock*: Probably while he was praying (see 3.1 and the note there).

some men to Joppa for a man named Simon Peter.
⁶He is visiting with Simon the leather maker, who
lives in a house near the sea." ⁷After saying this, the
angel left.

Cornelius called in two of his servants and one of
his soldiers who worshiped God. ⁸He explained
everything to them and sent them off to Joppa.

9 The next day about noon these men were coming
near Joppa. Peter went up on the roof*f* of the house to
pray ¹⁰and became very hungry. While the food was
being prepared, he fell sound asleep and had a vision.
¹¹He saw heaven open, and something came down
like a huge sheet held up by its four corners. ¹²In it
were all kinds of animals, snakes, and birds. ¹³A
voice said to him, "Peter, get up! Kill these and eat
them."

14 But Peter said, "Lord, I can't do that! I've never
eaten anything that is unclean and not fit to eat."*g*

15 The voice spoke to him again, "When God says
that something can be used for food, don't say it isn't
fit to eat."

16 This happened three times before the sheet was
suddenly taken back to heaven.

17 Peter was still wondering what all of this meant,
when the men sent by Cornelius came and stood at the
gate. They had found their way to Simon's house
¹⁸and were asking if Simon Peter was staying there.

---

f *roof*: In Palestine the houses usually had a flat roof.
Stairs on the outside led up to the roof, which was made
of beams and boards covered with packed earth.

g *unclean and not fit to eat*: The Law of Moses taught that
some foods were not fit to eat.

19 While Peter was still thinking about the vision, the Holy Spirit said to him, "Three[h] men are here looking for you. 20Hurry down and go with them. Don't worry, I sent them."

21 Peter went down and said to the men, "I am the one you are looking for. Why have you come?"

22 They answered, "Captain Cornelius sent us. He is a good man who worships God and is liked by the Jewish people. One of God's holy angels told Cornelius to send for you, so he could hear what you have to say." 23Peter invited them to spend the night.

The next morning, Peter and some of the Lord's followers in Joppa left with the men who had come from Cornelius. 24The next day they arrived in Caesarea where Cornelius was waiting for them. He had also invited his relatives and close friends.

25 When Peter arrived, Cornelius greeted him. Then he knelt at Peter's feet and started worshiping him. 26But Peter took hold of him and said, "Stand up! I am nothing more than a human."

27 As Peter entered the house, he was still talking with Cornelius. Many people were there, 28and Peter said to them, "You know that we Jews are not allowed to have anything to do with other people. But God has shown me that he doesn't think anyone is unclean or unfit. 29I agreed to come here, but I want to know why you sent for me."

30 Cornelius answered:

Four days ago at about three o'clock in the afternoon I was praying at home. Suddenly a man

---

[h] *Three*: Some manuscripts have "two;" one manuscript has "some."

in bright clothes stood in front of me. 31He said, "Cornelius, God has heard your prayers, and he knows about your gifts to the poor. 32Now send to Joppa for Simon Peter. He is visiting in the home of Simon the leather maker, who lives near the sea."

33 I sent for you right away, and you have been good enough to come. All of us are here in the presence of the Lord God, so that we can hear what he has to say.

34 Peter then said:

Now I am certain that God treats all people alike. 35God is pleased with everyone who worships him and does right, no matter what nation they come from. 36This is the same message that God gave to the people of Israel, when he sent Jesus Christ, the Lord of all, to offer peace to them.

37 You surely know what happened[i] everywhere in Judea. It all began in Galilee after John had told everyone to be baptized. 38God gave the Holy Spirit and power to Jesus from Nazareth. He was with Jesus, as he went around doing good and healing everyone who was under the power of the devil. 39We all saw what Jesus did both in Israel and in the city of Jerusalem.

Jesus was put to death on a cross. 40But three days later, God raised him to life and let him be seen. 41Not everyone saw him. He was seen only by us, who ate and drank with him after he

---

[i] *what happened*: Or "the message that went."

was raised from death. We were the ones God chose to tell others about him.

42 God told us to announce clearly to the people that Jesus is the one he has chosen to judge the living and the dead. 43Every one of the prophets has said that all who have faith in Jesus will have their sins forgiven in his name.

44 While Peter was still speaking, the Holy Spirit took control of everyone who was listening. 45Some Jewish followers of the Lord had come with Peter, and they were surprised that the Holy Spirit had been given to Gentiles. 46Now they were hearing Gentiles speaking unknown languages and praising God.

Peter said, 47"These Gentiles have been given the Holy Spirit, just as we have! I am certain that no one would dare stop us from baptizing them." 48Peter ordered them to be baptized in the name of Jesus Christ, and they asked him to stay on for a few days.

Peter Reports to the Church in Jerusalem

11 The apostles and the followers in Judea heard that Gentiles had accepted God's message. 2So when Peter came to Jerusalem, some of the Jewish followers started arguing with him. They wanted Gentile followers to be circumcised, and 3they said, "You stayed in the homes of Gentiles, and you even ate with them!"

4 Then Peter told them exactly what had happened:

5 I was in the town of Joppa and was praying when I fell sound asleep and had a vision. I saw heaven open, and something like a huge sheet held by its four corners came down to me. 6When I looked in it, I saw animals, wild beasts,

snakes, and birds. 7I heard a voice saying to me, "Peter, get up! Kill these and eat them."

8 But I said, "Lord, I can't do that! I've never taken a bite of anything that is unclean and not fit to eat."*j*

9 The voice from heaven spoke to me again, "When God says that something can be used for food, don't say it isn't fit to eat." 10This happened three times before it was all taken back into heaven.

11 Suddenly three men from Caesarea stood in front of the house where I was staying. 12The Holy Spirit told me to go with them and not to worry. Then six of the Lord's followers went with me to the home of a man 13who told us that an angel had appeared to him. The angel had ordered him to send to Joppa for someone named Simon Peter. 14Then Peter would tell him how he and everyone in his house could be saved.

15 After I started speaking, the Holy Spirit was given to them, just as the Spirit had been given to us at the beginning. 16I remembered that the Lord had said, "John baptized with water, but you will be baptized with the Holy Spirit." 17God gave those Gentiles the same gift that he gave us when we put our faith in the Lord Jesus Christ. So how could I have gone against God?

18 When they heard Peter say this, they stopped arguing and started praising God. They said, "God

---

j unclean and not fit to eat: See the note at 10.14.

has now let Gentiles turn to him, and he has given life to them!"

The Church in Antioch

19 Some of the Lord's followers had been scattered because of the terrible trouble that started when Stephen was killed. They went as far as Phoenicia, Cyprus, and Antioch, but they told the message only to the Jews.

20 Some of the followers from Cyprus and Cyrene went to Antioch and started telling Gentiles[k] the good news about the Lord Jesus. 21 The Lord's power was with them, and many people turned to the Lord and put their faith in him. 22 News of what was happening reached the church in Jerusalem. Then they sent Barnabas to Antioch.

23 When Barnabas got there and saw what God had been kind enough to do for them, he was very glad. So he begged them to remain faithful to the Lord with all their hearts. 24 Barnabas was a good man of great faith, and he was filled with the Holy Spirit. Many more people turned to the Lord.

25 Barnabas went to Tarsus to look for Saul. 26 He found Saul and brought him to Antioch, where they met with the church for a whole year and taught many of its people. There in Antioch the Lord's followers were first called Christians.

---

k Gentiles: This translates a Greek word that may mean "people who speak Greek" or "people who live as Greeks do." Here the word seems to mean "people who are not Jews." Some manuscripts have "Greeks," which also seems to mean "people who are not Jews."

27 During this time some prophets from Jerusalem came to Antioch. 28One of them was Agabus. Then with the help of the Spirit, he told that there would be a terrible famine everywhere in the world. And it happened when Claudius was Emperor.[l] 29The followers in Antioch decided to send whatever help they could to the followers in Judea. 30So they had Barnabas and Saul take their gifts to the church leaders in Jerusalem.

Herod Causes Trouble for the Church

12 At that time King Herod[m] caused terrible suffering for some members of the church. 2He ordered soldiers to cut off the head of James, the brother of John. 3When Herod saw that this pleased the Jewish people, he had Peter arrested during the Festival of Thin Bread. 4He put Peter in jail and ordered four squads of soldiers to guard him. Herod planned to put him on trial in public after the festival.

5 While Peter was being kept in jail, the church never stopped praying to God for him.

Peter Is Rescued

6 The night before Peter was to be put on trial, he was asleep and bound by two chains. A soldier was guarding him on each side, and two other soldiers were guarding the entrance to the jail. 7Suddenly an angel from the Lord appeared, and light flashed around in the cell. The angel poked Peter in the side and woke him up. Then he said, "Quick! Get up!"

---

[l] *when Claudius was Emperor*: A.D. 41-54.

[m] *Herod*: Herod Agrippa I, the grandson of Herod the Great.

The chains fell off his hands, [8]and the angel said, "Get dressed and put on your sandals." Peter did what he was told. Then the angel said, "Now put on your coat and follow me." [9]Peter left with the angel, but he thought everything was only a dream. [10]They went past the two groups of soldiers, and when they came to the iron gate to the city, it opened by itself. They went out and were going along the street, when all at once the angel disappeared.

[11] Peter now realized what had happened, and he said, "I am certain that the Lord sent his angel to rescue me from Herod and from everything the Jewish leaders planned to do to me." [12]Then Peter went to the house of Mary the mother of John whose other name was Mark. Many of the Lord's followers had come together there and were praying.

[13] Peter knocked on the gate, and a servant named Rhoda came to answer. [14]When she heard Peter's voice, she was too excited to open the gate. She ran back into the house and said that Peter was standing there.

[15] "You are crazy!" everyone told her. But she kept saying that it was Peter. Then they said, "It must be his angel."[n] [16]But Peter kept on knocking, until finally they opened the gate. They saw him and were completely amazed.

[17] Peter motioned for them to keep quiet. Then he told how the Lord had led him out of jail. He also said, "Tell James[o] and the others what has happened." After that, he left and went somewhere else.

---

[n] *his angel*: Probably meaning "his guardian angel."

[o] *James*: The brother of the Lord.

18 The next morning the soldiers who had been on guard were terribly worried and wondered what had happened to Peter. 19 Herod ordered his own soldiers to search for him, but they could not find him. Then he questioned the guards and had them put to death. After this, Herod left Judea to stay in Caesarea for a while.

Herod Dies

20 Herod and the people of Tyre and Sidon were very angry with each other. But their country got its food supply from the region that he ruled. So a group of them went to see Blastus, who was one of Herod's high officials. They convinced Blastus that they wanted to make peace between their cities and Herod, 21 and a day was set for them to meet with him.

Herod came dressed in his royal robes. He sat down on his throne and made a speech. 22 The people shouted, "You speak more like a god than a man!" 23 At once an angel from the Lord struck him down because he took the honor that belonged to God. Later, Herod was eaten by worms and died.

24 God's message kept spreading. 25 And after Barnabas and Saul had done the work they were sent to do, they went back to Jerusalem[p] with John, whose other name was Mark.

Barnabas and Saul Are Chosen and Sent

13 The church at Antioch had several prophets and teachers. They were Barnabas, Simeon,

---

[p] went back to Jerusalem: Some manuscripts have "left Jerusalem," and others have "went to Antioch."

also called Niger, Lucius from Cyrene, Manaen, who was Herod's[q] close friend, and Saul. [2]While they were worshiping the Lord and going without eating,[r] the Holy Spirit told them, "Appoint Barnabas and Saul to do the work for which I have chosen them." [3]Everyone prayed and went without eating for a while longer. Next, they placed their hands on Barnabas and Saul to show that they had been appointed to do this work. Then everyone sent them on their way.

Barnabas and Saul in Cyprus

4 After Barnabas and Saul had been sent by the Holy Spirit, they went to Seleucia. From there they sailed to the island of Cyprus. [5]They arrived at Salamis and began to preach God's message in the Jewish meeting places. They also had John[s] as a helper.

6 Barnabas and Saul went all the way to the city of Paphos on the other end of the island, where they met a Jewish man named Bar-Jesus. He practiced witchcraft and was a false prophet. [7]He also worked for Sergius Paulus, who was very smart and was the governor of the island. Sergius Paulus wanted to hear God's message, and he sent for Barnabas and Saul. [8]But Bar-Jesus, whose other name was Elymas, was against them. He even tried to keep the governor from having faith in the Lord.

---

[q] *Herod's*: Herod Antipas, the son of Herod the Great.

[r] *going without eating*: The Jews often went without eating as a way of showing how much they loved God. This is also called "fasting."

[s] *John*: Whose other name was Mark (see 12.12,25).

9 Then Saul, better known as Paul, was filled with the Holy Spirit. He looked straight at Elymas [10]and said, "You son of the devil! You are a liar, a crook, and an enemy of everything that is right. When will you stop speaking against the true ways of the Lord? [11]The Lord is going to punish you by making you completely blind for a while."

Suddenly the man's eyes were covered by a dark mist, and he went around trying to get someone to lead him by the hand. [12]When the governor saw what had happened, he was amazed at this teaching about the Lord. So he put his faith in the Lord.

Paul and Barnabas in Antioch of Pisidia

13 Paul and the others left Paphos and sailed to Perga in Pamphylia. But John[t] left them and went back to Jerusalem. [14]The rest of them went on from Perga to Antioch in Pisidia. Then on the Sabbath they went to the Jewish meeting place and sat down.

15 After the reading of the Law and the Prophets,[u] the leaders sent someone over to tell Paul and Barnabas, "Friends, if you have anything to say that will help the people, please say it."

16 Paul got up. He motioned with his hand and said:

People of Israel, and everyone else who worships God, listen! [17]The God of Israel chose our ancestors, and he let our people prosper while they were living in Egypt. Then with his mighty

---

[t] *John:* Whose other name was Mark (see 12.12,25).
[u] *the Law and the Prophets:* The Jewish Scriptures, that is, the Old Testament.

power he led them out, 18and for about forty years he took care of[v] them in the desert. 19He destroyed seven nations in the land of Canaan and gave their land to our people. 20All this happened in about 450 years.

Then God gave our people judges until the time of the prophet Samuel, 21but the people demanded a king. So for forty years God gave them King Saul, the son of Kish from the tribe of Benjamin. 22Later, God removed Saul and let David rule in his place. God said about him, "David the son of Jesse is the kind of person who pleases me most! He does everything I want him to do."

23 God promised that someone from David's family would come to save the people of Israel, and that one is Jesus. 24But before Jesus came, John was telling everyone in Israel to turn back to God and be baptized. 25Then, when John's work was almost done, he said, "Who do you people think I am? Do you think I am the Promised One? He will come later, and I am not good enough to untie his sandals."

26 Now listen, you descendants of Abraham! Pay attention, all of you Gentiles who are here to worship God! Listen to this message about how to be saved, because it is for everyone. 27The people of Jerusalem and their leaders didn't realize who Jesus was. And they didn't understand the words of the prophets that they read each Sabbath. So they condemned Jesus just as the prophets had said.

---

[v] took care of: Some manuscripts have "put up with."

28-29 They did exactly what the Scriptures said they would. Even though they couldn't find any reason to put Jesus to death, they still asked Pilate to have him killed.

After Jesus had been put to death, he was taken down from the cross [w] and placed in a tomb. 30 But God raised him from death! 31 Then for many days Jesus appeared to his followers who had gone with him from Galilee to Jerusalem. Now they are telling our people about him.

32 God made a promise to our ancestors. And we are here to tell you the good news 33 that he has kept this promise to us. It is just as the second Psalm says about Jesus,

"You are my son because today
I have become your Father."

34 God raised Jesus from death and will never let his body decay. It is just as God said,

"I will make to you
the same holy promise
that I made to David."

35 And in another psalm it says, "God will never let the body of his Holy One decay."

36 When David was alive, he obeyed God. Then after he died, he was buried in the family grave, and his body decayed. 37 But God raised Jesus from death, and his body did not decay.

38 My friends, the message is that Jesus can forgive your sins! The Law of Moses could not

---

[w] *cross*: This translates a Greek word that means "wood," "pole," or "tree."

set you free from all your sins. ³⁹But everyone who has faith in Jesus is set free. ⁴⁰Make sure that what the prophets have said doesn't happen to you. They said,

⁴¹ "Look, you people
who make fun of God!
Be amazed and disappear.
I will do something today
that you won't believe,
even if someone tells you about it!"

42 As Paul and Barnabas were leaving the meeting, the people begged them to say more about these same things on the next Sabbath. ⁴³After the service, many Jews and a lot of Gentiles who worshiped God went with them. Paul and Barnabas begged them all to remain faithful to God, who had been so kind to them.

44 The next Sabbath almost everyone in town came to hear the message about the Lord.^x ⁴⁵When the Jewish people saw the crowds, they were very jealous. They insulted Paul and spoke against everything he said.

46 But Paul and Barnabas bravely said:

We had to tell God's message to you before we told it to anyone else. But you rejected the message! This proves that you don't deserve eternal life. Now we are going to the Gentiles. ⁴⁷The Lord has given us this command,

"I have placed you here
as a light for the Gentiles.
You are to take the saving power of God
to people everywhere on earth."

---

^x *the Lord*: Some manuscripts have "God."

48 This message made the Gentiles glad, and they praised what they had heard about the Lord.[y] Everyone who had been chosen for eternal life then put their faith in the Lord.

49 The message about the Lord spread all over that region. [50]But the Jewish leaders went to some of the important men in the town and to some respected women who were religious. They turned them against Paul and Barnabas and started making trouble for them. They even chased them out of that part of the country.

51 Paul and Barnabas shook the dust from that place off their feet[z] and went on to the city of Iconium.

52 But the Lord's followers in Antioch were very happy and were filled with the Holy Spirit.

Paul and Barnabas in Iconium

14 Paul and Barnabas spoke in the Jewish meeting place in Iconium, just as they had done at Antioch, and many Jews and Gentiles[a] put their faith in the Lord. [2]But the Jews who did not have faith in him made the other Gentiles angry and turned them against the Lord's followers.

3 Paul and Barnabas stayed there for a while, having faith in the Lord and bravely speaking his message.

---

[y] *the Lord*: Some manuscripts have "God."

[z] *shook the dust from that place off their feet*: This was a way of showing rejection.

[a] *Gentiles*: The Greek text has "Greeks," which probably means people who were not Jews. But it may mean Gentiles who worshiped with the Jews.

The Lord gave them the power to work miracles and wonders, and he showed that their message about his great kindness was true.

4 The people of Iconium did not know what to think. Some of them believed the Jewish group, and others believed the apostles. ⁵Finally, some Gentiles and Jews, together with their leaders, decided to make trouble for Paul and Barnabas and to stone them to death.

6-7 But when the two apostles found out what was happening, they escaped to the region of Lycaonia. They preached the good news there in the towns of Lystra and Derbe and in the nearby countryside.

Paul and Barnabas in Lystra

8 In Lystra there was a man who had been born with crippled feet and had never been able to walk. ⁹The man was listening to Paul speak, when Paul saw that he had faith in Jesus and could be healed. So he looked straight at the man ¹⁰and shouted, "Stand up!" The man jumped up and started walking around.

11 When the crowd saw what Paul had done, they yelled out in the language of Lycaonia, "The gods have turned into humans and have come down to us!" ¹²The people then gave Barnabas the name Zeus, and they gave Paul the name Hermes,ᵇ because he did the talking.

13 The temple of Zeus was near the entrance to the city. Its priest and the crowds wanted to offer a sacrifice to Barnabas and Paul. So the priest brought some bulls and flowers to the city gates. ¹⁴When the two apostles

---

ᵇ *Hermes*: The Greeks thought of Hermes as the messenger of the other gods, especially of Zeus, their chief god.

found out about this, they tore their clothes in horror and ran to the crowd, shouting:

15 Why are you doing this? We are humans just like you. Please give up all this foolishness. Turn to the living God, who made the sky, the earth, the sea, and everything in them. ¹⁶In times past, God let each nation go its own way. ¹⁷But he showed that he was there by the good things he did. God sends rain from heaven and makes your crops grow. He gives food to you and makes your hearts glad.

18 Even after Paul and Barnabas had said all this, they could hardly keep the people from offering a sacrifice to them.

19 Some Jewish leaders from Antioch and Iconium came and turned the crowds against Paul. They hit him with stones and dragged him out of the city, thinking he was dead. ²⁰But when the Lord's followers gathered around Paul, he stood up and went back into the city. The next day he and Barnabas went to Derbe.

Paul and Barnabas Return to Antioch in Syria

21 Paul and Barnabas preached the good news in Derbe and won some people to the Lord. Then they went back to Lystra, Iconium, and Antioch in Pisidia. ²²They encouraged the followers and begged them to remain faithful. They told them, "We have to suffer a lot before we can get into God's kingdom." ²³Paul and Barnabas chose some leaders for each of the churches. Then they went without eating ᶜ and prayed that the Lord would take good care of these leaders.

ᶜ *went without eating*: See the note at 13.2.

I will build it from its ruins
        and set it up again.
17 Then other nations will turn to me
        and be my chosen ones.
    I, the Lord, say this.
18   I promised it long ago."

19 And so, my friends, I don't think we should place burdens on the Gentiles who are turning to God. 20 We should simply write and tell them not to eat anything that has been offered to idols. They should be told not to eat the meat of any animal that has been strangled or that still has blood in it. They must also not commit any terrible sexual sins.[g]

21 We must remember that the Law of Moses has been preached in city after city for many years, and every Sabbath it is read at our meeting.

A Letter to Gentiles Who Had Faith in the Lord

22 The apostles, the leaders, and all the church members decided to send some men to Antioch along with Paul and Barnabas. They chose Silas and Judas Barsabbas,[h] who were two leaders of the Lord's followers. 23 They wrote a letter that said:

---

[g] not commit any terrible sexual sins: This probably refers to the laws about the wrong kind of marriages that are forbidden in Leviticus 18.6-18 or to some serious sexual sin.

[h] Judas Barsabbas: He may have been a brother of Joseph Barsabbas (see 1.23), but the name "Barsabbas" was often used by the Jewish people.

We apostles and leaders send friendly greetings to all of you Gentiles who are followers of the Lord in Antioch, Syria, and Cilicia.

24 We have heard that some people from here have terribly upset you by what they said. But we did not send them! 25So we met together and decided to choose some men and to send them to you along with our good friends Barnabas and Paul. 26These men have risked their lives for our Lord Jesus Christ. 27We are also sending Judas and Silas, who will tell you in person the same things that we are writing.

28 The Holy Spirit has shown us that we should not place any extra burden on you. 29But you should not eat anything offered to idols. You should not eat any meat that still has the blood in it or any meat of any animal that has been strangled. You must also not commit any terrible sexual sins. If you follow these instructions, you will do well.

We send our best wishes.

30 The four men left Jerusalem and went to Antioch. Then they called the church members together and gave them the letter. 31When the letter was read, everyone was pleased and greatly encouraged. 32Judas and Silas were prophets, and they spoke a long time, encouraging and helping the Lord's followers.

33 The men from Jerusalem stayed on in Antioch for a while. And when they left to return to the ones who had sent them, the followers wished them well. 34-35But Paul and Barnabas stayed on in Antioch,

where they and many others taught and preached about the Lord.[i]

Paul and Barnabas Go Their Separate Ways

36 Sometime later Paul said to Barnabas, "Let's go back and visit the Lord's followers in the cities where we preached his message. Then we will know how they are doing." [37]Barnabas wanted to take along John, whose other name was Mark. [38]But Paul did not want to, because Mark had left them in Pamphylia and had stopped working with them.

39 Paul and Barnabas argued, then each of them went his own way. Barnabas took Mark and sailed to Cyprus, [40]but Paul took Silas and left after the followers had placed them in God's care. [41]They traveled through Syria and Cilicia, encouraging the churches.

Timothy Works with Paul and Silas

16 Paul and Silas went back to Derbe and Lystra, where there was a follower named Timothy. His mother was also a follower. She was Jewish, and his father was Greek. [2]The Lord's followers in Lystra and Iconium said good things about Timothy, [3]and Paul wanted him to go with them. But Paul first had him circumcised, because all the Jewish people around there knew that Timothy's father was Greek.[j]

---

[i] *Verse 34, which says that Silas decided to stay on in Antioch, is not in some manuscripts.*

[j] *had him circumcised…Timothy's father was Greek:* Timothy would not have been acceptable to the Jews unless he had been circumcised, and Greeks did not circumcise their sons.

4 As Paul and the others went from city to city, they told the followers what the apostles and leaders in Jerusalem had decided, and they urged them to follow these instructions. [5]The churches became stronger in their faith, and each day more people put their faith in the Lord.

Paul's Vision in Troas

6 Paul and his friends went through Phrygia and Galatia, but the Holy Spirit would not let them preach in Asia. [7]After they arrived in Mysia, they tried to go into Bithynia, but the Spirit of Jesus would not let them. [8]So they went on through[k] Mysia until they came to Troas.

9 During the night, Paul had a vision of someone from Macedonia who was standing there and begging him, "Come over to Macedonia and help us!" [10]After Paul had seen the vision, we began looking for a way to go to Macedonia. We were sure that God had called us to preach the good news there.

Lydia Becomes a Follower of the Lord

11 We sailed straight from Troas to Samothrace, and the next day we arrived in Neapolis. [12]From there we went to Philippi, which is a Roman colony in the first district of Macedonia.[l]

We spent several days in Philippi. [13]Then on the Sabbath we went outside the city gate to a place by the river, where we thought there would be a Jewish

---

[k] went on through: Or "passed by."
[l] in the first district of Macedonia: Some manuscripts have "and the leading city of Macedonia."

meeting place for prayer. We sat down and talked with the women who came. 14One of them was Lydia, who was from the city of Thyatira and sold expensive purple cloth. She was a worshiper of the Lord God, and he made her willing to accept what Paul was saying. 15Then after she and her family were baptized, she kept on begging us, "If you think I really do have faith in the Lord, come stay in my home." Finally, we accepted her invitation.

Paul and Silas Are Put in Jail

16 One day on our way to the place of prayer, we were met by a slave girl. She had a spirit in her that gave her the power to tell the future. By doing this she made a lot of money for her owners. 17The girl followed Paul and the rest of us and kept yelling, "These men are servants of the Most High God! They are telling you how to be saved."

18 This went on for several days. Finally, Paul got so upset that he turned and said to the spirit, "In the name of Jesus Christ, I order you to leave this girl alone!" At once the evil spirit left her.

19 When the girl's owners realized that they had lost all chances for making more money, they grabbed Paul and Silas and dragged them into court. 20They told the officials, "These Jews are upsetting our city! 21They are telling us to do things we Romans are not allowed to do."

22 The crowd joined in the attack on Paul and Silas. Then the officials tore the clothes off the two men and ordered them to be beaten with a whip. 23After they had been badly beaten, they were put in jail, and the jailer was told to guard them carefully.

²⁴The jailer did as he was told. He put them deep inside the jail and chained their feet to heavy blocks of wood.

25 About midnight Paul and Silas were praying and singing praises to God, while the other prisoners listened. ²⁶Suddenly a strong earthquake shook the jail to its foundations. The doors opened, and the chains fell from all the prisoners.

27 When the jailer woke up and saw that the doors were open, he thought that the prisoners had escaped. He pulled out his sword and was about to kill himself. ²⁸But Paul shouted, "Don't harm yourself! No one has escaped."

29 The jailer asked for a torch and went into the jail. He was shaking all over as he knelt down in front of Paul and Silas. ³⁰After he had led them out of the jail, he asked, "What must I do to be saved?"

31 They replied, "Have faith in the Lord Jesus and you will be saved! This is also true for everyone who lives in your home."

32 Then Paul and Silas told him and everyone else in his house about the Lord. ³³While it was still night, the jailer took them to a place where he could wash their cuts and bruises. Then he and everyone in his home were baptized. ³⁴They were very glad that they had put their faith in God. After this, the jailer took Paul and Silas to his home and gave them something to eat.

35 The next morning the officials sent some police with orders for the jailer to let Paul and Silas go. ³⁶The jailer told Paul, "The officials have ordered me to set you free. Now you can leave in peace."

37 But Paul told the police, "We are Roman citizens,^{m} and the Roman officials had us beaten in public without giving us a trial. They threw us into jail. Now do they think they can secretly send us away? No, they cannot! They will have to come here themselves and let us out."

38 When the police told the officials that Paul and Silas were Roman citizens, the officials were afraid. 39 So they came and apologized. They led them out of the jail and asked them to please leave town. 40 But Paul and Silas went straight to the home of Lydia, where they saw the Lord's followers and encouraged them. Then they left.

Trouble in Thessalonica

17 After Paul and his friends had traveled through Amphipolis and Apollonia, they went on to Thessalonica. A Jewish meeting place was in that city. 2 So as usual, Paul went there to worship, and on three Sabbaths he spoke to the people. He used the Scriptures 3 to show them that the Messiah had to suffer, but that he would rise from death. Paul also told them that Jesus is the Messiah he was preaching about. 4 Some of them believed what Paul had said, and they became followers with Paul and Silas. Some Gentiles^{n} and many important women also believed the message.

5 The Jewish leaders were jealous and got some worthless bums who hung around the marketplace to

---

^{m} *Roman citizens:* Only a small number of the people living in the Roman Empire were citizens, and they had special rights and privileges.

^{n} *Gentiles:* See the note at 14.1.

start a riot in the city. They wanted to drag Paul and Silas out to the mob, and so they went straight to Jason's home. 6But when they did not find them there, they dragged out Jason and some of the Lord's followers. They took them to the city authorities and shouted, "Paul and Silas have been upsetting things everywhere. Now they have come here, 7and Jason has welcomed them into his home. All of them break the laws of the Roman Emperor by claiming that someone named Jesus is king."

8 The officials and the people were upset when they heard this. 9So they made Jason and the other followers pay bail before letting them go.

People in Berea Welcome the Message

10 That same night the Lord's followers sent Paul and Silas on to Berea, and after they arrived, they went to the Jewish meeting place. 11The people in Berea were much nicer than those in Thessalonica, and they gladly accepted the message. Day after day they studied the Scriptures to see if these things were true. 12Many of them put their faith in the Lord, including some important Greek women and several men.

13 When the Jewish leaders in Thessalonica heard that Paul had been preaching God's message in Berea, they went there and caused trouble by turning the crowds against Paul.

14 Right away the followers sent Paul down to the coast, but Silas and Timothy stayed in Berea. 15Some men went with Paul as far as Athens, and then returned with instructions for Silas and Timothy to join him as soon as possible.

Paul in Athens

16 While Paul was waiting in Athens, he was upset to see all the idols in the city. 17He went to the Jewish meeting place to speak to the Jews and to anyone who worshiped with them. Day after day he also spoke to everyone he met in the market. 18Some of them were Epicureans*o* and some were Stoics,*p* and they started arguing with him.

People were asking, "What is this know-it-all trying to say?"

Some even said, "Paul must be preaching about foreign gods! That's what he means when he talks about Jesus and about people rising from death."*q*

19 They brought Paul before a council called the Areopagus, and said, "Tell us what your new teaching is all about. 20We have heard you say some strange things, and we want to know what you mean."

21 More than anything else the people of Athens and the foreigners living there loved to hear and to talk about anything new. 22So Paul stood up in front of the council and said:

People of Athens, I see that you are very religious. 23As I was going through your city

---

o Epicureans: People who followed the teaching of a man named Epicurus, who taught that happiness should be the main goal in life.

p Stoics: Followers of a man named Zeno, who taught that people should learn self-control and be guided by their consciences.

q people rising from death: Or "a goddess named 'Rising from Death.'"

and looking at the things you worship, I found an altar with the words, "To an Unknown God." You worship this God, but you don't really know him. So I want to tell you about him. 24This God made the world and everything in it. He is Lord of heaven and earth, and he doesn't live in temples built by human hands. 25He doesn't need help from anyone. He gives life, breath, and everything else to all people. 26From one person God made all nations who live on earth, and he decided when and where every nation would be.

27 God has done all this, so that we will look for him and reach out and find him. He isn't far from any of us, 28and he gives us the power to live, to move, and to be who we are. "We are his children," just as some of your poets have said.

29 Since we are God's children, we must not think that he is like an idol made out of gold or silver or stone. He isn't like anything that humans have thought up and made. 30In the past, God forgave all this because people did not know what they were doing. But now he says that everyone everywhere must turn to him. 31He has set a day when he will judge the world's people with fairness. And he has chosen the man Jesus to do the judging for him. God has given proof of this to all of us by raising Jesus from death.

32 As soon as the people heard Paul say that a man had been raised from death, some of them started laughing. Others said, "We will hear you talk about

this some other time." [33]When Paul left the council meeting, [34]some of the men put their faith in the Lord and went with Paul. One of them was a council member named Dionysius. A woman named Damaris and several others also put their faith in the Lord.

Paul in Corinth

18 Paul left Athens and went to Corinth, [2]where he met Aquila, a Jewish man from Pontus. Not long before this, Aquila had come from Italy with his wife Priscilla, because Emperor Claudius had ordered the Jewish people to leave Rome.[r] Paul went to see Aquila and Priscilla [3]and found out that they were tent makers. Paul was a tent maker too. So he stayed with them, and they worked together.

[4]Every Sabbath, Paul went to the Jewish meeting place. He spoke to Jews and Gentiles[s] and tried to win them over. [5]But after Silas and Timothy came from Macedonia, he spent all his time preaching to the Jews about Jesus the Messiah. [6]Finally, they turned against him and insulted him. So he shook the dust from his clothes[t] and told them, "Whatever happens to you will be your own fault! I am not to

---

[r] *Emperor Claudius had ordered the Jewish people to leave Rome*: Probably A.D. 49, though it may have been A.D. 41.

[s] *Gentiles*: Here the word is "Greeks." But see the note at 14.1.

[t] *shook the dust from his clothes*: This means the same as shaking dust from the feet (see the note at 13.51).

blame. From now on I am going to preach to the Gentiles."

7 Paul then moved into the house of a man named Titius Justus, who worshiped God and lived next door to the meeting place. 8Crispus was the leader of the meeting place. He and everyone in his family put their faith in the Lord. Many others in Corinth also heard the message, and all the people who had faith in the Lord were baptized.

9 One night, Paul had a vision, and in it the Lord said, "Don't be afraid to keep on preaching. Don't stop! 10I am with you, and you won't be harmed. Many people in this city belong to me." 11Paul stayed on in Corinth for a year and a half, teaching God's message to the people.

12 While Gallio was governor of Achaia, some of the Jewish leaders got together and grabbed Paul. They brought him into court 13and said, "This man is trying to make our people worship God in a way that is against our Law!"

14 Even before Paul could speak, Gallio said, "If you were charging this man with a crime or some other wrong, I would have to listen to you. 15But since this concerns only words, names, and your own law, you will have to take care of it. I refuse to judge such matters." 16Then he sent them out of the court. 17The crowd grabbed Sosthenes, the Jewish leader, and beat him up in front of the court. But none of this mattered to Gallio.

Paul Returns to Antioch in Syria

18 After Paul had stayed for a while with the Lord's followers in Corinth, he told them good-by and

sailed on to Syria with Aquila and Priscilla. But before he left, he had his head shaved *u* at Cenchreae because he had made a promise to God.

19 The three of them arrived in Ephesus, where Paul left Priscilla and Aquila. He then went into the Jewish meeting place to talk with the people there. 20 They asked him to stay longer, but he refused. 21 He told them good-by and said, "If God lets me, I will come back."

22 Paul sailed to Caesarea, where he greeted the church. Then he went on to Antioch. 23 After staying there for a while, he left and visited several places in Galatia and Phrygia. He helped the followers there to become stronger in their faith.

Apollos in Ephesus

24 A Jewish man named Apollos came to Ephesus. Apollos had been born in the city of Alexandria. He was a very good speaker and knew a lot about the Scriptures. 25 He also knew much about the Lord's Way, *v* and he spoke about it with great excitement. What he taught about Jesus was right, but all he knew was John's message about baptism.

26 Apollos started speaking bravely in the Jewish meeting place. But when Priscilla and Aquila heard him, they took him to their home and helped him understand God's Way even better.

---

u *he had his head shaved*: Paul had promised to be a "Nazirite" for a while. This meant that for the time of the promise, he could not cut his hair or drink wine. When the time was over, he would have to cut his hair and offer a sacrifice to God.

v *the Lord's Way*: See the note at 9.2.

27 Apollos decided to travel through Achaia. So the Lord's followers wrote letters, encouraging the followers there to welcome him. After Apollos arrived in Achaia, he was a great help to everyone who had put their faith in the Lord Jesus because of God's kindness. 28 He got into fierce arguments with the Jewish people, and in public he used the Scriptures to prove that Jesus is the Messiah.

Paul in Ephesus

19 While Apollos was in Corinth, Paul traveled across the hill country to Ephesus, where he met some of the Lord's followers. 2 He asked them, "When you put your faith in Jesus, were you given the Holy Spirit?"

"No!" they answered. "We have never even heard of the Holy Spirit."

3 "Then why were you baptized?" Paul asked.

They answered, "Because of what John taught." w

4 Paul replied, "John baptized people so that they would turn to God. But he also told them that someone else was coming, and that they should put their faith in him. Jesus is the one that John was talking about." 5 After the people heard Paul say this, they were baptized in the name of the Lord Jesus. 6 Then Paul placed his hands on them. The Holy Spirit was given to them, and they spoke unknown languages and prophesied. 7 There were about twelve men in this group.

---

w *Then why were you baptized? ... Because of what John taught:* Or "In whose name were you baptized? ... We were baptized in John's name."

8 For three months Paul went to the Jewish meeting place and talked bravely with the people about God's kingdom. He tried to win them over, 9but some of them were stubborn and refused to believe. In front of everyone they said terrible things about God's Way. Paul left and took the followers with him to the lecture hall of Tyrannus. He spoke there every day 10for two years, until every Jew and Gentile x in Asia had heard the Lord's message.

The Sons of Sceva

11 God gave Paul the power to work great miracles. 12People even took handkerchiefs and aprons that had touched Paul's body, and they carried them to everyone who was sick. All of the sick people were healed, and the evil spirits went out.

13 Some Jewish men started going around trying to force out evil spirits by using the name of the Lord Jesus. They said to the spirits, "Come out in the name of that same Jesus that Paul preaches about!"

14 Seven sons of a high priest named Sceva were doing this, 15when an evil spirit said to them, "I know Jesus! And I have heard about Paul. But who are you?" 16Then the man with the evil spirit jumped on them and beat them up. They ran out of the house, naked and bruised.

17 When the Jews and Gentiles x in Ephesus heard about this, they were so frightened that they praised the name of the Lord Jesus. 18Many who were followers now started telling everyone about the evil things they had been doing. 19Some who had

x Gentile(s): The text has "Greek(s)" (see the note at 14.1).

been practicing witchcraft even brought their books and burned them in public. These books were worth about fifty thousand silver coins. 20So the Lord's message spread and became even more powerful.

The Riot in Ephesus

21 After all of this had happened, Paul decided[y] to visit Macedonia and Achaia on his way to Jerusalem. Paul had said, "From there I will go on to Rome." 22So he sent his two helpers, Timothy and Erastus, to Macedonia. But he stayed on in Asia for a while.

23 At that time there was serious trouble because of the Lord's Way.[z] 24A silversmith named Demetrius had a business that made silver models of the temple of the goddess Artemis. Those who worked for him earned a lot of money. 25Demetrius brought together everyone who was in the same business and said:

Friends, you know that we make a good living at this. 26But you have surely seen and heard how this man Paul is upsetting a lot of people, not only in Ephesus, but almost everywhere in Asia. He claims that the gods we humans make are not really gods at all. 27Everyone will start saying terrible things about our business. They will stop respecting the temple of the goddess Artemis, who is worshiped in Asia and all over the world. Our great goddess will be forgotten!

28 When the workers heard this, they got angry and started shouting, "Great is Artemis, the goddess of the Ephesians!" 29Soon the whole city was in a riot,

---

[y] Paul decided: Or "Paul was led by the Holy Spirit."
[z] the Lord's Way: See the note at 9.2.

and some men grabbed Gaius and Aristarchus, who had come from Macedonia with Paul. Then everyone in the crowd rushed to the place where the town meetings were held.

30 Paul wanted to go out and speak to the people, but the Lord's followers would not let him. 31 A few of the local officials were friendly to Paul, and they sent someone to warn him not to go.

32 Some of the people in the meeting were shouting one thing, and others were shouting something else. Everyone was completely confused, and most of them did not even know why they were there.

33 Several of the Jewish leaders pushed a man named Alexander to the front of the crowd and started telling him what to say. He motioned with his hand and tried to explain what was going on. 34 But when the crowd saw that he was Jewish, they all shouted for two hours, "Great is Artemis, the goddess of the Ephesians!"

35 Finally, a town official made the crowd be quiet. Then he said:

People of Ephesus, who in the world doesn't know that our city is the center for worshiping the great goddess Artemis? Who doesn't know that her image which fell from heaven is right here? 36 No one can deny this, and so you should calm down and not do anything foolish. 37 You have brought men in here who have not robbed temples or spoken against our goddess.

38 If Demetrius and his workers have a case against these men, we have courts and judges. Let them take their complaints there. 39 But if you want to do more than that, the matter will

have to be brought before the city council. ⁴⁰We could easily be accused of starting a riot today. There is no excuse for it! We cannot even give a reason for this uproar.

41 After saying this, he told the people to leave.

Paul Goes through Macedonia and Greece

20 When the riot was over, Paul sent for the followers and encouraged them. He then told them good-by and left for Macedonia. ²As he traveled from place to place, he encouraged the followers with many messages. Finally, he went to Greece*a* ³and stayed there for three months.

Paul was about to sail to Syria. But some of the Jewish leaders plotted against him, so he decided to return by way of Macedonia. ⁴With him were Sopater, son of Pyrrhus from Berea, and Aristarchus and Secundus from Thessalonica. Gaius from Derbe was also with him, and so were Timothy and the two Asians, Tychicus and Trophimus. ⁵They went on ahead to Troas and waited for us there. ⁶After the Festival of Thin Bread, we sailed from Philippi. Five days later we met them in Troas and stayed there for a week.

Paul's Last Visit to Troas

7 On the first day of the week*b* we met to break bread together.*c* Paul spoke to the people until midnight because he was leaving the next morning.

---

a Greece: Probably Corinth.
b On the first day of the week: Since the Jewish day began at sunset, the meeting would have begun in the evening.
c break bread together: See the note at 2.46.

⁸In the upstairs room where we were meeting, there were a lot of lamps. ⁹A young man by the name of Eutychus was sitting on a window sill. While Paul was speaking, the young man got very sleepy. Finally, he went to sleep and fell three floors all the way down to the ground. When they picked him up, he was dead.

10 Paul went down and bent over Eutychus. He took him in his arms and said, "Don't worry! He's alive." ¹¹After Paul had gone back upstairs, he broke bread, and ate with us. He then spoke until dawn and left. ¹²Then the followers took the young man home alive and were very happy.

The Voyage from Troas to Miletus

13 Paul decided to travel by land to Assos. The rest of us went on ahead by ship, and we were to take him aboard there. ¹⁴When he met us in Assos, he came aboard, and we sailed on to Mitylene. ¹⁵The next day we came to a place near Chios, and the following day we reached Samos. The day after that we sailed to Miletus. ¹⁶Paul had decided to sail on past Ephesus, because he did not want to spend too much time in Asia. He was in a hurry and wanted to be in Jerusalem in time for Pentecost.*d*

Paul Says Good-By to the Church Leaders of Ephesus

17 From Miletus, Paul sent a message for the church leaders at Ephesus to come and meet with him. ¹⁸When they got there, he said:

---

d in time for Pentecost: The Jewish people liked to be in Jerusalem for this festival (see the note at 2.1).

You know everything I did during the time I was with you when I first came to Asia. ¹⁹Some of the Jews plotted against me and caused me a lot of sorrow and trouble. But I served the Lord and was humble. ²⁰When I preached in public or taught in your homes, I didn't hold back from telling anything that would help you. ²¹I told Jews and Gentiles to turn to God and have faith in our Lord Jesus.

22 I don't know what will happen to me in Jerusalem, but I must obey God's Spirit and go there. ²³In every city I visit, I am told by the Holy Spirit that I will be put in jail and will be in trouble in Jerusalem. ²⁴But I don't care what happens to me, as long as I finish the work that the Lord Jesus gave me to do. And that work is to tell the good news about God's great kindness.

25 I have gone from place to place, preaching to you about God's kingdom, but now I know that none of you will ever see me again. ²⁶I tell you today that I am no longer responsible for any of you! ²⁷I have told you everything God wants you to know. ²⁸Look after yourselves and everyone the Holy Spirit has placed in your care. Be like shepherds to God's church. It is the flock that he bought with the blood of his own Son.^h

29 I know that after I am gone, others will come like fierce wolves to attack you. ³⁰Some of your own people will tell lies to win over the Lord's followers. ³¹Be on your guard!

---

^e *the blood of his own Son*: Or "his own blood."

Remember how day and night for three years I kept warning you with tears in my eyes.

32 I now place you in God's care. Remember the message about his great kindness! This message can help you and give you what belongs to you as God's people. 33 I have never wanted anyone's money or clothes. 34 You know how I have worked with my own hands to make a living for myself and my friends. 35 By everything I did, I showed how you should work to help everyone who is weak. Remember that our Lord Jesus said, "More blessings come from giving than from receiving."

36 After Paul had finished speaking, he knelt down with all of them and prayed. 37 Everyone cried and hugged and kissed him. 38 They were especially sad because Paul had told them, "You will never see me again."

Then they went with him to the ship.

Paul Goes to Jerusalem

21 After saying good-by, we sailed straight to Cos. The next day we reached Rhodes and from there sailed on to Patara. 2 We found a ship going to Phoenicia, so we got on board and sailed off.

3 We came within sight of Cyprus and then sailed south of it on to the port of Tyre in Syria, where the ship was going to unload its cargo. 4 We looked up the Lord's followers and stayed with them for a week. The Holy Spirit had told them to warn Paul not to go on to Jerusalem. 5 But when the week was over, we started on our way again. All the men, together with their wives and children, walked with us from the

town to the seashore. We knelt on the beach and prayed. 6Then after saying good-by to each other, we got into the ship, and they went back home.

7 We sailed from Tyre to Ptolemais, where we greeted the followers and stayed with them for a day. 8The next day we went to Caesarea and stayed with Philip, the preacher. He was one of the seven men who helped the apostles, 9and he had four unmarried*f* daughters who prophesied.

10 We had been in Caesarea for several days, when the prophet Agabus came to us from Judea. 11He took Paul's belt, and with it he tied up his own hands and feet. Then he told us, "The Holy Spirit says that some of the Jewish leaders in Jerusalem will tie up the man who owns this belt. They will also hand him over to the Gentiles." 12After Agabus said this, we and the followers living there begged Paul not to go to Jerusalem.

13 But Paul answered, "Why are you crying and breaking my heart? I am not only willing to be put in jail for the Lord Jesus. I am even willing to die for him in Jerusalem!"

14 Since we could not get Paul to change his mind, we gave up and prayed, "Lord, please make us willing to do what you want."

15 Then we got ready to go to Jerusalem. 16Some of the followers from Caesarea went with us and took us to stay in the home of Mnason. He was from Cyprus and had been a follower from the beginning.

Paul Visits James

17 When we arrived in Jerusalem, the Lord's followers

---

f unmarried: Or "virgin."

gladly welcomed us. ¹⁸Paul went with us to see James*g* the next day, and all the church leaders were present. ¹⁹Paul greeted them and told how God had used him to help the Gentiles. ²⁰Everyone who heard this praised God and said to Paul:

My friend, you can see how many tens of thousands of our people have become followers! And all of them are eager to obey the Law of Moses. ²¹But they have been told that you are teaching those who live among the Gentiles to disobey this Law. They claim that you are telling them not to circumcise their sons or to follow our customs.

22 What should we do now that our people have heard that you are here? ²³Please do what we ask, because four of our men have made special promises to God. ²⁴Join with them and prepare yourself for the ceremony that goes with the promises. Pay the cost for their heads to be shaved. Then everyone will learn that the reports about you are not true. They will know that you do obey the Law of Moses.

25 Some while ago we told the Gentile followers what we think they should do. We instructed them not to eat anything offered to idols. They were told not to eat any meat with blood still in it or the meat of an animal that has been strangled. They were also told not to commit any terrible sexual sins.*h*

---

g James: The Lord's brother.

h not to commit any terrible sexual sins: See the note at 15.20.

26 The next day Paul took the four men with him and got himself ready at the same time they did. Then he went into the temple and told when the final ceremony would take place and when an offering would be made for each of them.

Paul Is Arrested

27 When the period of seven days for the ceremony was almost over, some of the Jewish people from Asia saw Paul in the temple. They got a large crowd together and started attacking him. 28 They were shouting, "Friends, help us! This man goes around everywhere, saying bad things about our nation and about the Law of Moses and about this temple. He has even brought shame to this holy temple by bringing in Gentiles." 29 Some of them thought that Paul had brought Trophimus from Ephesus into the temple, because they had seen them together in the city.

30 The whole city was in an uproar, and the people turned into a mob. They grabbed Paul and dragged him out of the temple. Then suddenly the doors were shut. 31 The people were about to kill Paul when the Roman army commander heard that all Jerusalem was starting to riot. 32 So he quickly took some soldiers and officers and ran to where the crowd had gathered.

As soon as the mob saw the commander and soldiers, they stopped beating Paul. 33 The army commander went over and arrested him and had him bound with two chains. Then he tried to find out who Paul was and what he had done. 34 Part of the crowd shouted one thing, and part of them shouted something else. But they were making so much noise that the commander could not find out a thing. Then he ordered Paul to be taken into the fortress. ³⁵As they reached the steps, the crowd became so wild that the soldiers had to lift Paul up and carry him. ³⁶The crowd followed and kept shouting, "Kill him! Kill him!"

Paul Speaks to the Crowd

37 When Paul was about to be taken into the fortress, he asked the commander, "Can I say something to you?"

"How do you know Greek?" the commander asked. ³⁸"Aren't you that Egyptian who started a riot not long ago and led four thousand terrorists into the desert?"

39 "No!" Paul replied. "I am a Jew from Tarsus, an important city in Cilicia. Please let me speak to the crowd."

40 The commander told him he could speak, so Paul stood on the steps and motioned to the people. When they were quiet, he spoke to them in Aramaic:

22 "My friends and leaders of our nation, listen as I explain what happened!" ²When the crowd heard Paul speak to them in Aramaic, they became even quieter. Then Paul said:

3 I am a Jew, born and raised in the city of Tarsus in Cilicia. I was a student of Gamaliel and was taught to follow every single law of our ancestors. In fact, I was just as eager to obey God as any of you are today.

4 I made trouble for everyone who followed the Lord's Way,ⁱ and I even had some of them killed. I had others arrested and put in jail. I didn't care if they were men or women.

ⁱ *followed the Lord's Way*: See the note at 9.2.

5The high priest and all the council members can tell you that this is true. They even gave me letters to the Jewish leaders in Damascus, so that I could arrest people there and bring them to Jerusalem to be punished.

6 One day about noon I was getting close to Damascus, when a bright light from heaven suddenly flashed around me. 7I fell to the ground and heard a voice asking, "Saul, Saul, why are you so cruel to me?"

8 "Who are you?" I answered.

The Lord replied, "I am Jesus from Nazareth! I am the one you are so cruel to." 9The men who were traveling with me saw the light, but did not hear the voice.

10 I asked, "Lord, what do you want me to do?"

Then he told me, "Get up and go to Damascus. When you get there, you will be told what to do." 11The light had been so bright that I couldn't see. And the other men had to lead me by the hand to Damascus.

12 In that city there was a man named Ananias, who faithfully obeyed the Law of Moses and was well liked by all the Jewish people living there. 13He came to me and said, "Saul, my friend, you can now see again!"

At once I could see. 14Then Ananias told me, "The God that our ancestors worshiped has chosen you to know what he wants done. He has chosen you to see the One Who Obeys God*j* and to hear his voice. 15You must tell everyone

---

j *One Who Obeys God*: See the note at 7.52.

what you have seen and heard. ¹⁶What are you waiting for? Get up! Be baptized, and wash away your sins by praying to the Lord."

17 After this I returned to Jerusalem and went to the temple to pray. There I had a vision ¹⁸of the Lord who said to me, "Hurry and leave Jerusalem! The people won't listen to what you say about me."

19 I replied, "Lord, they know that in many of our meeting places I arrested and beat people who had faith in you. ²⁰Stephen was killed because he spoke for you, and I stood there and cheered them on. I even guarded the clothes of the men who murdered him."

21 But the Lord told me to go, and he promised to send me far away to the Gentiles.

22 The crowd listened until Paul said this. Then they started shouting, "Get rid of this man! He doesn't deserve to live." ²³They kept shouting. They waved their clothes around and threw dust into the air.

Paul and the Roman Army Commander

24 The Roman commander ordered Paul to be taken into the fortress and beaten with a whip. He did this to find out why the people were screaming at Paul.

25 While the soldiers were tying Paul up to be beaten, he asked the officer standing there, "Is it legal to beat a Roman citizen before he has been tried in court?"

26 When the officer heard this, he went to the commander and said, "What are you doing? This man is a Roman citizen!"

27 The commander went to Paul and asked, "Tell me, are you a Roman citizen?"

"Yes," Paul answered.

28 The commander then said, "I paid a lot of money to become a Roman citizen."[k]

But Paul replied, "I was born a Roman citizen."

29 The men who were about to beat and question Paul quickly backed off. And the commander himself was frightened when he realized that he had put a Roman citizen in chains.

Paul Is Tried by the Council

30 The next day the commander wanted to know the real reason why the Jewish leaders had brought charges against Paul. So he had Paul's chains removed, and he ordered the chief priests and the whole council to meet. Then he had Paul led in and made him stand in front of them.

23 Paul looked straight at the council members and said, "My friends, to this day I have served God with a clear conscience!"

2 Then Ananias the high priest ordered the men standing beside Paul to hit him on the mouth. 3Paul turned to the high priest and said, "You whitewashed wall![l] God will hit you. You sit there to judge me by the Law of Moses. But at the same time you order men to break the Law by hitting me."

4 The men standing beside Paul asked, "Don't you know you are insulting God's high priest?"

---

[k] *Roman citizen:* See the note at 16.37.

[l] *whitewashed wall:* Someone who pretends to be good, but really isn't.

5 Paul replied, "Oh! I didn't know he was the high priest. The Scriptures do tell us not to speak evil about a leader of our people."

6 When Paul saw that some of the council members were Sadducees and others were Pharisees, he shouted, "My friends, I am a Pharisee and the son of a Pharisee. I am on trial simply because I believe that the dead will be raised to life."

7 As soon as Paul said this, the Pharisees and the Sadducees got into a big argument, and the council members started taking sides. 8 The Sadducees do not believe in angels or spirits or that the dead will rise to life. But the Pharisees believe in all of these, 9 and so there was a lot of shouting. Some of the teachers of the Law of Moses were Pharisees. Finally, they became angry and said, "We don't find anything wrong with this man. Maybe a spirit or an angel really did speak to him."

10 The argument became fierce, and the commander was afraid that Paul would be pulled apart. So he ordered the soldiers to go in and rescue Paul. Then they took him back into the fortress.

11 That night the Lord stood beside Paul and said, "Don't worry! Just as you have told others about me in Jerusalem, you must also tell about me in Rome."

A Plot To Kill Paul

12-13 The next morning more than forty Jewish men got together and vowed that they would not eat or drink anything until they had killed Paul. 14 Then some of them went to the chief priests and the nation's leaders and said, "We have promised God that we would not eat a thing until we have killed

Paul. 15 You and everyone in the council must go to the commander and pretend that you want to find out more about the charges against Paul. Ask for him to be brought before your court. Meanwhile, we will be waiting to kill him before he gets there."

16 When Paul's nephew heard about the plot, he went to the fortress and told Paul about it. 17 So Paul said to one of the army officers, "Take this young man to the commander. He has something to tell him."

18 The officer took him to the commander and said, "The prisoner named Paul asked me to bring this young man to you, because he has something to tell you."

19 The commander took the young man aside and asked him in private, "What do you want to tell me?"

20 He answered, "Some men are planning to ask you to bring Paul down to the Jewish council tomorrow. They will claim that they want to find out more about him. 21 But please don't do what they say. More than forty men are going to attack Paul. They have made a vow not to eat or drink anything until they have killed him. Even now they are waiting to hear what you decide."

22 The commander sent the young man away after saying to him, "Don't let anyone know that you told me this."

Paul Is Sent to Felix the Governor

23 The commander called in two of his officers and told them, "By nine o'clock tonight have two hundred soldiers ready to go to Caesarea. Take along seventy men on horseback and two hundred foot soldiers with spears. 24 Get a horse ready for Paul and make sure that he gets safely through to Felix the governor."

25 The commander wrote a letter that said:

26 Greetings from Claudius Lysias to the Honorable Governor Felix:

27 Some Jews grabbed this man and were about to kill him. But when I found out that he was a Roman citizen, I took some soldiers and rescued him.

28 I wanted to find out what they had against him. So I brought him before their council [29]and learned that the charges concern only their religious laws. This man isn't guilty of anything for which he should die or even be put in jail.

30 As soon as I learned that there was a plot against him, I sent him to you and told their leaders to bring charges against him in your court.

31 The soldiers obeyed the commander's orders, and that same night they took Paul to the city of Antipatris. [32]The next day the foot soldiers returned to the fortress and let the soldiers on horseback take him the rest of the way. [33]When they came to Caesarea, they gave the letter to the governor and handed Paul over to him.

34 The governor read the letter. Then he asked Paul and found out that he was from Cilicia. [35]The governor said, "I will listen to your case as soon as the people come to bring their charges against you." After saying this, he gave orders for Paul to be kept as a prisoner in Herod's palace.[m]

---

[m] *Herod's palace*: The palace built by Herod the Great and used by the Roman governors of Palestine.

Paul Is Accused in the Court of Felix

24 Five days later Ananias the high priest, together with some of their leaders and a lawyer named Tertullus, went to the governor to present their case against Paul. [2]So Paul was called in, and Tertullus stated the case against him:[n]

Honorable Felix, you have brought our people a long period of peace, and because of your concern our nation is much better off. [3]All of us are always grateful for what you have done. [4]I don't want to bother you, but please be patient with us and listen to me for just a few minutes.

[5] This man has been found to be a real pest and troublemaker for our people all over the world. He is also a leader of a group called Nazarenes. [6-8]When he tried to disgrace the temple, we arrested him.[o] If you question him, you will find out for yourself that our charges are true.

[9]The Jewish crowd spoke up and agreed with what Tertullus had said.

Paul Defends Himself

[10] The governor motioned for Paul to speak, and he began:

---

[n] *Paul was called in, and Tertullus stated the case against him:* Or "Tertullus was called in and stated the case against Paul."

[o] *we arrested him:* Some manuscripts add, "We wanted to judge him by our own laws. But Lysias the commander took him away from us by force. Then Lysias ordered us to bring our charges against this man in your court."

I know that you have judged the people of our nation for many years, and I am glad to defend myself in your court.

11 It was no more than twelve days ago that I went to worship in Jerusalem. You can find this out easily enough. 12 Never once did the Jews find me arguing with anyone in the temple. I didn't cause trouble in their meeting places or in the city itself. 13 There is no way that they can prove these charges that they are now bringing against me.

14 I admit that their leaders think that the Lord's Way*p* which I follow is based on wrong beliefs. But I still worship the same God that my ancestors worshiped. And I believe everything written in the Law of Moses and in the Prophets.*q* 15 I am just as sure as these people are that God will raise from death everyone who is good or evil. 16 And because I am sure, I try my best to have a clear conscience in whatever I do for God or for people.

17 After being away for several years, I returned here to bring gifts for the poor people of my nation and to offer sacrifices. 18 This is what I was doing when I was found going through a ceremony in the temple. I wasn't with a crowd, and there was no uproar.

19 Some Jews from Asia were there at that time, and if they have anything to say against me, they should be here now. 20 Or ask the ones who are here. They can tell you that they didn't

---

p *the Lord's Way:* See the note at 9.2.
q *Law of Moses . . . the Prophets:* The Jewish Scriptures, that is, the Old Testament.

find me guilty of anything when I was tried by their own council. ²¹The only charge they can bring against me is what I shouted out in court, when I said, "I am on trial today because I believe that the dead will be raised to life!"

22 Felix knew a lot about the Lord's Way.^r But he brought the trial to an end and said, "I will make my decision after Lysias the commander arrives." ²³He then ordered the army officer to keep Paul under guard, but not to lock him up or to stop his friends from helping him.

Paul Is Kept under Guard

24 Several days later Felix and his wife Drusilla, who was Jewish, went to the place where Paul was kept under guard. They sent for Paul and listened while he spoke to them about having faith in Christ Jesus. ²⁵But Felix was frightened when Paul started talking to them about doing right, about self-control, and about the coming judgment. So he said to Paul, "That's enough for now. You may go. But when I have time I will send for you." ²⁶After this, Felix often sent for Paul and talked with him, because he hoped that Paul would offer him a bribe.

27 Two years later Porcius Festus became governor in place of Felix. But since Felix wanted to do the Jewish leaders a favor, he kept Paul in jail.

Paul Asks To Be Tried by the Roman Emperor

25 Three days after Festus had become governor, he went from Caesarea to Jerusalem.

^r the Lord's Way: See the note at 9.2.

2There the chief priests and some Jewish leaders told him about their charges against Paul. They also asked Festus 3if he would be willing to bring Paul to Jerusalem. They begged him to do this because they were planning to attack and kill Paul on the way. 4But Festus told them, "Paul will be kept in Caesarea, and I am soon going there myself. 5If he has done anything wrong, let your leaders go with me and bring charges against him there."

6 Festus stayed in Jerusalem for eight or ten more days before going to Caesarea. Then the next day he took his place as judge and had Paul brought into court. 7As soon as Paul came in, the leaders from Jerusalem crowded around him and said he was guilty of many serious crimes. But they could not prove anything. 8Then Paul spoke in his own defense, "I have not broken the Law of my people. And I have not done anything against either the temple or the Emperor."

9 Festus wanted to please the leaders. So he asked Paul, "Are you willing to go to Jerusalem and be tried by me on these charges?"

10 Paul replied, "I am on trial in the Emperor's court, and that's where I should be tried. You know very well that I have not done anything to harm the Jewish nation. 11If I had done something deserving death, I would not ask to escape the death penalty. But I am not guilty of any of these crimes, and no one has the right to hand me over to these people. I now ask to be tried by the Emperor himself."

12 After Festus had talked this over with members of his council, he told Paul, "You have asked to be tried by the Emperor, and to the Emperor you will go!"

Paul Speaks to Agrippa and Bernice

13 A few days later King Agrippa and Bernice came to Caesarea to visit Festus. 14They had been there for several days, when Festus told the king about the charges against Paul. He said:

Felix left a man here in jail, 15and when I went to Jerusalem, the chief priests and the Jewish leaders came and asked me to find him guilty. 16I told them that it isn't the Roman custom to hand a man over to people who are bringing charges against him. He must first have the chance to meet them face to face and to defend himself against their charges.

17 So when they came here with me, I wasted no time. On the very next day I took my place on the judge's bench and ordered him to be brought in. 18But when the men stood up to make their charges against him, they did not accuse him of any of the crimes that I thought they would. 19Instead, they argued with him about some of their beliefs and about a dead man named Jesus, who Paul said was alive.

20 Since I did not know how to find out the truth about all this, I asked Paul if he would be willing to go to Jerusalem and be put on trial there. 21But Paul asked to be kept in jail until the Emperor could decide his case. So I ordered him to be kept here until I could send him to the Emperor.

22 Then Agrippa said to Festus, "I would also like to hear what this man has to say."

Festus answered, "You can hear him tomorrow."

23 The next day Agrippa and Bernice made a big show as they came into the meeting room. High ranking army officers and leading citizens of the town were also there. Festus then ordered Paul to be brought in 24and said:

King Agrippa and other guests, look at this man! Every Jew from Jerusalem and Caesarea has come to me, demanding for him to be put to death. 25I have not found him guilty of any crime deserving death. But because he has asked to be judged by the Emperor, I have decided to send him to Rome.

26 I have to write some facts about this man to the Emperor. So I have brought him before all of you, but especially before you, King Agrippa. After we have talked about his case, I will then have something to write. 27It makes no sense to send a prisoner to the Emperor without stating the charges against him.

Paul's Defense before Agrippa

26 Agrippa told Paul, "You may now speak for yourself."

Paul stretched out his hand and said:

2 King Agrippa, I am glad for this chance to defend myself before you today on all these charges that my own people have brought against me. 3You know a lot about our religious customs and the beliefs that divide us. So I ask you to listen patiently to me.

4-5 All the Jews have known me since I was a child. They know what kind of life I have lived in my own country and in Jerusalem.

And if they were willing, they could tell you that I was a Pharisee, a member of a group that is stricter than any other. 6Now I am on trial because I believe the promise God made to our people long ago.

7 Day and night our twelve tribes have earnestly served God, waiting for his promised blessings. King Agrippa, because of this hope, some of their leaders have brought charges against me. 8Why should any of you doubt that God raises the dead to life?

9 I once thought that I should do everything I could to oppose Jesus from Nazareth. 10I did this first in Jerusalem, and with the authority of the chief priests I put many of God's people in jail. I even voted for them to be killed. 11I often had them punished in our meeting places, and I tried to make them give up their faith. In fact, I was so angry with them, that I went looking for them in foreign cities.

12 King Agrippa, one day I was on my way to Damascus with the authority and permission of the chief priests. 13About noon I saw a light brighter than the sun. It flashed from heaven on me and on everyone traveling with me. 14We all fell to the ground. Then I heard a voice say to me in Aramaic, "Saul, Saul, why are you so cruel to me? It's foolish to fight against me!"

15 "Who are you?" I asked.

Then the Lord answered, "I am Jesus! I am the one you are so cruel to. 16Now stand up. I have appeared to you, because I have chosen you to be my servant. You are to tell others what you have learned about me and what I will show you later."

17 The Lord also said, "I will protect you from the Jews and from the Gentiles that I am sending you to. 18I want you to open their eyes, so that they will turn from darkness to light and from the power of Satan to God. Then their sins will be forgiven, and by faith in me they will become part of God's holy people."

19 King Agrippa, I obeyed this vision from heaven. 20First I preached to the people in Damascus, and then I went to Jerusalem and all over Judea. Finally, I went to the Gentiles and said, "Stop sinning and turn to God! Then prove what you have done by the way you live."

21 That is why some men grabbed me in the temple and tried to kill me. 22But all this time God has helped me, and I have preached both to the rich and to the poor. I have told them only what the prophets and Moses said would happen. 23I told them how the Messiah would suffer and be the first to be raised from death, so that he could bring light to his own people and to the Gentiles.

24 Before Paul finished defending himself, Festus shouted, "Paul, you're crazy! Too much learning has driven you out of your mind."

25 But Paul replied, "Honorable Festus, I am not crazy. What I am saying is true, and it makes sense. 26None of these things happened off in a corner somewhere. I am sure that King Agrippa knows what I am talking about. That's why I can speak so plainly to him."

27 Then Paul said to Agrippa, "Do you believe what the prophets said? I know you do."

28 Agrippa asked Paul, "In such a short time do you think you can talk me into being a Christian?"

29 Paul answered, "Whether it takes a short time or a long time, I wish you and everyone else who hears me today would become just like me! Except, of course, for these chains."

30 Then King Agrippa, Governor Festus, Bernice, and everyone who was with them got up. 31But before they left, they said, "This man isn't guilty of anything. He doesn't deserve to die or to be put in jail."

32 Agrippa told Festus, "Paul could have been set free, if he had not asked to be tried by the Roman Emperor."

Paul Is Taken to Rome

27 When it was time for us to sail to Rome, Captain Julius from the Emperor's special troops was put in charge of Paul and the other prisoners. 2We went aboard a ship from Adramyttium that was about to sail to some ports along the coast of Asia. Aristarchus from Thessalonica in Macedonia sailed on the ship with us.

3 The next day we came to shore at Sidon. Captain Julius was very kind to Paul. He even let him visit his friends, so they could give him whatever he needed. 4When we left Sidon, the winds were blowing against us, and we sailed close to the island of Cyprus to be safe from the wind. 5Then we sailed south of Cilicia and Pamphylia until we came to the port of Myra in Lycia. 6There the army captain found a ship from Alexandria that was going to Italy. So he ordered us to board that ship.

7 We sailed along slowly for several days and had a hard time reaching Cnidus. The wind would not let us go any farther in that direction, so we sailed past Cape Salmone, where the island of Crete would protect us from the wind. 8 We went slowly along the coast and finally reached a place called Fair Havens, not far from the town of Lasea.

9 By now we had already lost a lot of time, and sailing was no longer safe. In fact, even the Great Day of Forgiveness[s] was past. 10 Then Paul spoke to the crew of the ship, "Men, listen to me! If we sail now, our ship and its cargo will be badly damaged, and many lives will be lost." 11 But Julius listened to the captain of the ship and its owner, rather than to Paul.

12 The harbor at Fair Havens wasn't a good place to spend the winter. Because of this, almost everyone agreed that we should at least try to sail along the coast of Crete as far as Phoenix. It had a harbor that opened toward the southwest and northwest,[t] and we could spend the winter there.

The Storm at Sea

13 When a gentle wind from the south started blowing, the men thought it was a good time to do what they had planned. So they pulled up the anchor, and we sailed along the coast of Crete. 14 But soon a

---

[s] *Great Day of Forgiveness*: This Jewish festival took place near the end of September. The sailing season was dangerous after the middle of September, and it was stopped completely between the middle of November and the middle of March.

[t] *southwest and northwest*: Or "northeast and southeast."

strong wind called "The Northeaster" blew against us from the island. [15]The wind struck the ship, and we could not sail against it. So we let the wind carry the ship.

16 We went along the island of Cauda on the side that was protected from the wind. We had a hard time holding the lifeboat in place, [17]but finally we got it where it belonged. Then the sailors wrapped ropes around the ship to hold it together. They lowered the sail and let the ship drift along, because they were afraid it might hit the sandbanks in the gulf of Syrtis.

18 The storm was so fierce that the next day they threw some of the ship's cargo overboard. [19]Then on the third day, with their bare hands they threw overboard some of the ship's gear. [20]For several days we could not see either the sun or the stars. A strong wind kept blowing, and we finally gave up all hope of being saved.

21 Since none of us had eaten anything for a long time, Paul stood up and told the men:

You should have listened to me! If you had stayed on in Crete, you would not have had this damage and loss. [22]But now I beg you to cheer up, because you will be safe. Only the ship will be lost.

23 I belong to God, and I worship him. Last night he sent an angel [24]to tell me, "Paul, don't be afraid! You will stand trial before the Emperor. And because of you, God will save the lives of everyone on the ship." [25]Cheer up! I am sure that God will do exactly what he promised. [26]But we will first be shipwrecked on some island.

27 For fourteen days and nights we had been blown around over the Mediterranean Sea. But about midnight the sailors realized that we were getting near land. 28They measured and found that the water was about one hundred twenty feet deep. A little later they measured again and found it was only about ninety feet. 29The sailors were afraid that we might hit some rocks, and they let down four anchors from the back of the ship. Then they prayed for daylight.

30 The sailors wanted to escape from the ship. So they lowered the lifeboat into the water, pretending that they were letting down an anchor from the front of the ship. 31But Paul said to Captain Julius and the soldiers, "If the sailors don't stay on the ship, you won't have any chance to save your lives." 32The soldiers then cut the ropes that held the lifeboat and let it fall into the sea.

33 Just before daylight Paul begged the people to eat something. He told them, "For fourteen days you have been so worried that you haven't eaten a thing. 34I beg you to eat something. Your lives depend on it. Do this and not one of you will be hurt."

35 After Paul had said this, he took a piece of bread and gave thanks to God. Then in front of everyone, he broke the bread and ate some. 36They all felt encouraged, and each of them ate something. 37There were 276 people on the ship, 38and after everyone had eaten, they threw the cargo of wheat into the sea to make the ship lighter.

The Shipwreck

39 Morning came, and the ship's crew saw a coast that they did not recognize. But they did see a cove

with a beach. So they decided to try to run the ship aground on the beach. 40They cut the anchors loose and let them sink into the sea. At the same time they untied the ropes that were holding the rudders. Next, they raised the sail at the front of the ship and let the wind carry the ship toward the beach. 41But it ran aground on a sandbank. The front of the ship stuck firmly in the sand, and the rear was being smashed by the force of the waves.

42 The soldiers decided to kill the prisoners to keep them from swimming away and escaping. 43But Captain Julius wanted to save Paul's life, and he did not let the soldiers do what they had planned. Instead, he ordered everyone who could swim to dive into the water and head for shore. 44Then he told the others to hold on to planks of wood or parts of the ship. At last, everyone safely reached shore.

On the Island of Malta

28 When we came ashore, we learned that the island was called Malta. 2The local people were very friendly, and they welcomed us by building a fire, because it was rainy and cold.

3 After Paul had gathered some wood and had put it on the fire, the heat caused a snake to crawl out, and it bit him on the hand. 4When the local people saw the snake hanging from Paul's hand, they said to each other, "This man must be a murderer! He didn't drown in the sea, but the goddess of justice will kill him anyway."

5 Paul shook the snake off into the fire and wasn't harmed. 6The people kept thinking that Paul would either swell up or suddenly drop dead. They watched

him for a long time, and when nothing happened to him, they changed their minds and said, "This man is a god."

7 The governor of the island was named Publius, and he owned some of the land around there. Publius was very friendly and welcomed us into his home for three days. [8] His father was in bed, sick with fever and stomach trouble, and Paul went to visit him. Paul healed the man by praying and placing his hands on him.

9 After this happened, everyone on the island brought their sick people to Paul, and they were all healed. [10] The people were very respectful to us, and when we sailed, they gave us everything we needed.

From Malta to Rome

11 Three months later we sailed in a ship that had been docked at Malta for the winter. The ship was from Alexandria in Egypt and was known as "The Twin Gods." [u] [12] We arrived in Syracuse and stayed for three days. [13] From there we sailed to Rhegium. The next day a south wind began to blow, and two days later we arrived in Puteoli. [14] There we found some of the Lord's followers, who begged us to stay with them. A week later we left for the city of Rome.

15 Some of the followers in Rome heard about us and came to meet us at the Market of Appius and at the Three Inns. When Paul saw them, he thanked God and was encouraged.

---

[u] known as "The Twin Gods": Or "carried on its bow a wooden carving of the Twin Gods." These gods were Castor and Pollux, two of the favorite gods among sailors.

Paul in Rome

16 We arrived in Rome, and Paul was allowed to live in a house by himself with a soldier to guard him.

17 Three days after we got there, Paul called together some of the Jewish leaders and said:

My friends, I have never done anything to hurt our people, and I have never gone against the customs of our ancestors. But in Jerusalem I was handed over as a prisoner to the Romans. 18They looked into the charges against me and wanted to release me. They found that I had not done anything deserving death. 19The Jewish leaders disagreed, so I asked to be tried by the Emperor. But I don't have anything to say against my own nation. 20I am bound by these chains because of what we people of Israel hope for. That's why I have called you here to talk about this hope of ours.

21 The leaders replied, "No one from Judea has written us a letter about you. And not one of them has come here to report on you or to say anything against you. 22But we would like to hear what you have to say. We understand that people everywhere are against this new group."

23 They agreed on a time to meet with Paul, and many of them came to his house. From early morning until late in the afternoon, Paul talked to them about God's kingdom. He used the Law of Moses and the Books of the Prophets ^{v} to try to win them over to Jesus.

---

^{v} Law of Moses and the Books of the Prophets: The Jewish Bible, that is, the Old Testament.

24 Some of the leaders agreed with what Paul said, but others did not. 25Since they could not agree among themselves, they started leaving. But Paul said, "The Holy Spirit said the right thing when he sent Isaiah the prophet 26to tell our ancestors,

'Go to these people and tell them:
You will listen and listen,
    but never understand.
You will look and look,
    but never see.
27 All of you have stubborn hearts.
Your ears are stopped up,
    and your eyes are covered.
You cannot see or hear or understand.
If you could,
    you would turn to me,
    and I would heal you.'"

28-29 Paul said, "You may be sure that God wants to save the Gentiles! And they will listen."*w*

30 For two years Paul stayed in a rented house and welcomed everyone who came to see him. 31He bravely preached about God's kingdom and taught about the Lord Jesus Christ, and no one tried to stop him.

---

w And they will listen: Some manuscripts add, "After Paul said this, the people left, but they got into a fierce argument among themselves."

Paul's Letter
to the Church in Rome

ABOUT THIS LETTER

Paul wrote this letter to introduce himself and his message to the church at Rome. He had never been to this important city, although he knew the names of many Christians there and hoped to visit them soon (15.22–16.21). Paul tells them that he is an apostle, chosen to preach the good news (1.1). And the message he proclaims "is God's powerful way of saving all people who have faith, whether they are Jews or Gentiles" (1.16).

Paul reminds his readers, "All of us have sinned and fallen short of God's glory" (3.23). But how can we be made acceptable to God? This is the main question that Paul answers in this letter. He begins by showing how everyone has failed to do what God requires. The Jews have not obeyed the Law of Moses, and the Gentiles have refused even to think about God, although God has spoken to them in many different ways (1.18–3.20).

Now we see how God does make us acceptable to him.... He accepts people only because they have faith in Jesus Christ.... God treats us much better than we deserve, and because of Christ Jesus, he freely accepts us and sets us free from our sins. (3.21a,22b,24)

486

*God gave Jesus to die for our sins, and he raised
him to life, so that we would be made acceptable to
God. (4.25)*

A QUICK LOOK AT THIS LETTER

1 From Paul, a servant of Christ Jesus.
  God chose me to be an apostle, and he appointed
me to preach the good news ²that he promised long
ago by what his prophets said in the holy Scriptures.
³⁻⁴This good news is about his Son, our Lord Jesus
Christ! As a human, he was from the family of David.
But the Holy Spirit*ᵃ* proved that Jesus is the powerful
Son of God,*ᵇ* because he was raised from death.

5 Jesus was kind to me and chose me to be an
apostle,*ᶜ* so that people of all nations would obey and
have faith. ⁶You are some of those people chosen by
Jesus Christ.

7 This letter is to all of you in Rome. God loves
you and has chosen you to be his very own people.

ᵃ the Holy Spirit: Or "his own spirit of holiness."
ᵇ proved that Jesus is the powerful Son of God: Or "proved
   in a powerful way that Jesus is the Son of God."
ᶜ Jesus was kind to me and chose me to be an apostle:
   Or "Jesus was kind to us and chose us to be his apostles."

I pray that God our Father and our Lord Jesus Christ will be kind to you and will bless you with peace!

A Prayer of Thanks

8 First, I thank God in the name of Jesus Christ for all of you. I do this because people everywhere in the world are talking about your faith. ⁹God has seen how I never stop praying for you, while I serve him with all my heart and tell the good news about his Son.

10 In all my prayers, I ask God to make it possible for me to visit you. ¹¹I want to see you and share with you the same blessings that God's Spirit has given me. Then you will grow stronger in your faith. ¹²What I am saying is that we can encourage each other by the faith that is ours.

13 My friends, I want you to know that I have often planned to come for a visit. But something has always kept me from doing it. I want to win followers to Christ in Rome, as I have done in many other places. ¹⁴⁻¹⁵It doesn't matter if people are civilized and educated, or if they are uncivilized and uneducated. I must tell the good news to everyone. That's why I am eager to visit all of you in Rome.

The Power of the Good News

16 I am proud of the good news! It is God's powerful way of saving all people who have faith, whether they are Jews or Gentiles. ¹⁷The good news tells how God accepts everyone who has faith, but only those who have faith.ᵈ It is just as the Scriptures

---

ᵈ *but only those who have faith*: Or "and faith is all that matters."

say, "The people God accepts because of their faith will live."[e]

Everyone Is Guilty

18 From heaven God shows how angry he is with all the wicked and evil things that sinful people do to crush the truth. [19]They know everything that can be known about God, because God has shown it all to them. [20]God's eternal power and character cannot be seen. But from the beginning of creation, God has shown what these are like by all he has made. That's why those people don't have any excuse. [21]They know about God, but they don't honor him or even thank him. Their thoughts are useless, and their stupid minds are in the dark. [22]They claim to be wise, but they are fools. [23]They don't worship the glorious and eternal God. Instead, they worship idols that are made to look like humans who cannot live forever, and like birds, animals, and reptiles.

24 So God let these people go their own way. They did what they wanted to do, and their filthy thoughts made them do shameful things with their bodies. [25]They gave up the truth about God for a lie, and they worshiped God's creation instead of God, who will be praised forever. Amen.

26 God let them follow their own evil desires. Women no longer wanted to have sex in a natural way, and they did things with each other that were not natural. [27]Men behaved in the same way. They stopped

---

[e] *The people God accepts because of their faith will live*: Or "The people God accepts will live because of their faith."

wanting to have sex with women and had strong desires for sex with other men. They did shameful things with each other, and what has happened to them is punishment for their foolish deeds.

28 Since these people refused even to think about God, he let their useless minds rule over them. That's why they do all sorts of indecent things. 29They are evil, wicked, and greedy, as well as mean in every possible way. They want what others have, and they murder, argue, cheat, and are hard to get along with. They gossip, 30say cruel things about others, and hate God. They are proud, conceited, and boastful, always thinking up new ways to do evil.

These people don't respect their parents. 31They are stupid, unreliable, and don't have any love or pity for others. 32They know God has said that anyone who acts this way deserves to die. But they keep on doing evil things, and they even encourage others to do them.

God's Judgment Is Fair

2 Some of you accuse others of doing wrong. But there is no excuse for what you do. When you judge others, you condemn yourselves, because you are guilty of doing the very same things. 2We know that God is right to judge everyone who behaves in this way. 3Do you really think God won't punish you, when you behave exactly like the people you accuse? 4You surely don't think much of God's wonderful goodness or of his patience and willingness to put up with you. Don't you know that the reason God is good to you is because he wants you to turn to him?

5 But you are stubborn and refuse to turn to God. So you are making things even worse for yourselves on

that day when he will show how angry he is and will judge the world with fairness. 6God will reward each of us for what we have done. 7He will give eternal life to everyone who has patiently done what is good in the hope of receiving glory, honor, and life that lasts forever. 8But he will show how angry and furious he can be with every selfish person who rejects the truth and wants to do evil. 9All who are wicked will be punished with trouble and suffering. It doesn't matter if they are Jews or Gentiles. 10But all who do right will be rewarded with glory, honor, and peace, whether they are Jews or Gentiles. 11God doesn't have any favorites!

12 Those people who don't know about God's Law will still be punished for what they do wrong. And the Law will be used to judge everyone who knows what it says. 13God accepts those who obey his Law, but not those who simply hear it.

14 Some people naturally obey the Law's commands, even though they don't have the Law. 15This proves that the conscience is like a law written in the human heart. And it will show whether we are forgiven or condemned, 16when God has Jesus Christ judge everyone's secret thoughts, just as my message says.

The Jews and the Law

17 Some of you call yourselves Jews. You trust in the Law and take pride in God. 18By reading the Scriptures you learn how God wants you to behave, and you discover what is right. 19You are sure that you are a guide for the blind and a light for all who are in the dark. 20And since there is knowledge and truth in God's Law, you think you can instruct fools and teach young people.

21 But how can you teach others when you refuse to learn? You preach that it is wrong to steal. But do you steal? 22 You say people should be faithful in marriage. But are you faithful? You hate idols, yet you rob their temples. 23 You take pride in the Law, but you disobey the Law and bring shame to God. 24 It is just as the Scriptures tell us, "You have made foreigners say insulting things about God."

25 Being circumcised is worthwhile, if you obey the Law. But if you don't obey the Law, you are no better off than people who are not circumcised. 26 In fact, if they obey the Law, they are as good as anyone who is circumcised. 27 So everyone who obeys the Law, but has never been circumcised, will condemn you. Even though you are circumcised and have the Law, you still don't obey its teachings.

28 Just because you live like a Jew and are circumcised doesn't make you a real Jew. 29 To be a real Jew you must obey the Law. True circumcision is something that happens deep in your heart, not something done to your body. And besides, you should want praise from God and not from humans.

3 What good is it to be a Jew? What good is it to be circumcised? 2 It is good in a lot of ways! First of all, God's messages were spoken to the Jews. 3 It is true that some of them did not believe the message. But does this mean that God cannot be trusted, just because they did not have faith? 4 No, indeed! God tells the truth, even if everyone else is a liar. The Scriptures say about God,

"Your words will be proven true,
    and in court you will win your case."

5 If our evil deeds show how right God is, then what can we say? Is it wrong for God to become angry and punish us? What a foolish thing to ask. 6But the answer is, "No." Otherwise, how could God judge the world? 7Since your lies bring great honor to God by showing how truthful he is, you may ask why God still says you are a sinner. 8You might as well say, "Let's do something evil, so that something good will come of it!" Some people even claim that we are saying this. But God is fair and will judge them as well.

No One Is Good

9 What does all this mean? Does it mean that we Jews are better off *f* than the Gentiles? No, it doesn't! Jews, as well as Gentiles, are ruled by sin, just as I have said. 10The Scriptures tell us,

"No one is acceptable to God!
11 Not one of them understands
      or even searches for God.
12 They have all turned away
      and are worthless.
    There isn't one person who does right.
13 Their words are like an open pit,
      and their tongues are good
      only for telling lies.
    Each word is as deadly
      as the fangs of a snake,
14 and they say nothing but bitter curses.
15 These people quickly become violent.
16 Wherever they go,
      they leave ruin and destruction.

---

f *better off*: Or "worse off."

¹⁷ They don't know how to live in peace.
¹⁸　　They don't even fear God."

19 We know that everything in the Law was written for those who are under its power. The Law says these things to stop anyone from making excuses and to let God show that the whole world is guilty. ²⁰God doesn't accept people simply because they obey the Law. No, indeed! All the Law does is to point out our sin.

God's Way of Accepting People

21 Now we see how God does make us acceptable to him. The Law and the Prophets^g tell how we become acceptable, and it isn't by obeying the Law of Moses. ²²God treats everyone alike. He accepts people only because they have faith in Jesus Christ. ²³All of us have sinned and fallen short of God's glory. ²⁴But God treats us much better than we deserve,^h and because of Christ Jesus, he freely accepts us and sets us free from our sins. ²⁵⁻²⁶God sent Christ to be our sacrifice. Christ offered his life's blood, so that by faith in him we could come to God. And God did this to show that in the past he was right to be patient and forgive sinners. This also shows that God is right when he accepts people who have faith in Jesus.

---

^g *The Law and the Prophets*: The Jewish Scriptures, that is, the Old Testament.
^h *treats us much better than we deserve*: The Greek word *charis*, traditionally rendered "grace," is translated here and other places in the CEV to express the overwhelming kindness of God.

27 What is left for us to brag about? Not a thing! Is it because we obeyed some law? No! It is because of faith. 28We see that people are acceptable to God because they have faith, and not because they obey the Law. 29Does God belong only to the Jews? Isn't he also the God of the Gentiles? Yes, he is! 30There is only one God, and he accepts Gentiles as well as Jews, simply because of their faith. 31Do we destroy the Law by our faith? Not at all! We make it even more powerful.

The Example of Abraham

4 Well then, what can we say about our ancestor Abraham? 2If he became acceptable to God because of what he did, then he would have something to brag about. But he would never be able to brag about it to God. 3The Scriptures say, "God accepted Abraham because Abraham had faith in him."

4 Money paid to workers isn't a gift. It is something they earn by working. 5But you cannot make God accept you because of something you do. God accepts sinners only because they have faith in him. 6In the Scriptures David talks about the blessings that come to people who are acceptable to God, even though they don't do anything to deserve these blessings. David says,

7 "God blesses people
      whose sins are forgiven
      and whose evil deeds are forgotten.
8 The Lord blesses people
      whose sins are erased from his book."
9 Are these blessings meant for circumcised people

or for those who are not circumcised? Well, the Scriptures say that God accepted Abraham because Abraham had faith in him. ¹⁰But when did this happen? Was it before or after Abraham was circumcised? Of course, it was before.

11 Abraham let himself be circumcised to show that he had been accepted because of his faith even before he was circumcised. This makes Abraham the father of all who are acceptable to God because of their faith, even though they are not circumcised. ¹²This also makes Abraham the father of everyone who is circumcised and has faith in God, as Abraham did before he was circumcised.

The Promise Is for All Who Have Faith

13 God promised Abraham and his descendants that he would give them the world. This promise wasn't made because Abraham had obeyed a law, but because his faith in God made him acceptable. ¹⁴If Abraham and his descendants were given this promise because they had obeyed a law, then faith would mean nothing, and the promise would be worthless.

15 God becomes angry when his Law is broken. But where there isn't a law, it cannot be broken. ¹⁶Everything depends on having faith in God, so that God's promise is assured by his great kindness. This promise isn't only for Abraham's descendants who have the Law. It is for all who are Abraham's descendants because they have faith, just as he did. Abraham is the ancestor of us all. ¹⁷The Scriptures say that Abraham would become the ancestor of many nations. This promise was made to Abraham because

he had faith in God, who raises the dead to life and creates new things.

18 God promised Abraham a lot of descendants. And when it all seemed hopeless, Abraham still had faith in God and became the ancestor of many nations. 19 Abraham's faith never became weak, not even when he was nearly a hundred years old. He knew that he was almost dead and that his wife Sarah could not have children. 20 But Abraham never doubted or questioned God's promise. His faith made him strong, and he gave all the credit to God.

21 Abraham was certain that God could do what he had promised. 22 So God accepted him, 23 just as we read in the Scriptures. But these words were not written only for Abraham. 24 They were written for us, since we will also be accepted because of our faith in God, who raised our Lord Jesus to life. 25 God gave Jesus to die for our sins, and he raised him to life, so that we would be made acceptable to God.

What It Means To Be Acceptable to God

5 By faith we have been made acceptable to God. And now, because of our Lord Jesus Christ, we live at peace[i] with God. 2 Christ has also introduced us[j] to God's undeserved kindness on which we take our stand. So we are happy, as we look forward to sharing in the glory of God. 3 But that's not all! We gladly suffer,[k] because we know that suffering helps

---

[i] *we live at peace*: Some manuscripts have "let us live at peace."

[j] *introduced us*: Some manuscripts add "by faith."

[k] *We gladly suffer*: Or "Let us gladly suffer."

us to endure. ⁴And endurance builds character, which gives us a hope ⁵that will never disappoint us. All of this happens because God has given us the Holy Spirit, who fills our hearts with his love.

⁶Christ died for us at a time when we were helpless and sinful. ⁷No one is really willing to die for an honest person, though someone might be willing to die for a truly good person. ⁸But God showed how much he loved us by having Christ die for us, even though we were sinful.

⁹But there is more! Now that God has accepted us because Christ sacrificed his life's blood, we will also be kept safe from God's anger. ¹⁰Even when we were God's enemies, he made peace with us, because his Son died for us. Yet something even greater than friendship is ours. Now that we are at peace with God, we will be saved by his Son's life. ¹¹And in addition to everything else, we are happy because God sent our Lord Jesus Christ to make peace with us.

Adam and Christ

¹²Adam sinned, and that sin brought death into the world. Now everyone has sinned, and so everyone must die. ¹³Sin was in the world before the Law came. But no record of sin was kept, because there was no Law. ¹⁴Yet death still had power over all who lived from the time of Adam to the time of Moses. This happened, though not everyone disobeyed a direct command from God, as Adam did.

In some ways Adam is like Christ who came later. ¹⁵But the gift that God was kind enough to give was very different from Adam's sin. That one sin brought death to many others. Yet in an even greater way,

Jesus Christ alone brought God's gift of kindness to many people.

16 There is a lot of difference between Adam's sin and God's gift. That one sin led to punishment. But God's gift made it possible for us to be acceptable to him, even though we have sinned many times. 17 Death ruled like a king because Adam had sinned. But that cannot compare with what Jesus Christ has done. God has been so kind to us, and he has accepted us because of Jesus. And so we will live and rule like kings.

18 Everyone was going to be punished because Adam sinned. But because of the good thing that Christ has done, God accepts us and gives us the gift of life. 19 Adam disobeyed God and caused many others to be sinners. But Jesus obeyed him and will make many people acceptable to God.

20 The Law came, so that the full power of sin could be seen. Yet where sin was powerful, God's kindness was even more powerful. 21 Sin ruled by means of death. But God's kindness now rules, and God has accepted us because of Jesus Christ our Lord. This means that we will have eternal life.

Dead to Sin but Alive because of Christ

6 What should we say? Should we keep on sinning, so that God's wonderful kindness will show up even better? 2 No, we should not! If we are dead to sin, how can we go on sinning? 3 Don't you know that all who share in Christ Jesus by being baptized also share in his death? 4 When we were baptized, we died and were buried with Christ. We were baptized, so that we would live a new life, as Christ was raised to life by the glory of God the Father.

5 If we shared in Jesus' death by being baptized, we will be raised to life with him. 6We know that the persons we used to be were nailed to the cross with Jesus. This was done, so that our sinful bodies would no longer be the slaves of sin. 7We know that sin doesn't have power over dead people.

8 As surely as we died with Christ, we believe we will also live with him. 9We know that death no longer has any power over Christ. He died and was raised to life, never again to die. 10When Christ died, he died for sin once and for all. But now he is alive, and he lives only for God. 11In the same way, you must think of yourselves as dead to the power of sin. But Christ Jesus has given life to you, and you live for God.

12 Don't let sin rule your body. After all, your body is bound to die, so don't obey its desires 13or let any part of it become a slave of evil. Give yourselves to God, as people who have been raised from death to life. Make every part of your body a slave that pleases God. 14Don't let sin keep ruling your lives. You are ruled by God's kindness and not by the Law.

Slaves Who Do What Pleases God

15 What does all this mean? Does it mean we are free to sin, because we are ruled by God's wonderful kindness and not by the Law? Certainly not! 16Don't you know that you are slaves of anyone you obey? You can be slaves of sin and die, or you can be obedient slaves of God and be acceptable to him. 17You used to be slaves of sin. But I thank God that with all your heart you obeyed the teaching you received from me. 18Now you are set free from sin and are slaves who please God.

19 I am using these everyday examples, because in some ways you are still weak. You used to let the different parts of your body be slaves of your evil thoughts. But now you must make every part of your body serve God, so that you will belong completely to him.

20 When you were slaves of sin, you didn't have to please God. ²¹But what good did you receive from the things you did? All you have to show for them is your shame, and they lead to death. ²²Now you have been set free from sin, and you are God's slaves. This will make you holy and will lead you to eternal life. ²³Sin pays off with death. But God's gift is eternal life given by Jesus Christ our Lord.

An Example from Marriage

7 My friends, you surely understand enough about law to know that laws only have power over people who are alive. ²For example, the Law says that a man's wife must remain his wife as long as he lives. But once her husband is dead, she is free ³to marry someone else. However, if she goes off with another man while her husband is still alive, she is said to be unfaithful.

4 That is how it is with you, my friends. You are now part of the body of Christ and are dead to the power of the Law. You are free to belong to Christ, who was raised to life so that we could serve God. ⁵When we thought only of ourselves, the Law made us have sinful desires. It made every part of our bodies into slaves who are doomed to die. ⁶But the Law no longer rules over us. We are like dead people, and it cannot have any power over us. Now we can serve God in a new way by obeying his Spirit, and not in the old way by obeying the written Law.

The Battle with Sin

7 Does this mean that the Law is sinful? Certainly not! But if it had not been for the Law, I would not have known what sin is really like. For example, I would not have known what it means to want something that belongs to someone else, unless the Law had told me not to do that. ⁸It was sin that used this command as a way of making me have all kinds of desires. But without the Law, sin is dead.

9 Before I knew about the Law, I was alive. But as soon as I heard that command, sin came to life, ¹⁰and I died. The very command that was supposed to bring life to me, instead brought death. ¹¹Sin used this command to trick me, and because of it I died. ¹²Still, the Law and its commands are holy and correct and good.

13 Am I saying that something good caused my death? Certainly not! It was sin that killed me by using something good. Now we can see how terrible and evil sin really is. ¹⁴We know that the Law is spiritual. But I am merely a human, and I have been sold as a slave to sin. ¹⁵In fact, I don't understand why I act the way I do. I don't do what I know is right. I do the things I hate. ¹⁶Although I don't do what I know is right, I agree that the Law is good. ¹⁷So I am not the one doing these evil things. The sin that lives in me is what does them.

18 I know that my selfish desires won't let me do anything that is good. Even when I want to do right, I cannot. ¹⁹Instead of doing what I know is right, I do wrong. ²⁰And so, if I don't do what I know is right, I am no longer the one doing these evil things. The sin that lives in me is what does them.

21 The Law has shown me that something in me keeps me from doing what I know is right. 22With my whole heart I agree with the Law of God. 23But in every part of me I discover something fighting against my mind, and it makes me a prisoner of sin that controls everything I do. 24What a miserable person I am. Who will rescue me from this body that is doomed to die? 25Thank God! Jesus Christ will rescue me.

So with my mind I serve the Law of God, although my selfish desires make me serve the law of sin.

Living by the Power of God's Spirit

8 If you belong to Christ Jesus, you won't be punished. 2The Holy Spirit will give you life that comes from Christ Jesus and will set you[1] free from sin and death. 3The Law of Moses cannot do this, because our selfish desires make the Law weak. But God set you free when he sent his own Son to be like us sinners and to be a sacrifice for our sin. God used Christ's body to condemn sin. 4He did this, so that we would do what the Law commands by obeying the Spirit instead of our own desires.

5 People who are ruled by their desires think only of themselves. Everyone who is ruled by the Holy Spirit thinks about spiritual things. 6If our minds are ruled by our desires, we will die. But if our minds are ruled by the Spirit, we will have life and peace. 7Our desires fight against God, because they do not and cannot obey God's laws. 8If we follow our desires, we cannot please God.

---

[1] *you*: Some manuscripts have "me."

9 You are no longer ruled by your desires, but by God's Spirit, who lives in you. People who don't have the Spirit of Christ in them don't belong to him. 10But Christ lives in you. So you are alive because God has accepted you, even though your bodies must die because of your sins. 11Yet God raised Jesus to life! God's Spirit now lives in you, and he will raise you to life by his Spirit.

12 My dear friends, we must not live to satisfy our desires. 13If you do, you will die. But you will live, if by the help of God's Spirit you say "No" to your desires. 14Only those people who are led by God's Spirit are his children. 15God's Spirit doesn't make us slaves who are afraid of him. Instead, we become his children and call him our Father.*m* 16God's Spirit makes us sure that we are his children. 17His Spirit lets us know that together with Christ we will be given what God has promised. We will also share in the glory of Christ, because we have suffered with him.

A Wonderful Future for God's People

18 I am sure that what we are suffering now cannot compare with the glory that will be shown to us. 19In fact, all creation is eagerly waiting for God to show who his children are. 20Meanwhile, creation is confused, but not because it wants to be confused. God made it this way in the hope 21that creation would be set free from decay and would share in the glorious

---

m our Father: The Greek text uses the Aramaic word "Abba" (meaning "father"), which shows the close relation between the children and their father.

freedom of his children. 22We know that all creation is still groaning and is in pain, like a woman about to give birth.

23 The Spirit makes us sure about what we will be in the future. But now we groan silently, while we wait for God to show that we are his children.[n] This means that our bodies will also be set free. 24And this hope is what saves us. But if we already have what we hope for, there is no need to keep on hoping. 25However, we hope for something we have not yet seen, and we patiently wait for it.

26 In certain ways we are weak, but the Spirit is here to help us. For example, when we don't know what to pray for, the Spirit prays for us in ways that cannot be put into words. 27All of our thoughts are known to God. He can understand what is in the mind of the Spirit, as the Spirit prays for God's people. 28We know that God is always at work for the good of everyone who loves him.[o] They are the ones God has chosen for his purpose, 29and he has always known who his chosen ones would be. He had decided to let them become like his own Son, so that his Son would be the first of many children. 30God then accepted the people he had already decided to choose, and he has shared his glory with them.

---

[n] *to show that we are his children*: These words are not in some manuscripts. The translation of the remainder of the verse would then read, "while we wait for God to set our bodies free."

[o] *God is always at work for the good of everyone who loves him*: Or "All things work for the good of everyone who loves God" or "God's Spirit always works for the good of everyone who loves God."

God's Love

31 What can we say about all this? If God is on our side, can anyone be against us? 32God did not keep back his own Son, but he gave him for us. If God did this, won't he freely give us everything else? 33If God says his chosen ones are acceptable to him, can anyone bring charges against them? 34Or can anyone condemn them? No indeed! Christ died and was raised to life, and now he is at God's right side,*p* speaking to him for us. 35Can anything separate us from the love of Christ? Can trouble, suffering, and hard times, or hunger and nakedness, or danger and death? 36It is exactly as the Scriptures say,

"For you we face death all day long.
   We are like sheep
      on their way to be butchered."

37In everything we have won more than a victory because of Christ who loves us. 38I am sure that nothing can separate us from God's love–not life or death, not angels or spirits, not the present or the future, 39and not powers above or powers below. Nothing in all creation can separate us from God's love for us in Christ Jesus our Lord!

God's Choice of Israel

9 I am a follower of Christ, and the Holy Spirit is a witness to my conscience. So I tell the truth and I am not lying when I say 2my heart is broken and I am in great sorrow. 3I would gladly be placed under God's curse and be separated from Christ for the

---

p *right side*: The place of power and honor.

good of my own people. ⁴They are the descendants of Israel, and they are also God's chosen people. God showed them his glory. He made agreements with them and gave them his Law. The temple is theirs and so are the promises that God made to them. ⁵They have those famous ancestors, who were also the ancestors of Jesus Christ. I pray that God, who rules over all, will be praised forever!*q* Amen.

6 It cannot be said that God broke his promise. After all, not all of the people of Israel are the true people of God. ⁷⁻⁸In fact, when God made the promise to Abraham, he meant only Abraham's descendants by his son Isaac. God was talking only about Isaac when he promised ⁹Sarah, "At this time next year I will return, and you will already have a son."

10 Don't forget what happened to the twin sons of Isaac and Rebecca. ¹¹⁻¹²Even before they were born or had done anything good or bad, the Lord told Rebecca that her older son would serve the younger one. The Lord said this to show that he makes his own choices and that it wasn't because of anything either of them had done. ¹³That's why the Scriptures say that the Lord liked Jacob more than Esau.

14 Are we saying that God is unfair? Certainly not! ¹⁵The Lord told Moses that he has pity and mercy on anyone he wants to. ¹⁶Everything then depends on God's mercy and not on what people

---

q Christ. I pray that God, who rules over all, will be praised forever: Or "Christ, who rules over all. I pray that God will be praised forever" or "Christ. And I pray that Christ, who is God and rules over all, will be praised forever."

want or do. ¹⁷In the Scriptures the Lord says to the king of Egypt, "I let you become king, so that I could show you my power and be praised by all people on earth." ¹⁸Everything depends on what God decides to do, and he can either have pity on people or make them stubborn.

God's Anger and Mercy

19 Someone may ask, "How can God blame us, if he makes us behave in the way he wants us to?" ²⁰But, my friend, I ask, "Who do you think you are to question God? Does the clay have the right to ask the potter why he shaped it the way he did? ²¹Doesn't a potter have the right to make a fancy bowl and a plain bowl out of the same lump of clay?"

22 God wanted to show his anger and reveal his power against everyone who deserved to be destroyed. But instead, he patiently put up with them. ²³He did this by showing how glorious he is when he has pity on the people he has chosen to share in his glory. ²⁴Whether Jews or Gentiles, we are those chosen ones, ²⁵just as the Lord says in the book of Hosea,

"Although they are not my people,
    I will make them my people.
I will treat with love those nations
    that have never been loved.

26 "Once they were told,
    'You are not my people.'
But in that very place they will be called
    children of the living God."

27 And this is what the prophet Isaiah said about the people of Israel,

"The people of Israel are as many
　　as the grains of sand along the beach.
　But only a few who are left will be saved.
28 The Lord will be quick and sure
　　to do on earth
　　what he has warned he will do."
29 Isaiah also said,
　　"If the Lord All-Powerful
　　　had not spared some of our descendants,
　we would have been destroyed
　　like the cities of Sodom
　　　and Gomorrah."[r]

Israel and the Good News

30 What does all of this mean? It means that the Gentiles were not trying to be acceptable to God, but they found that he would accept them if they had faith. 31-32 It also means that the people of Israel were not acceptable to God. And why not? It was because they were trying[s] to be acceptable by obeying the Law instead of by having faith in God. The people of Israel fell over the stone that makes people stumble, 33just as God says in the Scriptures,

　　"Look! I am placing in Zion
　　　a stone to make people stumble and fall.
　But those who have faith in that one
　　will never be disappointed."

---

r *Sodom and Gomorrah*: During the time of Abraham
　the Lord destroyed these two cities because their people
　were so sinful.
s *because they were trying*: Or "while they were trying" or
　"even though they were trying."

10 Dear friends, my greatest wish and my prayer to God is for the people of Israel to be saved. [2]I know they love God, but they don't understand [3]what makes people acceptable to him. So they refuse to trust God, and they try to be acceptable by obeying the Law. [4]But Christ makes the Law no longer necessary[t] for those who become acceptable to God by faith.

Anyone Can Be Saved

[5] Moses said that a person could become acceptable to God by obeying the Law. He did this when he wrote, "If you want to live, you must do all that the Law commands."

[6] But people whose faith makes them acceptable to God will never ask, "Who will go up to heaven to bring Christ down?" [7]Neither will they ask, "Who will go down into the world of the dead to raise him to life?"

[8] All who are acceptable because of their faith simply say, "The message is as near as your mouth or your heart." And this is the same message we preach about faith. [9]So you will be saved, if you honestly say, "Jesus is Lord," and if you believe with all your heart that God raised him from death. [10]God will accept you and save you, if you truly believe this and tell it to others.

[11] The Scriptures say that no one who has faith will be disappointed, [12]no matter if that person is a Jew or a Gentile. There is only one Lord, and he is generous to everyone who asks for his help. [13]All who call out to the Lord will be saved.

---

[t] *But Christ makes the Law no longer necessary*: Or "But Christ gives the full meaning to the Law."

14 How can people have faith in the Lord and ask him to save them, if they have never heard about him? And how can they hear, unless someone tells them? 15 And how can anyone tell them without being sent by the Lord? The Scriptures say it is a beautiful sight to see even the feet of someone coming to preach the good news. 16 Yet not everyone has believed the message. For example, the prophet Isaiah asked, "Lord, has anyone believed what we said?"

17 No one can have faith without hearing the message about Christ. 18 But am I saying that the people of Israel did not hear? No, I am not! The Scriptures say,

"The message was told
    everywhere on earth.
It was announced all over the world."

19 Did the people of Israel understand or not? Moses answered this question when he told that the Lord had said,

"I will make Israel jealous of people
    who are a nation of nobodies.
I will make them angry at people
    who don't understand a thing."

20 Isaiah was fearless enough to tell that the Lord had said,

"I was found by people
    who were not looking for me.
I appeared to the ones
    who were not asking about me."

21 And Isaiah said about the people of Israel,

"All day long the Lord has reached out
    to people who are stubborn
    and refuse to obey."

God Has Not Rejected His People

11 Am I saying that God has turned his back on his people? Certainly not! I am one of the people of Israel, and I myself am a descendant of Abraham from the tribe of Benjamin. ²God did not turn his back on his chosen people. Don't you remember reading in the Scriptures how Elijah complained to God about the people of Israel? ³He said, "Lord, they killed your prophets and destroyed your altars. I am the only one left, and now they want to kill me."

⁴ But the Lord told Elijah, "I still have seven thousand followers who have not worshiped Baal." ⁵It is the same way now. God was kind to the people of Israel, and so a few of them are still his followers. ⁶This happened because of God's undeserved kindness and not because of anything they have done. It could not have happened except for God's kindness.

⁷ This means that only a chosen few of the people of Israel found what all of them were searching for. And the rest of them were stubborn, ⁸just as the Scriptures say,

"God made them so stupid
        that their eyes are blind,
        and their ears are still deaf."

⁹ Then David said,

"Turn their meals into bait for a trap,
        so that they will stumble
        and be given what they deserve.
¹⁰ Blindfold their eyes! Don't let them see.
    Bend their backs beneath a burden
        that will never be lifted."

Gentiles Will Be Saved

11 Do I mean that the people of Israel fell, never to get up again? Certainly not! Their failure made it possible for the Gentiles to be saved, and this will make the people of Israel jealous. 12 But if the rest of the world's people were helped so much by Israel's sin and loss, they will be helped even more by their full return.

13 I am now speaking to you Gentiles, and as long as I am an apostle to you, I will take pride in my work. 14 I hope in this way to make some of my own people jealous enough to be saved. 15 When Israel rejected God,^{u} the rest of the people in the world were able to turn to him. So when God makes friends with Israel, it will be like bringing the dead back to life. 16 If part of a batch of dough is made holy by being offered to God, then all of the dough is holy. If the roots of a tree are holy, the rest of the tree is holy too.

17 You Gentiles are like branches of a wild olive tree that were made to be part of a cultivated olive tree. You have taken the place of some branches that were cut away from it. And because of this, you enjoy the blessings that come from being part of that cultivated tree. 18 But don't think you are better than the branches that were cut away. Just remember that you are not supporting the roots of that tree. Its roots are supporting you.

19 Maybe you think those branches were cut away, so that you could be put in their place. 20 That's true enough. But they were cut away because they did not

---

^{u} *When Israel rejected God*: Or "When Israel was rejected."

have faith, and you are where you are because you do have faith. So don't be proud, but be afraid. [21] If God cut away those natural branches, couldn't he do the same to you?

22 Now you see both how kind and how hard God can be. He was hard on those who fell, but he was kind to you. And he will keep on being kind to you, if you keep on trusting in his kindness. Otherwise, you will be cut away too.

23 If those other branches will start having faith, they will be made a part of that tree again. God has the power to put them back. [24] After all, it wasn't natural for branches to be cut from a wild olive tree and to be made part of a cultivated olive tree. So it is much more likely that God will join the natural branches back to the cultivated olive tree.

The People of Israel Will Be Brought Back

25 My friends, I don't want you Gentiles to be too proud of yourselves. So I will explain the mystery of what has happened to the people of Israel. Some of them have become stubborn, and they will stay like that until the complete number of you Gentiles has come in. [26] In this way all of Israel will be saved, as the Scriptures say,

"From Zion someone will come
to rescue us.
Then Jacob's descendants
will stop being evil.
[27] This is what the Lord has promised to do
when he forgives their sins."

28 The people of Israel are treated as God's enemies, so that the good news can come to you Gentiles.

But they are still the chosen ones, and God loves them because of their famous ancestors. 29God doesn't take back the gifts he has given or forget about the people he has chosen.

30 At one time you Gentiles rejected God. But now Israel has rejected God, and you have been shown mercy. 31And because of the mercy shown to you, they will also be shown mercy. 32All people have disobeyed God, and that's why he treats them as prisoners. But he does this, so that he can have mercy on all of them.

33 Who can measure the wealth and wisdom and knowledge of God? Who can understand his decisions or explain what he does?

> 34 "Has anyone known the thoughts of the Lord
> or given him advice?
> 35 Has anyone loaned something to the Lord
> that must be repaid?"

36Everything comes from the Lord. All things were made because of him and will return to him. Praise the Lord forever! Amen.

Christ Brings New Life

12 Dear friends, God is good. So I beg you to offer your bodies to him as a living sacrifice, pure and pleasing. That's the most sensible way to serve God. 2Don't be like the people of this world, but let God change the way you think. Then you will know how to do everything that is good and pleasing to him.

3 I realize how kind God has been to me, and so I tell each of you not to think you are better than you really are. Use good sense and measure yourself by the amount of faith that God has given you. 4A body

is made up of many parts, and each of them has its own use. ⁵That's how it is with us. There are many of us, but we each are part of the body of Christ, as well as part of one another.

6 God has also given each of us different gifts to use. If we can prophesy, we should do it according to the amount of faith we have. ⁷If we can serve others, we should serve. If we can teach, we should teach. ⁸If we can encourage others, we should encourage them. If we can give, we should be generous. If we are leaders, we should do our best. If we are good to others, we should do it cheerfully.

Rules for Christian Living

9 Be sincere in your love for others. Hate everything that is evil and hold tight to everything that is good. ¹⁰Love each other as brothers and sisters and honor others more than you do yourself. ¹¹Never give up. Eagerly follow the Holy Spirit and serve the Lord. ¹²Let your hope make you glad. Be patient in time of trouble and never stop praying. ¹³Take care of God's needy people and welcome strangers into your home.

14 Ask God to bless everyone who mistreats you. Ask him to bless them and not to curse them. ¹⁵When others are happy, be happy with them, and when they are sad, be sad. ¹⁶Be friendly with everyone. Don't be proud and feel that you are smarter than others. Make friends with ordinary people.ᵛ ¹⁷Don't mistreat someone who has mistreated you. But try to earn the respect of others, ¹⁸and do your best to live at peace with everyone.

ᵛ *Make friends with ordinary people*: Or "Do ordinary jobs."

19 Dear friends, don't try to get even. Let God take revenge. In the Scriptures the Lord says,

"I am the one to take revenge
  and pay them back."

20 The Scriptures also say,

"If your enemies are hungry,
  give them something to eat.
And if they are thirsty,
  give them something to drink.
This will be the same
  as piling burning coals on their heads."

21 Don't let evil defeat you, but defeat evil with good.

Obey Rulers

13 Obey the rulers who have authority over you. Only God can give authority to anyone, and he puts these rulers in their places of power. 2 People who oppose the authorities are opposing what God has done, and they will be punished. 3 Rulers are a threat to evil people, not to good people. There is no need to be afraid of the authorities. Just do right, and they will praise you for it. 4 After all, they are God's servants, and it is their duty to help you.

If you do something wrong, you ought to be afraid, because these rulers have the right to punish you. They are God's servants who punish criminals to show how angry God is. 5 But you should obey the rulers because you know it is the right thing to do, and not just because of God's anger.

6 You must also pay your taxes. The authorities are God's servants, and it is their duty to take care of these matters. 7 Pay all that you owe, whether it is taxes and fees or respect and honor.

Love

8 Let love be your only debt! If you love others, you have done all that the Law demands. ⁹In the Law there are many commands, such as, "Be faithful in marriage. Do not murder. Do not steal. Do not want what belongs to others." But all of these are summed up in the command that says, "Love others as much as you love yourself." ¹⁰No one who loves others will harm them. So love is all that the Law demands.

The Day When Christ Returns

11 You know what sort of times we live in, and so you should live properly. It is time to wake up. You know that the day when we will be saved is nearer now than when we first put our faith in the Lord. ¹²Night is almost over, and day will soon appear. We must stop behaving as people do in the dark and be ready to live in the light. ¹³So behave properly, as people do in the day. Don't go to wild parties or get drunk or be vulgar or indecent. Don't quarrel or be jealous. ¹⁴Let the Lord Jesus Christ be as near to you as the clothes you wear. Then you won't try to satisfy your selfish desires.

Don't Criticize Others

14 Welcome all the Lord's followers, even those whose faith is weak. Don't criticize them for having beliefs that are different from yours. ²Some think it is all right to eat anything, while those whose faith is weak will eat only vegetables. ³But you should not criticize others for eating or for not eating. After all, God welcomes everyone. ⁴What right do you

have to criticize someone else's servants? Only their Lord can decide if they are doing right, and the Lord will make sure that they do right.

5 Some of the Lord's followers think one day is more important than another. Others think all days are the same. But each of you should make up your own mind. 6 Any followers who count one day more important than another day do it to honor their Lord. And any followers who eat meat give thanks to God, just like the ones who don't eat meat.

7 Whether we live or die, it must be for God, rather than for ourselves. 8 Whether we live or die, it must be for the Lord. Alive or dead, we still belong to the Lord. 9 This is because Christ died and rose to life, so that he would be the Lord of the dead and of the living. 10 Why do you criticize other followers of the Lord? Why do you look down on them? The day is coming when God will judge all of us. 11 In the Scriptures God says,

"I swear by my very life
    that everyone will kneel down
    and praise my name!"

12 And so, each of us must give an account to God for what we do.

Don't Cause Problems for Others

13 We must stop judging others. We must also make up our minds not to upset anyone's faith. 14 The Lord Jesus has made it clear to me that God considers all foods fit to eat. But if you think some foods are unfit to eat, then for you they are not fit.

15 If you are hurting others by the foods you eat, you are not guided by love. Don't let your appetite

destroy someone Christ died for. ¹⁶Don't let your right to eat bring shame to Christ. ¹⁷God's kingdom isn't about eating and drinking. It is about pleasing God, about living in peace, and about true happiness. All this comes from the Holy Spirit. ¹⁸If you serve Christ in this way, you will please God and be respected by people. ¹⁹We should try*ʷ* to live at peace and help each other have a strong faith.

20 Don't let your appetite destroy what God has done. All foods are fit to eat, but it is wrong to cause problems for others by what you eat. ²¹It is best not to eat meat or drink wine or do anything else that causes problems for other followers of the Lord. ²²What you believe about these things should be kept between you and God. You are fortunate, if your actions don't make you have doubts. ²³But if you do have doubts about what you eat, you are going against your beliefs. And you know that is wrong, because anything you do against your beliefs is sin.

Please Others and Not Yourself

15 If our faith is strong, we should be patient with the Lord's followers whose faith is weak. We should try to please them instead of ourselves. ²We should think of their good and try to help them by doing what pleases them. ³Even Christ did not try to please himself. But as the Scriptures say, "The people who insulted you also insulted me." ⁴And the Scriptures were written to teach and encourage us by giving us hope. ⁵God is the one who makes us patient and cheerful. I pray that he will help you live

---

ʷ *We should try*: Some manuscripts have "We try."

at peace with each other, as you follow Christ. [6]Then all of you together will praise God, the Father of our Lord Jesus Christ.

The Good News Is for Jews and Gentiles

7 Honor God by accepting each other, as Christ has accepted you. [8]I tell you that Christ came as a servant of the Jews to show that God has kept the promises he made to their famous ancestors. Christ also came, [9]so that the Gentiles would praise God for being kind to them. It is just as the Scriptures say,

"I will tell the nations about you,
    and I will sing praises to your name."

10 The Scriptures also say to the Gentiles, "Come and celebrate with God's people."

11 Again the Scriptures say,

"Praise the Lord, all you Gentiles.
    All you nations, come and worship him."

12 Isaiah says,

"Someone from David's family
    will come to power.
He will rule the nations,
    and they will put their hope in him."

13 I pray that God, who gives hope, will bless you with complete happiness and peace because of your faith. And may the power of the Holy Spirit fill you with hope.

Paul's Work as a Missionary

14 My friends, I am sure that you are very good and that you have all the knowledge you need to teach each other. [15]But I have spoken to you plainly and have tried to remind you of some things. God was

so kind to me! [16]He chose me to be a servant of Christ Jesus for the Gentiles and to do the work of a priest in the service of his good news. God did this so that the Holy Spirit could make the Gentiles into a holy offering, pleasing to him.

17 Because of Christ Jesus, I can take pride in my service for God. [18]In fact, all I will talk about is how Christ let me speak and work, so that the Gentiles would obey him. [19]Indeed, I will tell how Christ worked miracles and wonders by the power of the Holy Spirit. I have preached the good news about him all the way from Jerusalem to Illyricum. [20]But I have always tried to preach where people have never heard about Christ. I am like a builder who doesn't build on anyone else's foundation. [21]It is just as the Scriptures say,

"All who haven't been told about him
   will see him,
and those who haven't heard about him
   will understand."

Paul's Plan To Visit Rome

22 My work has always kept me from coming to see you. [23]Now there is nothing left for me to do in this part of the world, and for years I have wanted to visit you. [24]So I plan to stop off on my way to Spain. Then after a short, but refreshing, visit with you, I hope you will quickly send me on.

25-26 I am now on my way to Jerusalem to deliver the money that the Lord's followers in Macedonia and Achaia collected for God's needy people. [27]This is something they really wanted to do. But sharing their money with the Jews was also like paying back a debt, because the Jews had already shared their spiritual blessings with the Gentiles. ²⁸After I have safely delivered this money, I will visit you and then go on to Spain. ²⁹And when I do arrive in Rome, I know it will be with the full blessings of Christ.

30 My friends, by the power of the Lord Jesus Christ and by the love that comes from the Holy Spirit, I beg you to pray sincerely with me and for me. ³¹Pray that God will protect me from the unbelievers in Judea, and that his people in Jerusalem will be pleased with what I am doing. ³²Ask God to let me come to you and have a pleasant and refreshing visit. ³³I pray that God, who gives peace, will be with all of you. Amen.

Personal Greetings

16 I have good things to say about Phoebe, who is a leader in the church at Cenchreae. ²Welcome her in a way that is proper for someone who has faith in the Lord and is one of God's own people. Help her in any way you can. After all, she has proved to be a respected leader for many others, including me.

3 Give my greetings to Priscilla and Aquila. They have not only served Christ Jesus together with me, ⁴but they have even risked their lives for me. I am grateful for them and so are all the Gentile churches. ⁵Greet the church that meets in their home.

Greet my dear friend Epaenetus, who was the first person in Asia to have faith in Christ.

6 Greet Mary, who has worked so hard for you.

7 Greet my relatives ˣ Andronicus and Junias, who were in jail with me. They are highly respected by the apostles and were followers of Christ before I was.

ˣ *relatives:* Or *"Jewish friends."*

8 Greet Ampliatus, my dear friend whose faith is in the Lord.

9 Greet Urbanus, who serves Christ along with us. Greet my dear friend Stachys.

10 Greet Apelles, a faithful servant of Christ. Greet Aristobulus and his family.

11 Greet Herodion, who is a relative [y] of mine. Greet Narcissus and the others in his family, who have faith in the Lord.

12 Greet Tryphaena and Tryphosa, who work hard for the Lord.

Greet my dear friend Persis. She also works hard for the Lord.

13 Greet Rufus, that special servant of the Lord, and greet his mother, who has been like a mother to me.

14 Greet Asyncritus, Phlegon, Hermes, Patrobas, and Hermas, as well as our friends who are with them.

15 Greet Philologus, Julia, Nereus and his sister, and Olympas, and all of God's people who are with them.

16 Be sure to give each other a warm greeting. All of Christ's churches greet you.

17 My friends, I beg you to watch out for anyone who causes trouble and divides the church by refusing to do what all of you were taught. Stay away from them! 18 They want to serve themselves and not Christ the Lord. Their flattery and fancy talk fool people who don't know any better. 19 I am glad that everyone knows how well you obey the Lord. But still, I want you to understand what is good and not have anything

y relative: Or "Jewish friend."

to do with evil. [20]Then God, who gives peace, will soon crush Satan under your feet. I pray that our Lord Jesus will be kind to you.

21 Timothy, who works with me, sends his greetings, and so do my relatives,[z] Lucius, Jason, and Sosipater.

22 I, Tertius, also send my greetings. I am a follower of the Lord, and I wrote this letter.[a]

23-24 Gaius welcomes me and the whole church into his home, and he sends his greetings.

Erastus, the city treasurer, and our dear friend Quartus send their greetings too.[b]

Paul's Closing Prayer

25 Praise God! He can make you strong by means of my good news, which is the message about[c] Jesus Christ. For ages and ages this message was kept secret, [26]but now at last it has been told. The eternal God commanded his prophets to write about the good news, so that all nations would obey and have faith. [27]And now, because of Jesus Christ, we can praise the only wise God forever! Amen.[d]

---

[z] *relatives*: Or "Jewish friends."

[a] *I wrote this letter*: Paul probably dictated this letter to Tertius.

[b] *send their greetings, too*: Some manuscripts add, "I pray that our Lord Jesus Christ will always be kind to you. Amen."

[c] *about*: Or "from."

[d] *Amen*: Some manuscripts have verses 25-27 after 14.23. Others have the verses here and after 14.23, and one manuscript has them after 15.33.

Paul's First Letter
to the Church in Corinth

ABOUT THIS LETTER

Although this letter is called the First Letter to the Corinthians, it is not really the first one that Paul wrote to this church. We know this because he mentions in this letter that he had written one before (5.9). The Christians in Corinth had also written to him (7.1), and part of First Corinthians contains Paul's answers to questions they had asked.

Corinth is a large port city in southern Greece. Paul began his work there in a Jewish meeting place, but he had to move next door to the home of a Gentile who had become a follower of Jesus (Acts 18.1-17). Most of the followers in Corinth were poor people (1 Corinthians 1.26-29), though some of them were wealthy (1 Corinthians 11.18-21), and one was even the city treasurer (Romans 16.23). While he was in Corinth, Paul worked as a tentmaker to earn a living (Acts 18.3; 1 Corinthians 4.12; 9.1-18).

Paul was especially concerned about the way the Corinthian Christians were always arguing and dividing themselves into groups (1.10-4.21) and about the way they treated one another (5.1-6.20). These are two of Paul's main concerns as he writes this letter. But he also wants to answer the questions they asked him about marriage (7.1-40) and food offered to idols (8.1-13). Paul encourages them to worship God the

526

right way (10.1–14.40) and to be firm in their belief that God has given them victory over death (15.1-58).

Love, Paul tells them, is even more important than faith or hope. All of the problems in the church could be solved, if all the members would love one another, as Christians should:

> Love is kind and patient,
>   never jealous, boastful,
>   proud, or rude.
> Love rejoices in the truth,
>   but not in evil.
> Love is always supportive,
>   loyal, hopeful,
>   and trusting.
> Love never fails! (13.4, 5, 6-8)

A QUICK LOOK AT THIS LETTER

1 From Paul, chosen by God to be an apostle of Christ Jesus, and from Sosthenes, who is also a follower.

2 To God's church in Corinth. Christ Jesus chose you to be his very own people, and you worship in his name, as we and all others do who call him Lord.

3 My prayer is that God our Father and the Lord Jesus Christ will be kind to you and will bless you with peace!

4 I never stop thanking my God for being kind enough to give you Christ Jesus, 5who helps you speak and understand so well. 6Now you are certain that everything we told you about our Lord Christ Jesus is true. 7You are not missing out on any blessings, as you wait for him to return. 8And until the day Christ does return, he will keep you completely innocent. 9God can be trusted, and he chose you to be partners with his Son, our Lord Jesus Christ.

Taking Sides

10 My dear friends, as a follower of our Lord Jesus Christ, I beg you to get along with each other. Don't take sides. Always try to agree in what you think. 11Several people from Chloe's family*a* have already reported to me that you keep arguing with each other. 12They have said that some of you claim to follow me, while others claim to follow Apollos or Peter*b* or Christ.

13 Has Christ been divided up? Was I nailed to a cross for you? Were you baptized in my name? 14I thank God*c* that I didn't baptize any of you except Crispus and Gaius. 15Not one of you can say that you

---

a *family*: Family members and possibly slaves and others who may have lived in the house.

b *Peter*: The Greek text has "Cephas," which is an Aramaic name meaning "rock." Peter is the Greek name with the same meaning.

c *I thank God*: Some manuscripts have "I thank my God."

were baptized in my name. ¹⁶I did baptize the family *d* of Stephanas, but I don't remember if I baptized anyone else. ¹⁷Christ did not send me to baptize. He sent me to tell the good news without using big words that would make the cross of Christ lose its power.

Christ Is God's Power and Wisdom

18 The message about the cross doesn't make any sense to lost people. But for those of us who are being saved, it is God's power at work. ¹⁹As God says in the Scriptures,

"I will destroy the wisdom
    of all who claim to be wise.
I will confuse those
    who think they know so much."

20 What happened to those wise people? What happened to those experts in the Scriptures? What happened to the ones who think they have all the answers? Didn't God show that the wisdom of this world is foolish? ²¹God was wise and decided not to let the people of this world use their wisdom to learn about him.

Instead, God chose to save only those who believe the foolish message we preach. ²²Jews ask for miracles, and Greeks want something that sounds wise. ²³But we preach that Christ was nailed to a cross. Most Jews have problems with this, and most Gentiles think it is foolish. ²⁴Our message is God's power and wisdom for the Jews and the Greeks that he has chosen. ²⁵Even when God is foolish, he is wiser than everyone else, and even when God is weak, he is stronger than everyone else.

---

d family: See the note at 1.11.

26 My dear friends, remember what you were when God chose you. The people of this world didn't think that many of you were wise. Only a few of you were in places of power, and not many of you came from important families. 27 But God chose the foolish things of this world to put the wise to shame. He chose the weak things of this world to put the powerful to shame.

28 What the world thinks is worthless, useless, and nothing at all is what God has used to destroy what the world considers important. 29 God did all this to keep anyone from bragging to him. 30 You are God's children. He sent Christ Jesus to save us and to make us wise, acceptable, and holy. 31 So if you want to brag, do what the Scriptures say and brag about the Lord.

Telling about Christ and the Cross

2 Friends, when I came and told you the mystery*e* that God had shared with us, I didn't use big words or try to sound wise. 2 In fact, while I was with you, I made up my mind to speak only about Jesus Christ, who had been nailed to a cross.

3 At first, I was weak and trembling with fear. 4 When I talked with you or preached, I didn't try to prove anything by sounding wise. I simply let God's Spirit show his power. 5 That way you would have faith because of God's power and not because of human wisdom.

6 We do use wisdom when speaking to people who are mature in their faith. But it isn't the wisdom

---

e mystery: Some manuscripts have "testimony."

of this world or of its rulers, who will soon disappear.
⁷We speak of God's hidden and mysterious wisdom
that God decided to use for our glory long before the
world began. ⁸The rulers of this world didn't know
anything about this wisdom. If they had known about
it, they would not have nailed the glorious Lord to a
cross. ⁹But it is just as the Scriptures say,

"What God has planned
    for people who love him
is more than eyes have seen
    or ears have heard.
It has never even entered our minds!"

10 God's Spirit has shown you everything. His
Spirit finds out everything, even what is deep in the
mind of God. ¹¹You are the only one who knows
what is in your own mind, and God's Spirit is the only
one who knows what is in God's mind. ¹²But God has
given us his Spirit. That's why we don't think the
same way that the people of this world think. That's
also why we can recognize the blessings that God has
given us.

13 Every word we speak was taught to us by God's
Spirit, not by human wisdom. And this same Spirit
helps us teach spiritual things to spiritual people.ᶠ
¹⁴That's why only someone who has God's Spirit can
understand spiritual blessings. Anyone who doesn't
have God's Spirit thinks these blessings are foolish.
¹⁵People who are guided by the Spirit can make all
kinds of judgments, but they cannot be judged by others.
¹⁶The Scriptures ask,

ᶠ *teach spiritual things to spiritual people*: Or "compare
spiritual things with spiritual things."

"Has anyone ever known
    the thoughts of the Lord
    or given him advice?"
But we understand what Christ is thinking.[g]

Working Together for God

3 My friends, you are acting like the people of this
world. That's why I could not speak to you as
spiritual people. You are like babies as far as your
faith in Christ is concerned. [2]So I had to treat you like
babies and feed you milk. You could not take solid
food, and you still cannot, [3]because you are not yet
spiritual. You are jealous and argue with each other.
This proves that you are not spiritual and that you are
acting like the people of this world.

4 Some of you say that you follow me, and others
claim to follow Apollos. Isn't that how ordinary people
behave? [5]Apollos and I are merely servants who
helped you to have faith. It was the Lord who made it
all happen. [6]I planted the seeds, Apollos watered them,
but God made them sprout and grow. [7]What matters
isn't those who planted or watered, but God who made
the plants grow. [8]The one who plants is just as important as the one who waters. And each one will be paid
for what they do. [9]Apollos and I work together for
God, and you are God's garden and God's building.

Only One Foundation

10 God was kind and let me become an expert
builder. I laid a foundation on which others have

---

[g] *we understand what Christ is thinking*: Or "we think as
    Christ does."

built. But we must each be careful how we build, [11] because Christ is the only foundation. [12-13] Whatever we build on that foundation will be tested by fire on the day of judgment. Then everyone will find out if we have used gold, silver, and precious stones, or wood, hay, and straw. [14] We will be rewarded if our building is left standing. [15] But if it is destroyed by the fire, we will lose everything. Yet we ourselves will be saved, like someone escaping from flames.

16 All of you surely know that you are God's temple and that his Spirit lives in you. [17] Together you are God's holy temple, and God will destroy anyone who destroys his temple.

18 Don't fool yourselves! If any of you think you are wise in the things of this world, you will have to become foolish before you can be truly wise. [19] This is because God considers the wisdom of this world to be foolish. It is just as the Scriptures say, "God catches the wise when they try to outsmart him." [20] The Scriptures also say, "The Lord knows that the plans made by wise people are useless." [21-22] So stop bragging about what anyone has done. Paul and Apollos and Peter[h] all belong to you. In fact, everything is yours, including the world, life, death, the present, and the future. Everything belongs to you, [23] and you belong to Christ, and Christ belongs to God.

The Work of the Apostles

4 Think of us as servants of Christ who have been given the work of explaining God's mysterious ways. [2] And since our first duty is to be faithful to the

---

[h] *Peter*: See the note at 1.12.

one we work for, ³it doesn't matter to me if I am judged by you or even by a court of law. In fact, I don't judge myself. ⁴I don't know of anything against me, but that doesn't prove that I am right. The Lord is my judge. ⁵So don't judge anyone until the Lord returns. He will show what is hidden in the dark and what is in everyone's heart. Then God will be the one who praises each of us.

6 Friends, I have used Apollos and myself as examples to teach you the meaning of the saying, "Follow the rules." I want you to stop saying that one of us is better than the other. ⁷What is so special about you? What do you have that you were not given? And if it was given to you, how can you brag? ⁸Are you already satisfied? Are you now rich? Have you become kings while we are still nobodies? I wish you were kings. Then we could have a share in your kingdom.

9 It seems to me that God has put us apostles in the worst possible place. We are like prisoners on their way to death. Angels and the people of this world just laugh at us. ¹⁰Because of Christ we are thought of as fools, but Christ has made you wise. We are weak and hated, but you are powerful and respected. ¹¹Even today we go hungry and thirsty and don't have anything to wear except rags. We are mistreated and don't have a place to live. ¹²We work hard with our own hands, and when people abuse us, we wish them well. When we suffer, we are patient. ¹³When someone curses us, we answer with kind words. Until now we are thought of as nothing more than the trash and garbage of this world.

14 I am not writing to embarrass you. I want to help you, just as parents help their own dear children.

[15]Ten thousand people may teach you about Christ, but I am your only father. You became my children when I told you about Christ Jesus, [16]and I want you to be like me. [17]That's why I sent Timothy to you. I love him like a son, and he is a faithful servant of the Lord. Timothy will tell you what I do to follow Christ and how it agrees with what I always teach about Christ in every church.

18 Some of you think I am not coming for a visit, and so you are bragging. [19]But if the Lord lets me come, I will soon be there. Then I will find out if the ones who are doing all this bragging really have any power. [20]God's kingdom isn't just a lot of words. It is power. [21]What do you want me to do when I arrive? Do you want me to be hard on you or to be kind and gentle?

Immoral Followers

5 I have heard terrible things about some of you. In fact, you are behaving worse than the Gentiles. A man is even sleeping with his own stepmother.[i] [2]You are proud, when you ought to feel bad enough to chase away anyone who acts like that.

3-4 I am with you only in my thoughts. But in the name of our Lord Jesus I have already judged this man, as though I were with you in person. So when you meet together and the power of the Lord Jesus is with you, I will be there too. [5]You must then hand that man over to Satan. His body will be destroyed, but his spirit will be saved when the Lord Jesus returns.

---

[i] *is even sleeping with his own stepmother*: Or "has even married his own stepmother."

6 Stop being proud! Don't you know how a little yeast can spread through the whole batch of dough? 7Get rid of the old yeast! Then you will be like fresh bread made without yeast, and that is what you are. Our Passover lamb is Christ, who has already been sacrificed. 8So don't celebrate the festival by being evil and sinful, which is like serving bread made with yeast. Be pure and truthful and celebrate by using bread made without yeast.

9 In my other letter*j* I told you not to have anything to do with immoral people. 10But I wasn't talking about the people of this world. You would have to leave this world to get away from everyone who is immoral or greedy or who cheats or worships idols. 11I was talking about your own people who are immoral or greedy or worship idols or curse others or get drunk or cheat. Don't even eat with them! 12Why should I judge outsiders? Aren't we supposed to judge only church members? 13God judges everyone else. The Scriptures say, "Chase away any of your own people who are evil."

Taking Each Other to Court

6 When one of you has a complaint against another, do you take your complaint to a court of sinners? Or do you take it to God's people? 2Don't you know that God's people will judge the world? And if you are going to judge the world, can't you settle small problems? 3Don't you know that we will judge angels? And if that is so, we can surely judge everyday matters.

---

j other letter: An unknown letter that Paul wrote to the Christians at Corinth before he wrote this one.

⁴Why do you take everyday complaints to judges who are not respected by the church? ⁵I say this to your shame. Aren't any of you wise enough to act as a judge between one follower and another? ⁶Why should one of you take another to be tried by unbelievers?

7 When one of you takes another to court, all of you lose. It would be better to let yourselves be cheated and robbed. ⁸But instead, you cheat and rob other followers.

9 Don't you know that evil people won't have a share in the blessings of God's kingdom? Don't fool yourselves! No one who is immoral or worships idols or is unfaithful in marriage or is a pervert or behaves like a homosexual ¹⁰will share in God's kingdom. Neither will any thief or greedy person or drunkard or anyone who curses and cheats others. ¹¹Some of you used to be like that. But now the name of our Lord Jesus Christ and the power of God's Spirit have washed you and made you holy and acceptable to God.

Honor God with Your Body

12 Some of you say, "We can do anything we want to." But I tell you that not everything is good for us. So I refuse to let anything have power over me. ¹³You also say, "Food is meant for our bodies, and our bodies are meant for food." But I tell you that God will destroy them both. We are not supposed to do indecent things with our bodies. We are to use them for the Lord who is in charge of our bodies. ¹⁴God will raise us from death by the same power that he used when he raised our Lord to life.

15 Don't you know that your bodies are part of the body of Christ? Is it right for me to join part of the body of Christ to a prostitute? No, it isn't! ¹⁶Don't

you know that a man who does that becomes part of her body? The Scriptures say, "The two of them will be like one person." [17]But anyone who is joined to the Lord is one in spirit with him.

18 Don't be immoral in matters of sex. That is a sin against your own body in a way that no other sin is. [19]You surely know that your body is a temple where the Holy Spirit lives. The Spirit is in you and is a gift from God. You are no longer your own. [20]God paid a great price for you. So use your body to honor God.

Questions about Marriage

7 Now I will answer the questions that you asked in your letter. You asked, "Is it best for people not to marry?"[k] [2]Well, having your own husband or wife should keep you from doing something immoral. [3]Husbands and wives should be fair with each other about having sex. [4]A wife belongs to her husband instead of to herself, and a husband belongs to his wife instead of to himself. [5]So don't refuse sex to each other, unless you agree not to have sex for a little while, in order to spend time in prayer. Then Satan won't be able to tempt you because of your lack of self-control. [6]In my opinion that is what should be done, though I don't know of anything the Lord said about this matter. [7]I wish that all of you were like me, but God has given different gifts to each of us.

8 Here is my advice for people who have never been married and for widows. You should stay single,

---

[k] *people not to marry*: Or "married couples not to have sex."

just as I am. 9But if you don't have enough self-control, then go ahead and get married. After all, it is better to marry than to burn with desire.*

10 I instruct married couples to stay together, and this is exactly what the Lord himself taught. A wife who leaves her husband 11should either stay single or go back to her husband. And a husband should not leave his wife.

12 I don't know of anything else the Lord said about marriage. All I can do is to give you my own advice. If your wife isn't a follower of the Lord, but is willing to stay with you, don't divorce her. 13If your husband isn't a follower, but is willing to stay with you, don't divorce him. 14Your husband or wife who isn't a follower is made holy by having you as a mate. This also makes your children holy and keeps them from being unclean in God's sight.

15 If your husband or wife isn't a follower of the Lord and decides to divorce you, then you should agree to it. You are no longer bound to that person. After all, God chose you and wants you to live at peace. 16And besides, how do you know if you will be able to save your husband or wife who isn't a follower?

Obeying the Lord at All Times

17 In every church I tell the people to stay as they were when the Lord Jesus chose them and God called them to be his own. Now I say the same thing to you. 18If you are already circumcised, don't try to change it. If you are not circumcised, don't get circumcised. 19Being circumcised or uncircumcised isn't really

—

¹ with desire: Or "in the flames of hell."

what matters. The important thing is to obey God's commands. [20]So don't try to change what you were when God chose you. [21]Are you a slave? Don't let that bother you. But if you can win your freedom, you should. [22]When the Lord chooses slaves, they become his free people. And when he chooses free people, they become slaves of Christ. [23]God paid a great price for you. So don't become slaves of anyone else. [24]Stay what you were when God chose you.

Unmarried People

25 I don't know of anything that the Lord said about people who have never been married.[m] But I will tell you what I think. And you can trust me, because the Lord has treated me with kindness. [26]We are now going through hard times, and I think it is best for you to stay as you are. [27]If you are married, stay married. If you are not married, don't try to get married. [28]It isn't wrong to marry, even if you have never been married before. But those who marry will have a lot of trouble, and I want to protect you from that.

29 My friends, what I mean is that the Lord will soon come,[n] and it won't matter if you are married or not. [30]It will be all the same if you are crying or laughing, or if you are buying or are completely broke. [31]It won't make any difference how much good you are getting from this world or how much you like it. This world as we know it is now passing away.

---

[m] *people who have never been married:* Or "virgins."

[n] *the Lord will soon come:* Or "there's not much time left" or "the time for decision comes quickly."

32 I want all of you to be free from worry. An unmarried man worries about how to please the Lord. 33But a married man has more worries. He must worry about the things of this world, because he wants to please his wife. 34So he is pulled in two directions. Unmarried women and women who have never been married[o] worry only about pleasing the Lord, and they keep their bodies and minds pure. But a married woman worries about the things of this world, because she wants to please her husband. 35What I am saying is for your own good—it isn't to limit your freedom. I want to help you to live right and to love the Lord above all else.

36 But suppose you are engaged to someone old enough to be married, and you want her so much that all you can think about is getting married. Then go ahead and marry.[p] There is nothing wrong with that. 37But it is better to have self-control and to make up your mind not to marry. 38It is perfectly all right to marry, but it is better not to get married at all.

39 A wife should stay married to her husband until he dies. Then she is free to marry again, but only to a man who is a follower of the Lord. 40However, I think I am obeying God's Spirit when I say she would be happier to stay single.

---

o *women who have never been married*: Or "virgins."
p *But suppose you are engaged … go ahead and marry*:
  Verses 36-38 may also be translated: 36"If you feel that
  you are not treating your grown daughter right by keeping
  her from getting married, then let her marry. You won't
  be doing anything wrong. 37But it is better to have self-
  control and make up your mind not to let your daughter
  get married. 38It is all right for you to let her marry. But it
  is better if you don't let her marry at all."

Food Offered to Idols

8 In your letter you asked me about food offered to idols. All of us know something about this subject. But knowledge makes us proud of ourselves, while love makes us helpful to others. ²In fact, people who think they know so much don't know anything at all. ³But God has no doubts about who loves him.

4 Even though food is offered to idols, we know that none of the idols in this world are alive. After all, there is only one God. ⁵Many things in heaven and on earth are called gods and lords, but none of them really are gods or lords. ⁶We have only one God, and he is the Father. He created everything, and we live for him. Jesus Christ is our only Lord. Everything was made by him, and by him life was given to us.

7 Not everyone knows these things. In fact, many people have grown up with the belief that idols have life in them. So when they eat meat offered to idols, they are bothered by a weak conscience. ⁸But food doesn't bring us any closer to God. We are no worse off if we don't eat, and we are no better off if we do.

9 Don't cause problems for someone with a weak conscience, just because you have the right to eat anything. ¹⁰You know all this, and so it doesn't bother you to eat in the temple of an idol. But suppose a person with a weak conscience sees you and decides to eat food that has been offered to idols. ¹¹Then what you know has destroyed someone Christ died for. ¹²When you sin by hurting a follower with a weak conscience, you sin against Christ. ¹³So if I hurt one of the Lord's followers by what I eat, I will never eat meat as long as I live.

The Rights of an Apostle

9 I am free. I am an apostle. I have seen the Lord Jesus and have led you to have faith in him. ²Others may think that I am not an apostle, but you are proof that I am an apostle to you.

3 When people question me, I tell them ⁴that Barnabas and I have the right to our food and drink. ⁵We each have the right to marry one of the Lord's followers and to take her along with us, just as the other apostles and the Lord's brothers and Peter*q* do. ⁶Are we the only ones who have to support ourselves by working at another job? ⁷Do soldiers pay their own salaries? Don't people who raise grapes eat some of what they grow? Don't shepherds get milk from their own goats?

8-9 I am not saying this on my own authority. The Law of Moses tells us not to muzzle an ox when it is grinding grain. But was God concerned only about an ox? ¹⁰No, he wasn't! He was talking about us. This was written in the Scriptures so that all who plow and all who grind the grain will look forward to sharing in the harvest.

11 When we told the message to you, it was like planting spiritual seed. So we have the right to accept material things as our harvest from you. ¹²If others have the right to do this, we have an even greater right. But we haven't used this right of ours. We are willing to put up with anything to keep from causing trouble for the message about Christ.

13 Don't you know that people who work in the temple make their living from what is brought to the

---

q Peter: See the note at 1.12.

temple? Don't you know that a person who serves at the altar is given part of what is offered? ¹⁴In the same way, the Lord wants everyone who preaches the good news to make a living from preaching this message.

15 But I have never used these privileges of mine, and I am not writing this because I want to start now. I would rather die than have someone rob me of the right to take pride in this. ¹⁶I don't have any reason to brag about preaching the good news. Preaching is something God told me to do, and if I don't do it, I am doomed. ¹⁷If I preach because I want to, I will be paid. But even if I don't want to, it is still something God has sent me to do. ¹⁸What pay am I given? It is the chance to preach the good news free of charge and not to use the privileges that are mine because I am a preacher.

19 I am not anyone's slave. But I have become a slave to everyone, so that I can win as many people as possible. ²⁰When I am with the Jews, I live like a Jew to win Jews. They are ruled by the Law of Moses, and I am not. But I live by the Law to win them. ²¹And when I am with people who are not ruled by the Law, I forget about the Law to win them. Of course, I never really forget about the law of God. In fact, I am ruled by the law of Christ. ²²When I am with people whose faith is weak, I live as they do to win them. I do everything I can to win everyone I possibly can. ²³I do all this for the good news, because I want to share in its blessings.

A Race and a Fight

24 You know that many runners enter a race, and only one of them wins the prize. So run to win! ²⁵Athletes work hard to win a crown that cannot last,

but we do it for a crown that will last forever. ²⁶I don't run without a goal. And I don't box by beating my fists in the air. ²⁷I keep my body under control and make it my slave, so I won't lose out after telling the good news to others.

Don't Worship Idols

10 Friends, I want to remind you that all of our ancestors walked under the cloud and went through the sea. ²This was like being baptized and becoming followers of Moses. ³All of them also ate the same spiritual food ⁴and drank the same spiritual drink, which flowed from the spiritual rock that followed them. That rock was Christ. ⁵But most of them did not please God. So they died, and their bodies were scattered all over the desert.

6 What happened to them is a warning to keep us from wanting to do the same evil things. ⁷They worshiped idols, just as the Scriptures say, "The people sat down to eat and drink. Then they got up to dance around." So don't worship idols. ⁸Some of those people did shameful things, and in a single day about twenty-three thousand of them died. Don't do shameful things as they did. ⁹And don't try to test Christ,^r as some of them did and were later bitten by poisonous snakes. ¹⁰Don't even grumble, as some of them did and were killed by the destroying angel. ¹¹These things happened to them as a warning to us. All this was written in the Scriptures to teach us who live in these last days.

12 Even if you think you can stand up to temptation, be careful not to fall. ¹³You are tempted in the same

---

^r *Christ:* Some manuscripts have "the Lord."

way that everyone else is tempted. But God can be trusted not to let you be tempted too much, and he will show you how to escape from your temptations.

14 My friends, you must keep away from idols. 15I am speaking to you as people who have enough sense to know what I am talking about. 16When we drink from the cup that we ask God to bless, isn't that sharing in the blood of Christ? When we eat the bread that we break, isn't that sharing in the body of Christ? 17By sharing in the same loaf of bread, we become one body, even though there are many of us.

18 Aren't the people of Israel sharing in the worship when they gather around the altar and eat the sacrifices offered there? 19Am I saying that either the idols or the food sacrificed to them is anything at all? 20No, I am not! That food is really sacrificed to demons and not to God. I don't want you to have anything to do with demons. 21You cannot drink from the cup of demons and still drink from the Lord's cup. You cannot eat at the table of demons and still eat at the Lord's table. 22We would make the Lord jealous if we did that. And we are not stronger than the Lord.

Always Honor God

23 Some of you say, "We can do whatever we want to!" But I tell you that not everything may be good or helpful. 24We should think about others and not about ourselves. 25However, when you buy meat in the market, go ahead and eat it. Keep your conscience clear by not asking where the meat came from. 26The Scriptures say, "The earth and everything in it belong to the Lord."

27 If an unbeliever invites you to dinner, and you want to go, then go. Eat whatever you are served.

Don't cause a problem for someone's conscience by asking where the food came from. 28-29But if you are told that it has been sacrificed to idols, don't cause a problem by eating it. I don't mean a problem for yourself, but for the one who told you. Why should my freedom be limited by someone else's conscience? 30If I give thanks for what I eat, why should anyone accuse me of doing wrong?

31 When you eat or drink or do anything else, always do it to honor God. 32Don't cause problems for Jews or Greeks or anyone else who belongs to God's church. 33I always try to please others instead of myself, in the hope that many of them will be saved.

11 You must follow my example, as I follow the example of Christ.

Rules for Worship

2 I am proud of you, because you always remember me and obey the teachings I gave you. 3Now I want you to know that Christ is the head over all men, and a man is the head over a woman. But God is the head over Christ. 4This means that any man who prays or prophesies with something on his head brings shame to his head.

5 But any woman who prays or prophesies without something on her head brings shame to her head. In fact, she may as well shave her head.⁵ 6A woman should wear something on her head. It is a disgrace

---

⁵ *she may as well shave her head*: A woman's hair was a mark of beauty, and it was shameful for a woman to cut her hair short or to shave her head, so that she looked like a man.

for a woman to shave her head or cut her hair. But if she refuses to wear something on her head, let her cut off her hair.

7 Men were created to be like God and to bring honor to God. This means that a man should not wear anything on his head. Women were created to bring honor to men. [8]It was the woman who was made from a man, and not the man who was made from a woman. [9]He wasn't created for her. She was created for him. [10]And so, because of this, and also because of the angels, a woman ought to wear something on her head, as a sign of her authority.[t]

11 As far as the Lord is concerned, men and women need each other. [12]It is true that the first woman came from a man, but all other men have been given birth by women. Yet God is the one who created everything. [13]Ask yourselves if it is proper for a woman to pray without something on her head. [14]Isn't it unnatural and disgraceful for men to have long hair? [15]But long hair is a beautiful way for a woman to cover her head. [16]This is how things are done in all of God's churches,[u] and that's why none of you should argue about what I have said.

Rules for the Lord's Supper

17 Your worship services do you more harm than good. I am certainly not going to praise you for this. [18]I am told that you can't get along with each other

---

[t] *as a sign of her authority*: Or "as a sign that she is under someone's authority."

[u] *This is how things are done in all of God's churches*: Or "There is no set rule for this in any of God's churches."

when you worship, and I am sure that some of what I have heard is true. 19 You are bound to argue with each other, but it is easy to see which of you have God's approval.

20 When you meet together, you don't really celebrate the Lord's Supper. 21 You even start eating before everyone gets to the meeting, and some of you go hungry, while others get drunk. 22 Don't you have homes where you can eat and drink? Do you hate God's church? Do you want to embarrass people who don't have anything? What can I say to you? I certainly cannot praise you.

The Lord's Supper
(Matthew 26.26-29; Mark 14.22-25; Luke 22.14-20)

23 I have already told you what the Lord Jesus did on the night he was betrayed. And it came from the Lord himself.

He took some bread in his hands. 24 Then after he had given thanks, he broke it and said, "This is my body, which is given for you. Eat this and remember me."

25 After the meal, Jesus took a cup of wine in his hands and said, "This is my blood, and with it God makes his new agreement with you. Drink this and remember me."

26 The Lord meant that when you eat this bread and drink from this cup, you tell about his death until he comes.

27 But if you eat the bread and drink the wine in a way that isn't worthy of the Lord, you sin against his body and blood. 28 That's why you must examine the way you eat and drink. 29 If you fail to understand that

you are the body of the Lord, you will condemn yourselves by the way you eat and drink. ³⁰That's why many of you are sick and weak and why a lot of others have died. ³¹If we carefully judge ourselves, we won't be punished. ³²But when the Lord judges and punishes us, he does it to keep us from being condemned with the rest of the world.

33 My dear friends, you should wait until everyone gets there before you start eating. ³⁴If you really are hungry, you can eat at home. Then you won't condemn yourselves when you meet together.

After I arrive, I will instruct you about the other matters.

Spiritual Gifts

12 My friends, you asked me about spiritual gifts. ²I want you to remember that before you became followers of the Lord, you were led in all the wrong ways by idols that cannot even talk. ³Now I want you to know that if you are led by God's Spirit, you will say that Jesus is Lord, and you will never curse Jesus.

4 There are different kinds of spiritual gifts, but they all come from the same Spirit. ⁵There are different ways to serve the same Lord, ⁶and we can each do different things. Yet the same God works in all of us and helps us in everything we do.

7 The Spirit has given each of us a special way of serving others. ⁸Some of us can speak with wisdom, while others can speak with knowledge, but these gifts come from the same Spirit. ⁹To others the Spirit has given great faith or the power to heal the sick ¹⁰or the power to work mighty miracles. Some of us are

prophets, and some of us recognize when God's Spirit is present.ᵛ Others can speak different kinds of languages, and still others can tell what these languages mean. ¹¹But it is the Spirit who does all this and decides which gifts to give to each of us.

One Body with Many Parts

12 The body of Christ has many different parts, just as any other body does. ¹³Some of us are Jews, and others are Gentiles. Some of us are slaves, and others are free. But God's Spirit baptized each of us and made us part of the body of Christ. Now we each drink from that same Spirit.ʷ

14 Our bodies don't have just one part. They have many parts. ¹⁵Suppose a foot says, "I'm not a hand, and so I'm not part of the body." Wouldn't the foot still belong to the body? ¹⁶Or suppose an ear says, "I'm not an eye, and so I'm not part of the body." Wouldn't the ear still belong to the body? ¹⁷If our bodies were only an eye, we couldn't hear a thing. And if they were only an ear, we couldn't smell a thing. ¹⁸But God has put all parts of our body together in the way that he decided is best.

19 A body isn't really a body, unless there is more than one part. ²⁰It takes many parts to make a single

---

ᵛ *and some of us…present*: Or "and some of us recognize the difference between God's Spirit and other spirits."

ʷ *Some of us are Jews…that same Spirit*: Verse 13 may also be translated, "God's Spirit is inside each of us, and all around us as well. So it doesn't matter that some of us are Jews and others are Gentiles and that some are slaves and others are free. Together we are one body."

body. [21]That's why the eyes cannot say they don't need the hands. That's also why the head cannot say it doesn't need the feet. [22]In fact, we cannot get along without the parts of the body that seem to be the weakest. [23]We take special care to dress up some parts of our bodies. We are modest about our personal parts, [24]but we don't have to be modest about other parts.

God put our bodies together in such a way that even the parts that seem the least important are valuable. [25]He did this to make all parts of the body work together smoothly, with each part caring about the others. [26]If one part of our body hurts, we hurt all over. If one part of our body is honored, the whole body will be happy.

27 Together you are the body of Christ. Each one of you is part of his body. [28]First, God chose some people to be apostles and prophets and teachers for the church. But he also chose some to work miracles or heal the sick or help others or be leaders or speak different kinds of languages. [29]Not everyone is an apostle. Not everyone is a prophet. Not everyone is a teacher. Not everyone can work miracles. [30]Not everyone can heal the sick. Not everyone can speak different kinds of languages. Not everyone can tell what these languages mean. [31]I want you to desire the best gifts.[x] So I will show you a much better way.

Love

13 What if I could speak all languages of humans and of angels?

---

[x] *I want you to desire the best gifts:* Or "You desire the best gifts."

If I did not love others,
  I would be nothing more
    than a noisy gong or a clanging cymbal.
2 What if I could prophesy
    and understand all secrets
    and all knowledge?
And what if I had faith
    that moved mountains?
  I would be nothing, unless I loved others.
3 What if I gave away all that I owned
  and let myself be burned alive?[y]
    I would gain nothing, unless I loved others.
4 Love is kind and patient,
    never jealous, boastful, proud, or 5rude.
  Love isn't selfish or quick tempered.
  It doesn't keep a record of wrongs
    that others do.
6 Love rejoices in the truth, but not in evil.
7 Love is always supportive,
    loyal, hopeful, and trusting.
8 Love never fails!

Everyone who prophesies will stop,
  and unknown languages
    will no longer be spoken.
  All that we know will be forgotten.
9 We don't know everything,
    and our prophecies are not complete.
10 But what is perfect will someday appear,
    and what isn't perfect will then disappear.

---

y *and let myself be burned alive*: Some manuscripts have
"so that I could brag."

¹¹ When we were children,
    we thought and reasoned as children do.
But when we grew up,
    we quit our childish ways.
¹² Now all we can see of God
    is like a cloudy picture in a mirror.
Later we will see him face to face.
We don't know everything,
    but then we will,
        just as God completely understands us.
¹³ For now there are faith, hope, and love.
    But of these three, the greatest is love.

Speaking Unknown Languages and Prophesying

14 Love should be your guide. Be eager to have the gifts that come from the Holy Spirit, especially the gift of prophecy. ²If you speak languages that others don't know, God will understand what you are saying, though no one else will know what you mean. You will be talking about mysteries that only the Spirit understands. ³But when you prophesy, you will be understood, and others will be helped. They will be encouraged and made to feel better.

4 By speaking languages that others don't know, you help only yourself. But by prophesying you help everyone in the church. ⁵I am glad for you to speak unknown languages, although I had rather for you to prophesy. In fact, prophesying does much more good than speaking unknown languages, unless someone can help the church by explaining what you mean.

6 My friends, what good would it do, if I came and spoke unknown languages to you and didn't explain what I meant? How would I help you, unless I told you

what God had shown me or gave you some knowledge or prophecy or teaching? 7If all musical instruments sounded alike, how would you know the difference between a flute and a harp? 8If a bugle call isn't clear, how would you know to get ready for battle?

9 That's how it is when you speak unknown languages. If no one can understand what you are talking about, you will only be talking to the wind. 10There are many different languages in this world, and all of them make sense. 11But if I don't understand the language that someone is using, we will be like foreigners to each other. 12If you really want spiritual gifts, choose the ones that will be most helpful to the church.

13 When we speak languages that others don't know, we should pray for the power to explain what we mean. 14For example, if I use an unknown language in my prayers, my spirit prays but my mind is useless. 15Then what should I do? There are times when I should pray with my spirit, and times when I should pray with my mind. Sometimes I should sing with my spirit, and at other times I should sing with my mind.

16 Suppose some strangers are in your worship service, when you are praising God with your spirit. If they don't understand you, how will they know to say, "Amen"? 17You may be worshiping God in a wonderful way, but no one else will be helped. 18I thank God that I speak unknown languages more than any of you. 19But words that make sense can help the church. That's why in church I had rather speak five words that make sense than to speak ten thousand words in a language that others don't know.

20 My friends, stop thinking like children. Think like mature people and be as innocent as tiny babies.

21In the Scriptures the Lord says,
> "I will use strangers
> who speak unknown languages
> to talk to my people.
> They will speak to them in foreign languages,
> but still my people won't listen to me."

22 Languages that others don't know may mean something to unbelievers, but not to the Lord's followers. Prophecy, on the other hand, is for followers, not for unbelievers. 23Suppose everyone in your worship service started speaking unknown languages, and some outsiders or some unbelievers come in. Won't they think you are crazy? 24But suppose all of you are prophesying when those unbelievers and outsiders come in. They will realize that they are sinners, and they will want to change their ways because of what you are saying. 25They will tell what is hidden in their hearts. Then they will kneel down and say to God, "We are certain that you are with these people."

Worship Must Be Orderly

26 My friends, when you meet to worship, you must do everything for the good of everyone there. That's how it should be when someone sings or teaches or tells what God has said or speaks an unknown language or explains what the language means. 27No more than two or three of you should speak unknown languages during the meeting. You must take turns, and someone should always be there to explain what you mean. 28If no one can explain, you must keep silent in church and speak only to yourself and to God.

29 Two or three persons may prophesy, and everyone else must listen carefully. 30If someone sitting

there receives a message from God, the speaker must stop and let the other person speak. [31]Let only one person speak at a time, then all of you will learn something and be encouraged. [32]A prophet should be willing to stop and let someone else speak. [33]God wants everything to be done peacefully and in order.

When God's people meet in church, [34]the women must not be allowed to speak. They must keep quiet and listen, as the Law of Moses teaches. [35]If there is something they want to know, they can ask their husbands when they get home. It is disgraceful for women to speak in church. [36]God's message did not start with you people, and you are not the only ones it has reached.

[37] If you think of yourself as a prophet or a spiritual person, you will know that I am writing only what the Lord has commanded. [38]So don't pay attention to anyone who ignores what I am writing. [39]My friends, be eager to prophesy and don't stop anyone from speaking languages that others don't know. [40]But do everything properly and in order.

Christ Was Raised to Life

15 My friends, I want you to remember the message that I preached and that you believed and trusted. [2]You will be saved by this message, if you hold firmly to it. But if you don't, your faith was all for nothing.

[3] I told you the most important part of the message exactly as it was told to me. That part is:

> Christ died for our sins,
>   as the Scriptures say.
> [4] He was buried,
>   and three days later he was raised to life,
>   as the Scriptures say.

⁵ Christ appeared to Peter,ᶻ
then to the twelve.
⁶ After this, he appeared
to more than five hundred other followers.
Most of them are still alive,
but some have died.
⁷ He also appeared to James,
and then to all of the apostles.

8 Finally, he appeared to me, even though I am like someone who was born at the wrong time.ᵃ

9 I am the least important of all the apostles. In fact, I caused so much trouble for God's church that I don't even deserve to be called an apostle. ¹⁰But God was kind! He made me what I am, and his wonderful kindness wasn't wasted. I worked much harder than any of the other apostles, although it was really God's kindness at work and not me. ¹¹But it doesn't matter if I preached or if they preached. All of you believed the message just the same.

God's People Will Be Raised to Life

12 If we preach that Christ was raised from death, how can some of you say that the dead will not be raised to life? ¹³If they won't be raised to life, Christ himself wasn't raised to life. ¹⁴And if Christ wasn't raised to life, our message is worthless, and so is your faith. ¹⁵If the dead won't be raised to life, we have told lies about God by saying that he raised Christ to life, when he really did not.

ᶻ *Peter*: See the note at 1.12.
ᵃ *who was born at the wrong time*: The meaning of these words in Greek is not clear.

16 So if the dead won't be raised to life, Christ wasn't raised to life. 17Unless Christ was raised to life, your faith is useless, and you are still living in your sins. 18And those people who died after putting their faith in him are completely lost. 19If our hope in Christ is good only for this life, we are worse off than anyone else.

20 But Christ has been raised to life! And he makes us certain that others will also be raised to life. 21Just as we will die because of Adam, we will be raised to life because of Christ. 22Adam brought death to all of us, and Christ will bring life to all of us. 23But we must each wait our turn. Christ was the first to be raised to life, and his people will be raised to life when he returns. 24Then after Christ has destroyed all powers and forces, the end will come, and he will give the kingdom to God the Father.

25 Christ will rule until he puts all his enemies under his power, 26and the last enemy he destroys will be death. 27When the Scriptures say that he will put everything under his power, they don't include God. It was God who put everything under the power of Christ. 28After everything is under the power of God's Son, he will put himself under the power of God, who put everything under his Son's power. Then God will mean everything to everyone.

29 If the dead are not going to be raised to life, what will people do who are being baptized for them? Why are they being baptized for those dead people? 30And why do we always risk our lives 31and face death every day? The pride that I have in you because of Christ Jesus our Lord is what makes me say this. 32What do you think I gained by fighting wild animals in Ephesus? If the dead are not raised to life,

"Let's eat and drink.
Tomorrow we die."

33Don't fool yourselves. Bad friends will destroy you. 34Be sensible and stop sinning. You should be embarrassed that some people still don't know about God.

What Our Bodies Will Be Like

35 Some of you have asked, "How will the dead be raised to life? What kind of bodies will they have?" 36Don't be foolish. A seed must die before it can sprout from the ground. 37Wheat seeds and all other seeds look different from the sprouts that come up. 38This is because God gives everything the kind of body he wants it to have. 39People, animals, birds, and fish are each made of flesh, but none of them are alike. 40Everything in the heavens has a body, and so does everything on earth. But each one is very different from all the others. 41The sun isn't like the moon, the moon isn't like the stars, and each star is different.

42 That's how it will be when our bodies are raised to life. These bodies will die, but the bodies that are raised will live forever. 43These ugly and weak bodies will become beautiful and strong. 44As surely as there are physical bodies, there are spiritual bodies. And our physical bodies will be changed into spiritual bodies.

45 The first man was named Adam, and the Scriptures tell us that he was a living person. But Jesus, who may be called the last Adam, is a life-giving spirit. 46We see that the one with a spiritual body did not come first. He came after the one who had a physical body. 47The first man was made from

the dust of the earth, but the second man came from heaven. ⁴⁸Everyone on earth has a body like the body of the one who was made from the dust of the earth. And everyone in heaven has a body like the body of the one who came from heaven. ⁴⁹Just as we are like the one who was made out of earth, we will be like the one who came from heaven.

50 My friends, I want you to know that our bodies of flesh and blood will decay. This means that they cannot share in God's kingdom, which lasts forever. ⁵¹I will explain a mystery to you. Not every one of us will die, but we will all be changed. ⁵²It will happen suddenly, quicker than the blink of an eye. At the sound of the last trumpet the dead will be raised. We will all be changed, so that we will never die again. ⁵³Our dead and decaying bodies will be changed into bodies that won't die or decay. ⁵⁴The bodies we now have are weak and can die. But they will be changed into bodies that are eternal. Then the Scriptures will come true,

"Death has lost the battle!
⁵⁵   Where is its victory? Where is its sting?"

⁵⁶Sin is what gives death its sting, and the Law is the power behind sin. ⁵⁷But thank God for letting our Lord Jesus Christ give us the victory!

58 My dear friends, stand firm and don't be shaken. Always keep busy working for the Lord. You know that everything you do for him is worthwhile.

A Collection for God's People

16 When you collect money for God's people, I want you to do exactly what I told the churches in Galatia to do. ²That is, each Sunday each of you must put aside part of what you have earned. If you do this, you won't have to take up a collection when I come. ³Choose some followers to take the money to Jerusalem. I will send them on with the money and with letters which show that you approve of them. ⁴If you think I should go along, they can go with me.

Paul's Travel Plans

5 After I have gone through Macedonia, I hope to see you ⁶and visit with you for a while. I may even stay all winter, so that you can help me on my way to wherever I will be going next. ⁷If the Lord lets me, I would rather come later for a longer visit than to stop off now for only a short visit. ⁸I will stay in Ephesus until Pentecost, ⁹because there is a wonderful opportunity for me to do some work here. But there are also many people who are against me.

10 When Timothy arrives, give him a friendly welcome. He is doing the Lord's work, just as I am. ¹¹Don't let anyone mistreat him. I am looking for him to return to me together with the other followers. So when he leaves, send him off with your blessings.

12 I have tried hard to get our friend Apollos to visit you with the other followers. He doesn't want to come just now, but he will come when he can.

Personal Concerns and Greetings

13 Keep alert. Be firm in your faith. Stay brave and strong. ¹⁴Show love in everything you do.

15 You know that Stephanas and his family were the first in Achaia to have faith in the Lord. They have done all they can for God's people. My friends, I ask you

¹⁶to obey leaders like them and to do the same for all others who work hard with you.

17 I was glad to see Stephanas and Fortunatus and Achaicus. Having them here was like having you. ¹⁸They made me feel much better, just as they made you feel better. You should appreciate people like them.

19 Greetings from the churches in Asia.

Aquila and Priscilla, together with the church that meets in their house, send greetings in the name of the Lord.

20 All of the Lord's followers send their greetings. Give each other a warm greeting.

21 I am signing this letter myself: PAUL.

22 I pray that God will put a curse on everyone who doesn't love the Lord. And may the Lord come soon.

23 I pray that the Lord Jesus will be kind to you.

24 I love everyone who belongs to Christ Jesus.

Paul's Second Letter to the Church in Corinth

ABOUT THIS LETTER

In the beginning of this letter Paul answers the concerns of the Christians in Corinth who accused him of not living up to his promise to visit them. Paul had changed his mind for a good reason. He had stayed away from Corinth so that he would not seem to be too hard and demanding (1.23). He also wanted to see if they would follow his instructions about forgiving and comforting people who had sinned (2.5-11).

Paul reminds the Corinthians that God is generous and wants them to be just as generous in their giving to help God's people in Jerusalem and Judea (8.1–9.15).

Paul is a servant of God's new agreement (3.1-17). He is faithful in trying to bring people to God, even if it means terrible suffering for himself (4.1–6.13; 10.1–12.10). And what has God done to make it possible for us to come to him?

> *God has done it all! He sent Christ to make peace between himself and us, and he has given us the work of making peace between himself and others. What we mean is that God was in Christ, offering peace and forgiveness to the people of this world. And he has given us the work of sharing his message about peace. (5.18,19)*

1 From Paul, chosen by God to be an apostle of Jesus Christ, and from Timothy, who is also a follower.

To God's church in Corinth and to all of God's people in Achaia.

2 I pray that God our Father and the Lord Jesus Christ will be kind to you and will bless you with peace!

Paul Gives Thanks

3 Praise God, the Father of our Lord Jesus Christ! The Father is a merciful God, who always gives us comfort. 4He comforts us when we are in trouble, so that we can share that same comfort with others in trouble. 5We share in the terrible sufferings of Christ, but also in the wonderful comfort he gives. 6We suffer in the hope that you will be comforted and saved. And because we are comforted, you will also be comforted, as you patiently endure suffering like ours. 7You never disappoint us. You suffered as much as we did, and we know that you will be comforted as we were.

8 My friends, I want you to know what a hard time we had in Asia. Our sufferings were so horrible and so unbearable that death seemed certain. 9In fact, we felt sure that we were going to die. But this made us stop trusting in ourselves and start trusting God, who

raises the dead to life. [10]God saved us from the threat of death,[a] and we are sure that he will do it again and again. [11]Please help us by praying for us. Then many people will give thanks for the blessings we receive in answer to all these prayers.

Paul's Change of Plans

12 We can be proud of our clear conscience. We have always lived honestly and sincerely, especially when we were with you. And we were guided by God's wonderful kindness instead of by the wisdom of this world. [13]I am not writing anything you cannot read and understand. I hope you will understand it completely, [14]just as you already partly understand us. Then when our Lord Jesus returns, you can be as proud of us as we are of you.

15 I was so sure of your pride in us that I had planned to visit you first of all. In this way you would have the blessing of two visits from me. [16]Once on my way to Macedonia and again on my return from there. Then you could send me on to Judea. [17]Do you think I couldn't make up my mind about what to do? Or do I seem like someone who says "Yes" or "No" simply to please others? [18]God can be trusted, and so can I, when I say that our answer to you has always been "Yes" and never "No." [19]This is because Jesus Christ the Son of God is always "Yes" and never "No." And he is the one that Silas,[b] Timothy, and I told you about.

---

[a] *the threat of death*: Some manuscripts have "many threats of death."

[b] *Silas*: The Greek text has "Silvanus," which is another form of the name Silas.

20 Christ says "Yes" to all of God's promises. That's why we have Christ to say "Amen"[c] for us to the glory of God. 21And so God makes it possible for you and us to stand firmly together with Christ. God is also the one who chose us 22and put his Spirit in our hearts to show that we belong only to him.

23 God is my witness that I stayed away from Corinth, just to keep from being hard on you. 24We are not bosses who tell you what to believe. We are working with you to make you glad, because your faith is strong.

2 I have decided not to make my next visit with you so painful. 2If I make you feel bad, who would be left to cheer me up, except the people I had made to feel bad? 3The reason I want to be happy is to make you happy. I wrote as I did because I didn't want to visit you and be made to feel bad, when you should make me feel happy. 4At the time I wrote, I was suffering terribly. My eyes were full of tears, and my heart was broken. But I didn't want to make you feel bad. I only wanted to let you know how much I cared for you.

Forgiveness

5 I don't want to be hard on you. But if one of you has made someone feel bad, I am not really the one who has been made to feel bad. Some of you are the ones. 6Most of you have already pointed out the wrong that person did, and that is punishment enough for what was done.

---

[c] Amen: The word "amen" is used here with the meaning of "yes."

7 When people sin, you should forgive and comfort them, so they won't give up in despair. [8] You should make them sure of your love for them.

9 I also wrote because I wanted to test you and find out if you would follow my instructions. [10]I will forgive anyone you forgive. Yes, for your sake and with Christ as my witness, I have forgiven whatever needed to be forgiven. [11]I have done this to keep Satan from getting the better of us. We all know what goes on in his mind.

12 When I went to Troas to preach the good news about Christ, I found that the Lord had already prepared the way. [13]But I was worried when I didn't find my friend Titus there. So I left the other followers and went on to Macedonia.

14 I am grateful that God always makes it possible for Christ to lead us to victory. God also helps us spread the knowledge about Christ everywhere, and this knowledge is like the smell of perfume. [15-16]In fact, God thinks of us as a perfume that brings Christ to everyone. For people who are being saved, this perfume has a sweet smell and leads them to a better life. But for people who are lost, it has a bad smell and leads them to a horrible death.

No one really has what it takes to do this work. [17]A lot of people try to get rich from preaching God's message. But we are God's sincere messengers, and by the power of Christ we speak our message with God as our witness.

God's New Agreement

3 Are we once again bragging about ourselves? Do we need letters to you or from you to tell others

about us? Some people do need letters that tell about them. [2]But you are our letter, and you are in our[d] hearts for everyone to read and understand. [3]You are like a letter written by Christ and delivered by us. But you are not written with pen and ink or on tablets made of stone. You are written in our hearts by the Spirit of the living God.

4 We are sure about all this. Christ makes us sure in the very presence of God. [5]We don't have the right to claim that we have done anything on our own. God gives us what it takes to do all that we do. [6]He makes us worthy to be the servants of his new agreement that comes from the Holy Spirit and not from a written Law. After all, the Law brings death, but the Spirit brings life.

7 The Law of Moses brought only the promise of death, even though it was carved on stones and given in a wonderful way. Still the Law made Moses' face shine so brightly that the people of Israel could not look at it, even though it was a fading glory. [8]So won't the agreement that the Spirit brings to us be even more wonderful? [9]If something that brings the death sentence is glorious, won't something that makes us acceptable to God be even more glorious? [10]In fact, the new agreement is so wonderful that the Law is no longer glorious at all. [11]The Law was given with a glory that faded away. But the glory of the new agreement is much greater, because it will never fade away.

12 This wonderful hope makes us feel like speaking freely. [13]We are not like Moses. His face was shining,

---

[d] our: Some manuscripts have "your."

but he covered it to keep the people of Israel from seeing the brightness fade away. [14]The people were stubborn, and something still keeps them from seeing the truth when the Law is read. Only Christ can take away the covering that keeps them from seeing.

15 When the Law of Moses is read, they have their minds covered over [16]with a covering that is removed only for those who turn to the Lord. [17]The Lord and the Spirit are one and the same, and the Lord's Spirit sets us free. [18]So our faces are not covered. They show the bright glory of the Lord, as the Lord's Spirit makes us more and more like our glorious Lord.

Treasure in Clay Jars

4 God has been kind enough to trust us with this work. That's why we never give up. [2]We don't do shameful things that must be kept secret. And we don't try to fool anyone or twist God's message around. God is our witness that we speak only the truth, so others will be sure that we can be trusted. [3]If there is anything hidden about our message, it is hidden only to someone who is lost.

4 The god who rules this world has blinded the minds of unbelievers. They cannot see the light, which is the good news about our glorious Christ, who shows what God is like. [5]We are not preaching about ourselves. Our message is that Jesus Christ is Lord. He also sent us to be your servants. [6]The Scriptures say, "God commanded light to shine in the dark." Now God is shining in our hearts to let you know that his glory is seen in Jesus Christ.

7 We are like clay jars in which this treasure is stored. The real power comes from God and not

from us. 8We often suffer, but we are never crushed. Even when we don't know what to do, we never give up. 9In times of trouble, God is with us, and when we are knocked down, we get up again. 10-11We face death every day because of Jesus. Our bodies show what his death was like, so that his life can also be seen in us. 12This means that death is working in us, but life is working in you.

13 In the Scriptures it says, "I spoke because I had faith." We have that same kind of faith. So we speak 14because we know that God raised the Lord Jesus to life. And just as God raised Jesus, he will also raise us to life. Then he will bring us into his presence together with you. 15All of this has been done for you, so that more and more people will know how kind God is and will praise and honor him.

Faith in the Lord

16 We never give up. Our bodies are gradually dying, but we ourselves are being made stronger each day. 17These little troubles are getting us ready for an eternal glory that will make all our troubles seem like nothing. 18Things that are seen don't last forever, but things that are not seen are eternal. That's why we keep our minds on the things that cannot be seen.

5 Our bodies are like tents that we live in here on earth. But when these tents are destroyed, we know that God will give each of us a place to live. These homes will not be buildings that someone has made, but they are in heaven and will last forever. 2While we are here on earth, we sigh because we want to live in that heavenly home. 3We want to put it on like clothes and not be naked.

4 These tents we now live in are like a heavy burden, and we groan. But we don't do this just because we want to leave these bodies that will die. It is because we want to change them for bodies that will never die. 5God is the one who makes all of this possible. He has given us his Spirit to make us certain that he will do it. 6So always be cheerful!

As long as we are in these bodies, we are away from the Lord. 7But we live by faith, not by what we see. 8We should be cheerful, because we would rather leave these bodies and be at home with the Lord. 9But whether we are at home with the Lord or away from him, we still try our best to please him. 10After all, Christ will judge each of us for the good or the bad that we do while living in these bodies.

Bringing People to God

11 We know what it means to respect the Lord, and we encourage everyone to turn to him. God himself knows what we are like, and I hope you also know what kind of people we are. 12We are not trying once more to brag about ourselves. But we want you to be proud of us, when you are with those who are not sincere and brag about what others think of them.

13 If we seem out of our minds, it is between God and us. But if we are in our right minds, it is for your good. 14We are ruled by Christ's love for us. We are certain that if one person died for everyone else, then all of us have died. 15And Christ did die for all of us. He died so we would no longer live for ourselves, but for the one who died and was raised to life for us.

16 We are careful not to judge people by what they seem to be, though we once judged Christ in that way.

¹⁷Anyone who belongs to Christ is a new person. The past is forgotten, and everything is new. ¹⁸God has done it all! He sent Christ to make peace between himself and us, and he has given us the work of making peace between himself and others.

19 What we mean is that God was in Christ, offering peace and forgiveness to the people of this world. And he has given us the work of sharing his message about peace. ²⁰We were sent to speak for Christ, and God is begging you to listen to our message. We speak for Christ and sincerely ask you to make peace with God. ²¹Christ never sinned! But God treated him as a sinner, so that Christ could make us acceptable to God.

6 We work together with God, and we beg you to make good use of God's kindness to you. ²In the Scriptures God says,

> "When the time came,
>   I listened to you,
> and when you needed help,
>   I came to save you."

That time has come. This is the day for you to be saved.

3 We don't want anyone to find fault with our work, and so we try hard not to cause problems. ⁴But in everything and in every way we show that we truly are God's servants. We have always been patient, though we have had a lot of trouble, suffering, and hard times. ⁵We have been beaten, put in jail, and hurt in riots. We have worked hard and have gone without sleep or food. ⁶But we have kept ourselves pure and have been understanding, patient, and kind. The Holy Spirit has been with us, and our love has been real. ⁷We have spoken the truth, and God's power has

worked in us. In all our struggles we have said and done only what is right.

8 Whether we were honored or dishonored or praised or cursed, we always told the truth about ourselves. But some people said we did not. 9We are unknown to others, but well known to you. We seem to be dying, and yet we are still alive. We have been punished, but never killed, 10and we are always happy, even in times of suffering. Although we are poor, we have made many people rich. And though we own nothing, everything is ours.

11 Friends in Corinth, we are telling the truth when we say that there is room in our hearts for you. 12We are not holding back on our love for you, but you are holding back on your love for us. 13I speak to you as I would speak to my own children. Please make room in your hearts for us.

The Temple of the Living God

14 Stay away from people who are not followers of the Lord! Can someone who is good get along with someone who is evil? Are light and darkness the same? 15Is Christ a friend of Satan?*e* Can people who follow the Lord have anything in common with those who don't? 16Do idols belong in the temple of God? We are the temple of the living God, as God himself says,

"I will live with these people
    and walk among them.

---

e Satan: The Greek text has "Beliar," which is another form of the Hebrew word "Belial," meaning "wicked" or "useless." The Jewish people sometimes used this as a name for Satan.

> I will be their God,
>> and they will be my people."

[17]The Lord also says,

> "Leave them and stay away!
>> Don't touch anything that isn't clean.
> Then I will welcome you
> [18] and be your Father.
> You will be my sons and my daughters,
>> as surely as I am God,
>> the All-Powerful."

7 My friends, God has made us these promises. So we should stay away from everything that keeps our bodies and spirits from being clean. We should honor God and try to be completely like him.

The Church Makes Paul Happy

2 Make a place for us in your hearts! We haven't mistreated or hurt anyone. We haven't cheated anyone. [3]I am not saying this to be hard on you. But, as I have said before, you will always be in our thoughts, whether we live or die. [4]I trust you completely.[f] I am always proud of you, and I am greatly encouraged. In all my trouble I am still very happy.

5 After we came to Macedonia, we didn't have any chance to rest. We were faced with all kinds of problems. We were troubled by enemies and troubled by fears. [6]But God cheers up people in need, and that is what he did when he sent Titus to us. [7]Of course, we were glad to see Titus, but what really made us glad is the way you cheered him up. He told how sorry you

---

f *I trust you completely*: Or "I have always spoken the truth to you" or "I can speak freely to you."

were and how concerned you were about me. And this made me even happier.

8 I don't feel bad anymore, even though my letter[g] hurt your feelings. I did feel bad at first, but I don't now. I know that the letter hurt you for a while. [9]Now I am happy, but not because I hurt your feelings. It is because God used your hurt feelings to make you turn back to him, and none of you were harmed by us. [10]When God makes you feel sorry enough to turn to him and be saved, you don't have anything to feel bad about. But when this world makes you feel sorry, it can cause your death.

11 Just look what God has done by making you feel sorry! You sincerely want to prove that you are innocent. You are angry. You are shocked. You are eager to see that justice is done. You have proved that you were completely right in this matter. [12]When I wrote you, it wasn't to accuse the one who was wrong or to take up for the one who was hurt. I wrote, so that God would show you how much you do care for us. [13]And we were greatly encouraged.

Although we were encouraged, we felt even better when we saw how happy Titus was, because you had shown that he had nothing to worry about. [14]We had told him how much we thought of you, and you did not disappoint us. Just as we have always told you the truth, so everything we told him about you has also proved to be true. [15]Titus loves all of you very much, especially when he remembers how you obeyed him and how you trembled with fear when

---

[g] *my letter*: There is no copy of this letter that Paul wrote to the church at Corinth.

you welcomed him. ¹⁶It makes me really glad to know that I can depend on you.

Generous Giving

8 My friends, we want you to know that the churches in Macedonia*ʰ* have shown others how kind God is. ²Although they were going through hard times and were very poor, they were glad to give generously. ³They gave as much as they could afford and even more, simply because they wanted to. ⁴They even asked and begged us to let them have the joy of giving their money for God's people. ⁵And they did more than we had hoped. They gave themselves first to the Lord and then to us, just as God wanted them to do.

6 Titus was the one who got you started doing this good thing, so we begged him to have you finish what you had begun. ⁷You do everything better than anyone else. You have stronger faith. You speak better and know more. You are eager to give, and you love us better.*ⁱ* Now you must give more generously than anyone else.

8 I am not ordering you to do this. I am simply testing how real your love is by comparing it with the concern that others have shown. ⁹You know that our Lord Jesus Christ was kind enough to give up all his riches and become poor, so that you could become rich.

ʰ *churches in Macedonia:* The churches that Paul had started in Philippi and Thessalonica. The church in Berea is probably also meant.

ⁱ *you love us better:* Some manuscripts have "we love you better."

10 A year ago you were the first ones to give, and you gave because you wanted to. So listen to my advice. ¹¹I think you should finish what you started. If you give according to what you have, you will prove that you are as eager to give as you were to think about giving. ¹²It doesn't matter how much you have. What matters is how much you are willing to give from what you have.

13 I am not trying to make life easier for others by making life harder for you. But it is only fair ¹⁴for you to share with them when you have so much, and they have so little. Later, when they have more than enough, and you are in need, they can share with you. Then everyone will have a fair share, ¹⁵just as the Scriptures say,

> "Those who gathered too much
>   had nothing left.
> Those who gathered only a little
>   had all they needed."

Titus and His Friends

16 I am grateful that God made Titus care as much about you as we do. ¹⁷When we begged Titus to visit you, he said he would. He wanted to because he cared so much for you. ¹⁸With Titus we are also sending one of the Lord's followers who is well known in every church for spreading the good news. ¹⁹The churches chose this follower to travel with us while we carry this gift that will bring praise to the Lord and show how much we hope to help. ²⁰We don't want anyone to find fault with the way we handle your generous gift. ²¹But we want to do what pleases the Lord and what people think is right.

22 We are also sending someone else with Titus and the other follower. We approve of this man. In fact, he has already shown us many times that he wants to help. And now he wants to help even more than ever, because he trusts you so much. 23Titus is my partner, who works with me to serve you. The other two followers are sent by the churches, and they bring honor to Christ. 24Treat them in such a way that the churches will see your love and will know why we bragged about you.

The Money for God's People

9 I don't need to write you about the money you plan to give for God's people. 2I know how eager you are to give. And I have proudly told the Lord's followers in Macedonia that you people in Achaia have been ready for a whole year. Now your desire to give has made them want to give. 3That's why I am sending Titus and the two others to you. I want you to be ready, just as I promised. This will prove that we were not wrong to brag about you.

4 Some followers from Macedonia may come with me, and I want them to find that you have the money ready. If you don't, I would be embarrassed for trusting you to do this. But you would be embarrassed even more. 5So I have decided to ask Titus and the others to spend some time with you before I arrive. This way they can arrange to collect the money you have promised. Then you will have the chance to give because you want to, and not because you feel forced to.

6 Remember this saying,

"A few seeds make a small harvest,
    but a lot of seeds make a big harvest."

7 Each of you must make up your own mind about how much to give. But don't feel sorry that you must give and don't feel that you are forced to give. God loves people who love to give. 8God can bless you with everything you need, and you will always have more than enough to do all kinds of good things for others. 9The Scriptures say,

> "God freely gives his gifts to the poor,
>   and always does right."

10God gives seed to farmers and provides everyone with food. He will increase what you have, so that you can give even more to those in need. 11You will be blessed in every way, and you will be able to keep on being generous. Then many people will thank God when we deliver your gift.

12 What you are doing is much more than a service that supplies God's people with what they need. It is something that will make many others thank God. 13The way in which you have proved yourselves by this service will bring honor and praise to God. You believed the message about Christ, and you obeyed it by sharing generously with God's people and with everyone else. 14Now they are praying for you and want to see you, because God used you to bless them so very much. 15Thank God for his gift that is too wonderful for words!

Paul Defends His Work for Christ

10 Do you think I am a coward when I am with you and brave when I am far away? Well, I ask you to listen, because Christ himself was humble and gentle. 2Some people have said that we act like the people of this world. So when I arrive, I expect I will

have to be firm and forceful in what I say to them. Please don't make me treat you that way. ³We live in this world, but we don't act like its people ⁴or fight our battles with the weapons of this world. Instead, we use God's power that can destroy fortresses. We destroy arguments ⁵and every bit of pride that keeps anyone from knowing God. We capture people's thoughts and make them obey Christ. ⁶And when you completely obey him, we will punish anyone who refuses to obey.

7 You judge by appearances.ʲ If any of you think you are the only ones who belong to Christ, then think again. We belong to Christ as much as you do. ⁸Maybe I brag a little too much about the authority that the Lord gave me to help you and not to hurt you. Yet I am not embarrassed to brag. ⁹And I am not trying to scare you with my letters. ¹⁰Some of you are saying, "Paul's letters are harsh and powerful. But in person, he is a weakling and has nothing worth saying." ¹¹Those people had better understand that when I am with you, I will do exactly what I say in my letters.

12 We won't dare compare ourselves with those who think so much of themselves. But they are foolish to compare themselves with themselves. ¹³We won't brag about something we don't have a right to brag about. We will only brag about the work that God has sent us to do, and you are part of that work. ¹⁴We are not bragging more than we should. After all, we did bring the message about Christ to you.

15 We don't brag about what others have done, as if we had done those things ourselves. But I hope that

---

ʲ *You judge by appearances*: Or "Take a close look at yourselves."

as you become stronger in your faith, we will be able to reach many more of the people around you.[k] That has always been our goal. [16]Then we will be able to preach the good news in other lands where we cannot take credit for work someone else has already done. [17]The Scriptures say, "If you want to brag, then brag about the Lord." [18]You may brag about yourself, but the only approval that counts is the Lord's approval.

Paul and the False Apostles

11 Please put up with a little of my foolishness. [2]I am as concerned about you as God is. You were like a virgin bride I had chosen only for Christ. [3]But now I fear that you will be tricked, just as Eve was tricked by that lying snake. I am afraid that you might stop thinking about Christ in an honest and sincere way. [4]We told you about Jesus, and you received the Holy Spirit and accepted our message. But you let some people tell you about another Jesus. Now you are ready to receive another spirit and accept a different message. [5]I think I am as good as any of those super apostles. [6]I may not speak as well as they do, but I know as much. And this has already been made perfectly clear to you.

[7] Was it wrong for me to lower myself and honor you by preaching God's message free of charge? [8]I robbed other churches by taking money from them to serve you. [9]Even when I was in need, I still didn't bother you. In fact, some of the Lord's followers

---

[k] we will be able to reach many more of the people around you: Or "you will praise us even more because of our work among you."

from Macedonia brought me what I needed. I have not been a burden to you in the past, and I will never be a burden. ¹⁰As surely as I speak the truth about Christ, no one in Achaia can stop me from bragging about this. ¹¹And it isn't because I don't love you. God himself knows how much I do love you.

12 I plan to go on doing just what I have always done. Then those people won't be able to brag about doing the same things we are doing. ¹³Anyway, they are no more than false apostles and dishonest workers. They only pretend to be apostles of Christ. ¹⁴And it is no wonder. Even Satan tries to make himself look like an angel of light. ¹⁵So why does it seem strange for Satan's servants to pretend to do what is right? Someday they will get exactly what they deserve.

Paul's Sufferings for Christ

16 I don't want any of you to think that I am a fool. But if you do, then let me be a fool and brag a little. ¹⁷When I do all this bragging, I do it as a fool and not for the Lord. ¹⁸Yet if others want to brag about what they have done, so will I. ¹⁹And since you are so smart, you will gladly put up with a fool. ²⁰In fact, you let people make slaves of you and cheat you and steal from you. Why, you even let them strut around and slap you in the face. ²¹I am ashamed to say that we are too weak to behave in such a way.

If they can brag, so can I, but it is a foolish thing to do. ²²Are they Hebrews? So am I. Are they Jews? So am I. Are they from the family of Abraham?

Well, so am I. 23Are they servants of Christ? I am a fool to talk this way, but I serve him better than they do. I have worked harder and have been put in jail more times. I have been beaten with whips more and more and have been in danger of death more often.

24 Five times my own people gave me thirty-nine lashes with a whip. 25Three times the Romans beat me with a big stick, and once my enemies stoned me. I have been shipwrecked three times, and I even had to spend a night and a day in the sea. 26During my many travels, I have been in danger from rivers, robbers, my own people, and foreigners. My life has been in danger in cities, in deserts, at sea, and with people who only pretended to be the Lord's followers.

27 I have worked and struggled and spent many sleepless nights. I have gone hungry and thirsty and often had nothing to eat. I have been cold from not having enough clothes to keep me warm. 28Besides everything else, each day I am burdened down, worrying about all the churches. 29When others are weak, I am weak too. When others are tricked into sin, I get angry.[1]

30 If I have to brag, I will brag about how weak I am. 31God, the Father of our Lord Jesus, knows I am not lying. And God is to be praised forever! 32The governor of Damascus at the time of King Aretas had the city gates guarded, so that he could capture me. 33But I escaped by being let down in a basket through a window in the city wall.

---

[1] *When others are tricked into sin, I get angry:* Or "When others stumble into sin, I hurt for them."

Visions from the Lord

12 I have to brag. There is nothing to be gained by it, but I must brag about the visions and other things that the Lord has shown me. [2]I know about one of Christ's followers who was taken up into the third heaven fourteen years ago. I don't know if the man was still in his body when it happened, but God certainly knows.

3 As I said, only God really knows if this man was in his body at the time. [4]But he was taken up into paradise,[m] where he heard things that are too wonderful to tell. [5]I will brag about that man, but not about myself, except to say how weak I am.

6 Yet even if I did brag, I would not be foolish. I would simply be speaking the truth. But I will try not to say too much. That way, none of you will think more highly of me than you should because of what you have seen me do and say. [7]Of course, I am now referring to the wonderful things I saw. One of Satan's angels was sent to make me suffer terribly, so that I would not feel too proud.[n]

8 Three times I begged the Lord to make this suffering go away. [9]But he replied, "My kindness is all you need. My power is strongest when you are weak."

---

[m] *paradise*: In the Greek translation of the Old Testament, this word is used for the Garden of Eden. In New Testament times it was sometimes used for the place where God's people are happy and at rest, as they wait for the final judgment.

[n] *Of course...too proud*: Or "Because of the wonderful things that I saw, one of Satan's angels was sent to make me suffer terribly, so that I would not feel too proud."

So if Christ keeps giving me his power, I will gladly brag about how weak I am. [10]Yes, I am glad to be weak or insulted or mistreated or to have troubles and sufferings, if it is for Christ. Because when I am weak, I am strong.

Paul's Concern for the Lord's Followers at Corinth

11 I have been making a fool of myself. But you forced me to do it, when you should have been speaking up for me. I may be nothing at all, but I am as good as those super apostles. [12]When I was with you, I was patient and worked all the powerful miracles and signs and wonders of a true apostle. [13]You missed out on only one blessing that the other churches received. That is, you didn't have to support me. Forgive me for doing you wrong.

14 I am planning to visit you for the third time. But I still won't make a burden of myself. What I really want is you, and not what you have. Children are not supposed to save up for their parents, but parents are supposed to take care of their children. [15]So I will gladly give all that I have and all that I am. Will you love me less for loving you too much? [16]You agree that I wasn't a burden to you. Maybe that's because I was trying to catch you off guard and trick you. [17]Were you cheated by any of those I sent to you? [18]I urged Titus to visit you, and I sent another follower with him. But Titus didn't cheat you, and we felt and behaved the same way he did.

19 Have you been thinking all along that we have been defending ourselves to you? Actually, we have been speaking to God as followers of Christ. But, my friends, we did it all for your good.

20 I am afraid that when I come, we won't be pleased with each other. I fear that some of you may be arguing or jealous or angry or selfish or gossiping or insulting each other. I even fear that you may be proud and acting like a mob. 21I am afraid God will make me ashamed when I visit you again. I will feel like crying because many of you have never given up your old sins. You are still doing things that are immoral, indecent, and shameful.

Final Warnings and Greetings

13 I am on my way to visit you for the third time. And as the Scriptures say, "Any charges must be proved true by at least two or three witnesses." 2During my second visit I warned you that I would punish you and anyone else who doesn't stop sinning. I am far away from you now, but I give you the same warning. 3This should prove to you that I am speaking for Christ. When he corrects you, he won't be weak. He will be powerful! 4Although he was weak when he was nailed to the cross, he now lives by the power of God. We are weak, just as Christ was. But you will see that we will live by the power of God, just as Christ does.

5 Test yourselves and find out if you really are true to your faith. If you pass the test, you will discover that Christ is living in you. But if Christ isn't living in you, you have failed. 6I hope you will discover that we have not failed. 7We pray that you will stop doing evil things. We don't pray like this to make ourselves look good, but to get you to do right, even if we are failures.

8 All we can do is to follow the truth and not fight against it. 9Even though we are weak, we are glad

that you are strong, and we pray that you will do even better. ¹⁰I am writing these things to you before I arrive. This way I won't have to be hard on you when I use the authority that the Lord has given me. I was given this authority, so that I could help you and not destroy you.

11 Good-by, my friends. Do better and pay attention to what I have said. Try to get along and live peacefully with each other.

Now I pray that God, who gives love and peace, will be with you. ¹²Give each other a warm greeting. All of God's people send their greetings.

13 I pray that the Lord Jesus Christ will bless you and be kind to you! May God bless you with his love, and may the Holy Spirit join all your hearts together.

Paul's Letter
to the Churches in Galatia

From the very beginning of this letter to the churches in the region of Galatia (in central Asia Minor), Paul makes two things clear to his readers: he is a true apostle, and his message is the only true message (1.1-10). These statements were very important, because some people claimed that Paul was a false apostle with a false message.

Paul was indeed a true apostle, and his mission to the Gentiles was given to him by the Lord and approved by the apostles in Jerusalem (1.18–2.10). Paul had even corrected the apostle Peter, when he had stopped eating with Gentile followers who were not obeying the Law of Moses (2.1-18).

Faith is the only way to be saved. Paul insists that this was true already for Abraham, who had received God's promise by faith. And Paul leaves no doubt about what his own faith means to him:

I have been nailed to the cross with Christ. I have died, but Christ lives in me. And I now live by faith in the Son of God, who loved me and gave his life for me. (2.19b,20)

A QUICK LOOK AT THIS LETTER

589

1 1-2From the apostle Paul and from all the Lord's followers with me.

I was chosen to be an apostle by Jesus Christ and by God the Father, who raised him from death. No mere human chose or appointed me to this work.

To the churches in Galatia.

3 I pray that God the Father and our Lord Jesus Christ will be kind to you and will bless you with peace! 4Christ obeyed God our Father and gave himself as a sacrifice for our sins to rescue us from this evil world. 5God will be given glory forever and ever. Amen.

The Only True Message

6 I am shocked that you have so quickly turned from God, who chose you because of his wonderful kindness.*a* You have believed another message, 7when there is really only one true message. But some people are causing you trouble and want to make you turn away from the good news about Christ. 8I pray that God will punish anyone who preaches anything different from our message to you! It doesn't matter if that person is one of us or an angel from heaven. 9I have said it before, and I will say it again. I hope God will punish anyone who preaches anything different from what you have already believed.

---

a his wonderful kindness: Some manuscripts have "the wonderful kindness of Christ."

10 I am not trying to please people. I want to please God. Do you think I am trying to please people? If I were doing that, I would not be a servant of Christ.

How Paul Became an Apostle

11 My friends, I want you to know that no one made up the message I preach. 12It wasn't given or taught to me by some mere human. My message came directly from Jesus Christ when he appeared to me.

13 You know how I used to live as a Jew. I was cruel to God's church and even tried to destroy it. 14I was a much better Jew than anyone else my own age, and I obeyed every law that our ancestors had given us. 15But even before I was born, God had chosen me. He was kind and had decided 16to show me his Son, so that I would announce his message to the Gentiles. I didn't talk this over with anyone. 17I didn't say a word, not even to the men in Jerusalem who were apostles before I was. Instead, I went at once to Arabia, and afterwards I returned to Damascus.

18 Three years later I went to visit Peter[b] in Jerusalem and stayed with him for fifteen days. 19The only other apostle I saw was James, the Lord's brother. 20And in the presence of God I swear I am telling the truth.

21 Later, I went to the regions of Syria and Cilicia. 22But no one who belonged to Christ's churches in Judea had ever seen me in person. 23They had only

---

[b] *Peter*: The Greek text has "Cephas," which is an Aramaic name meaning "rock." Peter is the Greek name with the same meaning.

heard that the one who had been cruel to them was now preaching the message that he had once tried to destroy. [24] And because of me, they praised God.

2 Fourteen years later I went to Jerusalem with Barnabas. I also took along Titus. [2] But I went there because God had told me to go, and I explained the good news that I had been preaching to the Gentiles. Then I met privately with the ones who seemed to be the most important leaders. I wanted to make sure that my work in the past and my future work would not be for nothing.

[3] Titus went to Jerusalem with me. He was a Greek, but still he wasn't forced to be circumcised. [4] We went there because of those who pretended to be followers and had sneaked in among us as spies. They had come to take away the freedom that Christ Jesus had given us, and they were trying to make us their slaves. [5] But we wanted you to have the true message. That's why we didn't give in to them, not even for a second.

[6] Some of them were supposed to be important leaders, but I didn't care who they were. God doesn't have any favorites! None of these so-called special leaders added anything to my message. [7] They realized that God had sent me with the good news for Gentiles, and that he had sent Peter with the same message for Jews. [8] God, who had sent Peter on a mission to the Jews, was now using me to preach to the Gentiles.

[9] James, Peter,[c] and John realized that God had given me the message about his undeserved kindness.

---

[c] *Peter*: The Greek text has "Cephas," which is an Aramaic name meaning "rock." Peter is the Greek name with the same meaning.

And these men are supposed to be the backbone of the church. They even gave Barnabas and me a friendly handshake. This was to show that we would work with Gentiles and that they would work with Jews. [10]They only asked us to remember the poor, and that was something I had always been eager to do.

Paul Corrects Peter at Antioch

11 When Peter came to Antioch, I told him face-to-face that he was wrong. [12]He used to eat with Gentile followers of the Lord, until James sent some Jewish followers. Peter was afraid of the Jews and soon stopped eating with Gentiles. [13]He and the others hid their true feelings so well that even Barnabas was fooled. [14]But when I saw that they were not really obeying the truth that is in the good news, I corrected Peter in front of everyone and said:

Peter, you are a Jew, but you live like a Gentile. So how can you force Gentiles to live like Jews?

15 We are Jews by birth and are not sinners like Gentiles. [16]But we know that God accepts only those who have faith in Jesus Christ. No one can please God by simply obeying the Law. So we put our faith in Christ Jesus, and God accepted us because of our faith.

17 When we Jews started looking for a way to please God, we discovered that we are sinners too. Does this mean that Christ is the one who makes us sinners? No, it doesn't! [18]But if I tear down something and then build it again, I prove that I was wrong at first. [19]It was the Law itself

that killed me and freed me from its power, so that I could live for God.

I have been nailed to the cross with Christ. 20I have died, but Christ lives in me. And I now live by faith in the Son of God, who loved me and gave his life for me. 21I don't turn my back on God's undeserved kindness. If we can be acceptable to God by obeying the Law, it was useless for Christ to die.

Faith Is the Only Way

3 You stupid Galatians! I told you exactly how Jesus Christ was nailed to a cross. Has someone now put an evil spell on you? 2I want to know only one thing. How were you given God's Spirit? Was it by obeying the Law of Moses or by hearing about Christ and having faith in him? 3How can you be so stupid? Do you think that by yourself you can complete what God's Spirit started in you? 4Have you gone through all of this for nothing? Is it all really for nothing? 5God gives you his Spirit and works miracles in you. But does he do this because you obey the Law of Moses or because you have heard about Christ and have faith in him?

6 The Scriptures say that God accepted Abraham because Abraham had faith. 7And so, you should understand that everyone who has faith is a child of Abraham.*d* 8Long ago the Scriptures said that God would accept the Gentiles because of their faith. That's why God told Abraham the good news that all nations

---

d a child of Abraham: God chose Abraham, and so it was believed that anyone who was a child of Abraham was also a child of God (see the note at 3.29).

would be blessed because of him. ⁹This means that everyone who has faith will share in the blessings that were given to Abraham because of his faith.

10 Anyone who tries to please God by obeying the Law is under a curse. The Scriptures say, "Everyone who doesn't obey everything in the Law is under a curse." ¹¹No one can please God by obeying the Law. The Scriptures also say, "The people God accepts because of their faith will live."ᵉ

12 The Law isn't based on faith. It promises life only to people who obey its commands. ¹³But Christ rescued us from the Law's curse, when he became a curse in our place. This is because the Scriptures say that anyone who is nailed to a tree is under a curse. ¹⁴And because of what Jesus Christ has done, the blessing that was promised to Abraham was taken to the Gentiles. This happened so that by faith we would be given the promised Holy Spirit.

The Law and the Promise

15 My friends, I will use an everyday example to explain what I mean. Once someone agrees to something, no one else can change or cancel the agreement.ᶠ ¹⁶That is how it is with the promises God made to Abraham and his descendant.ᵍ The promises were not

---

ᵉ *The people God accepts because of their faith will live*: Or "The people God accepts will live because of their faith."

ᶠ *Once someone…cancel the agreement*: Or "Once a person makes out a will, no one can change or cancel it."

ᵍ *descendant*: The Greek text has "seed," which may mean one or many descendants. In this verse Paul says it means Christ.

made to many descendants, but only to one, and that one is Christ. ¹⁷What I am saying is that the Law cannot change or cancel God's promise that was made 430 years before the Law was given. ¹⁸If we have to obey the Law in order to receive God's blessings, those blessings don't really come to us because of God's promise. But God was kind to Abraham and made him a promise.

19 What is the use of the Law? It was given later to show that we sin. But it was only supposed to last until the coming of that descendant[h] who was given the promise. In fact, angels gave the Law to Moses, and he gave it to the people. ²⁰There is only one God, and the Law did not come directly from him.

Slaves and Children

21 Does the Law disagree with God's promises? No, it doesn't! If any law could give life to us, we could become acceptable to God by obeying that law. ²²But the Scriptures say that sin controls everyone, so that God's promises will be for anyone who has faith in Jesus Christ.

23 The Law controlled us and kept us under its power until the time came when we would have faith. ²⁴In fact, the Law was our teacher. It was supposed to teach us until we had faith and were acceptable to God. ²⁵But once a person has learned to have faith, there is no more need to have the Law as a teacher.

26 All of you are God's children because of your faith in Christ Jesus. ²⁷And when you were baptized, it was as though you had put on Christ in the same

---

[h] *that descendant*: Jesus.

way you put on new clothes. ²⁸Faith in Christ Jesus is what makes each of you equal with each other, whether you are a Jew or a Greek, a slave or a free person, a man or a woman. ²⁹So if you belong to Christ, you are now part of Abraham's family,*i* and you will be given what God has promised.

4 Children who are under age are no better off than slaves, even though everything their parents own will someday be theirs. ²This is because children are placed in the care of guardians and teachers until the time their parents have set. ³That is how it was with us. We were like children ruled by the powers of this world. ⁴But when the time was right, God sent his Son, and a woman gave birth to him. His Son obeyed the Law, ⁵so he could set us free from the Law, and we could become God's children. ⁶Now that we are his children, God has sent the Spirit of his Son into our hearts. And his Spirit tells us that God is our Father. ⁷You are no longer slaves. You are God's children, and you will be given what he has promised.

Paul's Concern for the Galatians

⁸Before you knew God, you were slaves of gods that are not real. ⁹But now you know God, or better still, God knows you. How can you turn back and become the slaves of those weak and pitiful powers?*j*

---

i *you are now part of Abraham's family*: Paul tells the Galatians that faith in Jesus Christ is what makes someone a true child of Abraham and of God (see the note at 3.7).

j *powers*: Spirits were thought to control human lives and were believed to be connected with the movements of the stars.

10You even celebrate certain days, months, seasons, and years. 11I am afraid I have wasted my time working with you.

12 My friends, I beg you to be like me, just as I once tried to be like you. Did you mistreat me 13when I first preached to you? No you didn't, even though you knew I had come there because I was sick. 14My illness must have caused you some trouble, but you didn't hate me or turn me away because of it. You welcomed me as though I were one of God's angels or even Christ Jesus himself. 15Where is that good feeling now? I am sure that if it had been possible, you would have taken out your own eyes and given them to me. 16Am I now your enemy, just because I told you the truth?

17 Those people may be paying you a lot of attention, but it isn't for your good. They only want to keep you away from me, so you will pay them a lot of attention. 18It is always good to give your attention to something worthwhile, even when I am not with you. 19My children, I am in terrible pain until Christ may be seen living in you. 20I wish I were with you now. Then I would not have to talk this way. You really have me puzzled.

Hagar and Sarah

21 Some of you would like to be under the rule of the Law of Moses. But do you know what the Law says? 22In the Scriptures we learn that Abraham had two sons. The mother of one of them was a slave, while the mother of the other one had always been free. 23The son of the slave woman was born in the usual way. But the son of the free woman was born because of God's promise.

24 All of this has another meaning as well. Each of the two women stands for one of the agreements God made with his people. Hagar, the slave woman, stands for the agreement that was made at Mount Sinai. Everyone born into her family is a slave. ²⁵Hagar also stands for Mount Sinai in Arabia[k] and for the present city of Jerusalem. She[l] and her children are slaves.

26 But our mother is the city of Jerusalem in heaven above, and she isn't a slave. ²⁷The Scriptures say about her,

"You have never had children,
    but now you can be glad.
You have never given birth,
    but now you can shout.
Once you had no children,
    but now you will have more children
        than a woman
           who has been married for a long time."

28 My friends, you were born because of this promise, just as Isaac was. ²⁹But the child who was born in the natural way made trouble for the child who was born because of the Spirit. The same thing is happening today. ³⁰The Scriptures say, "Get rid of the slave woman and her son! He won't be given anything. The son of the free woman will receive everything."

---

^k *Hagar also stands for Mount Sinai in Arabia*: Some manuscripts have "Sinai is a mountain in Arabia." This sentence would then be translated: "Sinai is a mountain in Arabia, and Hagar stands for the present city of Jerusalem."

^l *She*: "Hagar" or "Jerusalem."

³¹My friends, we are children of the free woman and not of the slave.

Christ Gives Freedom

5 Christ has set us free! This means we are really free. Now hold on to your freedom and don't ever become slaves of the Law again.

2 I, Paul, promise you that Christ won't do you any good if you get circumcised. ³If you do, you must obey the whole Law. ⁴And if you try to please God by obeying the Law, you have cut yourself off from Christ and his wonderful kindness. ⁵But the Spirit makes us sure that God will accept us because of our faith in Christ. ⁶If you are a follower of Christ Jesus, it makes no difference whether you are circumcised or not. All that matters is your faith that makes you love others.

7 You were doing so well until someone made you turn from the truth. ⁸And that person was certainly not sent by the one who chose you. ⁹A little yeast can change a whole batch of dough, ¹⁰but you belong to the Lord. That makes me certain that you will do what I say, instead of what someone else tells you to do. Whoever is causing trouble for you will be punished.

11 My friends, if I still preach that people need to be circumcised, why am I in so much trouble? The message about the cross would no longer be a problem, if I told people to be circumcised. ¹²I wish that everyone who is upsetting you would not only get circumcised, but would cut off much more!

13 My friends, you were chosen to be free. So don't use your freedom as an excuse to do anything

you want. Use it as an opportunity to serve each other with love. [14] All that the Law says can be summed up in the command to love others as much as you love yourself. [15] But if you keep attacking each other like wild animals, you had better watch out or you will destroy yourselves.

God's Spirit and Our Own Desires

16 If you are guided by the Spirit, you won't obey your selfish desires. [17] The Spirit and your desires are enemies of each other. They are always fighting each other and keeping you from doing what you feel you should. [18] But if you obey the Spirit, the Law of Moses has no control over you.

19 People's desires make them give in to immoral ways, filthy thoughts, and shameful deeds. [20] They worship idols, practice witchcraft, hate others, and are hard to get along with. People become jealous, angry, and selfish. They not only argue and cause trouble, but they are [21] envious. They get drunk, carry on at wild parties, and do other evil things as well. I told you before, and I am telling you again: No one who does these things will share in the blessings of God's kingdom.

22 God's Spirit makes us loving, happy, peaceful, patient, kind, good, faithful, [23] gentle, and self-controlled. There is no law against behaving in any of these ways. [24] And because we belong to Christ Jesus, we have killed our selfish feelings and desires. [25] God's Spirit has given us life, and so we should follow the Spirit. [26] But don't be conceited or make others jealous by claiming to be better than they are.

Help Each Other

6 My friends, you are spiritual. So if someone is trapped in sin, you should gently lead that person back to the right path. But watch out, and don't be tempted yourself. ²You obey the law of Christ when you offer each other a helping hand.

3 If you think you are better than others, when you really aren't, you are wrong. ⁴Do your own work well, and then you will have something to be proud of. But don't compare yourself with others. ⁵We each must carry our own load.

6 Share every good thing you have with anyone who teaches you what God has said.

7 You cannot fool God, so don't make a fool of yourself! You will harvest what you plant. ⁸If you follow your selfish desires, you will harvest destruction, but if you follow the Spirit, you will harvest eternal life. ⁹Don't get tired of helping others. You will be rewarded when the time is right, if you don't give up. ¹⁰We should help people whenever we can, especially if they are followers of the Lord.

Final Warnings

11 You can see what big letters I make when I write with my own hand.

12 Those people who are telling you to get circumcised are only trying to show how important they are. And they don't want to get into trouble for preaching about the cross of Christ. ¹³They are circumcised, but they don't obey the Law of Moses. All they want is to brag about having you circumcised. ¹⁴But I will never brag about anything except the cross of our Lord Jesus

Christ. Because of his cross, the world is dead as far as I am concerned, and I am dead as far as the world is concerned.

15 It doesn't matter if you are circumcised or not. All that matters is that you are a new person.

16 If you follow this rule, you will belong to God's true people. God will treat you with undeserved kindness and will bless you with peace.

17 On my own body are scars that prove I belong to Christ Jesus. So I don't want anyone to bother me anymore.

18 My friends, I pray that the Lord Jesus Christ will be kind to you! Amen.

Paul's Letter to the Church in Ephesus

"Praise the God and Father of our Lord Jesus Christ for the spiritual blessings that Christ has brought us from heaven!" (1.3). Paul begins his letter to the Christians in Ephesus with a powerful reminder of the main theme of his message. Christ died on the cross to set us free (1.7,8). But God raised Christ from death, and he now sits at God's right side in heaven, where he rules over this world. And he will rule over the future world as well (1.20,21).

Christ brought Jews and Gentiles together by "breaking down the wall of hatred" that separated them (2.14) and he united them all as part of that holy temple where God's Spirit lives (2.22). This was according to God's eternal plan (3.11).

There is only one Lord, one Spirit of God, and one God, who is the Father of all people (4.4,5). This means that Christians must let the Spirit keep their hearts united, so they can live at peace with each other (4.3). The idea of all Christians being one with Christ is so central to this letter that it occurs twenty times. There is one faith and one baptism by which believers become one body.

Ephesus was a port city on the western shore of Asia Minor (modern-day Turkey). In Paul's time this was the fourth largest city in the Roman empire. It was also an ancient center of nature religion where the goddess Artemis was widely worshiped (Acts 19).

Paul lets the Ephesians know that much is expected of people who are called to a new life (4.17–5.20). Followers of the Lord are God's dear children, and they must do as God does (5.1). They used to live in the dark, but they must now live in the light and make their light shine (5.8,9).

Paul then teaches husbands and wives, children and parents, and slaves and masters how to live as Christians (5.21–6.9).

Paul never forgets how kind God is:

God was merciful! We were dead because of our sins, but God loved us so much that he made us alive with Christ, and God's wonderful kindness is what saves you. (2.4,5)

You were saved by faith in God, who treats us much better than we deserve. This is God's gift to you, and not anything you have done on your own. (2.8)

A QUICK LOOK AT THIS LETTER

1. Greetings   (1.1,2)
2. Christ Brings Spiritual Blessings   (1.3–3.21)
3. A New Life in Unity with Christ   (4.1–6.20)
4. Final Greetings   (6.21-24)

1 From Paul, chosen by God to be an apostle of Christ Jesus.

To God's people who live in Ephesus and*a* are faithful followers of Christ Jesus.

---

a live in Ephesus and: Some manuscripts do not have these words.

2 I pray that God our Father and our Lord Jesus Christ will be kind to you and will bless you with peace!

Christ Brings Spiritual Blessings

3 Praise the God and Father of our Lord Jesus Christ for the spiritual blessings that Christ has brought us from heaven! [4]Before the world was created, God had Christ choose us to live with him and to be his holy and innocent and loving people. [5]God was kind[b] and decided that Christ would choose us to be God's own adopted children. [6]God was very kind to us because of the Son he dearly loves, and so we should praise God.

7-8 Christ sacrificed his life's blood to set us free, which means that our sins are now forgiven. Christ did this because God was so kind to us. God has great wisdom and understanding, [9]and by what Christ has done, God has shown us his own mysterious ways. [10]Then when the time is right, God will do all that he has planned, and Christ will bring together everything in heaven and on earth.

11 God always does what he plans, and that's why he had Christ choose us. [12]He did this so that we Jews would bring honor to him and be the first ones to have hope because of him. [13]Christ also brought you the truth, which is the good news about how you can be saved. You put your faith in Christ and were given the promised Holy Spirit to show that you belong to God. [14]The Spirit also makes us sure that

---

[b] *holy and innocent and loving people.* [5]*God was kind*: Or "holy and innocent people. God was loving [5]and kind."

we will be given what God has stored up for his people. Then we will be set free, and God will be honored and praised.

Paul's Prayer

15 I have heard about your faith in the Lord Jesus and your love for all of God's people. 16So I never stop being grateful for you, as I mention you in my prayers. 17I ask the glorious Father and God of our Lord Jesus Christ to give you his Spirit. The Spirit will make you wise and let you understand what it means to know God. 18My prayer is that light will flood your hearts and that you will understand the hope that was given to you when God chose you. Then you will discover the glorious blessings that will be yours together with all of God's people.

19 I want you to know about the great and mighty power that God has for us followers. It is the same wonderful power he used 20when he raised Christ from death and let him sit at his right side*c* in heaven. 21There Christ rules over all forces, authorities, powers, and rulers. He rules over all beings in this world and will rule in the future world as well. 22God has put all things under the power of Christ, and for the good of the church he has made him the head of everything. 23The church is Christ's body and is filled with Christ who completely fills everything.*d*

---

c *right side*: The place of power and honor.

d *and is filled with Christ who completely fills everything*: Or "which completely fills Christ and fully completes his work."

From Death to Life

2 In the past you were dead because you sinned and fought against God. ²You followed the ways of this world and obeyed the devil. He rules the world, and his spirit has power over everyone who doesn't obey God. ³Once we were also ruled by the selfish desires of our bodies and minds. We had made God angry, and we were going to be punished like everyone else.

4-5 But God was merciful! We were dead because of our sins, but God loved us so much that he made us alive with Christ, and God's wonderful kindness is what saves you. ⁶God raised us from death to life with Christ Jesus, and he has given us a place beside Christ in heaven. ⁷God did this so that in the future world he could show how truly good and kind he is to us because of what Christ Jesus has done. ⁸You were saved by faith in God, who treats us much better than we deserve.ᵉ This is God's gift to you, and not anything you have done on your own. ⁹It isn't something you have earned, so there is nothing you can brag about. ¹⁰God planned for us to do good things and to live as he has always wanted us to live. That's why he sent Christ to make us what we are.

United by Christ

11 Don't forget that you are Gentiles. In fact, you used to be called "uncircumcised" by those who take pride in being circumcised. ¹²At that time you did not

---

ᵉ *treats us much better than we deserve*: The Greek word *charis*, traditionally rendered "grace," is translated here and other places in the CEV to express the overwhelming kindness of God.

know about Christ. You were foreigners to the people of Israel, and you had no part in the promises that God had made to them. You were living in this world without hope and without God, 13 and you were far from God. But Christ offered his life's blood as a sacrifice and brought you near God.

14 Christ has made peace between Jews and Gentiles, and he has united us by breaking down the wall of hatred that separated us. Christ gave his own body 15 to destroy the Law of Moses with all its rules and commands. He even brought Jews and Gentiles together as though we were only one person, when he united us in peace. 16 On the cross Christ did away with our hatred for each other. He also made peace *f* between us and God by uniting Jews and Gentiles in one body. 17 Christ came and preached peace to you Gentiles, who were far from God, and peace to us Jews, who were near God. 18 And because of Christ, all of us can come to the Father by the same Spirit.

19 You Gentiles are no longer strangers and foreigners. You are citizens with everyone else who belongs to the family of God. 20 You are like a building with the apostles and prophets as the foundation and with Christ as the most important stone. 21 Christ is the one who holds the building together and makes it grow into a holy temple for the Lord. 22 And you are part of that building Christ has built as a place for God's own Spirit to live.

Paul's Mission to the Gentiles

3 Christ Jesus made me his prisoner, so that I could help you Gentiles. 2 You have surely heard about

---

f He also made peace: Or "The cross also made peace."

God's kindness in choosing me to help you. ³In fact, this letter tells you a little about how God has shown me his mysterious ways. ⁴As you read the letter, you will also find out how well I really do understand the mystery about Christ. ⁵No one knew about this mystery until God's Spirit told it to his holy apostles and prophets. ⁶And the mystery is this: Because of Christ Jesus, the good news has given the Gentiles a share in the promises that God gave to the Jews. God has also let the Gentiles be part of the same body.

7 God treated me with kindness. His power worked in me, and it became my job to spread the good news. ⁸I am the least important of all God's people. But God was kind and chose me to tell the Gentiles that because of Christ there are blessings that cannot be measured. ⁹God, who created everything, wanted me to help everyone understand the mysterious plan that had always been hidden in his mind. ¹⁰Then God would use the church to show the powers and authorities in the spiritual world that he has many different kinds of wisdom.

11 God did this according to his eternal plan. And he was able to do what he had planned because of all that Christ Jesus our Lord had done. ¹²Christ now gives us courage and confidence, so that we can come to God by faith. ¹³That's why you should not be discouraged when I suffer for you. After all, it will bring honor to you.

Christ's Love for Us

14 I kneel in prayer to the Father. ¹⁵All beings in heaven and on earth receive their life from him.ᵍ

ᵍ *receive their life from him*: Or "know who they really are because of him."

16God is wonderful and glorious. I pray that his Spirit will make you become strong followers 17and that Christ will live in your hearts because of your faith. Stand firm and be deeply rooted in his love. 18I pray that you and all of God's people will understand what is called wide or long or high or deep.*h* 19I want you to know all about Christ's love, although it is too wonderful to be measured. Then your lives will be filled with all that God is.

20-21 I pray that Christ Jesus and the church will forever bring praise to God. His power at work in us can do far more than we dare ask or imagine. Amen.

Unity with Christ

4 As a prisoner of the Lord, I beg you to live in a way that is worthy of the people God has chosen to be his own. 2Always be humble and gentle. Patiently put up with each other and love each other. 3Try your best to let God's Spirit keep your hearts united. Do this by living at peace. 4All of you are part of the same body. There is only one Spirit of God, just as you were given one hope when you were chosen to be God's people. 5We have only one Lord, one faith, and one baptism. 6There is one God who is the Father of all people. Not only is God above all others, but he works by using all of us, and he lives in all of us.

7 Christ has generously divided out his gifts to us. 8As the Scriptures say,

---

h what is called wide or long or high or deep: This may refer to the heavenly Jerusalem or to God's love or wisdom or to the meaning of the cross.

"When he went up to the highest place,
he led away many prisoners
and gave gifts to people."

9 When it says, "he went up," it means that Christ had been deep in the earth. 10This also means that the one who went deep into the earth is the same one who went into the highest heaven, so that he would fill the whole universe.

11 Christ chose some of us to be apostles, prophets, missionaries, pastors, and teachers, 12so that his people would learn to serve and his body would grow strong. 13This will continue until we are united by our faith and by our understanding of the Son of God. Then we will be mature, just as Christ is, and we will be completely like him.*i*

14 We must stop acting like children. We must not let deceitful people trick us by their false teachings, which are like winds that toss us around from place to place. 15Love should always make us tell the truth. Then we will grow in every way and be more like Christ, the head 16of the body. Christ holds it together and makes all of its parts work perfectly, as it grows and becomes strong because of love.

The Old Life and the New Life

17 As a follower of the Lord, I order you to stop living like stupid, godless people. 18Their minds are in the dark, and they are stubborn and ignorant and have missed out on the life that comes from God. They no longer have any feelings about what is right,

---

i and we will be completely like him: Or "and he is completely perfect."

¹⁹and they are so greedy that they do all kinds of indecent things.

20-21 But that isn't what you were taught about Jesus Christ. He is the truth, and you heard about him and learned about him. ²²You were told that your foolish desires will destroy you and that you must give up your old way of life with all its bad habits. ²³Let the Spirit change your way of thinking ²⁴and make you into a new person. You were created to be like God, and so you must please him and be truly holy.

Rules for the New Life

25 We are part of the same body. Stop lying and start telling each other the truth. ²⁶Don't get so angry that you sin. Don't go to bed angry ²⁷and don't give the devil a chance.

28 If you are a thief, quit stealing. Be honest and work hard, so you will have something to give to people in need.

29 Stop all your dirty talk. Say the right thing at the right time and help others by what you say.

30 Don't make God's Spirit sad. The Spirit makes you sure that someday you will be free from your sins.

31 Stop being bitter and angry and mad at others. Don't yell at one another or curse each other or ever be rude. ³²Instead, be kind and merciful, and forgive others, just as God forgave you because of Christ.

5 Do as God does. After all, you are his dear children. ²Let love be your guide. Christ loved us*ʲ* and offered his life for us as a sacrifice that pleases God.

ʲ us: Some manuscripts have "you."

3 You are God's people, so don't let it be said that any of you are immoral or indecent or greedy. 4Don't use dirty or foolish or filthy words. Instead, say how thankful you are. 5Being greedy, indecent, or immoral is just another way of worshiping idols. You can be sure that people who behave in this way will never be part of the kingdom that belongs to Christ and to God.

Living as People of Light

6 Don't let anyone trick you with foolish talk. God punishes everyone who disobeys him and says*k* foolish things. 7So don't have anything to do with anyone like that.

8 You used to be like people living in the dark, but now you are people of the light because you belong to the Lord. So act like people of the light 9and make your light shine. Be good and honest and truthful, 10as you try to please the Lord. 11Don't take part in doing those worthless things that are done in the dark. Instead, show how wrong they are. 12It is disgusting even to talk about what is done in the dark. 13But the light will show what these things are really like. 14Light shows up everything,*l* just as the Scriptures say,

"Wake up from your sleep
and rise from death.
Then Christ will shine on you."

15 Act like people with good sense and not like fools. 16These are evil times, so make every minute count.

---

k says: Or "does."
l Light shows up everything: Or "Everything that is seen in the light becomes light itself."

17Don't be stupid. Instead, find out what the Lord wants you to do. 18Don't destroy yourself by getting drunk, but let the Spirit fill your life. 19When you meet together, sing psalms, hymns, and spiritual songs, as you praise the Lord with all your heart. 20Always use the name of our Lord Jesus Christ to thank God the Father for everything.

Wives and Husbands

21 Honor Christ and put others first. 22A wife should put her husband first, as she does the Lord. 23A husband is the head of his wife, as Christ is the head and the Savior of the church, which is his own body. 24Wives should always put their husbands first, as the church puts Christ first.

25 A husband should love his wife as much as Christ loved the church and gave his life for it. 26He made the church holy by the power of his word, and he made it pure by washing it with water. 27Christ did this, so that he would have a glorious and holy church, without faults or spots or wrinkles or any other flaws.

28 In the same way, a husband should love his wife as much as he loves himself. A husband who loves his wife shows that he loves himself. 29None of us hate our own bodies. We provide for them and take good care of them, just as Christ does for the church, 30because we are each part of his body. 31As the Scriptures say, "A man leaves his father and mother to get married, and he becomes like one person with his wife." 32This is a great mystery, but I understand it to mean Christ and his church. 33So each husband should love his wife as much as he loves himself, and each wife should respect her husband.

Children and Parents

6 Children, you belong to the Lord, and you do the right thing when you obey your parents. The first commandment with a promise says, 2"Obey your father and your mother, 3and you will have a long and happy life."

4 Parents, don't be hard on your children. Raise them properly. Teach them and instruct them about the Lord.

Slaves and Masters

5 Slaves, you must obey your earthly masters. Show them great respect and be as loyal to them as you are to Christ. 6Try to please them at all times, and not just when you think they are watching. You are slaves of Christ, so with your whole heart you must do what God wants you to do. 7Gladly serve your masters, as though they were the Lord himself, and not simply people. 8You know that you will be rewarded for any good things you do, whether you are slaves or free.

9 Slave owners, you must treat your slaves with this same respect. Don't threaten them. They have the same Master in heaven that you do, and he doesn't have any favorites.

The Fight against Evil

10 Finally, let the mighty strength of the Lord make you strong. 11Put on all the armor that God gives, so you can defend yourself against the devil's tricks. 12We are not fighting against humans. We are fighting against forces and authorities and against rulers of

darkness and powers in the spiritual world. [13]So put on all the armor that God gives. Then when that evil day[m] comes, you will be able to defend yourself. And when the battle is over, you will still be standing firm.

14 Be ready! Let the truth be like a belt around your waist, and let God's justice protect you like armor. [15]Your desire to tell the good news about peace should be like shoes on your feet. [16]Let your faith be like a shield, and you will be able to stop all the flaming arrows of the evil one. [17]Let God's saving power be like a helmet, and for a sword use God's message that comes from the Spirit.

18 Never stop praying, especially for others. Always pray by the power of the Spirit. Stay alert and keep praying for God's people. [19]Pray that I will be given the message to speak and that I may fearlessly explain the mystery about the good news. [20]I was sent to do this work, and that's the reason I am in jail. So pray that I will be brave and will speak as I should.

Final Greetings

21-22 I want you to know how I am getting along and what I am doing. That's why I am sending Tychicus to you. He is a dear friend, as well as a faithful servant of the Lord. He will tell you how I am doing, and he will cheer you up.

23 I pray that God the Father and the Lord Jesus Christ will give peace, love, and faith to every follower! [24]May God be kind to everyone who keeps on loving our Lord Jesus Christ.

---

[m] *that evil day*: Either the present (see 5.16) or "the day of death" or "the day of judgment."

Paul's Letter to the Church in Philippi

ABOUT THIS LETTER

Paul wrote this letter from jail (1.7) to thank the Lord's followers at Philippi for helping him with their gifts and prayers (1.5; 4.10-19). He hopes to be set free, so that he can continue preaching the good news (3.17-19). But he knows that he might be put to death (1.21; 2.17; 3.10).

The city of Philippi is in the part of northern Greece known as Macedonia. It was at Philippi that Paul had entered Europe for the first time, and there he preached the good news and began a church (Acts 16). He now warns the Christians at Philippi that they may have to suffer, just as Christ suffered and Paul is now suffering. If this happens, the Philippians should count it a blessing that comes from having faith in Christ (1.28-30).

There were problems in the church at Philippi, because some of the members claimed that people must obey the law of Moses, or they could not be saved. But Paul has no patience with such members and warns the church, "Watch out for those people who behave like dogs!" (3.2-11). This letter is also filled with joy. Even in jail, Paul is happy because he has discovered how to make the best of a bad situation and because he remembers all the kindness shown to him by the people in the church at Philippi.

Paul reminds them that God's people are to live in harmony (2.2; 4.2,3) and to think the same way that Christ Jesus did:

> *Christ was truly God.*
> *But he did not try to remain*
>   *equal with God.*
> *He gave up everything*
>   *and became a slave,*
> *when he became*
>   *like one of us. (2.6, 7)*

A QUICK LOOK AT THIS LETTER

1. Greetings and a Prayer (1.1-11)
2. What Life Means to Paul (1.12-30)
3. Christ's Example of True Humility (2.1-18)
4. News about Paul's Friends (2.19-30)
5. Being Acceptable to God (3.1-4.9)
6. Paul Thanks the Philippians (4.10-20)
7. Final Greetings (4.21-23)

1 From Paul and Timothy, servants of Christ Jesus. To all of God's people who belong to Christ Jesus at Philippi and to all of your church officials and officers.[a]

2 I pray that God our Father and the Lord Jesus Christ will be kind to you and will bless you with peace!

Paul's Prayer for the Church in Philippi

3 Every time I think of you, I thank my God. 4 And whenever I mention you in my prayers, it makes me happy. 5 This is because you have taken part with me in

---

[a] *church officials and officers*: Or "bishops and deacons."

spreading the good news from the first day you heard about it. [6]God is the one who began this good work in you, and I am certain that he won't stop before it is complete on the day that Christ Jesus returns.

7 You have a special place in my heart. So it is only natural for me to feel the way I do. All of you have helped in the work that God has given me, as I defend the good news and tell about it here in jail. [8]God himself knows how much I want to see you. He knows that I care for you in the same way that Christ Jesus does.

9 I pray that your love will keep on growing and that you will fully know and understand [10]how to make the right choices. Then you will still be pure and innocent when Christ returns. And until that day, [11]Jesus Christ will keep you busy doing good deeds that bring glory and praise to God.

What Life Means to Paul

12 My dear friends, I want you to know that what has happened to me has helped to spread the good news. [13]The Roman guards and all the others know that I am here in jail because I serve Christ. [14]Now most of the Lord's followers have become brave and are fearlessly telling the message.[b]

15 Some are preaching about Christ because they are jealous and envious of us. Others are preaching because they want to help. [16]They love Christ and know that I am here to defend the good news about him. [17]But the ones who are jealous of us are not sincere. They just want to cause trouble for me while I am in jail.

---

[b] the message: Some manuscripts have "the Lord's message," and others have "God's message."

18 But that doesn't matter. All that matters is that people are telling about Christ, whether they are sincere or not. That is what makes me glad.

I will keep on being glad, 19 because I know that your prayers and the help that comes from the Spirit of Christ Jesus will keep me safe. 20 I honestly expect and hope that I will never do anything to be ashamed of. Whether I live or die, I always want to be as brave as I am now and bring honor to Christ.

21 If I live, it will be for Christ, and if I die, I will gain even more. 22 I don't know what to choose. I could keep on living and doing something useful. 23 It is a hard choice to make. I want to die and be with Christ, because that would be much better. 24-25 But I know that all of you still need me. That's why I am sure I will stay on to help you grow and be happy in your faith. 26 Then, when I visit you again, you will have good reason to take great pride in Christ Jesus because of me.[c]

27 Above all else, you must live in a way that brings honor to the good news about Christ. Then, whether I visit you or not, I will hear that all of you think alike. I will know that you are working together and that you are struggling side by side to get others to believe the good news.

28 Be brave when you face your enemies. Your courage will show them that they are going to be destroyed, and it will show you that you will be saved. God will make all of this happen, 29 and he has blessed you. Not only do you have faith in Christ, but you suffer for him. 30 You saw me suffer, and you still

---

[c] take great pride in Christ Jesus because of me: Or "take great pride in me because of Christ Jesus."

hear about my troubles. Now you must suffer in the same way.

True Humility

2 Christ encourages you, and his love comforts you. God's Spirit unites you, and you are concerned for others. ²Now make me completely happy! Live in harmony by showing love for each other. Be united in what you think, as if you were only one person. ³Don't be jealous or proud, but be humble and consider others more important than yourselves. ⁴Care about them as much as you care about yourselves ⁵and think the same way that Christ Jesus thought:*d*

> ⁶ Christ was truly God.
>   But he did not try
>   to remain*e* equal with God.
> ⁷ He gave up everything*f* and became a slave,
>   when he became like one of us.
>
> ⁸ Christ was humble. He obeyed God
>   and even died on a cross.
> ⁹ Then God gave Christ the highest place
>   and honored his name above all others.
>
> ¹⁰ So at the name of Jesus
>   everyone will bow down,
>   those in heaven, on earth,
>   and under the earth.

---

d think the same way that Christ Jesus thought: Or "think the way you should because you belong to Christ Jesus."

e remain: Or "become."

f He gave up everything: Greek, "He emptied himself."

¹¹ And to the glory of God the Father
    everyone will openly agree,
        "Jesus Christ is Lord!"

Lights in the World

12 My dear friends, you always obeyed when I was
with you. Now that I am away, you should obey even
more. So work with fear and trembling to discover
what it really means to be saved. ¹³God is working in
you to make you willing and able to obey him.

14 Do everything without grumbling or arguing.
¹⁵Then you will be the pure and innocent children of
God. You live among people who are crooked and
evil, but you must not do anything that they can say is
wrong. Try to shine as lights among the people of this
world, ¹⁶as you hold firmly to[g] the message that gives
life. Then on the day when Christ returns, I can take
pride in you. I can also know that my work and efforts
were not useless.

17 Your faith in the Lord and your service are like a
sacrifice offered to him. And my own blood may have
to be poured out with the sacrifice.[h] If this happens, I
will be glad and rejoice with you. ¹⁸In the same way,
you should be glad and rejoice with me.

Timothy and Epaphroditus

19 I want to be encouraged by news about you. So
I hope the Lord Jesus will soon let me send Timothy

g *hold firmly to*: Or "offer them."
h *my own blood may have to be poured out with the
  sacrifice*: Offerings of water or wine were sometimes
  poured out when animals were sacrificed on the altar.

to you. [20]I don't have anyone else who cares about you as much as he does. [21]The others think only about what interests them and not about what concerns Christ Jesus. [22]But you know what kind of person Timothy is. He has worked with me like a son in spreading the good news. [23]I hope to send him to you, as soon as I find out what is going to happen to me. [24]And I feel sure that the Lord will also let me come soon.

[25] I think I ought to send my dear friend Epaphroditus back to you. He is a follower and a worker and a soldier of the Lord, just as I am. You sent him to look after me, [26]but now he is eager to see you. He is worried, because you heard he was sick. [27]In fact, he was very sick and almost died. But God was kind to him, and also to me, and he kept me from being burdened down with sorrow.

[28] Now I am more eager than ever to send Epaphroditus back again. You will be glad to see him, and I won't have to worry any longer. [29]Be sure to give him a cheerful welcome, just as people who serve the Lord deserve. [30]He almost died working for Christ, and he risked his own life to do for me what you could not.

Being Acceptable to God

3 Finally, my dear friends, be glad that you belong to the Lord. It doesn't bother me to write the same things to you that I have written before. In fact, it is for your own good.

[2] Watch out for those people who behave like dogs! They are evil and want to do more than just circumcise you. [3]But we are the ones who are truly circumcised,

because we worship by the power of God's Spirit[i] and take pride in Christ Jesus. We don't brag about what we have done, 4although I could. Others may brag about themselves, but I have more reason to brag than anyone else. 5I was circumcised when I was eight days old,[j] and I am from the nation of Israel and the tribe of Benjamin. I am a true Hebrew. As a Pharisee, I strictly obeyed the Law of Moses. 6And I was so eager that I even made trouble for the church. I did everything the Law demands in order to please God.

7 But Christ has shown me that what I once thought was valuable is worthless. 8Nothing is as wonderful as knowing Christ Jesus my Lord. I have given up everything else and count it all as garbage. All I want is Christ 9and to know that I belong to him. I could not make myself acceptable to God by obeying the Law of Moses. God accepted me simply because of my faith in Christ. 10All I want is to know Christ and the power that raised him to life. I want to suffer and die as he did, 11so that somehow I also may be raised to life.

Running toward the Goal

12 I have not yet reached my goal, and I am not perfect. But Christ has taken hold of me. So I keep on running and struggling to take hold of the prize. 13My friends, I don't feel that I have already arrived. But I forget what is behind, and I struggle for what is ahead. 14I run toward the goal, so that I can win the prize of being called to heaven. This is the prize that God

---

i *by the power of God's Spirit*: Or "sincerely."
j *when I was eight days old*: Jewish boys are circumcised eight days after birth.

offers because of what Christ Jesus has done. [15]All of us who are mature should think in this same way. And if any of you think differently, God will make it clear to you. [16]But we must keep going in the direction that we are now headed.

17 My friends, I want you to follow my example and learn from others who closely follow the example we set for you. [18]I often warned you that many people are living as enemies of the cross of Christ. And now with tears in my eyes, I warn you again [19]that they are headed for hell! They worship their stomachs and brag about the disgusting things they do. All they can think about are the things of this world.

20 But we are citizens of heaven and are eagerly waiting for our Savior to come from there. Our Lord Jesus Christ [21]has power over everything, and he will make these poor bodies of ours like his own glorious body.

4 Dear friends, I love you and long to see you. Please keep on being faithful to the Lord. You are my pride and joy.

Paul Encourages the Lord's Followers

2 Euodia and Syntyche, you belong to the Lord, so I beg you to stop arguing with each other. [3]And, my true partner,[k] I ask you to help them. These women have worked together with me and with Clement and with the others in spreading the good news. Their names are now written in the book of life.[l]

---

[k] *partner*: Or "Syzygus," a person's name.
[l] *the book of life*: A book in which the names of God's people are written.

4 Always be glad because of the Lord! I will say it again: Be glad. ⁵Always be gentle with others. The Lord will soon be here. ⁶Don't worry about anything, but pray about everything. With thankful hearts offer up your prayers and requests to God. ⁷Then, because you belong to Christ Jesus, God will bless you with peace that no one can completely understand. And this peace will control the way you think and feel.

8 Finally, my friends, keep your minds on whatever is true, pure, right, holy, friendly, and proper. Don't ever stop thinking about what is truly worthwhile and worthy of praise. ⁹You know the teachings I gave you, and you know what you heard me say and saw me do. So follow my example. And God, who gives peace, will be with you.

Paul Gives Thanks for the Gifts He Was Given

10 The Lord has made me very grateful that at last you have thought about me once again. Actually, you were thinking about me all along, but you didn't have any chance to show it. ¹¹I am not complaining about having too little. I have learned to be satisfied with*m* whatever I have. ¹²I know what it is to be poor or to have plenty, and I have lived under all kinds of conditions. I know what it means to be full or to be hungry, to have too much or too little. ¹³Christ gives me the strength to face anything.

14 It was good of you to help me when I was having such a hard time. ¹⁵My friends at Philippi, you remember what it was like when I started preaching the good

---

m be satisfied with: Or "get by on."

news in Macedonia.[n] After I left there, you were the only church that became my partner by giving blessings and by receiving them in return. [16]Even when I was in Thessalonica, you helped me more than once. [17]I am not trying to get something from you, but I want you to receive the blessings that come from giving.

18 I have been paid back everything, and with interest. I am completely satisfied with the gifts that you had Epaphroditus bring me. They are like a sweet-smelling offering or like the right kind of sacrifice that pleases God. [19]I pray that God will take care of all your needs with the wonderful blessings that come from Christ Jesus! [20]May God our Father be praised forever and ever. Amen.

Final Greetings

21 Give my greetings to all who are God's people because of Christ Jesus.

The Lord's followers here with me send you their greetings.

22 All of God's people send their greetings, especially those in the service of the Emperor.

23 I pray that our Lord Jesus Christ will be kind to you and will bless your life!

---

[n] *when I started preaching the good news in Macedonia*: Paul is talking about his first visit to Philippi (see Acts 16.12-40).

Paul's Letter to the Church in Colossae

ABOUT THIS LETTER

Colossae was an important city in western Asia Minor, about 100 miles east of the port city of Ephesus. Paul had never been to Colossae, but he was pleased to learn that the Christians there were strong in their faith (1.3-7; 2.6,7). They had heard the good news from a man named Epaphras who had lived there (1.7; 4.12,13), but was in jail with Paul (Philemon 23) at the time that Paul wrote this letter (1.14; 4.3,10,18).

Many of the church members in Colossae were Gentiles (1.27), and some of them were influenced by strange religious ideas and practices (2.16-23). They thought that to obey God fully they must give up certain physical desires and worship angels and other spiritual powers. But Paul wanted them to know that Christ was with God in heaven, ruling over all powers in the universe (3.1). And so, their worship should be directed to Christ.

Paul quotes a beautiful hymn that explains who Christ is:

> Christ is exactly like God,
>   who cannot be seen.
> He is the first-born Son,
>   superior to all creation.
> God himself was pleased
>   to live fully in his Son.

And God was pleased
for him to make peace
by sacrificing his blood
on the cross. (1.15, 19, 20a)

A QUICK LOOK AT THIS LETTER

1. Greetings (1.1, 2)
2. A Prayer of Thanks (1.3-8)
3. The Person and Work of Christ (1.9–2.19)
4. New Life with Christ (2.20–4.6)
5. Final Greetings (4.7-18)

1 From Paul, chosen by God to be an apostle of Christ Jesus, and from Timothy, who is also a follower.

2 To God's people who live in Colossae and are faithful followers of Christ.

I pray that God our Father will be kind to you and will bless you with peace!

A Prayer of Thanks

3 Each time we pray for you, we thank God, the Father of our Lord Jesus Christ. 4We have heard of your faith in Christ and of your love for all of God's people, 5because what you hope for is kept safe for you in heaven. You first heard about this hope when you believed the true message, which is the good news.

6 The good news is spreading all over the world with great success. It has spread in that same way among you, ever since the first day you learned the truth about God's wonderful kindness 7from our good friend Epaphras. He works together with us for Christ and is

a faithful worker for you.[a] 8He is also the one who told us about the love that God's Spirit has given you.

The Person and Work of Christ

9 We have not stopped praying for you since the first day we heard about you. In fact, we always pray that God will show you everything he wants you to do and that you may have all the wisdom and understanding that his Spirit gives. 10Then you will live a life that honors the Lord, and you will always please him by doing good deeds. You will come to know God even better. 11His glorious power will make you patient and strong enough to endure anything, and you will be truly happy.

12 I pray that you will be grateful to God for letting you[a] have part in what he has promised his people in the kingdom of light. 13God rescued us from the dark power of Satan and brought us into the kingdom of his dear Son, 14who forgives our sins and sets us free.

15 Christ is exactly like God,
    who cannot be seen.
He is the first-born Son,
    superior to all creation.
16 Everything was created by him,
    everything in heaven and on earth,
        everything seen and unseen,
    including all forces and powers,
        and all rulers and authorities.
All things were created by God's Son,
    and everything was made for him.

---

[a] you: Some manuscripts have "us."

¹⁷ God's Son was before all else,
and by him everything is held together.
¹⁸ He is the head of his body,
which is the church.

He is the very beginning,
the first to be raised from death,
so that he would be above all others.

¹⁹ God himself was pleased
to live fully in his Son.
²⁰ And God was pleased for him to make peace
by sacrificing his blood on the cross,
so that all beings in heaven and on earth
would be brought back to God.

21 You used to be far from God. Your thoughts made you his enemies, and you did evil things. ²²But his Son became a human and died. So God made peace with you, and now he lets you stand in his presence as people who are holy and faultless and innocent. ²³But you must stay deeply rooted and firm in your faith. You must not give up the hope you received when you heard the good news. It was preached to everyone on earth, and I myself have become a servant of this message.

Paul's Service to the Church

24 I am glad that I can suffer for you. I am pleased also that in my own body I can continue*ᵇ* the suffering of Christ for his body, the church. ²⁵God's plan was to make me a servant of his church and to send me to preach his complete message to you. ²⁶For ages and

ᵇ *continue*: Or "complete."

ages this message was kept secret from everyone, but now it has been explained to God's people. ²⁷God did this because he wanted you Gentiles to understand his wonderful and glorious mystery. And the mystery is that Christ lives in you, and he is your hope of sharing in God's glory.

28 We announce the message about Christ, and we use all our wisdom to warn and teach everyone, so that all of Christ's followers will grow and become mature. ²⁹That's why I work so hard and use the mighty power he gives me.

2 I want you to know what a struggle I am going through for you, for God's people at Laodicea, and for all of those followers who have never met me. ²I do it to encourage them. Then as their hearts are joined together in love, they will be wonderfully blessed with complete understanding. And they will truly know Christ. Not only is he the key to God's mystery, ³but all wisdom and knowledge are hidden away in him. ⁴I tell you these things to keep you from being fooled by fancy talk. ⁵Even though I am not with you, I keep thinking about you. I am glad to know that you are living as you should and that your faith in Christ is strong.

Christ Brings Real Life

6 You have accepted Christ Jesus as your Lord. Now keep on following him. ⁷Plant your roots in Christ and let him be the foundation for your life. Be strong in your faith, just as you were taught. And be grateful.

8 Don't let anyone fool you by using senseless arguments. These arguments may sound wise, but

they are only human teachings. They come from the powers of this world[c] and not from Christ.

9 God lives fully in Christ. [10]And you are fully grown because you belong to Christ, who is over every power and authority. [11]Christ has also taken away your selfish desires, just as circumcision removes flesh from the body. [12]And when you were baptized, it was the same as being buried with Christ. Then you were raised to life because you had faith in the power of God, who raised Christ from death. [13]You were dead, because you were sinful and were not God's people. But God let Christ make you[d] alive, when he forgave all our sins.

14 God wiped out the charges that were against us for disobeying the Law of Moses. He took them away and nailed them to the cross. [15]There Christ defeated all powers and forces. He let the whole world see them being led away as prisoners when he celebrated his victory.

16 Don't let anyone tell you what you must eat or drink. Don't let them say that you must celebrate the New Moon festival, the Sabbath, or any other festival. [17]These things are only a shadow of what was to come. But Christ is real!

18 Don't be cheated by people who make a show of acting humble and who worship angels.[e] They brag

---

[c] *powers of this world*: Spirits and unseen forces were thought to control human lives and were believed to be connected with the movements of the stars.

[d] *you*: See the note at 1.7.

[e] *worship angels*: Or "worship with angels (in visions of heaven)."

about seeing visions. But it is all nonsense, because their minds are filled with selfish desires. ¹⁹They are no longer part of Christ, who is the head of the whole body. Christ gives the body its strength, and he uses its joints and muscles to hold it together, as it grows by the power of God.

Christ Brings New Life

20 You died with Christ. Now the forces of the universe*f* don't have any power over you. Why do you live as if you had to obey such rules as, ²¹"Don't handle this. Don't taste that. Don't touch this."? ²²After these things are used, they are no longer good for anything. So why be bothered with the rules that humans have made up? ²³Obeying these rules may seem to be the smart thing to do. They appear to make you love God more and to be very humble and to have control over your body. But they don't really have any power over our desires.

3 You have been raised to life with Christ. Now set your heart on what is in heaven, where Christ rules at God's right side.*g* ²Think about what is up there, not about what is here on earth. ³You died, which means that your life is hidden with Christ, who sits beside God. ⁴Christ gives meaning to your*h* life, and when he appears, you will also appear with him in glory.

5 Don't be controlled by your body. Kill every desire for the wrong kind of sex. Don't be immoral or

---

f forces of the universe: See the note at 2.8.

g right side: The place of power and honor.

h your: Some manuscripts have "our."

indecent or have evil thoughts. Don't be greedy, which is the same as worshiping idols. 6God is angry with people who disobey him by doing*i* these things. 7And that is exactly what you did, when you lived among people who behaved in this way. 8But now you must stop doing such things. You must quit being angry, hateful, and evil. You must no longer say insulting or cruel things about others. 9And stop lying to each other. You have given up your old way of life with its habits.

10 Each of you is now a new person. You are becoming more and more like your Creator, and you will understand him better. 11It doesn't matter if you are a Greek or a Jew, or if you are circumcised or not. You may even be a barbarian or a Scythian,*j* and you may be a slave or a free person. Yet Christ is all that matters, and he lives in all of us.

12 God loves you and has chosen you as his own special people. So be gentle, kind, humble, meek, and patient. 13Put up with each other, and forgive anyone who does you wrong, just as Christ has forgiven you. 14Love is more important than anything else. It is what ties everything completely together.

15 Each one of you is part of the body of Christ, and you were chosen to live together in peace. So let the peace that comes from Christ control your thoughts.

---

i *people who disobey him by doing*: Some manuscripts do not have these words.

j *a barbarian or a Scythian*: Barbarians were people who could not speak Greek and would be in the lower class of society. Scythians were people who were known for their cruelty.

And be grateful. 16Let the message about Christ completely fill your lives, while you use all your wisdom to teach and instruct each other. With thankful hearts, sing psalms, hymns, and spiritual songs to God. 17Whatever you say or do should be done in the name of the Lord Jesus, as you give thanks to God the Father because of him.

Some Rules for Christian Living

18 A wife must put her husband first. This is her duty as a follower of the Lord.

19 A husband must love his wife and not abuse her.

20 Children must always obey their parents. This pleases the Lord.

21 Parents, don't be hard on your children. If you are, they might give up.

22 Slaves, you must always obey your earthly masters. Try to please them at all times, and not just when you think they are watching. Honor the Lord and serve your masters with your whole heart. 23Do your work willingly, as though you were serving the Lord himself, and not just your earthly master. 24In fact, the Lord Christ is the one you are really serving, and you know that he will reward you. 25But Christ has no favorites! He will punish evil people, just as they deserve.

4 Slave owners, be fair and honest with your slaves. Don't forget that you have a Master in heaven.

2 Never give up praying. And when you pray, keep alert and be thankful. 3Be sure to pray that God will make a way for us to spread his message and explain the mystery about Christ, even though I am in jail for doing this. 4Please pray that I will make the message as clear as possible.

5 When you are with unbelievers, always make good use of the time. 6Be pleasant and hold their interest when you speak the message. Choose your words carefully and be ready to give answers to anyone who asks questions.

Final Greetings

7 Tychicus is the dear friend, who faithfully works and serves the Lord with us, and he will give you the news about me. 8I am sending him to cheer you up by telling you how we are getting along. 9Onesimus, that dear and faithful follower from your own group, is coming with him. The two of them will tell you everything that has happened here.

10 Aristarchus is in jail with me. He sends greetings to you, and so does Mark, the cousin of Barnabas. You have already been told to welcome Mark, if he visits you. 11Jesus, who is known as Justus, sends his greetings. These three men are the only Jewish followers who have worked with me for the kingdom of God. They have given me much comfort.

12 Your own Epaphras, who serves Christ Jesus, sends his greetings. He always prays hard that you may fully know what the Lord wants you to do and that you may do it completely. 13I have seen how much trouble he has gone through for you and for the followers in Laodicea and Hierapolis.

14 Our dear doctor Luke sends you his greetings, and so does Demas.

15 Give my greetings to the followers at Laodicea, especially to Nympha and the church that meets in her home.

16 After this letter has been read to your people, be sure to have it read in the church at Laodicea. And you should read the letter that I have sent to them.[k]

17 Remind Archippus to do the work that the Lord has given him to do.

18 I am signing this letter myself: PAUL.

Don't forget that I am in jail.

I pray that God will be kind to you.

---

[k] *the letter that I have sent to them*: This is the only mention of the letter to the church at Laodicea.

Paul's First Letter to the Church in Thessalonica

ABOUT THIS LETTER

Paul started the church in Thessalonica (2.13,14), while working hard to support himself (2.9). In this important city of northern Greece, many of the followers had worshiped idols before becoming Christians (1.9). But they were faithful to the Lord, and because of them the Lord's message had spread everywhere in that region (1.8). This letter may have been the first one that Paul wrote, and maybe even the first of all the New Testament writings.

Some people in Thessalonica began to oppose Paul, and he had to escape to Athens. But he sent his young friend Timothy to find out how the Christians were doing (3.1-5). When Timothy returned, he gave Paul good reports of their faith and love (3.6-10).

The church itself had problems. Some of its members had quit working, since they thought that the Lord would soon return (4.11,12). Others were worried because relatives and friends had already died before Christ's return. So Paul tried to explain to them more clearly what would happen when the Lord returns (4.13-15), and then told them how they should live in the meanwhile (5.1-11).

Paul's final instructions are well worth remembering: *Always be joyful and never stop praying. Whatever happens, keep thanking God because of Jesus Christ. This is what God wants you to do. (5.16-18)*

1 From Paul, Silas,[a] and Timothy.
To the church in Thessalonica, the people of God
the Father and of the Lord Jesus Christ.
I pray that God will be kind to you and will bless
you with peace!

2 We thank God for you and always mention you
in our prayers. Each time we pray, [3] we tell God our
Father about your faith and loving work and about
your firm hope in our Lord Jesus Christ.

The Thessalonians' Faith and Example

4 My dear friends, God loves you, and we know he
has chosen you to be his people. [5] When we told you the
good news, it was with the power and assurance that
come from the Holy Spirit, and not simply with words.
You knew what kind of people we were and how we
helped you. [6] So, when you accepted the message, you
followed our example and the example of the Lord. You
suffered, but the Holy Spirit made you glad.

7 You became an example for all the Lord's followers in Macedonia and Achaia. [8] And because of
you, the Lord's message has spread everywhere in

---

[a] *Silas*: The Greek text has "Silvanus," another form of
the name Silas.

those regions. Now the news of your faith in God is
known all over the world, and we don't have to say a
thing about it. [9]Everyone is talking about how you
welcomed us and how you turned away from idols to
serve the true and living God. [10]They also tell how
you are waiting for his Son Jesus to come from heaven.
God raised him from death, and on the day of judgment
Jesus will save us from God's anger.

Paul's Work in Thessalonica

2 My friends, you know that our time with you
wasn't wasted. [2]As you remember, we had been
mistreated and insulted at Philippi. But God gave us
the courage to tell you the good news about him, even
though many people caused us trouble. [3]We didn't
have any hidden motives when we won you over, and
we didn't try to fool or trick anyone. [4]God was pleased
to trust us with his message. We didn't speak to please
people, but to please God who knows our motives.

[5] You also know that we didn't try to flatter anyone.
God himself knows that what we did wasn't a cover-up
for greed. [6]We were not trying to get you or anyone else
to praise us. [7]But as apostles, we could have demanded
help from you. After all, Christ is the one who sent us.
We chose to be like children or like a mother[b] nursing
her baby. [8]We cared so much for you, and you became
so dear to us, that we were willing to give our lives for
you when we gave you God's message.

[9] My dear friends, you surely haven't forgotten our
hard work and hardships. You remember how night

---

[b] *like children or like a mother*: Some manuscripts have
   "as gentle as a mother."

and day we struggled to make a living, so that we could tell you God's message without being a burden to anyone. ¹⁰Both you and God are witnesses that we were pure and honest and innocent in our dealings with you followers of the Lord. ¹¹You also know we did everything for you that parents would do for their own children. ¹²We begged, encouraged, and urged each of you to live in a way that would honor God. He is the one who chose you to share in his own kingdom and glory.

13 We always thank God that you believed the message we preached. It came from him, and it isn't something made up by humans. You accepted it as God's message, and now he is working in you. ¹⁴My friends, you did just like God's churches in Judea and like the other followers of Christ Jesus there. And so, you were mistreated by your own people, in the same way they were mistreated by their people.

15 Those evil people killed the Lord Jesus and the prophets, and they even chased us away. God doesn't like what they do and neither does anyone else. ¹⁶They keep us from speaking his message to the Gentiles and from leading them to be saved. They have always gone too far with their sins. Now God has finally become angry and will punish them.

Paul Wants To Visit the Church Again

17 My friends, we were kept from coming to you for a while, but we never stopped thinking about you. We were eager to see you and tried our best to visit you in person. ¹⁸We really wanted to come. I myself tried several times, but Satan always stopped us. ¹⁹After all, when the Lord Jesus appears, who else but

you will give us hope and joy and be like a glorious crown for us? [20] You alone are our glory and joy!

3 Finally, we couldn't stand it any longer. We decided to stay in Athens by ourselves [2] and send our friend Timothy to you. He works with us as God's servant and preaches the good news about Christ. We wanted him to make you strong in your faith and to encourage you. [3] We didn't want any of you to be discouraged by all these troubles. You knew we would have to suffer, [4] because when we were with you, we told you this would happen. And we did suffer, as you well know. [5] At last, when I could not wait any longer, I sent Timothy to find out about your faith. I hoped that Satan had not tempted you and made all our work useless.

[6] Timothy has come back from his visit with you and has told us about your faith and love. He also said that you always have happy memories of us and that you want to see us as much as we want to see you.

[7] My friends, even though we have a lot of trouble and suffering, your faith makes us feel better about you. [8] Your strong faith in the Lord is like a breath of new life. [9] How can we possibly thank God enough for all the happiness you have brought us? [10] Day and night we sincerely pray that we will see you again and help you to have an even stronger faith.

[11] We pray that God our Father and our Lord Jesus will let us visit you. [12] May the Lord make your love for each other and for everyone else grow by leaps and bounds. That's how our love for you has grown. [13] And when our Lord comes with all of his people, I pray that he will make your hearts pure and innocent in the sight of God the Father.

A Life That Pleases God

4 Finally, my dear friends, since you belong to the Lord Jesus, we beg and urge you to live as we taught you. Then you will please God. You are already living that way, but try even harder. ²Remember the instructions we gave you as followers of the Lord Jesus. ³God wants you to be holy, so don't be immoral in matters of sex. ⁴Respect and honor your wife.ᶜ ⁵Don't be a slave of your desires or live like people who don't know God. ⁶You must not cheat any of the Lord's followers in matters of sex.ᵈ Remember, we warned you that he punishes everyone who does such things. ⁷God didn't choose you to be filthy, but to be pure. ⁸So if you don't obey these rules, you are not really disobeying us. You are disobeying God, who gives you his Holy Spirit.

9 We don't have to write you about the need to love each other. God has taught you to do this, ¹⁰and you already have shown your love for all of his people in Macedonia. But, my dear friends, we ask you to do even more. ¹¹Try your best to live quietly, to mind your own business, and to work hard, just as we taught you to do. ¹²Then you will be respected by people who are not followers of the Lord, and you won't have to depend on anyone.

The Lord's Coming

13 My friends, we want you to understand how it will be for those followers who have already died.

ᶜ *your wife*: Or "your body."
ᵈ *in matters of sex*: Or "in business."

Then you won't grieve over them and be like people who don't have any hope. [14]We believe that Jesus died and was raised to life. We also believe that when God brings Jesus back again, he will bring with him all who had faith in Jesus before they died. [15]Our Lord Jesus told us that when he comes, we won't go up to meet him ahead of his followers who have already died.

16 With a loud command and with the shout of the chief angel and a blast of God's trumpet, the Lord will return from heaven. Then those who had faith in Christ before they died will be raised to life. [17]Next, all of us who are still alive will be taken up into the clouds together with them to meet the Lord in the sky. From that time on we will all be with the Lord forever. [18]Encourage each other with these words.

5 I don't need to write you about the time or date when all this will happen. [2]You surely know that the Lord's return[e] will be as a thief coming at night. [3]People will think they are safe and secure. But destruction will suddenly strike them like the pains of a woman about to give birth. And they won't escape.

4 My dear friends, you don't live in darkness, and so that day won't surprise you like a thief. [5]You belong to the light and live in the day. We don't live in the night or belong to the dark. [6]Others may sleep, but we should stay awake and be alert. [7]People sleep during the night, and some even get drunk. [8]But we belong to the day. So we must stay sober and let our faith and love be like a suit of armor. Our firm hope that we will be saved is our helmet.

---

[e] *the Lord's return*: The Greek text has "the day of the Lord."

9 God doesn't intend to punish us, but to have our Lord Jesus Christ save us. 10Christ died for us, so that we could live with him, whether we are alive or dead when he comes. 11That's why you must encourage and help each other, just as you are already doing.

Final Instructions and Greetings

12 My friends, we ask you to be thoughtful of your leaders who work hard and tell you how to live for the Lord. 13Show them great respect and love because of their work. Try to get along with each other. 14My friends, we beg you to warn anyone who isn't living right. Encourage anyone who feels left out, help all who are weak, and be patient with everyone. 15Don't be hateful to people, just because they are hateful to you. Rather, be good to each other and to everyone else.

16 Always be joyful 17and never stop praying. 18Whatever happens, keep thanking God because of Jesus Christ. This is what God wants you to do.

19 Don't turn away God's Spirit 20or ignore prophecies. 21Put everything to the test. Accept what is good 22and don't have anything to do with evil.

23 I pray that God, who gives peace, will make you completely holy. And may your spirit, soul, and body be kept healthy and faultless until our Lord Jesus Christ returns. 24The one who chose you can be trusted, and he will do this.

25 Friends, please pray for us.

26 Give the Lord's followers a warm greeting.

27 In the name of the Lord I beg you to read this letter to all his followers.

28 I pray that our Lord Jesus Christ will be kind to you!

Paul's Second Letter to the Church in Thessalonica

ABOUT THIS LETTER

In this letter to the believers in Thessalonica, Paul begins by thanking God that their faith and love keep growing all the time (1.3). They were going through a lot of troubles, but Paul insists that this is God's way of testing their faith, not a way of punishing them (1.4,5).

Someone in Thessalonica claimed to have a letter from Paul, saying that the Lord had already returned (2.2). But Paul warns the church not to be fooled! The Lord will not return until after the "wicked one" has appeared (2.3).

Paul also warns against laziness (3.6-10), and he tells the church to guard against any followers who refuse to obey what he has written in this letter.

The letter closes with a prayer:

I pray that the Lord, who gives peace, will always bless you with peace. May the Lord be with all of you. (3.16)

A QUICK LOOK AT THIS LETTER

1. Greetings (1.1,2)
2. The Lord's Return Will Bring Justice   (1.3-12)
3. The Lord Has Not Returned Yet (2.1-12)
4. Be Faithful (2.13-17)
5. Pray and Work (3.1-15)
6. A Final Prayer (3.16-18)

648

1 From Paul, Silas,[a] and Timothy.
To the church in Thessalonica, the people of God
our Father and of the Lord Jesus Christ.

2 I pray that God our Father and the Lord Jesus
Christ will be kind to you and will bless you with
peace!

When Christ Returns

3 My dear friends, we always have good reason to
thank God for you, because your faith in God and
your love for each other keep growing all the time.
4That's why we brag about you to all of God's
churches. We tell them how patient you are and how
you keep on having faith, even though you are going
through a lot of trouble and suffering.

5 All of this shows that God judges fairly and that
he is making you fit to share in his kingdom for which
you are suffering. 6It is only right for God to punish
everyone who is causing you trouble, 7but he will
give you relief from your troubles. He will do the same
for us, when the Lord Jesus comes from heaven with
his powerful angels 8and with a flaming fire.

Our Lord Jesus will punish anyone who doesn't
know God and won't obey his message. 9Their punishment will be eternal destruction, and they will be kept
far from the presence of our Lord and his glorious
strength. 10This will happen on that day when the Lord
returns to be praised and honored by all who have faith
in him and belong to him. This includes you, because
you believed what we said.

---

a *Silas*: The Greek text has "Silvanus," which is another
   form of the name Silas.

11 God chose you, and we keep praying that God will make you worthy of being his people. We pray for God's power to help you do all the good things that you hope to do and that your faith makes you want to do. [12]Then, because God and our Lord Jesus Christ are so kind, you will bring honor to the name of our Lord Jesus, and he will bring honor to you.

The Lord's Return

2 When our Lord Jesus returns, we will be gathered up to meet him. So I ask you, my friends, [2]not to be easily upset or disturbed by people who claim that the Lord[b] has already come. They may say that they heard this directly from the Holy Spirit, or from someone else, or even that they read it in one of our letters. [3]But don't be fooled! People will rebel against God. Then before the Lord returns, the wicked[c] one who is doomed to be destroyed will appear. [4]He will brag and oppose everything that is holy or sacred. He will even sit in God's temple and claim to be God. [5]Don't you remember that I told you this while I was still with you?

6 You already know what is holding this wicked one back until it is time for him to come. [7]His mysterious power is already at work, but someone is holding him back. And the wicked one won't appear until that someone is out of the way. [8]Then he will appear, but the Lord Jesus will kill him simply by breathing on him. He will be completely destroyed by the Lord's glorious return.

---

[b] *Lord*: The Greek text has "day of the Lord."
[c] *wicked*: Some manuscripts have "sinful."

9 When the wicked one appears, Satan will pretend to work all kinds of miracles, wonders, and signs. 10Lost people will be fooled by his evil deeds. They could be saved, but they will refuse to love the truth and accept it. 11So God will make sure that they are fooled into believing a lie. 12All of them will be punished, because they would rather do evil than believe the truth.

Be Faithful

13 My friends, the Lord loves you, and it is only natural for us to thank God for you. God chose you to be the first ones to be saved.*d* His Spirit made you holy, and you put your faith in the truth. 14God used our preaching as his way of inviting you to share in the glory of our Lord Jesus Christ. 15My friends, that's why you must remain faithful and follow closely what we taught you in person and by our letters.

16 God our Father loves us. He is kind and has given us eternal comfort and a wonderful hope. We pray that our Lord Jesus Christ and God our Father 17will encourage you and help you always to do and say the right thing.

Pray for Us

3 Finally, our friends, please pray for us. This will help the message about the Lord to spread quickly, and others will respect it, just as you do. 2Pray that we may be kept safe from worthless and evil people.

---

d *God chose you to be the first ones to be saved*: Some manuscripts have "From the beginning God chose you to be saved."

After all, not everyone has faith. ³But the Lord can be trusted to make you strong and protect you from harm. ⁴He has made us sure that you are obeying what we taught you and that you will keep on obeying. ⁵I pray that the Lord will guide you to be as loving as God and as patient as Christ.

Warnings against Laziness

6 My dear friends, in the name of[e] the Lord Jesus, I beg you not to have anything to do with any of your people who loaf around and refuse to obey the instructions we gave you. ⁷You surely know that you should follow our example. We didn't waste our time loafing, ⁸and we didn't accept food from anyone without paying for it. We didn't want to be a burden to any of you, so night and day we worked as hard as we could.

9 We had the right not to work, but we wanted to set an example for you. ¹⁰We also gave you the rule that if you don't work, you don't eat. ¹¹Now we learn that some of you just loaf around and won't do any work, except the work of a busybody. ¹²So, for the sake of our Lord Jesus Christ, we ask and beg these people to settle down and start working for a living. ¹³Dear friends, you must never become tired of doing right.

14 Be on your guard against any followers who refuse to obey what we have written in this letter. Put them to shame by not having anything to do with them. ¹⁵Don't consider them your enemies, but speak kindly to them as you would to any other follower.

---

e *in the name of*: Or "as a follower of."

Final Prayer

16 I pray that the Lord, who gives peace, will always bless you with peace. May the Lord be with all of you.

17 I always sign my letters as I am now doing: PAUL.

18 I pray that our Lord Jesus Christ will be kind to all of you.

Paul's First Letter to Timothy

ABOUT THIS LETTER

Timothy traveled and worked with Paul (Romans 16.21; 1 Corinthians 16.10; Philippians 2.19), and because of their shared faith, Timothy was like a son to Paul (1.2). Timothy became one of Paul's most faithful co-workers, and Paul mentions Timothy in five of his letters.

Although this letter is addressed to Timothy personally, it actually addresses many of the concerns Paul had with the life of the entire church. Guidelines are given for choosing church officials (3.1-7), officers (3.8-13), and leaders (5.17-20).

Christians are to pray for everyone and to remember:

> There is only one God,
> and Christ Jesus is the only one
>   who can bring us to God. (2.5)

A QUICK LOOK AT THIS LETTER

1. Greetings (1.1,2)
2. Instructions for Church Life (1.3–3.13)
3. The Mystery of Our Religion (3.14–4.5)
4. Paul's Advice to Timothy (4.6–6.21)

1 From Paul.
    God our Savior and Christ Jesus commanded me to be an apostle of Christ Jesus, who gives us hope.

2 Timothy, because of our faith, you are like a son to me. I pray that God our Father and our Lord Jesus Christ

will be kind and merciful to you. May they bless you with peace!

Warning against False Teaching

3 When I was leaving for Macedonia, I asked you to stay on in Ephesus and warn certain people there to stop spreading their false teachings. ⁴You needed to warn them to stop wasting their time on senseless stories and endless lists of ancestors. Such things only cause arguments. They don't help anyone to do God's work that can only be done by faith.

5 You must teach people to have genuine love, as well as a good conscience and true faith. ⁶There are some who have given up these for nothing but empty talk. ⁷They want to be teachers of the Law of Moses. But they don't know what they are talking about, even though they think they do.

8 We know that the Law is good, if it is used in the right way. ⁹We also understand that it wasn't given to control people who please God, but to control law-breakers, criminals, godless people, and sinners. It is for wicked and evil people, and for murderers, who would even kill their own parents. ¹⁰The Law was written for people who are sexual perverts or who live as homosexuals or are kidnappers or liars or won't tell the truth in court. It is for anything else that opposes the correct teaching ¹¹of the good news that the glorious and wonderful God has given me.

Being Thankful for God's Kindness

12 I thank Christ Jesus our Lord. He has given me the strength for my work because he knew that he could trust me. ¹³I used to say terrible and insulting

things about him, and I was cruel. But he had mercy on me because I didn't know what I was doing, and I had not yet put my faith in him. [14]Christ Jesus our Lord was very kind to me. He has greatly blessed my life with faith and love just like his own.

15 "Christ Jesus came into the world to save sinners." This saying is true, and it can be trusted. I was the worst sinner of all! [16]But since I was worse than anyone else, God had mercy on me and let me be an example of the endless patience of Christ Jesus. He did this so that others would put their faith in Christ and have eternal life. [17]I pray that honor and glory will always be given to the only God, who lives forever and is the invisible and eternal King! Amen.

18 Timothy, my son, the instructions I am giving you are based on what some prophets[a] once said about you. If you follow these instructions, you will fight like a good soldier. [19]You will be faithful and have a clear conscience. Some people have made a mess of their faith because they didn't listen to their consciences. [20]Two of them are Hymenaeus and Alexander. I have given these men over to the power of Satan, so they will learn not to oppose God.

How To Pray

2 First of all, I ask you to pray for everyone. Ask God to help and bless them all, and tell God how thankful you are for each of them. [2]Pray for kings and others in power, so that we may live quiet and peaceful lives as we worship and honor God.

[a] prophets: Probably the Christian prophets referred to in 4.14.

³This kind of prayer is good, and it pleases God our Savior. ⁴God wants everyone to be saved and to know the whole truth, which is,

   ⁵ There is only one God,
      and Christ Jesus is the only one
         who can bring us to God.
      Jesus was truly human,
         and he gave himself to rescue all of us.
   ⁶ God showed us this at the right time.

⁷This is why God chose me to be a preacher and an apostle of the good news. I am telling the truth. I am not lying. God sent me to teach the Gentiles about faith and truth.

8 I want everyone everywhere to lift innocent hands toward heaven and pray, without being angry or arguing with each other.

9 I would like for women to wear modest and sensible clothes. They should not have fancy hairdos, or wear expensive clothes, or put on jewelry made of gold or pearls. ¹⁰Women who claim to love God should do helpful things for others, ¹¹and they should learn by being quiet and paying attention. ¹²They should be silent and not be allowed to teach or to tell men what to do. ¹³After all, Adam was created before Eve, ¹⁴and the man Adam wasn't the one who was fooled. It was the woman Eve who was completely fooled and sinned. ¹⁵But women will be saved by having children,ᵇ if they stay faithful, loving, holy, and modest.

ᵇ *saved by having children*: Or "brought safely through childbirth" or "saved by the birth of a child" (that is, by the birth of Jesus) or "saved by being good mothers."

Church Officials

3 It is true that[c] anyone who desires to be a church official[d] wants to be something worthwhile. [2]That's why officials must have a good reputation and be faithful in marriage.[e] They must be self-controlled, sensible, well-behaved, friendly to strangers, and able to teach. [3]They must not be heavy drinkers or troublemakers. Instead, they must be kind and gentle and not love money.

[4] Church officials must be in control of their own families, and they must see that their children are obedient and always respectful. [5]If they don't know how to control their own families, how can they look after God's people?

[6] They must not be new followers of the Lord. If they are, they might become proud and be doomed along with the devil. [7]Finally, they must be well-respected by people who are not followers. Then they won't be trapped and disgraced by the devil.

Church Officers

[8] Church officers[f] should be serious. They must not be liars, heavy drinkers, or greedy for money. [9]And they must have a clear conscience and hold

---

[c] *It is true that*: These words may be taken with 2.15. If so, that verse would be translated: "It is true that women will be saved...holy, and modest." And 3.1 would be translated, "Anyone who desires...something worthwhile."

[d] *church official*: Or "bishop."

[e] *be faithful in marriage*: Or "be the husband of only one wife" or "have never been divorced."

[f] *Church officers*: Or "Deacons."

firmly to what God has shown us about our faith. [10]They must first prove themselves. Then if no one has anything against them, they can serve as officers.

11 Women[g] must also be serious. They must not gossip or be heavy drinkers, and they must be faithful in everything they do.

12 Church officers must be faithful in marriage.[h] They must be in full control of their children and everyone else in their home. [13]Those who serve well as officers will earn a good reputation and will be highly respected for their faith in Christ Jesus.

The Mystery of Our Religion

14 I hope to visit you soon. But I am writing these instructions, [15]so that if I am delayed, you will know how everyone who belongs to God's family ought to behave. After all, the church of the living God is the strong foundation of truth.

16 Here is the great mystery of our religion:

> Christ[i] came as a human.
> The Spirit proved that he pleased God,
>   and he was seen by angels.
>
> Christ was preached to the nations.
> People in this world put their faith in him,
>   and he was taken up to glory.

---

g *Women*: Either church officers or the wives of church officers.

h *be faithful in marriage*: See the note at 3.2.

i *Christ*: The Greek text has "he," probably meaning "Christ." Some manuscripts have "God."

People Will Turn from Their Faith

4 God's Spirit clearly says that in the last days many people will turn from their faith. They will be fooled by evil spirits and by teachings that come from demons. [2]They will also be fooled by the false claims of liars whose consciences have lost all feeling. These liars [3]will forbid people to marry or to eat certain foods. But God created these foods to be eaten with thankful hearts by his followers who know the truth. [4]Everything God created is good. And if you give thanks, you may eat anything. [5]What God has said and your prayer will make it fit to eat.

Paul's Advice to Timothy

[6] If you teach these things to other followers, you will be a good servant of Christ Jesus. You will show that you have grown up on the teachings about our faith and on the good instructions you have obeyed. [7]Don't have anything to do with worthless, senseless stories. Work hard to be truly religious. [8-9]As the saying goes,

"Exercise is good for your body,
    but religion helps you in every way.
    It promises life now and forever."

These words are worthwhile and should not be forgotten. [10]We have put our hope in the living God, who is the Savior of everyone, but especially of those who have faith. That's why we work and struggle so hard.[j]

[11] Teach these things and tell everyone to do what you say. [12]Don't let anyone make fun of you,

---

[j] *struggle so hard*: Some manuscripts have "are treated so badly."

just because you are young. Set an example for other followers by what you say and do, as well as by your love, faith, and purity.

13 Until I arrive, be sure to keep on reading the Scriptures in worship, and don't stop preaching and teaching. 14Use the gift you were given when the prophets spoke and the group of church leaders[k] blessed you by placing their hands on you. 15Remember these things and think about them, so everyone can see how well you are doing. 16Be careful about the way you live and about what you teach. Keep on doing this, and you will save not only yourself, but the people who hear you.

How To Act toward Others

5 Don't correct an older man. Encourage him, as you would your own father. Treat younger men as you would your own brother, 2and treat older women as you would your own mother. Show the same respect to younger women that you would to your sister.

3 Take care of any widow who is really in need. 4But if a widow has children or grandchildren, they should learn to serve God by taking care of her, as she once took care of them. This is what God wants them to do. 5A widow who is really in need is one who doesn't have any relatives. She has faith in God, and she keeps praying to him night and day, asking for his help.

---

[k] *group of church leaders*: Or "group of elders" or "group of presbyters" or "group of priests." This translates one Greek word, and it is related to the one used in 5.17, 19.

6 A widow who thinks only about having a good time is already dead, even though she is still alive.

7 Tell all of this to everyone, so they will do the right thing. 8People who don't take care of their relatives, and especially their own families, have given up their faith. They are worse than someone who doesn't have faith in the Lord.

9 For a widow to be put on the list of widows, she must be at least sixty years old, and she must have been faithful in marriage.[l] 10She must also be well-known for doing all sorts of good things, such as raising children, giving food to strangers, welcoming God's people into her home,[m] helping people in need, and always making herself useful.

11 Don't put young widows on the list. They may later have a strong desire to get married. Then they will turn away from Christ 12and become guilty of breaking their promise to him. 13Besides, they will become lazy and get into the habit of going from house to house. Next, they will start gossiping and become busybodies, talking about things that are none of their business.

14 I would prefer that young widows get married, have children, and look after their families. Then the enemy won't have any reason to say insulting things

---

[l] *been faithful in marriage*: Or "been the wife of only one husband" or "never been divorced."

[m] *welcoming God's people into her home*: The Greek text has "washing the feet of God's people." In New Testament times most people either went barefoot or wore sandals, and a host would often wash the feet of special guests.

about us. ¹⁵Look what's already happened to some of the young widows! They have turned away to follow Satan.

16 If a woman who is a follower has any widows in her family, she*ⁿ* should help them. This will keep the church from having that burden, and then the church can help widows who are really in need.

Church Leaders

17 Church leaders*ᵒ* who do their job well deserve to be paid*ᵖ* twice as much, especially if they work hard at preaching and teaching. ¹⁸It is just as the Scriptures say, "Don't muzzle an ox when you are using it to grind grain." You also know the saying, "Workers are worth their pay."

19 Don't listen to any charge against a church leader, unless at least two or three people bring the same charges. ²⁰But if any of the leaders should keep on sinning, they must be corrected in front of the whole group, as a warning to everyone else.

21 In the presence of God and Christ Jesus and their chosen angels, I order you to follow my instructions! Be fair with everyone, and don't have any favorites.

22 Don't be too quick to accept people into the service of the Lord*q* by placing your hands on them.

ⁿ *woman...she*: Some manuscripts have "man...he," and others have "man or woman...that person."

ᵒ *leaders*: Or "elders" or "presbyters" or "priests."

ᵖ *paid*: Or "honored" or "respected."

q *to accept people into the service of the Lord*: Or "to forgive people."

Don't sin because others do, but stay close to God.

23 Stop drinking only water. Take a little wine to help your stomach trouble and the other illnesses you always have.

24 Some people get caught in their sins right away, even before the time of judgment. But other people's sins don't show up until later. 25It is the same with good deeds. Some are easily seen, but none of them can be hidden.

6 If you are a slave, you should respect and honor your owner. This will keep people from saying bad things about God and about our teaching. 2If any of you slaves have owners who are followers, you should show them respect. After all, they are also followers of Christ, and he loves them. So you should serve and help them the best you can.

False Teaching and True Wealth

These are the things you must teach and tell the people to do. 3Anyone who teaches something different disagrees with the correct and godly teaching of our Lord Jesus Christ. 4Those people who disagree are proud of themselves, but they don't really know a thing. Their minds are sick, and they like to argue over words. They cause jealousy, disagreements, unkind words, evil suspicions, 5and nasty quarrels. They have wicked minds and have missed out on the truth.

These people think religion is supposed to make you rich. 6And religion does make your life rich, by making you content with what you have. 7We didn't bring anything into this world, and we won't[r] take

---

[r] we won't: Some manuscripts have "we surely won't."

anything with us when we leave. ⁸So we should be satisfied just to have food and clothes. ⁹People who want to be rich fall into all sorts of temptations and traps. They are caught by foolish and harmful desires that drag them down and destroy them. ¹⁰The love of money causes all kinds of trouble. Some people want money so much that they have given up their faith and caused themselves a lot of pain.

Fighting a Good Fight for the Faith

11 Timothy, you belong to God, so keep away from all these evil things. Try your best to please God and to be like him. Be faithful, loving, dependable, and gentle. ¹²Fight a good fight for the faith and claim eternal life. God offered it to you when you clearly told about your faith, while so many people listened. ¹³Now I ask you to make a promise. Make it in the presence of God, who gives life to all, and in the presence of Jesus Christ, who openly told Pontius Pilate about his faith. ¹⁴Promise to obey completely and fully all that you have been told until our Lord Jesus Christ returns.

¹⁵ The glorious God is the only Ruler,
    the King of kings and Lord of lords.
  At the time that God has already decided,
    he will send Jesus Christ back again.

¹⁶ Only God lives forever!
  And he lives in light
    that no one can come near.
  No human has ever seen God
    or ever can see him.
  God will be honored,
    and his power will last forever. Amen.

17 Warn the rich people of this world not to be proud or to trust in wealth that is easily lost. Tell them to have faith in God, who is rich and blesses us with everything we need to enjoy life. 18 Instruct them to do as many good deeds as they can and to help everyone. Remind the rich to be generous and share what they have. 19 This will lay a solid foundation for the future, so that they will know what true life is like.

20 Timothy, guard what God has placed in your care! Don't pay any attention to that godless and stupid talk that sounds smart but really isn't. 21 Some people have even lost their faith by believing this talk.

I pray that the Lord will be kind to all of you!

Paul's Second Letter to Timothy

In his second letter to Timothy, Paul is more personal than in his first one. Timothy is like a "dear child" to Paul, and Paul always mentions him in his prayers (1.2,3) because he wants Timothy to be a "good soldier" of Christ Jesus and to learn to endure suffering (2.1,3). Paul mentions Timothy's mother and grandmother by name in this letter and reminds Timothy how he had placed his hands on him as a special sign that the Spirit was guiding his work.

Some who claimed to be followers of the Lord had already been trapped by the devil, and Paul warns Timothy to run from those temptations that often catch young people (2.20-26; 3.1-9). He tells Timothy to keep preaching God's message, even if it is not the popular thing to do (4.2). He should also beware of false teachers.

Paul knows that he will soon die for his faith, but he will be rewarded for his faithfulness (4.6-8), and he reminds Timothy of the true message:

> If we died with Christ,
> we will live with him.
> If we don't give up,
> we will rule with him. (2.11, 12a)

1 From Paul, an apostle of Christ Jesus.
God himself chose me to be an apostle, and he gave me the promised life that Jesus Christ makes possible.

2 Timothy, you are like a dear child to me. I pray that God our Father and our Lord Christ Jesus will be kind and merciful to you and will bless you with peace!

Do Not Be Ashamed of the Lord

3 Night and day I mention you in my prayers. I am always grateful for you, as I pray to the God my ancestors and I have served with a clear conscience. 4I remember how you cried, and I want to see you, because that will make me truly happy. 5I also remember the genuine faith of your mother Eunice. Your grandmother Lois had the same sort of faith, and I am sure that you have it as well. 6So I ask you to make full use of the gift that God gave you when I placed my hands on you.[a] Use it well. 7God's Spirit[b]

---

[a] *when I placed my hands on you*: Church leaders placed their hands on people who were being appointed to preach or teach (see 1 Timothy 4.14).

[b] *God's Spirit*: Or "God."

doesn't make cowards out of us. The Spirit gives us power, love, and self-control.

8 Don't be ashamed to speak for our Lord. And don't be ashamed of me, just because I am in jail for serving him. Use the power that comes from God and join with me in suffering for telling the good news.

9 God saved us and chose us
    to be his holy people.
We did nothing to deserve this,
    but God planned it because he is so kind.
Even before time began
God planned for Christ Jesus
    to show kindness to us.

10 Now Christ Jesus has come
    to show us the kindness of God.
Christ our Savior defeated death
    and brought us the good news.
It shines like a light
    and offers life that never ends.

11 My work is to be a preacher, an apostle, and a teacher.[c] 12 That's why I am suffering now. But I am not ashamed! I know the one I have faith in, and I am sure that he can guard until the last day what he has trusted me with.[d] 13 Now follow the example of the correct teaching I gave you, and let the faith and love of Christ Jesus be your model. 14 You have been trusted with a wonderful treasure. Guard it with the help of the Holy Spirit, who lives within you.

---

c *teacher*: Some manuscripts add "of the Gentiles."
d *what he has trusted me with*: Or "what I have trusted him with."

15 You know that everyone in Asia has turned against me, especially Phygelus and Hermogenes.

16 I pray that the Lord will be kind to the family of Onesiphorus. He often cheered me up and wasn't ashamed of me when I was put in jail. 17Then after he arrived in Rome, he searched everywhere until he found me. 18I pray that the Lord Jesus will ask God to show mercy to Onesiphorus on the day of judgment. You know how much he helped me in Ephesus.

A Good Soldier of Christ Jesus

2 Timothy, my child, Christ Jesus is kind, and you must let him make you strong. 2You have often heard me teach. Now I want you to tell these same things to followers who can be trusted to tell others.

3 As a good soldier of Christ Jesus you must endure your share of suffering. 4Soldiers on duty don't work at outside jobs. They try only to please their commanding officer. 5No one wins an athletic contest without obeying the rules. 6And farmers who work hard are the first to eat what grows in their field. 7If you keep in mind what I have told you, the Lord will help you understand completely.

8 Keep your mind on Jesus Christ! He was from the family of David and was raised from death, just as my good news says. 9And because of this message, I am locked up in jail and treated like a criminal. But God's good news isn't locked in jail, 10and so I am willing to put up with anything. Then God's special people will be saved. They will be given eternal glory because they belong to Christ Jesus. 11Here is a true message:

"If we died with Christ,
   we will live with him.

> 12 If we don't give up,
>   we will rule with him.
>   If we deny that we know him,
>   he will deny that he knows us.
> 13 If we are not faithful,
>   he will still be faithful.
>   Christ cannot deny who he is."

An Approved Worker

14 Don't let anyone forget these things. And with God[e] as your witness, you must warn them not to argue about words. These arguments don't help anyone. In fact, they ruin everyone who listens to them. 15Do your best to win God's approval as a worker who doesn't need to be ashamed and who teaches only the true message.

16 Keep away from worthless and useless talk. It only leads people farther away from God. 17That sort of talk is like a sore that won't heal. And Hymenaeus and Philetus have been talking this way 18by teaching that the dead have already been raised to life. This is far from the truth, and it is destroying the faith of some people.

19 But the foundation that God has laid is solid. On it is written, "The Lord knows who his people are. So everyone who worships the Lord must turn away from evil."

20 In a large house some dishes are made of gold or silver, while others are made of wood or clay. Some of these are special, and others are not. 21That's also how

---

e *God*: Some manuscripts have "the Lord," and others have "Christ."

it is with people. The ones who stop doing evil and make themselves pure will become special. Their lives will be holy and pleasing to their Master, and they will be able to do all kinds of good deeds.

22 Run from temptations that capture young people. Always do the right thing. Be faithful, loving, and easy to get along with. Worship with people whose hearts are pure. 23Stay away from stupid and senseless arguments. These only lead to trouble, 24and God's servants must not be troublemakers. They must be kind to everyone, and they must be good teachers and very patient.

25 Be humble when you correct people who oppose you. Maybe God will lead them to turn to him and learn the truth. 26They have been trapped by the devil, and he makes them obey him, but God may help them escape.

What People Will Be Like in the Last Days

3 You can be certain that in the last days there will be some very hard times. 2People will love only themselves and money. They will be proud, stuck-up, rude, and disobedient to their parents. They will also be ungrateful, godless, 3heartless, and hateful. Their words will be cruel, and they will have no self-control or pity. These people will hate everything that is good. 4They will be sneaky, reckless, and puffed up with pride. Instead of loving God, they will love pleasure. 5Even though they will make a show of being religious, their religion won't be real. Don't have anything to do with such people.

6 Some men fool whole families, just to get power over those women who are slaves of sin and

are controlled by all sorts of desires. 7These women always want to learn something new, but they never can discover the truth. 8Just as Jannes and Jambres *f* opposed Moses, these people are enemies of the truth. Their minds are sick, and their faith isn't real. 9But they won't get very far with their foolishness. Soon everyone will know the truth about them, just as Jannes and Jambres were found out.

Paul's Last Instructions to Timothy

10 Timothy, you know what I teach and how I live. You know what I want to do and what I believe. You have seen how patient and loving I am, and how in the past I put up with 11trouble and suffering in the cities of Antioch, Iconium, and Lystra. Yet the Lord rescued me from all those terrible troubles. 12Anyone who belongs to Christ Jesus and wants to live right will have trouble from others. 13But evil people who pretend to be what they are not will become worse than ever, as they fool others and are fooled themselves.

14 Keep on being faithful to what you were taught and to what you believed. After all, you know who taught you these things. 15Since childhood, you have known the Holy Scriptures that are able to make you wise enough to have faith in Christ Jesus and be saved. 16Everything in the Scriptures is God's Word. All of it is useful for teaching and helping people and

---

f Jannes and Jambres: These names are not found in the Old Testament. But many believe these were the names of the two Egyptian magicians who opposed Moses when he wanted to lead the people of Israel out of Egypt (see Exodus 7.11, 22).

for correcting them and showing them how to live.
[17]The Scriptures train God's servants to do all kinds
of good deeds.

4 When Christ Jesus comes as king, he will be the
judge of everyone, whether they are living or dead.
So with God and Christ as witnesses, I command you [2]to
preach God's message. Do it willingly, even if it isn't the
popular thing to do. You must correct people and point
out their sins. But also cheer them up, and when you
instruct them, always be patient. [3]The time is coming
when people won't listen to good teaching. Instead, they
will look for teachers who will please them by telling
them only what they are itching to hear. [4]They will turn
from the truth and eagerly listen to senseless stories. [5]But
you must stay calm and be willing to suffer. You must
work hard to tell the good news and to do your job well.

[6] Now the time has come for me to die. My life is
like a drink offering[g] being poured out on the altar. [7]I
have fought well. I have finished the race, and I have
been faithful. [8]So a crown will be given to me for
pleasing the Lord. He judges fairly, and on the day of
judgment he will give a crown to me and to everyone
else who wants him to appear with power.

Personal Instructions

[9] Come to see me as soon as you can. [10]Demas
loves the things of this world so much that he left me
and went to Thessalonica. Crescens has gone to
Galatia, and Titus has gone to Dalmatia. [11]Only Luke
has stayed with me.

---

[g] *drink offering*: Water or wine was sometimes poured out
as an offering when an animal sacrifice was made.

Mark can be very helpful to me, so please find him and bring him with you. ¹²I sent Tychicus to Ephesus.

13 When you come, bring the coat I left at Troas with Carpus. Don't forget to bring the scrolls, especially the ones made of leather.ʰ

14 Alexander, the metalworker, has hurt me in many ways. But the Lord will pay him back for what he has done. ¹⁵Alexander opposes what we preach. You had better watch out for him.

16 When I was first put on trial, no one helped me. In fact, everyone deserted me. I hope it won't be held against them. ¹⁷But the Lord stood beside me. He gave me the strength to tell his full message, so that all Gentiles would hear it. And I was kept safe from hungry lions. ¹⁸The Lord will always keep me from being harmed by evil, and he will bring me safely into his heavenly kingdom. Praise him forever and ever! Amen.

Final Greetings

19 Give my greetings to Priscilla and Aquila and to the family of Onesiphorus.

20 Erastus stayed at Corinth.

Trophimus was sick when I left him at Miletus.

21 Do your best to come before winter.

Eubulus, Pudens, Linus, and Claudia send you their greetings, and so do the rest of the Lord's followers.

22 I pray that the Lord will bless your life and will be kind to you.

ʰ *the ones made of leather*: A scroll was a kind of rolled up book, and it could be made out of paper (called "papyrus") or leather (that is, animal skin) or even copper.

Paul's Letter to Titus

ABOUT THIS LETTER

Paul mentions Titus several times in his letters as someone who worked with him in Asia Minor and Greece (2 Corinthians 2.13; 7.6, 13; 8.6, 16, 23; 12.18; Galatians 2.3). He is told by Paul to appoint church leaders and officials in Crete.

Paul instructs Titus to make sure that church leaders and officials have good reputations (1.5-9) and that all of the Lord's followers keep themselves pure and avoid arguments (1.10-2.9).

Paul includes special instructions for the different groups within the church in Crete. He reminds Titus that a new way of life is possible because of what God has done by sending Jesus Christ: God has saved them, washed them by the power of the Holy Spirit, and given them a fresh start and the hope of eternal life.

Paul also tells how we are saved:

> God our Savior showed us
> how good and kind he is.
> He saved us because
> of his mercy,
> and not because
> of any good things
> that we have done. (3.4, 5)

A QUICK LOOK AT THIS LETTER

1. Greetings and a Prayer for Titus (1.1-4)
2. Instructions for Church Officials (1.5-16)
3. Instructions for Church People (2.1–3.11)
4. Personal Advice and Final Greetings (3.12-15)

1 From Paul, a servant of God and an apostle of Jesus Christ.

I encourage God's own people to have more faith and to understand the truth about religion. ²Then they will have the hope of eternal life that God promised long ago. And God never tells a lie! ³So, at the proper time, God our Savior gave this message and told me to announce what he had said.

4 Titus, because of our faith, you are like a son to me. I pray that God our Father and Christ Jesus our Savior will be kind to you and will bless you with peace!

What Titus Was To Do in Crete

5 I left you in Crete to do what had been left undone and to appoint leaders *a* for the churches in each town. As I told you, ⁶they must have a good reputation and be faithful in marriage.*b* Their children must be followers of the Lord and not have a reputation for being wild and disobedient.

7 Church officials *c* are in charge of God's work, and so they must also have a good reputation. They must not

---

a leaders: Or "elders" or "presbyters" or "priests."
b be faithful in marriage: Or "be the husband of only one wife" or "have never been divorced."
c Church officials: Or "Bishops."

be bossy, quick-tempered, heavy drinkers, bullies, or dishonest in business. 8Instead, they must be friendly to strangers and enjoy doing good things. They must also be sensible, fair, pure, and self-controlled. 9They must stick to the true message they were taught, so that their good teaching can help others and correct everyone who opposes it.

10 There are many who don't respect authority, and they fool others by talking nonsense. This is especially true of some Jewish followers. 11But you must make them be quiet. They are after money, and they upset whole families by teaching what they should not. 12It is like one of their own prophets once said,

"The people of Crete always tell lies.
They are greedy and lazy
like wild animals."

13 That surely is a true saying. And you should be hard on such people, so you can help them grow stronger in their faith. 14Don't pay any attention to any of those senseless Jewish stories and human commands. These are made up by people who won't obey the truth.

15 Everything is pure for someone whose heart is pure. But nothing is pure for an unbeliever with a dirty mind. That person's mind and conscience are destroyed. 16Such people claim to know God, but their actions prove that they really don't. They are disgusting. They won't obey God, and they are too worthless to do anything good.

Instructions for Different Groups of People

2 Titus, you must teach only what is correct. 2Tell the older men to have self-control and to be serious and sensible. Their faith, love, and patience must never fail.

3 Tell the older women to behave as those who love the Lord should. They must not gossip about others or be slaves of wine. They must teach what is proper, 4so the younger women will be loving wives and mothers. 5Each of the younger women must be sensible and kind, as well as a good homemaker, who puts her own husband first. Then no one can say insulting things about God's message.

6 Tell the young men to have self-control in everything.

7 Always set a good example for others. Be sincere and serious when you teach. 8Use clean language that no one can criticize. Do this, and your enemies will be too ashamed to say anything against you.

9 Tell slaves always to please their owners by obeying them in everything. Slaves must not talk back to their owners 10or steal from them. They must be completely honest and trustworthy. Then everyone will show great respect for what is taught about God our Savior.

God's Kindness and the New Life

11 God has shown us how kind he is by coming to save all people. 12He taught us to give up our wicked ways and our worldly desires and to live decent and honest lives in this world. 13We are filled with hope, as we wait for the glorious return of our great God and Savior Jesus Christ.[d] 14He gave himself to rescue

---

[d] *the glorious return of our great God and Savior Jesus Christ*: Or "the glorious return of our great God and our Savior Jesus Christ" or "the return of Jesus Christ, who is the glory of our great God and Savior."

us from everything that is evil and to make our hearts
pure. He wanted us to be his own people and to be
eager to do right.

15 Teach these things, as you use your full authority to encourage and correct people. Make sure you
earn everyone's respect.

Doing Helpful Things

3 Remind your people to obey the rulers and
authorities and not to be rebellious. They must
always be ready to do something helpful 2and not say
cruel things or argue. They should be gentle and kind
to everyone. 3We used to be stupid, disobedient, and
foolish, as well as slaves of all sorts of desires and
pleasures. We were evil and jealous. Everyone hated
us, and we hated everyone.

4 God our Savior showed us
　　how good and kind he is.
5 He saved us because of his mercy,
　　and not because of any good things
　　that we have done.

God washed us
　　by the power of the Holy Spirit.
He gave us new birth and a fresh beginning.
6 God sent Jesus Christ our Savior
　　to give us his Spirit.

7 Jesus treated us
　　much better than we deserve.
He made us acceptable to God
　　and gave us the hope of eternal life.
8This message is certainly true.

These teachings are useful and helpful for everyone. I want you to insist that the people follow them, so that all who have faith in God will be sure to do good deeds. ⁹But don't have anything to do with stupid arguments about ancestors. And stay away from disagreements and quarrels about the Law of Moses. Such arguments are useless and senseless.

10 Warn troublemakers once or twice. Then don't have anything else to do with them. ¹¹You know that their minds are twisted, and their own sins show how guilty they are.

Personal Instructions and Greetings

12 I plan to send Artemas or Tychicus to you. After he arrives, please try your best to meet me at Nicopolis. I have decided to spend the winter there.

13 When Zenas the lawyer and Apollos get ready to leave, help them as much as you can, so they won't have need of anything.

14 Our people should learn to spend their time doing something useful and worthwhile.

15 Greetings to you from everyone here. Greet all of our friends who share in our faith.

I pray that the Lord will be kind to all of you!

Paul's Letter to Philemon

ABOUT THIS LETTER

Philemon was a wealthy man who owned slaves and who used his large house for church meetings (2). He probably lived in Colossae, since Paul's letter to the Colossians mentions Onesimus, a slave of Philemon, and Archippus (Colossians 4.9, 17).

Paul is writing from jail on behalf of Onesimus, a runaway slave owned by Philemon. Onesimus had become a follower of the Lord and a valuable friend to Paul, and Paul is writing to encourage Philemon to accept Onesimus also as a friend and follower of the Lord.

This letter is an excellent example of the art of letter-writing in the Roman world, and it is the most personal of all Paul's letters. The way the letter is written suggests that Paul and Philemon were close friends.

A QUICK LOOK AT THIS LETTER

1 From Paul, who is in jail for serving Christ Jesus, and from Timothy, who is like a brother because of our faith.

Philemon, you work with us and are very dear to us. This letter is to you ²and to the church that meets in your home. It is also to our dear friend Apphia and to Archippus, who serves the Lord as we do.

3 I pray that God our Father and our Lord Jesus Christ will be kind to you and will bless you with peace!

Philemon's Love and Faith

4 Philemon, each time I mention you in my prayers, I thank God. 5I hear about your faith in our Lord Jesus and about your love for all of God's people. 6As you share your faith with others, I pray that they may come to know all the blessings Christ has given us. 7My friend, your love has made me happy and has greatly encouraged me. It has also cheered the hearts of God's people.

Paul Speaks to Philemon about Onesimus

8 Christ gives me the courage to tell you what to do. 9But I would rather ask you to do it simply because of love. Yes, as someone[a] in jail for Christ, 10I beg you to help Onesimus![b] He is like a son to me because I led him to Christ here in jail. 11Before this, he was useless to you, but now he is useful both to you and to me.

12 Sending Onesimus back to you makes me very sad. 13I would like to keep him here with me, where he could take your place in helping me while I am here in prison for preaching the good news. 14But I won't do anything unless you agree to it first. I want your act of kindness to come from your heart, and not be something you feel forced to do.

---

[a] *someone*: Greek "a messenger" or "an old man."

[b] *Onesimus*: In Greek this name means "useful."

15 Perhaps Onesimus was taken from you for a little while so that you could have him back for good, 16but not as a slave. Onesimus is much more than a slave. To me he is a dear friend, but to you he is even more, both as a person and as a follower of the Lord.

17 If you consider me a friend because of Christ, then welcome Onesimus as you would welcome me. 18If he has cheated you or owes you anything, charge it to my account. 19With my own hand I write: I, PAUL, WILL PAY YOU BACK. But don't forget that you owe me your life. 20My dear friend and follower of Christ our Lord, please cheer me up by doing this for me.

21 I am sure you will do all I have asked, and even more. 22Please get a room ready for me. I hope your prayers will be answered, and I can visit you.

23 Epaphras is also here in jail for being a follower of Christ Jesus. He sends his greetings, 24and so do Mark, Aristarchus, Demas, and Luke, who work together with me.

25 I pray that the Lord Jesus Christ will be kind to you!

The Letter to the Hebrews

ABOUT THIS LETTER

Many religious people in the first century after Jesus' birth, both Jews and Gentiles, had questions about the religion of the early Christians. They were looking for evidence that this new faith was genuine. Jews had the miracle of crossing the Red Sea and the agreement made with God at Mount Sinai to support their faith. But what miracles did Christians have? Jews had beautiful worship ceremonies and a high priest who offered sacrifices in the temple so that the people would be forgiven. But what did Christians have? How could this new Christian faith, centered in Jesus, offer forgiveness of sins and friendship with God?

The letter to the Hebrews was written to answer exactly these kinds of questions. In it the author tells the readers how important Jesus really is. He is greater than any of God's angels (1.5-14), greater than any prophet, and greater even than Moses and Joshua (2.1–4.14). Jesus is the perfect high priest because he never sinned, and by offering his own life he has made the perfect sacrifice for sin once for all time (9.23–10.18). By his death and return from death he has opened the way for all people to come to God (4.14–5.10; 7.1–8.13).

This letter has much to say about the importance of faith. The writer points out that what Jesus offers comes only by faith. And this faith makes his followers sure of what they hope for and gives them proof of things that cannot be seen. The writer praises God's faithful people of the past (11.1-40) and encourages those who follow Jesus now to keep their eyes on him as they run the race (12.1-3).

What does it mean to have a high priest like Jesus? *Jesus understands every weakness of ours, because he was tempted in every way that we are. But he did not sin! So whenever we are in need, we should come bravely before the throne of our merciful God. There we will be treated with undeserved kindness, and we will find help. (4.15,16)*

A QUICK LOOK AT THIS LETTER

1. The Greatness of God's Son (1.1-4)
2. Jesus Is Greater than Angels (1.5-2.18)
3. Jesus Is Greater than Moses and Joshua (3.1-4.13)
4. Jesus Is the Great High Priest (4.14-7.28)
5. Jesus Brings a Better Agreement (8.1-9.22)
6. Jesus' Sacrifice Is Once and for All (9.23-10.31)
7. Some of God's People Who Had Great Faith (11.1-40)
8. Follow the Example of Jesus (12.1-13.19)
9. Final Prayers and Greetings (13.20-25)

1 Long ago in many ways and at many times God's prophets spoke his message to our ancestors. ²But now at last, God sent his Son to bring his message to us. God created the universe by his Son, and everything will someday belong to the Son. ³God's Son has all the brightness of God's own glory and is like him in every way. By his own mighty word, he holds the universe together.

After the Son had washed away our sins, he sat

down at the right side[a] of the glorious God in heaven. [4]He had become much greater than the angels, and the name he was given is far greater than any of theirs.

God's Son Is Greater than Angels

[5] God has never said to any of the angels,

"You are my Son,
because today I have become your Father!"
Neither has God said to any of them,
"I will be his Father,
and he will be my Son!"

[6] When God brings his first-born Son[b] into the world, he commands all of his angels to worship him. [7] And when God speaks about the angels, he says,

"I change my angels into wind
and my servants into flaming fire."

[8] But God says about his Son,

"You are God,
and you will rule as King forever!
Your[c] royal power brings about justice.
[9] You loved justice and hated evil,
and so I, your God, have chosen you.
I appointed you
and made you happier
than any of your friends."

---

[a] *right side*: The place of honor and power.
[b] *first-born Son*: The first son born into a family had certain privileges that the other children did not have. In 12.23 "first-born" refers to God's special people.
[c] *Your*: Some manuscripts have "His."

10 The Scriptures also say,
>"In the beginning, Lord, you were the one
>who laid the foundation of the earth
>and created the heavens.
>11 They will all disappear
>and wear out like clothes,
>but you will last forever.
>12 You will roll them up like a robe
>and change them like a garment.
>But you are always the same,
>and you will live forever."

13 God never said to any of the angels,
>"Sit at my right side
>until I make your enemies
>into a footstool for you!"

14 Angels are merely spirits sent to serve people who are going to be saved.

This Great Way of Being Saved

2 We must give our full attention to what we were told, so that we won't drift away. ²The message spoken by angels proved to be true, and all who disobeyed or rejected it were punished as they deserved. ³So if we refuse this great way of being saved, how can we hope to escape? The Lord himself was the first to tell about it, and people who heard the message proved to us that it was true. ⁴God himself showed that his message was true by working all kinds of powerful miracles and wonders. He also gave his Holy Spirit to anyone he chose to.

The One Who Leads Us To Be Saved

5 We know that God did not put the future world under the power of angels. 6Somewhere in the Scriptures someone says to God,

> "What makes you care about us humans?
> Why are you concerned for weaklings
> such as we?
>
> 7 You made us lower than the angels
> for a while.
> Yet you have crowned us
> with glory and honor.[d]
>
> 8 And you have put everything
> under our power!"

God has put everything under our power and has not left anything out of our power. But we still don't see it all under our power. 9What we do see is Jesus, who for a little while was made lower than the angels. Because of God's wonderful kindness, Jesus died for everyone. And now that Jesus has suffered and died, he is crowned with glory and honor!

10 Everything belongs to God, and all things were created by his power. So God did the right thing when he made Jesus perfect by suffering, as Jesus led many of God's children to be saved and to share in his glory. 11Jesus and the people he makes holy all belong to the same family. That is why he isn't ashamed to call them his brothers and sisters. 12He even said to God,

---

d and honor: Some manuscripts add "and you have placed us in charge of all you created."

> "I will tell them your name
> and sing your praises
> > when they come together to worship."

13 He also said,

> "I will trust God."

Then he said,

> "Here I am with the children
> > God has given me."

14 We are people of flesh and blood. That is why Jesus became one of us. He died to destroy the devil, who had power over death. 15 But he also died to rescue all of us who live each day in fear of dying. 16 Jesus clearly did not come to help angels, but he did come to help Abraham's descendants. 17 He had to be one of us, so that he could serve God as our merciful and faithful high priest and sacrifice himself for the forgiveness of our sins. 18 And now that Jesus has suffered and was tempted, he can help anyone else who is tempted.

Jesus Is Greater than Moses

3 My friends, God has chosen you to be his holy people. So think about Jesus, the one we call our apostle and high priest! 2 Jesus was faithful to God, who appointed him, just as Moses was faithful in serving all of[e] God's people. 3 But Jesus deserves more honor than Moses, just as the builder of a house deserves more honor than the house. 4 Of course, every house is built by someone, and God is really the one who built everything.

5 Moses was a faithful servant and told God's people what would be said in the future. 6 But Christ is

---

[e] *all of*: Some manuscripts do not have these words.

the Son in charge of God's people. And we are those people, if we keep on being brave and don't lose hope.

A Rest for God's People

7 It is just as the Holy Spirit says,

"If you hear God's voice today,
8   don't be stubborn!
Don't rebel like those people
     who were tested in the desert.
9 For forty years your ancestors tested God
     and saw the things he did.

10 "Then God got tired of them and said,
     'You people never show good sense,
     and you don't understand
          what I want you to do.'
11 God became angry and told the people,
     'You will never enter my place of rest!'"

12 My friends, watch out! Don't let evil thoughts or doubts make any of you turn from the living God. 13You must encourage one another each day. And you must keep on while there is still a time that can be called "today." If you don't, then sin may fool some of you and make you stubborn. 14We were sure about Christ when we first became his people. So let's hold tightly to our faith until the end. 15The Scriptures say,

"If you hear his voice today,
     don't be stubborn like those who rebelled."

16 Who were those people that heard God's voice and rebelled? Weren't they the same ones that came out of Egypt with Moses? 17Who were the people that made God angry for forty years? Weren't they the

ones that sinned and died in the desert? ¹⁸And who did God say would never enter his place of rest? Weren't they the ones that disobeyed him? ¹⁹We see that those people did not enter the place of rest because they did not have faith.

4 The promise to enter the place of rest is still good, and we must take care that none of you miss out. ²We have heard the message, just as they did. But they failed to believe what they heard, and the message did not do them any good. ³Only people who have faith will enter the place of rest. It is just as the Scriptures say,

> "God became angry and told the people,
>   'You will never enter my place of rest!'"

God said this, even though everything has been ready from the time of creation. ⁴In fact, somewhere the Scriptures say that by the seventh day, God had finished his work, and so he rested. ⁵We also read that he later said, "You people will never enter my place of rest!" ⁶This means that the promise to enter is still good, because those who first heard about it disobeyed and did not enter. ⁷Much later God told David to make the promise again, just as I have already said,

> "If you hear his voice today,
>   don't be stubborn!"

8 If Joshua had really given the people rest, there would not be any need for God to talk about another day of rest. ⁹But God has promised us a Sabbath when we will rest, even though it has not yet come. ¹⁰On that day God's people will rest from their work, just as God rested from his work.

11 We should do our best to enter that place of rest, so that none of us will disobey and miss going there, as they did. 12What God has said isn't only alive and active! It is sharper than any double-edged sword. His word can cut through our spirits and souls and through our joints and marrow, until it discovers the desires and thoughts of our hearts. 13Nothing is hidden from God! He sees through everything, and we will have to tell him the truth.

Jesus Is the Great High Priest

14 We have a great high priest, who has gone into heaven, and he is Jesus the Son of God. That is why we must hold on to what we have said about him. 15Jesus understands every weakness of ours, because he was tempted in every way that we are. But he did not sin! 16So whenever we are in need, we should come bravely before the throne of our merciful God. There we will be treated with undeserved kindness, and we will find help.

5 Every high priest is appointed to help others by offering gifts and sacrifices to God because of their sins. 2A high priest has weaknesses of his own, and he feels sorry for foolish and sinful people. 3That is why he must offer sacrifices for his own sins and for the sins of others. 4But no one can have the honor of being a high priest simply by wanting to be one. Only God can choose a priest, and God is the one who chose Aaron.

5 That is how it was with Christ. He became a high priest, but not just because he wanted the honor of being one. It was God who told him,

"You are my Son,
    because today I have become your Father!"

[6]In another place, God says,

> "You are a priest forever
>   just like Melchizedek."[f]

7 God had the power to save Jesus from death. And while Jesus was on earth, he begged God with loud crying and tears to save him. He truly worshiped God, and God listened to his prayers. [8]Jesus is God's own Son, but still he had to suffer before he could learn what it really means to obey God. [9]Suffering made Jesus perfect, and now he can save forever all who obey him. [10]This is because God chose him to be a high priest like Melchizedek.

Warning against Turning Away

11 Much more could be said about this subject. But it is hard to explain, and all of you are slow to understand. [12]By now you should have been teachers, but once again you need to be taught the simplest things about what God has said. You need milk instead of solid food. [13]People who live on milk are like babies who don't really know what is right. [14]Solid food is for mature people who have been trained to know right from wrong.

6 We must try to become mature and start thinking about more than just the basic things we were taught about Christ. We shouldn't need to keep talking about why we ought to turn from deeds that bring death and why we ought to have faith in God.

---

[f] *Melchizedek*: When Melchizedek is mentioned in the Old Testament, he is described as a priest who lived before Aaron. Nothing is said about his ancestors or his death (see 7.3 and Genesis 14.17-20).

²And we shouldn't need to keep teaching about baptisms*ᵍ* or about the laying on of hands*ʰ* or about people being raised from death and the future judgment. ³Let's grow up, if God is willing.

4-6 But what about people who turn away after they have already seen the light and have received the gift from heaven and have shared in the Holy Spirit? What about those who turn away after they have received the good message of God and the powers of the future world? There is no way to bring them back. What they are doing is the same as nailing the Son of God to a cross and insulting him in public!

7 A field is useful to farmers, if there is enough rain to make good crops grow. In fact, God will bless that field. ⁸But land that produces only thornbushes is worthless. It is likely to fall under God's curse, and in the end it will be set on fire.

9 My friends, we are talking this way. But we are sure that you are doing those really good things that people do when they are being saved. ¹⁰God is always fair. He will remember how you helped his people in the past and how you are still helping them. You belong to God, and he won't forget the love you have shown his people. ¹¹We wish that each of you would always be eager to show how strong and lasting your hope really is. ¹²Then you would never be lazy. You would

---

ᵍ *baptisms*: Or "ceremonies of washing."

ʰ *laying on of hands*: This was a ceremony in which church leaders and others put their hands on people to show that those people were chosen to do some special kind of work.

be following the example of those who had faith and were patient until God kept his promise to them.

God's Promise Is Sure

13 No one is greater than God. So he made a promise in his own name when he said to Abraham, ¹⁴"I, the Lord, will bless you with many descendants!" ¹⁵Then after Abraham had been very patient, he was given what God had promised. ¹⁶When anyone wants to settle an argument, they make a vow by using the name of someone or something greater than themselves. ¹⁷So when God wanted to prove for certain that his promise to his people could not be broken, he made a vow. ¹⁸God cannot tell lies! And so his promises and vows are two things that can never be changed.

We have run to God for safety. Now his promises should greatly encourage us to take hold of the hope that is right in front of us. ¹⁹This hope is like a firm and steady anchor for our souls. In fact, hope reaches behind the curtain *i* and into the most holy place. ²⁰Jesus has gone there ahead of us, and he is our high priest forever, just like Melchizedek.*j*

The Priestly Family of Melchizedek

7 Melchizedek was both king of Salem and priest of God Most High. He was the one who went out and gave Abraham his blessing, when Abraham

---

i *behind the curtain*: In the tent that was used for worship, a curtain separated the "holy place" from the "most holy place," which only the high priest could enter.

j *Melchizedek*: See the note at 5.6.

returned from killing the kings. ²Then Abraham gave him a tenth of everything he had.

The meaning of the name Melchizedek is "King of Justice." But since Salem means "peace," he is also "King of Peace." ³We are not told that he had a father or mother or ancestors or beginning or end. He is like the Son of God and will be a priest forever.*ᵏ*

4 Notice how great Melchizedek is! Our famous ancestor Abraham gave him a tenth of what he had taken from his enemies. ⁵The Law teaches that even Abraham's descendants must give a tenth of what they possess. And they are to give this to their own relatives, who are the descendants of Levi and are priests. ⁶Although Melchizedek wasn't a descendant of Levi, Abraham gave him a tenth of what he had. Then Melchizedek blessed Abraham, who had been given God's promise. ⁷Everyone agrees that a person who gives a blessing is greater than the one who receives the blessing.

8 Priests are given a tenth of what people earn. But all priests die, except Melchizedek, and the Scriptures teach that he is alive. ⁹Levi's descendants are now the ones who receive a tenth from people. We could even say that when Abraham gave Melchizedek a tenth, Levi also gave him a tenth. ¹⁰This is because Levi was born later into the family of Abraham, who gave a tenth to Melchizedek.

11 Even though the Law of Moses says that the priests must be descendants of Levi, those priests cannot make anyone perfect. So there needs to be a priest like Melchizedek, rather than one from the priestly

---

ᵏ will be a priest forever: See the note at 5.6.

family of Aaron.[1] 12And when the rules for selecting a priest are changed, the Law must also be changed.

13 The person we are talking about is our Lord, who came from a tribe that had never had anyone to serve as a priest at the altar. 14Everyone knows he came from the tribe of Judah, and Moses never said that priests would come from that tribe.

15 All of this becomes clearer, when someone who is like Melchizedek is appointed to be a priest. 16That person wasn't appointed because of his ancestors, but because his life can never end. 17The Scriptures say about him,

"You are a priest forever,
just like Melchizedek."

18In this way a weak and useless command was put aside, 19because the Law cannot make anything perfect. At the same time, we are given a much better hope, and it can bring us close to God.

20-21 God himself made a promise when this priest was appointed. But he did not make a promise like this when the other priests were appointed. The promise he made is,

"I, the Lord, promise
that you will be a priest forever!
And I will never change my mind!"

22 This means that Jesus guarantees us a better agreement with God. 23There have been a lot of other priests, and all of them have died. 24But Jesus

---

[1] descendants of Levi…from the priestly family of Aaron: Levi was the ancestor of the tribe from which priests and their helpers (called "Levites") were chosen. Aaron was the first high priest.

will never die, and so he will be a priest forever! [25]He is forever able to save*m* the people he leads to God, because he always lives to speak to God for them.

26 Jesus is the high priest we need. He is holy and innocent and faultless, and not at all like us sinners. Jesus is honored above all beings in heaven, [27]and he is better than any other high priest. Jesus doesn't need to offer sacrifices each day for his own sins and then for the sins of the people. He offered a sacrifice once for all, when he gave himself. [28]The Law appoints priests who have weaknesses. But God's promise, which came later than the Law, appoints his Son. And he is the perfect high priest forever.

A Better Promise

8 What I mean is that we have a high priest who sits at the right side*n* of God's great throne in heaven. [2]He also serves as the priest in the most holy place*o* inside the real tent there in heaven. This tent of worship was set up by the Lord, not by humans.

3 Since all priests must offer gifts and sacrifices, Christ also needed to have something to offer. [4]If he were here on earth, he would not be a priest at all, because here the Law appoints other priests to offer sacrifices. [5]But the tent where they serve is just a copy and a shadow of the real one in heaven. Before Moses made the tent, he was told, "Be sure to make it exactly

---

m forever able to save: Or "able to save forever."

n right side: See the note at 1.3.

o most holy place: See the note at 6.19.

like the pattern you were shown on the mountain!"
⁶Now Christ has been appointed to serve as a priest in
a much better way, and he has given us much assurance
of a better agreement.

7 If the first agreement with God had been all right,
there would not have been any need for another one.
⁸But the Lord found fault with it and said,

> "I tell you the time will come,
>   when I will make a new agreement
>   with the people of Israel
>   and the people of Judah.
> ⁹ It won't be like the agreement
>   that I made with their ancestors,
>   when I took them by the hand
>   and led them out of Egypt.
> They broke their agreement with me,
>   and I stopped caring about them!

> ¹⁰ "But now I tell the people of Israel
>   this is my new agreement:
> 'The time will come
>   when I, the Lord, will write my laws
>   on their minds and hearts.
> I will be their God,
>   and they will be my people.
> ¹¹ Not one of them will have to teach another
>   to know me, their Lord.'

> "All of them will know me,
>   no matter who they are.
> ¹² I will treat them with kindness,
>   even though they are wicked.
> I will forget their sins."

13 When the Lord talks about a new agreement, he means that the first one is out of date. And anything that is old and useless will soon disappear.

The Tent in Heaven

9 The first promise that was made included rules for worship and a tent for worship here on earth. [2]The first part of the tent was called the holy place, and a lampstand, a table, and the sacred loaves of bread were kept there.

3 Behind the curtain was the most holy place. [4]The gold altar that was used for burning incense was in this holy place. The gold-covered sacred chest was also there, and inside it were three things. First, there was a gold jar filled with manna.[p] Then there was Aaron's walking stick that sprouted.[q] Finally, there were the flat stones with the Ten Commandments written on them. [5]On top of the chest were the glorious creatures with wings[r] opened out above the place of mercy.[s]

---

[p] *manna*: When the people of Israel were wandering through the desert, the Lord provided them with food that could be made into thin wafers. This food was called manna, which in Hebrew means "What is it?"

[q] *Aaron's walking stick that sprouted*: According to Numbers 17.1-11, Aaron's walking stick sprouted and produced almonds to show that the Lord was pleased with him and Moses.

[r] *glorious creatures with wings*: Two of these creatures (called "cherubim" in Hebrew and Greek) with outspread wings were on top of the sacred chest and were symbols of God's throne.

[s] *place of mercy*: The lid of the sacred chest, which was thought to be God's throne on earth.

Now isn't the time to go into detail about these things. [6]But this is how everything was when the priests went each day into the first part of the tent to do their duties. [7]However, only the high priest could go into the second part of the tent, and he went in only once a year. Each time he carried blood to offer for his sins and for any sins that the people had committed without meaning to.

8 All of this is the Holy Spirit's way of saying that no one could enter the most holy place while the tent was still the place of worship. [9]This also has a meaning for today. It shows that we cannot make our consciences clear by offering gifts and sacrifices. [10]These rules are merely about such things as eating and drinking and ceremonies for washing ourselves. And rules about physical things will last only until the time comes to change them for something better.

11 Christ came as the high priest of the good things that are now here.[f] He also went into a much better tent that wasn't made by humans and that doesn't belong to this world. [12]Then Christ went once for all into the most holy place and freed us from sin forever. He did this by offering his own blood instead of the blood of goats and bulls.

13 According to the Law of Moses, those people who become unclean are not fit to worship God. Yet they will be considered clean, if they are sprinkled with the blood of goats and bulls and with the ashes of a sacrificed calf. [14]But Christ was sinless, and he offered himself as an eternal and spiritual sacrifice to God. That's why his blood is much more powerful

---

[f] *that are now here*: Some manuscripts have "that were coming."

and makes our[u] consciences clear. Now we can serve the living God and no longer do things that lead to death.

15 Christ died to rescue those who had sinned and broken the old agreement. Now he brings his chosen ones a new agreement with its guarantee of God's eternal blessings! [16]In fact, making an agreement of this kind is like writing a will. This is because the one who makes the will must die before it is of any use. [17]In other words, a will doesn't go into effect as long as the one who made it is still alive.

18 Blood was also used[v] to put the first agreement into effect. [19]Moses told the people all that the Law said they must do. Then he used red wool and a hyssop plant to sprinkle the people and the book of the Law with the blood of bulls and goats[w] and with water. [20]He told the people, "With this blood God makes his agreement with you." [21]Moses also sprinkled blood on the tent and on everything else that was used in worship. [22]The Law says that almost everything must be sprinkled with blood, and no sins can be forgiven unless blood is offered.

Christ's Great Sacrifice

23 These things are only copies of what is in heaven, and so they had to be made holy by these ceremonies. But the real things in heaven must be made holy by

---

[u] *our*: Some manuscripts have "your," and others have "their."

[v] *Blood was also used*: Or "There also had to be a death."

[w] *blood of bulls and goats*: Some manuscripts do not have "and goats."

something better. 24This is why Christ did not go into a tent that had been made by humans and was only a copy of the real one. Instead, he went into heaven and is now there with God to help us.

25 Christ did not have to offer himself many times. He wasn't like a high priest who goes into the most holy place each year to offer the blood of an animal. 26If he had offered himself every year, he would have suffered many times since the creation of the world. But instead, near the end of time he offered himself once and for all, so that he could be a sacrifice that does away with sin.

27 We die only once, and then we are judged. 28So Christ died only once to take away the sins of many people. But when he comes again, it will not be to take away sin. He will come to save everyone who is waiting for him.

10 The Law of Moses is like a shadow of the good things to come. This shadow isn't the good things themselves, because it cannot free people from sin by the sacrifices that are offered year after year. 2If there were worshipers who already have their sins washed away and their consciences made clear, there would not be any need to go on offering sacrifices. 3-4But the blood of bulls and goats cannot take away sins. It only reminds people of their sins from one year to the next.

5 When Christ came into the world, he said to God,

"Sacrifices and offerings
are not what you want,
        but you have given me my body.
6 No, you are not pleased with animal sacrifices
        and offerings for sin."

7 Then Christ said,

"And so, my God,

I have come to do what you want,

as the Scriptures say."

8 The Law teaches that offerings and sacrifices must be made because of sin. But why did Christ mention these things and say that God did not want them? 9 Well, it was to do away with offerings and sacrifices and to replace them. That is what he meant by saying to God, "I have come to do what you want." 10 So we are made holy because Christ obeyed God and offered himself once for all.

11 The priests do their work each day, and they keep on offering sacrifices that can never take away sins. 12 But Christ offered himself as a sacrifice that is good forever. Now he is sitting at God's right side,[x] 13 and he will stay there until his enemies are put under his power. 14 By his one sacrifice he has forever set free from sin the people he brings to God.

15 The Holy Spirit also speaks of this by telling us that the Lord said,

16 "When the time comes,

I will make an agreement with them.

I will write my laws on their minds and hearts.

17 Then I will forget about their sins

and no longer remember their evil deeds."

18 When sins are forgiven, there is no more need to offer sacrifices.

Encouragement and Warning

19 My friends, the blood of Jesus gives us courage

---

x *right side*: See the note at 1.3.

to enter the most holy place ²⁰by a new way that leads to life! And this way takes us through the curtain that is Christ himself.

21 We have a great high priest who is in charge of God's house. ²²So let's come near God with pure hearts and a confidence that comes from having faith. Let's keep our hearts pure, our consciences free from evil, and our bodies washed with clean water. ²³We must hold tightly to the hope that we say is ours. After all, we can trust the one who made the agreement with us. ²⁴We should keep on encouraging each other to be thoughtful and to do helpful things. ²⁵Some people have gotten out of the habit of meeting for worship, but we must not do that. We should keep on encouraging each other, especially since you know that the day of the Lord's coming is getting closer.

26 No sacrifices can be made for people who decide to sin after they find out about the truth. ²⁷They are God's enemies, and all they can look forward to is a terrible judgment and a furious fire. ²⁸If two or more witnesses accused someone of breaking the Law of Moses, that person could be put to death. ²⁹But it is much worse to dishonor God's Son and to disgrace the blood of the promise that made us holy. And it is just as bad to insult the Holy Spirit, who shows us mercy. ³⁰We know that God has said he will punish and take revenge. We also know that the Scriptures say the Lord will judge his people. ³¹It is a terrible thing to fall into the hands of the living God!

32 Don't forget all the hard times you went through when you first received the light. ³³Sometimes you were abused and mistreated in public, and at other times you shared in the sufferings of others. ³⁴You were kind

to people in jail. And you gladly let your possessions be taken away, because you knew you had something better, something that would last forever.

35 Keep on being brave! It will bring you great rewards. 36 Learn to be patient, so that you will please God and be given what he has promised. 37 As the Scriptures say,

> "God is coming soon!
>   It won't be very long.
> 38 The people God accepts
>   will live because of their faith.*
> But he isn't pleased
>   with anyone who turns back."

39 We are not like those people who turn back and get destroyed. We will keep on having faith until we are saved.

The Great Faith of God's People

11 Faith makes us sure of what we hope for and gives us proof of what we cannot see. 2 It was their faith that made our ancestors pleasing to God.

3 Because of our faith, we know that the world was made at God's command. We also know that what can be seen was made out of what cannot be seen.

4 Because Abel had faith, he offered God a better sacrifice than Cain did. God was pleased with him and his gift, and even though Abel is now dead, his faith still speaks for him.

5 Enoch had faith and did not die. He pleased God, and God took him up to heaven. That's why his body

---

y The people God accepts will live because of their faith:
   Or "The people God accepts because of their faith will
   live."

was never found. 6But without faith no one can please God. We must believe that God is real and that he rewards everyone who searches for him.

7 Because Noah had faith, he was warned about something that had not yet happened. He obeyed and built a boat that saved him and his family. In this way the people of the world were judged, and Noah was given the blessings that come to everyone who pleases God.

8 Abraham had faith and obeyed God. He was told to go to the land that God had said would be his, and he left for a country he had never seen. 9Because Abraham had faith, he lived as a stranger in the promised land. He lived there in a tent, and so did Isaac and Jacob, who were later given the same promise. 10Abraham did this, because he was waiting for the eternal city that God had planned and built.

11 Even when Sarah was too old to have children, she had faith that God would do what he had promised, and she had a son. 12Her husband Abraham was almost dead, but he became the ancestor of many people. In fact, there are as many of them as there are stars in the sky or grains of sand along the beach.

13 Every one of those people died. But they still had faith, even though they had not received what they had been promised. They were glad just to see these things from far away, and they agreed just that they were only strangers and foreigners on this earth. 14When people talk this way, it is clear that they are looking for a place to call their own. 15If they had been talking about the land where they had once lived, they could have gone back at any time. 16But they were looking forward to a better home in heaven.

That's why God wasn't ashamed for them to call him their God. He even built a city for them.

17-18 Abraham had been promised that Isaac, his only son,[z] would continue his family. But when Abraham was tested, he had faith and was willing to sacrifice Isaac, [19]because he was sure that God could raise people to life. This was just like getting Isaac back from death.

20 Isaac had faith, and he promised blessings to Jacob and Esau. [21]Later, when Jacob was about to die, he leaned on his walking stick and worshiped. Then because of his faith he blessed each of Joseph's sons. [22]And right before Joseph died, he had faith that God would lead the people of Israel out of Egypt. So he told them to take his bones with them.

23 Because Moses' parents had faith, they kept him hidden until he was three months old. They saw that he was a beautiful child, and they were not afraid to disobey the king's orders.[a] [24]Then after Moses grew up, his faith made him refuse to be called the king's grandson. [25]He chose to be mistreated with God's people instead of having the good time that sin could bring for a little while. [26]Moses knew that the treasures of Egypt were not as wonderful as what he would receive from suffering for the Messiah,[b] and he looked forward to his reward.

---

[z] *his only son*: Although Abraham had a son by a slave woman, his son Isaac was considered his only son, because he was born as a result of God's promise to Abraham.

[a] *the king's orders*: The king of Egypt ordered all Israelite baby boys to be left outside of their homes, so they would die or be killed.

[b] *the Messiah*: Or "Christ."

27 Because of his faith, Moses left Egypt. Moses had seen the invisible God and wasn't afraid of the king's anger. 28His faith also made him celebrate Passover. He sprinkled the blood of animals on the doorposts, so that the first-born sons of the people of Israel would not be killed by the destroying angel.

29 Because of their faith, the people walked through the Red Sea[c] on dry land. But when the Egyptians tried to do it, they were drowned.

30 God's people had faith, and when they had walked around the city of Jericho for seven days, its walls fell down.

31 Rahab had been a prostitute, but she had faith and welcomed the spies. So she wasn't killed with the people who disobeyed.

32 What else can I say? There isn't enough time to tell about Gideon, Barak, Samson, Jephthah, David, Samuel, and the prophets. 33Their faith helped them conquer kingdoms, and because they did right, God made promises to them. They closed the jaws of lions 34and put out raging fires and escaped from the swords of their enemies. Although they were weak, they were given the strength and power to chase foreign armies away.

35 Some women received their loved ones back from death. Many of these people were tortured,

---

[c] *Red Sea*: This name comes from the Bible of the early Christians, a translation made into Greek about 200 B.C. It refers to the body of water that the Israelites crossed and was one of the marshes or fresh water lakes near the eastern part of the Nile Delta, where they lived and where the towns of Exodus 13.17–14.9 were located.

but they refused to be released. They were sure that they would get a better reward when the dead are raised to life. 36Others were made fun of and beaten with whips, and some were chained in jail. 37Still others were stoned to death or sawed in two[d] or killed with swords. Some had nothing but sheep skins or goat skins to wear. They were poor, mistreated, and tortured. 38The world did not deserve these good people, who had to wander in deserts and on mountains and had to live in caves and holes in the ground.

39 All of them pleased God because of their faith! But still they died without being given what had been promised. 40This was because God had something better in store for us. And he did not want them to reach the goal of their faith without us.

A Large Crowd of Witnesses

12 Such a large crowd of witnesses is all around us! So we must get rid of everything that slows us down, especially the sin that just won't let go. And we must be determined to run the race that is ahead of us. 2We must keep our eyes on Jesus, who leads us and makes our faith complete. He endured the shame of being nailed to a cross, because he knew that later on he would be glad he did. Now he is seated at the right side[e] of God's throne! 3So keep your mind on Jesus, who put up with many insults from sinners. Then you won't get discouraged and give up.

---

[d] *sawed in two*: Some manuscripts have "tested" or "tempted."

[e] *right side*: See the note at 1.3.

4 None of you have yet been hurt[f] in your battle against sin. 5But you have forgotten that the Scriptures say to God's children,

"When the Lord punishes you,
    don't make light of it,
and when he corrects you,
    don't be discouraged.
6 The Lord corrects the people he loves
    and disciplines those he calls his own."

7 Be patient when you are being corrected! This is how God treats his children. Don't all parents correct their children? 8God corrects all of his children, and if he doesn't correct you, then you don't really belong to him. 9Our earthly fathers correct us, and we still respect them. Isn't it even better to be given true life by letting our spiritual Father correct us?

10 Our human fathers correct us for a short time, and they do it as they think best. But God corrects us for our own good, because he wants us to be holy, as he is. 11It is never fun to be corrected. In fact, at the time it is always painful. But if we learn to obey by being corrected, we will do right and live at peace.

12 Now stand up straight! Stop your knees from shaking 13and walk a straight path. Then lame people will be healed, instead of getting worse.

Warning against Turning from God

14 Try to live at peace with everyone! Live a clean life. If you don't, you will never see the Lord. 15Make sure that no one misses out on God's wonderful kindness. Don't let anyone become bitter and cause trouble

---

f hurt: Or "killed."

for the rest of you. ¹⁶Watch out for immoral and ungodly people like Esau, who sold his future blessing*g* for only one meal. ¹⁷You know how he later wanted it back. But there was nothing he could do to change things, even though he begged his father and cried.

18 You have not come to a place like Mount Sinai*h* that can be seen and touched. There is no flaming fire or dark cloud or storm ¹⁹or trumpet sound. The people of Israel heard a voice speak. But they begged it to stop, ²⁰because they could not obey its commands. They were even told to kill any animal that touched the mountain. ²¹The sight was so frightening that Moses said he shook with fear.

22 You have now come to Mount Zion and to the heavenly Jerusalem. This is the city of the living God, where thousands and thousands of angels have come to celebrate. ²³Here you will find all of God's dearest children,*i* whose names are written in heaven. And you will find God himself, who judges everyone. Here also are the spirits of those good people who have been made perfect. ²⁴And Jesus is here! He is the one who makes God's new agreement with us, and his sprinkled blood says much better things than the blood of Abel.*j*

---

g *sold his future blessing*: As the first-born son, Esau had certain privileges that were known as a "birthright."

h *a place like Mount Sinai*: The Greek text has "a place," but the writer is referring to the time that the Lord spoke to the people of Israel from Mount Sinai (see Exodus 19.16-25).

i *all of God's dearest children*: The Greek text has "the gathering of the first-born children" (see the note at 1.6).

j *blood of Abel*: Cain and Abel were the two sons of Adam and Eve. Cain murdered Abel (see Genesis 4.1-16).

25 Make sure that you obey the one who speaks to you. The people did not escape, when they refused to obey the one who spoke to them at Mount Sinai. Do you think you can possibly escape, if you refuse to obey the one who speaks to you from heaven? 26When God spoke the first time, his voice shook only the earth. This time he has promised to shake the earth once again, and heaven too.

27 The words "once again" mean that these created things will someday be shaken and removed. Then what cannot be shaken will last. 28We should be grateful that we were given a kingdom that cannot be shaken. And in this kingdom we please God by worshiping him and by showing him great honor and respect. 29Our God is like a destructive fire!

Service That Pleases God

13 Keep being concerned about each other as the Lord's followers should.

2 Be sure to welcome strangers into your home. By doing this, some people have welcomed angels as guests, without even knowing it.

3 Remember the Lord's people who are in jail and be concerned for them. Don't forget those who are suffering, but imagine that you are there with them.

4 Have respect for marriage. Always be faithful to your partner, because God will punish anyone who is immoral or unfaithful in marriage.

5 Don't fall in love with money. Be satisfied with what you have. The Lord has promised that he will not leave us or desert us. 6That should make you feel like saying,

"The Lord helps me!
Why should I be afraid
of what people can do to me?"

7 Don't forget about your leaders who taught you God's message. Remember what kind of lives they lived and try to have faith like theirs.

8 Jesus Christ never changes! He is the same yesterday, today, and forever. 9Don't be fooled by any kind of strange teachings. It is better to receive strength from God's undeserved kindness than to depend on certain foods. After all, these foods don't really help the people who eat them. 10But we have an altar where even the priests who serve in the place of worship have no right to eat.

11 After the high priest offers the blood of animals as a sin offering, the bodies of those animals are burned outside the camp. 12Jesus himself suffered outside the city gate, so that his blood would make people holy. 13That's why we should go outside the camp to Jesus and share in his disgrace. 14On this earth we don't have a city that lasts forever, but we are waiting for such a city.

15 Our sacrifice is to keep offering praise to God in the name of Jesus. 16But don't forget to help others and to share your possessions with them. This too is like offering a sacrifice that pleases God.

17 Obey your leaders and do what they say. They are watching over you, and they must answer to God. So don't make them sad as they do their work. Make them happy. Otherwise, they won't be able to help you at all.

18 Pray for us. Our consciences are clear, and we always try to live right. 19I especially want you to pray that I can visit you again soon.

Final Prayers and Greetings

20 God gives peace, and he raised our Lord Jesus Christ from death. Now Jesus is like a Great Shepherd whose blood was used to make God's eternal agreement with his flock.[k] 21I pray that God will make you ready to obey him and that you will always be eager to do right. May Jesus help you do what pleases God. To Jesus Christ be glory forever and ever! Amen.

22 My friends, I have written only a short letter to encourage you, and I beg you to pay close attention to what I have said.

23 By now you surely must know that our friend Timothy is out of jail. If he gets here in time, I will bring him with me when I come to visit you.

24 Please give my greetings to your leaders and to the rest of the Lord's people.

His followers from Italy send you their greetings.

25 I pray that God will be kind to all of you![l]

---

[k] whose blood was used to make God's eternal agreement with his flock: See 9.18-22.

[l] to all of you!: Some manuscripts add "Amen."

A Letter from James

ABOUT THIS LETTER

This is a good example of a general letter, because it is addressed to Christians scattered throughout the Roman empire. Though written as a letter, it is more like a short book of instructions for daily living.

For James faith means action! In fact, the entire book is a series of examples that show faith in action in wise and practical ways.

His advice was clear and to the point: If you are poor, don't despair! Don't give up when your faith is being tested. Don't get angry quickly. Don't favor the rich over the poor. Do good things for others. Control your tongue and desires. Surrender to God and rely on his wisdom. Resist the devil. Don't brag about what you are going to do. If you are rich, use your money to help the poor. Be patient and kind, and pray for those who need God's help.

A QUICK LOOK AT THIS LETTER

717

1 From James, a servant of God and of our Lord Jesus Christ.

Greetings to the twelve tribes scattered all over the world.*

Faith and Wisdom

2 My friends, be glad, even if you have a lot of trouble. ³You know that you learn to endure by having your faith tested. ⁴But you must learn to endure everything, so that you will be completely mature and not lacking in anything.

5 If any of you need wisdom, you should ask God, and it will be given to you. God is generous and won't correct you for asking. ⁶But when you ask for something, you must have faith and not doubt. Anyone who doubts is like an ocean wave tossed around in a storm. ⁷⁻⁸If you are that kind of person, you can't make up your mind, and you surely can't be trusted. So don't expect the Lord to give you anything at all.

Poor People and Rich People

9 Any of God's people who are poor should be glad that he thinks so highly of them. ¹⁰But any who are rich should be glad when God makes them humble. Rich people will disappear like wild flowers ¹¹scorched by the burning heat of the sun. The flowers lose their blossoms, and their beauty is destroyed. That is how the rich will disappear, as they go about their business.

---

a twelve tribes scattered all over the world: James is saying that the Lord's followers are like the tribes of Israel that were scattered everywhere by their enemies.

Trials and Temptations

12 God will bless you, if you don't give up when your faith is being tested. He will reward you with a glorious life,[b] just as he rewards everyone who loves him.

13 Don't blame God when you are tempted! God cannot be tempted by evil, and he doesn't use evil to tempt others. 14We are tempted by our own desires that drag us off and trap us. 15Our desires make us sin, and when sin is finished with us, it leaves us dead.

16 Don't be fooled, my dear friends. 17Every good and perfect gift comes down from the Father who created all the lights in the heavens. He is always the same and never makes dark shadows by changing. 18He wanted us to be his own special people,[c] and so he sent the true message to give us new birth.

Hearing and Obeying

19 My dear friends, you should be quick to listen and slow to speak or to get angry. 20If you are angry, you cannot do any of the good things that God wants done. 21You must stop doing anything immoral or evil. Instead be humble and accept the message that is planted in you to save you.

---

[b] *a glorious life*: The Greek text has "the crown of life." In ancient times an athlete who had won a contest was rewarded with a crown of flowers as a sign of victory.

[c] *his own special people*: The Greek text has "the first of his creatures." The Law of Moses taught that the first-born of all animals and the first part of the harvest were special and belonged to the Lord.

22 Obey God's message! Don't fool yourselves by just listening to it. [23]If you hear the message and don't obey it, you are like people who stare at themselves in a mirror [24]and forget what they look like as soon as they leave. [25]But you must never stop looking at the perfect law that sets you free. God will bless you in everything you do, if you listen and obey, and don't just hear and forget.

26 If you think you are being religious, but can't control your tongue, you are fooling yourself, and everything you do is useless. [27]Religion that pleases God the Father must be pure and spotless. You must help needy orphans and widows, and not let this world make you evil.

Warning against Having Favorites

2 My friends, if you have faith in our glorious Lord Jesus Christ, you won't treat some people better than others. [2]Suppose a rich person wearing fancy clothes and a gold ring comes to one of your meetings. And suppose a poor person dressed in worn-out clothes also comes. [3]You must not give the best seat to the one in fancy clothes and tell the one who is poor to stand at the side or sit on the floor. [4]That is the same as saying that some people are better than others, and you would be acting like a crooked judge.

5 My dear friends, pay attention. God has given a lot of faith to the poor people in this world. He has also promised them a share in his kingdom that he will give to everyone who loves him. [6]You mistreat the poor. But isn't it the rich who boss you around and drag you off to court? [7]Aren't they the ones who make fun of your Lord?

8 You will do all right, if you obey the most important law *d* in the Scriptures. It is the law that commands us to love others as much as we love ourselves. 9But if you treat some people better than others, you have done wrong, and the Scriptures teach that you have sinned.

10 If you obey every law except one, you are still guilty of breaking them all. 11The same God who told us to be faithful in marriage also told us not to murder. So even if you are faithful in marriage, but murder someone, you still have broken God's Law.

12 Speak and act like people who will be judged by the law that sets us free. 13Do this, because on the day of judgment there will be no pity for those who have not had pity on others. But even in judgment, God is merciful! *e*

Faith and Works

14 My friends, what good is it to say you have faith, when you don't do anything to show that you really do have faith? Can that kind of faith save you? 15If you know someone who doesn't have any clothes or food, 16you shouldn't just say, "I hope all goes well for you. I hope you will be warm and have plenty to eat." What good is it to say this, unless you do something to help? 17Faith that doesn't lead us to do good deeds is all alone and dead!

---

d most important law: The Greek text has "royal law," meaning the one given by the king (that is, God).

e But even in judgment, God is merciful!: Or "So be merciful, and you will be shown mercy on the day of judgment."

18 Suppose someone disagrees and says, "It is possible to have faith without doing kind deeds."

I would answer, "Prove that you have faith without doing kind deeds, and I will prove that I have faith by doing them." 19 You surely believe there is only one God. That's fine. Even demons believe this, and it makes them shake with fear.

20 Does some stupid person want proof that faith without deeds is useless? 21 Well, our ancestor Abraham pleased God by putting his son Isaac on the altar to sacrifice him. 22 Now you see how Abraham's faith and deeds worked together. He proved that his faith was real by what he did. 23 This is what the Scriptures mean by saying, "Abraham had faith in God, and God was pleased with him." That's how Abraham became God's friend.

24 You can now see that we please God by what we do and not only by what we believe. 25 For example, Rahab had been a prostitute. But she pleased God when she welcomed the spies and sent them home by another way.

26 Anyone who doesn't breathe is dead, and faith that doesn't do anything is just as dead!

The Tongue

3 My friends, we should not all try to become teachers. In fact, teachers will be judged more strictly than others. 2 All of us do many wrong things. But if you can control your tongue, you are mature and able to control your whole body.

3 By putting a bit into the mouth of a horse, we can turn the horse in different directions. 4 It takes strong winds to move a large sailing ship, but the captain uses

only a small rudder to make it go in any direction. [5]Our tongues are small too, and yet they brag about big things.

It takes only a spark to start a forest fire! [6]The tongue is like a spark. It is an evil power that dirties the rest of the body and sets a person's entire life on fire with flames that come from hell itself. [7]All kinds of animals, birds, reptiles, and sea creatures can be tamed and have been tamed. [8]But our tongues get out of control. They are restless and evil, and always spreading deadly poison.

9-10 My dear friends, with our tongues we speak both praises and curses. We praise our Lord and Father, and we curse people who were created to be like God, and this isn't right. [11]Can clean water and dirty water both flow from the same spring? [12]Can a fig tree produce olives or a grapevine produce figs? Does fresh water come from a well full of salt water?

Wisdom from Above

13 Are any of you wise or sensible? Then show it by living right and by being humble and wise in everything you do. [14]But if your heart is full of bitter jealousy and selfishness, don't brag or lie to cover up the truth. [15]That kind of wisdom doesn't come from above. It is earthly and selfish and comes from the devil himself. [16]Whenever people are jealous or selfish, they cause trouble and do all sorts of cruel things. [17]But the wisdom that comes from above leads us to be pure, friendly, gentle, sensible, kind, helpful, genuine, and sincere. [18]When peacemakers plant seeds of peace, they will harvest justice.

Friendship with the World

4 Why do you fight and argue with each other? Isn't it because you are full of selfish desires that fight to control your body? ² You want something you don't have, and you will do anything to get it. You will even kill! But you still cannot get what you want, and you won't get it by fighting and arguing. You should pray for it. ³ Yet even when you do pray, your prayers are not answered, because you pray just for selfish reasons.

4 You people aren't faithful to God! Don't you know that if you love the world, you are God's enemies? And if you decide to be a friend of the world, you make yourself an enemy of God. ⁵ Do you doubt the Scriptures that say, "God truly cares about the Spirit he has put in us"?ᶠ ⁶ In fact, God treats us with even greater kindness, just as the Scriptures say,

"God opposes everyone who is proud,
   but he is kind to everyone who is humble."

7 Surrender to God! Resist the devil, and he will run from you. ⁸ Come near to God, and he will come near to you. Clean up your lives, you sinners. Purify your hearts, you people who can't make up your mind. ⁹ Be sad and sorry and weep. Stop laughing and start crying. Be gloomy instead of glad. ¹⁰ Be humble in the Lord's presence, and he will honor you.

ᶠ *God truly cares about the Spirit he has put in us:* One possible meaning for the difficult Greek text; other translations are possible, such as, "the Spirit that God put in us truly cares."

Saying Cruel Things about Others

11 My friends, don't say cruel things about others! If you do, or if you condemn others, you are condemning God's Law. And if you condemn the Law, you put yourself above the Law and refuse to obey either it 12 or God who gave it. God is our judge, and he can save or destroy us. What right do you have to condemn anyone?

Warning against Bragging

13 You should know better than to say, "Today or tomorrow we will go to the city. We will do business there for a year and make a lot of money!" 14 What do you know about tomorrow? How can you be so sure about your life? It is nothing more than mist that appears for only a little while before it disappears. 15 You should say, "If the Lord lets us live, we will do these things." 16 Yet you are stupid enough to brag, and it is wrong to be so proud. 17 If you don't do what you know is right, you have sinned.

Warning to the Rich

5 You rich people should cry and weep! Terrible things are going to happen to you. 2 Your treasures have already rotted, and moths have eaten your clothes. 3 Your money has rusted, and the rust will be evidence against you, as it burns your body like fire. Yet you keep on storing up wealth in these last days. 4 You refused to pay the people who worked in your fields, and now their unpaid wages are shouting out against you. The Lord All-Powerful has surely heard the cries of the workers who harvested your crops.

5 While here on earth, you have thought only of filling your own stomachs and having a good time. But now you are like fat cattle on their way to be butchered. 6 You have condemned and murdered innocent people, who couldn't even fight back.

Be Patient and Kind

7 My friends, be patient until the Lord returns. Think of farmers who wait patiently for the spring and summer rains to make their valuable crops grow. 8 Be patient like those farmers and don't give up. The Lord will soon be here! 9 Don't grumble about each other or you will be judged, and the judge is right outside the door.

10 My friends, follow the example of the prophets who spoke for the Lord. They were patient, even when they had to suffer. 11 In fact, we praise the ones who endured the most. You remember how patient Job was and how the Lord finally helped him. The Lord did this because he is so merciful and kind.

12 My friends, above all else, don't take an oath. You must not swear by heaven or by earth or by anything else. "Yes" or "No" is all you need to say. If you say anything more, you will be condemned.

13 If you are having trouble, you should pray. And if you are feeling good, you should sing praises. 14 If you are sick, ask the church leaders [g] to come and pray for you. Ask them to put olive oil [h] on you in the name of the Lord. 15 If you have faith when you pray for sick

---

[g] *church leaders*: Or "elders" or "presbyters" or "priests."

[h] *olive oil*: The Jewish people used olive oil for healing.

people, they will get well. The Lord will heal them, and if they have sinned, he will forgive them.

16 If you have sinned, you should tell each other what you have done. Then you can pray for one another and be healed. The prayer of an innocent person is powerful, and it can help a lot. 17Elijah was just as human as we are, and for three and a half years his prayers kept the rain from falling. 18But when he did pray for rain, it fell from the skies and made the crops grow.

19 My friends, if any followers have wandered away from the truth, you should try to lead them back. 20If you turn sinners from the wrong way, you will save them from death, and many of their sins will be forgiven.

Peter's First Letter

ABOUT THIS LETTER

In this letter Peter has much to say about suffering. He shows how it can be a way of serving the Lord, of sharing the faith, and of being tested. The letter was written to Christians scattered all over the northern part of Asia Minor. In this part of the Roman empire many Christians had already suffered unfair treatment from people who did not believe in Jesus. And they could expect to suffer even more.

Peter was quick to offer encouragement. His letter reminds the readers that some of the Lord's followers may have to go through times of hard testing. But this should make them glad, Peter declares, because it will strengthen their faith and bring them honor on the day when Jesus Christ returns (1.6, 7).

Peter reminds them that Christ suffered here on earth, and when his followers suffer for doing right they are sharing his sufferings (2.18-25; 4.12-17). In fact, Christians should expect to suffer for their faith (3.8–4.19).

But because of who God is and because of what God has done by raising Jesus Christ from death, Christians can have hope in the future. Just as Christ suffered before he received honor from God, so will Christians be tested by suffering before they receive honor when the Lord returns. Peter uses poetic language to remind his readers of what Christ has done:

Christ died once for our sins.
An innocent person died
   for those who are guilty.
Christ did this
   to bring you to God,
when his body
    was put to death
and his spirit
    was made alive. (3.18)

A QUICK LOOK AT THIS LETTER

1. Greetings and Prayer (1.1,2)
2. A Real Reason for Hope (1.3-12)
3. Living as God's Holy People (1.13–2.17)
4. The Example of Christ's Suffering (2.18-25)
5. Being a Christian and Suffering (3.1–4.19)
6. Advice for Church Leaders (5.1-11)
7. Final Greetings (5.12-14)

1 From Peter, an apostle of Jesus Christ.
   To God's people who are scattered like foreigners in Pontus, Galatia, Cappadocia, Asia, and Bithynia.

2 God the Father decided to choose you as his people, and his Spirit has made you holy. You have obeyed Jesus Christ and are sprinkled with his blood.[a]

I pray that God will be kind to you and will keep on giving you peace!

---

[a] *sprinkled with his blood*: According to Exodus 24.3-8, the people of Israel were sprinkled with the blood of cows to show they would keep their agreement with God. Peter says that it is the blood of Jesus that seals the agreement between God and his people (see Hebrews 9.18-21).

A Real Reason for Hope

3 Praise God, the Father of our Lord Jesus Christ. God is so good, and by raising Jesus from death, he has given us new life and a hope that lives on. ⁴God has something stored up for you in heaven, where it will never decay or be ruined or disappear.

5 You have faith in God, whose power will protect you until the last day.*ᵇ* Then he will save you, just as he has always planned to do. ⁶On that day you will be glad, even if you have to go through many hard trials for a while. ⁷Your faith will be like gold that has been tested in a fire. And these trials will prove that your faith is worth much more than gold that can be destroyed. They will show that you will be given praise and honor and glory when Jesus Christ returns.

8 You have never seen Jesus, and you don't see him now. But still you love him and have faith in him, and no words can tell how glad and happy ⁹you are to be saved. That's why you have faith.

10 Some prophets told how kind God would be to you, and they searched hard to find out more about the way you would be saved. ¹¹The Spirit of Christ was in them and was telling them how Christ would suffer and would then be given great honor. So they searched to find out exactly who Christ would be and when this would happen. ¹²But they were told that they were serving you and not themselves. They preached to you by the power of the Holy Spirit, who was sent from heaven. And their message was only for you, even though angels would like to know more about it.

ᵇ the last day: When God will judge all people.

Chosen To Live a Holy Life

13 Be alert and think straight. Put all your hope in how kind God will be to you when Jesus Christ appears. ¹⁴Behave like obedient children. Don't let your lives be controlled by your desires, as they used to be. ¹⁵Always live as God's holy people should, because God is the one who chose you, and he is holy. ¹⁶That's why the Scriptures say, "I am the holy God, and you must be holy too."

17 You say that God is your Father, but God doesn't have favorites! He judges all people by what they do. So you must honor God while you live as strangers here on earth. ¹⁸You were rescued*ᶜ* from the useless way of life that you learned from your ancestors. But you know that you were not rescued by such things as silver or gold that don't last forever. ¹⁹You were rescued by the precious blood of Christ, that spotless and innocent lamb. ²⁰Christ was chosen even before the world was created, but because of you, he did not come until these last days. ²¹And when he did come, it was to lead you to have faith in God, who raised him from death and honored him in a glorious way. That's why you have put your faith and hope in God.

22 You obeyed the truth,*ᵈ* and your souls were made pure. Now you sincerely love each other. But you must keep on loving with all your heart. ²³Do this because

---

ᶜ rescued: The Greek word often, though not always, means payment of a price to free a slave or prisoner.
ᵈ You obeyed the truth: Some manuscripts add "by the power of the Spirit."

God has given you new birth by his message that lives on forever. 24The Scriptures say,

> "Humans wither like grass,
>> and their glory fades like wild flowers.
> Grass dries up,
>> and flowers fall to the ground.
> 25 But what the Lord has said
>> will stand forever."

Our good news to you is what the Lord has said.

A Living Stone and a Holy Nation

2 Stop being hateful! Quit trying to fool people, and start being sincere. Don't be jealous or say cruel things about others. 2Be like newborn babies who are thirsty for the pure spiritual milk that will help you grow and be saved. 3You have already found out how good the Lord really is.

4 Come to Jesus Christ. He is the living stone that people have rejected, but which God has chosen and highly honored. 5And now you are living stones that are being used to build a spiritual house. You are also a group of holy priests, and with the help of Jesus Christ you will offer sacrifices that please God. 6It is just as God says in the Scriptures,

> "Look! I am placing in Zion
>> a choice and precious cornerstone.
> No one who has faith in that one
>> will be disappointed."

7 You are followers of the Lord, and that stone is precious to you. But it isn't precious to those who refuse to follow him. They are the builders who tossed aside the stone that turned out to be the most important one of all. 8They disobeyed the message

and stumbled and fell over that stone, because they were doomed.

9 But you are God's chosen and special people. You are a group of royal priests and a holy nation. God has brought you out of darkness into his marvelous light. Now you must tell all the wonderful things that he has done. The Scriptures say,

10 "Once you were nobody.
Now you are God's people.
At one time no one had pity on you.
Now God has treated you with kindness.

Live as God's Servants Should

11 Dear friends, you are foreigners and strangers on this earth. So I beg you not to surrender to those desires that fight against you. 12 Always let others see you behaving properly, even though they may still accuse you of doing wrong. Then on the day of judgment, they will honor God by telling the good things they saw you do.

13 The Lord wants you to obey all human authorities, especially the Emperor, who rules over everyone. 14 You must also obey governors, because they are sent by the Emperor to punish criminals and to praise good citizens. 15 God wants you to silence stupid and ignorant people by doing right. 16 You are free, but still you are God's servants, and you must not use your freedom as an excuse for doing wrong. 17 Respect everyone and show special love for God's people. Honor God and respect the Emperor.

The Example of Christ's Suffering

18 Servants, you must obey your masters and always show respect to them. Do this, not only to

those who are kind and thoughtful, but also to those
who are cruel. ¹⁹God will bless you, even if others
treat you unfairly for being loyal to him. ²⁰You
don't gain anything by being punished for some
wrong you have done. But God will bless you, if
you have to suffer for doing something good.
²¹After all, God chose you to suffer as you follow
in the footsteps of Christ, who set an example by
suffering for you.

> ²² Christ did not sin or ever tell a lie.
> ²³ Although he was abused,
>   he never tried to get even.
> And when he suffered,
>   he made no threats.
> Instead, he had faith in God,
>   who judges fairly.
> ²⁴ Christ carried the burden of our sins.
> He was nailed to the cross,
>   so that we would stop sinning
>   and start living right.
> By his cuts and bruises you are healed.
> ²⁵ You had wandered away like sheep.
> Now you have returned to the one
>   who is your shepherd and protector.

Wives and Husbands

3 If you are a wife, you must put your husband first.
Even if he opposes your message, you will win
him over by what you do. No one else will have to say
anything to him, ²because he will see how you honor
God and live a pure life. ³Don't depend on things like
fancy hairdos or gold jewelry or expensive clothes to
make you look beautiful. ⁴Be beautiful in your heart

by being gentle and quiet. This kind of beauty will last, and God considers it very special.

5 Long ago those women who worshiped God and put their hope in him made themselves beautiful by putting their husbands first. 6For example, Sarah obeyed Abraham and called him her master. You are her true children, if you do right and don't let anything frighten you.

7 If you are a husband, you should be thoughtful of your wife. Treat her with honor, because she isn't as strong as you are, and she shares with you in the gift of life. Then nothing will stand in the way of your prayers.

Suffering for Doing Right

8 Finally, all of you should agree and have concern and love for each other. You should also be kind and humble. 9Don't be hateful and insult people just because they are hateful and insult you. Instead, treat everyone with kindness. You are God's chosen ones, and he will bless you. The Scriptures say,

10 "Do you really love life?
   Do you want to be happy?
      Then stop saying cruel things
         and quit telling lies.
11 Give up your evil ways and do right,
      as you find and follow the road
         that leads to peace.
12 The Lord watches over everyone
   who obeys him,
      and he listens to their prayers.
   But he opposes everyone who does evil."

13 Can anyone really harm you for being eager to do good deeds? 14Even if you have to suffer for doing

good things, God will bless you. So stop being afraid and don't worry about what people might do. ¹⁵Honor Christ and let him be the Lord of your life.

Always be ready to give an answer when someone asks you about your hope. ¹⁶Give a kind and respectful answer and keep your conscience clear. This way you will make people ashamed for saying bad things about your good conduct as a follower of Christ. ¹⁷You are better off to obey God and suffer for doing right than to suffer for doing wrong.

¹⁸ Christ died once for our sins.
An innocent person died
for those who are guilty.
Christ did this to bring you to God,
when his body was put to death
and his spirit was made alive.

19 Christ then preached to the spirits that were being kept in prison. ²⁰They had disobeyed God while Noah was building the boat, but God had been patient with them. Eight people went into that boat and were brought safely through the flood.

21 Those flood waters were like baptism that now saves you. But baptism is more than just washing your body. It means turning to God with a clear conscience, because Jesus Christ was raised from death. ²²Christ is now in heaven, where he sits at the right side*^e of God. All angels, authorities, and powers are under his control.

Being Faithful to God

4 Christ suffered here on earth. Now you must be ready to suffer as he did, because suffering shows

---

^e *right side*: The place of honor and power.

that you have stopped sinning. ²It means you have turned from your own desires and want to obey God for the rest of your life. ³You have already lived long enough like people who don't know God. You were immoral and followed your evil desires. You went around drinking and partying and carrying on. In fact, you even worshiped disgusting idols. ⁴Now your former friends wonder why you have stopped running around with them, and they curse you for it. ⁵But they will have to answer to God, who judges the living and the dead. ⁶The good news has even been preached to the dead,*f* so that after they have been judged for what they have done in this life, their spirits will live with God.

7 Everything will soon come to an end. So be serious and be sensible enough to pray.

8 Most important of all, you must sincerely love each other, because love wipes away many sins.

9 Welcome people into your home and don't grumble about it.

10 Each of you has been blessed with one of God's many wonderful gifts to be used in the service of others. So use your gift well. ¹¹If you have the gift of speaking, preach God's message. If you have the gift of helping others, do it with the strength that God supplies. Everything should be done in a way that will bring honor to God because of Jesus Christ, who is glorious and powerful forever. Amen.

Suffering for Being a Christian

12 Dear friends, don't be surprised or shocked that

---

f *the dead*: Either people who died after becoming followers of Christ or the people of Noah's day (see 3.19).

you are going through testing that is like walking through fire. 13Be glad for the chance to suffer as Christ suffered. It will prepare you for even greater happiness when he makes his glorious return.

14 Count it a blessing when you suffer for being a Christian. This shows that God's glorious Spirit is with you. 15But you deserve to suffer if you are a murderer, a thief, a crook, or a busybody. 16Don't be ashamed to suffer for being a Christian. Praise God that you belong to him. 17God has already begun judging his own people. And if his judgment begins with us, imagine how terrible it will be for those who refuse to obey his message. The Scriptures say,

18 "If good people barely escape,
      what will happen to sinners
      and to others who don't respect God?"

19 If you suffer for obeying God, you must have complete faith in your faithful Creator and keep on doing right.

Helping Christian Leaders

5 Church leaders,*g* I am writing to encourage you. I too am a leader, as well as a witness to Christ's suffering, and I will share in his glory when it is shown to us.

2 Just as shepherds watch over their sheep, you must watch over everyone God has placed in your care. Do it willingly in order to please God, and not simply because you think you must. Let it be something you want to do, instead of something you do merely to make money. 3Don't be bossy to those people

---

g Church leaders: Or "Elders" or "Presbyters" or "Priests."

who are in your care, but set an example for them. [4]Then when Christ the Chief Shepherd returns, you will be given a crown that will never lose its glory.

5 All of you young people should obey your elders. In fact, everyone should be humble toward everyone else. The Scriptures say,

"God opposes proud people,
    but he helps everyone who is humble."

6 Be humble in the presence of God's mighty power, and he will honor you when the time comes. [7]God cares for you, so turn all your worries over to him.

8 Be on your guard and stay awake. Your enemy, the devil, is like a roaring lion, sneaking around to find someone to attack. [9]But you must resist the devil and stay strong in your faith. You know that all over the world the Lord's followers are suffering just as you are. [10]But God shows undeserved kindness to everyone. That's why he had Christ Jesus choose you to share in his eternal glory. You will suffer for a while, but God will make you complete, steady, strong, and firm. [11]God will be in control forever! Amen.

Final Greetings

12 Silvanus helped me write this short letter, and I consider him a faithful follower of the Lord. I wanted to encourage you and tell you how kind God really is, so that you will keep on having faith in him.

13 Greetings from the Lord's followers in Babylon.[h] They are God's chosen ones.

Mark, who is like a son to me, sends his greetings too.

---

[h] *Babylon:* This may be a secret name for the city of Rome.

14 Give each other a warm greeting. I pray that God will give peace to everyone who belongs to Christ.[i]

---

[i] *Christ*: Some manuscripts add "Amen."

Peter's Second Letter

ABOUT THIS LETTER

The writer of this letter wants the readers to know that Christians must live in a way that pleases God (1.3) and hold firmly to the truth they were given (1.12).

He warns them that false prophets and teachers had entered the Christian community and were trying to lead the Lord's followers away from the truth. But they will be punished for their evil deeds (2.1-22). When false teachers are at work, Christians must stick to their faith and be examples for others of right living. They must have understanding, self-control and patience, and they should show love for God and all people.

The readers must never forget that the Lord's return is certain, no matter what others may say (3.1-18):

> *Don't forget that for the Lord one day is the same as a thousand years, and a thousand years is the same as one day. The Lord isn't slow about keeping his promises, as some people think he is. In fact, God is patient, because he wants everyone to turn from sin and no one to be lost. (3.8,9)*

A QUICK LOOK AT THIS LETTER

1 From Simon Peter, a servant and an apostle of Jesus Christ.

To everyone who shares with us in the privilege of believing that our God and Savior Jesus Christ will do what is just and fair.[a]

2 I pray that God will be kind to you and will let you live in perfect peace! May you keep learning more and more about God and our Lord Jesus.

Living as the Lord's Followers

3 We have everything we need to live a life that pleases God. It was all given to us by God's own power, when we learned that he had invited us to share in his wonderful goodness. [4]God made great and marvelous promises, so that his nature would become part of us. Then we could escape our evil desires and the corrupt influences of this world.

5 Do your best to improve your faith. You can do this by adding goodness, understanding, [6]self-control, patience, devotion to God, [7]concern for others, and love. [8]If you keep growing in this way, it will show that what you know about our Lord Jesus Christ has made your lives useful and meaningful. [9]But if you don't grow, you are like someone who is nearsighted or blind, and you have forgotten that your past sins are forgiven.

10 My friends, you must do all you can to show that God has really chosen and selected you. If you keep on doing this, you won't stumble and fall. [11]Then our

---

[a] *To everyone who ... just and fair:* Or "To everyone whose faith in the justice and fairness of our God and Savior Jesus Christ is as precious as our own faith."

Lord and Savior Jesus Christ will give you a glorious welcome into his kingdom that will last forever.

12 You are holding firmly to the truth that you were given. But I am still going to remind you of these things. 13In fact, I think I should keep on reminding you until I leave this body. 14And our Lord Jesus Christ has already told me that I will soon leave it behind. 15That is why I am doing my best to make sure that each of you remembers all of this after I am gone.

The Message about the Glory of Christ

16 When we told you about the power and the return of our Lord Jesus Christ, we were not telling clever stories that someone had made up. But with our own eyes we saw his true greatness. 17God, our great and wonderful Father, truly honored him by saying, "This is my own dear Son, and I am pleased with him." 18We were there with Jesus on the holy mountain and heard this voice speak from heaven.

19 All of this makes us even more certain that what the prophets said is true. So you should pay close attention to their message, as you would to a lamp shining in some dark place. You must keep on paying attention until daylight comes and the morning star rises in your hearts. 20But you need to realize that no one alone can understand any of the prophecies in the Scriptures. 21The prophets did not think these things up on their own, but they were guided by the Spirit of God.

False Prophets and Teachers

2 Sometimes false prophets spoke to the people of Israel. False teachers will also sneak in and speak

harmful lies to you. But these teachers don't really belong to the Master who paid a great price for them, and they will quickly destroy themselves. ²Many people will follow their evil ways and cause others to tell lies about the true way. ³They will be greedy and cheat you with smooth talk. But long ago God decided to punish them, and God doesn't sleep.

4 God did not have pity on the angels that sinned. He had them tied up and thrown into the dark pits of hell until the time of judgment. ⁵And during Noah's time, God did not have pity on the ungodly people of the world. He destroyed them with a flood, though he did save eight people, including Noah, who preached the truth.

6 God punished the cities of Sodom and Gomorrah*ᵇ* by burning them to ashes, and this is a warning to anyone else who wants to sin.

7-8 Lot lived right and was greatly troubled by the terrible way those wicked people were living. He was a good man, and day after day he suffered because of the evil things he saw and heard. So the Lord rescued him. ⁹This shows that the Lord knows how to rescue godly people from their sufferings and to punish evil people while they wait for the day of judgment.

10 The Lord is especially hard on people who disobey him and don't think of anything except their own filthy desires. They are reckless and proud and are not afraid of cursing the glorious beings in heaven. ¹¹Although angels are more powerful than these evil

---

ᵇ *Sodom and Gomorrah*: During the time of Abraham the Lord destroyed these cities because the people there were so evil (see Genesis 19.24).

beings,[c] even the angels don't dare to accuse them to the Lord.

12 These people are no better than senseless animals that live by their feelings and are born to be caught and killed. They speak evil of things they don't know anything about. But their own corrupt deeds will destroy them. 13 They have done evil, and they will be rewarded with evil.

They think it is fun to have wild parties during the day. They are immoral, and the meals they eat with you are spoiled by the shameful and selfish way they carry on.[d] 14 All they think about is having sex with someone else's husband or wife. There is no end to their wicked deeds. They trick people who are easily fooled, and their minds are filled with greedy thoughts. But they are headed for trouble!

15 They have left the true road and have gone down the wrong path by following the example of the prophet Balaam. He was the son of Beor and loved what he got from being a crook. 16 But a donkey corrected him for this evil deed. It spoke to him with a human voice and made him stop his foolishness.

17 These people are like dried up water holes and clouds blown by a windstorm. The darkest part of hell is waiting for them. 18 They brag out loud about their stupid nonsense. And by being vulgar and crude,

---

[c] *evil beings*: or "evil teachers."

[d] *and the meals they eat with you are spoiled by the shameful and selfish way they carry on*: Some manuscripts have "and the meals they eat with you are spoiled by the shameful way they carry on during your feasts of Christian love."

they trap people who have barely escaped from living the wrong kind of life. [19]They promise freedom to everyone. But they are merely slaves of filthy living, because people are slaves of whatever controls them.

20 When they learned about our Lord and Savior Jesus Christ, they escaped from the filthy things of this world. But they are again caught up and controlled by these filthy things, and now they are in worse shape than they were at first. [21]They would have been better off if they had never known about the right way. Even after they knew what was right, they turned their backs on the holy commandments that they were given. [22]What happened to them is just like the true saying,

"A dog will come back
to lick up its own vomit.
A pig that has been washed
will roll in the mud."

The Lord Will Return

3 My dear friends, this is the second letter I have written to encourage you to do some honest thinking. I don't want you to forget [2]what God's prophets said would happen. You must never forget what the holy prophets taught in the past. And you must remember what the apostles told you our Lord and Savior has commanded us to do.

3 But first you must realize that in the last days some people won't think about anything except their own selfish desires. They will make fun of you [4]and say, "Didn't your Lord promise to come back? Yet the first leaders have already died, and the world hasn't changed a bit."

5 They will say this because they want to forget that long ago the heavens and the earth were made at God's command. The earth came out of water and was made from water. ⁶Later it was destroyed by the waters of a mighty flood. ⁷But God has commanded the present heavens and earth to remain until the day of judgment. Then they will be set on fire, and ungodly people will be destroyed.

8 Dear friends, don't forget that for the Lord one day is the same as a thousand years, and a thousand years is the same as one day. ⁹The Lord isn't slow about keeping his promises, as some people think he is. In fact, God is patient, because he wants everyone to turn from sin and no one to be lost.

10 The day of the Lord's return will surprise us like a thief. The heavens will disappear with a loud noise, and the heat will melt the whole universe.ᵉ Then the earth and everything on it will be seen for what they are.ᶠ

11 Everything will be destroyed. So you should serve and honor God by the way you live. ¹²You should look forward to the day when God judges everyone, and you should try to make it come soon.ᵍ On that day the heavens will be destroyed by fire, and everything else will melt in the heat. ¹³But God has promised us a new heaven and a new earth, where justice will rule. We are really looking forward to that!

ᵉ *the whole universe*: Probably the sun, moon, and stars, or the elements that everything in the universe is made of.

ᶠ *will be seen for what they are*: Some manuscripts have "will go up in flames."

ᵍ *and you should try to make it come soon*: Or "and you should eagerly desire for that day to come."

14 My friends, while you are waiting, you should make certain that the Lord finds you pure, spotless, and living at peace. 15Don't forget that the Lord is patient because he wants people to be saved. This is also what our dear friend Paul said when he wrote you with the wisdom that God had given him. 16Paul talks about these same things in all his letters, but part of what he says is hard to understand. Some ignorant and unsteady people even destroy themselves by twisting what he said. They do the same thing with other Scriptures too.

17 My dear friends, you have been warned ahead of time! So don't let the errors of evil people lead you down the wrong path and make you lose your balance. 18Let the wonderful kindness and the understanding that come from our Lord and Savior Jesus Christ help you to keep on growing. Praise Jesus now and forever! Amen.*h*

---

h Amen: Some manuscripts do not have "Amen."

John's First Letter

ABOUT THIS LETTER

John wants Christian believers to know that when we tell God about our sins, God will forgive us and take them away (1.9).

The true test of faith is love for each other (3.11-24). Because God is love, his people must be like him (4.1-21). For a complete victory over sin, we must not only love others, but we must believe that Jesus, the Son of God, is truly Christ, and that his death for us was real (5.1-12).

Remember:

> *The Word that gives life*
> *was from the beginning,*
> *and this is the one*
> *our message is about. (1.1a)*

1
The Word that gives life
was from the beginning,
and this is the one our message is about.

Our ears have heard, our own eyes have seen,
and our hands touched this Word.

2 The one who gives life appeared! We saw it happen,
and we are witnesses to what we have seen. Now we are
telling you about this eternal life that was with the Father
and appeared to us. [3]We are telling you what we have
seen and heard, so that you may share in this life with us.
And we share in it with the Father and with his Son Jesus
Christ. [4]We are writing to tell you these things, because
this makes us[a] truly happy.

God Is Light

5 Jesus told us that God is light and doesn't have
any darkness in him. Now we are telling you.

6 If we say that we share in life with God and keep
on living in the dark, we are lying and are not living by
the truth. [7]But if we live in the light, as God does, we
share in life with each other. And the blood of his Son
Jesus washes all our sins away. [8]If we say that we have
not sinned, we are fooling ourselves, and the truth isn't
in our hearts. [9]But if we confess our sins to God, he can
always be trusted to forgive us and take our sins away.

10 If we say that we have not sinned, we make God
a liar, and his message isn't in our hearts.[b]

Christ Helps Us

2 My children, I am writing this so that you won't
sin. But if you do sin, Jesus Christ always does
the right thing, and he will speak to the Father for us.

---

[a] *us*: Some manuscripts have "you."

[b] *and his message isn't in our hearts*: Or "because we
have not accepted his message."

²Christ is the sacrifice that takes away our sins and the sins of all the world's people.

3 When we obey God, we are sure that we know him. ⁴But if we claim to know him and don't obey him, we are lying and the truth isn't in our hearts. ⁵We truly love God only when we obey him as we should, and then we know that we belong to him. ⁶If we say we are his, we must follow the example of Christ.

The New Commandment

7 My dear friends, I am not writing to give you a new commandment. It is the same one that you were first given, and it is the message you heard. ⁸But it really is a new commandment, and you know its true meaning, just as Christ does. You can see the darkness fading away and the true light already shining.

9 If we claim to be in the light and hate someone, we are still in the dark. ¹⁰But if we love others, we are in the light, and we don't cause problems for them.ᶜ ¹¹If we hate others, we are living and walking in the dark. We don't know where we are going, because we can't see in the dark.

¹² Children, I am writing you,
>> because your sins have been forgiven
>> in the name of Christ.

¹³ Parents, I am writing you,
>> because you have known the one
>> who was there from the beginning.

> Young people, I am writing you,
>> because you have defeated the evil one.

ᶜ *and we don't cause problems for them*: Or "and we can see anything that might make us fall."

¹⁴ Children, I am writing you,
    because you have known the Father.
Parents, I am writing you,
    because you have known the one
    who was there from the beginning.
Young people, I am writing you,
    because you are strong.
God's message is firm in your hearts,
    and you have defeated the evil one.

15 Don't love the world or anything that belongs to the world. If you love the world, you cannot love the Father. ¹⁶Our foolish pride comes from this world, and so do our selfish desires and our desire to have everything we see. None of this comes from the Father. ¹⁷The world and the desires it causes are disappearing. But if we obey God, we will live forever.

The Enemy of Christ

18 Children, this is the last hour. You heard that the enemy of Christ would appear at this time, and many of Christ's enemies have already appeared. So we know that the last hour is here. ¹⁹These people came from our own group, yet they were not part of us. If they had been part of us, they would have stayed with us. But they left, which proves that they did not belong to our group. 20 Christ, the Holy One,ᵈ has blessedᵉ you, and

---

ᵈ *Christ, the Holy One*: The Greek text has "the Holy One" which may refer either to Christ or to God the Father.

ᵉ *blessed*: This translates a word which means "to pour olive oil on (someone's head)." In Old Testament times now all of you understand.[f] [21] I did not need to write you about the truth, since you already know it. You also know that liars do not belong to the truth. [22] And a liar is anyone who says that Jesus isn't truly Christ. Anyone who says this is an enemy of Christ and rejects both the Father and the Son. [23] If we reject the Son, we reject the Father. But if we say that we accept the Son, we have the Father. [24] Keep thinking about the message you first heard, and you will always be one in your heart with the Son and with the Father. [25] The Son[g] has promised us[h] eternal life.

[26] I am writing to warn you about those people who are misleading you. [27] But Christ has blessed you with the Holy Spirit.[i] Now the Spirit stays in you, and you don't need any teachers. The Spirit is truthful and teaches you everything. So stay one in your heart with Christ, just as the Spirit has taught you to do.

---

it was the custom to pour olive oil on a person's head when that person was chosen to be a priest or a king. Here the meaning is not clear. It may refer to the ceremony of pouring olive oil on the followers of the Lord right before they were baptized or it may refer to the gift of the Holy Spirit which they were given at baptism (see verse 27).

[f] *now all of you understand*: Some manuscripts have "you understand all things."

[g] *The Son*: The Greek text has "he" and may refer to God the Father.

[h] *us*: Some manuscripts have "you."

[i] *Christ has blessed you with the Holy Spirit*: The Greek text has "You received a pouring on of olive oil from him" (see verse 20). The "pouring on of olive oil" is here taken to refer to the gift of the Holy Spirit, and "he" may refer either to Christ or to the Father.

Children of God

28 Children, stay one in your hearts with Christ. Then when he returns, we will have confidence and won't have to hide in shame. [29]You know that Christ always does right and that everyone who does right is a child of God.

3 Think how much the Father loves us. He loves us so much that he lets us be called his children, as we truly are. But since the people of this world did not know who Christ[j] is, they don't know who we are. [2]My dear friends, we are already God's children, though what we will be hasn't yet been seen. But we do know that when Christ returns, we will be like him, because we will see him as he truly is. [3]This hope makes us keep ourselves holy, just as Christ[k] is holy.

4 Everyone who sins breaks God's law, because sin is the same as breaking God's law. [5]You know that Christ came to take away sins. He isn't sinful, [6]and people who stay one in their hearts with him won't keep on sinning. If they do keep on sinning, they don't know Christ, and they have never seen him.

7 Children, don't be fooled. Anyone who does right is good, just like Christ himself. [8]Anyone who keeps on sinning belongs to the devil. He has sinned from the beginning, but the Son of God came to destroy all that he has done. [9]God's children cannot keep on being sinful. His life-giving power[l] lives in

---

[j] *Christ*: The Greek text has "he" and may refer to God.

[k] *Christ*: The Greek text has "that one" and may refer to God.

[l] *His life-giving power*: The Greek text has "his seed."

them and makes them his children, so that they cannot keep on sinning. [10]You can tell God's children from the devil's children, because those who belong to the devil refuse to do right or to love each other.

Love Each Other

11 From the beginning you were told that we must love each other. [12]Don't be like Cain, who belonged to the devil and murdered his own brother. Why did he murder him? He did it because his brother was good, and he was evil. [13]My friends, don't be surprised if the people of this world hate you. [14]Our love for each other proves that we have gone from death to life. But if you don't love each other, you are still under the power of death.

15 If you hate each other, you are murderers, and we know that murderers do not have eternal life. [16]We know what love is because Jesus gave his life for us. That's why we must give our lives for each other. [17]If we have all we need and see one of our own people in need, we must have pity on that person, or else we cannot say we love God. [18]Children, you show love for others by truly helping them, and not merely by talking about it.

19 When we love others, we know that we belong to the truth, and we feel at ease in the presence of God. [20]But even if we don't feel at ease, God is greater than our feelings, and he knows everything. [21]Dear friends, if we feel at ease in the presence of God, we will have the courage to come near him. [22]He will give us whatever we ask, because we obey him and do what pleases him. [23]God wants us to have faith in his Son Jesus Christ and to love each other.

This is also what Jesus taught us to do. [24]If we obey
God's commandments, we will stay one in our hearts
with him, and he will stay one with us. The Spirit that
he has given us is proof that we are one with him.

God Is Love

4 Dear friends, don't believe everyone who claims
to have the Spirit of God. Test them all to find out
if they really do come from God. Many false prophets
have already gone out into the world, [2]and you can
know which ones come from God. His Spirit says that
Jesus Christ had a truly human body. [3]But when
someone doesn't say this about Jesus, you know that
person has a spirit that doesn't come from God and is
the enemy of Christ. You knew that this enemy was
coming into the world and now is already here.

4 Children, you belong to God, and you have
defeated these enemies. God's Spirit[m] is in you and is
more powerful than the one that is in the world.
[5]These enemies belong to this world, and the world
listens to them, because they speak its language. [6]We
belong to God, and everyone who knows God will
listen to us. But the people who don't know God
won't listen to us. That is how we can tell the Spirit
that speaks the truth from the one that tells lies.

7 My dear friends, we must love each other. Love
comes from God, and when we love each other, it
shows that we have been given new life. We are now
God's children, and we know him. [8]God is love, and
anyone who doesn't love others has never known

---

[m] *God's Spirit*: The Greek text has "he" and may refer to
the Spirit or to God or to Jesus.

him. [9]God showed his love for us when he sent his only Son into the world to give us life. [10]Real love isn't our love for God, but his love for us. God sent his Son to be the sacrifice by which our sins are forgiven. [11]Dear friends, since God loved us this much, we must love each other.

12 No one has ever seen God. But if we love each other, God lives in us, and his love is truly in our hearts.

13 God has given us his Spirit. That is how we know that we are one with him, just as he is one with us. [14]God sent his Son to be the Savior of the world. We saw his Son and are now telling others about him. [15]God stays one with everyone who openly says that Jesus is the Son of God. That's how we stay one with God [16]and are sure that God loves us.

God is love. If we keep on loving others, we will stay one in our hearts with God, and he will stay one with us. [17]If we truly love others and live as Christ did in this world, we won't be worried about the day of judgment. [18]A real love for others will chase those worries away. The thought of being punished is what makes us afraid. It shows that we have not really learned to love.

19 We love because God loved us first. [20]But if we say we love God and don't love each other, we are liars. We cannot see God. So how can we love God, if we don't love the people we can see? [21]The commandment that God has given us is: "Love God and love each other!"

Victory over the World

5 If we believe that Jesus is truly Christ, we are God's children. Everyone who loves the Father

will also love his children. 2If we love and obey God, we know that we will love his children. 3We show our love for God by obeying his commandments, and they are not hard to follow.

4 Every child of God can defeat the world, and our faith is what gives us this victory. 5No one can defeat the world without having faith in Jesus as the Son of God.

Who Jesus Is

6 Water and blood came out from the side of Jesus Christ. It wasn't just water, but water and blood.[n] The Spirit tells about this, because the Spirit is truthful. 7In fact, there are three who tell about it. 8They are the Spirit, the water, and the blood, and they all agree.

9 We believe what people tell us. But we can trust what God says even more, and God is the one who has spoken about his Son. 10If we have faith in God's Son, we have believed what God has said. But if we don't believe what God has said about his Son, it is the same as calling God a liar. 11God has also said that he gave us eternal life and that this life comes to us from his Son. 12And so, if we have God's Son, we have this life. But if we don't have the Son, we don't have this life.

---

[n] *Water and blood came out from the side of Jesus Christ. It wasn't just water, but water and blood*: See John 19.34. It is also possible to translate, "Jesus Christ came by the water of baptism and by the blood of his death! He was not only baptized, but he bled and died." The purpose of the verse is to tell that Jesus was truly human and that he really died.

Knowing about Eternal Life

13 All of you have faith in the Son of God, and I have written to let you know that you have eternal life. [14]We are certain that God will hear our prayers when we ask for what pleases him. [15]And if we know that God listens when we pray, we are sure that our prayers have already been answered.

16 Suppose you see one of our people commit a sin that isn't a deadly sin. You can pray, and that person will be given eternal life. But the sin must not be one that is deadly. [17]Everything that is wrong is sin, but not all sins are deadly.

18 We are sure that God's children do not keep on sinning. God's own Son protects them, and the devil cannot harm them.

19 We are certain that we come from God and that the rest of the world is under the power of the devil.

20 We know that Jesus Christ the Son of God has come and has shown us the true God. And because of Jesus, we now belong to the true God who gives eternal life.

21 Children, you must stay away from idols.

John's Second Letter

1 From the church leader.[a]

To a very special woman and her children.[b] I truly love all of you, and so does everyone else who knows the truth. 2 We love you because the truth is now in our hearts, and it will be there forever.

3 I pray that God the Father and Jesus Christ his Son will be kind and merciful to us! May they give us peace and truth and love.

---

[a] *church leader*: Or "elder" or "presbyter" or "priest."
[b] *very special woman and her children*: A group of the Lord's followers who met together for worship. "The children of your ... sister" (see verse 13) is another group of followers. "Very special" (here and verse 13) probably means "chosen (by the Lord)."

Truth and Love

4 I was very glad to learn that some of your children are obeying the truth, as the Father told us to do. 5Dear friend, I am not writing to tell you and your children to do something you have not done before. I am writing to tell you to love each other, which is the first thing you were told to do. 6Love means that we do what God tells us. And from the beginning, he told you to love him.

7 Many liars have gone out into the world. These deceitful liars are saying that Jesus Christ did not have a truly human body. But they are liars and the enemies of Christ. 8So be sure not to lose what we*c* have worked for. If you do, you won't be given your full reward. 9Don't keep changing what you were taught about Christ, or else God will no longer be with you. But if you hold firmly to what you were taught, both the Father and the Son will be with you. 10If people won't agree to this teaching, don't welcome them into your home or even greet them. 11Greeting them is the same as taking part in their evil deeds.

Final Greetings

12 I have much more to tell you, but I don't want to write it with pen and ink. I want to come and talk to you in person, because that will make us*d* really happy.

13 Greetings from the children of your very special sister.*e*

---

c we: Some manuscripts have "you."

d us: Some manuscripts have "you."

e sister: See the note at verse 1.

John's Third Letter

ABOUT THIS LETTER

In this letter the writer reminds Christian readers that they should help support those who go to other parts of the world to tell others about the Lord. The letter is written to an important church member named Gaius, who had been very helpful to Christians who traveled around and preached the good news.

A QUICK LOOK AT THIS LETTER

1. Greetings to Gaius (1-4)
2. The Importance of Working Together (5-12)
3. Final Greetings (13-15)

1 From the church leader.*

To my dear friend Gaius.

I love you because we follow the truth, ²dear friend, and I pray that all goes well for you. I hope that you are as strong in body, as I know you are in spirit. ³It makes me very happy when the Lord's followers come by and speak openly of how you obey the truth. ⁴Nothing brings me greater happiness than to hear that my children* are obeying the truth.

---

* *church leader*: Or "elder" or "presbyter" or "priest."

* *children*: Probably persons that the leader had led to be followers of the Lord.

Working Together

5 Dear friend, you have always been faithful in helping other followers of the Lord, even the ones you didn't know before. 6They have told the church about your love. They say you were good enough to welcome them and to send them on their mission in a way that God's servants deserve. 7When they left to tell others about the Lord, they decided not to accept help from anyone who wasn't a follower. 8We must support people like them, so that we can take part in what they are doing to spread the truth.

9 I wrote to the church. But Diotrephes likes to be the number-one leader, and he won't pay any attention to us. 10So if I come, I will remind him of how he has been attacking us with gossip. Not only has he been doing this, but he refuses to welcome any of the Lord's followers who come by. And when other church members want to welcome them, he puts them out of the church.

11 Dear friend, don't copy the evil deeds of others! Follow the example of people who do kind deeds. They are God's children, but those who are always doing evil have never seen God.

12 Everyone speaks well of Demetrius, and so does the true message that he teaches. I also speak well of him, and you know what I say is true.

Final Greetings

13 I have much more to say to you, but I don't want to write it with pen and ink. 14I hope to see you soon, and then we can talk in person.

15 I pray that God will bless you with peace!

Your friends send their greetings. Please give a personal greeting to each of our friends.

A Letter from Jude

ABOUT THIS LETTER

Jude has much to say about false teachers. They are evil! God will punish them, and Christians should not follow their teaching or imitate the way they live.

Jude ends with a beautiful prayer-like blessing:
Offer praise to God our Savior because of our Lord Jesus Christ! Only God can keep you from falling and make you pure and joyful in his glorious presence. Before time began and now and forevermore, God is worthy of glory, honor, power, and authority. Amen. (24, 25)

1 From Jude, a servant of Jesus Christ and the brother of James.

To all who are chosen and loved by God the Father and are kept safe by Jesus Christ.

2 I pray that God will greatly bless you with kindness, peace, and love!

False Teachers

3 My dear friends, I really wanted to write you about God's saving power at work in our lives. But instead, I must write and ask you to defend the faith

that God has once for all given to his people. ⁴Some godless people have sneaked in among us and are saying, "God treats us much better than we deserve, and so it is all right to be immoral." They even deny that we must obey Jesus Christ as our only Master and Lord. But long ago the Scriptures warned that these godless people were doomed.

5 Don't forget what happened to those people that the Lord rescued from Egypt. Some of them did not have faith, and he later destroyed them. ⁶You also know about the angels*ᵃ* who didn't do their work and left their proper places. God chained them with everlasting chains and is now keeping them in dark pits until the great day of judgment. ⁷We should also be warned by what happened to the cities of Sodom and Gomorrah*ᵇ* and the nearby towns. Their people became immoral and did all sorts of sexual sins. Then God made an example of them and punished them with eternal fire.

8 The people I am talking about are behaving just like those dreamers who destroyed their own bodies. They reject all authority and insult angels. ⁹Even Michael, the chief angel, didn't dare to insult the devil, when the two of them were arguing about the body of Moses.*ᶜ* All Michael said was, "The Lord will punish you!"

ᵃ *angels*: This may refer to the angels who liked the women on earth so much that they came down and married them (see Genesis 6.2).

ᵇ *Sodom and Gomorrah*: During the time of Abraham the Lord destroyed these cities because the people there were so evil.

ᶜ *Michael … the body of Moses*: This refers to what was said in an ancient Jewish book about Moses.

10 But these people insult powers they don't know anything about. They are like senseless animals that end up getting destroyed, because they live only by their feelings. [11]Now they are in for real trouble. They have followed Cain's example[d] and have made the same mistake that Balaam[e] did by caring only for money. They have also rebelled against God, just as Korah did.[f] Because of all this, they will be destroyed.

12 These people are filthy minded, and by their shameful and selfish actions they spoil the meals you eat together. They are like clouds blown along by the wind, but never bringing any rain. They are like leafless trees, uprooted and dead, and unable to produce fruit. [13]Their shameful deeds show up like foam on wild ocean waves. They are like wandering stars forever doomed to the darkest pits of hell.

14 Enoch was the seventh person after Adam, and he was talking about these people when he said:

Look! The Lord is coming with thousands and thousands of holy angels [15]to judge everyone. He will punish all those ungodly people for all the evil things they have done. The Lord will

---

[d] *Cain's example*: Cain murdered his brother Abel.

[e] *Balaam*: According to the biblical account, Balaam refused to curse the people of Israel for profit (see Numbers 22.18; 24.13), though he led them to be unfaithful to the Lord (see Numbers 25.1-3; 31.16). But by New Testament times, some Jewish teachers taught that Balaam was greedy and did accept money to curse them.

[f] *just as Korah did*: Together with Dathan and Abiram, Korah led a rebellion against Moses and Aaron (see Numbers 16.1-35; 26.9,10).

surely punish those ungodly sinners for every
evil thing they have ever said about him.

16 These people grumble and complain and live by
their own selfish desires. They brag about themselves
and flatter others to get what they want.

More Warnings

17 My dear friends, remember the warning you
were given by the apostles of our Lord Jesus Christ.
18 They told you that near the end of time, selfish and
godless people would start making fun of God. 19 And
now these people are already making you turn against
each other. They think only about this life, and they
don't have God's Spirit.

20 Dear friends, keep building on the foundation of
your most holy faith, as the Holy Spirit helps you to
pray. 21 And keep in step with God's love, as you wait
for our Lord Jesus Christ to show how kind he is by
giving you eternal life. 22 Be helpful to g all who may
have doubts. 23 Rescue any who need to be saved, as
you would rescue someone from a fire. Then with
fear in your own hearts, have mercy on everyone
who needs it. But hate even the clothes of those who
have been made dirty by their filthy deeds.

Final Prayer

24-25 Offer praise to God our Savior because of our
Lord Jesus Christ! Only God can keep you from falling
and make you pure and joyful in his glorious presence.
Before time began and now and forevermore, God is
worthy of glory, honor, power, and authority. Amen.

---

g *Be helpful to*: Some manuscripts have "Correct."

Revelation

ABOUT THIS BOOK

This book tells what John had seen in a vision about
God's message and about what Jesus Christ had said
and done (1.2). The message has three main parts:
(1) There are evil forces at work in the world, and
Christians may have to suffer and die; (2) Jesus is Lord,
and he will conquer all people and powers who oppose
God; and (3) God has wonderful rewards in store for his
faithful people, who remain faithful to him, especially
for those who lose their lives in his service.

This was a powerful message of hope for those early
Christians who had to suffer or die for their faith. In this
book they learned that, in spite of the cruel power of the
Roman Empire, the Lamb of God would win the final
victory. And this gave them the courage to be faithful.

Because this book is so full of visions that use
ideas and word pictures from the Old Testament, it
was like a book with secret messages for the early
Christians. The book could be passed around and be
understood by Christians, but an official of the Roman
Empire would not be able to understand it. For example,
when the fall of Babylon is described (chapter 18), the
early Christians knew that this pointed to the fall of the
Roman Empire. This knowledge gave them hope.

At the beginning of this book there are seven letters
to seven churches. These letters show what different
groups of the Lord's followers will do in times of
persecution (2.1–3.22).

The author uses many powerful images to describe God's power and judgment. The vision of God's throne (4.1-11) and of the scroll and the Lamb (5.1-14) show that God and Christ are in control of all human and supernatural events. Opening seven seals (6.1-8.5), blowing the seven trumpets (8.6-11.19), and emptying the seven bowls (16.1-21) are among the visions that show God's fierce judgment on the world.

After the suffering has ended, God's faithful people will receive the greatest blessing of all:

> God's home is now with his people. He will live with them, and they will be his own. Yes, God will make his home among his people. He will wipe all tears from their eyes, and there will be no more death, suffering, crying, or pain. These things of the past are gone forever. (21.3b,4)

A QUICK LOOK AT THIS BOOK

1 This is what God showed to Jesus Christ, so that he could tell his servants what must happen soon. Christ then sent his angel with the message to his servant John. ²And John told everything that he had seen about God's message and about what Jesus Christ had said and done.

3 God will bless everyone who reads this prophecy to others,ᵃ and he will bless everyone who hears and obeys it. The time is almost here.

4 From John to the seven churches in Asia.ᵇ

I pray that you will be blessed
    with kindness and peace from God,
    who is and was and is coming.
May you receive kindness and peace
    from the seven spirits
    before the throne of God.
⁵ May kindness and peace be yours
    from Jesus Christ, the faithful witness.

Jesus was the first to conquer death,
    and he is the ruler of all earthly kings.
Christ loves us, and by his blood
    he set us free from our sins.
⁶ He lets us rule as kings
    and serve God his Father as priests.
To him be glory and power
    forever and ever! Amen.

ᵃ *who reads this prophecy to others*: A public reading, in a worship service.
ᵇ *Asia*: The section 1.4–3.22 is in the form of a letter. Asia was in the eastern part of the Roman empire and is present day Turkey.

⁷ Look! He is coming with the clouds.
　Everyone will see him,
　　even the ones
　　who stuck a sword through him.
　All people on earth will weep
　　because of him.
　Yes, it will happen! Amen.

8 The Lord God says, "I am Alpha and Omega,^c the one who is and was and is coming. I am God All-Powerful!"

A Vision of the Risen Lord

9 I am John, a follower together with all of you. We suffer because Jesus is our king, but he gives us the strength to endure. I was sent to Patmos Island,^d because I had preached God's message and had told about Jesus. ¹⁰On the Lord's day the Spirit took control of me, and behind me I heard a loud voice that sounded like a trumpet. ¹¹The voice said, "Write in a book what you see. Then send it to the seven churches in Ephesus, Smyrna, Pergamum, Thyatira, Sardis, Philadelphia, and Laodicea."^e

12 When I turned to see who was speaking to me, I saw seven gold lampstands. ¹³There with the lampstands was someone who seemed to be the Son of Man.^f

---

^c *Alpha and Omega*: The first and last letters of the Greek alphabet, which sometimes mean "first" and "last."

^d *Patmos Island*: A small island where prisoners were sometimes kept by the Romans.

^e *Ephesus…Laodicea*: Ephesus was in the center with the six other cities forming a half-circle around it.

^f *Son of Man*: That is, Jesus.

He was wearing a robe that reached down to his feet, and a gold cloth was wrapped around his chest. ¹⁴His head and his hair were white as wool or snow, and his eyes looked like flames of fire. ¹⁵His feet were glowing like bronze being heated in a furnace, and his voice sounded like the roar of a waterfall. ¹⁶He held seven stars in his right hand, and a sharp double-edged sword was coming from his mouth. His face was shining as bright as the sun at noon.

17 When I saw him, I fell at his feet like a dead person. But he put his right hand on me and said:

Don't be afraid! I am the first, the last, ¹⁸and the living one. I died, but now I am alive forevermore, and I have the keys to death and the world of the dead.ᵍ ¹⁹Write what you have seen and what is and what will happen after these things. ²⁰I will explain the mystery of the seven stars that you saw at my right side and the seven gold lampstands. The seven stars are the angelsʰ of the seven churches, and the lampstands are the seven churches.

The Letter to Ephesus

2 This is what you must write to the angel of the church in Ephesus:

I am the one who holds the seven stars in my right hand, and I walk among the seven gold lampstands. Listen to what I say.

ᵍ *keys to death and the world of the dead*: That is, power over death and the world of the dead.

ʰ *angels*: Perhaps guardian angels that represent the churches, or they may be church leaders or messengers sent to the churches.

2 I know everything you have done, including your hard work and how you have endured. I know you won't put up with anyone who is evil. When some people pretended to be apostles, you tested them and found out that they were liars. ³You have endured and gone through hard times because of me, and you have not given up.

4 But I do have something against you! And it is this: You don't have as much love as you used to. ⁵Think about where you have fallen from, and then turn back and do as you did at first. If you don't turn back, I will come and take away your lampstand. ⁶But there is one thing you are doing right. You hate what the Nicolaitans*i* are doing, and so do I.

7 If you have ears, listen to what the Spirit says to the churches. I will let everyone who wins the victory eat from the life-giving tree in God's wonderful garden.

The Letter to Smyrna

8 This is what you must write to the angel of the church in Smyrna:

I am the first and the last. I died, but now I am alive! Listen to what I say.

9 I know how much you suffer and how poor you are, but you are rich. I also know the cruel things being said about you by people

---

i Nicolaitans: Nothing else is known about these people, though it is possible that they claimed to be followers of Nicolaus from Antioch (see Acts 6.5).

who claim to be God's people. But they are really not. They are a group that belongs to Satan.

10 Don't worry about what you will suffer. The devil will throw some of you into jail, and you will be tested and made to suffer for ten days. But if you are faithful until you die, I will reward you with a glorious life.*j*

11 If you have ears, listen to what the Spirit says to the churches. Whoever wins the victory will not be hurt by the second death.*k*

The Letter to Pergamum

12 This is what you must write to the angel of the church in Pergamum:

I am the one who has the sharp double-edged sword! Listen to what I say.

13 I know that you live where Satan has his throne.*l* But you have kept true to my name. Right there where Satan lives, my faithful witness Antipas*m* was taken from you and put to death. Even then you did not give up your faith in me.

---

j *a glorious life*: The Greek text has "a crown of life." In ancient times an athlete who had won a contest was rewarded with a crown of flowers as a sign of victory.

k *second death*: The first death is physical death, and the "second death" is eternal death.

l *where Satan has his throne*: The meaning is uncertain, but it may refer to the city as a center of pagan worship or of Emperor worship.

m *Antipas*: Nothing else is known about this man, who is mentioned only here in the New Testament.

14 I do have a few things against you. Some of you are following the teaching of Balaam.[n] Long ago he told Balak to teach the people of Israel to eat food that had been offered to idols and to be immoral. [15]Now some of you are following the teaching of the Nicolaitans.[o] [16]Turn back! If you don't, I will come quickly and fight against these people. And my words will cut like a sword.

17 If you have ears, listen to what the Spirit says to the churches. To everyone who wins the victory, I will give some of the hidden food.[p] I will also give each one a white stone[q] with a new name[r] written on it. No one will know that name except the one who is given the stone.

---

[n] *Balaam*: According to Numbers 22–24, Balaam refused to disobey the Lord. But in other books of the Old Testament, he is spoken of as evil (see Deuteronomy 23.4,5; Joshua 13.22; 24.9,10; Nehemiah 13.2).

[o] *Nicolaitans*: See the note at 2.6.

[p] *hidden food*: When the people of Israel were going through the desert, the Lord provided a special food for them. Some of this was placed in a jar and stored in the sacred chest (see Exodus 16). According to later Jewish teaching, the prophet Jeremiah rescued the sacred chest when the temple was destroyed by the Babylonians. He hid the chest in a cave, where it would stay until God came to save his people.

[q] *white stone*: The meaning of this is uncertain, though it may be the same as a ticket that lets a person into God's banquet where the "hidden food" is eaten. Or it may be a symbol of victory.

[r] *a new name*: Either the name of Christ or God or the name of the follower who is given the stone.

The Letter to Thyatira

18 This is what you must write to the angel of the church in Thyatira:

I am the Son of God! My eyes are like flames of fire, and my feet are like bronze. Listen to what I say.

19 I know everything about you, including your love, your faith, your service, and how you have endured. I know that you are doing more now than you have ever done before. 20But I still have something against you because of that woman Jezebel.[s] She calls herself a prophet, and you let her teach and mislead my servants to do immoral things and to eat food offered to idols. 21I gave her a chance to turn from her sins, but she did not want to stop doing these immoral things.

22 I am going to strike down Jezebel. Everyone who does these immoral things with her will also be punished, if they don't stop. 23I will even kill her followers.[t] Then all the churches will see that I know everyone's thoughts and feelings. I will treat each of you as you deserve.

24 Some of you in Thyatira don't follow Jezebel's teaching. You don't know anything about what her followers call the "deep secrets

---

[s] *Jezebel*: Nothing else is known about her. This may have been her real name or a name that was given to her because she was like Queen Jezebel, who opposed the Lord (see 1 Kings 19.1,2; 21.1-26).

[t] *her followers*: Or "her children."

of Satan." So I won't burden you down with any other commands. 25But until I come, you must hold firmly to the teaching you have.

26 I will give power over the nations to everyone who wins the victory and keeps on obeying me until the end. 27-28I will give each of them the same power that my Father has given me. They will rule the nations with an iron rod and smash those nations to pieces like clay pots. I will also give them the morning star.*

29 If you have ears, listen to what the Spirit says to the churches.

The Letter to Sardis

3 This is what you must write to the angel of the church in Sardis:

I have the seven spirits of God and the seven stars. Listen to what I say.

I know what you are doing. Everyone may think you are alive, but you are dead. 2Wake up! You have only a little strength left, and it is almost gone. So try to become stronger. I have found that you are not completely obeying God. 3Remember the teaching that you were given and that you heard. Hold firmly to it and turn from your sins. If you don't wake up, I will come when you least expect it, just as a thief does.

4 A few of you in Sardis have not dirtied your clothes with sin. You will walk with me in white

---

* *the morning star*: Probably thought of as the star that signals the end of night and the beginning of day. In 22.16 Christ is called the "morning star."

clothes, because you are worthy. [5]Everyone who wins the victory will wear white clothes. Their names will not be erased from the book of life,[v] and I will tell my Father and his angels that they are my followers.

6 If you have ears, listen to what the Spirit says to the churches.

The Letter to Philadelphia

7 This is what you must write to the angel of the church in Philadelphia:

I am the one who is holy and true, and I have the keys that belonged to David.[w] When I open a door, no one can close it. And when I close a door, no one can open it. Listen to what I say.

8 I know everything you have done. And I have placed before you an open door that no one can close. You were not very strong, but you obeyed my message and did not deny that you are my followers.[x] [9]Now you will see what I will do with those people who belong to Satan's group. They claim to be God's people, but they are liars. I will make them come and kneel down at your feet. Then they will know that I love you.

10 You obeyed my message and endured. So I will protect you from the time of testing that

---

[v] *book of life*: The book in which the names of God's people are written.

[w] *the keys that belonged to David*: The keys stand for authority over David's kingdom.

[x] *did not deny that you are my followers*: Or "did not say evil things about me."

everyone in all the world must go through. [11]I am coming soon. So hold firmly to what you have, and no one will take away the crown that you will be given as your reward.

12 Everyone who wins the victory will be made into a pillar in the temple of my God, and they will stay there forever. I will write on each of them the name of my God and the name of his city. It is the new Jerusalem that my God will send down from heaven. I will also write on them my own new name.

13 If you have ears, listen to what the Spirit says to the churches.

The Letter to Laodicea

14 This is what you must write to the angel of the church in Laodicea:

I am the one called Amen! [y] I am the faithful and true witness and the source [z] of God's creation. Listen to what I say.

15 I know everything you have done, and you are not cold or hot. I wish you were either one or the other. [16]But since you are lukewarm and neither cold nor hot, I will spit you out of my mouth. [17]You claim to be rich and successful and to have everything you need. But you don't know how bad off you are. You are pitiful, poor, blind, and naked.

18 Buy your gold from me. It has been refined in a fire, and it will make you rich. Buy white

---

[y] *Amen*: Meaning "Trustworthy."
[z] *source*: Or "beginning."

on the outside. And it was sealed in seven places. ²I saw a mighty angel ask with a loud voice, "Who is worthy to open the scroll and break its seals?" ³No one in heaven or on earth or under the earth was able to open the scroll or see inside it.

4 I cried hard because no one was found worthy to open the scroll or see inside it. ⁵Then one of the elders said to me, "Stop crying and look! The one who is called both the 'Lion from the Tribe of Judah' *e* and 'King David's Great Descendant' *f* has won the victory. He will open the book and its seven seals."

6 Then I looked and saw a Lamb standing in the center of the throne that was surrounded by the four living creatures and the elders. The Lamb looked as if it had once been killed. It had seven horns and seven eyes, which are the seven spirits *g* of God, sent out to all the earth.

7 The Lamb went over and took the scroll from the right hand of the one who sat on the throne. ⁸After he had taken it, the four living creatures and the twenty-four elders knelt down before him. Each of them had a harp and a gold bowl full of incense, *h* which are the prayers of God's people. ⁹Then they sang a new song,

---

e *'Lion from the Tribe of Judah'*: In Genesis 49.9 the tribe of Judah is called a young lion, and King David was from Judah.

f *'King David's Great Descendant'*: The Greek text has "the root of David" which is a title for the Messiah based on Isaiah 11.1,10.

g *the seven spirits*: Some manuscripts have "the spirits."

h *incense*: A material that produces a sweet smell when burned. Sometimes it is a symbol for the prayers of God's people.

"You are worthy
    to receive the scroll and open its seals,
    because you were killed.
And with your own blood you bought for God
        people from every tribe,
    language, nation, and race.
¹⁰ You let them become kings
        and serve God as priests,
    and they will rule on earth."

11 As I looked, I heard the voices of a lot of angels around the throne and the voices of the living creatures and of the elders. There were millions and millions of them, ¹²and they were saying in a loud voice,

"The Lamb who was killed is worthy
    to receive power, riches, wisdom,
    strength, honor, glory, and praise."

13 Then I heard all beings in heaven and on the earth and under the earth and in the sea offer praise. Together, all of them were saying,

"Praise, honor, glory, and strength
        forever and ever
    to the one who sits on the throne
        and to the Lamb!"

14 The four living creatures said "Amen," while the elders knelt down and worshiped.

Opening the Seven Seals

6 At the same time that I saw the Lamb open the first of the seven seals, I heard one of the four living creatures shout with a voice like thunder.

It said, "Come out!" 2Then I saw a white horse. Its rider carried a bow and was given a crown. He had already won some victories, and he went out to win more.

3 When the Lamb opened the second seal, I heard the second living creature say, "Come out!" 4Then another horse came out. It was fiery red. And its rider was given the power to take away all peace from the earth, so that people would slaughter one another. He was also given a big sword.

5 When the Lamb opened the third seal, I heard the third living creature say, "Come out!" Then I saw a black horse, and its rider had a balance scale in one hand. 6I heard what sounded like a voice from somewhere among the four living creatures. It said, "A quart of wheat will cost you a whole day's wages! Three quarts of barley will cost you a day's wages too. But don't ruin the olive oil or the wine."

7 When the Lamb opened the fourth seal, I heard the voice of the fourth living creature say, "Come out!" 8Then I saw a pale green horse. Its rider was named Death, and Death's Kingdom followed behind. They were given power over one fourth of the earth, and they could kill its people with swords, famines, diseases, and wild animals.

9 When the Lamb opened the fifth seal, I saw under the altar the souls of everyone who had been killed for speaking God's message and telling about their faith. 10They shouted, "Master, you are holy and faithful! How long will it be before you judge and punish the people of this earth who killed us?"

11 Then each of those who had been killed was given a white robe and told to rest for a little while.

They had to wait until the complete number of the Lord's other servants and followers would be killed.

12 When I saw the Lamb open the sixth seal, I looked and saw a great earthquake. The sun turned as dark as sackcloth,[i] and the moon became as red as blood. [13]The stars in the sky fell to earth, just like figs shaken loose by a windstorm. [14]Then the sky was rolled up like a scroll,[j] and all mountains and islands were moved from their places.

15 The kings of the earth, its famous people, and its military leaders hid in caves or behind rocks on the mountains. They hid there together with the rich and the powerful and with all the slaves and free people. [16]Then they shouted to the mountains and the rocks, "Fall on us! Hide us from the one who sits on the throne and from the anger of the Lamb. [17]That terrible day has come! God and the Lamb will show their anger, and who can face it?"

The 144,000 Are Marked for God

7 1-2 After this I saw four angels. Each one was standing on one of the earth's four corners. The angels held back the four winds, so that no wind would blow on the earth or on the sea or on any tree. These angels had also been given the power to harm the earth and the sea. Then I saw another angel come up from where the sun rises in the east, and he was ready to put the mark of the living God on people.

---

[i] *sackcloth*: A rough, dark-colored cloth made from goat or camel hair and used to make grain sacks. It was worn in times of trouble or sorrow.

[j] *scroll*: See the note at 5.1.

He shouted to the four angels, ³"Don't harm the earth or the sea or any tree! Wait until I have marked the foreheads of the servants of our God."

4 Then I heard how many people had been marked on the forehead. There were one hundred forty-four thousand, and they came from every tribe of Israel:

> ⁵ 12,000 from Judah,
> 12,000 from Reuben,
> 12,000 from Gad,
> ⁶ 12,000 from Asher,
> 12,000 from Naphtali,
> 12,000 from Manasseh,
> ⁷ 12,000 from Simeon,
> 12,000 from Levi,
> 12,000 from Issachar,
> ⁸ 12,000 from Zebulun,
> 12,000 from Joseph, and
> 12,000 from Benjamin.

People from Every Nation

9 After this, I saw a large crowd with more people than could be counted. They were from every race, tribe, nation, and language, and they stood before the throne and before the Lamb. They wore white robes and held palm branches in their hands, ¹⁰as they shouted,

> "Our God, who sits upon the throne,
>   has the power to save his people,
> and so does the Lamb."

11 The angels who stood around the throne knelt in front of it with their faces to the ground. The elders and the four living creatures knelt there with them.

Then they all worshiped God ¹²and said,

> "Amen! Praise, glory, wisdom,
> thanks, honor, power, and strength
>   belong to our God forever and ever!
> Amen!"

13 One of the elders asked me, "Do you know who these people are that are dressed in white robes? Do you know where they come from?"

14 "Sir," I answered, "you must know."

Then he told me:

> "These are the ones
>   who have gone through the great suffering.
> They have washed their robes
>   in the blood of the Lamb
>   and have made them white.
> ¹⁵ And so they stand before the throne of God
>   and worship him in his temple
>   day and night.
> The one who sits on the throne
>   will spread his tent over them.
> ¹⁶ They will never hunger or thirst again,
>   and they won't be troubled
>   by the sun or any scorching heat.
>
> ¹⁷ The Lamb in the center of the throne
>   will be their shepherd.
> He will lead them
>   to streams of life-giving water,
>   and God will wipe all tears from their eyes."

The Seventh Seal Is Opened

8 When the Lamb opened the seventh seal, there was silence in heaven for about half an hour. ²I noticed that the seven angels who stood before God were each given a trumpet.

3 Another angel, who had a gold container for incense,[k] came and stood at the altar. This one was given a lot of incense to offer with the prayers of God's people on the gold altar in front of the throne. 4 Then the smoke of the incense, together with the prayers of God's people, went up to God from the hand of the angel.

5 After this, the angel filled the incense container with fire from the altar and threw it on the earth. Thunder roared, lightning flashed, and the earth shook.

The Trumpets

6 The seven angels now got ready to blow their trumpets.

7 When the first angel blew his trumpet, hail and fire mixed with blood were thrown down on the earth. A third of the earth, a third of the trees, and a third of all green plants were burned.

8 When the second angel blew his trumpet, something like a great fiery mountain was thrown into the sea. A third of the sea turned to blood, 9 a third of the living creatures in the sea died, and a third of the ships were destroyed.

10 When the third angel blew his trumpet, a great star fell from heaven. It was burning like a torch, and it fell on a third of the rivers and on a third of the springs of water. 11 The name of the star was Bitter, and a third of the water turned bitter. Many people died because the water was so bitter.

---

[k] *incense*: See the note at 5.8.

12 When the fourth angel blew his trumpet, a third of the sun, a third of the moon, and a third of the stars were struck. They each lost a third of their light. So during a third of the day there was no light, and a third of the night was also without light.

13 Then I looked and saw a lone eagle flying across the sky. It was shouting, "Trouble, trouble, trouble to everyone who lives on earth! The other three angels are now going to blow their trumpets."

9 When the fifth angel blew his trumpet, I saw a star*l* fall from the sky to earth. It was given the key to the tunnel that leads down to the deep pit. ²As it opened the tunnel, smoke poured out like the smoke of a great furnace. The sun and the air turned dark because of the smoke. ³Locusts*m* came out of the smoke and covered the earth. They were given the same power that scorpions have.

4 The locusts were told not to harm the grass on the earth or any plant or any tree. They were to punish only those people who did not have God's mark on their foreheads. ⁵The locusts were allowed to make them suffer for five months, but not to kill them. The suffering they caused was like the sting of a scorpion. ⁶In those days people will want to die, but they will not be able to. They will hope for death, but it will escape from them.

7 These locusts looked like horses ready for battle. On their heads they wore something like gold crowns,

---

l star: In the ancient world, stars were often thought of as living beings, such as angels.

m Locusts: A type of grasshopper that comes in swarms and causes great damage to crops.

and they had human faces. [8]Their hair was like a woman's long hair, and their teeth were like those of a lion. [9]On their chests they wore armor made of iron. Their wings roared like an army of horse-drawn chariots rushing into battle. [10]Their tails were like a scorpion's tail with a stinger that had the power to hurt someone for five months. [11]Their king was the angel in charge of the deep pit. In Hebrew his name was Abaddon, and in Greek it was Apollyon.[n]

12 The first horrible thing has now happened! But wait. Two more horrible things will happen soon.

13 Then the sixth angel blew his trumpet. I heard a voice speak from the four corners of the gold altar that stands in the presence of God. [14]The voice spoke to this angel and said, "Release the four angels who are tied up beside the great Euphrates River." [15]The four angels had been prepared for this very hour and day and month and year. Now they were set free to kill a third of all people.

16 By listening, I could tell there were more than two hundred million of these war horses. [17]In my vision their riders wore fiery-red, dark-blue, and yellow armor on their chests. The heads of the horses looked like lions, with fire and smoke and sulphur coming out of their mouths. [18]One third of all people were killed by the three terrible troubles caused by the fire, the smoke, and the sulphur. [19]The horses had powerful mouths, and their tails were like poisonous snakes that bite and hurt.

20 The people who lived through these terrible troubles did not turn away from the idols they had made,

---

[n] *Abaddon...Apollyon*: The Hebrew word "Abaddon" and the Greek word "Apollyon" each mean "destruction."

and they did not stop worshiping demons. They kept on worshiping idols that were made of gold, silver, bronze, stone, and wood. Not one of these idols could see, hear, or walk. 21No one stopped murdering or practicing witchcraft or being immoral or stealing.

The Angel and the Little Scroll

10 I saw another powerful angel come down from heaven. This one was covered with a cloud, and a rainbow was over his head. His face was like the sun, his legs were like columns of fire, 2and with his hand he held a little scroll*o* that had been unrolled. He stood there with his right foot on the sea and his left foot on the land. 3Then he shouted with a voice that sounded like a growling lion. Thunder roared seven times.

4 After the thunder stopped, I was about to write what it had said. But a voice from heaven shouted, "Keep it secret! Don't write these things."

5 The angel I had seen standing on the sea and the land then held his right hand up toward heaven. 6He made a promise in the name of God who lives forever and who created heaven, earth, the sea, and every living creature. The angel said, "You won't have to wait any longer. 7God told his secret plans to his servants the prophets, and it will all happen by the time the seventh angel sounds his trumpet."

8 Once again the voice from heaven spoke to me. It said, "Go and take the open scroll from the hand of the angel standing on the sea and the land."

9 When I went over to ask the angel for the little scroll, the angel said, "Take the scroll and eat it! Your

---

o scroll: See the note at 5.1.

stomach will turn sour, but the taste in your mouth will be as sweet as honey." ¹⁰I took the little scroll from the hand of the angel and ate it. The taste was as sweet as honey, but my stomach turned sour.

11 Then some voices said, "Keep on telling what will happen to the people of many nations, races, and languages, and also to kings."

The Two Witnesses

11 An angel gave me a measuring stick and said: Measure around God's temple. Be sure to include the altar and everyone worshiping there. ²But don't measure the courtyard outside the temple building. Leave it out. It has been given to those people who don't know God, and they will trample all over the holy city for forty-two months. ³My two witnesses will wear sackcloth,ᵖ while I let them preach for one thousand two hundred sixty days.

4 These two witnesses are the two olive trees and the two lampstands that stand in the presence of the Lord who rules the earth. ⁵Any enemy who tries to harm them will be destroyed by the fire that comes out of their mouths. ⁶They have the power to lock up the sky and to keep rain from falling while they are prophesying. And whenever they want to, they can turn water to blood and cause all kinds of terrible troubles on earth.

7 After the two witnesses have finished preaching God's message, the beast that lives in the deep pit will come up and fight against them. It will win the battle

---

ᵖ *sackcloth*: See the note at 6.12.

and kill them. ⁸Their bodies will be left lying in the streets of the same great city where their Lord was nailed to a cross. And that city is spiritually like the city of Sodom or the country of Egypt.

9 For three and a half days the people of every nation, tribe, language, and race will stare at the bodies of these two witnesses and refuse to let them be buried. ¹⁰Everyone on earth will celebrate and be happy. They will give gifts to each other, because of what happened to the two prophets who caused them so much trouble. ¹¹But three and a half days later, God will breathe life into their bodies. They will stand up, and everyone who sees them will be terrified.

12 The witnesses then heard a loud voice from heaven, saying, "Come up here." And while their enemies were watching, they were taken up to heaven in a cloud. ¹³At that same moment there was a terrible earthquake that destroyed a tenth of the city. Seven thousand people were killed, and the rest were frightened and praised the God who rules in heaven.

14 The second horrible thing has now happened! But the third one will be here soon.

The Seventh Trumpet

15 At the sound of the seventh trumpet, loud voices were heard in heaven. They said,

"Now the kingdom of this world
    belongs to our Lord
    and to his Chosen One!
And he will rule forever and ever!"

16 Then the twenty-four elders, who were seated on thrones in God's presence, knelt down and worshiped him. ¹⁷They said,

"Lord God All-Powerful,
　　you are and you were,
　　　and we thank you.
You used your great power
　　and started ruling.
  18 When the nations got angry,
　　　you became angry too!
Now the time has come
　　for the dead to be judged.
It is time for you to reward
　　your servants the prophets
and all of your people
　　who honor your name,
　　　no matter who they are.
It is time to destroy everyone
　　who has destroyed the earth."

19 The door to God's temple in heaven was then
opened, and the sacred chest[q] could be seen inside the
temple. I saw lightning and heard roars of thunder.
The earth trembled and huge hailstones fell to the
ground.

The Woman and the Dragon

12 Something important appeared in the sky.
It was a woman whose clothes were the sun.
The moon was under her feet, and a crown made of
twelve stars was on her head. 2She was about to give
birth, and she was crying because of the great pain.

_____

q sacred chest: In Old Testament times the sacred chest was
　kept in the tent used for worship. It was the symbol of
　God's presence with his people and also of his agreement
　with them.

3 Something else appeared in the sky. It was a huge red dragon with seven heads and ten horns, and a crown on each of its seven heads. 4With its tail, it dragged a third of the stars from the sky and threw them down to the earth. Then the dragon turned toward the woman, because it wanted to eat her child as soon as it was born.

5 The woman gave birth to a son, who would rule all nations with an iron rod. The boy was snatched away. He was taken to God and placed on his throne. 6The woman ran into the desert to a place that God had prepared for her. There she would be taken care of for one thousand two hundred sixty days.

Michael Fights the Dragon

7 A war broke out in heaven. Michael and his angels were fighting against the dragon and its angels. 8But the dragon lost the battle. It and its angels were forced out of their places in heaven 9and were thrown down to the earth. Yes, that old snake and his angels were thrown out of heaven! That snake, who fools everyone on earth, is known as the devil and Satan. 10Then I heard a voice from heaven shout,

> "Our God has shown his saving power,
>   and his kingdom has come!
> God's own Chosen One
>   has shown his authority.
> Satan accused our people
>   in the presence of God day and night.
> Now he has been thrown out!

11 Our people defeated Satan
    because of the blood[r] of the Lamb
    and the message of God.
  They were willing to give up their lives.

12 The heavens should rejoice,
    together with everyone who lives there.
  But pity the earth and the sea,
    because the devil was thrown down
    to the earth.
  He knows his time is short,
    and he is very angry."

13 When the dragon realized that it had been thrown down to the earth, it tried to make trouble for the woman who had given birth to a son. 14But the woman was given two wings like those of a huge eagle, so that she could fly into the desert. There she would escape from the snake and be taken care of for a time, two times, and half a time.

15 The snake then spewed out water like a river to sweep the woman away. 16But the earth helped her and swallowed the water that had come from the dragon's mouth. 17This made the dragon terribly angry with the woman. So it started a war against the rest of her children. They are the people who obey God and are faithful to what Jesus did and taught. 18The dragon[s] stood on the beach beside the sea.

---

[r] blood: Or "death."
[s] The dragon: The text has "he," and some manuscripts have "I."

The Two Beasts

13 I looked and saw a beast coming up from the sea. This one had ten horns and seven heads, and a crown was on each of its ten horns. On each of its heads were names that were an insult to God. ²The beast that I saw had the body of a leopard, the feet of a bear, and the mouth of a lion. The dragon handed over its own power and throne and great authority to this beast. ³One of its heads seemed to have been fatally wounded, but now it was well. Everyone on earth marveled at this beast, ⁴and they worshiped the dragon who had given its authority to the beast. They also worshiped the beast and said, "No one is like this beast! No one can fight against it."

5 The beast was allowed to brag and claim to be God, and for forty-two months it was allowed to rule. ⁶The beast cursed God, and it cursed the name of God. It even cursed the place where God lives, as well as everyone who lives in heaven with God. ⁷It was allowed to fight against God's people and defeat them. It was also given authority over the people of every tribe, nation, language, and race. ⁸The beast was worshiped by everyone whose name wasn't written before the time of creation in the book of the Lamb who was killed.ᶠ

9 If you have ears, then listen!

10 If you are doomed to be captured,
    you will be captured.

If you are doomed to be killed by a sword,
    you will be killed by a sword.

ᶠ *wasn't written…was killed*: Or "not written in the book of the Lamb who was killed before the time of creation."

This means that God's people must learn to endure and be faithful!

11 I now saw another beast. This one came out of the ground. It had two horns like a lamb, but spoke like a dragon. [12] It worked for the beast whose fatal wound had been healed. And it used all its authority to force the earth and its people to worship that beast. [13] It worked mighty miracles, and while people watched, it even made fire come down from the sky.

14 This second beast fooled people on earth by working miracles for the first one. Then it talked them into making an idol in the form of the beast that did not die after being wounded by a sword. [15] It was allowed to put breath into the idol, so that it could speak. Everyone who refused to worship the idol of the beast was put to death. [16] All people were forced to put a mark on their right hand or forehead. Whether they were powerful or weak, rich or poor, free people or slaves, [17] they all had to have this mark, or else they could not buy or sell anything. This mark stood for the name of the beast and for the number of its name.

18 You need wisdom to understand the number of the beast! But if you are smart enough, you can figure this out. Its number is six hundred sixty-six, and it stands for a person.

The Lamb and His 144,000 Followers

14 I looked and saw the Lamb standing on Mount Zion![u] With him were a hundred forty-four thousand, who had his name and his Father's name written on their foreheads. [2] Then I heard a sound

---

[u] *Mount Zion*: Another name for Jerusalem.

from heaven that was like a roaring flood or loud thunder or even like the music of harps. ³And a new song was being sung in front of God's throne and in front of the four living creatures and the elders. No one could learn that song, except the one hundred forty-four thousand who had been rescued from the earth. ⁴All of these are pure virgins, and they follow the Lamb wherever he leads. They have been rescued to be presented to God and the Lamb as the most precious people ᵛ on earth. ⁵They never tell lies, and they are innocent.

The Messages of the Three Angels

6 I saw another angel. This one was flying across the sky and had the eternal good news to announce to the people of every race, tribe, language, and nation on earth. ⁷The angel shouted, "Worship and honor God! The time has come for him to judge everyone. Kneel down before the one who created heaven and earth, the oceans, and every stream."

8 A second angel followed and said, "The great city of Babylon has fallen! This is the city that made all nations drunk and immoral. Now God is angry, and Babylon has fallen."

9 Finally, a third angel came and shouted:

Here is what will happen if you worship the beast and the idol and have the mark of the beast on your hand or forehead. ¹⁰You will have to drink

---

ᵛ *the most precious people*: The Greek text has "the first people." The Law of Moses taught that the first-born of all animals and the first part of the harvest were special and belonged to the Lord.

the wine that God gives to everyone who makes him angry. You will feel his mighty anger, and you will be tortured with fire and burning sulphur, while the holy angels and the Lamb look on.

11 If you worship the beast and the idol and accept the mark of its name, you will be tortured day and night. The smoke from your torture will go up forever and ever, and you will never be able to rest.

12 God's people must learn to endure. They must also obey his commands and have faith in Jesus.

13 Then I heard a voice from heaven say, "Put this in writing. From now on, the Lord will bless everyone who has faith in him when they die."

The Spirit answered, "Yes, they will rest from their hard work, and they will be rewarded for what they have done."

The Earth Is Harvested

14 I looked and saw a bright cloud, and someone who seemed to be the Son of Man [w] was sitting on the cloud. He wore a gold crown on his head and held a sharp sickle [x] in his hand. 15 An angel came out of the temple and shouted, "Start cutting with your sickle! Harvest season is here, and all crops on earth are ripe." 16 The one on the cloud swung his sickle and harvested the crops.

17 Another angel with a sharp sickle then came out of the temple in heaven. 18 After this, an angel with

---

[w] *Son of Man*: See the note at 1.13.

[x] *sickle*: A knife with a long curved blade, used to cut grain and other crops.

power over fire came from the altar and shouted to the angel who had the sickle. He said, "All grapes on earth are ripe! Harvest them with your sharp sickle." [19]The angel swung his sickle on earth and cut off its grapes. He threw them into a pit[y] where they were trampled on as a sign of God's anger. [20]The pit was outside the city, and when the grapes were mashed, blood flowed out. The blood turned into a river that was about two hundred miles long and almost deep enough to cover a horse.

The Last of the Terrible Troubles

15 After this, I looked at the sky and saw something else that was strange and important. Seven angels were bringing the last seven terrible troubles. When these are ended, God will no longer be angry.

2 Then I saw something that looked like a glass sea mixed with fire, and people were standing on it. They were the ones who had defeated the beast and the idol and the number that tells the name of the beast. God had given them harps, [3]and they were singing the song that his servant Moses and the Lamb had sung. They were singing,

"Lord God All-Powerful,
    you have done great and marvelous things.
You are the ruler of all nations,
    and you do what is right and fair.
[4] Lord,
    who doesn't honor and praise your name?

---

[y] pit: It was the custom to put grapes in a pit (called a wine press) and stomp on them to make juice that would later turn to wine.

You alone are holy,
and all nations will come and worship you,
because you have shown
that you judge with fairness."

5 After this, I noticed something else in heaven.
The sacred tent used for a temple was open. 6 And the
seven angels who were bringing the terrible troubles
were coming out of it. They were dressed in robes of
pure white linen and wore belts made of pure gold.
7 One of the four living creatures gave each of the
seven angels a bowl made of gold. These bowls were
filled with the anger of God who lives forever and
ever. 8 The temple quickly filled with smoke from the
glory and power of God. No one could enter it until
the seven angels had finished pouring out the seven
last troubles.

The Bowls of God's Anger

16 From the temple I heard a voice shout to the
seven angels, "Go and empty the seven bowls
of God's anger on the earth."

2 The first angel emptied his bowl on the earth. At
once ugly and painful sores broke out on everyone
who had the mark of the beast and worshiped the idol.

3 The second angel emptied his bowl on the sea.
Right away the sea turned into blood like that of a
dead person, and every living thing in the sea died.

4 The third angel emptied his bowl into the rivers
and streams. At once they turned to blood. 5 Then I
heard the angel, who has power over water, say,

"You have always been,
and you always will be the holy God.
You had the right to judge in this way.

⁶ They poured out the blood[z] of your people
and your prophets.
So you gave them blood to drink,
as they deserve!"
⁷ After this, I heard the altar shout,
"Yes, Lord God All-Powerful,
your judgments are honest and fair."

8 The fourth angel emptied his bowl on the sun, and it began to scorch people like fire. ⁹Everyone was scorched by its great heat, and all of them cursed the name of God who had power over these terrible troubles. But no one turned to God and praised him.

10 The fifth angel emptied his bowl on the throne of the beast. At once darkness covered its kingdom, and its people began biting their tongues in pain. ¹¹And because of their painful sores, they cursed the God who rules in heaven. But still they did not stop doing evil things.

12 The sixth angel emptied his bowl on the great Euphrates River, and it completely dried up to make a road for the kings from the east. ¹³An evil spirit that looked like a frog came out of the mouth of the dragon. One also came out of the mouth of the beast, and another out of the mouth of the false prophet. ¹⁴These evil spirits had the power to work miracles. They went to every king on earth, to bring them together for a war against God All-Powerful. But that will be the day of God's great victory.

15 Remember that Christ says, "When I come, it will surprise you like a thief! But God will bless you,

---

[z] *They poured out the blood*: A way of saying "They murdered."

if you are awake and ready. Then you won't have to walk around naked and be ashamed."

16 Those armies came together in a place that in Hebrew is called Armagedon.[a]

17 As soon as the seventh angel emptied his bowl in the air, a loud voice from the throne in the temple shouted, "It's done!" 18 There were flashes of lightning, roars of thunder, and the worst earthquake in all history. 19 The great city of Babylon split into three parts, and the cities of other nations fell. So God made Babylon drink from the wine cup that was filled with his anger. 20 Every island ran away, and the mountains disappeared. 21 Hailstones, weighing about a hundred pounds each, fell from the sky on people. Finally, the people cursed God, because the hail was so terrible.

The Prostitute and the Beast

17 One of the seven angels who had emptied the bowls came over and said to me, "Come on! I will show you how God will punish that shameless prostitute who sits on many oceans. 2 Every king on earth has slept with her, and her shameless ways are like wine that has made everyone on earth drunk."

3 With the help of the Spirit, the angel took me into the desert, where I saw a woman sitting on a red beast. The beast was covered with names that were an insult to God, and it had seven heads and ten horns. 4 The

---

[a] Armagedon: The Hebrew form of the name would be "Har Megeddo," meaning "Hill of Megeddo," where many battles were fought in ancient times (see Judges 5.19; 2 Kings 23.29, 30).

woman was dressed in purple and scarlet robes, and she wore jewelry made of gold, precious stones, and pearls. In her hand she held a gold cup filled with the filthy and nasty things she had done. [5]On her forehead a mysterious name was written:

I AM THE GREAT CITY OF BABYLON,
THE MOTHER OF EVERY IMMORAL
AND FILTHY THING ON EARTH.

[6]I could tell that the woman was drunk on the blood of God's people who had given their lives for Jesus. This surprising sight amazed me, [7]and the angel said:

Why are you so amazed? I will explain the mystery about this woman and about the beast she is sitting on, with its seven heads and ten horns. [8]The beast you saw is one that used to be and no longer is. It will come back from the deep pit, but only to be destroyed. Everyone on earth whose names were not written in the book of life[b] before the time of creation will be amazed. They will see this beast that used to be and no longer is, but will be once more.

9 Anyone with wisdom can figure this out. The seven heads that the woman is sitting on stand for seven hills. These heads are also seven kings. [10]Five of the kings are dead. One is ruling now, and the other one has not yet come. But when he does, he will rule for only a little while.

11 You also saw a beast that used to be and no longer is. That beast is one of the seven kings

[b] *book of life*: See the note at 3.5.

who will return as the eighth king, but only to be destroyed.

12 The ten horns that you saw are ten more kings, who have not yet come into power, and they will rule with the beast for only a short time. 13 They all think alike and will give their power and authority to the beast. 14 These kings will go to war against the Lamb. But he will defeat them, because he is Lord over all lords and King over all kings. His followers are chosen and special and faithful.

15 The oceans that you saw the prostitute sitting on are crowds of people from all races and languages. 16 The ten horns and the beast will start hating the shameless woman. They will strip off her clothes and leave her naked. Then they will eat her flesh and throw the rest of her body into a fire. 17 God is the one who made these kings all think alike and decide to give their power to the beast. And they will do this until what God has said comes true.

18 The woman you saw is the great city that rules over all kings on earth.

The Fall of Babylon

18 I saw another angel come from heaven. This one had great power, and the earth was bright because of his glory. 2 The angel shouted,

> "Fallen! Powerful Babylon has fallen
>   and is now the home of demons.
> It is the den of every filthy spirit
>   and of all unclean birds,
>   and every dirty and hated animal.

³ Babylon's evil and immoral wine
    has made all nations drunk.
Every king on earth has slept with her,
    and every merchant on earth is rich
        because of her evil desires."

⁴Then I heard another voice from heaven shout,
    "My people,
    you must escape from Babylon.
Don't take part in her sins
    and share her punishment.
⁵ Her sins are piled as high as heaven.
God has remembered the evil
    she has done.
⁶ Treat her as she has treated others.
Make her pay double for what she has done.
Make her drink twice as much
    of what she mixed for others.
⁷ That woman honored herself
    with a life of luxury.
Reward her now with suffering and pain.

"Deep in her heart Babylon said,
    'I am the queen!
Never will I be a widow
    or know what it means to be sad.'
⁸ And so, in a single day
    she will suffer the pain
    of sorrow, hunger, and death.
Fire will destroy her dead body,
    because her judge
    is the powerful Lord God."

9 Every king on earth who slept with her and shared in her luxury will mourn. They will weep, when they see the smoke from that fire. ¹⁰Her sufferings will frighten them, and they will stand at a distance and say,

"Pity that great and powerful city!
     Pity Babylon!
          In a single hour her judgment has come."

11 Every merchant on earth will mourn, because there is no one to buy their goods. ¹²There won't be anyone to buy their gold, silver, jewels, pearls, fine linen, purple cloth, silk, scarlet cloth, sweet-smelling wood, fancy carvings of ivory and wood, as well as things made of bronze, iron, or marble. ¹³No one will buy their cinnamon, spices, incense, myrrh, frankincense,ᶜ wine, olive oil, fine flour, wheat, cattle, sheep, horses, chariots, slaves, and other humans.

¹⁴ Babylon, the things your heart desired
          have all escaped from you.
     Every luxury and all your glory
          will be lost forever.
     You will never get them back.

15 The merchants had become rich because of her. But when they saw her sufferings, they were terrified. They stood at a distance, crying and mourning. ¹⁶Then they shouted,

"Pity the great city of Babylon!

ᶜ *myrrh, frankincense*: Myrrh was a valuable sweet-smelling powder often used in perfume. Frankincense was a valuable powder that was burned to make a sweet smell.

She dressed in fine linen
and wore purple and scarlet cloth.
She had jewelry made of gold
and precious stones and pearls.
¹⁷ Yet in a single hour her riches disappeared."

Every ship captain and passenger and sailor stood at a distance, together with everyone who does business by traveling on the sea. ¹⁸When they saw the smoke from her fire, they shouted, "This was the greatest city ever!"

19 They cried loudly, and in their sorrow they threw dust on their heads, as they said,

"Pity the great city of Babylon!
Everyone who sailed the seas
became rich from her treasures.
But in a single hour the city was destroyed.
²⁰ The heavens should be happy
with God's people
and apostles and prophets.
God has punished her for them."

21 A powerful angel then picked up a huge stone and threw it into the sea. The angel said,

"This is how the great city of Babylon
will be thrown down, never to rise again.
²² The music of harps and singers
and of flutes and trumpets
will no longer be heard.
No workers will ever set up shop in that city,
and the sound of grinding grain
will be silenced forever.
²³ Lamps will no longer shine
anywhere in Babylon,

and couples
    will never again say wedding vows there.
Her merchants ruled the earth,
    and by her witchcraft
    she fooled all nations.
24 On the streets of Babylon
    is found the blood of God's people
    and of his prophets, and everyone else."

19 After this, I heard what sounded like a lot of
voices in heaven, and they were shouting,
    "Praise the Lord!
To our God
    belongs the glorious power to save,
2   because his judgments are honest and fair.
That filthy prostitute ruined the earth
    with shameful deeds.
But God has judged her
and made her pay the price
    for murdering his servants."

3 Then the crowd shouted,
    "Praise the Lord!
Smoke will never stop rising
    from her burning body."

4 After this, the twenty-four elders and the four
living creatures all knelt before the throne of God and
worshiped him. They said, "Amen! Praise the Lord!"

The Marriage Supper of the Lamb

5 From the throne a voice said,
    "If you worship and fear our God,
        give praise to him,
        no matter who you are."

6 Then I heard what seemed to be a large crowd that sounded like a roaring flood and loud thunder all mixed together. They were saying,

"Praise the Lord!
Our Lord God All-Powerful
    now rules as king.
7 So we will be glad and happy
    and give him praise.
The wedding day of the Lamb is here,
    and his bride is ready.
8 She will be given a wedding dress
    made of pure and shining linen.
This linen stands for the good things
    God's people have done."

9 Then the angel told me, "Put this in writing. God will bless everyone who is invited to the wedding feast of the Lamb." The angel also said, "These things that God has said are true."

10 I knelt at the feet of the angel and began to worship him. But the angel said, "Don't do that! I am a servant, just like you and everyone else who tells about Jesus. Don't worship anyone but God. Everyone who tells about Jesus does it by the power of the Spirit."

The Rider on the White Horse

11 I looked and saw that heaven was open, and a white horse was there. Its rider was called Faithful and True, and he is always fair when he judges or goes to war. 12 He had eyes like flames of fire, and he was wearing a lot of crowns. His name was written on him, but he was the only one who knew what the name meant.

13 The rider wore a robe that was covered with[d] blood, and he was known as "The Word of God." 14He was followed by armies from heaven that rode on horses and were dressed in pure white linen. 15From his mouth a sharp sword went out to attack the nations. He will rule them with an iron rod and will show the fierce anger of God All-Powerful by trampling the grapes in the pit where wine is made. 16On the part of the robe that covered his thigh was written, "KING OF KINGS AND LORD OF LORDS."

17 I then saw an angel standing on the sun, and he shouted to all the birds flying in the sky, "Come and join in God's great feast! 18You can eat the flesh of kings, rulers, leaders, horses, riders, free people, slaves, important people, and everyone else."

19 I also saw the beast and all kings of the earth come together. They fought against the rider on the white horse and against his army. 20But the beast was captured and so was the false prophet. This is the same prophet who had worked miracles for the beast, so that he could fool everyone who had the mark of the beast and worshiped the idol. The beast and the false prophet were thrown alive into a lake of burning sulphur. 21And the rest of their army was killed by the sword that came from the mouth of the rider on the horse. Then the birds stuffed themselves on the dead bodies.

The Thousand Years

20 I saw an angel come down from heaven, carrying the key to the deep pit and a big chain. He chained the dragon for a thousand years. It

---

[d] covered with: Some manuscripts have "sprinkled

old snake, who is also known as the devil and Satan.
³Then the angel threw the dragon into the pit. He
locked and sealed it, so that a thousand years would
go by before the dragon could fool the nations again.
But after that, it would have to be set free for a little
while.

4 I saw thrones, and sitting on those thrones were
the ones who had been given the right to judge. I also
saw the souls of the people who had their heads cut
off because they had told about Jesus and preached
God's message. They were the same ones who had
not worshiped the beast or the idol, and they had
refused to let its mark be put on their hands or foreheads. They will come to life and rule with Christ for
a thousand years.

5-6 These people are the first to be raised to life,
and they are especially blessed and holy. The second
death ^{e} has no power over them. They will be priests
for God and Christ and will rule with them for a
thousand years.

No other dead people were raised to life until a
thousand years later.

Satan Is Defeated

7 At the end of the thousand years, Satan will be
set free. ⁸He will fool the countries of Gog and
Magog, which are at the far ends of the earth, and
their people will follow him into battle. They will
have as many followers as there are grains of sand
along the beach, ⁹and they will march all the way
across the earth. They will surround the camp of

---

second death: See the note at 2.11.

God's people and the city that his people love. But fire will come down from heaven and destroy the whole army. ¹⁰Then the devil who fooled them will be thrown into the lake of fire and burning sulphur. He will be there with the beast and the false prophet, and they will be in pain day and night forever and ever.

The Judgment at the Great White Throne

11 I saw a great white throne with someone sitting on it. Earth and heaven tried to run away, but there was no place for them to go. ¹²I also saw all the dead people standing in front of that throne. Every one of them was there, no matter who they had once been. Several books were opened, and then the book of life*ᶠ* was opened. The dead were judged by what those books said they had done.

13 The sea gave up the dead people who were in it, and death and its kingdom also gave up their dead. Then everyone was judged by what they had done. ¹⁴Afterwards, death and its kingdom were thrown into the lake of fire. This is the second death.*ᵍ* ¹⁵Anyone whose name wasn't written in the book of life was thrown into the lake of fire.

The New Heaven and the New Earth

21 I saw a new heaven and a new earth. The first heaven and the first earth had disappeared, and so had the sea. ²Then I saw New Jerusalem, that holy city, coming down from God in heaven. It was

---

ᶠ book of life: See the note at 3.5.
ᵍ second death: See the note at 2.11.

like a bride dressed in her wedding gown and ready to meet her husband.

3 I heard a loud voice shout from the throne:

God's home is now with his people. He will live with them, and they will be his own. Yes, God will make his home among his people. [4]He will wipe all tears from their eyes, and there will be no more death, suffering, crying, or pain. These things of the past are gone forever.

5 Then the one sitting on the throne said:

I am making everything new. Write down what I have said. My words are true and can be trusted. [6]Everything is finished! I am Alpha and Omega,[h] the beginning and the end. I will freely give water from the life-giving fountain to everyone who is thirsty. [7]All who win the victory will be given these blessings. I will be their God, and they will be my people.

8 But I will tell you what will happen to cowards and to everyone who is unfaithful or dirty-minded or who murders or is sexually immoral or uses witchcraft or worships idols or tells lies. They will be thrown into that lake of fire and burning sulphur. This is the second death.[i]

The New Jerusalem

9 I saw one of the seven angels who had the bowls filled with the seven last terrible troubles. The angel came to me and said, "Come on! I will show you the one who will be the bride and wife of the Lamb."

---

[h] *Alpha and Omega*: See the note at 1.8.
[i] *second death*: See the note at 2.11.

¹⁰Then with the help of the Spirit, he took me to the top of a very high mountain. There he showed me the holy city of Jerusalem coming down from God in heaven.

11 The glory of God made the city bright. It was dazzling and crystal clear like a precious jasper stone. ¹²The city had a high and thick wall with twelve gates, and each one of them was guarded by an angel. On each of the gates was written the name of one of the twelve tribes of Israel. ¹³Three of these gates were on the east, three were on the north, three more were on the south, and the other three were on the west. ¹⁴The city was built on twelve foundation stones. On each of the stones was written the name of one of the Lamb's twelve apostles.

15 The angel who spoke to me had a gold measuring stick to measure the city and its gates and its walls. ¹⁶The city was shaped like a cube, because it was just as high as it was wide. When the angel measured the city, it was about fifteen hundred miles high and fifteen hundred miles wide. ¹⁷Then the angel measured the wall, and by our measurements it was about two hundred sixteen feet high.

18 The wall was built of jasper, and the city was made of pure gold, clear as crystal. ¹⁹Each of the twelve foundations was a precious stone. The first was jasper,ʲ

ʲ *jasper*: The precious and semi-precious stones mentioned in verses 19 and 20 are of different colors. *Jasper* is usually green or clear; *sapphire* is blue; *agate* has circles of brown and white; *emerald* is green; *onyx* has different bands of color; *carnelian* is deep-red or reddish-white; *chrysolite* is olive-green; *beryl* is green or bluish-green; *topaz* is yellow; *chrysoprase* is apple-green; *jacinth* is reddish-orange; and *amethyst* is deep purple.

the second was sapphire, the third was agate, the fourth was emerald, ²⁰the fifth was onyx, the sixth was carnelian, the seventh was chrysolite, the eighth was beryl, the ninth was topaz, the tenth was chrysoprase, the eleventh was jacinth, and the twelfth was amethyst. ²¹Each of the twelve gates was a solid pearl. The streets of the city were made of pure gold, clear as crystal.

22 I did not see a temple there. The Lord God All-Powerful and the Lamb were its temple. ²³And the city did not need the sun or the moon. The glory of God was shining on it, and the Lamb was its light.

24 Nations will walk by the light of that city, and kings will bring their riches there. ²⁵Its gates are always open during the day, and night never comes. ²⁶The glorious treasures of nations will be brought into the city. ²⁷But nothing unworthy will be allowed to enter. No one who is dirty-minded or who tells lies will be there. Only those whose names are written in the Lamb's book of life*k* will be in the city.

22 The angel showed me a river that was crystal clear, and its waters gave life. The river came from the throne where God and the Lamb were seated. ²Then it flowed down the middle of the city's main street. On each side of the river are trees*l* that grow a different kind of fruit each month of the year. The fruit gives life, and the leaves are used as medicine to heal the nations.

---

k *book of life*: See the note at 3.5.

l *trees*: The Greek has "tree," which is used in a collective sense of trees on both sides of the heavenly river.

3 God's curse will no longer be on the people of that city. He and the Lamb will be seated there on their thrones, and its people will worship God 4and will see him face to face. God's name will be written on the foreheads of the people. 5Never again will night appear, and no one who lives there will ever need a lamp or the sun. The Lord God will be their light, and they will rule forever.

The Coming of Christ

6 Then I was told:

These words are true and can be trusted. The Lord God controls the spirits of his prophets, and he is the one who sent his angel to show his servants what must happen right away. 7Remember, I am coming soon! God will bless everyone who pays attention to the message of this book.

8 My name is John, and I am the one who heard and saw these things. Then after I had heard and seen all this, I knelt down and began to worship at the feet of the angel who had shown it to me.

9 But the angel said,

Don't do that! I am a servant, just like you. I am the same as a follower or a prophet or anyone else who obeys what is written in this book. God is the one you should worship.

10 Don't keep the prophecies in this book a secret. These things will happen soon.

11 Evil people will keep on being evil, and everyone who is dirty-minded will still be dirty-minded. But good people will keep on doing right, and God's people will always be holy.

12 Then I was told:

I am coming soon! And when I come, I will reward everyone for what they have done. 13I am Alpha and Omega,*m* the first and the last, the beginning and the end.

14 God will bless all who have washed their robes. They will each have the right to eat fruit from the tree that gives life, and they can enter the gates of the city. 15But outside the city will be dogs, witches, immoral people, murderers, idol worshipers, and everyone who loves to tell lies and do wrong.

16 I am Jesus! And I am the one who sent my angel to tell all of you these things for the churches. I am David's Great Descendant,*n* and I am also the bright morning star.*o*

17 The Spirit and the bride say, "Come!" Everyone who hears this*p* should say, "Come!" If you are thirsty, come! If you want life-giving water, come and take it. It's free!

18 Here is my warning for everyone who hears the prophecies in this book:

If you add anything to them, God will make you suffer all the terrible troubles written in this book. 19If you take anything away from these prophecies, God will not let you have part in the

---

m Alpha and Omega: See the note at 1.8.

n David's Great Descendant: See the note at 5.5.

o the bright morning star: Probably thought of as the brightest star (see 2.27,28).

p who hears this: The reading of the book of Revelation in a service of worship.

life-giving tree and in the holy city described in this book.

20 The one who has spoken these things says, "I am coming soon!"

So, Lord Jesus, please come soon!

21 I pray that the Lord Jesus will be kind to all of you.

Psalms

ABOUT THIS BOOK

The book of Psalms is the longest book in the Bible. Psalms are poems that can either be sung as songs or spoken as prayers by individuals or groups. There are 150 psalms in this book, and many of them list King David as their author. They were collected over a long period of time and became a very important part of the worship of the people of Israel.

Some of the psalms tell the music leader what instruments should be used and what tunes should be followed. For example, look at Psalm 4 and Psalm 45.

Many of the Bible's main ideas are echoed in the Psalms: praise, thankfulness, faith, hope, sorrow for sin, God's loyalty and help. And at the heart of all the psalms there is a deep trust in God. The writers of the psalms always express their true feelings, whether they are praising God for his blessings or complaining in times of trouble.

In ancient Israel the psalms were used in several different ways: (1) to praise God, as in Psalm 105; (2) to express sorrow, as in Psalm 13; (3) to teach, as in Psalm 1; (4) to honor Israel's king and pray for fairness in his rule, as in Psalm 72; (5) to tell of God's power over all creation, as in Psalm 47; (6) to show love for Jerusalem, as in Psalm 46; and (7) to celebrate festivals, as in Psalm 121. Of course, many of the psalms could be used for more than one purpose.

Jesus used the psalms when he preached and taught, and they were often quoted by the writers of the New Testament. The earliest Christians also used the psalms in worship, teaching, and telling others the good news about what God has done through Jesus Christ. A verse from Psalm 118, for example, is directly referred to six times in the New Testament:

> *The stone that the builders tossed aside*
> *has now become the most important stone.*
>
> *(118.22)*

A QUICK LOOK AT THIS BOOK

The book of Psalms is divided into five sections or "books." Most of the psalms in Books I and II were written by David, while many in Book III were written by either Asaph or the people of Korah. Psalms 120-134 are all "celebration psalms." The five sections of the book of Psalms are:

Book I   (1–41)   Book II   (42–72)
Book III   (73–89)   Book IV   (90–106)
Book V   (107–150)

BOOK I
(Psalms 1–41)

Psalm 1

The Way to Happiness

¹ God blesses those people
who refuse evil advice and won't follow sinners
or join in sneering at God.

2 Instead, the Law of the LORD makes them happy,
   and they think about it day and night.

3 They are like trees growing beside a stream,
   trees that produce fruit in season
      and always have leaves.
   Those people succeed in everything they do.

4 That isn't true of those who are evil,
   because they are like straw blown by the wind.
5 Sinners won't have an excuse
      on the day of judgment,
   and they won't have a place
      with the people of God.
6 The LORD protects everyone who follows him,
   but the wicked follow a road that leads to ruin.

Psalm 2

The Lord's Chosen King

1 Why do the nations plot,[a]
   and why do their people make useless plans?[b]
2 The kings of this earth have all joined together
   to turn against the LORD and his chosen one.
3 They say, "Let's cut the ropes
   and set ourselves free!"

4 In heaven the LORD laughs as he sits on his throne,
   making fun of the nations.

---

[a] Why...plot?: Or "Why are the nations restless?"
[b] make useless plans: Or "grumble uselessly."

⁵ The LORD becomes furious and threatens them.
  His anger terrifies them as he says,
⁶   "I've put my king on Zion, my sacred hill."

⁷ I will tell the promise that the LORD made to me:
  "You are my son,
      because today I have become your father.
⁸ Ask me for the nations,
      and every nation on earth will belong to you.
⁹ You will smash them with an iron rod
      and shatter them like dishes of clay."

¹⁰ Be smart, all you rulers, and pay close attention.
¹¹   Serve and honor the LORD; be glad and tremble.
¹² Show respect to his son
  because if you don't,
      the LORD might become furious
      and suddenly destroy you.ᶜ
  But he blesses and protects
      everyone who runs to him.

Psalm 3

*[Written by David
when he was running from his son Absalom.]*

An Early Morning Prayer

¹ I have a lot of enemies, LORD.
  Many fight against ²me and say,
      "God won't rescue you!"

ᶜ *Serve . . . you*: One possible meaning for the difficult
Hebrew text of verses 11 and 12.

3 But you are my shield,
      and you give me victory and great honor.
4 I pray to you,
      and you answer from your sacred hill.

5 I sleep and wake up refreshed
      because you, LORD, protect me.
6 Ten thousand enemies attack from every side,
      but I am not afraid.

7 Come and save me, LORD God!
  Break my enemies' jaws and shatter their teeth,
8   because you protect and bless your people.

Psalm 4

*[A psalm by David for the music leader.
Use stringed instruments.]*

An Evening Prayer

1 You are my God and protector.
      Please answer my prayer.
  I was in terrible distress,
      but you set me free.
  Now have pity and listen as I pray.

2 How long will you people refuse to respect me?*d*
  You love foolish things,
      and you run after what is worthless.*e*

---

d me: Or "my God."
e foolish…worthless: This may refer to idols and false
  gods.

3 The LORD has chosen everyone who is faithful
    to be his very own,*f*
and he answers my prayers.
4 But each of you had better tremble
    and turn from your sins.
Silently search your heart as you lie in bed.
5   Offer the proper sacrifices and trust the LORD.

6 There are some who ask,
    "Who will be good to us?"
Let your kindness, LORD, shine brightly on us.
7 You brought me more happiness
    than a rich harvest of grain and grapes.
8 I can lie down and sleep soundly
    because you, LORD, will keep me safe.

Psalm 5

[A psalm by David for the music leader. Use flutes.]

A Prayer for Help

1 Listen, LORD, as I pray!
    Pay attention when I groan.*g*
2 You are my King and my God.
    Answer my cry for help because I pray to you.
3 Each morning you listen to my prayer,
    as I bring my requests*h* to you
    and wait for your reply.

---

f *has chosen... very own:* Some Hebrew manuscripts have
   "work miracles for his faithful people."
g *when I groan:* Or "to my thoughts" or "to my words."
h *requests:* Or "sacrifices."

4 You are not the kind of God
    who is pleased with evil.
  Sinners can't stay with you.
5 No one who boasts
    can stand in your presence, LORD,
  and you hate evil people.
6 You destroy every liar,
    and you despise violence and deceit.

7 Because of your great mercy,
    I come to your house, LORD,
  and I am filled with wonder
    as I bow down to worship at your holy temple.
8 You do what is right, and I ask you to guide me.
  Make your teaching clear
    because of my enemies.

9 Nothing they say is true!
    They just want to destroy.
  Their words are deceitful like a hidden pit,
    and their tongues are good only for telling lies.
10 Punish them, God,
    and let their own plans bring their downfall.
  Get rid of them!
    They keep committing crimes
    and turning against you.

11 Let all who run to you for protection
    always sing joyful songs.
  Provide shelter for those who truly love you
    and let them rejoice.
12 Our LORD, you bless those who live right,
    and you shield them with your kindness.

Psalm 6

[A psalm by David for the music leader.
Use stringed instruments.[i]]

A Prayer in Time of Trouble

¹ Don't punish me, LORD, or even correct me
    when you are angry!
² Have pity on me and heal my feeble body.
    My bones tremble with fear,
³   and I am in deep distress.
    How long will it be?

⁴ Turn and come to my rescue.
    Show your wonderful love and save me, LORD.
⁵ If I die, I cannot praise you
    or even remember you.
⁶ My groaning has worn me out.
    At night my bed and pillow
    are soaked with tears.
⁷ Sorrow has made my eyes dim,
    and my sight has failed because of my enemies.

⁸ You, LORD, heard my crying,
    and those hateful people
    had better leave me alone.
⁹ You have answered my prayer
    and my plea for mercy.
¹⁰ My enemies will be ashamed and terrified,
    as they quickly run away in complete disgrace.

---

[i] *instruments:* The Hebrew text adds "according to the
sheminith," which may refer to a musical instrument
with eight strings.

Psalm 7

[Written by David.^{j} He sang this to the LORD because of Cush from the tribe of Benjamin.]

The LORD Always Does Right

1 You, LORD God, are my protector.
Rescue me and keep me safe
     from all who chase me.
2 Or else they will rip me apart
     like lions attacking a victim,
and no one will save me.

3 I am innocent, LORD God!
4 I have not betrayed a friend
     or had pity on an enemy^k
     who attacks for no reason.
5 If I have done any of this,
     then let my enemies chase and capture me.
Let them stomp me to death and leave me in the dirt.

6 Get angry, LORD God! Do something!
Attack my furious enemies.
     See that justice is done.
7 Make the nations come to you,
     as you sit on your throne^l above them all.

8 Our LORD, judge the nations! Judge me
     and show that I am honest and innocent.

---

^{j} *Written by David*: The Hebrew text has "a shiggaion by David," which may refer to a psalm of mourning.
^{k} *had pity on an enemy*: Or "failed to have pity on an enemy."
^{l} *sit...throne*: Or "return to your place."

⁹ You know every heart and mind,
　　and you always do right.
Now make violent people stop,
　　but protect all of us who obey you.

¹⁰ You, God, are my shield,
　　the protector of everyone whose heart is right.
¹¹ You see that justice is done,
　　and each day you take revenge.
¹² Whenever your enemies refuse to change their ways,
　　you sharpen your sword and string your bow.
¹³ Your deadly arrows are ready with flaming tips.

¹⁴ An evil person is like a woman about to give birth
　　to a hateful, deceitful, and rebellious child.
¹⁵ Such people dig a deep hole,
　　then fall in it themselves.
¹⁶ The trouble they cause comes back on them,
　　and their heads are crushed
　　　by their own evil deeds.

¹⁷ I will praise you, LORD! You always do right.
　I will sing about you, the LORD Most High.

Psalm 8

[A psalm by David for the music leader.ᵐ]

The Wonderful Name of the LORD

¹ Our LORD and Ruler,
　　your name is wonderful everywhere on earth!

―――――――――――

ᵐ *leader*: The Hebrew text adds "according to the gittith,"
　which may refer to either a musical instrument or a tune.

You let your glory be seen[n] in the heavens above.
2 With praises from children and from tiny infants,
    you have built a fortress.
It makes your enemies silent,
    and all who turn against you are left speechless.

3 I often think of the heavens your hands have made,
    and of the moon and stars you put in place.
4 Then I ask, "Why do you care about us humans?
    Why are you concerned for us weaklings?"
5 You made us a little lower than you yourself,[o]
    and you have crowned us with glory and honor.

6 You let us rule everything your hands have made.
    And you put all of it under our power
7   the sheep and the cattle, and every wild animal,
8   the birds in the sky, the fish in the sea,
        and all ocean creatures.

9 Our LORD and Ruler,
    your name is wonderful everywhere on earth!

Psalm 9

*[A psalm by David for the music leader.
To the tune "The Death of the Son."]*

Sing Praises to the LORD

1 I will praise you, LORD, with all my heart
    and tell about the wonders you have worked.

---

[n] *You... seen*: Or "I will worship your glory."
[o] *you yourself*: Or "the angels" or "the beings in heaven."

2 God Most High, I will rejoice;
    I will celebrate and sing because of you.

3 When my enemies face you,
    they run away and stumble and are destroyed.
4 You take your seat as judge,
    and your fair decisions prove
    that I was in the right.
5 You warn the nations and destroy evil people;
    you wipe out their names forever and ever.
6 Our enemies are destroyed completely for all time.
  Their cities are torn down,
    and they will never be remembered again.

7 You rule forever, LORD,
    and you are on your throne,
    ready for judgment.
8 You judge the world fairly
    and treat all nations with justice.
9 The poor can run to you
    because you are a fortress in times of trouble.
10 Everyone who honors your name can trust you,
    because you are faithful
    to all who depend on you.

11 You rule from Zion, LORD, and we sing about you
    to let the nations know
    everything you have done.
12 You did not forget to punish the guilty
    or listen to the cries of those in need.

13 Please have mercy, LORD!
    My enemies mistreat me.

Keep me from the gates that lead to death,
14   and I will sing about you at the gate to Zion.
I will be happy there because you rescued me.

15 Our LORD, the nations fell into their own pits,
        and their feet were caught in their own traps.
16 You showed what you are like,
            and you made certain that justice is done,
    but evil people are trapped
        by their own evil deeds.
17 The wicked will go down to the world of the dead
        to be with those nations that forgot about you.

18 The poor and the homeless
        won't always be forgotten and without hope.

19 Do something, LORD! Don't let the nations win.
        Make them stand trial in your court of law.
20 Make the nations afraid and let them all discover
        just how weak they are.

Psalm 10

A Prayer for Help

1 Why are you far away, LORD?
Why do you hide yourself
        when I am in trouble?
2 Proud and brutal people hunt down the poor.
        But let them get caught by their own evil plans!

3 The wicked brag about their deepest desires.
        Those greedy people hate and curse you, LORD.

4 The wicked are too proud to turn to you
   or even think about you.
5 They are always successful,
   though they can't understand your teachings,
      and they keep sneering at their enemies.

6 In their hearts they say, "Nothing can hurt us!
      We'll always be happy and free from trouble."
7 They curse and tell lies,
   and all they talk about
      is how to be cruel or how to do wrong.

8 They hide outside villages, waiting to strike
      and murder some innocent victim.
9 They are hungry lions hiding in the bushes,
      hoping to catch some helpless passerby.
   They trap the poor in nets and drag them away.
10 They crouch down and wait to grab a victim.
11 They say, "God can't see!
      He's got on a blindfold."

12 Do something, LORD God,
      and use your powerful arm
         to help those in need.
13 The wicked don't respect you.
      In their hearts they say, "God won't punish us!"

14 But you see the trouble and the distress,
      and you will do something.
   The poor can count on you, and so can orphans.
15 Now break the arms of all merciless people.
   Punish them for doing wrong
      and make them stop.

16 Our LORD, you will always rule,
   but nations will vanish from the earth.
17 You listen to the longings of those who suffer.
   You offer them hope,
     and you pay attention to their cries for help.
18 You defend orphans and everyone else in need,
   so that no one on earth
     can terrify others again.

Psalm 11

[A psalm by David for the music leader.]

Trusting the LORD

1 The LORD is my fortress!
   Don't say to me,
     "Escape like a bird to the mountains!"
2 You tell me,
     "Watch out!
   Those evil people
     have put their arrows on their bows,
   and they are standing in the shadows,
     aiming at good people.
3 What can an honest person do
     when everything crumbles?"

4 The LORD is sitting in his sacred temple
     on his throne in heaven.
   He knows everything we do
     because he sees us all.
5 The LORD tests honest people,
   but despises those who are cruel
     and love violence.

⁶ He will send fiery coals*p* and flaming sulphur
        down on the wicked,
    and they will drink nothing but a scorching wind.

⁷ The LORD always does right
        and wants justice done.
    Everyone who does right will see his face.

Psalm 12

*[A psalm by David for the music leader.*q*]*

A Prayer for Help

¹ Please help me, LORD!
    All who were faithful
        and all who were loyal have disappeared.
² Everyone tells lies, and no one is sincere.
³ Won't you chop off all flattering tongues
        that brag so loudly?
⁴ They say to themselves, "We are great speakers.
    No one else has a chance."

⁵ But you, LORD, tell them, "I will do something!
    The poor are mistreated
        and helpless people moan.
    I'll rescue all who suffer."

⁶ Our LORD, you are true to your promises,
    and your word is like silver

---

p fiery coals: Or "trouble, fire."

q leader: The Hebrew text adds "according to the sheminith,"
which may be a musical instrument with eight strings.

heated seven times in a fiery furnace.*r*

7 You will protect us
　　and always keep us safe from those people.
8 But all who are wicked will keep on strutting,
　　while everyone praises their shameless deeds.*s*

Psalm 13

[A psalm by David for the music leader.]

A Prayer for the LORD's Help

1 How much longer, LORD, will you forget about me?
　　Will it be forever? How long will you hide?
2 How long must I be confused
　　and miserable all day?
　　How long will my enemies keep beating me down?

3 Please listen, LORD God, and answer my prayers.
　　Make my eyes sparkle again,
　　　　or else I will fall into the sleep of death.
4 My enemies will say, "Now we've won!"
　　They will be greatly pleased when I am defeated.

5 I trust your love, and I feel like celebrating
　　because you rescued me.
6 You have been good to me, LORD,
　　and I will sing about you.

---

r in a fiery furnace: The Hebrew text has "in a furnace to
the ground," which may describe part of a process for
refining silver in Old Testament times.
s while ... deeds: One possible meaning for the difficult
Hebrew text.

Psalm 14

[A psalm by David for the music leader.]

No One Can Ignore the LORD

¹Only a fool would say, "There is no God!"
People like that are worthless;
   they are heartless and cruel and never do right.

² From heaven the LORD looks down to see
   if anyone is wise enough to search for him.
³ But all of them are corrupt; no one does right.

⁴ Won't you evil people learn? You refuse to pray,
   and you gobble down the LORD's people.
⁵ But you will be frightened,
   because God is on the side
   of every good person.
⁶ You may spoil the plans of the poor,
   but the LORD protects them.

⁷ I long for someone from Zion
   to come and save Israel!
Our LORD, when you bless your people again,
   Jacob's family will be glad,
   and Israel will celebrate.

Psalm 15

[A psalm by David.]

Who May Worship the LORD?

¹ Who may stay in God's temple
   or live on the holy mountain of the LORD?

2 Only those who obey God and do as they should.
  They speak the truth 3and don't spread gossip;
    they treat others fairly
      and don't say cruel things.

4 They hate worthless people,
    but show respect for all who worship the LORD.
  And they keep their promises,
    no matter what the cost.
5 They lend their money without charging interest,
    and they don't take bribes to hurt the innocent.

Those who do these things will always stand firm.

Psalm 16

[A special psalm by David.]

The Best Choice

1 Protect me, LORD God!
    I run to you for safety,
2 and I have said, "Only you are my Lord!
    Every good thing I have is a gift from you."

3 Your people are wonderful,
    and they make me happy,*t*
4 but worshipers of other gods
    will have much sorrow.*u*

---

t *Your people . . . happy*: Or "I was happy worshiping gods I
thought were powerful."
u *but . . . sorrow*: One possible meaning for the difficult
Hebrew text.

I refuse to offer sacrifices of blood to those gods
      or worship in their name.

5 You, LORD, are all I want!
      You are my choice, and you keep me safe.
6 You make my life pleasant, and my future is bright.

7 I praise you, LORD, for being my guide.
   Even in the darkest night,
      your teachings fill my mind.
8 I will always look to you,
      as you stand beside me
      and protect me from fear.
9 With all my heart, I will celebrate,
      and I can safely rest.

10 I am your chosen one.
   You won't leave me in the grave
      or let my body decay.
11 You have shown me the path to life,
      and you make me glad by being near to me.
   Sitting at your right side,[y] I will always be joyful.

Psalm 17

[A prayer by David.]

The Prayer of an Innocent Person

1 I am innocent, LORD!
   Won't you listen as I pray and beg for help?
      I am honest! Please hear my prayer.

---

[y] *right side*: The place of power and honor.

2 Only you can say that I am innocent,
   because only your eyes can see the truth.

3 You know my heart,
   and even during the night you have tested me
      and found me innocent.
   I have made up my mind never to tell a lie.
4   I don't do like others.
   I obey your teachings and am not cruel.
5   I have followed you, without ever stumbling.

6 I pray to you, God, because you will help me.
   Listen and answer my prayer!
7   Show your wonderful love.
   Your mighty arm protects those
      who run to you for safety from their enemies.
8 Protect me as you would your very own eyes;
   hide me in the shadow of your wings.

9 Don't let my brutal enemies
   attack from all sides and kill me.
10 They refuse to show mercy, and they keep bragging.

11 They have caught up with me!
   My enemies are everywhere,
      eagerly hoping to smear me in the dirt.
12 They are like hungry lions hunting for food,
   or like young lions hiding in ambush.

13 Do something, LORD! Attack and defeat them.
   Take your sword and save me
      from those evil people.
14 Use your powerful arm and rescue me

from the hands of mere humans
    whose world won't last.[w]

You provide food for those you love.
Their children have plenty,
    and their grandchildren
      will have more than enough.

15 I am innocent, LORD, and I will see your face!
    When I awake,
      all I want is to see you as you are.

Psalm 18

[For the music leader.
A psalm by David, the LORD's servant.
David sang this to the LORD after the LORD had rescued
him from his enemies, but especially from Saul.]

David's Song of Thanks

1 I love you, LORD God, and you make me strong.
2 You are my mighty rock,[x] my fortress, my protector,
    the rock where I am safe, my shield,
      my powerful weapon,[y] and my place of shelter.

---

[w] *last:* One possible meaning for the difficult Hebrew text
of verse 14.

[x] *mighty rock:* The Hebrew text has "rock," which is sometimes used in poetry to compare the Lord to a mountain
where his people can run for protection from their enemies.

[y] *my powerful weapon:* The Hebrew text has "the horn,"
which refers to the horn of a bull, one of the most powerful
animals in ancient Palestine.

3 I praise you, LORD!
   I prayed, and you rescued me from my enemies.
4 Death had wrapped its ropes around me,
   and I was almost swallowed
      by its flooding waters.

5 Ropes from the world of the dead
   had coiled around me,
and death had set a trap in my path.
6 I was in terrible trouble when I called out to you,
   but from your temple you heard me
      and answered my prayer.
7 The earth shook and shivered,
   and the mountains trembled down to their roots.
   You were angry 8and breathed out smoke.
   Scorching heat and fiery flames
      spewed from your mouth.

9 You opened the heavens like curtains,
   and you came down
      with storm clouds under your feet.
10 You rode on the backs of flying creatures
   and swooped down with the wind as wings.
11 Darkness was your robe;
   thunderclouds filled the sky,
      hiding you from sight.
12 Hailstones and fiery coals
   lit up the sky in front of you.

13 LORD Most High,
   your voice thundered from the heavens,
      as hailstones and fiery coals
         poured down like rain.

¹⁴ You scattered your enemies
        with arrows of lightning.
¹⁵ You roared at the sea,
        and its deepest channels could be seen.
    You snorted,
        and the earth shook to its foundations.

¹⁶ You reached down from heaven,
        and you lifted me from deep in the ocean.
¹⁷ You rescued me from enemies,
        who were hateful and too powerful for me.
¹⁸ On the day disaster struck, they came and attacked,
        but you defended me.
¹⁹ When I was fenced in,
        you freed and rescued me because you love me.

²⁰ You are good to me, LORD, because I do right,
        and you reward me because I am innocent.
²¹ I do what you want and never turn to do evil.
²² I keep your laws in mind
        and never look away from your teachings.
²³ I obey you completely and guard against sin.
²⁴ You have been good to me because I do right;
    you have rewarded me
        for being innocent by your standards.

²⁵ You are always loyal to your loyal people,
        and you are faithful to the faithful.
²⁶ With all who are sincere, you are sincere,
    but you treat the unfaithful
        as their deeds deserve.
²⁷ You rescue the humble,
        but you put down all who are proud.

²⁸ You, the LORD God, keep my lamp burning
      and turn darkness to light.
²⁹ You help me defeat armies and capture cities.

³⁰ Your way is perfect, LORD,
      and your word is correct.
   You are a shield for those who run to you for help.
³¹ You alone are God!
      Only you are a mighty rock.ᶻ
³² You give me strength and guide me right.
³³ You make my feet run as fast as those of a deer,
      and you help me stand on the mountains.

³⁴ You teach my hands to fight
      and my arms to use a bow of bronze.
³⁵ You alone are my shield.
   Your right hand supports me,
      and by coming to help me,
      you have made me famous.
³⁶ You clear the way for me, and now I won't stumble.

³⁷ I kept chasing my enemies,
      until I caught them and destroyed them.
³⁸ I stuck my sword through my enemies,
      and they were crushed under my feet.
³⁹ You helped me win victories,
      and you forced my attackers to fall victim to me.

⁴⁰ You made my enemies run, and I killed them.
⁴¹ They cried out for help, but no one saved them;
      they called out to you, but there was no answer.

ᶻ *mighty rock*: See the note at 18.2.

42 I ground them to dust blown by the wind,
    and I poured them out like mud in the streets.

43 You rescued me from stubborn people,
    and you made me the leader of foreign nations,
    who are now my slaves.
44 They obey and come crawling.
45 They have lost all courage,
    and from their fortresses, they come trembling.

46 You are the living LORD! I will praise you.
    You are a mighty rock.[a]
    I will honor you for keeping me safe.
47 You took revenge for me,
    and you put nations in my power.
48 You protected me from violent enemies
    and made me much greater than all of them.

49 I will praise you, LORD,
    and I will honor you among the nations.
50 You give glorious victories to your chosen king.
    Your faithful love for David
    and for his descendants will never end.

Psalm 19

[A psalm by David for the music leader.]

The Wonders of God and the Goodness of His Law

1 The heavens keep telling the wonders of God,
    and the skies declare what he has done.

---

a mighty rock: See the note at 18.2.

2 Each day informs the following day;
   each night announces to the next.
3 They don't speak a word,
   and there is never the sound of a voice.
4 Yet their message reaches all the earth,
   and it travels around the world.

In the heavens a tent is set up for the sun.
5 It rises like a bridegroom
   and gets ready like a hero
   eager to run a race.
6 It travels all the way across the sky.
   Nothing hides from its heat.

7 The Law of the LORD is perfect;
   it gives us new life.
His teachings last forever,
   and they give wisdom to ordinary people.
8 The LORD's instruction is right;
   it makes our hearts glad.
His commands shine brightly,
   and they give us light.

9 Worshiping the LORD is sacred;
   he will always be worshiped.
All of his decisions are correct and fair.
10 They are worth more than the finest gold
   and are sweeter than honey from a honeycomb.

11 By your teachings, Lord, I am warned;
   by obeying them, I am greatly rewarded.
12 None of us know our faults.
   Forgive me when I sin without knowing it.

¹³ Don't let me do wrong on purpose, Lord,
      or let sin have control over my life.
Then I will be innocent,
      and not guilty of some terrible fault.

¹⁴ Let my words and my thoughts
   be pleasing to you, LORD,
      because you are my mighty rock[b]
      and my protector.

Psalm 20

[A psalm by David for the music leader.]

A Prayer for Victory

¹I pray that the LORD will listen
when you are in trouble,
      and that the God of Jacob will keep you safe.
² May the LORD send help from his temple
      and come to your rescue from Mount Zion.
³ May he remember your gifts
      and be pleased with what you bring.

⁴ May God do what you want most
      and let all go well for you.
⁵ Then you will win victories, and we will celebrate,
      while raising our banners
      in the name of our God.
   May the LORD answer all of your prayers!

⁶ I am certain, LORD,

----

b mighty rock: See the note at 18.2.

that you will help your chosen king.
You will answer my prayers
from your holy place in heaven,
    and you will save me with your mighty arm.

7 Some people trust the power of chariots or horses,
    but we trust you, LORD God.
8 Others will stumble and fall,
    but we will be strong and stand firm.

9 Give the king victory, LORD, and answer our prayers.*c*

Psalm 21

[A psalm by David for the music leader.]

Thanking the LORD for Victory

1 Our LORD, your mighty power makes the king glad,
    and he celebrates victories
        that you have given him.
2 You did what he wanted most
    and never told him "No."
3 You truly blessed the king,
    and you placed on him a crown of finest gold.
4 He asked to live a long time,
    and you promised him life that never ends.

5 The king is highly honored.
   You have let him win victories
      that have made him famous.

---

c victory...prayers: Or "victory. He (God or the king) answers us."

6 You have given him blessings that will last forever,
and you have made him glad
by being so near to him.
7 LORD Most High, the king trusts you,
and your kindness keeps him from defeat.

8 With your mighty arm, LORD,
you will strike down
all of your hateful enemies.
9 They will be destroyed by fire once you are here,
and because of your anger,
flames will swallow them.
10 You will wipe their families from the earth,
and they will disappear.
11 All their plans to harm you will come to nothing.
12 You will make them run away
by shooting your arrows at their faces.

13 Show your strength, LORD,
so that we may sing and praise your power.

Psalm 22

*[A psalm by David for the music leader.
To the tune "A Deer at Dawn."]*

Suffering and Praise

1 My God, my God, why have you deserted me?
Why are you so far away?
Won't you listen to my groans
and come to my rescue?
2 I cry out day and night, but you don't answer,
and I can never rest.

³ Yet you are the holy God,
   ruling from your throne
   and praised by Israel.
⁴ Our ancestors trusted you,
   and you rescued them.
⁵ When they cried out for help, you saved them,
   and you did not let them down
   when they depended on you.

⁶ But I am merely a worm, far less than human,
   and I am hated and rejected
   by people everywhere.
⁷ Everyone who sees me makes fun and sneers.
   They shake their heads, ⁸and say,
"Trust the LORD! If you are his favorite,
   let him protect you and keep you safe."

⁹ You, LORD, brought me safely through birth,
   and you protected me
   when I was a baby at my mother's breast.
¹⁰ From the day I was born, I have been in your care,
   and from the time of my birth,
   you have been my God.

¹¹ Don't stay far off
   when I am in trouble with no one to help me.
¹² Enemies are all around like a herd of wild bulls,
   Powerful bulls from Bashan*d* are everywhere.
¹³ My enemies are like lions
   roaring and attacking with jaws open wide.

---

d Bashan: A land east of the Jordan River, where there
   were pastures suitable for raising fine cattle.

¹⁴ I have no more strength than a few drops of water.
   All my bones are out of joint;
      my heart is like melted wax.
¹⁵ My strength has dried up like a broken clay pot,
      and my tongue sticks to the roof of my mouth.
   You, God, have left me to die in the dirt.

¹⁶ Brutal enemies attack me like a pack of dogs,
      tearing at*ᵉ* my hands and my feet.
¹⁷ I can count all my bones,
      and my enemies just stare and sneer at me.
¹⁸ They took my clothes and gambled for them.

¹⁹ Don't stay far away, LORD!
      My strength comes from you, so hurry and help.
²⁰ Rescue me from enemy swords
      and save me from those dogs.
²¹ Don't let lions eat me.
   You rescued me from the horns of wild bulls,
²²   and when your people meet,
         I will praise you, LORD.

²³ All who worship the LORD, now praise him!
   You belong to Jacob's family
   and to the people of Israel,
      so fear and honor the LORD!
²⁴ The LORD doesn't hate or despise the helpless
      in all of their troubles.
   When I cried out,
      he listened and did not turn away.

ᵉ *tearing at*: One possible meaning for the difficult Hebrew
text.

25 When your people meet,
    you will fill my heart with your praises, LORD,
and everyone will see me keep
    my promises to you.
26 The poor will eat and be full,
    and all who worship you will be thankful
    and live in hope.

27 Everyone on this earth will remember you, LORD.
People all over the world
    will turn and worship you,
28 because you are in control,
    the ruler of all nations.

29 All who are rich and have more than enough
    will bow down to you, Lord.
Even those who are dying and almost in the grave
    will come and bow down.
30 In the future, everyone will worship
    and learn about you, our Lord.
31 People not yet born will be told,
    "The Lord has saved us!"

Psalm 23

[A psalm by David.]

The Good Shepherd

1 You, LORD, are my shepherd.
    I will never be in need.
2 You let me rest in fields of green grass.
You lead me to streams of peaceful water,
3   and you refresh my life.

You are true to your name,
and you lead me along the right paths.
4 I may walk through valleys as dark as death,
but I won't be afraid.
You are with me,
and your shepherd's rod ^{f} makes me feel safe.

5 You treat me to a feast, while my enemies watch.
You honor me as your guest,
and you fill my cup until it overflows.
6 Your kindness and love
will always be with me each day of my life,
and I will live forever in your house, LORD.

Psalm 24

[A psalm by David.]

Who Can Enter the LORD's Temple?

1 The earth and everything on it belong to the LORD.
The world and its people belong to him.
2 The LORD placed it all on the oceans and rivers.

3 Who may climb the LORD's hill ^{g}
or stand in his holy temple?
4 Only those who do right for the right reasons,
and don't worship idols or tell lies under oath.

---

^{f} *shepherd's rod*: The Hebrew text mentions two objects
carried by the shepherd: a club to defend against wild
animals and a long pole to guide and control the sheep.
^{g} *the LORD's hill*: The hill in Jerusalem where the temple
was built.

5 The LORD God, who saves them,
   will bless and reward them,
6   because they worship and serve
     the God of Jacob.[h]
7 Open the ancient gates,
   so that the glorious king may come in.

8 Who is this glorious king?
   He is our LORD, a strong and mighty warrior.

9 Open the ancient gates,
   so that the glorious king may come in.

10 Who is this glorious king?
   He is our LORD, the All-Powerful!

Psalm 25

[By David.]

A Prayer for Guidance and Help

1 I offer you my heart, LORD God, 2and I trust you.
   Don't make me ashamed
   or let enemies defeat me.
3 Don't disappoint any of your worshipers,
   but disappoint all deceitful liars.
4 Show me your paths and teach me to follow;
5   guide me by your truth and instruct me.
   You keep me safe, and I always trust you.

---

[h] *worship...Jacob*: Two ancient translations; Hebrew
"worship God and serve the descendants of Jacob."

⁶ Please, LORD, remember,
   you have always been patient and kind.
⁷ Forget each wrong I did when I was young.
   Show how truly kind you are and remember me.
⁸ You are honest and merciful,
   and you teach sinners how to follow your path.

⁹ You lead humble people to do what is right
   and to stay on your path.
¹⁰ In everything you do, you are kind and faithful
   to everyone who keeps our agreement with you.

¹¹ Be true to your name, LORD,
   by forgiving each one of my terrible sins.
¹² You will show the right path
   to all who worship you.
¹³ They will have plenty,
   and then their children will receive the land.

¹⁴ Our LORD, you are the friend of your worshipers,
   and you make an agreement with all of us.
¹⁵ I always look to you,
   because you rescue me from every trap.
¹⁶ I am lonely and troubled.
   Show that you care and have pity on me.
¹⁷ My awful worries keep growing.
   Rescue me from sadness.
¹⁸ See my troubles and misery
   and forgive my sins.

¹⁹ Look at all my enemies!
   See how much they hate me.
²⁰ I come to you for shelter.

Protect me, keep me safe,
  and don't disappoint me.
21 I obey you with all my heart,
  and I trust you, knowing that you will save me.

22 Our God, please save Israel from all of its troubles.

Psalm 26

[By David.]

The Prayer of an Innocent Person

1 Show that I am right, LORD!
I stay true to myself,
  and I have trusted you without doubting.
2 Test my thoughts and find out what I am like.
3 I never forget your kindness,
  and I am always faithful to you.*i*
4 I don't spend my time with worthless liars
5   or go with evil crowds.

6 I wash my hands, LORD, to show my innocence,
  and I worship at your altar,
7   while gratefully singing about your wonders.
8 I love the temple where you live,
  and where your glory shines.
9 Don't sweep me away, as you do sinners.
Don't punish me with death
as you do those people
    who are brutal 10or full of meanness
    or who bribe others.

---

i *I am...to you*: Or "I trust your faithfulness."

¹¹ I stay true to myself. Be kind and rescue me.

¹² Now I stand on solid ground!
And when your people meet,
I will praise you, LORD.

Psalm 27

[By David.]

A Prayer of Praise

¹ You, LORD, are the light that keeps me safe.
I am not afraid of anyone.
You protect me, and I have no fears.
² Brutal people may attack and try to kill me,
but they will stumble.
Fierce enemies may attack, but they will fall.
³ Armies may surround me, but I won't be afraid;
war may break out, but I will trust you.

⁴ I ask only one thing, LORD:
Let me live in your house every day of my life
to see how wonderful you are
and to pray in your temple.

⁵ In times of trouble, you will protect me.
You will hide me in your tent
and keep me safe on top of a mighty rock.ʲ
⁶ You will let me defeat all of my enemies.
Then I will celebrate, as I enter your tent
with animal sacrifices and songs of praise.

ʲ *mighty rock*: See the note at 18.2.

7 Please listen when I pray!
　　Have pity. Answer my prayer.
8 My heart tells me to pray.
I am eager to see your face,
9   so don't hide from me.
I am your servant, and you have helped me.
　　Don't turn from me in anger.
You alone keep me safe.
　　Don't reject or desert me.
10 Even if my father and mother should desert me,
　　you will take care of me.

11 Teach me to follow, LORD,
　　and lead me on the right path
　　　because of my enemies.
12 Don't let them do to me what they want.
People tell lies about me
　　and make terrible threats,
13 but I know I will live to see how kind you are.

14 Trust the LORD!
　　Be brave and strong and trust the LORD.

Psalm 28

[By David.]

A Prayer for Help

1 Only you, LORD, are a mighty rock!*k*
　　Don't refuse to help me when I pray.
　　If you don't answer me, I will soon be dead.

---

k *mighty rock*: See the note at 18.2.

² Please listen to my prayer and my cry for help,
    as I lift my hands toward your holy temple.

³ Don't drag me away, LORD, with those cruel people,
    who speak kind words, while planning trouble.
⁴ Treat them as they deserve!
    Punish them for their sins.
⁵ They don't pay any attention
    to your wonderful deeds.
Now you will destroy them
    and leave them in ruin.

⁶ I praise you, LORD, for answering my prayers.
⁷ You are my strong shield,
    and I trust you completely.
You have helped me,
    and I will celebrate and thank you in song.

⁸ You give strength to your people, LORD,
    and you save and protect your chosen ones.
⁹ Come save us and bless us.
Be our shepherd
    and always carry us in your arms.

Psalm 29

[A psalm by David.]

The Voice of the LORD in a Storm

¹ All of you angels¹ in heaven,
    honor the glory and power of the LORD!

---

¹ *angels*: Or "supernatural beings" or "gods."

2 Honor the wonderful name of the LORD,
    and worship the LORD most holy and glorious.*m*

3 The voice of the LORD echoes over the oceans.
  The glorious LORD God thunders
      above the roar of the raging sea,
4   and his voice is mighty and marvelous.
5 The voice of the LORD destroys the cedar trees;
    the LORD shatters cedars on Mount Lebanon.
6 God makes Mount Lebanon skip like a calf
    and Mount Hermon jump like a wild ox.

7 The voice of the LORD makes lightning flash
8   and the desert tremble.
  And because of the LORD,
      the desert near Kadesh shivers and shakes.

9 The voice of the LORD makes deer give birth
      before their time.*n*
  Forests are stripped of leaves,
      and the temple is filled with shouts of praise.

10 The LORD rules on his throne,
      king of the flood*o* forever.
11 Pray that our LORD will make us strong
      and give us peace.

---

m most … glorious: Or "in his holy place" or "and wear
  your glorious clothes."
n makes … time: Or "twists the oak trees around."
o king of the flood: In ancient times the people of Israel
  believed that a mighty ocean surrounded all of creation,
  and that God could release the water to flood the earth.

Psalm 30

[A psalm by David for the dedication of the temple.]

A Prayer of Thanks

1 I will praise you, LORD! You saved me from the grave
and kept my enemies from celebrating my death.
2 I prayed to you, LORD God, and you healed me,
3 saving me from death and the grave.

4 Your faithful people, LORD, will praise you with songs
and honor your holy name.
5 Your anger lasts a little while,
but your kindness lasts for a lifetime.
At night we may cry,
but when morning comes we will celebrate.

6 I was carefree and thought, "I'll never be shaken!"
7 You, LORD, were my friend,
and you made me strong as a mighty mountain.
But when you hid your face, I was crushed.

8 I prayed to you, LORD, and in my prayer I said,
9 "What good will it do you if I am in the grave?
Once I have turned to dust,
how can I praise you or tell how loyal you are?
10 Have pity, LORD! Help!"

11 You have turned my sorrow into joyful dancing.
No longer am I sad and wearing sackcloth.*p*

---

p sackcloth: A rough, dark-colored cloth made from goat or
camel hair and used to make grain sacks. It was worn in
times of trouble or sorrow.

12 I thank you from my heart,
  and I will never stop singing your praises,
    my LORD and my God.

Psalm 31

[A psalm by David for the music leader.]

A Prayer for Protection

1 I come to you, LORD, for protection.
  Don't let me be ashamed.
    Do as you have promised and rescue me.
2 Listen to my prayer and hurry to save me.
  Be my mighty rock*q* and the fortress where I am safe.

3 You, LORD God, are my mighty rock and my fortress.
  Lead me and guide me,
    so that your name will be honored.
4 Protect me from hidden traps and keep me safe.
5 You are faithful,
    and I trust you because you rescued me.

6 I hate the worshipers of worthless idols,
    but I trust you, LORD.
7 I celebrate and shout because you are kind.
    You saw all my suffering, and you cared for me.
8 You kept me from the hands of my enemies,
    and you set me free.

9 Have pity, LORD! I am hurting and almost blind.
    My whole body aches.

---

q **mighty rock**: See the note at 18.2.

¹⁰ I have known only sorrow all my life long,
and I suffer year after year.
I am weak from sin, and my bones are limp.

¹¹ My enemies insult me. Neighbors are even worse,
and I disgust my friends.
People meet me on the street, and they turn and run.
¹² I am completely forgotten like someone dead.
I am merely a broken dish.
¹³ I hear the crowds whisper, "Everyone is afraid!"
They are plotting and scheming to murder me.

¹⁴ But I trust you, LORD, and I claim you as my God.
¹⁵ My life is in your hands.
Save me from enemies who hunt me down.
¹⁶ Smile on me, your servant.
Have pity and rescue me.

¹⁷ I pray only to you. Don't disappoint me.
Disappoint my cruel enemies
until they lie silent in their graves.
¹⁸ Silence those proud liars!
Make them stop bragging
and insulting your people.

¹⁹ You are wonderful, and while everyone watches,
you store up blessings for all
who honor and trust you.
²⁰ You are their shelter from harmful plots,
and you are their protection from vicious gossip.

²¹ I will praise you, LORD, for showing great kindness
when I was like a city under attack.

22 I was terrified and thought,
  "They've chased me far away from you!"
But you answered my prayer when I shouted for help.

23 All who belong to the LORD, show how you love him.
The LORD protects the faithful,
  but he severely punishes everyone who is proud.
24 All who trust the LORD, be cheerful and strong.

Psalm 32

[A special psalm by David.]

The Joy of Forgiveness

1 Our God, you bless everyone
  whose sins you forgive and wipe away.
2 You bless them by saying,
  "You told me your sins, without trying to hide them,
    and now I forgive you."

3 Before I confessed my sins, my bones felt limp,
  and I groaned all day long.
4 Night and day your hand weighed heavily on me,
  and my strength was gone as in the summer heat.

5 So I confessed my sins and told them all to you.
  I said, "I'll tell the LORD each one of my sins."
Then you forgave me and took away my guilt.

6 We worship you, Lord, and we should always pray
  whenever we find out that we have sinned.*r*

---

r *whenever . . . sinned*: Hebrew "at a time of finding only."

Then we won't be swept away by a raging flood.
⁷ You are my hiding place!
   You protect me from trouble,
and you put songs in my heart
   because you have saved me.

⁸ You said to me, "I will point out the road
   that you should follow.
I will be your teacher and watch over you.
⁹ Don't be stupid like horses and mules
   that must be led with ropes to make them obey."

¹⁰ All kinds of troubles will strike the wicked,
   but your kindness shields those
   who trust you, LORD.
¹¹ And so your good people
   should celebrate and shout.

Psalm 33

Sing Praises to the LORD

¹ You are the LORD's people.
   Obey him and celebrate!
   He deserves your praise.
² Praise the LORD with harps!
   Use harps with ten strings to make music for him.
³   Sing a new song. Shout!
   Play beautiful music.

⁴ The LORD is truthful; he can be trusted.
⁵ He loves justice and fairness,
   and he is kind to everyone everywhere on earth.

⁶ The LORD made the heavens
       and everything in them by his word.
⁷ He scooped up the ocean and stored the water.
⁸ Everyone in this world should worship
       and honor the LORD!
⁹ As soon as he spoke the world was created;
       at his command, the earth was formed.

¹⁰ The LORD destroys the plans
       and spoils the schemes of the nations.
¹¹ But what the LORD has planned will stand forever.
       His thoughts never change.
¹² The LORD blesses each nation
       that worships only him.
       He blesses his chosen ones.
¹³ The LORD looks at the world
¹⁴   from his throne in heaven, and he watches us all.
¹⁵ The LORD gave us each a mind,
       and nothing we do can be hidden from him.

¹⁶ Mighty armies alone cannot win wars for a king;
       great strength by itself cannot keep a soldier safe.
¹⁷ In war the strength of a horse cannot be trusted
       to take you to safety.
¹⁸ But the LORD watches over all
       who honor him and trust his kindness.
¹⁹ He protects them from death and starvation.

²⁰ We depend on you, LORD, to help and protect us.
²¹ You make our hearts glad
       because we trust you, the only God.
²² Be kind and bless us!
       We depend on you.

Psalm 34

[Written by David when he pretended to be crazy in front of Abimelech, so that Abimelech would send him away, and David could leave.]

Honor the LORD

1 I will always praise the LORD.
2 With all my heart, I will praise the LORD.
   Let all who are helpless, listen and be glad.
3 Honor the LORD with me!
   Celebrate his great name.

4 I asked the LORD for help,
   and he saved me from all my fears.
5 Keep your eyes on the LORD!
   You will shine like the sun
   and never blush with shame.
6 I was a nobody, but I prayed,
   and the LORD saved me from all my troubles.
7 If you honor the LORD,
   his angel will protect you.
8 Discover for yourself that the LORD is kind.
   Come to him for protection,
   and you will be glad.

9 Honor the LORD!
   You are his special people.
   No one who honors the LORD
   will ever be in need.
10 Young lions[s] may go hungry or even starve,

---

[s] *Young lions*: In the Psalms wild animals often stand for God's enemies.

but if you trust the LORD,
  you will never miss out on anything good.

11 Come, my children, listen
   as I teach you to respect the LORD.
12 Do you want to live and enjoy a long life?
13   Then don't say cruel things and don't tell lies.
14 Do good instead of evil
   and try to live at peace.

15 If you obey the LORD,
   he will watch over you
   and answer your prayers.
16 But God despises evil people,
   and he will wipe them all from the earth,
     till they are forgotten.
17 When his people pray for help,
   he listens and rescues them from their troubles.
18 The LORD is there to rescue all
   who are discouraged
   and have given up hope.

19 The LORD's people may suffer a lot,
   but he will always bring them safely through.
20 Not one of their bones will ever be broken.

21 Wicked people are killed
   by their own evil deeds,
   and if you hate God's people
   you will be punished.
22 The LORD saves the lives of his servants.
   Run to him for protection,
   and you won't be punished.

Psalm 35

[A psalm by David.]

A Prayer for Protection from Enemies

¹ Fight my enemies, LORD! Attack my attackers!
²   Shield me and help me.
³ Aim your spear at everyone who hunts me down,
    but promise to save me.

⁴ Let all who want to kill me
    be disappointed and disgraced.
  Chase away and confuse all who plan to harm me.
⁵ Send your angel after them
    and let them be like straw in the wind.
⁶ Make them run in the dark on a slippery road,
    as your angel chases them.
⁷ I did them no harm,
    but they hid a net to trap me,
    and they dug a deep pit to catch and kill me.
⁸ Surprise them with disaster!
  Trap them in their own nets
    and let them fall and rot in the pits they have dug.

⁹ I will celebrate and be joyful
    because you, LORD, have saved me.
¹⁰ Every bone in my body will shout:
    "No one is like the LORD!"
  You protect the helpless from those in power;
  you save the poor and needy
    from those who hurt them.

¹¹ Liars accuse me of crimes I know nothing about.
¹²   They repay evil for good, and I feel all alone.

13 When they were sick, I wore sackcloth[t]
    and went without food.[u]
  I truly prayed for them,[v]
14   as I would for a friend or a relative.
  I was in sorrow and mourned,
      as I would for my mother.

15 I have stumbled,
    and worthless liars I don't even know
      surround me and sneer.
16 Worthless people make fun[w] and never stop laughing.
17 But all you do is watch!
    When will you do something?
      Save me from the attack of those vicious lions.
18 And when your people meet,
    I will praise you and thank you, Lord,
      in front of them all.

19 Don't let my brutal enemies
    be glad because of me.
  They hate me for no reason.
    Don't let them wink behind my back.
20 They say hurtful things, and they lie to people
    who want to live in peace.
21 They are quick to accuse me.
    They say, "You did it! We saw you ourselves."

---

t *sackcloth*: See the note at 30.11.
u *went without food*: People sometimes went without food
   (called "fasting") to show sorrow.
v *I...them*: Or "My prayer wasn't answered, but I prayed."
w *Worthless...fun*: One possible meaning for the difficult
   Hebrew text.

22 You see everything, LORD!
  Please don't keep silent
  or stay so far away.
23 Fight to defend me, Lord God,
24   and prove that I am right by your standards.
  Don't let them laugh at me 25 or say to each other,
    "Now we've got what we want!
    We'll gobble him down!"

26 Disappoint and confuse all
  who are glad to see me in trouble,
  but disgrace and embarrass my proud enemies
  who say to me,
    "You are nothing!"

27 Let all who want me to win be happy and joyful.
  From now on let them say,
    "The LORD is wonderful!
    God is glad when all goes well for his servant."
28 Then I will shout all day,
    "Praise the LORD God!
    He did what was right."

Psalm 36

[For the music leader by David, the LORD's servant.]

Human Sin and God's Goodness

1 Sinners don't respect God;
  sin is all they think about.
2 They like themselves too much
  to hate their own sins
  or even to see them.

³ They tell deceitful lies,
    and they don't have the sense to live right.
⁴ Those people stay awake, thinking up mischief,
  and they follow the wrong road,
    refusing to turn from sin.

⁵ Your love is faithful, LORD,
  and even the clouds in the sky
    can depend on you.
⁶ Your decisions are always fair.
  They are firm like mountains, deep like the sea,
    and all people and animals are under your care.

⁷ Your love is a treasure,
  and everyone finds shelter
    in the shadow of your wings.
⁸ You give your guests a feast in your house,
  and you serve a tasty drink
    that flows like a river.
⁹ The life-giving fountain belongs to you,
    and your light gives light to each of us.

¹⁰ Our LORD, keep showing love
    to everyone who knows you,
  and use your power to save
    all whose thoughts please you.
¹¹ Don't let those proud and merciless people
    kick me around or chase me away.

¹² Look at those wicked people!
  They are knocked down,
    never to get up again.

Psalm 37

[By David.]

Trust the LORD

1 Don't be annoyed by anyone who does wrong,
   and don't envy them.
2 They will soon disappear like grass without rain.

3 Trust the LORD and live right!
   The land will be yours, and you will be safe.
4 Do what the LORD wants,
   and he will give you your heart's desire.

5 Let the LORD lead you and trust him to help.
6 Then it will be as clear as the noonday sun
   that you were right.

7 Be patient and trust the LORD.
   Don't let it bother you when all goes well
   for those who do sinful things.
8 Don't be angry or furious. Anger can lead to sin.
9 All sinners will disappear,
   but if you trust the LORD, the land will be yours.

10 Sinners will soon disappear, never to be found,
11 but the poor will take the land
   and enjoy a big harvest.

12 Merciless people make plots against good people
   and snarl like animals,
13 but the Lord laughs and knows
   their time is coming soon.
14 The wicked kill with swords and shoot arrows

to murder the poor and the needy
and all who do right.
¹⁵ But they will be killed by their own swords,
and their arrows will be broken.

¹⁶ It is better to live right and be poor
than to be sinful and rich.
¹⁷ The wicked will lose all of their power,
but the LORD gives strength
to everyone who is good.

¹⁸ Those who obey the LORD are daily in his care,
and what he has given them will be theirs forever.
¹⁹ They won't be in trouble when times are bad,
and they will have plenty when food is scarce.

²⁰ Wicked people are enemies of the LORD
and will vanish like smoke from a field on fire.

²¹ An evil person borrows and never pays back;
a good person is generous and never stops giving.
²² Everyone the LORD blesses will receive the land;
everyone the LORD curses will be destroyed.

²³ If you do what the LORD wants,
he will make certain each step you take is
²⁴ The LORD will hold your hand,
and if you stumble, you still won't fall.

²⁵ As long as I can remember,
good people have never been left helple
and their children
have never gone begging for food

²⁶ They gladly give and lend,
    and their children turn out good.

²⁷ If you stop sinning and start doing right,
    you will keep living and be secure forever.
²⁸ The LORD loves justice,
    and he won't ever desert his faithful people.
He always protects them,
    but destroys the children of the wicked.
²⁹ God's people will own the land
    and live here forever.

³⁰ Words of wisdom come
    when good people speak for justice.
³¹ They remember God's teachings,
    and they never take a wrong step.

³² The wicked try to trap and kill good people,
³³ but the LORD is on their side,
    and he will defend them when they are on trial.

³⁴ Trust the LORD and follow him.
He will give you the land,
    and you will see the wicked destroyed.

³⁵ I have seen brutal people abuse others
    and grow strong like trees in rich soil.^x
³⁶ Suddenly they disappeared!
I looked,
    but they were gone and no longer there.

---

ke . . . soil: One possible meaning for the difficult Hebrew
·xt.

37 Think of the bright future waiting
for all the families of honest
and innocent and peace-loving people.
38 But not a trace will be left
of the wicked or their families.

39 The LORD protects his people,
and they can come to him in times of trouble.
40 The LORD helps them
and saves them from the wicked
because they run to him.

Psalm 38

[A psalm by David to be used when an offering is made.]

A Prayer in Times of Trouble

1 When you are angry, LORD,
please don't punish me
or even correct me.

2 You shot me with your arrows,
and you struck me with your hand.

3 My body hurts all over because of your anger.
Even my bones are in pain,
and my sins 4are so heavy that I am crushed.

5 Because of my foolishness,
I am covered with sores that stink and spread.
6 My body is twisted and bent,
and I groan all day long.
7 Fever has my back in flames,
and I hurt all over.

⁸ I am worn out and weak,
 moaning and in distress.

⁹ You, Lord, know every one of my deepest desires,
 and my noisy groans are no secret to you.
¹⁰ My heart is beating fast.
 I feel weak all over, and my eyes are red.

¹¹ Because of my sickness,
 no friends or neighbors will come near me.
¹² All who want me dead set traps to catch me,
 and those who want to harm and destroy me
 plan and plot all day.

¹³ I am not able to hear or speak a word;
¹⁴   I am completely deaf and can't make a sound.

¹⁵ I trust you, LORD God, and you will do something.
¹⁶ I said, "Don't let them laugh
 or brag because I slip."

¹⁷ I am about to collapse from constant pain.
¹⁸   I told you my sins, and I am sorry for them.
¹⁹ Many deadly and powerful enemies hate me,
²⁰ and they repay evil for good
 because I try to do right.

²¹ You are the LORD God!
 Stay nearby and don't desert me.
²² You are the one who saves me.
 Please hurry and help.

Psalm 39

[A psalm by David for Jeduthun, the music leader.]

A Prayer for Forgiveness

¹ I told myself,
  "I'll be careful not to sin by what I say,
      and I'll muzzle my mouth
      when evil people are near."
² I kept completely silent, but it did no good,*ʸ*
      and I hurt even worse.

³ I felt a fire burning inside,
  and the more I thought,
      the more it burned, until at last I said:
⁴ "Please, LORD, show me my future.
  Will I soon be gone?
⁵ You made my life short,
      so brief that the time means nothing to you.

  "Human life is but a breath,
⁶   and it disappears like a shadow.
  Our struggles are senseless;
  we store up more and more,
      without ever knowing who will get it all.

⁷ "What am I waiting for? I depend on you, Lord!
⁸   Save me from my sins.
  Don't let fools sneer at me.
⁹ You treated me like this,
      and I kept silent, not saying a word.

ʸ but … good: One possible meaning for the difficult Hebrew text.

10 "Won't you stop punishing me?
   You have worn me down.
11 You punish us severely because of our sins.
   Like a moth, you destroy what we treasure most.
      We are as frail as a breath.

12 "Listen, LORD, to my prayer!
   My eyes are flooded with tears, as I pray to you.
   I am merely a stranger visiting in your home
      as my ancestors did.
13 Stop being angry with me and let me smile again
   before I am dead and gone."

Psalm 40

[A psalm by David for the music leader.]

A Prayer for Help

1 I patiently waited, LORD,
      for you to hear my prayer.
   You listened 2and pulled me from a lonely pit
      full of mud and mire.
   You let me stand on a rock with my feet firm,
3 and you gave me a new song,
      a song of praise to you.
   Many will see this,
      and they will honor and trust you, the LORD God.

4 You bless all of those who trust you, LORD,
      and refuse to worship idols or follow false gods.
5 You, LORD God, have done many wonderful things,
   and you have planned marvelous things for us.
      No one is like you!

I would never be able to tell all you have done.

6 Sacrifices and offerings are not what please you;
    gifts and payment for sin
        are not what you demand.
But you made me willing to listen and obey.
7 And so, I said, "I am here to do what is written
        about me in the book, where it says,
8 'I enjoy pleasing you.
    Your Law is in my heart.'"

9 When your people worshiped, you know I told them,
    "Our LORD always helps!"
10 When all your people met, I did not keep silent.
I said, "Our LORD is kind.
    He is faithful and caring, and he saves us."

11 You, LORD, never fail to have pity on me;
    your love and faithfulness
        always keep me secure.

12 I have more troubles than I can count.
My sins are all around me,
    and I can't find my way.
My sins outnumber the hairs on my head,
    and I feel weak.
13 Please show that you care and come to my rescue.
    Hurry and help me!

14 Disappoint and confuse all who want me dead;
    turn away and disgrace all who want to hurt me.
15 Embarrass and shame all of those who say,
    "Just look at you now!"

16 Our LORD, let your worshipers rejoice and be glad.
  They love you for saving them,
      so let them always say,
        "The LORD is wonderful!"

17 I am poor and needy,
  but, LORD God, you care about me,
    and you come to my rescue.
  Please hurry and help.

Psalm 41

[A psalm by David for the music leader.]

A Prayer in Time of Sickness

1 You, LORD God, bless everyone
      who cares for the poor,
  and you rescue those people in times of trouble.
2 You protect them and keep them alive.
  You make them happy here in this land,
      and you don't hand them over to their enemies.
3 You always heal them and restore their strength
      when they are sick.
4 I prayed, "Have pity, LORD! Heal me,
      though I have sinned against you."

5 My vicious enemies ask me,
      "When will you die and be forgotten?"
6 When visitors come,
      all they ever bring are worthless words,
  and when they leave, they spread gossip.

7 My enemies whisper about me.

They think the worst, ⁸and they say,
"You have some fatal disease!
You'll never get well."
⁹ My most trusted friend has turned against me,
though he ate at my table.

¹⁰ Have pity, LORD!
Heal me, so I can pay them back.
¹¹ Then my enemies won't defeat me,
and I will know that you really care.
¹² You have helped me because I am innocent,
and you will always be close to my side.

¹³ You, the LORD God of Israel, will be praised forever!
Amen and amen.

BOOK II
(Psalms 42–72)

Psalm 42

*[A special psalm for the people of Korah
and for the music leader.]*

Longing for God

¹ As a deer gets thirsty for streams of water,
I truly am thirsty for you, my God.
² In my heart, I am thirsty for you, the living God.
When will I see your face?
³ Day and night my tears are my only food,
as everyone keeps asking,
"Where is your God?"

⁴ Sorrow floods my heart, when I remember
  leading the worshipers to your house.^z
I can still hear them shout their joyful praises.
⁵ Why am I discouraged? Why am I restless?
I trust you! And I will praise you again
  because you help me, ⁶and you are my God.

I am deeply discouraged as I think about you
  from where the Jordan begins at Mount Hermon
  and from Mount Mizar.^a
⁷ Your vicious waves have swept over me
  like an angry ocean or a roaring waterfall.

⁸ Every day, you are kind,
and at night you give me a song
  as my prayer to you, the living LORD God.

⁹ You are my mighty rock.^b
Why have you forgotten me?
Why must enemies mistreat me
  and make me sad?
¹⁰ Even my bones are in pain,
while all day long my enemies sneer and ask,
  "Where is your God?"

¹¹ Why am I discouraged? Why am I restless?
I trust you! And I will praise you again
  because you help me, and you are my God.

---

^z *leading ... house*: One possible meaning for the difficult
  Hebrew text.
^a *Mount Mizar*: The location is not known.
^b *mighty rock*: See the note at 18.2.

Psalm 43

A Prayer in Times of Trouble

1 Show that I am right, God!
    Defend me against everyone
        who doesn't know you;
    rescue me from each of those deceitful liars.
2 I run to you for protection.
    Why have you turned me away?
        Why must enemies mistreat me
            and make me sad?

3 Send your light and your truth to guide me.
    Let them lead me to your house
        on your sacred mountain.
4 Then I will worship at your altar
        because you make me joyful.
    You are my God, and I will praise you.
        Yes, I will praise you as I play my harp.

5 Why am I discouraged? Why am I restless?
    I trust you! And I will praise you again
        because you help me, and you are my God.

Psalm 44

*[A special psalm for the people of Korah
and for the music leader.]*

A Prayer for Help

1 Our God, our ancestors told us
    what wonders you worked
    and we listened carefully.

2 You chased off the nations
    by causing them trouble with your powerful arm.
Then you let our ancestors take over their land.
3 Their strength and weapons were not
    what won the land and gave them victory!
You loved them and fought with your powerful arm
    and your shining glory.

4 You are my God and King,
    and you give victory*c* to the people of Jacob.
5 By your great power, we knocked our enemies down
    and stomped on them.
6 I don't depend on my arrows
    or my sword to save me.
7 But you saved us from our hateful enemies,
    and you put them to shame.
8 We boast about you, our God,
    and we are always grateful.

9 But now you have rejected us;
    you don't lead us into battle, and we look foolish.
10 You made us retreat,
    and our enemies have taken everything we own.
11 You let us be slaughtered like sheep,
    and you scattered us among the nations.
12 You sold your people for little or nothing,
    and you earned no profit.

13 You made us look foolish to our neighbors,
    and people who live nearby insult us and sneer.

---

c and... victory: One ancient translation; Hebrew "please give victory."

14 Foreigners joke about us and shake their heads.
15 I am embarrassed every day,
    and I blush with shame.
16 But others mock and sneer,
    as they watch my enemies take revenge on me.

17 All of this has happened to us,
    though we didn't forget you
    or break our agreement.
18 We always kept you in mind
    and followed your teaching.
19 But you crushed us,
    and you covered us with deepest darkness
    where wild animals live.

20 We did not forget you
    or lift our hands in prayer to foreign gods.
21 You would have known it
    because you discover every secret thought.
22 We face death all day for you.
    We are like sheep on their way to be slaughtered.

23 Wake up! Do something, Lord!
   Why are you sleeping?
    Don't desert us forever.
24 Why do you keep looking away?
   Don't forget our sufferings
    and all of our troubles.
25 We are flat on the ground,
    holding on to the dust.
26 Do something! Help us!
   Show how kind you are
    and come to our rescue.

Psalm 45

*[A special psalm for the people of Korah
and for the music leader. To the tune "Lilies." A love song.]*

For a Royal Wedding

1 My thoughts are filled
    with beautiful words for the king,
    and I will use my voice
        as a writer would use pen and ink.

2 No one is as handsome as you!
    Your words are always kind.
        That is why God will always bless you.

3 Mighty king, glorious ruler, strap on your sword
4   and ride out in splendor!
    Win victories for truth and mercy and justice.
        Do fearsome things with your powerful arm.

5 Send your sharp arrows through enemy hearts
    and make all nations fall at your feet.

6 You are God, and you will rule forever as king.*d*
    Your royal power brings about justice.

7 You love justice and hate evil.
    And so, your God chose you
    and made you happier than any of your friends.

8 The sweet aroma of the spices
    myrrh, aloes, and cassia,
        covers your royal robes.
    You enjoy the music of harps
        in palaces decorated with ivory.

---

d You...king: Or "God has made you king, and you will
rule forever."

9 Daughters of kings are here,
   and your bride stands at your right side,
      wearing a wedding gown
      trimmed with pure gold.*e*

10 Bride of the king, listen carefully to me.
      Forget your own people
      and your father's family.
11 The king is your husband, so do what he desires.
12 All of the richest people from the city of Tyre
      will try to influence you
13   with precious treasures.

   Your bride, my king, has inward beauty,*f*
   and her wedding gown is woven
      with threads of gold.
14 Wearing the finest garments, she is brought to you,
      followed by her young friends, the bridesmaids.
15 Everyone is excited,
      as they follow you to the royal palace.

16 Your sons and your grandsons will also be kings
      as your ancestors were.
   You will make them the rulers
      everywhere on earth.

17 I will make your name famous from now on,
      and you will be praised forever and ever.

---

e trimmed with pure gold: Hebrew has "with gold from
   Ophir," which may have been in Africa or India. Gold
   from there was considered the very best.
f has inward beauty: Or "is dressed in her room."

Psalm 46

*[A special song for the people of Korah
and for the music leader.]*

God Is Our Mighty Fortress

¹ God is our mighty fortress,
always ready to help in times of trouble.
² And so, we won't be afraid!
Let the earth tremble
and the mountains tumble
into the deepest sea.
³ Let the ocean roar and foam,
and its raging waves shake the mountains.

⁴ A river and its streams bring joy to the city,
which is the sacred home of God Most High.
⁵ God is in that city, and it won't be shaken.
He will help it at dawn.

⁶ Nations rage! Kingdoms fall!
But at the voice of God
the earth itself melts.
⁷ The LORD All-Powerful is with us.
The God of Jacob is our fortress.

⁸ Come! See the fearsome things
the LORD has done on earth.
⁹ God brings wars to an end all over the world.
He breaks the arrows,
shatters the spears,
and burns the shields.⁸

---

⁸ *shields*: Or "chariots."

10 Our God says,
  "Calm down, and learn that I am God!
   All nations on earth will honor me."

11 The LORD All-Powerful is with us.
   The God of Jacob is our fortress.

Psalm 47

*[A psalm for the people of Korah
and for the music leader.]*

God Rules the Nations

1 All of you nations, clap your hands
   and shout joyful praises to God.
2 The LORD Most High is fearsome,
   the ruler of all the earth.
3 God has put every nation under our power,
4 and he chose for us the land
   that was the pride of Jacob, his favorite.

5 God goes up to his throne,
   as people shout and trumpets blast.
6 Sing praises to God our King,
7   the ruler of all the earth!
  Praise God with songs.

8 God rules the nations from his sacred throne.
9 Their leaders come together
   and are now the people of Abraham's God.
   All rulers on earth surrender their weapons,
   and God is greatly praised!

Psalm 48

[A song and a psalm for the people of Korah.]

The City of God

¹ The LORD God is wonderful!
   He deserves all praise in the city where he lives.
His holy mountain, ²beautiful and majestic,
   brings joy to all on earth.
Mount Zion, truly sacred,
   is home for the Great King.
³ God is there to defend it
   and has proved to be its protector.

⁴ Kings joined forces to attack the city,
⁵ but when they saw it,
   they were terrified and ran away.
⁶ They trembled all over like women giving birth
⁷ or like seagoing ships *h*
   wrecked by eastern winds.
⁸ We heard about it, and now we have seen it
   in the city of our God, the LORD All-Powerful.
This is the city that God will let stand forever.

⁹ Our God, here in your temple
   we think about your love.
¹⁰ You are famous and praised everywhere on earth,
   as you win victories with your powerful arm.
¹¹ Mount Zion will celebrate,
   and all Judah will be glad,
   because you bring justice.

h seagoing ships: The Hebrew text has "ships of Tarshish,"
which probably means large, seagoing ships.

¹² Let's walk around Zion and count its towers.
¹³ We will see its strong walls
    and visit each fortress.
    Then you can say to future generations,
¹⁴ "Our God is like this forever
    and will always*ⁱ* guide us."

Psalm 49

*[A psalm for the people of Korah
and for the music leader.]*

Don't Depend on Wealth

¹ Everyone on this earth,
    now listen to what I say!
² Listen, no matter who you are, rich or poor.
³ I speak words of wisdom,
    and my thoughts make sense.
⁴ I have in mind a mystery
    that I will explain while playing my harp.

⁵ Why should I be afraid in times of trouble,
    when I am surrounded by vicious enemies?
⁶ They trust in their riches
    and brag about all of their wealth.
⁷ You cannot buy back your life
    or pay off God!
⁸ It costs far too much to buy back your life.
    You can never pay God enough
⁹   to stay alive forever and safe from death.

---

i always: One possible meaning for the difficult Hebrew
text.

¹⁰ We see that wise people die,
     and so do stupid fools.
          Then their money is left for someone else.
¹¹ The grave *ʲ* will be their home forever and ever,
     although they once had land of their own.
¹² Our human glory disappears,
     and, like animals, we die.

¹³ Here is what happens to fools
     and to those who trust the words of fools:
¹⁴ They are like sheep
   with death as their shepherd,
     leading them to the grave.*ᵏ*
   In the morning God's people will walk all over them,
     as their bodies lie rotting in their home, the grave.
¹⁵ But God will rescue me from the power of death.

¹⁶ Don't let it bother you
     when others get rich and live in luxury.
¹⁷ Soon they will die
     and all of their wealth will be left behind.

¹⁸ We humans are praised when we do well,
     and all of us are glad to be alive.
¹⁹ But we each will go down to our ancestors,
     never again to see the light of day.
²⁰ Our human glory disappears,
     and, like animals, we die.

ʲ The grave: Some ancient translations; Hebrew "Their inward thoughts."
ᵏ as their… grave: One possible meaning for the difficult Hebrew text.

Psalm 50

[A psalm by Asaph.]

What Pleases God

1 From east to west, the powerful LORD God
    has been calling together everyone on earth.
2 God shines brightly from Zion,
    the most beautiful city.

3 Our God approaches, but not silently;
    a flaming fire comes first,
    and a storm surrounds him.
4 God comes to judge his people.
    He shouts to the heavens and to the earth,
5 "Call my followers together!
    They offered me a sacrifice,
    and we made an agreement."

6 The heavens announce, "God is the judge,
    and he is always honest."

7 My people, I am God! Israel, I am your God.
    Listen to my charges against you.
8 Although you offer sacrifices and always bring gifts,
9   I won't accept your offerings of bulls and goats.

10 Every animal in the forest belongs to me,
    and so do the cattle on a thousand hills.
11 I know all the birds in the mountains,
    and every wild creature is in my care.

12 If I were hungry, I wouldn't tell you,
    because I own the world and everything in it.

¹³ I don't eat the meat of bulls
   or drink the blood of goats.
¹⁴ I am God Most High! The only sacrifice I want
   is for you to be thankful and to keep your word.
¹⁵ Pray to me in time of trouble.
   I will rescue you, and you will honor me.

¹⁶ But to the wicked I say:
   "You don't have the right to mention my laws
   or claim to keep our agreement!
¹⁷ You refused correction
   and rejected my commands.
¹⁸ You made friends with every crook you met,
   and you liked people
   who break their wedding vows.
¹⁹ You talked only about violence
   and told nothing but lies;
²⁰ you sat around gossiping,
   ruining the reputation of your own relatives."

²¹ When you did all of this, I didn't say a word,
   and you thought, "God is just like us!"
   But now I will accuse you.
²² You have ignored me! So pay close attention
   or I will tear you apart,
   and no one can help you.

²³ The sacrifice that honors me is a thankful heart.
   Obey me,*
   and I, your God, will show my power to save.

---

* *Obey me*: One possible meaning for the difficult Hebrew
text.

Psalm 51

[For the music leader. A psalm by David when the prophet Nathan came to him after David had been with Bathsheba.]

A Prayer for Forgiveness

1 You are kind, God! Please have pity on me.
 You are always merciful!
  Please wipe away my sins.
2 Wash me clean from all of my sin and guilt.
3 I know about my sins,
  and I cannot forget my terrible guilt.
4 You are really the one I have sinned against;
  I have disobeyed you and have done wrong.
 So it is right and fair for you
  to correct and punish me.

5 I have sinned and done wrong
  since the day I was born.
6 But you want complete honesty,
  so teach me true wisdom.
7 Wash me with hyssop*m*
  until I am clean and whiter than snow.
8 Let me be happy and joyful!
  You crushed my bones, now let them celebrate.
9 Turn your eyes from my sin and cover my guilt.
10 Create pure thoughts in me
  and make me faithful again.
11 Don't chase me away from you
  or take your Holy Spirit away from me.

---

m hyssop: A small bush with bunches of small, white flowers. It was sometimes used as a symbol for making a person clean from sin.

¹² Make me as happy as you did when you saved me;
    make me want to obey!
¹³ I will teach sinners your Law,
    and they will return to you.
¹⁴ Keep me from any deadly sin.
    Only you can save me!
Then I will shout and sing about your power to save.

¹⁵ Help me to speak,
    and I will praise you, Lord.
¹⁶ Offerings and sacrifices are not what you want.
¹⁷ The way to please you
    is to feel sorrow deep in our hearts.
This is the kind of sacrifice you won't refuse.

¹⁸ Please be willing, Lord, to help the city of Zion
    and to rebuild its walls.
¹⁹ Then you will be pleased with the proper sacrifices,
    and we will offer bulls on your altar once again.

Psalm 52

*[A special psalm by David for the music leader.
He wrote this when Doeg from Edom went to Saul and said,
   "David has gone to Ahimelech's house."]*

God Is in Control

¹ You people may be strong and brag about your sins,
    but God can be trusted day after day.
² You plan brutal crimes,
    and your lying words cut like a sharp razor.
³ You would rather do evil than good,
    and tell lies than speak the truth.

4 You love to say cruel things,
  and your words are a trap.

5 God will destroy you forever!
  He will grab you and drag you from your homes.
    You will be uprooted and left to die.

6 When good people see this fearsome sight,
  they will laugh and say,
7 "Just look at them now! Instead of trusting God,
  they trusted their wealth and their cruelty."

8 But I am like an olive tree growing in God's house,
  and I can count on his love forever and ever.
9 I will always thank God for what he has done;
  I will praise his good name when his people meet.

Psalm 53

*[A special psalm by David for the music leader.
To the tune "Mahalath." [n]]*

No One Can Ignore God

1 Only a fool would say, "There is no God!"
  People like that are worthless!
    They are heartless and cruel and never do right.

2 From heaven God looks down to see
  if anyone is wise enough to search for him.
3 But all of them are crooked and corrupt.
    Not one of them does right.

---

[n] *Mahalath*: Or "For flutes," one possible meaning for the
difficult Hebrew text.

⁴ Won't you lawbreakers learn?
    You refuse to pray,
        and you gobble down the people of God.
⁵ But you will be terrified worse than ever before.
    God will scatter the bones of his enemies,
        and you will be ashamed when God rejects you.

⁶ I long for someone from Zion
    to come and save Israel!
Our God, when you bless your people again,
    Jacob's family will be glad,
        and Israel will celebrate.

Psalm 54

*[For the music leader. Use with stringed instruments.
A special psalm that David wrote when the people of Ziph
went to Saul and said, "David is hiding here with us."]*

Trusting God in Times of Trouble

¹ Save me, God, by your power
    and prove that I am right.
² Listen to my prayer and hear what I say.
³ Cruel strangers have attacked and want me dead.
    Not one of them cares about you.

⁴ You will help me, Lord God,
    and keep me from falling;
⁵ you will punish my enemies for their evil deeds.
    Be my faithful friend and destroy them.

⁶ I will bring a gift and offer a sacrifice to you, LORD.
    I will praise your name because you are good.

7 You have rescued me from all of my troubles,
 and my own eyes have seen my enemies fall.

Psalm 55

*[A special psalm by David for the music leader.
Use with stringed instruments.]*

Betrayed by a Friend

1 Listen, God, to my prayer! Don't reject my request.
2   Please listen and help me.
My thoughts are troubled, and I keep groaning
3   because my loud enemies shout and attack.
They treat me terribly and hold angry grudges.
4 My heart is racing fast, and I am afraid of dying.
5   I am trembling with fear, completely terrified.

6 I wish I had wings like a dove,
 so I could fly far away and be at peace.
7 I would go and live in some distant desert.
8 I would quickly find shelter
 from howling winds and raging storms.

9 Confuse my enemies, Lord! Upset their plans.
Cruelty and violence are all I see in the city,
10   and they are like guards on patrol day and night.
The city is full of trouble, evil, 11and corruption.
 Troublemakers and liars freely roam the streets.

12 My enemies are not the ones
 who sneer and make fun.
I could put up with that or even hide from them.
13 But it was my closest friend, the one I trusted most.

¹⁴ We enjoyed being together,
      and we went with others to your house, our God.

¹⁵ All who hate me
      are controlled by the power of evil.
   Sentence them to death
   and send them down alive
      to the world of the dead.

¹⁶ I ask for your help, LORD God,
      and you will keep me safe.
¹⁷ Morning, noon, and night
      you hear my concerns and my complaints.
¹⁸ I am attacked from all sides,
      but you will rescue me unharmed by the battle.
¹⁹ You have always ruled, and you will hear me.
   You will defeat my enemies
      because they won't turn and worship you.

²⁰ My friend turned against me and broke his promise.
²¹ His words were smoother than butter,
      and softer than olive oil.
   But hatred filled his heart,
      and he was ready to attack with a sword.

²² Our LORD, we belong to you.
   We tell you what worries us,
      and you won't let us fall.
²³ But what about those people
      who are cruel and brutal?
   You will throw them down into the deepest pit
      long before their time.
   I trust you, LORD!

Psalm 56

[For the music leader. To the tune "A Silent Dove in the Distance." o *A special psalm by David when the Philistines captured him in Gath.]*

A Prayer of Trust in God

1 Have pity, God Most High!
     My enemies chase me all day.
2 Many of them are pursuing and attacking me,
3   but even when I am afraid, I keep on trusting you.
4 I praise your promises! I trust you and am not afraid.
     No one can harm me.

5 Enemies spend the whole day finding fault with me;
     all they think about is how to do me harm.
6 They attack from ambush,
     watching my every step and hoping to kill me.
7 They won't get away^p with these crimes, God,
     because when you get angry, you destroy people.

8 You have kept record of my days of wandering.
     You have stored my tears in your bottle
     and counted each of them.

9 When I pray, LORD God, my enemies will retreat,
     because I know for certain that you are with me.
10 I praise your promises!
11 I trust you and am not afraid. No one can harm me.

---

^{o} *A Silent...Distance*: One possible meaning for the difficult
Hebrew text.

^{p} *They...away*: One possible meaning for the difficult
Hebrew text.

¹² I will keep my promises to you, my God,
and bring you gifts.
¹³ You protected me from death
and kept me from stumbling,
so that I would please you
and follow the light that leads to life.

Psalm 57

[For the music leader. To the tune "Don't Destroy." �q
*A special psalm by David when he was in the cave
while running from Saul.]*

Praise and Trust in Times of Trouble

¹ God Most High, have pity on me!
Have mercy.
I run to you for safety.
In the shadow of your wings,
I seek protection till danger dies down.
² I pray to you, my protector.
³ You will send help from heaven and save me,
but you will bring trouble on my attackers.
You are faithful, and you can be trusted.

⁴ I live among lions, who gobble down people!
They have spears and arrows instead of teeth,
and they have sharp swords instead of tongues.

⁵ May you, my God, be honored above the heavens;
may your glory be seen everywhere on earth.

�q *Don't Destroy*: One possible meaning for the difficult
Hebrew text.

⁶ Enemies set traps for my feet and struck me down.
  They dug a pit in my path,
      but fell in it themselves.
⁷ I am faithful to you, and you can trust me.
      I will sing and play music for you, my God.
⁸ I feel wide awake!
  I will wake up my harp
      and wake up the sun.
⁹ I will praise you, Lord, for everyone to hear,
      and I will sing hymns to you in every nation.
¹⁰ Your love reaches higher than the heavens;
      your loyalty extends beyond the clouds.

¹¹ May you, my God, be honored above the heavens;
      may your glory be seen everywhere on earth.

Psalm 58

*[A special psalm by David for the music leader.
To the tune "Don't Destroy."ʳ]*

A Prayer When All Goes Wrong

¹ Do you mighty peopleˢ talk only to oppose justice?ᵗ
      Don't you ever judge fairly?
² You are always planning evil, and you are brutal.
³ You have done wrong and lied
      from the day you were born.

ʳ *Don't Destroy:* See the note at Psalm 57.
ˢ *mighty people:* Or "mighty rulers" or "mighty gods."
ᵗ *Do...justice:* One possible meaning for the difficult
  Hebrew text.

4 Your words spread poison like the bite of a cobra
5   that refuses to listen to the snake charmer.

6 My enemies are fierce as lions, LORD God!
    Shatter their teeth. Snatch out their fangs.
7 Make them disappear like leaking water,
    and make their arrows miss.
8 Let them dry up like snails
    or be like a child that dies before seeing the sun.
9 Wipe them out quicker than a pot can be heated
    by setting thorns on fire.*u*

10 Good people will be glad
  when they see the wicked getting what they deserve,
    and they will wash their feet
    in their enemies' blood.
11 Everyone will say, "It's true!
  Good people are rewarded.
    God does rule the earth with justice."

Psalm 59

[For the music leader. To the tune "Don't Destroy."v
A special psalm by David when Saul had David's house
watched so that he could kill him.]

A Prayer for Protection

1 Save me, God!
    Protect me from enemy attacks!

---

u Wipe…fire: One possible meaning for the difficult
Hebrew text.
v Don't Destroy: See the note at Psalm 57.

2 Keep me safe from brutal people
   who want to kill me.

3 Merciless enemies, LORD, are hiding and plotting,
   hoping to kill me.
I have not hurt them in any way at all.
4   But they are ready to attack.
Do something! Help me!
   Look at what's happening.
5 LORD God All-Powerful, you are the God of Israel.
Punish the other nations
   and don't pity those terrible
   and rebellious people.

6 My enemies return at evening,
   growling like dogs roaming the city.
7 They curse and their words cut like swords,
   as they say to themselves, "No one can hear us!"

8 You, LORD, laugh at them and sneer at the nations.
9 You are my mighty fortress, and I depend on you.
10 You love me
    and will let me see my enemies defeated.
11 Don't kill them, or everyone may forget!
Just use your mighty power
    to make them tremble and fall.

You are a shield for your people.
12 My enemies are liars!
    So let them be trapped by their boastful lies.
13 Get angry and destroy them.
    Leave them in ruin.
Then all the nations will know that you rule in Israel.

¹⁴ Those liars return at evening,
    growling like dogs roaming the city.
¹⁵ They search for scraps of food,
    and they snarl until they are stuffed.

¹⁶ But I will sing about your strength, my God,
    and I will celebrate because of your love.
You are my fortress,
    my place of protection in times of trouble.
¹⁷ I will sing your praises!
You are my mighty fortress,
    and you love me.

Psalm 60

[For the music leader. To the tune "Lily of the Promise."
A special psalm by David for teaching. He wrote it
during his wars with the Arameans of northern Syria,ʷ
when Joab came back and killed twelve thousand Edomitesˣ
in Salt Valley.]

You Can Depend on God

¹ You, God, are angry with us!
We are rejected and crushed.
    Make us strong again!
² You made the earth shake and split wide open;
    now heal its wounds and stop its trembling.
³ You brought hard times on your people,
    and you gave us wine that made us stagger.

ʷ *wars...Syria*: See 2 Samuel 8.3-8; 10.16-18; 1 Chronicles
    18.3-11; 19.6-19.
ˣ *killed...Edomites*: See 2 Samuel 8.13; 1 Chronicles 18.12.

4 You gave a signal to those who worship you,
    so they could escape from enemy arrows. [y]
5 Answer our prayers!
Use your powerful arm and give us victory.
    Then the people you love will be safe.

6 Our God, you solemnly promised,
    "I would gladly divide up the city of Shechem
        and give away Succoth Valley piece by piece.
7 The lands of Gilead and Manasseh are mine.
Ephraim is my war helmet,
    and Judah is the symbol of my royal power.
8 Moab is merely my washbasin. Edom belongs to me,
    and I shout in triumph over the Philistines."

9 Our God, who will bring me to the fortress,
    or lead me to Edom?
10 Have you rejected us and deserted our armies?
11 Help us defeat our enemies!
    No one else can rescue us.
12 You will give us victory and crush our enemies.

Psalm 61

*[A psalm by David for the music leader.
Use with stringed instruments.]*

Under the Protection of God

1 Please listen, God,
    and answer my prayer!

---

[y] *so...arrows*: Some ancient translations and one possible
meaning for the difficult Hebrew text.

² I feel hopeless,
>   and I cry out to you from a faraway land.

Lead me to the mighty rock^z high above me.
³ You are a strong tower,
>   where I am safe from my enemies.

⁴ Let me live with you forever
>   and find protection under your wings, my God.
⁵ You heard my promises, and you have blessed me,
>   just as you bless everyone who worships you.

⁶ Let the king have a long and healthy life.
⁷ May he always rule with you, God, at his side;
>   may your love and loyalty watch over him.

⁸ I will sing your praises forever
>   and will always keep my promises.

Psalm 62

[A psalm by David for Jeduthun, the music leader.]

God Is Powerful and Kind

¹ Only God can save me, and I calmly wait for^a him.
² God alone is the mighty rock^z that keeps me safe
>   and the fortress where I am secure.

³ I feel like a shaky fence or a sagging wall.
>   How long will all of you attack and assault me?

---

^z *mighty rock*: See the note at 18.2.
^a *calmly wait for*: Or "am at peace with."

4 You want to bring me down from my place of honor.
  You love to tell lies,
        and when your words are kind,
        hatred hides in your heart.

5 Only God gives inward peace, and I depend on him.
6 God alone is the mighty rock that keeps me safe,
        and he is the fortress where I feel secure.
7 God saves me and honors me.
        He is that mighty rock where I find safety.

8 Trust God, my friends,
        and always tell him each one of your concerns.
  God is our place of safety.

9 We humans are only a breath;
        none of us are truly great.
  All of us together weigh less than a puff of air.
10 Don't trust in violence or depend on dishonesty
        or rely on great wealth.

11 I heard God say two things:
        "I am powerful, 12and I am very kind."
   The Lord rewards each of us
        according to what we do.

Psalm 63

[A psalm by David when he was in the desert of Judah.]

God's Love Means More than Life

1 You are my God. I worship you.
  In my heart, I long for you,
        as I would long for a stream in a scorching desert.

² I have seen your power and your glory
    in the place of worship.
³ Your love means more than life to me,
    and I praise you.
⁴ As long as I live, I will pray to you.
⁵ I will sing joyful praises
    and be filled with excitement
    like a guest at a banquet.

⁶ I think about you before I go to sleep,
    and my thoughts turn to you during the night.
⁷ You have helped me,
    and I sing happy songs
    in the shadow of your wings.
⁸ I stay close to you,
    and your powerful arm supports me.

⁹ All who want to kill me
    will end up in the ground.
¹⁰ Swords will run them through,
    and wild dogs will eat them.

¹¹ Because of you, our God,
    the king will celebrate with your faithful followers,
    but liars will be silent.

Psalm 64

[A psalm by David for the music leader.]

Celebrate because of the LORD

¹ Listen to my concerns, God,
    and protect me from my terrible enemies.

² Keep me safe from secret plots
    of corrupt and evil gangs.
³ Their words cut like swords,
    and their cruel remarks
      sting like sharp arrows.
⁴ They fearlessly ambush
    and shoot innocent people.

⁵ They are determined to do evil,
    and they tell themselves,
    "Let's set traps! No one can see us."*b*
⁶ They make evil plans and say,
    "We'll commit a perfect crime.
    No one knows our thoughts."*c*

⁷ But God will shoot his arrows
    and quickly wound them.
⁸ They will be destroyed by their own words,
    and everyone who sees them
      will tremble with fear.*d*
⁹ They will be afraid and say,
    "Look at what God has done
    and keep it all in mind."

¹⁰ May the LORD bless his people
    with peace and happiness
    and let them celebrate.

---

b us: One ancient translation; Hebrew "them."
c thoughts: One possible meaning for the difficult Hebrew
text of verse 6.
d tremble with fear: Or "turn and run."

Psalm 65

[A psalm by David and a song for the music leader.]

God Answers Prayer

1 Our God, you deserve *e* praise in Zion,
   where we keep our promises to you.
2 Everyone will come to you
   because you answer prayer.
3 Our terrible sins get us down, but you forgive us.
4 You bless your chosen ones, and you invite them
   to live near you in your temple.
We will enjoy your house, the sacred temple.

5 Our God, you save us, and your fearsome deeds
   answer our prayers for justice!
You give hope to people everywhere on earth,
   even those across the sea.
6 You are strong,
and your mighty power
   put the mountains in place.
7 You silence the roaring waves
   and the noisy shouts of the nations.
8 People far away marvel at your fearsome deeds,
and all who live under the sun
   celebrate and sing because of you.

9 You take care of the earth and send rain
   to help the soil grow all kinds of crops.
Your rivers never run dry,
   and you prepare the earth to produce much grain.

---

e deserve: One possible meaning for the difficult Hebrew
text.

10 You water all of its fields
     and level the lumpy ground.
   You send showers of rain to soften the soil
     and help the plants sprout.
11 Wherever your footsteps touch the earth,
     a rich harvest is gathered.
12 Desert pastures blossom, and mountains celebrate.
13 Meadows are filled with sheep and goats;
     valleys overflow with grain
     and echo with joyful songs.

Psalm 66

[A song and a psalm for the music leader.]

Shout Praises to God

1 Tell everyone on this earth to shout praises to God!
2 Sing about his glorious name.
     Honor him with praises.
3 Say to God, "Everything you do is fearsome,
     and your mighty power
     makes your enemies come crawling.
4 You are worshiped by everyone!
     We all sing praises to you."

5 Come and see the fearsome things our God has done!
6 When God made the sea dry up,
     our people walked across,
     and because of him, we celebrated there.
7 His mighty power rules forever,
     and nothing the nations do
     can be hidden from him.
   So don't turn against God.

8 All of you people, come praise our God!
   Let his praises be heard.
9 God protects us from death and keeps us steady.

10 Our God, you tested us, just as silver is tested.
11 You trapped us in a net and gave us heavy burdens.
12   You sent war chariots to crush our skulls.
   We traveled through fire and through floods,
      but you brought us to a land of plenty.

13 I will bring sacrifices into your house, my God,
      and I will do what I promised
14   when I was in trouble.
15 I will sacrifice my best sheep
      and offer bulls and goats on your altar.

16 All who worship God, come here and listen;
      I will tell you everything God has done for me.
17 I prayed to the Lord, and I praised him.
18 If my thoughts had been sinful,
      he would have refused to hear me.
19 But God did listen and answered my prayer.
20 Let's praise God! He listened when I prayed,
      and he is always kind.

Psalm 67

*[A psalm and a song for the music leader.
Use with stringed instruments.]*

Tell the Nations To Praise God

1 Our God, be kind and bless us!
   Be pleased and smile.

2 Then everyone on earth will learn to follow you,
　　and all nations will see your power to save us.

3 Make everyone praise you
　　and shout your praises.
4 Let the nations celebrate with joyful songs,
　　because you judge fairly and guide all nations.
5 Make everyone praise you
　　and shout your praises.

6 Our God has blessed the earth
　　with a wonderful harvest!
7 Pray for his blessings to continue
　　and for everyone on earth to worship our God.

Psalm 68

[A psalm and a song by David for the music leader.]

God Will Win the Battle

1 Do something, God!
　　Scatter your hateful enemies.
　　　Make them turn and run.
2 　　Scatter them like smoke!
　　When you come near,
　　　make them melt like wax in a fire.
3 But let your people be happy
　　and celebrate because of you.

4 Our God, you are the one who rides on the clouds,
　　and we praise you.
　　Your name is the LORD,
　　　and we celebrate as we worship you.

5 Our God, from your sacred home
   you take care of orphans and protect widows.
6 You find families for those who are lonely.
   You set prisoners free and let them prosper,*f*
      but all who rebel will live in a scorching desert.

7 You set your people free,
   and you led them through the desert.
8 God of Israel, the earth trembled,
   and rain poured down.
   You alone are the God
      who rules from Mount Sinai.
9 When your land was thirsty,
   you sent showers to refresh it.
10 Your people settled there,
   and you were generous to everyone in need.

11 You gave the command,
   and a chorus of women told what had happened:
12 "Kings and their armies retreated and ran,
   and everything they left is now being divided.
13 And for those who stayed back to guard the sheep,
   there are metal doves with silver-coated wings
      and shiny gold feathers."

14 God All-Powerful, you scattered the kings
   like snow falling on Mount Zalmon.*g*

15 Our LORD and our God,
   Bashan is a mighty mountain covered with peaks.

---

f and let them prosper: Or "and give them a song."

g Mount Zalmon: The location of this mountain is not known.

16 Why is it jealous of Zion,
   the mountain you chose as your home forever?

17 When you, LORD God, appeared
    to your people [h] at Sinai,
       you came with thousands of mighty chariots.
18 When you climbed the high mountain,
       you took prisoners with you
       and were given gifts.
   Your enemies didn't want you to live there,
       but they gave you gifts.

19 We praise you, Lord God!
   You treat us with kindness day after day,
       and you rescue us.
20 You always protect us and save us from death.

21 Our Lord and our God,
    your terrible enemies are ready for war, [i]
       but you will crush their skulls.
22 You promised to bring them from Bashan
       and from the deepest sea.
23 Then we could stomp on their blood,
       and our dogs could chew on their bones.

24 We have seen crowds marching
       to your place of worship, our God and King.

---

[h] to your people: Or "in all your holiness" or "in your holy
    place."
[i] are ready for war: The Hebrew text has "have long hair,"
    which probably refers to the ancient custom of wearing
    long hair on special occasions, such as a "holy war."

25 The singers come first, and then the musicians,
    surrounded by young women
        playing tambourines.
26 They come shouting,
    "People of Israel, praise the LORD God!"
27 The small tribe of Benjamin leads the way,
    followed by the leaders from Judah.
    Then come the leaders from Zebulun and Naphtali.

28 Our God, show your strength! Show us once again.
29 Then kings will bring gifts
    to your temple in Jerusalem.*j*

30 Punish that animal that lives in the swamp!*k*
    Punish that nation
        whose leaders and people are like wild bulls.
    Make them come crawling with gifts of silver.
        Scatter those nations that enjoy making war.*l*
31 Force the Egyptians to bring gifts of bronze;
    make the Ethiopians*m* hurry to offer presents.*n*

32 Now sing praises to God!
    Every kingdom on earth, sing to the Lord!

---

j Our God...Jerusalem: One possible meaning for the
    difficult Hebrew text of verses 28 and 29.
k animal...swamp: Probably Egypt.
l war: One possible meaning for the difficult Hebrew text
    of verse 30.
m the Ethiopians: The Hebrew text has "the people of
    Cush," which was a region south of Egypt that included
    parts of the present countries of Ethiopia and Sudan.
n presents: One possible meaning for the difficult Hebrew
    text of verse 31.

33 Praise the one who rides across the ancient skies;
    listen as he speaks with a mighty voice.

34 Tell about God's power!
    He is honored in Israel, and he rules the skies.
35 The God of Israel is fearsome in his temple,
    and he makes us strong.
    Let's praise our God!

Psalm 69

[By David for the music leader. To the tune "Lilies."]

God Can Be Trusted

1 Save me, God! I am about to drown.
2 I am sinking deep in the mud,
    and my feet are slipping.
   I am about to be swept under by a mighty flood.
3 I am worn out from crying, and my throat is dry.
   I have waited for you till my eyes are blurred.

4 There are more people who hate me for no reason
    than there are hairs on my head.
  Many terrible enemies want to destroy me, God.
  Am I supposed to give back something I didn't steal?
5 You know my foolish sins.
    Not one is hidden from you.

6 LORD God All-Powerful, ruler of Israel,
  don't let me embarrass anyone
    who trusts and worships you.
7 It is for your sake alone
    that I am insulted and blush with shame.

⁸ I am like a stranger to my relatives
    and like a foreigner to my own family.

⁹ My love for your house burns in me like a fire,
  and when others insulted you,
    they insulted me as well.
¹⁰ I cried and went without food,*ᵒ*
  but they still insulted me.
¹¹ They sneered at me for wearing sackcloth*ᵖ*
  to show my sorrow.
¹² Rulers and judges gossip about me,
    and drunkards make up songs to mock me.

¹³ But I pray to you, LORD.
  So when the time is right, answer me
    and help me with your wonderful love.
¹⁴ Don't let me sink in the mud,
  but save me from my enemies
    and from the deep water.
¹⁵ Don't let me be swept away by a flood
  or drowned in the ocean or swallowed by death.

¹⁶ Answer me, LORD! You are kind and good.
  Pay attention to me! You are truly merciful.
¹⁷ Don't turn away from me.
  I am your servant, and I am in trouble.
  Please hurry and help!
¹⁸   Come and save me from my enemies.

¹⁹ You know how I am insulted, mocked, and disgraced;

ᵒ went without food: See the note at 35.13.
ᵖ sackcloth: See the note at 30.11.

you know every one of my enemies.

20 I am crushed by insults, and I feel sick.
I had hoped for mercy and pity,
but there was none.

21 Enemies poisoned my food,
and when I was thirsty, they gave me vinegar.

22 Make their table a trap for them and their friends.

23 Blind them with darkness
and make them tremble.

24 Show them how angry you are!
Be furious and catch them.

25 Destroy their camp
and don't let anyone live in their tents.

26 They cause trouble for people
you have already punished;
their gossip hurts those you have wounded.

27 Make them guiltier than ever
and don't forgive them.

28 Wipe their names from the book of the living;
remove them from the list of the innocent.

29 I am mistreated and in pain.
Protect me, God, and keep me safe!

30 I will praise the LORD God
with a song and a thankful heart.

31 This will please the LORD
better than offering an ox or a full-grown bull.

32 When those in need see this, they will be happy,
and the LORD's worshipers will be encouraged.

33 The LORD will listen when the homeless cry out,
and he will never forget his people in prison.

³⁴ Heaven and earth will praise our God,
    and so will the oceans and everything in them.
³⁵ God will rescue Jerusalem,
    and he will rebuild the towns of Judah.
His people will live there on their own land,
³⁶ and when the time comes,
    their children will inherit the land.
Then everyone who loves God
    will also settle there.

Psalm 70

[By David for the music leader.
To be used when an offering is made.]

God Is Wonderful

¹ Save me, LORD God! Hurry and help.
² Disappoint and confuse
    all who want to kill me.
Turn away and disgrace all who want to hurt me.
³ Embarrass and shame those who say,
    "We told you so!"

⁴ Let your worshipers celebrate and be glad
    because of you.
They love your saving power,
    so let them always say,
    "God is wonderful!"
⁵ I am poor and needy,
    but you, the LORD God, care about me.

You are the one who saves me.
    Please hurry and help!

Psalm 71

A Prayer for God's Protection

1 I run to you, LORD, for protection.
    Don't disappoint me.
2 You do what is right, so come to my rescue.
    Listen to my prayer and keep me safe.
3 Be my mighty rock,*q*
    the place where I can always run for protection.
Save me by your command!
    You are my mighty rock and my fortress.

4 Come and save me, LORD God,
    from vicious and cruel and brutal enemies!
5 I depend on you,
    and I have trusted you since I was young.
6 I have relied on you*r* from the day I was born.
You brought me safely through birth,
    and I always praise you.

7 Many people think of me as something evil.
    But you are my mighty protector,
8   and I praise and honor you all day long.
9 Don't throw me aside when I am old;
    don't desert me when my strength is gone.
10 My enemies are plotting
    because they want me dead.
11 They say, "Now we'll catch you!
    God has deserted you, and no one can save you."

---

q mighty rock: See the note at 18.2.
r I... you: One possible meaning for the difficult Hebrew text.

¹² Come closer, God! Please hurry and help.
¹³ Embarrass and destroy all who want me dead;
    disgrace and confuse all who want to hurt me.
¹⁴ I will never give up hope or stop praising you.
¹⁵ All day long I will tell
    the wonderful things you do
    to save your people.
But you have done much more
    than I could possibly know.
¹⁶ I will praise you, LORD God,
    for your mighty deeds and your power to save.

¹⁷ You have taught me since I was a child,
    and I never stop telling
    about your marvelous deeds.
¹⁸ Don't leave me when I am old
    and my hair turns gray.
    Let me tell future generations
    about your mighty power.
¹⁹ Your deeds of kindness are known in the heavens.
    No one is like you!

²⁰ You made me suffer a lot,
    but you will bring me back from this deep pit
    and give me new life.
²¹ You will make me truly great
    and take my sorrow away.

²² I will praise you, God, the Holy One of Israel.
    You are faithful.
    I will play the harp and sing your praises.
²³ You have rescued me! I will celebrate and shout,
    singing praises to you with all my heart.

²⁴ All day long I will announce your power to save.
   I will tell how you disgraced and disappointed
      those who wanted to hurt me.

Psalm 72

[By Solomon.]

A Prayer for God To Guide and Help the King

¹ Please help the king to be honest and fair
   just like you, our God.
² Let him be honest and fair with all your people,
   especially the poor.
³ Let peace and justice rule every mountain and hill.
⁴ Let the king defend the poor, rescue the homeless,
   and crush everyone who hurts them.
⁵ Let the king live*s* forever like the sun and the moon.
⁶ Let him be as helpful as rain
   that refreshes the meadows and the ground.
⁷ Let the king be fair with everyone,
   and let there be peace
      until the moon falls from the sky.

⁸ Let his kingdom reach from sea to sea,
   from the Euphrates River across all the earth.
⁹ Force the desert tribes to accept his rule,
   and make his enemies crawl in the dirt.
¹⁰ Force the rulers of Tarshish*t* and of the islands
   to pay taxes to him.

---

s Let the king live: One ancient translation; Hebrew "Let
them worship you."

t Tarshish: The exact location of this city is not known.

Make the kings of Sheba and of Seba[u] bring gifts.
11 Make other rulers bow down
    and all nations serve him.

12 Do this because the king rescues the homeless
    when they cry out,
        and he helps everyone who is poor and in need.
13 The king has pity on the weak and the helpless
    and protects those in need.
14 He cares when they hurt,
    and he saves them from cruel and violent deaths.

15 Long live the king!
    Give him gold from Sheba.
    Always pray for the king
    and praise him each day.
16 Let cities overflow with food
    and hills be covered with grain,
        just like Mount Lebanon.
    Let the people in the cities prosper
        like wild flowers.
17 May the glory of the king shine brightly forever
    like the sun in the sky.
    Let him make nations prosper
        and learn to praise him.

18 LORD God of Israel, we praise you.
    Only you can work miracles.
19 We will always praise your glorious name.

---

[u] *Sheba...Seba*: Sheba may have been a place in what is
now southwest Arabia, and Seba may have been in
southern Arabia.

Let your glory be seen everywhere on earth.
   Amen and amen.

20 This ends the prayers of David, the son of Jesse.

BOOK III
(Psalms 73–89)

Psalm 73
[A psalm by Asaph.]

God Is Good

1 God is truly good to Israel,[v]
   especially to everyone with a pure heart.
2 But I almost stumbled and fell,
3   because it made me jealous
   to see proud and evil people
   and to watch them prosper.
4 They never have to suffer,[w] they stay healthy,
5   and they don't have troubles like everyone else.

6 Their pride is like a necklace,
   and they commit sin
   more often than they dress themselves.
7 Their eyes poke out with fat,
   and their minds are flooded
   with foolish thoughts.
8 They sneer and say cruel things,

---

[v] *to Israel*: Or "to those who do right."
[w] *They…suffer*: Or "They die a painless death."

and because of their pride,
  they make violent threats.
⁹ They dare to speak against God
  and to order others around.

¹⁰ God will bring his people back,
  and they will drink the water he so freely gives.ˣ

¹¹ Only evil people would say,
  "God Most High cannot know everything!"
¹² Yet all goes well for them, and they live in peace.
¹³ What good did it do me to keep my thoughts pure
  and refuse to do wrong?
¹⁴ I am sick all day, and I am punished each morning.
¹⁵ If I had said evil things,
  I would not have been loyal to your people.

¹⁶ It was hard for me to understand all this!
¹⁷ Then I went to your temple, and there I understood
  what will happen to my enemies.
¹⁸ You will make them stumble, never to get up again.
¹⁹ They will be terrified,
  suddenly swept away and no longer there.
²⁰ They will disappear, Lord,
  despised like a bad dream the morning after.

²¹ Once I was bitter and brokenhearted.
²² I was stupid and ignorant,
  and I treated you as a wild animal would.
²³ But I never really left you,

ˣ *gives*: One possible meaning for the difficult Hebrew text
of verse 10.

and you hold my right hand.
24 Your advice has been my guide,
   and later you will welcome me in glory.[y]
25 In heaven I have only you,
   and on this earth you are all I want.
26 My body and mind may fail,
   but you are my strength and my choice forever.

27 Powerful LORD God,
   all who stay far from you will be lost,
   and you will destroy those who are unfaithful.
28 It is good for me to be near you.
   I choose you as my protector,
   and I will tell about your wonderful deeds.

Psalm 74

[A special psalm by Asaph.]

A Prayer for the Nation in Times of Trouble

1 Our God, why have you completely rejected us?
   Why are you so angry
   with the ones you care for?
2 Remember the people you rescued long ago,
   the tribe you chose to be your very own.
   Think of Mount Zion, your home;
3 walk over to the temple left in ruins forever
   by those who hate us.

4 Your enemies roared like lions in your holy temple,
   and they have placed their banners there.

---

[y] *in glory*: Or "with honor."

⁵ It looks like a forest chopped to pieces.ᶻ
⁶ They used axes and hatchets to smash the carvings.
⁷ They burned down your temple
      and badly disgraced it.
⁸ They said to themselves,
      "We'll crush them!"
Then they burned every one of your meeting places
      all over the country.
⁹ There are no more miracles and no more prophets.
      Who knows how long it will be like this?

¹⁰ Our God, how much longer will our enemies sneer?
      Won't they ever stop insulting you?
¹¹ Why don't you punish them?
      Why are you holding back?

¹² Our God and King,
      you have ruled since ancient times;
      you have won victories everywhere on this earth.
¹³ By your power you made a path through the sea,
      and you smashed the heads of sea monsters.
¹⁴ You crushed the heads of the monster Leviathan,ᵃ
      then fed him to wild creatures in the desert.
¹⁵ You opened the ground for streams and springs
      and dried up mighty rivers.
¹⁶ You rule the day and the night,
      and you put the moon and the sun in place.

ᶻ *pieces*: One meaning for the difficult Hebrew text of
verse 5.
ᵃ *Leviathan*: God's victory over this monster sometimes
stands for his power over all creation and sometimes for
his defeat of Egypt.

17 You made summer and winter
    and gave them to the earth.[b]

18 Remember your enemies, LORD!
    They foolishly sneer and won't respect you.
19 You treat us like pet doves, but they mistreat us.
    Don't keep forgetting us
        and letting us be fed to those wild animals.
20 Remember the agreement you made with us.
    Violent enemies are hiding
        in every dark corner of the earth.
21 Don't disappoint those in need
    or make them turn from you,
        but help the poor and homeless
        to shout your praises.
22 Do something, God! Defend yourself.
    Remember how those fools
        sneer at you all day long.
23 Don't forget the loud shouts of your enemies.

Psalm 75

*[A psalm and a song by Asaph for the music leader.
To the tune "Don't Destroy."[c]]*

Praise God for All He Has Done

1 Our God, we thank you for being so near to us!
    Everyone celebrates your wonderful deeds.

2 You have set a time to judge with fairness.

---

b *gave…earth*: Or "made boundaries for the earth."
c *Don't Destroy*: See the note at Psalm 57.

³ The earth trembles, and its people shake;
    you alone keep its foundations firm.

⁴ You tell every bragger, "Stop bragging!"
  And to the wicked you say,
    "Don't boast of your power!

⁵ Stop bragging! Quit telling me how great you are."

⁶ Our LORD and our God, victory doesn't come
    from the east or the west or from the desert.

⁷ You are the one who judges.
    You can take away power and give it to others.

⁸ You hold in your hand a cup filled with wine,^d
    strong and foaming.
You will pour out some
  for every sinful person on this earth,
    and they will have to drink until it is gone.

⁹ But I will always tell about you, the God of Jacob,
  and I will sing your praise.

¹⁰ Our Lord, you will destroy the power of evil people,
  but you will give strength to those who are good.

Psalm 76

*[A song and a psalm for the music leader.
Use stringed instruments.]*

God Always Wins

¹ You, our God, are famous in Judah
  and honored in Israel.

---

^d *a cup…wine*: In the Old Testament "a cup filled with
wine" sometimes stands for God's anger.

2 Your home is on Mount Zion in the city of peace.
3 There you destroyed fiery arrows, shields, swords,
    and all the other weapons.

4 You are more glorious than the eternal mountains.*e*
5 Brave warriors were robbed of what they had taken,
    and now they lie dead, unable to lift an arm.
6 God of Jacob, when you roar,
    enemy chariots and horses
    drop dead in their tracks.

7 Our God, you are fearsome,
   and no one can oppose you
    when you are angry.
8 From heaven you announced
    your decisions as judge!
And all who live on this earth
were terrified and silent
9   when you took over as judge,
    ready to rescue everyone in need.
10 Even the most angry people will praise you
    when you are furious.*f*

11 Everyone, make your promises
   to the LORD your God
   and do what you promise.
   The LORD is fearsome,
    and all of his servants should bring him gifts.

---

e the eternal mountains: One ancient translation; Hebrew
  "the mountains of victims (of wild animals)."
f furious: One possible meaning for the difficult Hebrew
  text of verse 10.

12 God destroys the courage of rulers and kings
   and makes cowards of them.

Psalm 77

[A psalm by Asaph for Jeduthun, the music leader.]

In Times of Trouble God Is with His People

1 I pray to you, Lord God, and I beg you to listen.
2   In days filled with trouble, I search for you.
   And at night I tirelessly lift my hands in prayer,
      refusing comfort.
3 When I think of you, I feel restless and weak.

4 Because of you, Lord God, I can't sleep.
   I am restless and can't even talk.
5   I think of times gone by, of those years long ago.
6 Each night my mind is flooded with questions: *8*
7   "Have you rejected me forever?
      Won't you be kind again?
8 Is this the end of your love and your promises?
9   Have you forgotten how to have pity?
   Do you refuse to show mercy
      because of your anger?"
10 Then I said, "God Most High, what hurts me most
   is that you no longer help us
      with your mighty arm."

11 Our LORD, I will remember
   the things you have done,

---

8 my mind . . . questions: One ancient translation; Hebrew
   "I remember my music."

your miracles of long ago.

12 I will think about each one of your mighty deeds.
13 Everything you do is right,
    and no other god compares with you.
14 You alone work miracles,
    and you have let nations see your mighty power.
15 With your own arm you rescued your people,
    the descendants of Jacob and Joseph.

16 The ocean looked at you, God,
    and it trembled deep down with fear.
17 Water flowed from the clouds.
    Thunder was heard above
    as your arrows of lightning flashed about.
18 Your thunder roared like chariot wheels.
    The world was made bright by lightning,
    and all the earth trembled.

19 You walked through the water of the mighty sea,
    but your footprints were never seen.
20 You guided your people like a flock of sheep,
    and you chose Moses and Aaron
    to be their leaders.

Psalm 78

[A special psalm by Asaph.]

What God Has Done for His People

1 My friends, I beg you to listen as I teach.
2 I will give instruction
  and explain the mystery
    of what happened long ago.

3 These are things we learned from our ancestors,
4   and we will tell them to the next generation.
  We won't keep secret the glorious deeds
      and the mighty miracles of the LORD.

5 God gave his Law to Jacob's descendants,
      the people of Israel.
  And he told our ancestors to teach their children,
6 so that each new generation would know his Law
      and tell it to the next.
7 Then they would trust God and obey his teachings,
      without forgetting anything God had done.
8 They would be different from their ancestors,
      who were stubborn, rebellious,
      and unfaithful to God.

9 The warriors from Ephraim
  were armed with arrows,
      but they ran away when the battle began.
10 They broke their agreement with God,
      and they turned their backs on his teaching.
11 They forgot all he had done,
      even the mighty miracles
12   he did for their ancestors near Zoan*h* in Egypt.

13 God made a path in the sea
      and piled up the water as he led them across.
14 He guided them during the day with a cloud,
      and each night he led them with a flaming fire.
15 God made water flow from rocks
  he split open in the desert,

---

h Zoan: A city in the eastern part of the Nile Delta.

⁴¹ They kept testing him
        and caused terrible pain
        for the Holy One of Israel.
⁴² They forgot about his power
        and how he had rescued them
        from their enemies.
⁴³ God showed them all kinds of wonderful miracles
        near Zoan*ᵏ* in Egypt.
⁴⁴ He turned the rivers of Egypt into blood,
        and no one could drink from the streams.
⁴⁵ He sent swarms of flies to pester the Egyptians,
        and he sent frogs to cause them trouble.

⁴⁶ God let worms and grasshoppers eat their crops.
⁴⁷ He destroyed their grapevines
        and their fig trees with hail and floods.*ˡ*
⁴⁸ Then he killed their cattle with hail
        and their other animals with lightning.

⁴⁹ God was so angry and furious
        that he went into a rage
and caused them great trouble
        by sending swarms of destroying angels.
⁵⁰ God gave in to his anger
        and slaughtered them in a terrible way.
⁵¹ He killed the first-born son of each Egyptian family.

⁵² Then God led his people out of Egypt
        and guided them in the desert
        like a flock of sheep.

ᵏ *Zoan*: See the note at 78.12.
ˡ *floods*: Or "frost."

53 He led them safely along,
   and they were not afraid,
but their enemies drowned in the sea.

54 God brought his people to the sacred mountain
   that he had taken by his own power.
55 He made nations run from the tribes of Israel,
   and he let the tribes take over their land.

56 But the people tested God Most High,
   and they refused to obey his laws.
57 They were as unfaithful as their ancestors,
   and they were as crooked as a twisted arrow.
58 God demanded all their love,
   but they made him angry
   by worshiping idols.

59 So God became furious
   and completely rejected the people of Israel.
60 Then he deserted his home at Shiloh,
   where he lived here on earth.
61 He let enemies capture the sacred chest*m*
   and let them dishonor him.

62 God took out his anger on his chosen ones
   and let them be killed by enemy swords.
63 Fire destroyed the young men,
   and the young women were left
   with no one to marry.

---

m sacred chest: The Hebrew text has "his power," which
refers to the sacred chest. In Psalm 132.8 it is called
"powerful."

64 Priests died violent deaths,
  but their widows were not allowed to mourn.
65 Finally the Lord woke up,
  and he shouted like a drunken soldier.
66 God scattered his enemies
  and made them ashamed forever.

67 Then the Lord decided not to make his home
  with Joseph's descendants in Ephraim.[n]
68 Instead he chose the tribe of Judah,
  and he chose Mount Zion,
    the place he loves.
69 There he built his temple
    as lofty as the mountains
  and as solid as the earth that he had made
    to last forever.

70 The Lord God chose David to be his servant
  and took him from tending sheep
71   and from caring for lambs.
  Then God made him the leader of Israel,
    his own nation.
72 David treated the people fairly
    and guided them with wisdom.

---

[n] *with...Ephraim*: Ephraim was Joseph's youngest son.
One of the twelve tribes was named after him, and sometimes the northern kingdom of Israel was also known
as Ephraim. The town of Shiloh was in the territory of
Ephraim, but the place where God was worshiped was
moved from there to Zion (Jerusalem) in the territory of
Judah.

Psalm 79

[A psalm by Asaph.]

Have Pity on Jerusalem

1 Our God, foreign nations have taken your land,
    disgraced your temple,
        and left Jerusalem in ruins.
2 They have fed the bodies of your servants
        to flesh-eating birds;
    your loyal people are food for savage animals.
3 All Jerusalem is covered with their blood,
        and there is no one left to bury them.
4 Every nation around us sneers and makes fun.

5 Our LORD, will you keep on being angry?
    Will your angry feelings
        keep flaming up like fire?
6 Get angry with those nations
        that don't know you
        and won't worship you!
7 They have gobbled down Jacob's descendants
        and left the land in ruins.

8 Don't make us pay for the sins of our ancestors.
    Have pity and come quickly!
        We are completely helpless.
9 Our God, you keep us safe.
        Now help us! Rescue us.
    Forgive our sins
        and bring honor to yourself.

10 Why should nations ask us,
        "Where is your God?"

Let us and the other nations see you take revenge
    for your servants who died a violent death.

11 Listen to the prisoners groan!
    Let your mighty power
        save all who are sentenced to die.
12 Each of those nations sneered at you, our Lord.
    Now let others sneer at them, seven times as much.
13   Then we, your people, will always thank you.
    We are like sheep with you as our shepherd,
        and all generations will hear us praise you.

Psalm 80

*[A psalm by Asaph for the music leader.
To the tune "Lilies of the Agreement."]*

Help Our Nation

1 Shepherd of Israel,
    you lead the descendants of Joseph,
and you sit on your throne
    above the winged creatures.*o*
Listen to our prayer and let your light shine
2   for the tribes of Ephraim, Benjamin,
        and Manasseh.
Save us by your power.

3 Our God, make us strong again!
    Smile on us and save us.

---

o winged creatures: Two winged creatures made of gold
were on the top of the sacred chest and were symbols of
the Lord's throne on earth (see Exodus 25.18).

4 LORD God All-Powerful,
  how much longer
    will the prayers of your people make you angry?
5 You gave us tears for food,
    and you made us drink them by the bowlful.
6 Because of you, our enemies who live nearby
    laugh and joke about us.
7 But if you smile on us, we will be saved.

8 We were like a grapevine you brought out of Egypt.
  You chased other nations away
    and planted us here.
9 Then you cleared the ground,
  and we put our roots deep,
    spreading over the land.

10 Shade from this vine covered the mountains.
   Its branches climbed the mighty cedars
11   and stretched to the sea;
   its new growth reached to the river.*p*

12 Our Lord, why have you torn down the wall
     from around the vineyard?
   You let everyone who walks by pick the grapes.
13 Now the vine is gobbled down
     by pigs from the forest and other wild animals.

14 God All-Powerful, please do something!
   Look down from heaven
     and see what's happening to this vine.

---

p *the sea…the river*: The Mediterranean Sea and the Euphrates
River were part of the ideal boundaries for Israel.

15 With your own hands you planted its roots,
    and you raised it as your very own.

16 Enemies chopped the vine down and set it on fire.
    Now show your anger and destroy them.
17 But help the one who sits at your right side,*q*
    the one you raised to be your own.
18 Then we will never turn away.
    Put new life into us, and we will worship you.

19 LORD God All-Powerful, make us strong again!
    Smile on us and save us.

Psalm 81

*[By Asaph for the music leader.*r*]*

God Makes Us Strong

1 Be happy and shout to God who makes us strong!
    Shout praises to the God of Jacob.
2 Sing as you play tambourines
    and the lovely sounding stringed instruments.
3 Sound the trumpets
    and start the New Moon Festival.*s*
  We must also celebrate when the moon is full.

---

q right side: See the note at 16.11.
r leader: See the note at Psalm 8.
s New Moon Festival: Celebrated on the first day of each
  new moon, which was the beginning of the month. But
  this may refer to either the New Year celebration or the
  Harvest Festival. "The moon is full" suggests a festival
  in the middle of the month.

⁴ This is the law in Israel,
    and it was given to us by the God of Jacob.
⁵ The descendants of Joseph were told to obey it,
    when God led them out from the land of Egypt.

In a language unknown to me, I heard someone say:
⁶ "I lifted the burden from your shoulder
    and took the heavy basket from your hands.
⁷ When you were in trouble, I rescued you,
    and from the thunderclouds,
        I answered your prayers.
Later I tested you at Meribah Spring.ᵗ

⁸ "Listen, my people, while I, the Lord, correct you!
    Israel, if you would only pay attention to me!
⁹ Don't worship foreign gods
    or bow down to gods you know nothing about.
¹⁰ I am the LORD your God. I rescued you from Egypt.
    Just ask, and I will give you whatever you need.

¹¹ "But, my people, Israel, you refused to listen,
    and you would have nothing to do with me!
¹² So I let you be stubborn
    and keep on following your own advice.

¹³ "My people, Israel, if only you would listen
    and do as I say!

ᵗ *Meribah Spring*: When the people of Israel complained to
Moses about the need for water, God commanded Moses
to strike a rock with his walking stick, and water came
out. The place was then named Massah ("test") and
Meribah ("complaining").

¹⁴ I, the LORD, would quickly defeat your enemies
    with my mighty power.
¹⁵ Everyone who hates me would come crawling,
    and that would be the end of them.
¹⁶ But I would feed you with the finest bread
    and with the best honey^u until you were full."

Psalm 82

[A psalm by Asaph.]

Please Do Something, God!

¹ When all of the other gods^v have come together,
    the Lord God judges them and says:
² "How long will you keep judging unfairly
    and favoring evil people?
³ Be fair to the poor and to orphans.
    Defend the helpless and everyone in need.
⁴ Rescue the weak and homeless
    from the powerful hands of heartless people.

⁵ "None of you know or understand a thing.
    You live in darkness,
      while the foundations of the earth tremble."^w

---

^u *the best honey*: The Hebrew text has "honey from rocks,"
  referring to honey taken from beehives in holes or cracks
  in large rocks.
^v *the other gods*: This probably refers to the gods of the
  nations that God defeated, but it could refer to God's
  servants (angels) in heaven or even to human rulers.
^w *foundations...tremble*: In ancient times it was believed
  that the earth was flat and supported by columns.

6 "I, the Most High God, say
    that all of you are gods [x]
    and also my own children.
7 But you will die, just like everyone else,
    including powerful rulers."

8 Do something, God!
  Judge the nations of the earth;
    they belong to you.

Psalm 83

[A song and a psalm by Asaph.]

God Rules All the Earth

1 Our God, don't just sit there,
    silently doing nothing!
2 Your hateful enemies
    are turning against you and rebelling.
3 They are sly,
    and they plot against those you treasure.
4 They say, "Let's wipe out the nation of Israel
    and make sure that no one remembers its name!"

5 All of them fully agree in their plans against you,
    and among them are
6 Edom and the Ishmaelites; Moab and the Hagrites;
7   Gebal, Ammon, and Amalek;
    Philistia and Phoenicia. [y]

---

[x] *all of you are gods*: See the note at 82.1.

[y] *Phoenicia*: The Hebrew text has "Tyre," the main city in
Phoenicia.

8 Even Assyria has joined forces
    with Moab and Ammon.ᶻ

9 Our Lord, punish all of them
    as you punished Midian.
  Destroy them,
    as you destroyed Sisera and Jabin
    at Kishon Creek 10near Endor,
and let their bodies rot.
11 Treat their leaders
    as you did Oreb and Zeeb,
    Zebah and Zalmunna.
12 All of them said,
    "We'll take God's valuable land!"

13 Our God, scatter them around
    like dust in a whirlwind.
14 Just as flames destroy forests on the mountains,
15   pursue and terrify them
    with storms of your own.
16 Make them blush with shame,
    until they turn and worship you, our LORD.
17 Let them be forever ashamed and confused.
    Let them die in disgrace.
18 Make them realize that you are
    the LORD Most High,
    the only ruler of earth!

ᶻ *Moab and Ammon*: The Hebrew text has "the descendants of Lot," whose older daughter was the mother of the Moabites and whose younger daughter was the mother of the Ammonites (see Genesis 19.30-38).

Psalm 84

[For the music leader.[a] A psalm for the people of Korah.]

The Joy of Worship

1 LORD God All-Powerful, your temple is so lovely!
2 Deep in my heart I long for your temple,
   and with all that I am, I sing joyful songs to you.

3 LORD God All-Powerful, my King and my God,
   sparrows find a home near your altars;
      swallows build nests there to raise their young.

4 You bless everyone who lives in your house,
   and they sing your praises.
5 You bless all who depend on you for their strength
   and all who deeply desire to visit your temple.
6 When they reach Dry Valley,[b]
      springs start flowing,
      and the autumn rain fills it with pools of water.[c]
7 Your people grow stronger,
   and you, the God of gods, will be seen in Zion.

8 LORD God All-Powerful, the God of Jacob,
   please answer my prayer!
9 You are the shield that protects your people,
   and I am your chosen one.
      Won't you smile on me?

---

[a] *leader*: See the note at Psalm 8.
[b] *Dry Valley*: Or "Balsam Tree Valley." The exact location
is not known.
[c] *and...water*: One possible meaning for the difficult
Hebrew text.

¹⁰ One day in your temple is better
  than a thousand anywhere else.
I would rather serve in your house,
  than live in the homes of the wicked.

¹¹ Our LORD and our God, you are like the sun
  and also like a shield.
You treat us with kindness and with honor,
  never denying any good thing
  to those who live right.

¹² LORD God All-Powerful,
  you bless everyone who trusts you.

Psalm 85

[A psalm by the people of Korah for the music leader.]

A Prayer for Peace

¹ Our LORD, you have blessed your land
  and made all go well for Jacob's descendants.
² You have forgiven the sin
  and taken away the guilt of your people.
³ Your fierce anger is no longer aimed at us.

⁴ Our LORD and our God,
  you save us!
Please bring us back home and don't be angry.
⁵ Will you always be angry
  with us and our families?
⁶ Won't you give us fresh life
  and let your people be glad because of you?
⁷ Show us your love and save us!

⁸ I will listen to you, LORD God,
    because you promise peace to those
        who are faithful and no longer foolish.
⁹ You are ready to rescue
    everyone who worships you,
        so that you will live with us in all of your glory.

¹⁰ Love and loyalty will come together;
    goodness and peace will unite.
¹¹ Loyalty will sprout from the ground;
    justice will look down from the sky above.

¹² Our LORD, you will bless us;
    our land will produce wonderful crops.
¹³ Justice will march in front,
    making a path for you to follow.

Psalm 86

[A prayer by David.]

A Prayer for Help

¹ Please listen, LORD,
    and answer my prayer!
I am poor and helpless.
² Protect me and save me because you are my God.
    I am your faithful servant, and I trust you.
³ Be kind to me! I pray to you all day.
⁴ Make my heart glad!
    I serve you, and my prayer is sincere.
⁵ You willingly forgive,
    and your love is always there
        for those who pray to you.

6 Please listen, LORD!
    Answer my prayer for help.
7 When I am in trouble,
    I pray, knowing you will listen.

8 No other gods are like you;
    only you work miracles.
9 You created each nation,
    and they will all bow down
    to worship and honor you.
10 You perform great wonders
    because you alone are God.

11 Teach me to follow you, and I will obey your truth.
    Always keep me faithful.
12 With all my heart I thank you.
    I praise you, LORD God.
13 Your love for me is so great
    that you protected me
    from death and the grave.

14 Proud and violent enemies,
    who don't care about you,
    have ganged up to attack and kill me.
15 But you, the Lord God,
    are kind and merciful.
    You don't easily get angry,
    and your love can always be trusted.
16 I serve you, LORD,
    and I am the child of one of your servants.
    Look on me with kindness.
    Make me strong and save me.
17 Show that you approve of me!

Then my hateful enemies will feel like fools,
  because you have helped and comforted me.

Psalm 87

[A psalm and a song by the people of Korah.]

The Glory of Mount Zion

1 Zion was built by the LORD on the holy mountain,
2 and he loves that city
      more than any other place in all of Israel.
3 Zion, you are the city of God,
      and wonderful things are told about you.

4 Egypt,*d* Babylonia, Philistia,
      Phoenicia,*e* and Ethiopia*f*
  are some of those nations that know you,
      and their people all say,
      "I was born in Zion."

5 God Most High will strengthen the city of Zion.
  Then everyone will say,
      "We were born here too."
6 The LORD will make a list of his people,
      and all who were born here will be included.

7 All who sing or dance will say,
      "I too am from Zion."

---

d *Egypt:* The Hebrew text has "Rahab," the name of a
  monster that stands for Egypt (see Isaiah 30.7).
e *Phoenicia:* See the note at 83.7.
f *Ethiopia:* See the note at 68.31.

Psalm 88

*[A song and a psalm by the people of Korah
for the music leader. To the tune "Mahalath Leannoth."[g]
A special psalm by Heman the Ezrahite.]*

A Prayer When You Can't Find the Way

1 You keep me safe, LORD God.
  So when I pray at night,
2   please listen carefully to each of my concerns.

3 I am deeply troubled and close to death;
4   I am as good as dead and completely helpless.
5 I am no better off than those in the grave,
  those you have forgotten and no longer help.

6 You have put me in the deepest and darkest grave;
7   your anger rolls over me like ocean waves.
8 You have made my friends turn in horror from me.
  I am a prisoner who cannot escape,
9   and I am almost blind because of my sorrow.

  Each day I lift my hands in prayer to you, LORD.
10   Do you work miracles for the dead?
  Do they stand up and praise you?
11 Are your love and loyalty announced
    in the world of the dead?
12 Do they know of your miracles
    or your saving power
  in the dark world below
    where all is forgotten?

---

[g] *To...Leannoth*: Or "For the flutes," one possible meaning
  for the difficult Hebrew text.

¹³ Each morning I pray to you, LORD.
¹⁴   Why do you reject me?
       Why do you turn from me?
¹⁵ Ever since I was a child,
       I have been sick and close to death.
       You have terrified me and made me helpless.[h]

¹⁶ Your anger is like a flood!
       And I am shattered by your furious attacks
¹⁷   that strike each day and from every side.
¹⁸ My friends and neighbors
       have turned against me because of you,
       and now darkness is my only companion.

Psalm 89

[A special psalm by Ethan the Ezrahite.]

The LORD's Agreement with David

¹ Our LORD, I will sing of your love forever.
   Everyone yet to be born
       will hear me praise your faithfulness.
² I will tell them,
   "God's love can always be trusted,
       and his faithfulness lasts as long as the heavens."

³ You said,
   "David, my servant, is my chosen one,
       and this is the agreement I made with him:
⁴ David, one of your descendants will always be king."

---

[h] *and made me helpless*: One possible meaning for the
difficult Hebrew text.

5 Our LORD,
   let the heavens now praise your miracles,
      and let all of your angels
      praise your faithfulness.

6 None who live in the heavens
   can compare with you.
7 You are the most fearsome
   of all who live in heaven;
  all the others fear and greatly honor you.
8 You are LORD God All-Powerful!
   No one is as loving and faithful as you are.
9 You rule the roaring sea and calm its waves.
10 You crushed the monster Rahab,[i]
  and with your powerful arm
     you scattered your enemies.
11 The heavens and the earth belong to you.
  And so does the world with all its people
    because you created them
12   and everything else.[j]

  Mount Tabor and Mount Hermon gladly praise you.
13   You are strong and mighty!
14 Your kingdom is ruled by justice and fairness
  with love and faithfulness leading the way.

---

i *Rahab*: Many people in the ancient world thought that the
  world was controlled by this sea monster that the Lord
  destroyed at the time of creation (see Isaiah 51.9).

j *and everything else*: The Hebrew text has "Zaphon and
  Yamin," which may either be the names of mountains or
  refer to the directions "north and south," with the meaning "everything from north to south."

¹⁵ Our LORD, you bless those who join in the festival
　　　and walk in the brightness of your presence.
¹⁶ We are happy all day because of you,
　　　and your saving power brings honor to us.
¹⁷ Your own glorious power makes us strong,
　　and because of your kindness,
　　　our strength increases.
¹⁸ Our LORD and our King, the Holy One of Israel,
　　　you are truly our shield.

¹⁹ In a vision, you once said to your faithful followers:
　　"I have helped a mighty hero.
　　　I chose him from my people
　　　and made him famous.
²⁰ David, my servant, is the one I chose to be king,
²¹　　and I will always be there
　　　to help and strengthen him.

²² "No enemy will outsmart David,
　　　and he won't be defeated by any hateful people.
²³ I will strike down
　　　and crush his troublesome enemies.
²⁴ He will always be able to depend on my love,
　　　and I will make him strong with my own power.
²⁵ I will let him rule the lands
　　　across the rivers and seas.
²⁶ He will say to me,
　　'You are my Father and my God,
　　　as well as the mighty rock^k where I am safe.'

²⁷ "I have chosen David as my first-born son,

---

^k *mighty rock*: See the note at 18.2.

and he will be the ruler of all kings on earth.
28 My love for him will last,
    and my agreement with him
        will never be broken.

29 "One of David's descendants will always be king,
    and his family will rule
        until the sky disappears.
30 Suppose some of his children
        should reject my Law
        and refuse my instructions.
31 Or suppose they should disobey
        all of my teachings.
32 Then I will correct and punish them
        because of their sins.
33 But I will always love David
    and faithfully keep all of my promises to him.

34 "I won't break my agreement
        or go back on my word.
35 I have sworn once and for all
    by my own holy name,
        and I won't lie to David.
36 His family will always rule.
    I will let his kingdom last
        as long as the sun 37and moon appear in the sky."

38 You are now angry, God,
    and you have turned your back
        on your chosen king.
39 You broke off your agreement
    with your servant, the king,
        and you completely destroyed his kingdom.

⁴⁰ The walls of his city have been broken through,
   and every fortress now lies in ruin.
⁴¹ All who pass by take what they want,
   and nations everywhere joke about the king.

⁴² You made his enemies powerful
   and let them celebrate.
⁴³ But you forced him to retreat
   because you did not fight on his side.
⁴⁴ You took his crown*l*
   and threw his throne in the dirt.
⁴⁵ You made an old man of him
   and put him to shame.

⁴⁶ How much longer, LORD?
   Will you hide forever?
   How long will your anger keep burning like fire?
⁴⁷ Remember, life is short!*m*
   Why did you empty our lives of all meaning?
⁴⁸ No one can escape the power
   of death and the grave.

⁴⁹ Our Lord,
   where is the love you have always shown
   and that you promised so faithfully to David?
⁵⁰ Remember your servant, Lord!
   People make jokes about me,
   and I suffer many insults.

---

l *You took…crown:* One possible meaning for the difficult
Hebrew text.

m *Remember…short:* One possible meaning for the difficult
Hebrew text.

51 I am your chosen one,
    but your enemies chase and make fun of me.

52 Our LORD, we praise you forever.
    Amen and amen.

BOOK IV
(Psalms 90–106)

Psalm 90

[A prayer by Moses, the man of God.]

God Is Eternal

1 Our Lord,
    in all generations you have been our home.

2 You have always been God
    long before the birth of the mountains,
    even before you created the earth and the world.

3 At your command we die and turn back to dust,
4   but a thousand years mean nothing to you!
  They are merely a day gone by
    or a few hours in the night.

5 You bring our lives to an end just like a dream.
  We are merely tender grass
6   that sprouts and grows in the morning,
    but dries up by evening.

7 Your furious anger frightens and destroys us,
8 and you know all of our sins,
    even those we do in secret.

⁹ Your anger is a burden each day we live,
    then life ends like a sigh.
¹⁰ We can expect seventy years,
    or maybe eighty, if we are healthy,
    but even our best years bring trouble and sorrow.
    Suddenly our time is up, and we disappear.
¹¹ No one knows the full power of your furious anger,
    but it is as great as the fear that we owe to you.
¹² Teach us to use wisely all the time we have.

¹³ Help us, LORD! Don't wait!
    Pity your servants.
¹⁴ When morning comes,
    let your love satisfy all our needs.
    Then we can celebrate
    and be glad for what time we have left.
¹⁵ Make us happy for as long
    as you caused us trouble and sorrow.
¹⁶ Do wonderful things for us, your servants,
    and show your mighty power to our children.
¹⁷ Our Lord and our God, treat us with kindness
    and let all go well for us.
    Please let all go well!

Psalm 91

The LORD Is My Fortress

¹ Live under the protection of God Most High
    and stay in the shadow of God All-Powerful.
² Then you will say to the LORD,
    "You are my fortress, my place of safety;
    you are my God, and I trust you."

3 The Lord will keep you safe from secret traps
    and deadly diseases.
4 He will spread his wings over you
    and keep you secure.
  His faithfulness is like a shield or a city wall.[n]

5 You won't need to worry about dangers at night
    or arrows during the day.
6 And you won't fear diseases that strike in the dark
    or sudden disaster at noon.

7 You will not be harmed,
    though thousands fall all around you.
8 And with your own eyes you will see
    the punishment of the wicked.
9 The LORD Most High is your fortress.
  Run to him for safety,
10   and no terrible disasters will strike you
    or your home.

11 God will command his angels to protect you
    wherever you go.
12 They will carry you in their arms,
    and you won't hurt your feet on the stones.
13 You will overpower the strongest lions
    and the most deadly snakes.

14 The Lord says,
    "If you love me and truly know who I am,
    I will rescue you and keep you safe.

---

[n] *city wall*: One possible meaning for a difficult Hebrew
    word; it may possibly mean some kind of shield or weapon.

¹⁵ When you are in trouble, call out to me.
I will answer and be there
to protect and honor you.
¹⁶ You will live a long life
and see my saving power."

Psalm 92

[A psalm and a song for the Sabbath.]

Sing Praises to the LORD

¹ It is wonderful to be grateful
and to sing your praises, LORD Most High!
² It is wonderful each morning to tell about your love
and at night to announce how faithful you are.
³ I enjoy praising your name to the music of harps,
⁴ because everything you do makes me happy,
and I sing joyful songs.

⁵ You do great things, LORD.
Your thoughts are too deep
⁶   for an ignorant fool to know or understand.
⁷ Though the wicked sprout and spread like grass,
they will be pulled up by their roots.
⁸ But you will rule over all of us forever,
⁹ and your hateful enemies will be scattered
and then destroyed.

¹⁰ You have given me the strength of a wild ox,
and you have chosen me to be your very own.
¹¹ My eyes have seen, and my ears have heard
the doom and destruction
of my terrible enemies.

12 Good people will prosper like palm trees,
   and they will grow strong
      like the cedars of Lebanon.
13 They will take root
   in your house, LORD God,
      and they will do well.
14 They will be like trees that stay healthy and fruitful,
   even when they are old.
15 And they will say about you,
   "The LORD always does right!
      God is our mighty rock."*o*

Psalm 93

The LORD Is King

1 Our LORD, you are King!
      Majesty and power are your royal robes.
   You put the world in place,
      and it will never be moved.
2 You have always ruled,
      and you are eternal.

3 The ocean is roaring, LORD!
      The sea is pounding hard.
4 Its mighty waves are majestic,
      but you are more majestic,
      and you rule over all.
5 Your decisions are firm,
      and your temple
         will always be beautiful and holy.

---

o mighty rock: See the note at 18.2.

Psalm 94

The LORD Punishes the Guilty

1 LORD God, you punish the guilty.
Show what you are like
    and punish them now.

2 You judge the earth. Come and help us!
Pay back those proud people
    for what they have done.

3 How long will the wicked celebrate and be glad?

4 All of those cruel people strut and boast,
5 and they crush and wound
    your chosen nation, LORD.
6 They murder widows, foreigners, and orphans.
7 Then they say,
    "The LORD God of Jacob doesn't see or know."

8 Can't you fools see? Won't you ever learn?
9 God gave us ears and eyes!
    Can't he hear and see?
10 God instructs the nations
    and gives knowledge to us all.
        Won't he also correct us?
11 The LORD knows how useless our plans really are.

12 Our LORD, you bless everyone
    that you instruct and teach by using your Law.
13 You give them rest from their troubles,
    until a pit can be dug for the wicked.
14 You won't turn your back on your chosen nation.
15 Justice and fairness will go hand in hand,
    and all who do right will follow along.

16 Who will stand up for me
        against those cruel people?
17 If you had not helped me, LORD,
        I would soon have gone to the land of silence.*p*
18 When I felt my feet slipping,
        you came with your love and kept me steady.
19 And when I was burdened with worries,
        you comforted me and made me feel secure.
20 But you are opposed to dishonest lawmakers
21   who gang up to murder innocent victims.

22 You, LORD God, are my fortress,
        that mighty rock*q* where I am safe.
23 You will pay back my enemies,
    and you will wipe them out
        for the evil they did.

Psalm 95

Worship and Obey the LORD

1 Sing joyful songs to the LORD!
        Praise the mighty rock*q* where we are safe.
2 Come to worship him with thankful hearts
        and songs of praise.

3 The LORD is the greatest God,
        king over all other gods.
4 He holds the deepest part of the earth in his hands,
        and the mountain peaks belong to him.

---

p land of silence: The grave or the world of the dead.
q mighty rock: See the note at 18.2.

⁵ The ocean is the Lord's because he made it,
    and with his own hands he formed the dry land.

⁶ Bow down and worship the LORD our Creator!
⁷ The LORD is our God, and we are his people,
    the sheep he takes care of in his own pasture.

Listen to God's voice today!
⁸ Don't be stubborn and rebel as your ancestors did
    at Meribah and Massah^r out in the desert.
⁹⁻¹⁰ For forty years they tested God
    and saw the things he did.
Then God got tired of them and said,
    "You never show good sense,
    and you don't understand what I want you to do."
¹¹ In his anger, God told them,
    "You people will never enter my place of rest."

Psalm 96

Sing a New Song to the LORD

¹ Sing a new song to the LORD!
    Everyone on this earth, sing praises to the LORD,
²   sing and praise his name.

Day after day announce, "The LORD has saved us!"
³ Tell every nation on earth, "The LORD is wonderful
    and does marvelous things!
⁴ The LORD is great and deserves our greatest praise!
    He is the only God worthy of our worship.

---

^r *Meribah and Massah*: See the note at 81.7.

¹² You are the LORD's people!
So celebrate and praise the only God.

Psalm 98

The LORD Works Miracles

¹ Sing a new song to the LORD!
He has worked miracles,
and with his own powerful arm,
he has won the victory.

² The LORD has shown the nations
that he has the power to save
and to bring justice.

³ God has been faithful in his love for Israel,
and his saving power is seen
everywhere on earth.

⁴ Tell everyone on this earth
to sing happy songs in praise of the LORD.

⁵ Make music for him on harps.
Play beautiful melodies!

⁶ Sound the trumpets and horns
and celebrate with joyful songs
for our LORD and King!

⁷ Command the ocean to roar
with all of its creatures,
and the earth to shout
with all of its people.

⁸ Order the rivers to clap their hands,
and all of the hills to sing together.

⁹ Let them worship the LORD!

He is coming to judge everyone on the earth,
   and he will be honest and fair.

Psalm 99

Our LORD Is King

¹ Our LORD, you are King!
  You rule from your throne
      above the winged creatures,ˢ
   as people tremble and the earth shakes.
² You are praised in Zion,
   and you control all nations.
³ Only you are God!
  And your power alone,
      so great and fearsome, is worthy of praise.
⁴ You are our mighty King,ᵗ a lover of fairness,
      who sees that justice is done
   everywhere in Israel.
⁵ Our LORD and our God, we praise you
      and kneel down to worship you,
   the God of holiness!

⁶ Moses and Aaron were two of your priests.
  Samuel was also one of those
      who prayed in your name,
   and you, our LORD, answered their prayers.
⁷ You spoke to them from a thick cloud,
      and they obeyed your laws.

ˢ *winged creatures*: See the note at 80.1.
ᵗ *You... King*: One possible meaning for the difficult
Hebrew text.

8 Our LORD and our God,
    you answered their prayers
      and forgave their sins,
  but when they did wrong, you punished them.
9 We praise you, LORD God,
    and we worship you at your sacred mountain.
  Only you are God!

Psalm 100

[A psalm of praise.]

The LORD Is God

1 Shout praises to the LORD, everyone on this earth.
2 Be joyful and sing
    as you come in to worship the LORD!

3 You know the LORD is God!
  He created us, and we belong to him;
    we are his people, the sheep in his pasture.

4 Be thankful and praise the LORD
    as you enter his temple.
5 The LORD is good!
    His love and faithfulness will last forever.

Psalm 101

[A psalm by David.]

A King and His Promises

1 I will sing to you, LORD!
    I will celebrate your kindness and your justice.

2 Please help me learn to do the right thing,
and I will be honest and fair in my own kingdom.
3 I refuse to be corrupt
or to take part in anything crooked,
4   and I won't be dishonest or deceitful.

5 Anyone who spreads gossip will be silenced,
and no one who is conceited will be my friend.

6 I will find trustworthy people
to serve as my advisers,
and only an honest person
will serve as an official.

7 No one who cheats or lies
will have a position in my royal court.
8 Each morning I will silence any lawbreakers I find
in the countryside or in the city of the LORD.

Psalm 102

*[A prayer for someone who hurts
and needs to ask the LORD for help.]*

A Prayer in Time of Trouble

1 I pray to you, LORD! Please listen.
2   Don't hide from me in my time of trouble.
Pay attention to my prayer
and quickly give an answer.

3 My days disappear like smoke,
and my bones are burning
as though in a furnace.

4 I am wasting away like grass,
    and my appetite is gone.
5 My groaning never stops,
    and my bones can be seen through my skin.
6 I am like a lonely owl in the desert
7   or a restless sparrow alone on a roof.

8 My enemies insult me all day,
    and they use my name for a curse word.
9 Instead of food,
  I have ashes to eat and tears to drink,
10   because you are furious
    and have thrown me aside.
11 My life fades like a shadow at the end of day
    and withers like grass.

12 Our LORD, you are King forever
    and will always be famous.
13 You will show pity to Zion
    because the time has come.
14 We, your servants, love each stone in the city,
    and we are sad to see them lying in the dirt.

15 Our LORD, the nations will honor you,
    and all kings on earth will praise your glory.
16 You will rebuild the city of Zion.
    Your glory will be seen,
17   and the prayers of the homeless will be answered.

18 Future generations must also praise the LORD,
    so write this for them:
19 "From his holy temple,
    the LORD looked down at the earth.

20 He listened to the groans of prisoners,
    and he rescued everyone
      who was doomed to die."

21 All Jerusalem should praise you, our LORD,
22   when people from every nation
      meet to worship you.

23 I should still be strong,
    but you, LORD, have made an old person of me.
24 You will live forever! Years mean nothing to you.
    Don't cut my life in half!

25 In the beginning, LORD,
    you laid the earth's foundation
      and created the heavens.
26 They will all disappear
    and wear out like clothes.
You change them, as you would a coat,
    but you last forever.
27 You are always the same. Years cannot change you.
28 Every generation of those who serve you
    will live in your presence.

Psalm 103

[By David.]

The LORD's Wonderful Love

1 With all my heart I praise the LORD,
    and with all that I am I praise his holy name!
2 With all my heart I praise the LORD!
    I will never forget how kind he has been.

3 The LORD forgives our sins,
   heals us when we are sick,
4   and protects us from death.
   His kindness and love are a crown on our heads.
5 Each day that we live,*ᵘ he provides for our needs
   and gives us the strength of a young eagle.

6 For all who are mistreated, the LORD brings justice.
7 He taught his Law to Moses
   and showed all Israel what he could do.

8 The LORD is merciful!
   He is kind and patient,
   and his love never fails.
9 The LORD won't always be angry
   and point out our sins;
10   he doesn't punish us as our sins deserve.

11 How great is God's love for all who worship him?
      Greater than the distance
   between heaven and earth!
12 How far has the LORD taken our sins from us?
      Farther than the distance
   from east to west!

13 Just as parents are kind to their children,
   the LORD is kind to all who worship him,
14   because he knows we are made of dust.
15 We humans are like grass
   or wild flowers that quickly bloom.

ᵘ *Each . . . live*: One possible meaning for the difficult
   Hebrew text.

¹⁶ But a scorching wind blows,
　　and they quickly wither to be forever forgotten.

¹⁷ The LORD is always kind
　　to those who worship him,
　and he keeps his promises to their descendants
¹⁸　who faithfully obey him.

¹⁹ God has set up his kingdom in heaven,
　　and he rules the whole creation.
²⁰ All of you mighty angels,
　who obey God's commands,
　　come and praise your LORD!
²¹ All of you thousands who serve and obey God,
　　come and praise your LORD!
²² All of God's creation and all that he rules,
　　come and praise your LORD!
　With all my heart I praise the LORD!

Psalm 104

The LORD Takes Care of His Creation

¹ I praise you, LORD God, with all my heart.
　You are glorious and majestic,
　　dressed in royal robes
²　and surrounded by light.
　You spread out the sky like a tent,
³　and you built your home over the mighty ocean.
　The clouds are your chariot
　　with the wind as its wings.
⁴ The winds are your messengers,
　　and flames of fire are your servants.

5 You built foundations for the earth,
    and it will never be shaken.
6 You covered the earth with the ocean
    that rose above the mountains.
7 Then your voice thundered!
    And the water flowed 8down the mountains
    and through the valleys
    to the place you prepared.
9 Now you have set boundaries,
    so that the water will never flood the earth again.

10 You provide streams of water
    in the hills and valleys,
11 so that the donkeys and other wild animals
    can satisfy their thirst.
12 Birds build their nests nearby
    and sing in the trees.
13 From your home above you send rain on the hills
    and water the earth.
14 You let the earth produce grass for cattle,
    plants for our food, 15wine to cheer us up,
    olive oil for our skin, and grain for our health.

16 Our LORD, your trees always have water,
    and so do the cedars you planted in Lebanon.
17 Birds nest in those trees,
    and storks make their home in the fir trees.
18 Wild goats find a home in the tall mountains,
    and small animals can hide between the rocks.

19 You created the moon to tell us the seasons.
    The sun knows when to set,
20   and you made the darkness,

so the animals in the forest
could come out at night.

21 Lions roar as they hunt for the food you provide.
22 But when morning comes, they return to their dens,
23   then we go out to work until the end of day.

24 Our LORD,
     by your wisdom you made so many things;
   the whole earth is covered
     with your living creatures.
25 But what about the ocean so big and wide?
     It is alive with creatures, large and small.
26 And there are the ships, as well as Leviathan,[v]
     the monster you created to splash in the sea.

27 All of these depend on you
     to provide them with food,
28 and you feed each one with your own hand,
     until they are full.
29 But when you turn away, they are terrified;
     when you end their life, they die and rot.
30 You created all of them by your Spirit,
     and you give new life to the earth.

31 Our LORD, we pray that your glory will last forever
   and that you will be pleased
     with what you have done.
32 You look at the earth, and it trembles.
     You touch the mountains, and smoke goes up.
33 As long as I live,
     I will sing and praise you, the LORD God.

---

[v] Leviathan: See the note at 74.14.

34 I hope my thoughts will please you,
   because you are the one who makes me glad.

35 Destroy all wicked sinners from the earth
   once and for all.
   With all my heart I praise you, LORD! I praise you!

Psalm 105

The LORD Can Be Trusted

1 Praise the LORD and pray in his name!
   Tell everyone what he has done.
2 Sing praises to the LORD! Tell about his miracles.
3 Celebrate and worship his holy name
   with all your heart.

4 Trust the LORD and his mighty power.
5 Remember his miracles and all his wonders
   and his fair decisions.
6 You belong to the family of Abraham, his servant;
   you are his chosen ones,
   the descendants of Jacob.

7 The LORD is our God,
   bringing justice everywhere on earth.
8 He will never forget his agreement
   or his promises,
   not in thousands of years.
9-10 God made an eternal promise
   to Abraham, Isaac, and Jacob,
11 when he said,
   "I'll give you the land of Canaan."

¹² At the time there were only a few of us,
  and we were homeless.
¹³ We wandered from nation to nation,
  from one country to another.
¹⁴ God did not let anyone mistreat our people.
  Instead he protected us
    by punishing rulers ¹⁵and telling them,
  "Don't touch my chosen leaders
    or harm my prophets!"

¹⁶ God kept crops from growing
  until food was scarce everywhere in the land.
¹⁷ But he had already sent Joseph,
  sold as a slave into Egypt,
¹⁸   with chains of iron around his legs and neck.

¹⁹ Joseph remained a slave
  until his own words had come true,
    and the LORD had finished testing him.
²⁰ Then the king of Egypt set Joseph free
²¹   and put him in charge of everything he owned.
²² Joseph was in command of the officials,
  and he taught the leaders how to use wisdom.

²³ Jacob and his family came
  and settled in Egypt as foreigners.
²⁴ They were the LORD's people,
  so he let them grow stronger than their enemies.
²⁵ They served the LORD,
  and he made the Egyptians plan
    hateful things against them.
²⁶ God sent his servant Moses.
  He also chose and sent Aaron

27   to his people in Egypt,
        and they worked miracles and wonders there.
28 Moses and Aaron obeyed God,
        and he sent darkness to cover Egypt.
29 God turned their rivers into streams of blood,
        and the fish all died.
30 Frogs were everywhere,
        even in the royal palace.
31 When God gave the command,
        flies and gnats swarmed all around.

32 In place of rain, God sent hailstones
        and flashes of lightning.
33 He destroyed their grapevines and their fig trees,
        and he made splinters of all the other trees.
34 God gave the command,
        and more grasshoppers came
        than could be counted.
35 They ate every green plant
        and all the crops that grew in the land of Egypt.
36 Then God took the life of every first-born son.

37 When God led Israel from Egypt,
        they took silver and gold,
        and no one was left behind.
38 The Egyptians were afraid and gladly let them go.
39 God hid them under a cloud
        and guided them by fire during the night.

40 When they asked for food,
        he sent more birds than they could eat.
41 God even split open a rock,
        and streams of water gushed into the desert.

⁴² God never forgot his sacred promise
to his servant Abraham.

⁴³ When the Lord rescued
his chosen people from Egypt,
they celebrated with songs.
⁴⁴ The Lord gave them the land
and everything else the nations had worked for.
⁴⁵ He did this so that his people
would obey all of his laws.
Shout praises to the LORD!

Psalm 106

A Nation Asks for Forgiveness

¹ We will celebrate and praise you, LORD!
You are good to us, and your love never fails.
² No one can praise you enough
for all of the mighty things you have done.
³ You bless those people who are honest and fair
in everything they do.

⁴ Remember me, LORD, when you show kindness
by saving your people.
⁵ Let me prosper with the rest of your chosen ones,
as they celebrate with pride
because they belong to you.

⁶ We and our ancestors have sinned terribly.
⁷ When they were in Egypt, they paid no attention
to your marvelous deeds
or your wonderful love.

And they turned against you at the Red Sea.[w]

8 But you were true to your name,
    and you rescued them
    to prove how mighty you are.
9 You said to the Red Sea,[w] "Dry up!"
    Then you led your people across
    on land as dry as a desert.
10 You saved all of them
11   and drowned every one of their enemies.
12 Then your people trusted you
    and sang your praises.

13 But they soon forgot what you had done
    and rejected your advice.
14 They became greedy for food
    and tested you there in the desert.
15 So you gave them what they wanted,
    but later you destroyed them
    with a horrible disease.

16 Everyone in camp was jealous of Moses
    and of Aaron, your chosen priest.
17 Dathan and Abiram rebelled,
    and the earth opened up and swallowed them.

---

[w] *Red Sea*: Hebrew *yam suph* "Sea of Reeds," one of the
marshes or fresh water lakes near the eastern part of the
Nile Delta. This identification is based on Exodus
13.17–14.9, which lists the towns on the route of the
Israelites before crossing the sea. In the Greek translation
of the Scriptures made about 200 B.C., the "Sea of Reeds"
was named "Red Sea."

¹⁸ Then fire broke out
      and destroyed all of their followers.

¹⁹ At Horeb your people made and worshiped
      the statue ²⁰of a bull,
      instead of you, their glorious God.
²¹ You worked powerful miracles
      to save them from Egypt,
    but they forgot about you
²²   and the fearsome things you did
      at the Red Sea.^x
²³ You were angry and started to destroy them,
      but Moses, your chosen leader,
      begged you not to do it.

²⁴ They would not trust you, LORD,
      and they did not like the promised land.
²⁵ They would not obey you,
      and they grumbled in their tents.
²⁶ So you threatened them by saying,
      "I'll kill you out here in the desert!
²⁷   I'll scatter your children
      everywhere in the world."

²⁸ Your people became followers
      of a god named Baal Peor,
      and they ate sacrifices offered to the dead.^y
²⁹ They did such terrible things
      that you punished them
      with a deadly disease.

---

^x *Red Sea*: See the note at 106.7.
^y *the dead*: Or "lifeless idols."

30 But Phinehas[z] helped them,
   and the sickness stopped.
31 Now he will always be highly honored.
32 At Meribah Spring[a] they turned against you
   and made you furious.
33 Then Moses got into trouble
   for speaking in anger.

34 Our LORD, they disobeyed you
   by refusing to destroy the nations.
35 Instead they were friendly
   with those foreigners
   and followed their customs.
36 Then they fell into the trap
   of worshiping idols.
37 They sacrificed their sons and their daughters
   to demons 38and to the gods of Canaan.
   Then they poured out the blood
   of these innocent children
   and made the land filthy.
39 By doing such gruesome things,
   they also became filthy.

40 Finally, LORD, you were angry
   and terribly disgusted with your people.
41 So you put them in the power of nations
   that hated them.

---

[z] *Phinehas*: The grandson of Aaron, who put two people
to death and kept the Lord from being angry with the rest
of his people (see Numbers 25.1-13).
[a] *Meribah Spring*: See the note at 81.7.

42 They were mistreated
    and abused by their enemies,
43   but you saved them time after time.
  They were determined to rebel,
    and their sins caused their downfall.

44 You answered their prayers
    when they were in trouble.
45 You kept your agreement and were so merciful
46   that their enemies had pity on them.

47 Save us, LORD God!
    Bring us back from among the nations.
  Let us celebrate and shout
    in praise of your holy name.

48 LORD God of Israel,
    you deserve to be praised forever and ever.
  Let everyone say, "Amen!
    Shout praises to the LORD!"

BOOK V

(Psalms 107–150)

Psalm 107

The LORD Is Good to His People

1 Shout praises to the LORD!
    He is good to us, and his love never fails.
2 Everyone the LORD has rescued from trouble
    should praise him,

3 everyone he has brought from the east and the west,
  the north and the south.[b]

4 Some of you were lost in the scorching desert,
  far from a town.
5 You were hungry and thirsty and about to give up.
6 You were in serious trouble,
  but you prayed to the LORD, and he rescued you.
7 Right away he brought you to a town.
8 You should praise the LORD for his love
  and for the wonderful things he does for all of us.
9 To everyone who is thirsty,
  he gives something to drink;
 to everyone who is hungry,
  he gives good things to eat.

10 Some of you were prisoners
   suffering in deepest darkness
   and bound by chains,
11 because you had rebelled against God Most High
   and refused his advice.
12 You were worn out from working like slaves,
   and no one came to help.
13 You were in serious trouble,
   but you prayed to the LORD, and he rescued you.
14 He brought you out of the deepest darkness
   and broke your chains.

15 You should praise the LORD for his love
   and for the wonderful things he does for all of us.

_____

b *south*: The Hebrew text has "sea," probably referring to
  the Mediterranean Sea.

¹⁶ He breaks down bronze gates
   and shatters iron locks.

¹⁷ Some of you had foolishly committed a lot of sins
   and were in terrible pain.
¹⁸ The very thought of food was disgusting to you,
   and you were almost dead.
¹⁹ You were in serious trouble,
   but you prayed to the LORD, and he rescued you.
²⁰ By the power of his own word, he healed you
   and saved you from destruction.

²¹ You should praise the LORD for his love
   and for the wonderful things he does for all of us.
²² You should celebrate by offering sacrifices
   and singing joyful songs to tell what he has done.

²³ Some of you made a living
   by sailing the mighty sea,
²⁴ and you saw the miracles
   the LORD performed there.
²⁵ At his command a storm arose,
   and waves covered the sea.
²⁶ You were tossed to the sky and to the ocean depths,
   until things looked so bad
   that you lost your courage.
²⁷ You staggered like drunkards and gave up all hope.
²⁸ You were in serious trouble,
   but you prayed to the LORD, and he rescued you.
²⁹ He made the storm stop and the sea be quiet.
³⁰ You were happy because of this,
   and he brought you to the port
   where you wanted to go.

31 You should praise the LORD for his love
  and for the wonderful things he does
   for all of us.
32 Honor the LORD when you
  and your leaders meet to worship.

33 If you start doing wrong,
 the LORD will turn rivers into deserts,
34   flowing streams into scorched land,
  and fruitful fields into beds of salt.

35 But the Lord can also turn deserts into lakes
  and scorched land into flowing streams.
36 If you are hungry,
  you can settle there and build a town.
37 You can plant fields and vineyards
  that produce a good harvest.
38 The LORD will bless you with many children
  and with herds of cattle.

39 Sometimes you may be crushed
 by troubles and sorrows,
  until only a few of you are left to survive.
40 But the LORD will take revenge
 on those who conquer you,
  and he will make them wander
  across desert sands.
41 When you are suffering and in need,
 he will come to your rescue,
  and your families will grow
  as fast as a herd of sheep.
42 You will see this because you obey the LORD,
  but everyone who is wicked will be silenced.

⁴³ Be wise! Remember this
　　and think about the kindness of the LORD.

Psalm 108

[A song and a psalm by David.]

With God on Our Side

¹ Our God, I am faithful to you with all my heart,
　　and you can trust me.
I will sing and play music for you
　　with all that I am.
² I will start playing my harps before the sun rises.
³ I will praise you, LORD,
　　for everyone to hear;
I will sing hymns to you in every nation.
⁴ Your love reaches higher than the heavens,
　　and your loyalty extends beyond the clouds.

⁵ Our God, may you be honored above the heavens;
　　may your glory be seen everywhere on earth.
⁶ Answer my prayers
and use your powerful arm to give us victory.
　　Then the people you love will be safe.

⁷ Our God, from your holy place
　　you made this promise:
"I will gladly divide up the city of Shechem
　　and give away Succoth Valley
　　piece by piece.
⁸ The lands of Gilead and Manasseh are mine.
Ephraim is my war helmet,
　　and Judah is my symbol of royal power.

9 Moab is merely my washbasin,
   and Edom belongs to me.
   I shout with victory over the Philistines."

10 Our God, who will bring me to the fortress
   or lead me to Edom?
11 Have you rejected us? You don't lead our armies.
12   Help us defeat our enemies!
      No one else can rescue us.
13 You are the one who gives us victory
   and crushes our enemies.

Psalm 109

[A psalm by David for the music leader.]

A Prayer for the LORD's Help

1 I praise you, God!
   Don't keep silent.
2 Destructive and deceitful lies are told about me,
3   and hateful things are said for no reason.
4 I had pity and prayed[c] for my enemies,
   but their words to me were harsh and cruel.
5 For being friendly and kind,
   they paid me back
   with meanness and hatred.
6 My enemies said,
   "Find some worthless fools
   to accuse him of a crime.
7 Try him and find him guilty!

---

c *and prayed*: One possible meaning for the difficult
Hebrew text.

Consider his prayers a lie.

8 Cut his life short
     and let someone else have his job.

9 Make orphans of his children
     and a widow of his wife;

10 make his children beg for food
     and live in the slums.

11 "Let the people he owes take everything he owns.
     Give it all to strangers.

12 Don't let anyone be kind to him
     or have pity on the children he leaves behind.

13 Bring an end to his family,
     and from now on let him be a forgotten man.

14 "Don't let the LORD forgive
     the sins of his parents and his ancestors.

15 Don't let the LORD forget the sins of his family,
     or let anyone remember his family ever lived.

16 He was so cruel to the poor, homeless,
     and discouraged
          that they died young.

17 "He cursed others. Now place a curse on him!
     He never wished others well.
          Wish only trouble for him!

18 He cursed others
     more often than he dressed himself.
     Let his curses strike him deep,
          just as water and olive oil
               soak through to our bones.

19 Let his curses surround him,
     just like the clothes he wears each day."

20 Those are the cruel things my enemies wish for me.
   Let it all happen to them!
21 Be true to your name, LORD God!
   Show your great kindness and rescue me.

22 I am poor and helpless,
   and I have lost all hope.
23 I am fading away like an evening shadow;
   I am tossed aside like a crawling insect.
24 I have gone without eating,*d*
   until my knees are weak,
   and my body is bony.
25 When my enemies see me,
   they say cruel things and shake their heads.

26 Please help me, LORD God!
   Come and save me because of your love.
27   Let others know that you alone have saved me.
28 I don't care if they curse me,
   as long as you bless me.
   You will make my enemies fail
   when they attack,
      and you will make me glad
      to be your servant.
29 You will cover them with shame,
   just as their bodies are covered with clothes.

30 I will sing your praises and thank you, LORD,
   when your people meet.
31 You help everyone in need,
   and you defend them when they are on trial.

---

d without eating: See the note at 35.13.

Psalm 110

[A psalm by David.]

The LORD Gives Victory

¹ The LORD said to my Lord,
    "Sit at my right side,*e*
        until I make your enemies
        into a footstool for you."

² The LORD will let your power reach out from Zion,
        and you will rule over your enemies.
³ Your glorious power will be seen
        on the day you begin to rule.
You will wear the sacred robes
        and shine like the morning sun
        in all of your strength.*f*
⁴ The LORD has made a promise
        that will never be broken:
    "You will be a priest forever, just like Melchizedek."

⁵ My Lord is at your right side,
        and when he gets angry
        he will crush the other kings.
⁶ He will judge the nations and crack their skulls,
        leaving piles of dead bodies all over the earth.
⁷ He will drink from any stream that he chooses,
        while winning victory after victory.*g*

----

e *right side*: See the note at 16.11.
f *You will... strength*: One possible meaning for the difficult
Hebrew text.
g *while... victory*: Or "God will give him victory after
victory."

Psalm 111

Praise the LORD for All He Has Done

1 Shout praises to the LORD!
  With all my heart I will thank the LORD
    when his people meet.

2 The LORD has done many wonderful things!
  Everyone who is pleased
  with God's marvelous deeds
    will keep them in mind.

3 Everything the LORD does is glorious and majestic,
    and his power to bring justice will never end.

4 The LORD God is famous for his wonderful deeds,
    and he is kind and merciful.

5 He gives food to his worshipers
    and always keeps his agreement with them.

6 He has shown his mighty power to his people
    and has given them the lands of other nations.

7 God is always honest and fair,
  and his laws can be trusted.

8   They are true and right and will stand forever.

9 God rescued his people,
  and he will never break his agreement with them.
    He is fearsome and holy.

10 Respect and obey the LORD!
  This is the first step to wisdom and good sense.[h]
    God will always be respected.

---

[h] *This... sense:* Or "This is what wisdom and good sense
  are all about."

Psalm 112

God Blesses His Worshipers

1 Shout praises to the LORD!
The LORD blesses everyone
who worships him
and gladly obeys his teachings.
2 Their descendants will have great power
in the land,
because the LORD blesses all who do right.
3 They will get rich and prosper
and will always be remembered
for their fairness.
4 They will be so kind and merciful and good,
that they will be a light in the dark
for others who do the right thing.

5 Life will go well for those who freely lend
and are honest in business.
6 They won't ever be troubled,
and the kind things they do
will never be forgotten.
7 Bad news won't bother them;
they have decided to trust the LORD.
8 They are dependable and not afraid,
and they will live to see their enemies defeated.
9 They will always be remembered
and greatly praised,
because they were kind
and freely gave to the poor.
10 When evil people see this,
they angrily bite their tongues and disappear.
They will never get what they really want.

18 I will keep my promise to you
    when your people 19gather
    at your temple in Jerusalem.
Shout praises to the LORD!

Psalm 117

Come Praise the LORD

1 All of you nations, come praise the LORD!
    Let everyone praise him.
2 His love for us is wonderful;
    his faithfulness never ends.
Shout praises to the LORD!

Psalm 118

The LORD Is Always Merciful

1 Tell the LORD how thankful you are,
    because he is kind and always merciful.

2 Let Israel shout, "God is always merciful!"
3 Let the family of Aaron the priest shout,
    "God is always merciful!"
4 Let every true worshiper of the LORD shout,
    "God is always merciful!"

5 When I was really hurting, I prayed to the LORD.
He answered my prayer,
    and took my worries away.
6 The LORD is on my side,
    and I am not afraid of what others can do to me.

7 With the LORD on my side,
    I will defeat all of my hateful enemies.
8 It is better to trust the LORD for protection
    than to trust anyone else,
9   including strong leaders.
10 Nations surrounded me,
    but I got rid of them by the power of the LORD.
11 They attacked from all sides,
    but I got rid of them by the power of the LORD.
12 They swarmed around like bees,
    but by the power of the LORD,
    I got rid of them and their fiery sting.
13 Their attacks were so fierce that I nearly fell,
    but the LORD helped me.
14 My power and my strength come from the LORD,
    and he has saved me.

15 From the tents of God's people
    come shouts of victory:
    "The LORD is powerful!
16 With his mighty arm the LORD wins victories!
    The LORD is powerful!"

17 And so my life is safe,
    and I will live to tell what the LORD has done.
18 He punished me terribly,
    but he did not let death lay its hands on me.
19 Open the gates of justice!
    I will enter
    and tell the LORD how thankful I am.

20 Here is the gate of the LORD!
    Everyone who does right may enter this gate.

21 I praise the LORD
    for answering my prayers
    and saving me.
22 The stone that the builders tossed aside
    has now become the most important stone.

23 The LORD has done this,
    and it is amazing to us.
24 This day belongs to the LORD!
    Let's celebrate and be glad today.
25 We'll ask the LORD to save us!
    We'll sincerely ask the LORD to let us win.

26 God bless the one who comes
    in the name of the LORD!
We praise you from here in the house of the LORD.

27 The LORD is our God,
    and he has given us light!
Start the celebration!
March with palm branches
    all the way to the altar. *i*

28 The LORD is my God!
I will praise him
    and tell him how thankful I am.

29 Tell the LORD how thankful you are,
    because he is kind and always merciful.

---

i Start...altar: One possible meaning for the difficult
  Hebrew text.

Psalm 119

In Praise of the Law of the LORD

¹ Our LORD, you bless everyone
　　who lives right and obeys your Law.
² You bless all of those
　　　who follow your commands
　　　from deep in their hearts
³　　and who never do wrong or turn from you.
⁴ You have ordered us always to obey your teachings;
⁵　I don't ever want to stray from your laws.
⁶ Thinking about your commands
　　will keep me from doing some foolish thing.
⁷ I will do right and praise you
　　by learning to respect your perfect laws.
⁸ I will obey all of them!
　　Don't turn your back on me.

⁹ Young people can live a clean life
　　by obeying your word.
¹⁰ I worship you with all my heart.
　　Don't let me walk away from your commands.
¹¹ I treasure your word above all else;
　　it keeps me from sinning against you.
¹² I praise you, LORD! Teach me your laws.
¹³ With my own mouth,
　　I tell others the laws that you have spoken.
¹⁴ Obeying your instructions
　　brings as much happiness as being rich.
¹⁵ I will study your teachings
　　and follow your footsteps.
¹⁶ I will take pleasure in your laws
　　and remember your words.

17 Treat me with kindness, LORD,
    so that I may live and do what you say.
18 Open my mind
    and let me discover the wonders of your Law.
19 I live here as a stranger.
    Don't keep me from knowing your commands.
20 What I want most of all and at all times
    is to honor your laws.
21 You punish those boastful, worthless nobodies
    who turn from your commands.
22 Don't let them sneer and insult me
    for following you.
23 I keep thinking about your teachings, LORD,
    even if rulers plot against me.
24 Your laws are my greatest joy!
    I follow their advice.

25 I am at the point of death.
    Let your teachings breathe new life into me.
26 When I told you my troubles,
    you answered my prayers.
    Now teach me your laws.
27 Help me to understand your teachings,
    and I will think about your marvelous deeds.
28 I am overcome with sorrow.
    Encourage me,
    as you have promised to do.
29 Keep me from being deceitful,
    and be kind enough to teach me your Law.
30 I am determined to be faithful
    and to respect your laws.
31 I follow your rules, LORD.
    Don't let me be ashamed.

³² I am eager to learn all that you want me to do;
    help me to understand more and more.

³³ Point out your rules to me,
    and I won't disobey even one of them.
³⁴ Help me to understand your Law;
    I promise to obey it with all my heart.
³⁵ Direct me by your commands!
    I love to do what you say.
³⁶ Make me want to obey you, rather than to be rich.
³⁷ Take away my foolish desires,
    and let me find life by walking with you.
³⁸ I am your servant!
    Do for me what you promised
    to those who worship you.
³⁹ Your wonderful teachings protect me
    from the insults that I hate so much.
⁴⁰ I long for your teachings.
    Be true to yourself and let me live.

⁴¹ Show me your love and save me, LORD,
    as you have promised.
⁴² Then I will have an answer for everyone
    who insults me for trusting your word.
⁴³ I rely on your laws!
    Don't take away my chance to speak your truth.
⁴⁴ I will keep obeying your Law forever and ever.
⁴⁵ I have gained perfect freedom
    by following your teachings,
⁴⁶   and I trust them so much
    that I tell them to kings.
⁴⁷ I love your commands!
    They bring me happiness.

48 I love and respect them
   and will keep them in mind.

49 Don't forget your promise to me, your servant.
   I depend on it.
50 When I am hurting,
   I find comfort in your promise that leads to life.
51 Conceited people sneer at me,
   but I obey your Law.
52 I find true comfort, LORD,
   because your laws have stood the test of time.
53 I get furious
   when evil people turn against your Law.
54 No matter where I am,
   your teachings fill me with songs.
55 Even in the night I think about you, LORD,
   and I obey your Law.
56 You have blessed me
   because I have always followed your teachings.

57 You, LORD, are my choice, and I will obey you.
58 With all my heart I beg you to be kind to me,
   just as you have promised.
59 I pay careful attention as you lead me,
   and I follow closely.
60 As soon as you command, I do what you say.
61   Evil people may set a trap, but I obey your Law.
62 Your laws are so fair that I wake up
   and praise you in the middle of the night.
63 I choose as my friends everyone who worships you
   and follows your teachings.
64 Our LORD, your love is seen all over the world.
   Teach me your laws.

⁶⁵ I am your servant, LORD,
     and you have kept your promise
       to treat me with kindness.
⁶⁶ Give me wisdom and good sense.
     I trust your commands.
⁶⁷ Once you corrected me for not obeying you,
     but now I obey.
⁶⁸ You are kindhearted, and you do good things,
     so teach me your laws.
⁶⁹ My reputation is being ruined by conceited liars,
     but with all my heart I follow your teachings.
⁷⁰ Those liars have no sense,
     but I find happiness in your Law.
⁷¹ When you corrected me, it did me good
     because it taught me to study your laws.
⁷² I would rather obey you
     than to have a thousand pieces of silver and gold.

⁷³ You created me and put me together.
  Make me wise enough to learn
     what you have commanded.
⁷⁴ Your worshipers will see me,
     and they will be glad that I trust your word.
⁷⁵ Your decisions are correct,
     and you were right to punish me.
⁷⁶ I serve you, LORD.
  Comfort me with your love,
     just as you have promised.
⁷⁷ I love to obey your Law!
     Have mercy and let me live.
⁷⁸ Put down those proud people
  who hurt me with their lies,
     because I have chosen to study your teachings.

79 Let your worshipers come to me,
    so they will learn to obey your rules.
80 Let me truly respect your laws,
    so I won't be ashamed.

81 I long for you to rescue me!
    Your word is my only hope.
82 I am worn out from waiting
    for you to keep your word.
    When will you have mercy?
83 My life is wasting away like a dried-up wineskin,*j*
    but I have not forgotten your teachings.
84 I am your servant!
    How long must I suffer?
    When will you punish those troublemakers?
85 Those proud people reject your teachings,
    and they dig pits for me to fall in.
86 Your laws can be trusted!
    Protect me from cruel liars.
87 They have almost killed me,
    but I have been faithful to your teachings.
88 Show that you love me and let me live,
    so that I may obey all of your commands.

89 Our LORD, you are eternal!
    Your word will last as long as the heavens.*k*

---

j a dried-up wineskin: The Hebrew text has "a wineskin in
the smoke." In ancient times bags were made from animal
skins to hold wine, but when the bags dried up they
cracked and could no longer be used.
k Our…heavens: Or "Our LORD, your word is eternal.
It will last as long as the heavens."

⁹⁰ You remain faithful in every generation,
  and the earth you created
  will keep standing firm.
⁹¹ All things are your servants,
  and the laws you made are still in effect today.
⁹² If I had not found happiness in obeying your Law,
  I would have died in misery.
⁹³ I won't ever forget your teachings,
  because you give me new life
  by following them.
⁹⁴ I belong to you, and I have respected your laws,
  so keep me safe.
⁹⁵ Brutal enemies are waiting to ambush
  and destroy me,
  but I obey your rules.
⁹⁶ Nothing is completely perfect,
  except your teachings.

⁹⁷ I deeply love your Law! I think about it all day.
⁹⁸ Your laws never leave my mind,
  and they make me much wiser
  than my enemies.
⁹⁹ Thinking about your teachings
  gives me better understanding than my teachers,
¹⁰⁰ and obeying your laws makes me wiser
  than those who have lived a long time.
¹⁰¹ I obey your word
  instead of following a way that leads to trouble.
¹⁰² You have been my teacher,
  and I won't reject your instructions.
¹⁰³ Your teachings are sweeter than honey.
¹⁰⁴   They give me understanding
  and make me hate all lies.

105 Your word is a lamp that gives light
    wherever I walk.
106 Your laws are fair,
    and I have given my word to respect them all.
107 I am in terrible pain!
    Save me, LORD,
        as you said you would.
108 Accept my offerings of praise
    and teach me your laws.
109 I never forget your teachings,
    although my life is always in danger.
110 Some merciless people are trying to trap me,
    but I never turn my back on your teachings.
111 They will always be my most prized possession
    and my source of joy.
112 I have made up my mind
    to obey your laws forever,
        no matter what.

113 I hate anyone whose loyalty is divided,
    but I love your Law.
114 You are my place of safety and my shield.
    Your word is my only hope.

115 All of you worthless people, get away from me!
    I am determined to obey
        the commands of my God.

116 Be true to your word, LORD.
    Keep me alive and strong;
        don't let me be ashamed because of my hope.
117 Keep me safe and secure,
    so that I will always respect your laws.

118 You reject all deceitful liars
        because they refuse your teachings.
119 As far as you are concerned,
    all evil people are[^l] garbage,
        and so I follow your rules.
120 I tremble all over when I think of you
        and the way you judge.

121 I did what was fair and right!
        Don't hand me over
        to those who want to mistreat me.
122 Take good care of me, your servant,
        and don't let me be harmed
        by those conceited people.
123 My eyes are weary from waiting
        to see you keep your promise
        to come and save me.
124 Show your love for me, your servant,
        and teach me your laws.
125 I serve you, so let me understand your teachings.
126 Do something, LORD!
        They have broken your Law.
127 Your laws mean more to me than the finest gold.
128 I follow all of your commands,[^m]
        but I hate anyone who leads me astray.

129 Your teachings are wonderful, and I respect them all.

[^l]: *As far as ... are*: A few Hebrew manuscripts and ancient
    translations. Most Hebrew manuscripts have "You get rid
    of evil people as if they were."
[^m]: *I ... commands*: One possible meaning for the difficult
    Hebrew text.

130 Understanding your word brings light
       to the minds of ordinary people.
131 I honestly want to know everything you teach.
132 Think about me and be kind,
       just as you are to everyone
       who loves your name.
133 Keep your promise and don't let me stumble
       or let sin control my life.
134 Protect me from abuse, so I can obey your laws.
135 Smile on me, your servant,
       and teach me your laws.
136 When anyone disobeys you,
       my eyes overflow with tears.

137 Our LORD, you always do right,
       and your decisions are fair.
138 All of your teachings are true and trustworthy.
139 It upsets me greatly
       when my enemies neglect your teachings.
140 Your word to me, your servant, is like pure gold;
       I treasure what you say.
141 Everyone calls me a nobody,
       but I remember your laws.
142 You will always do right,
       and your teachings are true.
143 I am in deep distress, but I love your teachings.
144 Your rules are always fair.
       Help me to understand them and live.

145 I pray to you, LORD! Please answer me.
    I promise to obey your laws.
146   I beg you to save me,
       so I can follow your rules.

¹⁴⁷ Even before sunrise, I pray for your help,
and I put my hope in what you have said.
¹⁴⁸ I lie awake at night, thinking of your promises.
¹⁴⁹ Show that you love me, LORD,
and answer my prayer.
Please do the right thing and save my life.
¹⁵⁰ People who disobey your Law
have made evil plans and want to hurt me,
¹⁵¹ but you are with me,
and all of your commands can be trusted.
¹⁵² From studying your laws, I found out long ago
that you made them to last forever.

¹⁵³ I have not forgotten your Law!
Look at the trouble I am in, and rescue me.
¹⁵⁴ Be my defender and protector!
Keep your promise and save my life.
¹⁵⁵ Evil people won't obey you,
and so they have no hope of being saved.
¹⁵⁶ You are merciful, LORD!
Please do the right thing and save my life.
¹⁵⁷ I have a lot of brutal enemies,
but still I never turn from your laws.
¹⁵⁸ All of those unfaithful people
who refuse to obey you
are disgusting to me.
¹⁵⁹ Remember how I love your laws,
and show your love for me
by keeping me safe.
¹⁶⁰ All you say can be trusted;
your teachings are true and will last forever.

¹⁶¹ Rulers are cruel to me for no reason.

But with all my heart I respect your words,
162   because they bring happiness
         like treasures taken in war.
163 I can't stand liars, but I love your Law.
164 I praise you seven times a day
         because your laws are fair.
165 You give peace of mind to all who love your Law.
         Nothing can make them fall.
166 You are my only hope for being saved, LORD,
         and I do all you command.
167 I love and obey your laws with all my heart.
168 You know everything I do.
         You know I respect every law you have given.

169 Please, LORD, hear my prayer
     and give me the understanding
         that comes from your word.
170 Listen to my concerns and keep me safe,
         just as you have promised.
171 If you will teach me your laws,
     I will praise you 172and sing about your promise,
         because all of your teachings
         are what they ought to be.
173 Be ready to protect me
         because I have chosen to obey your laws.
174 I am waiting for you to save me, LORD.
         Your Law makes me happy.
175 Keep me alive, so I can praise you,
         and let me find help in your teachings.
176 I am your servant,
         but I have wandered away like a lost sheep.
     Please come after me,
         because I have not forgotten your teachings.

Psalm 120

[A song for worship.]

A Prayer for the LORD's Help

1 When I am in trouble, I pray,
2   "Come and save me, LORD, from deceitful liars!"

3 What punishment is fitting for you deceitful liars?
4   Your reward should be sharp
     and flaming arrows!

5 But I must live as a foreigner
     among the people of Meshech
     and in the tents of Kedar.[n]
6 I have spent too much time
     living among people who hate peace.
7 I am in favor of peace, but when I speak of it,
     all they want is war.

Psalm 121

[A song for worship.]

The LORD Will Protect His People

1 I look to the hills! Where will I find help?
2 It will come from the LORD,
     who created the heavens and the earth.

3 The LORD is your protector,
     and he won't go to sleep or let you stumble.

---

[n] *Meshech... Kedar*: Meshech was a country near the Black Sea, and Kedar was a tribe of the Syrian desert.

4 The protector of Israel doesn't doze
   or ever get drowsy.

5 The LORD is your protector,
   there at your right side
   to shade you from the sun.
6 You won't be harmed by the sun during the day
   or by the moon*o* at night.

7 The LORD will protect you
   and keep you safe from all dangers.
8 The LORD will protect you
   now and always wherever you go.

Psalm 122

[A song by David for worship.]

A Song of Praise

1 It made me glad to hear them say,
   "Let's go to the house of the LORD!"
2   Jerusalem, we are standing inside your gates.

3 Jerusalem,
   what a strong and beautiful city you are!
4 Every tribe of the LORD obeys him
   and comes to you to praise his name.
5 David's royal throne is here where justice rules.

---

o harmed … sun … moon: In ancient times people saw the
harmful effects of the rays of the sun, and they thought
that certain illnesses (especially mental disorders) were
also caused by the rays of the moon.

[6] Jerusalem, we pray that you will have peace,
    and that all will go well for those who love you.
[7] May there be peace inside your city walls
    and in your palaces.
[8] Because of my friends and my relatives,
    I will pray for peace.
[9] And because of the house of the LORD our God,
    I will work for your good.

Psalm 123

[A song for worship.]

A Prayer for Mercy

[1] Our LORD and our God,
    I turn my eyes to you,
    on your throne in heaven.
[2] Servants look to their master,
    but we will look to you,
    until you have mercy on us.

[3] Please have mercy, LORD!
    We have been insulted more than we can stand,
[4] and we can't take more abuse
    from those proud, conceited people.

Psalm 124

[A song by David for worship.]

Thanking the LORD for Victory

[1] The LORD was on our side!
    Let everyone in Israel say:

2   "The LORD was on our side!
       Otherwise, the enemy attack
3 would have killed us all,
       because it was furious.
4 We would have been swept away
       in a violent flood 5 of high and roaring waves."

6 Let's praise the LORD!
       He protected us from enemies
         who were like wild animals,
7 and we escaped like birds
       from a hunter's torn net.

8 The LORD made heaven and earth,
       and he is the one who sends us help.

Psalm 125

[A song for worship.]

The LORD's People Are Safe

1 Everyone who trusts the LORD
       is like Mount Zion
         that cannot be shaken
         and will stand forever.
2 Just as Jerusalem is protected
       by mountains on every side,
     the LORD protects his people
       by holding them in his arms now and forever.
3 He won't let the wicked rule his people
       or lead them to do wrong.
4 Let's ask the LORD to be kind to everyone
       who is good and completely obeys him.

⁵ When the LORD punishes the wicked,
    he will punish everyone else
    who lives a crooked life.
Pray for peace in Israel!

Psalm 126

[A song for worship.]

Celebrating the Harvest

¹ It seemed like a dream
    when the LORD brought us back
    to the city of Zion.ᵖ
² We celebrated with laughter
    and joyful songs.
In foreign nations it was said,
    "The LORD has worked miracles for his people."
³ And so we celebrated
    because the LORD had indeed
    worked miracles for us.

⁴ Our LORD,
    we ask you to bless our people again,
    and let us be like streams
    in the Southern Desert.
⁵ We cried as we went out to plant our seeds.
    Now let us celebrate as we bring in the crops.
⁶ We cried on the way to plant our seeds,
    but we will celebrate and shout
    as we bring in the crops.

ᵖ *brought...Zion:* Or "made the city of Zion prosperous again."

Psalm 127

[A song by Solomon for worship.]

Only the LORD Can Bless a Home

1 Without the help of the LORD
      it is useless to build a home or to guard a city.
2 It is useless to get up early and stay up late
      in order to earn a living.
   God takes care of his own, even while they sleep.*q*

3 Children are a blessing and a gift from the LORD.
4 Having a lot of children
      to take care of you in your old age
   is like a warrior with a lot of arrows.
5 The more you have, the better off you will be,
      because they will protect you
         when your enemies attack with arguments.

Psalm 128

[A song for worship.]

The LORD Rewards His Faithful People

1 The LORD will bless you
      if you respect him and obey his laws.
2 Your fields will produce,
      and you will be happy and all will go well.
3 Your wife will be as fruitful as a grapevine,
      and just as an olive tree is rich with olives,
         your home will be rich with healthy children.

---

q God...sleep: One possible meaning for the difficult
   Hebrew text.

4 That is how the LORD will bless everyone
who respects him.

5 I pray that the LORD will bless you from Zion
and let Jerusalem prosper as long as you live.
6 May you live long enough
to see your grandchildren.
Let's pray for peace in Israel!

Psalm 129

[A song for worship.]

A Prayer for Protection

1 Since the time I was young,
enemies have often attacked!
Let everyone in Israel say:
2 "Since the time I was young,
enemies have often attacked!
But they have not defeated me,
3 though my back is like a field
that has just been plowed."

4 The LORD always does right,
and he has set me free
from the ropes of those cruel people.
5 I pray that all who hate the city of Zion
will be made ashamed and forced to turn and run.
6 May they be like grass on the flat roof of a house,
grass that dries up as soon as it sprouts.
7 Don't let them be like wheat gathered in bundles.
8 And don't let anyone who passes by
say to them,

"The Lord bless you!
    I give you my blessing in the name of the Lord."

Psalm 130

[A song for worship.]

Trusting the Lord in Times of Trouble

1 From a sea of troubles I call out to you, Lord.
2   Won't you please listen as I beg for mercy?

3 If you kept record of our sins, no one could last long.
4   But you forgive us, and so we will worship you.

5 With all my heart, I am waiting, Lord, for you!
    I trust your promises.
6 I wait for you more eagerly
        than a soldier on guard duty waits for the dawn.
    Yes, I wait more eagerly
        than a soldier on guard duty waits for the dawn.

7 Israel, trust the Lord! He is always merciful,
    and he has the power to save you.
8 Israel, the Lord will save you from all of your sins.

Psalm 131

[A song by David for worship.]

Trust the Lord!

1 I am not conceited, Lord,
        and I don't waste my time
        on impossible schemes.

² But I have learned to feel safe and satisfied,
    just like a young child on its mother's lap.

³ People of Israel,
    you must trust the LORD now and forever.

Psalm 132

[A song for worship.]

The LORD Is Always with His People

¹ Our LORD, don't forget David and how he suffered.
² Mighty God of Jacob,
    remember how he promised:
³ "I won't go home or crawl into bed
⁴ or close my eyelids, ⁵until I find a home for you,
    the mighty LORD God of Jacob."

⁶ When we were in Ephrathah, we heard
    that the sacred chest was somewhere near Jaar.
⁷ Then we said, "Let's go to the throne of the LORD
    and worship at his feet."

⁸ Come to your new home, LORD,
    you and the sacred chest with all of its power.
⁹ Let victory be like robes for the priests;
    let your faithful people celebrate and shout.
¹⁰ David is your chosen one, so don't reject him.
¹¹ You made a solemn promise to David,
    when you said,
    "I, the LORD, promise
        that someone in your family
        will always be king.

12 If they keep our agreement
and follow my teachings,
then someone in your family will rule forever."

13 You have gladly chosen Zion as your home,
our LORD.
14 You said, "This is my home!
I will live here forever.
15 I will bless Zion with food,
and even the poor will eat until they are full.
16 Victory will be like robes for the priests,
and its faithful people will celebrate and shout.
17 I will give mighty power to the kingdom of David.
Each one of my chosen kings will shine like a lamp
18   and wear a sparkling crown.
But I will disgrace their enemies."

Psalm 133

[A song for worship.]

Living Together in Peace

1 It is truly wonderful
when relatives live together in peace.
2 It is as beautiful as olive oil
poured on Aaron's head[r]
and running down his beard
and the collar of his robe.
3 It is like the dew from Mount Hermon,
falling on Zion's mountains,

---

r *head*: Olive oil was poured on Aaron's head to show that
God had chosen him to be the high priest.

where the LORD has promised to bless his people
with life forevermore.

Psalm 134

[A song for worship.]

Praising the LORD at Night

¹ Everyone who serves the LORD,
come and offer praises.
Everyone who has gathered in his temple tonight,
² lift your hands in prayer toward his holy place
and praise the LORD.

³ The LORD is the Creator of heaven and earth,
and I pray that the Lord
will bless you from Zion.

Psalm 135

In Praise of the LORD's Kindness

¹ Shout praises to the LORD!
You are his servants, so praise his name.
² All who serve in the temple of the LORD our God,
³ come and shout praises.
Praise the name of the LORD! He is kind and good.
⁴ He chose the family of Jacob
and the people of Israel for his very own.

⁵ The LORD is much greater than any other god.
⁶ He does as he chooses in heaven and on earth
and deep in the sea.

7 The LORD makes the clouds rise
    from far across the earth,
        and he makes lightning to go with the rain.
    Then from his secret place he sends out the wind.

8 The LORD killed the first-born
        of people and animals in the land of Egypt.
9 God used miracles and wonders
        to fight the king of Egypt
        and all of his officials.
10 He destroyed many nations
        and killed powerful kings,
11 including King Sihon of the Amorites
        and King Og of Bashan.
    He conquered every kingdom in the land of Canaan
12   and gave their property to his people Israel.

13 The name of the LORD
        will be remembered forever,
        and he will be famous for all time to come.
14 The LORD will bring justice and show mercy
        to all who serve him.

15 Idols of silver and gold
        are made and worshiped in other nations.
16 They have a mouth and eyes,
        but they can't speak or see.
17 They are completely deaf, and they can't breathe.
18 Everyone who makes idols
    and all who trust them
        will end up as helpless as their idols.

19 Everyone in Israel, come praise the LORD!

All the family of Aaron
20 and all the tribe of Levi,[s]
    come praise the LORD!
All of his worshipers, come praise the LORD.
21 Praise the LORD from Zion!
    He lives here in Jerusalem.
        Shout praises to the LORD!

Psalm 136

God's Love Never Fails

1 Praise the LORD! He is good.
    God's love never fails.
2 Praise the God of all gods.
    God's love never fails.
3 Praise the Lord of lords.
    God's love never fails.

4 Only God works great miracles.[t]
    God's love never fails.
5 With wisdom he made the sky.
    God's love never fails.
6 The Lord stretched the earth over the ocean.
    God's love never fails.
7 He made the bright lights in the sky.
    God's love never fails.

---

[s] *Aaron...Levi*: Aaron was from the tribe of Levi, and all priests were from his family. The temple helpers, singers, and musicians were also from the tribe of Levi.

[t] *great miracles*: One Hebrew manuscript and one ancient translation have "miracles."

2 You know when I am resting
  or when I am working,
      and from heaven you discover my thoughts.

3 You notice everything I do and everywhere I go.
4 Before I even speak a word,
    you know what I will say,
5 and with your powerful arm
    you protect me from every side.
6 I can't understand all of this!
    Such wonderful knowledge is far above me.

7 Where could I go to escape
    from your Spirit or from your sight?
8 If I were to climb up to the highest heavens,
    you would be there.
  If I were to dig down to the world of the dead
    you would also be there.

9 Suppose I had wings like the dawning day
    and flew across the ocean.
10 Even then your powerful arm
    would guide and protect me.
11 Or suppose I said, "I'll hide in the dark
    until night comes to cover me over."
12 But you see in the dark
    because daylight and dark
    are all the same to you.

13 You are the one who put me together
    inside my mother's body,
14 and I praise you
    because of the wonderful way you created me.

Everything you do is marvelous!
  Of this I have no doubt.

15 Nothing about me is hidden from you!
  I was secretly woven together
    deep in the earth below,
16 but with your own eyes
    you saw my body being formed.
  Even before I was born,
    you had written in your book
    everything I would do.

17 Your thoughts are far beyond my understanding,
    much more than I could ever imagine.
18 I try to count your thoughts,
    but they outnumber the grains of sand
    on the beach.
  And when I awake, I will find you nearby.

19 How I wish that you would kill
    all cruel and heartless people
    and protect me from them!
20 They are always rebelling
    and speaking evil of you.ᵃ
21 You know I hate anyone who hates you, LORD,
    and refuses to obey.
22 They are my enemies too, and I truly hate them.

23 Look deep into my heart, God,
    and find out everything I am thinking.

ᵃ you: One possible meaning for the difficult Hebrew text
of verse 20.

24 Don't let me follow evil ways,
    but lead me in the way that time has proven true.

Psalm 140

[A psalm by David for the music leader.]

A Prayer for the LORD's Help

1 Rescue me from cruel and violent enemies, LORD!
2 They think up evil plans
    and always cause trouble.
3 Their words bite deep
    like the poisonous fangs of a snake.

4 Protect me, LORD, from cruel and brutal enemies,
    who want to destroy me.
5 Those proud people have hidden traps and nets
    to catch me as I walk.

6 You, LORD, are my God! Please listen to my prayer.
7 You have the power to save me,
    and you keep me safe in every battle.

8 Don't let the wicked succeed
    in doing what they want,
    or else they might never stop planning evil.
9 They have me surrounded,
    but make them the victims
    of their own vicious lies.[b]
10 Dump flaming coals on them

---

[b] *or else… lies:* One possible meaning for the difficult
Hebrew text.

and throw them into pits
    where they can't climb out.
11 Chase those cruel liars away!
    Let trouble hunt them down.

12 Our LORD, I know that you defend the homeless
    and see that the poor are given justice.
13 Your people will praise you and will live with you
    because they do right.

Psalm 141

[A psalm by David.]

A Prayer for the LORD's Protection

1 I pray to you, LORD!
    Please listen when I pray
    and hurry to help me.
2 Think of my prayer as sweet-smelling incense,
    and think of my lifted hands
    as an evening sacrifice.

3 Help me to guard my words
    whenever I say something.
4 Don't let me want to do evil
    or waste my time doing wrong
    with wicked people.
    Don't let me even taste the good things they offer.

5 Let your faithful people correct and punish me.
    My prayers condemn the deeds
    of those who do wrong,
    so don't let me be friends with any of them.

6 Everyone will admit that I was right
　　when their rulers are thrown down a rocky cliff,
7 and their bones lie scattered
　　like broken rocks on top of a grave.*c*

8 You are my LORD and God,
　　and I look to you for safety.
　　Don't let me be harmed.
9 Protect me from the traps of those violent people,
10 and make them fall into their own traps
　　while you help me escape.

Psalm 142

*[A special psalm and a prayer by David
when he was in the cave.]*

A Prayer for Help

1 I pray to you, LORD. I beg for mercy.
2 I tell you all of my worries and my troubles,
3 　　and whenever I feel low,
　　you are there to guide me.

A trap has been hidden along my pathway.
4 Even if you look, you won't see anyone
　　who cares enough to walk beside me.
There is no place to hide,
　　and no one who really cares.

5 I pray to you, LORD!

---

c Let . . . grave: One possible meaning for the difficult
Hebrew text of verses 5-7.

You are my place of safety,
    and you are my choice in the land of the living.
Please answer my prayer.
    I am completely helpless.

6 Help! They are chasing me, and they are too strong.
7 Rescue me from this prison,
    so I can praise your name.
And when your people notice
your wonderful kindness to me,
    they will rush to my side.

Psalm 143

[A psalm by David.]

A Prayer in Time of Danger

1 Listen, LORD, as I pray!
You are faithful and honest
    and will answer my prayer.
2 I am your servant. Don't try me in your court,
    because no one is innocent by your standards.
3 My enemies are chasing me,
    crushing me in the ground.
I am in total darkness, like someone long dead.
4 I have given up all hope,
    and I feel numb all over.

5 I remember to think about the many things
    you did in years gone by.
6 Then I lift my hands in prayer,
    because my soul is a desert,
        thirsty for water from you.

7 Please hurry, LORD, and answer my prayer.
I feel hopeless.
> Don't turn away and leave me here to die.
8 Each morning let me learn more about your love
> because I trust you.
I come to you in prayer, asking for your guidance.

9 Please rescue me from my enemies, LORD!
> I come to you for safety.[d]
10 You are my God.
Show me what you want me to do,
> and let your gentle Spirit lead me
> in the right path.

11 Be true to your name, LORD,
> and keep my life safe.
Use your saving power
> to protect me from trouble.
12 I am your servant.
Show how much you love me
> by destroying my enemies.

Psalm 144

[By David.]

A Prayer for the Nation

1 I praise you, LORD!
You are my mighty rock,[e]
> and you teach me how to fight my battles.

---

[d] *I...safety*: Or "You are my hiding place."
[e] *mighty rock*: See the note at 18.2.

² You are my friend,
  and you are my fortress where I am safe.
You are my shield,
  and you made me the ruler of our people.*f*

³ Why do we humans mean anything to you,
  our LORD?
    Why do you care about us?
⁴ We disappear like a breath;
  we last no longer than a faint shadow.

⁵ Open the heavens like a curtain
  and come down, LORD.
Touch the mountains
  and make them send up smoke.
⁶ Use your lightning as arrows
  to scatter my enemies and make them run away.
⁷ Reach down from heaven and set me free.
Save me from the mighty flood
⁸   of those lying foreigners
  who can't tell the truth.

⁹ In praise of you, our God,
  I will sing a new song, while playing my harp.
¹⁰ By your power, kings win wars,
  and your servant David is saved
    from deadly swords.
¹¹ Won't you keep me safe
  from those lying foreigners
    who can't tell the truth?

---

f *of our people*: Some Hebrew manuscripts and ancient
translations have "of the nations."

¹² Let's pray that our young sons will grow
    like strong plants
and that our daughters will be as lovely
    as columns in the corner of a palace.
¹³ May our barns be filled with all kinds of crops.
May our fields be covered
    with sheep by the thousands,
¹⁴   and every cow have calves.^g
Don't let our city be captured
or any of us be taken away,
    and don't let cries of sorrow
    be heard in our streets.

¹⁵ Our LORD and our God,
    you give these blessings to all who worship you.

Psalm 145

[By David for praise.]

The LORD Is Kind and Merciful

¹ I will praise you, my God and King,
    and always honor your name.
² I will praise you each day
    and always honor your name.
³ You are wonderful, LORD, and you deserve all praise,
    because you are much greater
    than anyone can understand.

⁴ Each generation will announce to the next
    your wonderful and powerful deeds.

---

^g *have calves*: Or "grow fat."

⁵ I will keep thinking
    about your marvelous glory
    and your mighty miracles.ʰ
⁶ Everyone will talk about your fearsome deeds,
    and I will tell all nations how great you are.
⁷ They will celebrate and sing
    about your matchless mercy
    and your power to save.

⁸ You are merciful, LORD!
    You are kind and patient
    and always loving.
⁹ You are good to everyone,
    and you take care of all your creation.

¹⁰ All creation will thank you,
    and your loyal people will praise you.
¹¹ They will tell about
    your marvelous kingdom and your power.
¹² Then everyone will know about
    the mighty things you do
    and your glorious kingdom.
¹³ Your kingdom will never end,
    and you will rule forever.

Our LORD, you keep your word
    and do everything you say.ⁱ

ʰ *and…miracles*: One Hebrew manuscript and two ancient
translations have "as others tell about your mighty
miracles."

ⁱ *Our…say*: These words are found in one Hebrew
manuscript and in two ancient translations.

14 When someone stumbles or falls,
    you give a helping hand.
15 Everyone depends on you,
    and when the time is right,
       you provide them with food.
16 By your own hand
    you satisfy the desires of all who live.

17 Our LORD,
    everything you do is kind and thoughtful,
18   and you are near to everyone
       whose prayers are sincere.
19 You satisfy the desires of all your worshipers,
    and you come to save them
       when they ask for help.
20 You take care of everyone who loves you,
    but you destroy the wicked.

21 I will praise you, LORD,
    and everyone will respect
       your holy name forever.

Psalm 146

Shout Praises to the LORD

1 Shout praises to the LORD!
    With all that I am, I will shout his praises.
2 I will sing and praise the LORD God
    for as long as I live.

3 You can't depend on anyone,
    not even a great leader.

⁴ Once they die and are buried,
    that will be the end of all their plans.

⁵ The LORD God of Jacob blesses everyone
    who trusts him and depends on him.
⁶ God made heaven and earth;
    he created the sea and everything else.
God always keeps his word.
⁷   He gives justice to the poor
    and food to the hungry.

The LORD sets prisoners free ⁸and heals blind eyes.
    He gives a helping hand to everyone who falls.
The LORD loves good people
⁹   and looks after strangers.
He defends the rights of orphans and widows,
    but destroys the wicked.

¹⁰ The LORD God of Zion will rule forever!
    Shout praises to the LORD!

Psalm 147

Sing and Praise the LORD

¹ Shout praises to the LORD! Our God is kind,
    and it is right and good to sing praises to him.
² The LORD rebuilds Jerusalem
    and brings the people of Israel back home again.
³ He renews our hopes and heals our bodies.
⁴ He decided how many stars
    there would be in the sky
    and gave each one a name.

5 Our LORD is great and powerful!
   He understands everything.
6 The LORD helps the poor,
   but he smears the wicked in the dirt.

7 Celebrate and sing!
   Play your harps for the LORD our God.
8 He fills the sky with clouds
   and sends rain to the earth,
      so that the hills will be green with grass.
9 He provides food for cattle
   and for the young ravens, when they cry out.
10 The LORD doesn't care about the strength of horses
   or powerful armies.
11 The LORD is pleased only with those
   who worship him
   and trust his love.

12 Everyone in Jerusalem,
   come and praise the LORD your God!
13 He makes your city gates strong
   and blesses your people
      by giving them children.
14 God lets you live in peace,
   and he gives you the very best wheat.
15 As soon as God speaks, the earth obeys.
16 He covers the ground with snow
   like a blanket of wool,
      and he scatters frost like ashes on the ground.
17 God sends down hailstones like chips of rocks.
   Who can stand the cold?
18 At his command the ice melts, the wind blows,
   and streams begin to flow.

¹⁹ God gave his laws and teachings
  to the descendants of Jacob,
  the nation of Israel.
²⁰ But he has not given his laws to any other nation.
  Shout praises to the LORD!

Psalm 148

Come Praise the LORD

¹ Shout praises to the LORD!
  Shout the LORD's praises in the highest heavens.
² All of you angels, and all who serve him above,
  come and offer praise.

³ Sun and moon, and all of you bright stars,
  come and offer praise.
⁴ Highest heavens,
  and the water above the highest heavens,^j
  come and offer praise.

⁵ Let all things praise the name of the LORD,
  because they were created at his command.
⁶ He made them to last forever,
  and nothing can change what he has done.^k

⁷⁻⁸ All creatures on earth,
  you obey his commands,
  so come praise the Lord!

---

^j *the water…heavens*: It was believed that the earth and
the heavens were surrounded by water.
^k *nothing…done*: Or "his laws will never change."

Sea monsters and the deep sea, fire and hail,
snow and frost, and every stormy wind,
come praise the LORD!

9 All mountains and hills, fruit trees and cedars,
10 every wild and tame animal, all reptiles and birds,
come praise the LORD!

11 Every king and every ruler, all nations on earth,
12 every man and every woman, young people and old,
come praise the LORD!

13 All creation, come praise the name of the LORD.
Praise his name alone.
The glory of God is greater than heaven and earth.

14 Like a bull with mighty horns,
the LORD protects his faithful nation Israel,
because they belong to him.
Shout praises to the LORD!

Psalm 149

A New Song of Praise

1 Shout praises to the LORD!
Sing him a new song of praise
when his loyal people meet.
2 People of Israel, rejoice because of your Creator.
People of Zion, celebrate because of your King.
3 Praise his name by dancing
and playing music on harps and tambourines.
4 The LORD is pleased with his people,
and he gives victory to those who are humble.

⁵ All of you faithful people, praise our glorious Lord!
  Celebrate and worship.
⁶ Praise God with songs on your lips
  and a sword in your hand.
⁷ Take revenge and punish the nations.
⁸   Put chains of iron on their kings and rulers.
⁹ Punish them as they deserve;
  this is the privilege of God's faithful people.
  Shout praises to the LORD!

Psalm 150

The LORD Is Good to His People

¹ Shout praises to the LORD!
  Praise God in his temple.
    Praise him in heaven, his mighty fortress.
² Praise our God!
  His deeds are wonderful,
    too marvelous to describe.

³ Praise God with trumpets and all kinds of harps.
⁴ Praise him with tambourines and dancing,
    with stringed instruments and woodwinds.
⁵ Praise God with cymbals, with clashing cymbals.
⁶ Let every living creature praise the LORD.
    Shout praises to the LORD!

A
Mini Dictionary
for the Bible

A Mini Dictionary for the Bible

This dictionary is divided into 21 sections. The indexes below list all the sections and all of the entries in alphabetical order, so that you can find what you are looking for more easily.

Section Index

Alphabetical Index

1. A Few Basics

CEV The Contemporary English Version of the Bible.

Old Testament This part of the Bible is made up of the 39 books from Genesis through Malachi. They were written mostly in Hebrew, with a few passages in Aramaic.

New Testament This part of the Bible is made up of the 27 books from Matthew through Revelation. They were written in Greek.

Chapter and Verse Numbers These numbers were not part of the original books, but were added hundreds of years later as a way to refer to specific parts of the books of Scripture. For example, Genesis 1.3 means "the book of Genesis, chapter 1, verse 3." Genesis 2.4,5 means "the book of Genesis, chapter 2, verses 4 and 5." Genesis 2.4-6 means "the book of Genesis, chapter 2, verses 4 through 6." And Genesis 1–2 means, "the book of Genesis, chapters 1 through 2."

A few books are so short that they were not divided into chapters, and so these books only have verse numbers.

In the text of the CEV, verse numbers have sometimes been combined, for example, 3-4. One reason for this is that contemporary English expresses things in a different order than ancient Greek and Hebrew. And in lists, the verse numbers are often blended together into a single heading to avoid confusion. But all the meaning from the original Greek and Hebrew has been carefully included in the CEV translation.

2. Scriptures, Manuscripts

Ancient Translations The Old Testament was translated into Greek over the period 250–150 B.C. Later, the whole Bible was translated into Latin, Syriac, and some other languages. These ancient translations can sometimes show what the Hebrew or Greek text said at the time they were translated, and so the CEV notes will sometimes refer to them.

Commandments God's rules for his people to live by. The most famous are the Ten Commandments (see Exodus 20.1-17; Deuteronomy 5.6-21).

Dead Sea Scrolls Manuscripts found near the Dead Sea from 1947-1954. They date from about 250 B.C. to A.D. 68. These manuscripts include at least some parts of nearly all Old Testament books.

God's Law God's rules for his people to live by. They are found in the Old Testament, especially in the first five books.

Law and the Prophets A term used in New Testament times to refer to the sacred writings of the Jews. The Law and the Prophets were two of the three sections of the Old Testament, but the expression sometimes refers to the entire Old Testament.

Law of Moses and **Law of the Lord** Usually refers to the first five books of the Old Testament, but sometimes to the entire Old Testament.

Manuscript In ancient times, all books were copied by hand. A copy made this way is called "a manuscript."

Proverb A wise saying that is short and easy to remember.

Psalm A Hebrew poem. Psalms were often written in

such a way that they could be prayed or sung by an individual or a group. Some of the psalms thank and praise God, while others ask God to take away sins or to give protection, comfort, vengeance, or mercy.

Samaritan Hebrew Text The Hebrew text of Genesis through Deuteronomy used and preserved by the Samaritans (see also "Samaria"). This text uses forms of letters and many spellings that are different from the Standard Hebrew Text. It has traditionally been called "the Samaritan Pentateuch."

Scriptures Although this term now refers to the whole Bible, in the New Testament it refers to the Old Testament.

Standard Hebrew Text The Hebrew text that is found in most Hebrew manuscripts of the Old Testament. Almost all of these manuscripts were copied after A.D. 900 (but see also "Dead Sea Scrolls").

Wisdom Often refers to the common sense and practical skill needed to solve everyday problems, but sometimes involves trying to find answers to the hard questions about the meaning of life.

3. Languages

Aramaic A language closely related to Hebrew. In New Testament times, Aramaic was spoken by many Jews including Jesus. Ezra 4.8–6.18; 7.12-26; and Daniel 2.4b–7.28 were written in Aramaic.

Greek The language used throughout the Mediterranean world in New Testament times, and the language in which the New Testament was written.

Hebrew The language used by most of the people of Israel until the Exile. But after the people returned, more and more people spoke Aramaic instead. Most of the Old Testament was written in Hebrew.

4. People

Aaron The brother of Moses. Only he and his descendants were to serve as priests and offer sacrifices for the people of Israel (see Exodus 4.14-16; 28.1; Numbers 16.1–18.7).

Abel The second son of Adam and Eve and the younger brother of Cain. Abel was killed by Cain after God accepted Abel's offering and refused to accept Cain's (see Genesis 4.1-11).

Abraham The first of the three great ancestors of the people of Israel. Abraham was the husband of Sarah and the father of Isaac. At first Abraham's name was Abram, meaning "Great Father." Then, when Abram was ninety-nine years old, God changed Abram's name to Abraham, which means "Father of a Crowd." Abraham trusted God, and so God promised that Abraham and his wife Sarah would have a son and more descendants than could be counted. God also promised that Abraham would be a blessing to everyone on earth (see Genesis 12.1-7; 17.1–18.15).

Adam The first man and the husband of Eve (see Genesis 1.26–3.21).

Agrippa (1) Herod Agrippa was king of Judea A.D. 41–44 and mistreated Christians (see Acts 12.1-5). (2) Agrippa II was the son of Herod Agrippa and ruled parts of Palestine from A.D. 53 to A.D. 93 or later. He and his sister Bernice listened to Paul defend himself (see Acts 25.13–26.32).

Antipas (1) Herod Antipas, son of Herod the Great (see "Herod"). (2) An otherwise unknown Christian at Pergamum, who was killed because he was a follower of Christ (see Revelation 2.13).

Augustus A title meaning "honored," which was given to Octavian by the Romans when he began ruling the Roman world in 27 B.C. He was the Roman Emperor when Jesus was born.

Cain The first son of Adam and Eve; Cain killed his brother Abel after God accepted Abel's offering and refused to accept Cain's (see Genesis 4.1-17).

David King of Israel from about 1010–970 B.C. David was the most famous king Israel ever had, and many of the people of Israel hoped that one of his descendants would always be their king (see 1 Samuel 16–30; 2 Samuel; 1 Kings 12).

Esau The older son of Isaac and Rebekah, and the brother of Jacob. Esau was also known as Edom and as the ancestor of the Edomites (see Genesis 25.20-34; 26.34-46; 32.1–33.16).

Eve The first woman and the wife of Adam (see Genesis 1.26–3.21).

Felix The Roman governor of Palestine A.D. 52–60, who listened to Paul speak and kept him in jail (see Acts 23.24–24.27).

Festus The Roman governor after Felix, who sent Paul to stand trial in Rome (see Acts 24.27–26.32).

Hagar A slave of Sarah, the wife of Abraham. When Sarah could not have any children, she followed the ancient custom of letting her husband have a child by Hagar, her slave. The boy's name was Ishmael (see Genesis 16; 21.8-21).

Herod (1) Herod the Great was the king of all Palestine

Gilead. (2) West Manasseh lived west of the Jordan River and to the north of Ephraim.

Naphtali Occupied land north and west of Lake Galilee.

Reuben Occupied land east of the Dead Sea, from the Arnon River in the south to the northern end of the Dead Sea.

Simeon Occupied land southwest of Judah, and was later practically absorbed into Judah.

Zebulun Occupied land north of Manasseh from the eastern end of Mount Carmel to Mount Tabor.

7. Christ's Twelve Apostles

Apostle A person chosen and sent by Christ to take his message to others. Lists of the names of Christ's twelve apostles can be found in Matthew 10.2-4; Mark 3.16-19; Luke 6.14-16; Acts 1.12-13. Later, others such as Paul and James the brother of Jesus also became known as apostles.

Simon also known as Peter or Cephas

Andrew Simon Peter's brother

James the son of Zebedee

John the son of Zebedee (James and John were also known as "Thunderbolts")

Philip from Bethsaida, the hometown of Simon and Andrew

Bartholomew mentioned in all New Testament lists of apostles, but nowhere else

Thomas also known as "The Twin"

Matthew also known as Levi

James the son of Alphaeus

Thaddeus also known as Judas or Jude the son of James

Simon also known as "the Eager One".
Judas Iscariot who betrayed Jesus
Matthias who was chosen to replace Judas Iscariot

8. Groups of People, Cities, Nations

Amalekites A nomadic nation living mostly in the area south and east of the Dead Sea. They were enemies of Israel.

Ammon A nation that lived east of Israel. According to Genesis 19.30-38, the people of Ammon descended from Lot, a nephew of Abraham.

Amorites Usually a name for all the non-Israelite nations who lived in Canaan, but in some passages it may refer to one nation scattered in several areas of Canaan.

Anakim Perhaps a group of very large people who lived in Palestine before the Israelites (see Numbers 13.33 and Deuteronomy 2.10, 11, 20, 21).

Asia A Roman province in what is today the nation of Turkey.

Assyria An empire of Old Testament times, whose capital city Nineveh was located in what is today northern Iraq. In 722 B.C. Assyria conquered the kingdom of Israel and took many Israelites as captives. The Assyrians then forced people from other parts of its empire to settle on Israel's land (see 2 Kings 18.9-12).

Avvites A nation that lived along the Mediterranean seacoast before the Philistines came and took their land. The Avvites who survived lived south of the Philistines.

Babylonia A large empire of Old Testament times, whose capital city Babylon was a located in south-central Mesopotamia. The Babylonians defeated the southern kingdom of Judah in 586 B.C. and forced many of its people to live in Babylonia (see 2 Kings 25.1-12).

Canaanites The nations who lived in Canaan before the Israelites. Many Canaanites continued to live there even after the Israelites came.

Cush The Hebrew form for Ethiopia (see "Ethiopia" below).

Disciples Those who were followers of Jesus and learned from him. The term often refers to his twelve apostles.

Edomites A nation living in Edom or Seir, an area south and southeast of the Dead Sea. According to Genesis 36.1-43, the Edomites descended from Esau, Jacob's brother.

Empire A number of kingdoms ruled by one strong military power.

Epicureans People who followed the teachings of a man named Epicurus, who taught that happiness should be the main goal in life.

Ethiopia A region south of Egypt that included parts of the present countries of Ethiopia and Sudan.

Exiles Israelites who were taken away as prisoners to Babylonia (see also "Exile").

Gentiles Those people who are not Jews.

Girgashites One of the nations that lived in Canaan before the Israelites.

Hebrew An older term for "Israelite" or "Jewish."

Hittites A nation whose capital city was located in what is now Turkey. The Hittites had an empire that at times controlled some kingdoms in Canaan before 1200 B.C., and many Hittites remained in Canaan even after the Israelites came.

Hivites A nation that lived in Canaan before the Israelites, probably related to the Horites.

Horites A nation that lived in Canaan before the Israelites. The Horites were also known as "Hurrians."

Israel (1) The nation made up of the twelve tribes descended from Jacob (see Section 6, "Twelve Tribes of Israel"). (2) The northern kingdom, after the northern tribes broke away following the death of Solomon (see 1 Kings 12.1-20).

Jebusites A group of Canaanite people who lived at Jebus, also known as Jerusalem (see 2 Samuel 5.6-10).

Jews A name first used in referring to someone belonging to the tribe of Judah. Later, the term came to be used of any Israelite.

Kadesh A town in the desert of Paran southwest of the Dead Sea, near the southern border of Israel and the western border of Edom. Israel camped at Kadesh while the twelve tribal leaders explored Canaan (see Numbers 13–14).

Levites Those Israelites who belonged to the tribe of Levi. God chose the men of one Levite family, the descendants of Aaron, to be Israel's priests. The other men from this tribe helped with the work in the sacred tent and later in the temple (see Numbers 3.5-10).

Medes A nation that lived in what is today northwest Iran. Their kingdom, called "Media," later became one of the most important provinces of the Persian Empire, and Persian laws were referred to as the laws of the Medes and Persians (see Esther 1.19; Daniel 6.8, 12, 15).

Midianites A nomadic nation who lived mainly in the desert along the eastern shore of the Gulf of Aqaba.

Moab A nation that lived east of the Dead Sea.

According to Genesis 19.30-38, the people of Moab descended from Lot, the nephew of Abraham.

Nazarenes A name that was sometimes used for the followers of Jesus, who came from the small town of Nazareth (see Acts 24.5).

Perizzites A nation that lived in the central hill country of Canaan, before the Israelites.

Persia A large empire of Old Testament times, whose capital was located in what is now southern Iran. It is sometimes called "the Medo-Persian Empire," because of the importance of the province of Media.

Pharisees A group of Jews who thought they could best serve God by strictly obeying the laws of the Old Testament as well as their own rules, traditions, and teachings.

Philistines The land along the Mediterranean coast controlled by the Philistine people was called "Philistia." There were five main cities, each with its own ruler: Ashdod, Ashkelon, Ekron, Gath, and Gaza. The Philistines were often at war with Israel.

Phoenicia The territory along the Mediterranean Sea controlled by the cities of Tyre, Sidon, Arvad, and Byblos. The coast of modern Lebanon covers about the same area.

Rephaim Perhaps a group of very large people who lived in Palestine before the Israelites (see Deuteronomy 2.11,20).

Roman Empire Controlled the area around the Mediterranean Sea in New Testament times. Its capital was Rome.

Sadducees A small and powerful group of Jews in New Testament times. They were closely connected with the high priests and accepted only the first five books of the Old Testament as their Bible. They also did not believe in life after death.

Samaria (1) The capital city of the northern kingdom of Israel beginning with the rule of King Omri (ruled 885–874 B.C.). (2) In New Testament times, a district between Judea and Galilee, named for the city of Samaria. The people of this district, called "Samaritans," worshiped God differently from the Jews, and these two groups refused to have anything to do with one another.

Sidon See "Phoenicia."

Stoics Followers of a man named Zeno, who taught that people should learn self-control and be guided by their consciences.

Tyre See "Phoenicia."

9. Places

Bashan The flat highlands and wooded hills of southern Syria. Bashan was just north of the region of Gilead and was known for its fat cattle and fine grain.

Canaan The area now covered by Israel plus Gaza, the West Bank of Jordan, Lebanon, and southern Syria (see Numbers 34.1-12). Many passages use the term to refer only to the area south of Lebanon.

Gethsemane A garden or olive orchard on the Mount of Olives (see "Mount of Olives").

Gilead A region east of the Jordan River. The country of Moab lay to the south of Gilead, and the region of Bashan was to the north.

Hinnom Valley A valley west and south of Jerusalem, where human sacrifice was sometimes made in Old Testament times (see "Molech").

Mount of Olives A mountain just east of Jerusalem, across Kidron Valley from the temple. Gethsemane, a place where Jesus and his disciples often went to pray, was on this mountain, and so were the villages of Bethany, Bethphage, and Bahurim (see Matthew 26.36; Mark 14.32; Luke 22.39; John 18.1,2).

Palestine The area now covered by Israel, Gaza, and Jordan.

Peniel A place near the Jabbok River where Jacob wrestled with God. At that time God changed Jacob's name to Israel (see Genesis 32.22-32).

Zion Another name for Jerusalem. Zion can also refer to the hill in Jerusalem where the temple was built.

10. Objects

Chariot A two-wheeled cart that was open at the back and that was pulled by horses.

Cistern A hole or pit used for storing rainwater. Cisterns were sometimes dug in the ground and lined with stones and plaster, and at other times they were cut into the rock. The CEV sometimes translates "cistern" as "well."

Cross A device used by the Romans to put people to death. It was made of two pieces of lumber crossed in a "T," "†," or "X" shape.

Piece of Silver In the Old Testament, this usually refers to an amount of silver weighing about 0.4 oz. Coins were not invented until late Old Testament times, so when silver or gold was used to buy things, it was weighed. In traditional translations this amount is called "a shekel." Silver and gold were worth more in biblical times than they are today.

Sackcloth A rough, dark-colored cloth made from goat or camel hair. Sackcloth was usually used to make grain sacks, but clothing made from it was worn in times of trouble or sorrow.

Scroll In biblical times, writing was done on rolls of paper or special thin leather called "scrolls".

Scepter A decorated rod, often made of gold, that a king held in his hand as a symbol of royal power.

Sling A weapon used to throw rocks a little smaller than a tennis ball. A sling was made of a piece of leather that wrapped almost around the rock and had a leather strap at each end. The person would hold the ends of the straps and swing the sling around and around. When the person let go of one strap, the rock would fly out of the sling.

Tomb A burial place, often made by cutting a small room out of the rock.

11. Festivals and Holy Days

Many of these festivals are still celebrated by Jewish people.

Festival of Shelters A festival in the early fall celebrating the period of forty years when the people of Israel walked through the desert and lived in small shelters. This happy celebration began on the fifteenth day of Tishri, and for the next seven days, the people lived in small shelters made of tree branches. The name of this festival in Hebrew is "Sukkoth."

Festival of Thin Bread A seven-day festival right after Passover. During this festival the Israelites ate a thin, flat bread made without yeast to remind themselves how God freed the people of Israel from slavery in Egypt and made them into a nation. The name of this festival in Hebrew is "Mazzoth."

Festival of Trumpets See "New Moon Festival."

Great Day of Forgiveness The tenth day of the month of Tishri in the early fall. On this one day of the year, the high priest was allowed to go into the most holy part of the temple and sprinkle some of the blood of a sacrificed bull on the sacred chest. This was done so that the people's sins would be forgiven. In English this holy day has traditionally been called "the Day of Atonement," and its name in Hebrew is "Yom Kippur."

Harvest Festival See "Pentecost."

New Moon Festival A religious festival held on the day of the new moon, the day when only a thin edge of the moon can be seen. This day was always the first day of the month for the Hebrew calendar. The New Moon Festival was a time for rest from work, and a time for worship, sacrifices, celebration, and eating. The New Moon Festival in the month of Tishri in the early fall was also called "the Festival of Trumpets," and it involved even more sacrifices.

Passover A festival held on the fourteenth day of the month of Abib in the early spring. At Passover the Israelites celebrated the time God rescued them from slavery in Egypt. The name of this festival in Hebrew is "Pesach."

Pentecost A Jewish festival held in mid-spring, fifty days after Passover. At this festival Israelites celebrated the wheat harvest. Pentecost was also known as "the Harvest Festival" and has traditionally been called "the Feast of Weeks"; in Hebrew its name is "Shavuoth."

Festival of Purim A Jewish festival on the fourteenth and fifteenth of the month of Adar, near the end of winter, when the Jews celebrated how they were saved from Haman, the evil prime minister of Persia who wanted to have them killed (see Esther 9.20-32).

Sabbath The seventh day of the week, from sunset on Friday to sunset on Saturday. Israelites worshiped on the Sabbath and rested from their work in obedience to the third commandment.

Temple Festival In 165 B.C. the Jewish people recaptured the temple in Jerusalem from their enemies and made it fit for worship again. They celebrated this event each year by an eight-day festival that began on the twenty-fifth day of the month of Chislev in the late fall. This festival is traditionally called "the Festival of Dedication," or in Hebrew, "Hanukkah."

12. Sacrifice, Temple, Worship

Altar A raised structure where sacrifices and offerings were presented to God or to pagan gods. Altars could be made of rocks, packed earth, metal, or pottery.

Amen A Hebrew word used after a prayer or a blessing and meaning that what had been said was right and true.

Fire Pan A metal pan used for burning incense or carrying hot coals from the altar.

God's Tent See "Sacred Tent."

High Priest See "Priest."

Holy Place The main room of the sacred tent and of the temple. This room contained the sacred bread, the golden incense altar, and the golden lamp stand. A curtain or wall separated the holy place from the most holy place. A priest would go into the holy place once each morning and evening to burn incense on the golden altar (see also "Most Holy Place").

Incense A material that makes a sweet smell when burned. It was used in the worship of God.

Local Shrine See "Place of Worship."

Most Holy Place The inner room of the sacred tent and of the temple. In the sacred tent this room contained only the sacred chest; in Solomon's temple, the most holy place also held statues of winged creatures. Only the high priest could enter the most holy place, and even he could enter it only once a year on the Great Day of Forgiveness. The most holy place has traditionally been called "the holy of holies."

Offerings See "Sacrifices."

Place of Worship A place to worship God or pagan gods. These places were often on a hill outside of a town and have traditionally been called "high places." In the CEV they are sometimes called "local shrines."

Priest A man who led the worship in the sacred tent or in the temple and who offered sacrifices. Some of the more important priests were called "chief priests," and the most important priest was called the "high priest."

Sacred Chest The chest or box that contained the two flat stones with the Ten Commandments written on them. The chest was covered with gold, and two golden statues of winged creatures were on the lid of the chest. These winged creatures and the chest represented God's throne on earth. Two wooden poles, one on each side, were put through rings at the corners of the chest, so that the Levites could carry the chest without touching it. The chest was kept in the most holy place (see Exodus 25.10-22).

Sacred Tent The tent where the people of Israel worshiped God before the temple was built. It has traditionally been called "the tabernacle" (see Exodus 26).

Sacrifices These gifts to God included certain animals, grains, fruits, and sweet-smelling spices. Israelites offered sacrifices to give thanks to God, to ask for his forgiveness and his blessing, and to make a payment for a wrong. Some sacrifices were completely burned on the altar. In the case of other sacrifices, a portion was given to the Lord and burned on the altar, then the rest was eaten by the priests or the worshipers who had offered the sacrifice.

Sacrifices To Ask the Lord's Blessing Traditionally called "peace offerings" or "offerings of well-being." A main purpose was to ask for the Lord's blessing, and so in the CEV they are sometimes called "sacrifices to ask the Lord's blessing" (see Leviticus 3).

Sacrifices To Give Thanks to the Lord Traditionally called "grain offerings." A main purpose of such sacrifices was to thank the Lord with a gift of grain, and so in the CEV they are sometimes called "sacrifices to give thanks to the Lord" (see Leviticus 2).

Sacrifices To Make Things Right Traditionally called "guilt offerings." A main purpose was to make things right when a person had cheated someone or the LORD. These sacrifices were also made when a person had broken certain religious rules (see Leviticus 5.14–6.7).

Sacrifices To Please the LORD Traditionally called "whole burnt offerings" because the whole animal was burned on the altar. While these sacrifices did involve forgiveness for sin, a main purpose was to please the LORD with the smell of the smoke from the sacrifice, and so in the CEV they are often called "sacrifices to please the LORD" (see Leviticus 1).

Snuffer A small tool used for putting out the flame of an oil lamp, or for trimming off the charred part of the wick.

Temple A building used as a place of worship. The god that was worshiped in a particular temple was believed to be present there in a special way. The Lord's temple was in Jerusalem.

13. Customs

Ashes People put ashes, dust, or dirt on their heads, or they rolled in ash piles or dust or dirt, as a way of showing sorrow.

Circumcise To cut off the foreskin from the male organ. This was done for Israelite boys eight days after they were born. God commanded that all newborn Israelite boys be circumcised to show that they belonged to his people (see Genesis 17.9-14).

Clean and **Unclean** (1) In Old Testament times, a person who was acceptable to worship God was called "clean." A person who had certain kinds of diseases, who had touched a dead body, or who had broken certain laws became "unclean," and was unacceptable to worship God. If a person was unclean because of disease, the disease would have to be cured before the person could be clean again. And becoming clean involved performing certain ceremonies that sometimes included sacrifices. (2) Animals that were acceptable as food were called "clean." Those that were not acceptable were called "unclean" (see Leviticus 11.1-47; Deuteronomy 14.3-21). (3) Many things including tools, dishes, houses, and land could also become unclean and unusable, especially if they were touched by something unclean. Some unclean objects had to be destroyed, but others could be made clean by being washed or placed in a fire for a short time.

Going without Eating This was a way of showing sorrow, or of asking for God's help. It is also called "fasting."

Tearing Clothes A way of showing sorrow or anger, or of asking for God's help.

14. God, Jesus, Angels

Angel A supernatural being who tells God's messages to people or protects those who belong to God.

Christ A Greek word meaning "the Chosen One" and used to translate the Hebrew word "Messiah." In New Testament times, many of the Jews believed that God was going to send the Messiah to set them free from the power of their enemies. The term "Christ" is used in the New Testament both as a title and as a name for Jesus.

Eternal Life Life that is the gift of God and that never ends.

Glory Something seen, heard, or felt that shows a person or thing is important, wonderful, or powerful. When God appeared to people, his glory was often seen as a bright light or as fire and smoke. Jesus' glory was seen when he performed miracles, when he was lifted up on the cross, and when he was raised from death.

God's Kingdom God's rule over people, both in this life and in the next.

Holy One A name for the Savior that God had promised to send (see "Savior").

Kingdom of Heaven See "God's kingdom."

LORD In the Old Testament the word "LORD" in capital letters stands for the Hebrew consonants *YHWH*, the personal name of God. Ancient Hebrew did not have vowel letters, and so anyone reading Hebrew would have to know what vowels to put with the consonants. It is not known for certain what vowel sounds were originally used with the consonants YHWH. The word "Lord" represents the Hebrew term *Adonai*, the usual word for "lord." By late Old Testament times, Jews considered God's personal name too holy to be pronounced. So they said *Adonai*, "Lord," whenever they read *YHWH*. When the Jewish scribes first translated the Hebrew Scriptures into ancient Greek, they translated the personal name of God as *Kurios*, "Lord." Since that time, most translations, including the *Contemporary English Version* , have followed their example and have avoided using the personal name of God.

Messiah See "Christ."

Promised One A title for the Savior that God promised to send (see "Savior").

Save To rescue people from the power of their enemies or from the power of evil, and to give them new life and place them under God's care (see also "Savior").

Savior The one that God has chosen to rescue or save his people (see also "Save").

Sin Turning away from God and disobeying the teachings or commandments of God.

Son of Man A title often used by Jesus to refer to himself. This title is also found in the Hebrew text of Daniel 7.13 and Psalm 8.4, and God uses it numerous times in the book of Ezekiel to refer to Ezekiel.

Way In the book of Acts the Christian life is sometimes called "the Way" or "the Way of the Lord" or "God's Way."

Winged Creature(s) These supernatural beings represented the presence of God and supported his throne in Ezekiel 1.4-25; 10.1-22. Statues of winged creatures were on top of the sacred chest, and larger ones were in the most holy place in the temple built by Solomon. Wood carvings of winged creatures decorated the inside walls and doors of the temple, and figures of winged creatures were woven into the curtain separating the holy place from the most holy place in the sacred tent. The traditional term for winged creature is "cherub" (or "cherubim" for more than one).

15. Foreign Gods, Fortunetellers, Evil Spirits

Astarte A Canaanite goddess. Those who worshiped her believed that she gave them fertile land and many children, and that she helped their animals give birth to lots of young.

Baal A Canaanite god. The Canaanites believed that Baal was the most powerful of all the gods.

Dagon The chief god of the Philistines.

Demons and **Evil Spirits** Supernatural beings that do harmful things to people and sometimes cause them to do bad things. In the New Testament they are sometimes called "unclean spirits," because people under their power were thought to be unclean and unfit to worship God.

Devil The chief of the demons and evil spirits, also known as "Satan."

Evil Spirits See "Demons."

Fortunetellers Fortunetellers thought they could learn secrets or learn about the future by doing such things as watching the flight of birds, looking at the livers of animals, and rolling dice.

Hermes The Greek god of skillful speaking and the messenger of the other Greek gods.

Molech or **Milcom** The national god of the Ammonites. Some Israelites offered human sacrifices to Molech in Hinnom Valley near Jerusalem.

Satan See "Devil."

Zeus The chief god of the Greeks.

16. Plants, Animals, and Farming

Acacia A flowering tree that produces a hard, durable wood. The sacred chest, the altars, and certain other wooden objects in the sacred tent were made of acacia wood.

Aloes A sweet-smelling spice that was mixed with myrrh and used as a perfume.

Barley A grain that was used to make bread.

Cedar A tall tree once common in the Lebanon mountains and used for many of the royal building projects in Jerusalem.

Cumin A plant with small seeds used for seasoning food.

Flax The stalks of flax plants were harvested, soaked in water, and dried. Then their fibers were separated and spun into thread, which was woven to make linen cloth.

Hyssop A bush with clusters of small branches. In religious ceremonies, hyssop was sometimes dipped in a liquid and then used to sprinkle people or objects.

Jackal A wild desert animal related to wolves, but smaller.

Leviathan A legendary sea monster representing revolt and evil, also known from Canaanite writings.

Locust A type of grasshopper that comes in huge swarms and causes great damage to plant life.

Mint A garden plant used for seasoning and medicine.

Mustard A large plant with very small seeds, which were ground up and used as a spice.

Myrrh A valuable sweet-smelling powder used in perfume.

Pomegranate A reddish fruit with a hard rind. Figures of pomegranates were used as decorations on the high priest's robe and in the temple.

Reed Several kinds of tall plants related to the grass family can be called "reeds." Some varieties are hollow, and some grow in shallow water. The stems were strong and could be up to 18 feet long and 3 inches across at the base.

Rue A garden plant used for seasoning and medicine.

Threshing The process of separating grain from its husks. Grain was spread out at a "threshing place," a flat area of stone or packed earth. People or animals walked on the grain or dragged heavy boards across it to remove the husks. Then the grain and husks were tossed into the air with a special shovel called a "threshing fork." The wind would blow the light husks away, but the heavy grain would fall back to the surface of the threshing place.

Wine-pit A hollow place cut into the rock where the juice was squeezed from grapes to make wine.

Yoke A strong, heavy, wooden collar that fit around the neck of an ox, so that the ox could pull a plow or a cart.

17. Society and Its Leaders

Citizen A person who is given special rights and privileges by a nation or state. In return, a citizen was expected to be loyal to that nation or state.

Council (1) A group of leaders who meet and make decisions for their people. (2) The Old Testament refers to God's council as a group of angels who meet and talk with God in heaven.

Elders Men whose age and wisdom made them respected leaders.

Emperor The person who ruled an empire.

Generation One way of describing a group of people who live during the same period of time. In the Bible the time of one generation is often understood to be about forty years.

Judges Leaders chosen by the Lord for the people of Israel after the time of Joshua and before the time of the kings.

Tax Collectors See "Taxes."

Taxes Special fees collected by rulers. Taxes are usually part of the value of crops, property, or income. Taxes were collected at markets, city gates, ports, and border crossings. In New Testament times, Jews were hired by the Roman government to collect taxes from other Jews, and these tax collectors were hated by their own people.

18. Families, Relatives

Ancestor Someone born earlier in a family line, especially several generations earlier.

Clan A group of families who were related to each other and who often lived close to each other. A group of clans made up a tribe.

Descendant Someone born one or more generations later in a family line.

Tribe A large group of people descended from a common ancestor (see also "Clan" and Section 6, "Twelve Tribes of Israel").

19. Events

Exile The time in Israel's history (597-539 B.C.) when the Babylonians took away many of the people of Jerusalem and Judah as prisoners of war and made them live in Babylonia. The northern tribes had been taken away by Assyria in 722 B.C.

Exodus The people of Israel leaving Egypt, led by Moses and Aaron. This event is celebrated each year as Passover.

20. Dates

B.C. Before Christ. Used to date events that happened before Christ's birth. "B.C." is used after the number of the year.

A.D. *Anno Domini*, Latin for "In the year of the Lord." Used to date events that happened after Christ's birth. "A.D." is often used before the number of the year.[a]

931 B.C. The nation of Israel split into two parts: Israel, the northern kingdom, and Judah, the southern kingdom.

722 B.C. Samaria, the capital of the northern kingdom, was captured by the Assyrian army.

---

[a] The numbering system now in use was developed about A.D. 525. The plan was that the year of Christ's birth would be A.D. 1, and then the years would be numbered before and after. But an error was made in assigning A.D. 1, and by the time the error was discovered, the numbering system could not be changed. And so, the correct year of Christ's birth according to the numbering system is probably about 6 B.C.

586 B.C. Jerusalem, the capital of the southern kingdom, was captured by the Babylonian army.

538 B.C. Cyrus of Persia allowed the Jews to return to Judah.

333 B.C. Alexander the Great took control of Palestine.

323 B.C. Palestine was taken over by Ptolemy, who was one of Alexander's generals and who became the ruler of Egypt after Alexander's death.

198 B.C. Palestine was taken over by the Seleucids, the descendants of one of Alexander's generals. They had been the rulers of Syria since Alexander's death.

166 B.C. The Jews revolted, led by Judas Maccabeus and his brothers.

63 B.C. Rome took control of Palestine.

37 B.C. Herod the Great was appointed king of the Jews by the Roman government.

6 B.C. Jesus was born. (See the note following "A.D." above.)

A.D. 30 (or possibly A.D. 33) Jesus died and was raised to life.

21. The Hebrew Calendar

Nisan or **Abib** first month, about mid-March to mid-April

Iyyar or **Ziv** second month about mid-April to mid-May

Sivan third month, about mid-May to mid-June

Tammuz fourth month, about mid-June to mid-July

Ab fifth month, about mid-July to mid-August

Elul sixth month, about mid-August to mid-September

Tishri or **Ethanim** seventh month, about mid-September to mid-October

Marchesvan or **Bul** eighth month, about mid-October to mid-November

Chislev ninth month, about mid-November to mid-December

Tebeth tenth month, about mid-December to mid-January

Shebat eleventh month, about mid-January to mid-February

Adar twelfth month, about mid-February to mid-March

PALESTINE IN THE
TIME OF JESUS

Scale in Miles
0 — 40

Scale in Kilometers
0 — 40

MEDITERRANEAN

SEA

PHOENICIA

LEBANON MTS.

SYRIA

Sidon

Zarephath

Tyre

Ptolemais

MOUNT
CARMEL

Caesarea

GALILEE

Chorazin
Capernaum
Magadan
Cana
Nazareth
MT.
TABOR
Nain

Bethsaida
Lake Galilee
Tiberias

Gadara

TEN TOWNS

Abila
ABILENE
Damascus

MT. HERMON

Caesarea
Philippi

Joppa

Caesarea

SAMARIA

Samaria
MT. EBAL
MT. GERZIM
Sychar

Arimathea?

Emmaus
Jerusalem

Salim
Aenon

Ephraim
Jericho
Bethany
Qumran

Jordan River

Gerasa

PEREA

Azotus

Ascalon

Gaza

JUDEA

Bethlehem

Hebron

Dead
Sea

IDUMEA

NABATEA

WHERE TO LOOK

WHEN YOU ARE ...

Tired	- Matthew 11.28-30
Tense	- Psalm 91; James 5.7-11
Worried	- Psalm 46; Matthew 6.25-34
Discouraged	- Psalms 23; 42; 43
Frustrated	- Psalms 40; 90; 73; Hebrews 12
Jealous	- Psalm 49; James 3
Bored	- Psalms 103; 104; Ephesians 2.10; 3; 4.1-16
Bereaved	- 1 Corinthians 15; 1 Thessalonians 4.13–5.28; Revelation 21; 22
Bearing a grudge	- Luke 6; 2 Corinthians 4; Ephesians 4
Becoming lax and indifferent	- Matthew 25; Revelation 2; 3
Staying awake nights	- Psalms 4; 56; 130
Lonely or fearful	- Psalms 27; 91; Luke 8; 1 Peter 4
Feeling rejected	- Colossians 1; 1 Peter 1; Romans 8
Desiring inward peace	- John 14; Romans 8

WHERE TO LOOK

WHEN YOU ARE . . .

Anxious for dear ones	- Psalm 121; Luke 7
Overtaken by sorrow	- Psalm 46; Matthew 28
Tempted to do wrong	- Psalms 15; 19; Matthew 4; Hebrews 4.14-16; James 1.12-16
Angry with someone	- Matthew 18; Ephesians 4; James 4
Weary	- Psalm 95.1-7; Matthew 11
Building a new home	- Psalm 127; Ephesians 5; Colossians 3; 1 John 4.7-21
Assuming more responsibility	- 2 Corinthians 8.1-15
Sick or in pain	- Psalms 6; 39; 41; 67
Afraid of death	- John 11; 17; 20; 2 Corinthians 5; 1 John 3; Revelation 14
In need of forgiveness	- Psalm 51; Matthew 23; Luke 15; 1 John 1; Philemon
Weak in faith	- Psalms 126; 146; Matthew 9.20-22; Mark 9.14-29; Hebrews 11
Feeling that God is far away	- Psalms 25; 118; 125; 139; Luke 10; John 14; 17; Romans 8.31-39; Hebrews 10.19-39